D0701785

EUROPE, 1815-1914

THIRD EDITION

Gordon A. Craig

J. E. Wallace Sterling Professor of Humanities, Stanford University

Holt, Rinehart and Winston, Inc.
Fort Worth   Chicago   San Francisco   Philadelphia
Montreal   Toronto   London   Sydney   Tokyo

Copyright © 1961, 1966, 1971 by Holt, Rinehart and Winston, Inc.

All rights reserved. No part of this publication may be reproduced or transmitted in any form or by any means, electronic or mechanical, including photocopy, recording or any information storage and retrieval system, without permission in writing from the publisher.

Requests for permission to make copies of any part of the work should be mailed to: Permissions, Holt, Rinehart and Winston, Inc., 301 Commerce St., Fort Worth, TX 76102
Library of Congress Catalog Card Number: 77-140148
ISBN: 0-03-089194-9
Printed in the United States of America
0123   006   18

TO
SUSAN,
DEBORAH,
and
MARTHA
and their families

CONTENTS

Contents

Contents

Contents

Contents

Contents

PART ONE
1815-1850

GENERAL
OBSERVATIONS

Because our own age has been marked by bitter international rivalry and continual preoccupation with war, it is perhaps understandable that whenever we think of the general characteristics of an earlier period, we are apt to turn our attention first to the state of international politics during it. Regarded from this point of view, the years that stretch from 1815 to 1848 seem almost, in comparison with our own time, to have formed a golden age of harmony. There was no major conflict between the Great Powers of Europe, indeed, no war of any kind in which Great Powers were ranged against each other as enemies; and fewer Europeans died as a result of international war during these three and a half decades than in any comparable period since 1848.

Why were the European states able in the years after the Congress of Vienna to rise above their conflicting interests and their ideological differences and to resolve their disputes without going to war? Partly, no doubt, because after their long struggle against Napoleon, they were exhausted physically and psychologically by the long struggle and ready to agree that war was an unpleasant and unprofitable business which should be avoided wherever possible. But this is hardly a complete explanation, for wars are as often the result of blundering as they are of deliberate intent. It is more accurate to say that peace among the Great Powers was the result of a happy combination of determination to avoid war, self-restraint when opportunities for unilateral aggrandizement presented themselves, and skillful diplomacy. With respect to the last of these, the years from 1815 to 1848 were perhaps the last years in the modern period in which the pen was recognizably mightier than the sword; and twentieth-century statesmen could do much worse

3

than to study the methods of the diplomats of this period.

Because Europe was free of wars between the powers, it does not follow that these were entirely peaceful years, for they were not. The political and territorial settlement that had been effected at Vienna in 1814–1815 was not, after all, universally admired. Its most inveterate opponents were those who claimed that it violated what we would today call the principle of national self-determination. Believing that men who shared a common history, language, and culture should be permitted to form independent political units (or nations) under rulers of their own choice, these critics argued that the Vienna settlement denied this right to such peoples as the Belgians, the Germans, the Italians, the Poles, and the Greeks. If they themselves happened to be Belgians or Germans or Italians or Poles or Greeks, they often attempted to correct what they considered to be the deficiencies of the treaties, by means of propaganda, or agitation, or even resort to force.

The nationalism that inspired their efforts had little of the narrow arrogance or the frenetic jingoism that was to characterize nationalistic movements in the second half of the century. Early nineteenth-century nationalism was animated by an ardent, if idealistic, belief that a Europe based on truly national lines—that is, composed entirely of free nations—would be a healthier and a more peaceful Europe than one in which there were still subject nationalities living under alien rule. Granted the enlightened nature of this philosophy—which was preached by such disparate personalities as Mazzini and Napoleon III—attempts to apply it were usually violent in nature and unhappy in result.

Another and closely related source of turbulence in this period was the continuous struggle between the conservatism of the ruling classes of the various European states and the liberalism of the educated, professional, and commercial classes. Liberalism, as the word indicates, was a philosophy of freedom, and its adherents—whether in Spain or England, in Austria or France—wished to free the individual from the absolute control of his government and to secure fundamental liberties (like freedom of speech and assembly) for all citizens and a share in political power for a greater number than were permitted to participate in politics under the old regime. To the ruling classes of post-Vienna Europe, whose conservatism was for the most part a completely negative philosophy based on a panicky fear of revolution and an aversion to change of any kind, these liberal objectives were too repellent to admit of compromise. This inflexible opposition to even moderate proposals of reform, and the attempted persecution of the would-be reformers which often accompanied it, had the result of forcing the liberals (as they came to be called) to resort to underground activity, conspiracy, and, ultimately, revolution. Throughout this period, indeed, there was some kind of *coup de main* or insurrection somewhere in Europe every two or three years, while major explosions affecting several national capitals, occurred in 1820, 1830, and 1848. These uprisings did not always advance the cause of freedom; and they frequently jeopardized the peace that diplomacy was so bent on preserving, since their repercussions could not always be confined within the borders of the countries in which they took place.

Another development that contributed to the agitation of the period was the steady expansion of machine industry. The speed with which Europe was conquered by the machine should not, of course, be overestimated. Throughout the period under review the economy—even of England—remained primarily agrarian, as is demonstrated by the fact that all the economic crises before 1850 had their origins in agricultural disorders of one kind or another. The only sizable industrial area outside England in the two decades after 1815 was in Belgium, where English methods and techniques were introduced into the textile industry and began to transform the extractive and metallurgical industries as well. In France, significant industrial development did not get under way until after 1830, while in countries further east it came even later.

Nevertheless, as the period proceeded, industrial expansion was encouraged by several factors. Between 1750 and 1850, for reasons still obscure to historians, a virtual population explosion occurred,[1] and in the first half of the nineteenth century, there was a forty percent increase, from 188,000,000 in 1800 to 266,000,000 in 1850. This created a myriad of problems, but it also gave industry the labor force it needed and provided large numbers of potential customers as well. At the same time, currency reforms, the establishment of central banks to control the issue of paper money, and the encouragement of investment by new company and insurance laws made available the capital without which industrial growth would have been impossible. The revolution in transportation effected by the improvement and expansion of highways and canals, the promotion by all European governments of railroad construction, which began on a large scale in the 1840s, and the increasing use of steam transport in rivers and coastal waters and on the high seas improved access to raw materials and markets. Finally, industrial growth benefited from the removal of artificial hindrances to commercial intercourse by such things as the establishment of the Prussian Customs Union and the repeal of the Corn Laws by the British government in 1846. Thanks to these developments, conditions in all European countries—even in Russia, which was still virtually unaffected by the technological progress of the West—were infinitely more favorable for industrial expansion at the end of this period than they had been in 1815.

Moreover, if the scope and magnitude of industrialism was still small by twentieth-century standards, it was sufficiently great to contribute to the unrest of the age. Man was already becoming, as the greatest historian of the romantic age, Jules Michelet, said he would become, "the humble servant of these steel giants." This transformation was evident even in the sphere of foreign affairs, where industrial development sometimes complicated existing diplomatic problems or created new ones. There is little doubt that both Belgian opposition to Dutch domination in the years leading to 1830 and Lombard opposition to Austrian suzerainty throughout the whole period

---

[1] W. L. Langer has recently suggested that it was due to the higher marriage rate resulting from the relaxation of the controls of the seigneurial and guild systems and to the increase of the available food supply, effected primarily by the cultivation of the potato. For other factors, see chapter 4, p. 92.

were strongly influenced by conflicts of interest between the industrialists of the subject and the governing states.

Equally significant were the changes in social structure which the expansion of the industrial economy made inevitable. Land, which had formerly been the basis of social organization in all European states, became less important as industrialism advanced, and capital began slowly to take its place. Simultaneously, the old division of society began to break down. The position of the nobles and their clerical allies was challenged by an emergent and self-confident bourgeoisie, which made its way in life by the accumulation and manipulation of money and which believed that, to its economic power, political and social power must be added. The distinction between the upper and lower bourgeoisie or middle class, which was to assume great significance later in the century, was not yet obvious and, until the 1840s, the most striking characteristic of the bourgeoisie was unity of view and purpose. In politics, they were for the most part militantly liberal; in social attitude, they were in general agreement that the upper classes—that is, the older entrenched classes—must be put down. For this very reason, they were supported by the peasants, the artisans, and the industrial workers. Economically vulnerable and without direction, these groups accepted middle class leadership and participated in all the political struggles of this period; and it is doubtful whether the July revolution in France or the fight for the Great Reform Bill in England could have been successful without their support.

This combination of forces was not destined to last. On the one hand, the working classes discovered that the victories won by it brought greater material benefits to the middle class than to themselves, and the discovery led to disillusionment and resentment. On the other hand, the bourgeoisie, always uncomfortable with their lower class allies, grew alarmed over the increasingly radical nature of the reforms desired by them. The truth of the matter was, as the revolutions of 1848 were to show, that there was no real community of interest between the middle and lower classes. The lower classes were, by instinct, believers in the kind of political democracy that would give the vote to every man, as well as in a rudimentary socialism that held that it was the duty of the government to improve the lot of the lower classes by economic and social reform. These ideas were anathema to middle class liberals who believed that political power should be restricted to the propertied and educated classes and that the healthiest societies were those in which government intervened least in economic and social matters. It was no accident that classes with such contradictory conviction should have ceased to be allies.

As this happened, the homogeneity of the middle class itself began to break down and its wealthiest members—because of their fear of the working class but also as a result of the social opportunities which their riches brought them—began to modify their formerly hostile attitude toward the old aristocracy. By 1848 there were already indications that the future would bring an alliance, if not a merger, between the older ruling class and the upper bourgeoisie, and that the less wealthy bourgeoisie would find itself as a middle group between the working class and a new aristo-plutocracy. In any case, the stratification of society had, in all countries, become much less simple and clear-cut than it was in 1815, while conflict between classes—upon which Karl Marx placed so much emphasis in *The Communist Manifesto* in 1848—had greatly increased in intensity.

Despite all the nationalist risings and liberal agitations and the economic and social dislocations that industrialism brought in its train, these things were not enough to absorb the energy of the peoples of Europe completely. These were rich and exciting years in literature and the arts, for this is the period in which the movement known as romanticism reached its height. It would be difficult to find a universally satisfactory definition for this term, which has been used to characterize the work of such different people as Chateaubriand, Coleridge, Mendelssohn, Pushkin, Manzoni, and Delacroix. It is perhaps better merely to say, as Irving Babbitt once said, that in literature and the arts romanticism was a revolt against classicism, which seemed (at least to romantics) to stifle all that was creative and spontaneous in artistic expression, and that, in a more general sense it was an intellectual reaction against the rationalism and the sometimes barren logic of the eighteenth century. It was marked by a high degree of emotionalism; and, when one considers the great number of romantics who had visions or passed through religious frenzies or saw apparitions or were haunted by *Doppelgänger* or professed satanism, it is easy to understand why conservative critics held that romanticism was a malady similar to sleepwalking or epilepsy. It was characterized also by an exaggerated cult of nature and an excessive veneration of the remote past, as well as by an amazing amount of cloudy talk about solving the riddle of the universe and bridging the gulf between the real and the ideal. With all that, it was a lively

and a fertile movement which, as later chapters will attempt to show, produced a lot of good painting and music and poetry and had a healthy influence in other fields beside those of the arts and literature.

There can be little doubt, for instance, that the interest in the past that was awakened by romanticism helped revitalize historical studies. The new appreciation of the organic development of society made men curious about the origins of their own institutions and customs and this promoted research into the past, while simultaneously stimulating archaeology, philology, legal studies, and philosophy as well. It is surely not without significance that the most influential philosopher of this period, Georg Friedrich Hegel, and his most illustrious disciple, Karl Marx, should have placed such emphasis in their systems upon historical evolution and the laws that guide it.

Because romanticism was so rich and varied a movement, the political views of its adherents were marked by extreme diversity. The movement was one of the most important forces that fed the nationalism of the age, for one of the offshoots of the new interest in the past was national pride and self-consciousness. At the same time, romanticism was a European movement that forged close ties between its followers with little concern for their nationality and thus contributed as much to the spread of internationalism as the reverse. In the same way, although many of the best-known representatives of the movement were conservative and even reactionary in their views in the first years after the Vienna Congress, Stendhal noted in his diary in 1827 that romanticism was becoming the cult of liberal and democratic youth.

The revulsion against the rationalism of the eighteenth century that we find expressed in the romantic movement is seen also in the marked revival, among the intellectuals of this age and the upper classes, of religion. Those romantics who were enthusiastic about Gothic cathedrals discovered new enthusiasm for the faith those cathedrals had been built to celebrate. At the same time, an aristocracy whose position had been almost fatally shaken by the French revolution was no longer as tolerant of free thought as it had been in the previous century, but was inclined to regard religious orthodoxy as a valuable—indeed, a necessary—reinforcement of existing institutions.

It is doubtful whether the return to the faith of either of these groups helped the churches in the long run. The romantic intellectuals who were most vocal about their new faith placed more emphasis upon the trappings than upon the essentials of religion; and their enthusiasm was so excessive as to bring ridicule upon its object. More serious was the fact that the religiosity of court and aristocratic circles placed a conservative, if not a reactionary, stamp upon the churches which they found hard to shake off at a later date when they were under attack. This was unfortunate, because, as a matter of fact, the churches were not onesidedly conservative in the period before 1848, as the vigorous controversies between liberal and conservative groups inside both the Roman Catholic and the Protestant churches showed.

In general, the major religions reflected strength and vigor, and religion was practiced by the majority of the population. Industrialism and urbanization had not yet advanced so far as to weaken the ties that bound the masses to their traditional faith. As for the bourgeoisie, they were still, for the most part, churchgoers; and even the most doctrinaire liberals among them, who kept up a drumfire of criticism against religious obscurantism and church influence in education, did not deny that the churches had a legitimate and important role to play in society.

With respect to education, the period was not distinguished by notable advances. With some exceptions, notably in the German states, the governments of Europe neither made elementary education compulsory nor made it possible for the children of the poor to attend existing schools. As late as 1835 three Englishmen in ten could neither read nor write; in France, in 1830, 153,635 recruits out of 294,975 reporting for military service were in the same plight; and the situation was worse in southern and eastern Europe. As the years passed, the spread of industrialism was going to make the extension of popular education necessary (since machines require literate operators) and possible (by producing inexpensive books and bringing the masses into urban centers). But that time was not yet; and when one thinks of the appalling ignorance of the masses in these years, he finds it easier to understand why both the aristocracy and the middle classes feared and opposed democracy.

This dark picture is somewhat brightened by the flourishing state of institutions of higher learning in this period. It is perhaps true that some of the older universities—Oxford and Cambridge, for example, and the provincial universities of France—seemed content to rest on their laurels, but the Scottish universities, the newly founded universities in Berlin and Munich, the Collège de France in Paris, and many others that might be named were centers of intellectual vitality, inspired teaching, and enthusiastic scholarship. In the sciences in particular, revolutionary work was done by university savants in these years: in mathematics and astronomy, where the work of men like K. F. Gauss of Göttingen and Urbain Leverrier of Paris expanded human awareness of the nature and dimensions of the universe (Leverrier's determination of the position of the newly discovered planet Neptune was one of the great scientific coups of the midcentury); in physics, where the Germans Julius Mayer and Hermann Helmholtz conceived the idea of conservation of energy and laid the foundations of thermodynamics, and where the first basic work in the practical application of electricity was done by Hans Christian Oersted of Copenhagen, André Marie Ampère of Paris, and especially the Englishman Michael Faraday, whose formulation of the theory of electromagnetic induction was another of the century's most significant breakthroughs; in chemistry, where Jöns Jakob Berzelius of Stockholm drew up the first fairly accurate table of atomic weights and Justus Liebig's studies of plant physiology and soil analysis made clear the importance of chemicals in restoring fertility and increasing the production of food. In geology and in biology and its related sciences fewer basic discoveries were made, but here, too, research activity was systematic and energetic.

A special word concerning medicine may be added, for the period of which we are talking has been described as that in which modern medicine emerged. This may seem an exaggerated view to anyone who considers the ravages caused by diseases like smallpox, tuberculosis, and particularly Asiatic cholera, which raged across Europe

in 1831, claiming thousands of victims, including such notables as the philosopher Hegel, the French prime minister Casimir-Perier, Napoleon's great adversary the former Prussian chief of staff Gneisenau, the theorist of war Clausewitz, and Grand Duke Constantine and General Diebitch of Russia. Against the continuing failure to diagnose the causes of these diseases and to devise effective treatment must be placed such solid achievements as the progress made toward a localized pathology, the improvement of diagnostic methods by such advances as the invention of the stethoscope, Pierre Louis' demonstration of the value of medical statistics, the discovery of the uses of morphine and the isolation of strychnine and quinine, the beginning of serious experimentation with clinical thermometry and anesthesia, and the intensive study of cell structure made possible by the introduction of the achromatic microscope in the 1830s.

These accomplishments of European science and their practical applications were, like other European ideas and institutions, communicated to the outside world and inspired the developments that in the course of the century were to Europeanize the globe. In this connection European ideas were carried to the distant corners of the earth, not only by the merchant and the missionary but also by the colonial activities of the governments. This was not, to be sure, a period in which the expansion of European possessions overseas was even remotely comparable to that which was to take place in the fourth quarter of the century; and there was no great enthusiasm for colonial acquisition. Spain and Portugal were, indeed, losing their American empires in these years. On the other hand, the British and the Russians were advancing in the Middle and the Far East, and the French were establishing an empire in North Africa.

In his memoirs, the old and disappointed Chateaubriand wrote of his age: "After Napoleon nothing!" Yet this was a period crowded with developments as worthy of note as any of Napoleon's triumphs. Happily free from the ravages of large-scale war, it was characterized by political and intellectual ferment, economic growth, scientific progress, and literary and artistic vitality. It might be more accurate to describe it, as Victor Hugo did, as "a magnificent epoch ... the virile age of mankind."

Chapter 1 THE GREAT POWERS
AND THE
BALANCE OF POWER, 1815–1848

THE RECONSTRUCTION OF EUROPE, 1814–1815

The Great Powers and the Postwar Decisions   In March 1814 Austrian cavalry clattered over the cobblestones of Paris, and Prussian grenadiers bivouacked on the heights of Montmartre. An unaccustomed quiet settled over the country. After a spirited but brief struggle at the Clichy Gate, the organized resistance of French armies had collapsed, and Marshals Mortier and Marmont had capitulated to the Allies. At Fontainebleau Napoleon sat, almost alone, still grimly holding on to an imperial title that would have little meaning in the exile to which he was soon to be consigned. The Corsican still had one desperate throw to make, but in reality his day was done. After a quarter of a century of almost continuous war, revolutionary and imperialistic France, which had dominated the continent under Napoleon's leadership, had been defeated by Europe.

But what—or rather, who—was Europe? For all practical purposes, Europe meant the four states which, like France, were considered—by virtue of their military, economic, and other resources—to be great powers and which had done most to defeat Napoleon. It is true, of course, that many states and peoples had contributed to the combined effort that gradually sapped the strength of Bonaparte's armies; one thinks immediately of the Spanish guerrilla bands or of those South German patriots who died with Andreas Hofer. But essentially the victory had been won by the Great Powers and by the Grand Alliance that they had finally succeeded in forming in the spring of 1813. And now, in deciding the thorny questions involved in the process of restoring peace to the wartorn continent, those same Great Powers took the initiative and exercised preponderant, if not exclusive, influence.

11

The First Peace of Paris   From the outset, the powers recognized that there were two different jobs that had to be done before Europe could return to a peaceful footing. They had, first, to put a definitive end to hostilities by making some kind of arrangement with the defeated enemy, France. They had, in the second place, to reduce the confusion and disorder and solve the dynastic and territorial problems that had been created all over Europe by the collapse of the Napoleonic empire.

The first of these tasks was the easier and was completed with dispatch. The Allied Powers were no longer willing to tolerate Napoleon's continued presence on the throne of France. They had, therefore, to find a successor for him, and they decided—after an inconclusive consideration of such candidates as his son and the Swedish prince Bernadotte, who had won the favor of the tsar of Russia—that the easiest and most logical thing to do was to restore the old dynasty, the House of Bourbon, in the person of Louis XVIII. Once it had been agreed to place this representative of the old Europe on the throne, the Allies had the good sense to see that it would be illogical to saddle him with a punitive peace, which would probably delay the return of the security and repose that they so strongly desired.

The terms of the treaty concluded with Louis XVIII in May 1814—the so-called First Peace of Paris—were, therefore, lenient. France lost its recently acquired holdings in Italy, Germany, and the Low Countries, as well as such colonial possessions as Tobago, Santa Lucia, and Ile de France, which were ceded to Great Britain, and part of San Domingo, which was handed over to Spain. But these losses were no more than had been expected. On the other hand, France was not only permitted to keep the boundaries that it had had in January 1792 but was allowed to take over certain enclaves that had not formerly belonged to it. Moreover, despite some British interest in the idea of an indemnity to pay the costs of the war and strong Prussian demands that France be forced to restore certain monies extorted from the German states by Napoleon, the new French king let it be known that he was inflexibly opposed to any financial impositions and would submit to arrest rather than pay them. This firmness so impressed the Allies that they dropped the idea of financial reparations. They did not, in the end, even insist that France return the art treasures that Napoleon's agents had systematically looted from the museums and palaces of Europe.

The signing of the treaty marked the successful conclusion of the first phase of the reconstruction of Europe. The opening of the second phase, in which a general settlement was to be negotiated, was announced in one of the last paragraphs of the Paris Peace, which read: "All the Powers engaged on either side in the present war shall, within the space of two months, send Plenipotentiaries to Vienna for the purpose of regulating, in General Congress, the arrangements which are to complete the provisions of the present Treaty."

The Congress of Vienna: Organization   The first thing that has to be remembered about the Congress of Vienna is that it never met as a congress or deliberative body at all. Probably the only occasions on which anything like a majority of the delegates of the states represented at Vienna assembled in one place were ceremonial ones—the innumerable receptions, reviews, fêtes, and tournaments held for the entertainment of the notables who poured into Vienna in the last months of 1814. But there was nothing in the nature of a diplomatic assembly at which the great territorial questions and other issues affecting the future of Europe could be debated. If the term Congress of Vienna means anything at all, it refers only to the totality of negotiations that took place in the Austrian capital during the eight months following October 1, 1814.

These negotiations were controlled by the Great Powers. Indeed, if they could have managed it, the four Allied Powers would have settled everything before they ever came to Vienna and would simply have asked the other states to ratify their decisions. But, although there was almost continuous consultation between them during the three months that followed the conclusion of the Paris Peace, they were unable to agree on such questions as the way in which the map was to be redrawn; and, when they arrived in Vienna at the end of September, their real work was just beginning. In the long run, this did not make much difference in the way in which things were done at Vienna. Decisions on the important territorial questions the four powers reserved for themselves, although they eventually decided to admit France to their inner circle, partly to mediate their own differences of view, partly to prevent the French representative Talleyrand from organizing the lesser states into an anti-Great-Power bloc. To occupy the lesser powers and to ease their susceptibilities, there were ten special committees (on German affairs, on international rivers, and the like), while three of their number (Spain, Portugal, and Sweden) sat with the Great Powers on a Committee of Eight. This last body, however, met infrequently and accomplished little.

The delegations of the five Great Powers were strong and included some of the ablest negotiators of the nineteenth century. Chief among them was Clemens Prince Metternich, the Austrian foreign minister, whose carefully timed swing from alliance with Napoleon to union with his enemies had assured the success of the Grand Alliance and, at the same time, made his country its leader. Metternich was an inordinately vain man, who found it impossible to believe that he was capable of mistakes. "I say to myself twenty times a day," he once confessed, "how right I am and how wrong the others are. And yet it is so *easy* to be right." He could also be intolerably dull and pompous, especially when discoursing on his own excellent qualities. Yet he had become minister of foreign affairs in 1809 at the age of 36, and he continued in the post until 1848, a term unequaled by any other European diplomat in the modern period and one which indicates that Metternich possessed uncommon political gifts. Sir Llewellyn Woodward has written that his greatest talent was a "sensitiveness to the existence of general European interests." Far from being a narrow nationalist, he believed that the conflicting interests of national states should be reconciled for the sake of general peace and stability; and he showed genius in producing the formulas that made such reconciliation possible.

Metternich's interest in European order and in reconciling the interests of the powers was shared by the chief British delegate, Foreign Secretary Viscount Castlereagh. A shy and reserved man, the object of misunderstanding and even persistent denigration in his own country (when he died a suicide in 1822, some of his critics, including the poet Shelley, rejoiced in a wholly indecent manner), Castlereagh was certainly one of the great foreign secretaries of the modern era. Indeed, Lord Strang has recently suggested that, with his distrust of abstract ideas, overdefinition, ideological motivation, and his preference for flexibility and practical attention to concrete interests precisely defined, Castlereagh was the creator of a British style of diplomacy that has persisted to the present. It was largely because of his untiring efforts that the Grand Alliance had been able to survive the jealousy and mutual suspicion that had threatened to destroy it before Napoleon was definitively beaten. Now, he wished to restore the kind of balance of power in Europe that would give security and peace to all its members.

Both Metternich and Castlereagh had more freedom of decision than their Russian and Prussian colleagues, for those diplomats had to take account of the desires and prejudices of their sovereigns, who were present and active in Vienna. Thus, the Russian foreign minister, Nesselrode, whose views were "European" in the same sense that Castlereagh's and Metternich's were, had constantly to defer to the whims of his monarch, Tsar Alexander I. Alexander was neurotic and possibly schizophrenic. He went through life haunted by a sense of guilt incurred when he was elevated to the throne over the murdered corpse of his father, and his attempts to escape from this by posing alternately as the scourge and as the savior of Europe, by indulging in paroxysms of idealistic reform and frenzies of sexual excess, and, finally, by giving his support to experiments in religious mysticism, failed to ease his troubled spirit or to prevent his eventual collapse, ten years after Vienna, into the depths of manic depression. At Vienna Alexander was still a handsome, vigorous, and charming man, but he was also at his most volatile and unpredictable, changing his policies and his close advisers from day to day.

The Prussian delegation was headed by Prince Hardenberg, who, because of his advancing years and growing deafness, was assisted by Wilhelm von Humboldt, the former minister of culture who had been chiefly responsible for founding the University of Berlin in 1810 and had been serving since then as ambassador to the court of Vienna. Their efforts to promote Prussian interest by playing an independent role during the congress were seriously handicapped by the presence of their sovereign, Frederick William III, who, out of gratitude for Tsar Alexander's role in liberating Prussia in 1813, tended to side with the Russians rather more than was politic. Humboldt, who had spent much more of his life thinking and writing about problems of philosophy, philology, educational theory, and esthetics than about politics and diplomacy, nevertheless proved himself to be an indefatigable and efficient organizer at Vienna. He himself provided the procedural plan that prevented the negotiations from becoming hopelessly complicated, and his staff made almost all the statistical studies and calculations that served as the basis for the redrawing of the map of Europe. Since many of these turned out to be in support of Prussian claims, the other delegations showed little gratitude for Humboldt's energy, which merely strengthened their impression that the Prussians were both boring and greedy—a conclusion that was not wholly fair.

Finally, hovering on the sidelines at all the levées and balls in Vienna and never absent when great matters were to be decided was the chief of the French delegation, with his badly powdered hair and his club foot, his pendulous lips, and his lusterless but mocking eyes, Talleyrand-Périgord, Prince of Benevento. This was the man who had survived all the perilous storms of the revolution by knowing exactly when it was necessary to change sides, who had served and betrayed Napoleon, who had played a leading part in persuading the Allies to give the succession to the French throne to Louis XVIII, and who was to go on his blithe way for another fifteen years, finally ending a fantastically varied career as Louis Philippe's ambassador in London in 1830. One is never quite certain what Talleyrand's motives were at any given moment; but it would be unfair to him to deny that regard for his country and its national interest was among the strongest of the forces that determined his devious course. Because he believed, further, that France's best interest was to be served by recognizing the legitimate interests of others and by maintaining relations with them on the basis of reciprocal respect, Talleyrand had a point of contact with Metternich and Castlereagh that proved not without importance in the Vienna negotiations.

The Vienna Settlement: Basic Principles   It has been said that the territorial settlement reached at Vienna was based upon three principles: compensation for the victors, legitimacy, and balance of power. Provided too much is not made of these labels, they are useful in illustrating the main features of the Vienna treaties.

Despite their willingness to forego financial reparation from France, the Great Powers expected some form of compensation for their costly efforts against Napoleon, and they thought principally in terms of territorial expansion. Great Britain was no exception. If its representatives seemed to be more disinterested at Vienna than other delegates, this was only because they knew that their country had gotten most of what it wanted before the negotiations began. In the course of the wars, the British had seized such strategic outposts as Helgoland in the North Sea, Malta and the Ionian Islands in the Mediterranean, Cape Colony in South Africa, and Ceylon, Ile de France, Demerara, St. Lucia, Tobago, and Trinidad. These they retained.

The British gains were far exceeded by those of Austria. Metternich took advantage of the general reshuffling of territory that was taking place to disembarrass his country of certain of its former possessions in Belgium and South Germany, which were too far away for efficient administration or military defense; but, in place of them, he won the rich and conveniently situated provinces of Lombardy and Venetia in northern Italy. Austria also regained its Polish possessions and gained territory in the Tyrol and in Illyria, on the eastern coast of the Adriatic. All in all, by the end of the Vienna negotiations, Austria had a population four or five millions larger than it had had in 1792.

The process of adjusting the Great Powers' claims for compensation was not always amicable and sometimes involved bitter quarreling. The territorial ambitions of Prussia and Russia, for instance, caused a very ugly crisis in December 1814.

Russia was already assured of the possession of Finland, which it had conquered from Sweden, and of Bessarabia and other territories it had taken from the Turks, but Alexander wanted more. He burned to win new renown by standing before Europe as the restorer of the ancient kingdom of Poland (with

"The Congress of Vienna," 1814–1815, an engraving from a painting by the French portraitist Jean-Baptiste Isabey (1767–1855). The Duke of Wellington stands at the far left, with Hardenberg sitting in front of him. Castlereagh is seated with his legs crossed in the center and is looking toward Metternich, who is standing and pointing toward him. In the right foreground sits Talleyrand, with his forearm on the table. Immediately behind him is Gentz, with Humboldt standing to the right of him. (Graphische Sammlung Albertina, Vienna)

the understanding, of course, that once restored that kingdom would be placed under Russian control) and therefore demanded that Napoleon's Grand Duchy of Warsaw, which had included the Polish districts formerly belonging to Austria and Prussia, be handed over to him so that he might join them to his own Polish holdings. The Prussians were willing to give up their Polish territory if they were indemnified elsewhere. They proposed that suitable compensation would be the kingdom of Saxony, a populous and wealthy country that lay immediately south of Prussia. Alexander, remembering that the king of Saxony had remained loyal to Napoleon until after the battle of Leipzig, agreed that Saxony was fair game for the Prussians; and the Russian and Prussian delegations henceforth supported each other's claims.

Neither Austria nor Great Britain was very happy about this. Both powers were concerned over Alexander's Polish project, which would enormously enhance Russian power in central Europe. In addition, Metternich feared that if he permitted Prussia to annex Saxony, he would be attacked by his enemies in Vienna on the ground that he had increased Prussian influence in the affairs of Germany at the expense of his own country. Castlereagh had no real objection to Prussia's gaining territory, but he preferred to have it do so on the Rhine, where Prussian forces could, if necessary, be employed to prevent new adventures on the part of France. Both Castlereagh and Metternich were irritated by the intimate collaboration between the Russians and the Prussians and by the defiant and even menacing attitude they had adopted toward their allies. As their irritation grew, relations between the two sets of powers became so strained that by the end of December armed conflict between them did not seem unlikely.

This situation gave Talleyrand an opportunity to make the most startling coup of the Congress. For the sake of France's future position in Europe, he was anxious to end its isolation in face of the union of the other powers. He now took advantage of their differences to propose that England and Austria conclude a secret alliance with France, by which the three powers undertook to resist Prusso-Russian pretensions by force of arms if necessary. At first Castlereagh demurred, pointing out that such a combination "might augment the chances of war rather than of an amicable settlement"; but, as the Prussians persisted in their intransigence with respect to Saxony, he changed his mind and drafted the tripartite treaty that was concluded on January 3, 1815.

On the part of Metternich, who had no desire to resume hostilities, the promise to do so if necessary was probably a bluff; but, if so, it called the bluff of the other side. For Alexander was in no position to go to war either, since his troops were disorganized and disaffected and many of his officers were out of sympathy with his European plans. As a result of the secret treaty—the existence and purpose of which were soon known to everyone in Vienna—the crisis between the powers vanished, and an elaborate patching up followed which pleased everybody but the Prussians. The tsar was permitted to take the greater part of the Grand Duchy of Warsaw, but Prussia and Austria retained some of their Polish districts, and Cracow was made a free city. The king of Saxony remained on his throne and kept possession of his two most important cities, Dresden and Leipzig. The Prussians were, it is true, given almost half of Saxony, in addition to Swedish Pomerania and extensive holdings in the Rhineland, but this did not prevent their soldiers from grumbling that the diplomats were giving away all the fruits of victory.

Once the Polish-Saxon crisis was overcome and their own ambitions satisfied, the powers turned their attention to the arrangements that had to be made in the other liberated areas. Here, when it seemed expedient, they observed the principle of legitimacy, a term invented by Talleyrand and, in its widest sense, meaning that the rights of the pre-Napoleonic rulers of European states should be respected and their thrones restored to them if they had lost them in the course of the wars. The principle, however, was not applied automatically or consistently. The powers recognized that there was little point in restoring German states that had ceased to exist as far back as 1803, and they ignored legitimacy also in the case of Italian states that had disappeared before 1798. Nor did they allow legitimacy to worry them while they were making their own acquisitions.

They were more consistent in their application of the principle of the balance of power, of which Metternich, Castlereagh, and Talleyrand were devoted and eloquent champions. To each of them, balance of power meant what it had generally meant in the eighteenth century: an equilibrium of forces between the Great Powers of such a nature as to discourage unilateral aggression on the part of any of them. Talleyrand was more skeptical than his two associates concerning the possibility of ever attaining more than a precarious equilibrium, and he held that the only true preventive of aggression was a spirit of moderation and justice on the part of the powers. Metternich and Castlereagh, on the other hand, tended to think in almost mathematical terms and to seek an adjustment of territory, population, and resources that would reduce the danger of war to a minimum.

It was this that determined the course they took in all matters of Great Power compensation—Castlereagh, for instance, holding that if Russia increased its Polish holdings, both Prussia and Austria must be given equivalent accretions of strength, even if this necessitated violations of legitimacy. Their attitude on the German and Italian questions and on that of the Low Countries was inspired by the same desire to construct an equilibrium that would not be easily shaken.

In the Low Countries, the Belgians were united, much against their will, with their northern neighbors and placed under the rule of the House of Orange, largely because it was hoped that this arrangement might serve as an additional barrier against a possibly resurgent France. Germany was left divided into thirty-eight separate states, because any other solution would have complicated relations among the powers, whereas it was believed that a disunited block of territory in central Europe might serve them as a kind of shock absorber. This is what Wilhelm von Humboldt meant when he said that Germany's "true and actual purpose [was] to secure peace, and its whole existence [was] therefore based upon a preservation of balance through an inherent force of gravity." Finally, in Italy, while the king of Piedmont and the pope regained, and even enlarged, their territories, and while it was decided in principle that the kingdom of the Two Sicilies should be restored to the House of Bourbon, Austria was not only given Lombardy and Venetia but was permitted to extend its influence over the northern duchies of Parma, Modena, Lucca, and Tuscany. Here again the purpose was partly to keep Austrian strength in balance with that of the other powers and partly to place it in a position to make impossible a new French assault on Italy.

It was once the custom to regard the diplomats of the Congress of Vienna as reactionaries who wanted to turn the clock back and who flouted the principles of nationalism. Rather than accept these stereotypes, it would be more logical to think of them as men who had an enormously difficult job to do and who accomplished it in a way that satisfied the great majority of the politically conscious people affected by their decisions. In their work, they were often surprisingly enlightened: in their stipulation that all members of the Germanic Confederation should establish assemblies of estates, for instance; in their guarantee of Switzerland's neutrality and independence; and in their condemnation of the slave trade. In redrawing the map of Europe, they showed that they were not insensible to changes that had taken place since the beginning of the French

Revolution; and both the German and Italian settlements prove this. That they did not recognize or try to apply the principle of nationality should not seem strange. They felt that chaos would ensue if attempts were made to free the Italians or unite the Germans in 1815; and they were probably right. Finally, before the Vienna settlement is condemned, it should be noted that it did, in fact, provide a reasonable equilibrium among the Great Powers. It left no power seriously aggrieved and, thus, cannot be said to have contained in its provisions the seeds of a future major war. That in itself was a major accomplishment and deserves recognition.

The Hundred Days and the Second Peace of Paris   While the last details of the settlement were being worked out, the world was electrified by the news that Napoleon had escaped from his exile in Elba, had landed in France, and had seized the throne left vacant by Louis XVIII, who had fled at the first news of his coming. Bonaparte doubtless hoped to split the Allies and defeat them separately, but, if so, he was disappointed. The worst of the differences among the Allies were over before his adventure started; and his return restored the brotherhood in arms that defeated him at Leipzig in 1813. The Corsican, therefore, had only one hundred days of restored power, and their result was the crushing defeat at Waterloo on June 18, 1815, and a new and final exile on St. Helena. For France the consequences were even more serious, for Napoleon's last campaign destroyed most of what Talleyrand had accomplished at Vienna.

There was no longer any disposition on the part of the Allies to spare France the penalties usually imposed on defeated powers; nor were they much concerned about the feelings of Louis XVIII. That monarch was put back on the throne again, but this time over a smaller realm. The Second Peace of Paris (November 20, 1815) deprived France of a number of strategic posts in the north and east and reduced its over-all territory in such a way that it lost about half a million subjects. Moreover, it now had to pay a war indemnity of 700 million francs—by contemporary standards, a heavy burden—and to support an army of occupation for a minimum of three years. Despite all of Talleyrand's efforts at Vienna, his country was now isolated again and regarded with distrust and fear.

The Holy Alliance and the Concert of Europe   At the end of 1815 the powers signed two other engagements that had importance in the future: the Holy Alliance and the Quadruple Alliance.

The Holy Alliance was conceived by Alexander I and, in its original form, seems to have been an attempt to establish a new international order that would be based not on traditional diplomacy but on the principles of Christianity. Castlereagh refused to have anything to do with it. "The fact is," he wrote to his prime minister, "that the Emperor's mind is not completely sound." The Prussians and Austrians were less willing to offend Alexander by turning his project down; and, in the end, they signed, after Metternich had won some amendments in the text. As issued, the Holy Alliance announced that the "sublime truths taught by the eternal religion of God our Saviour" ought to guide not only the relations among nations but their domestic affairs as well. Henceforth, the treaty said, the signatories would consider themselves as delegates of Providence and "thinking of themselves in their relation to their subjects and armies as fathers of families, they will lead them, in the spirit with which they are animated, to protect Religion, Peace and Justice."

These last words were Metternich's addition to Alexander's original text. Their meaning was obscure, but their tone was suggestive. Here was an intimation of a kind of paternalism that promised to stifle and suppress freedom within the countries controlled by the three signatory powers and one that they might possibly seek to apply outside their boundaries as well.

The second engagement was the treaty of the Quadruple Alliance, signed on November 20, 1815. In this document, the four allied Great Powers undertook to use all their forces to prevent the general tranquillity from again being disturbed by France, to keep Napoleon and his family from the French throne, and to preserve France from new revolutionary convulsions. In addition, they agreed to hold periodic meetings "for the purpose of consulting upon their interests, or for the consideration of the measures which, at each of these periods, shall be considered the most salutary for the repose and prosperity of Nations and for the maintenance of the Peace of Europe."

Metternich's colleague, Friedrich von Gentz, who had served as secretary general of the Vienna Congress, may have had this alliance in mind when he wrote that the diplomatic negotiations of 1814 and 1815 had "the undeniable merit of having prepared the world for a more complete political structure." Back in the eighteenth century there had been some discussion among publicists of the idea of a federation or concert of Europe, although no one had taken any steps to realize it. With the signing of the Quadruple Alliance, the Concert of Europe became actual and operative. The Allied Powers—having just concluded a settlement that reconstructed the map of Europe according to the principles of compensation, legitimacy, and balance of power—now established themselves as a continuing European directorate, which would meet whenever necessary to see that their settlement was not endangered.

The only trouble was that there was no agreement among them about what was or was not a danger to their settlement or how far they were committed to take common action when revolutionary situations occurred.

FROM VIENNA TO THE REVOLUTIONS OF 1830

The Conference System   The postwar cooperation of the powers worked best as long as revolutionary France was its object. While the ambassadors of the occupying powers were sitting in Paris, holding weekly meetings to consider such things as projected laws of the French government, the provocative tactics of the Ultra-Royalists, and the contents of speeches made in the Chamber of Deputies, there were no important differences of opinion among them. It was only after 1818, when the occupation of France came to an end, and when other and more dangerous matters came to the fore, that serious disagreement arose, particularly between Great Britain on the one hand and the three signatories of the Holy Alliance on the other.

Signs of this appeared at the first major postwar conference, which was held at Aix-la-Chapelle in the autumn of 1818. This meeting was convened ostensibly to complete the settlement with France, by making a final adjustment of reparations and by authorizing the withdrawal of occupation troops. But the Russians took this opportunity to raise the question of the future of the alliance, now that France had apparently ceased to be a menace to the peace; and Tsar Alexander presented a memorandum to the conference in which he suggested that—given the dangerous temper in certain other areas of Europe—it might be advisable for the powers to clarify the nature of their existing engagements. They should make clear, he urged, that they were "bound in law and in fact" to a general association, the object of which was, first, to maintain the territorial settlement concluded at Vienna and, second, to guarantee all legitimate regimes existing at the present moment of time.

This proposal annoyed and disturbed the British. Castlereagh saw in Alexander's memorandum an attempt to substitute the vague but sweeping principles of the Holy Alliance for the carefully defined obligations of the Quadruple Alliance, and he objected. His government, he pointed out, was not prepared to honor engagements that it had never signed; and Britain's obligations, as laid down clearly in the treaty of the Quadruple Alliance, were simply to help prevent any new French attempt to disturb the peace. Alexander seemed to want to freeze the existing political situation by collecting pledges to support established power everywhere. No British government could give such a promise except in particular cases and even then only after considering the nature of the regime in question.

This was blunt enough to make Alexander withdraw his proposal; but, if he did so, it was not because he was persuaded that Castlereagh was right. At the beginning of 1820 he came back to his idea, this time with more determination. The occasion was a sudden explosion of revolutionary passion in Spain.

To call what happened in Spain in 1820 a liberal revolution is to attribute to liberalism a strength it did not possess in the Iberian peninsula. The revolution that began in January 1820 would more properly be described as a military revolt against a ruler who was stupid enough to neglect what should have been the strongest support of his throne, his army. Ferdinand VII, who had been restored to the throne by the Allies in 1814, was one of the least gifted rulers in Europe, and his only accomplishment since his accession had been to alienate completely the subjects of his American empire, who had declared their independence. The king had organized a large army to win his colonies back again, but he housed it in unspeakable quarters, fed and clothed it abominably, and paid it inadequately and infrequently. The result was a rising in Cadiz, where units were being assembled for shipment overseas. This was supported by riots and demonstrations in Madrid, Barcelona, and Saragossa, and the king—in a desperate attempt to get control of the situation—felt it necessary to proclaim the constitution of 1812 (a document that had been issued by the Cortes during the fight against Napoleon, was saturated with liberal and even democratic ideas, and had been revoked in 1814).

This was enough to bring the tsar back into the field; he now insisted that the Quadruple Alliance must intervene in Spain to check the tide of revolution before it engulfed all Europe. Once more Castlereagh objected. In a now famous memorandum of May 5, 1820, he warned his fellow allies that the original purpose of their alliance had been to maintain the peace of Europe and the balance of power. Great Britain would always be prepared to cooperate in fulfilling this, but it would neither intervene itself in the domestic affairs of other European states nor view with indifference the intervention of other powers. "The principle," he added tartly, "of one state interfering in the internal affairs of another in order to enforce obedience to the governing authority is always a question of the greatest moral, as well as political, delicacy.... To generalize such a principle, to think of reducing it to a system, or to impose it as an obligation, is a scheme utterly impracticable and objectionable."

But Alexander *wanted* to generalize the principle, and everything that was happening around him in 1820 convinced him that he was right. Not only did the Spanish disorders continue, but in July there was a military insurrection in Naples that forced the king to grant a constitution and gave enormous impetus to revolutionary agitation throughout the Italian peninsula; in August, a revolt broke out in Portugal as well. Metternich too was alarmed. If he had tried in the past to avoid siding with either Alexander or Castlereagh, he now urged that the powers concert on measures to meet the European emergency. At the conference at Troppau in October, he presented a memorandum, already approved by the Russians and the Prussians, which laid down the principle that changes brought about by revolutionary action would not be accepted as legal by the powers, and asserted the right of the powers to intervene wherever necessary to put such changes down.

Castlereagh had refused to go to Troppau, and he refused now to adhere to this so-called Troppau Protocol. This did not deter the three eastern powers from adjourning to Laibach, where they authorized the Austrian army to intervene in Naples, to restore the witless and treacherous Ferdinand I, and to revoke the constitution that had been imposed on him. The Austrians had no difficulty in executing this assignment or, a few months later, in intervening in Piedmont to put down a revolution that had broken out there in March 1821.

Successful in Italy, the eastern powers were determined to act in the same manner in Spain, and here they received the support of the French government, which, after the murder of the king's nephew, the Duke of Berry, in February 1820 (see pp. 70–71), had become almost fanatically conservative and found it both congenial and advantageous to collaborate with the Holy Alliance in suppressing disorders so close to their own borders. The Spanish affair was regulated at the conference of Verona, which met in October 1822. Castlereagh was now dead, but his arguments were restated by the Duke of Wellington, who staunchly opposed any intervention in Spanish affairs. The conference nevertheless concluded its labors by empowering the French government to restore order in Spain; and, in April 1823, Europe once more saw French armies on the march, as a force of 100,000 men under the Duke of Angoulême crossed the southern frontier. They met no serious resistance; within six months, Ferdinand VII was back on the throne and Spain was in the grip of a wave of savage reaction.

There were no more of the periodic conferences provided for in the treaty of the Quadruple Alliance, for the British, defeated at Verona, decided not to be represented at future meetings of this nature. This did not mean that Britain had seceded from the Concert of Europe. We shall see, later in this chapter, that her governments were willing to meet with the other powers on an *ad hoc* basis, when the peace of Europe was really threatened. But they had no desire to remain part of what now appeared to have degenerated into a witch-hunting organization.

Moreover, if their wishes were disregarded at Verona, they soon demonstrated that the Holy Alliance could not hope always to have its way. There can be no doubt that Alexander and Metternich would have liked to restore the New World to Spain. But the British, who had important trading connections with the former Spanish-American colonies and had poured £22,000,000 of private investments into them between 1821 and 1825, were not anxious to see Spanish control restored. Castlereagh's successor, George Canning, made it clear to all interested parties, therefore, that while Spain doubtless had the right to attempt to reassert its rule, Great Britain would oppose attempts by the other powers to intervene. Canning's attitude was given formidable support when the United States government announced, in the so-called Monroe Doctrine (December 1823), that any attempt on the part of the Holy Alliance to extend their system to any portion of the Western Hemisphere would be regarded as "dangerous to our peace and safety" and as "the manifestation of an unfriendly disposition towards the United States." Even before this, however, British firmness had made the French uncertain about the implications of their involvement in Spanish affairs, and Canning had been clever enough to discern this. In a series of conversations with the French ambassador Prince Jules de Polignac in October 1823, he secured an explicit abjuration of any French intention of intervening by force in the New World, giving in return an ambiguous, and indeed disingenuous, statement of possible British interest in a conference on Spain's American problems. The record of the London talks, which was known as the Polignac Memorandum, was soon bruited abroad and virtually ended the crisis, assuring the independence of Latin America.

The incident showed that the power of the Holy Alliance stopped at the water's edge. Moreover, despite its victories in Spain and Italy, it had other limitations which became apparent in the course of the revolution that had broken out in Greece.

The Greek Rising   The bloody events that took place in Greece during the 1820s marked the opening of a long series of disorders in the Balkans and the Near East which were made inevitable by the internal disintegration of the Ottoman Empire. At the beginning of the nineteenth century that empire still stretched from Asia Minor across Egypt and the southern shores of the Mediterranean to Tunis and Algeria and, to the northwest, across the Dardanelles to the southern borders of the Austrian and Russian empires. In Europe alone the Turks still claimed dominance over about 238,000 square miles of territory with some eight million inhabitants, most of them Christians. But in many parts of this great empire, the sultan's authority had become more nominal than real. Mehemet Ali in Egypt and Ali Pasha of Janina in Albania, while still recognizing his suzerainty, had become virtually independent; and their example was emulated by other local governors and military commanders.

This was one of the chief reasons for the troubles that began in the sultan's European provinces. Had Turkish administration been more efficient, the Christian subjects of those provinces would have had little to complain about. Legally they were allowed to observe their own religion and to educate their children without interference; they were permitted a not inconsiderable amount of self-government; and they were exempt from military service. But the decline of the imperial system was accompanied by a cessation of even a pretense at economic improvement and this made the subject peoples restive, while at the same time increasing their opposition to the numerous discriminatory taxes that they had to pay. Even worse, since the government at Constantinople could no longer always control its local governors or its garrison troops—the redoubtable but increasingly undisciplined Janissaries—the subject peoples were often harassed by these officials, who exacted special levies under duress or resorted to pointless outbursts of brutality against Christians and Jews.

It was resentment against the conduct of the Janissary garrison in Belgrade that touched off the first Christian revolt in the Balkans, when the Serbian peasants rose under Kara (Black) George in 1804 and expelled their oppressors. The Turks fought back, and, in 1813, succeeded in driving Kara George into exile and restoring order. But the fight was taken up again two years later under the leadership of Milos Obrenovitch and, although success was jeopardized by the beginning of a feud between the new leader and the old (one that was to last for a century), Serbian freedom was attained within two years. Its nature and limitations were not spelled out until the early 1830s, when Milos was acknowledged by the Turks to be hereditary prince of Serbia and when, in return for an annual tribute and some garrison rights in its fortresses, Serbia was recognized as an autonomous state.

All of this attracted little attention in the West. But when the Greeks followed the Serbian example, the European powers could not be so disinterested.

The Greek revolt, like that of the Serbs, arose in part from exasperation over the maladministration of Turkish officials; but there was an additional factor at work here. The leading spirits in the revolutionary movement were the merchants of the Aegean islands and the so-called *capitani*—commanders of ships or of bands of brigands in the mountains of the Morea. During the period of the French Revolution they had come into touch with French ideas—because of their activities in the carrying trade (Greek ships carried Russian grains to France during the Terror and after) or, later, because Napoleon found it useful to maintain contact with fighting bands in the Balkans—and they had been profoundly influenced by them. As was true in other parts of Europe, French influence stimulated national self-consciousness, which was further inflamed by the writings of propagandists and scholars, like the martyr poet Rhigas, killed by the Turks in 1798, and Koraes, the linguistic reformer who sought to awaken Greek pride in their national heritage, and by the activities of the secret society *Hetairia Philiké,* which worked for the expulsion of the Turks from Europe and which, by the end of 1820, claimed a membership of more than a hundred thousand.

In March 1821 the head of this society, a former general in the Russian army called Prince Alexander Ypsilanti, attempted to start a general rising against the

Turks in what is now Rumania. This was a fiasco, but it inspired imitation. A month later, the peasants of the Morea rose and slaughtered the local Turkish troops and officials, thus starting the struggle that was not to stop until Greek independence was won.

The long fight aroused widespread enthusiasm throughout western Europe. It made an immediate appeal to an age that had a vivid interest in antiquity and that was too ready to romanticize the conflict. Only a few years before, Lord Byron had sadly described the Greeks as a fallen race

> Trembling beneath the scourge of Turkish hand,
> From birth to death enslaved; in word, in deed, unmann'd.[1]

Now the poet seems to have concluded that the spirit of Marathon was revived and went himself to join and, as it turned out, to die at Missolonghi for the cause of freedom, and, in spirit at least, thousands of other young men went with him.

At a later date, another poet, Pushkin, wrote bitterly: "This enthusiasm of all cultured nations for Greece is unforgiveable childishness. The Jesuits have told us all that twaddle about Themistocles and Pericles, and so we imagine that the shabby nation of robbers and traders are their legitimate successors." Pushkin was not the only one who, in time, became disillusioned with a struggle that was marked by savagery on both sides. The best-known atrocity of the war was the massacre at Chios in April 1822, where the Turkish governor systematically executed the captured population, which, after the bloodletting, had been reduced from 120,000 to 30,000. But even before this, when the Turks had surrendered at Tripolitsa, 12,000 of them had been hanged, impaled, and roasted alive by their Greek captors, while 200 Jews, also in the town, had been killed, some of them by crucifixion.

The war was of interest to the Great Powers, not only because of its threat to the general peace but because all of them except Prussia had economic and political interests in the Near East. But, for most of the powers, the Greek affair was so complicated that they were hesitant to take a firm position with respect to it; and in the end it was the British who took the initiative, when George Canning announced Britain's recognition of Greek belligerency in March 1823.

If Canning had been thinking only in economic terms, he might well have sided with the Turks. His action seems to have been taken for three reasons. In the first place, by 1823 popular enthusiasm for the Greeks, inflamed by the agitations of dozens of Philhellenic societies and given new impetus by Byron's romantic death, was so strong in England that the government had to do something for them if it wanted to stay in office. In the second place, Canning expected that sooner or later the Russians would have to come to the aid of Greece and that, if they were alone in doing so, Greece might become a Russian satellite and the Turkish Empire might be destroyed. He wished to forestall both eventualities, neither of which would be in accord with British interests. Finally, the

---

[1] *Childe Harold's Pilgrimage,* canto II, stanza 74.

Eugene Delacroix: ''Greece Expiring on the Ruins of Missolonghi,'' 1827. (Musée des Beaux Arts, Bordeaux. Photo: A. Danvers)

British statesman seems to have wished to embarrass the Holy Alliance and, especially, to annoy Metternich, for whom he had conceived a strong personal dislike.

He certainly succeeded in the last objective. Metternich did not want to see Russia intervene in Greece because this would increase its influence in the Balkans and thus alter the balance of power. Moreover, as he told the tsar, Russian aid to Greece would be a betrayal of the Holy Alliance and a repudiation of the Troppau Protocol and would weaken the security of thrones everywhere, for—whatever one thought of the sultan—he was a legitimate ruler, while the Greeks were undeniably rebels. This argument deterred Alexander from action but had less effect upon his successor Nicholas, who took the throne in December 1825. By that date, it appeared likely that a strong Egyptian-Turkish army under Ibrahim Pasha, which had landed in the Morea in February 1825, might quell the revolt; and this inflamed Russian public opinion, which was pro-Greek for religious and other reasons. Despite Metternich's pleas, Nicholas gradually yielded to the popular temper, detached himself temporarily from the Holy Alliance, joined the British in calling upon the sultan to give the Greeks autonomy, and, when this was refused, concluded an alliance with Britain and France (July 6, 1827), with the declared object of securing Greek independence. The Turks fought on; but, in October, a joint Anglo-French-Russian fleet under the command of the British admiral Codrington encountered the bulk of the Egyptian navy off Navarino on the west coast of the Morea and destroyed it. The sultan still refused to yield, perhaps deceived by indications of differences among his opponents. This merely encouraged the Russians, supported by the French but not by the English, to open hostilities on the land as well. The war that followed dragged on for two years, with French troops clearing the Morea of Ibrahim's forces while one Russian army invaded Asia Minor and a second crossed the Balkan mountains and, on August 14, 1829, pushed its way into Adrianople. The Turkish government thereupon sued for peace.

Russo-Turkish relations were adjusted by the Treaty of Adrianople of September 14, 1829. The Turks were forced to give up control of the mouths of the Danube, to cede part of the Black Sea coast to Russia, and to pay a large indemnity within a period of ten years. Pending complete payment, the Danubian principalities (covering the area now called Rumania) were to be occupied by Russian troops. Moreover, all Moslems were to be expelled from the principalities and all Turkish fortresses to be destroyed. In effect, these measures spelled the end of Turkish influence in Rumania, which now became practically a Russian protectorate.

With respect to Greece, the treaty bound the Turkish government to accept the decisions of an ambassadorial conference in London, which had already tentatively agreed that Greece must be accorded autonomy. In the course of 1830 this grant was changed to one of outright independence, but the attempt by the conference to define the boundaries of the new state was rejected by the Greeks. Haggling among the interested parties continued until March 1832, when the powers extended the boundaries of the country and, at the same time, elected Prince Otto of Bavaria as Greece's first king.

The liberation of Greece made the first significant change in the map of Europe since the Congress of Vienna. For liberals this was heartening, for it had been accomplished in the face of Metternich's desire to freeze the status quo, and it seemed to represent a victory over legitimacy and reaction.

From the standpoint of relations among the Great Powers, the long struggle in Greece had subjected the Holy Alliance to a considerable amount of strain; while Russia's increased strength in eastern Europe as a result of the treaty of Adrianople aroused misgivings in Vienna, as it did in London, and caused anxious speculation about its effects on the balance of power.

FROM 1830 TO 1848

The Revolution in France and Its Consequences   In the last week of July 1830 civil war broke out in Paris and, at the end of three days of fighting, the Bourbon king Charles X was driven from power and the Duke of Orleans took the throne with the title Louis Philippe, *roi des Français*.[2] It was rumored that when the news reached St. Petersburg, Nicholas I said to his aides: "Gentlemen, saddle your horses! Revolution rules again in Paris!" In point of fact, even though what had happened in Paris made a breach in the Vienna settlement and flew in the face of the principle of legitimacy and the Troppau Protocol, no one marched against France. For the revolution in Paris inspired revolutions elsewhere, and soon the members of the Holy Alliance were occupied with troubles closer to their own doorsteps: Russia in Poland, Prussia in the German states, Austria in Italy. Unable to oppose the new French king effectively, therefore, they found it expedient to recognize him, although they did it rather sulkily.

The July revolution destroyed the system of absolutism that Charles X had been seeking to consolidate, and France became a state in which the wealthier bourgeoisie exercised political power. Two years after the events in Paris, a similar development took place in England, where the upper middle class was enfranchised by the passing of the Great Reform Bill.[3] Ideologically, Britain and France were now brought closer together and, at the same time, the difference between them and the members of the Holy Alliance became more pronounced. The result of the events of these years, in short, seemed to be to divide the Great Powers into two tightly organized diplomatic combinations that were firmly opposed to each other. This division impressed contemporary observers, Lord Melbourne, for instance, remarking that "the three and the two think differently and therefore they act differently."

It is important, however, not to make too much of this division or to regard the two combinations as cohesive and mutually exclusive leagues. In the years between the July revolution and 1848, ideological differences were ignored as often as they were honored; on occasion, Metternich and Nicholas could cooperate with Palmerston as effectively as Metternich and Alexander had cooperated with Castlereagh; and, when dangerous crises arose, the powers demonstrated that the Concert of Europe could still work. This can be illustrated by a brief consideration of their handling of the Belgian revolution.

The Belgian Revolution   The Belgian people had been placed under Dutch rule in 1815 as a matter of international convenience. Their own wishes were not considered and neither was the fact that there was little community of interest between them and the Dutch. The two countries had had a different historical evolution. They differed in language and in religion—the Belgians being predominantly Roman Catholic, the Dutch militantly Calvinist. Economically, their interests were opposed also, for the Dutch were an agricultural and commercial

---

[2] A more detailed account of the background and course of the revolution in France will be found in Chapter 3.

[3] For details and analysis, see Chapter 4.

people, holding to free trade, while Belgium was the home of a flourishing but still young industry, with most of the leading industrialists believing in tariff protection. In making the Belgians subjects of the king of the Netherlands, then, the powers succeeded in alienating the liberal intellectuals who took pride in their country's past, the Catholic clergy, and the manufacturers, as well as other groups, including those who would have liked to join the civil service but found all the best positions filled by Dutch officials.

Their resentment grew as years passed; and, in the late 1820s, they received increasing popular support, for the peasants were hurt by a series of bad harvests and the industrial workers suffered from a slow rise in the cost of living that was not balanced by any increase in pay. The crisis of overproduction which hit the textile industry at Verviers, Liège, and Tournai in the spring of 1830 probably had the effect of heightening passions further, since all economic troubles were, naturally if unreasonably, blamed on the Dutch. All that was needed now was something to touch off the explosion, and the rising in Paris did that. On August 25, 1830, rioting began in Brussels. Troops were brought into the city but could not restore order and, in September, they were again driven out. By that time, the revolutionary agitation had spread to other towns. The king, William I, who had taken a completely intransigent position at the outset, now tried to make concessions. It was too late. A provisional government had already been formed and, on October 4, it declared Belgium independent.

On October 1, the tsar of Russia had informed his allies that he was prepared to send an army of 60,000 men to extirpate the revolutionary infection and return Belgium to Dutch control; it was known that the king of Prussia had placed his army on a war footing, presumably for the same purpose. This raised the threat of war between the Great Powers. For, as the veteran Talleyrand, who had just been sent to London as ambassador, pointed out to the British government, France would not tolerate any intervention in a country so close to her own borders. The British government was sufficiently alarmed by this communication to urge the Eastern Powers to refrain from any action until representatives of all Great Powers could meet in London to discuss Belgian affairs.

The Eastern Powers accepted the invitation, hoping perhaps to be able to win the British over to their point of view. But the man who was now responsible for British policy was Henry Temple, Viscount Palmerston (1784–1865), who regretted the dissolution of the union of the Low Countries, which he considered "advantageous to the general interests of Europe," but felt that it was too late to restore it. As his long and notable career was to demonstrate, Palmerston had many faults as a diplomat, including an excessive fondness for sensation, an inclination to cocksureness, and a tendency to bully weaker opponents. But these were matched by quick and accurate judgment, rapidity of decision, force of will, an incredible capacity for work, and great skill in negotiation. He displayed these latter qualities now as—disavowing partisan motives and speaking in the name of peace and the balance of power—he pointed out to the powers that an attempt to restore Belgium to Dutch control would be unrealistic and, from the standpoint of Great-Power harmony, dangerous, and that it would be better to admit the fact of Belgian independence under conditions that would, as far as possible, repair the breach in the system of 1815.

Palmerston was aided in his efforts by the sudden rising of the Poles in November 1830 and by disorders in Germany and Italy, which began at the end of the year and reduced the ability of any of the Eastern Powers to act in the west. By the end of December 1830, at any rate, all powers had agreed to Belgian independence. There were many other problems that had to be solved before the affair was regulated definitively; and the agitation of annexationist groups in France and the stubborn efforts of the Dutch king to reimpose his will on his former subjects by force of arms caused ugly crises. But the first of these was met by the combination of Palmerston's firmness and Louis Philippe's moderation, while William I's military efforts were finally checked by a French intervention authorized by the powers. The important thing is that, despite frequent flurries of anxiety, the powers held together and made joint decisions.

In the end, by the treaty of November 15, 1831 (ratified in May 1832 but not accepted by the Dutch king until April 1839), Belgium was admitted to the family of nations as an independent state and with a ruler, Leopold of Saxe-Coburg, of its own choosing. In keeping with Palmerston's desire to make good the damage done to the Vienna settlement, the new nation was established as a neutral state. The old barrier fortresses were demolished, and the Great Powers guaranteed that they would all take action against any state that violated Belgian integrity. Whether this arrangement was as effective a means of securing this important strategical area as the continued union of the Low Countries would have been is debatable. It did not, in any case, discourage the aggressor in 1914.

The Italian, German, and Polish Risings   The willingness of the Eastern Powers to agree to Belgian independence was doubtless made easier by the restraint displayed by the British and French governments in the case of the disorders in southern and central Europe.

In Italy the suppression of the revolts of 1820–1821 had not put an end to revolutionary agitation. The number of secret societies had increased, and there was greater coordination between them. At the end of 1830 disorders began in central Italy. In a kind of chain reaction, revolution spread from Modena to Parma and to the papal states, bringing provisional governments and new charters in its train. But the revolutionary movement was not yet so strong that it could defeat the power of Austria without outside help. The rebels expected aid from France, but, in the end, Louis Philippe's government agreed with the English view that it would be dangerous for France either to intervene in Italy or to try to prevent Austria from doing so. The Western Powers, in short, concluded that peace and the balance of power would best be served by allowing Metternich to enforce the 1814 arrangements in Italy, which he proceeded to do.

The radical movement in Germany was suppressed in the same way, without Western interference or even much evidence of Western interest (see pp. 56–57). As for Poland, in 1831 as on several later occasions, the Poles received the sympathy of the West but no tangible assistance.

Russian Poland had been transformed by Tsar Alexander I into a country with undeniably liberal institutions. Bound to Russia by personal union (the tsar was the king of Poland), it had a constitution that provided for a bicameral parliament, religious toleration, and civil liberties. Polish was the official lan-guage, and all official positions had to be filled by Poles. The Poles, in fact, had everything they might reasonably expect except their independence; but it was independence that the politically conscious class wanted more than any-thing else, and without it, they took no satisfaction in their other privileges. Their diet began to disregard the tsar's wishes and to criticize the policies of his ministers. They fell increasingly under the influence of Western liberal and democratic ideas, which alarmed Alexander and his successor Nicholas and led them to restrict some of the liberties previously granted. By 1830 tempers had been brought to the breaking point; and in November of that year a group of discontented officers and university students started a revolt in Warsaw. It would probably have come to nothing if the Grand Duke Constantine, brother of the tsar and commander of the Polish army, had acted promptly. But Constantine was a man of indecision who was moved, moreover, by sympathy for the Polish cause. He tried to negotiate, and this sign of weakness strengthened the rebels and forced Constantine, in the end, to flee the city.

The usual succession of events followed: the calling of a provisional govern-ment, attempts at a compromise solution by moderates among the rebels, the ascendancy of the radicals, defiance of the imperial government, a declaration of independence, and counteraction by the imperial power. A Russian army under Diebitch, the conqueror of Adrianople, entered Poland in February 1831. The rebels had expected aid from the Western Powers. But neither Palmerston nor Louis Philippe approved their action or wished Europe to be torn by further complications. The only ally the Poles found was Asiatic cholera which swept across the whole of Europe in 1831. Cholera killed both Diebitch and Constan-tine, as well as thousands of soldiers on both sides of the line. It slowed the Russian advance, but it could not check it; and, meanwhile, the rebels fell to fighting among themselves and ruined what chances they might have had. On September 8, Diebitch's successor, the hard-bitten and resolute Paskévitch, was able to send Nicholas the message, "Warsaw is at Your Majesty's feet!"

The Polish revolt of 1830–1831 was a revolt of aristocrats and intellectuals. They had given little thought to the needs and desires of the Polish masses, who in turn had remained apathetic to the revolutionary cause. The result of the ill-considered Warsaw rising was the destruction of the autonomy that Poland had enjoyed since 1815 and the subjection of the country to military rule. While hundreds were put to death or imprisoned, thousands of intellectuals fled to Paris and London, where they lived in poverty and plotted new risings. It was in exile that a new messianic Polish nationalism was born under the inspiration of Joachim Lelewel, a historian and publicist, and Adam Mickiewicz, whose poetry, widely read in France, Germany, and England, created the picture of the Poles as a chosen people destined to lead Europe to freedom and democracy.

This had no immediate consequences. With the liquidation of the Polish revolt, calm was restored within the confines of Europe proper, except for the confusion caused by the increasingly complicated political situation in Portugal and Spain, in each of which there were, at the beginning of the 1830s, rival claimants to the throne. All that need be said here of politics in the Iberian peninsula is that the Eastern Powers found it expedient to refrain from inviting trouble with England or France by seeking to meddle there.

Two Egyptian Crises   Some final rays of light may be thrown on the workings of Great-Power politics in this period by a brief consideration of two crises in the Near East, each of which was precipitated by the pasha of Egypt, Mehemet Ali.

Mehemet was certainly one of the ablest rulers of this period. Originally an Albanian trader, he had entered Turkish military service at the time of Napoleon's expedition to Egypt and had risen rapidly, being made pasha by the sheiks of Cairo in 1805. In this capacity, he had rebuilt Alexandria and constructed the canal between that city and the Nile; he had carried through an extensive series of agricultural and medical reforms; and, finally, with French assistance, he had modernized the Egyptian army. It is understandable that a man who had risen so high should want to rise higher and that one who had lavished care on a military establishment should wish to test its efficiency. Mehemet Ali had long lusted after the control of Palestine, Syria, and Arabia; in the latter part of 1831 he set out to get them and sent his redoubtable son Ibrahim to invest Acre, an enterprise in which he was joined by the Emir of Lebanon, Bashir II, who also hoped to enlarge his domain and secure its independence. Sultan Mahmud II, long wearied by Mehemet Ali's complaints about the inadequate compensation that he had received for his past services to the empire, declared the pasha a rebel and set out to crush him. During the course of the year 1832, however, the Turkish forces reeled from one defeat to another and, in December, Egyptian and Lebanese troops threatened to overrun all of Asia Minor and to take Constantinople as well.

Metternich recognized the dangers implicit in this situation and tried to bring the Great Powers together to protect the legitimate ruler of Turkey against his rebellious vassal. But the British government was curiously uncertain concerning their interest in the area, and the French sympathized with Mehemet Ali; so Metternich's efforts were unavailing. The sultan appealed in vain to Britain for help and then, in desperation, turned to the Russians. Nicholas responded at once and dispatched an army and a fleet to the Porte. By May 1833, thanks to this intervention, peace had been restored, on terms that left Syria in Mehemet Ali's hands; and—what was infinitely more important—the Turks and the Russians had signed the treaty of Unkiar Skelessi (July 8, 1833), promising each other mutual assistance in case of attacks by other states, but agreeing (in a secret article) that Turkey need not send military aid to Russia in time of war provided she close the straits of the Dardanelles to all foreign naval units.

When this became known to the Western Powers, it was feared that the secret clause assured the Russians of exclusive freedom in the straits and that, indeed, there might be other secret clauses with other damaging concessions. In fact, neither of these fears was justified, the tsar having been persuaded by his foreign minister Nesselrode that any special privileges he might exact from the sultan would not be recognized by the other powers. The real importance of Unkiar Skelessi, in the eyes of Nicholas, was that it promised him a kind of protectorate over the Turks, who would now presumably consult him first on matters of importance and follow his advice.

But even this was a dubious gain, which attracted the liveliest suspicion among the other powers, and Nicholas was soon ready to divest himself of it, a fact that became clear during the second Egyptian crisis. In 1839, Sultan Mahmud II, warned by the build-up of Egyptian forces that Mehemet Ali was planning a new attack, sought to take the initiative. Attached to the staff of the army he sent against the Egyptians was a young Prussian captain named Helmuth von Moltke, who was to direct the victory of Prussian arms against Austria in 1866 and France in 1870. But the Turkish commanders paid no attention to Moltke's advice, with the result that, when they met Ibrahim Pasha's army at Nezib in June, they were utterly smashed. Once more the Egyptians stood at the gates of Constantinople. The situation of 1833 seemed about to be repeated.

This, however, was not true. The British government was no longer as aloof as it had been in 1833. Since that date, successful experiments with steam navigation on the Red Sea and the Euphrates had increased the importance of the overland routes to India in British eyes; and for this reason Palmerston was determined that neither Russia nor Mehemet Ali, whom Palmerston regarded as a French pawn, should be allowed to dominate them. The British foreign secretary wanted action by the Concert of Europe to check Mehemet Ali and to replace Unkiar Skelessi with a general guarantee of Turkish independence.

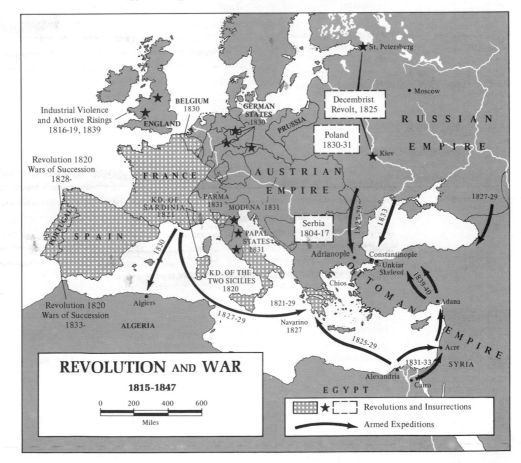

Metternich agreed with this idea as a matter of course. What is perhaps more surprising is that the tsar did too. But Nicholas seems to have reached the conclusion that Unkiar Skelessi was a burdensome arrangement which, if ever applied, would simply unite the other powers against him. In September he concluded an agreement with the British to make Mehemet Ali give up most of his gains and, once hostilities had ceased, to close both the Bosphorus and the Dardanelles to warships of all powers. To this the Austrians and the Prussians adhered.

After that it was simply a matter of getting the French to go along. This was not easy, for boulevard sentiment, tired of Louis Philippe's lackluster foreign policy and longing for Napoleonic triumphs (see pp. 81–82), was strongly pro-Egyptian, and the government in power, which was headed by Adolphe Thiers, dared not run counter to it. The other powers, therefore, acted alone. This touched off an ugly war scare as Paris mobs called for war against England and—rather illogically—against the Germans; but by October, when Thiers fell from office, passions had subsided and the danger had passed. Meanwhile, the powers had sent an ultimatum to Mehemet Ali, and that doughty ruler had decided that discretion was the better part of valor. He had to restore Syria, Crete, and Arabia, which he had conquered, to Turkey and to suffer the additional humiliation of seeing his Lebanese ally Bashir deposed; but he was confirmed in his possession of Egypt, at the price of an annual tribute to the sultan. Finally, in July 1841, the powers signed the famous Straits Convention, which stipulated that the straits of the Bosphorus and the Dardanelles must be closed to foreign warships while Turkey was at peace. This was more to Britain's advantage than to Russia's, but the tsar ratified the treaty; and the long series of Near Eastern troubles came to an end.

The Great Power Consensus   The last years before the explosion of 1848 were relatively free from international complications. From the standpoint of diplomatic history, the most arresting development was a curious tendency toward a reversal of alliances. On the one hand, as a result of political differences in Spain and economic friction everywhere, Britain and France grew less friendly, and Louis Philippe began to draw closer to Austria. Thus, we find his minister Guizot writing to Metternich in May 1847: "France is now disposed to a policy of conservatism." On the other hand, the most conservative of the powers sought the friendship of Britain. After trying in 1840 to induce Britain to become a member of the Holy Alliance (an offer that Palmerston adroitly sidestepped), Tsar Nicholas visited England in 1844 and urged that Russia and Britain pursue a common policy in Eastern affairs in the future.

This development should be enough to show that it is unwise to think of the powers as being divided into liberal and conservative combinations. The ideological differences, while present, were not as important as one might suppose. The diplomatic alignments that existed were fluid; single powers shifted their positions and their influence at crucial moments, when their interests were threatened or war seemed possible. And they were able to do so because, despite all their differences, there was a remarkable consensus among them.

With the possible exception of France, who did not dare admit her uniqueness, all powers accepted the balance of power—that is, the territorial arrangements made at Vienna and the broader principle that no single state should be allowed to increase its possessions except with the consent of the others. And acceptance of this implied certain other things: a high degree of self-restraint on the part of single powers; a willingness to accept the validity of existing treaties; a willingness—when single powers sought unilateral aggrandizement—to participate in concerted action to restrain them.

In their dealings with each other in the period between the Congress of Vienna and the revolutions of 1848, the Great Powers observed these rules. Liberal opinion in France would have welcomed open support of the Poles in 1830 or of Mehemet Ali in 1840; liberal opinion in England would have been enthusiastic if the British government had given aid to the rebels in the Romagna in 1831. But, on those occasions, the governments accepted the risk of losing public support at home in order to avoid embroiling the whole European system. Tsar Nicholas might well have asked a higher price for his aid to Turkey in 1833 and he might have insisted on acting alone in the Near East in 1840. He did not do so because he quite genuinely viewed unilateral action with reprobation.

It may be difficult for us, living as we do in a more lawless age, to believe that the powers were sincere in the respect they paid to treaties. But even in 1914 the world was shocked when a statesman referred to a specific treaty as a scrap of paper; and in the period from 1815 to 1848 it would have been even more so. In these years, at any rate, the powers did not lightly break their pledged word.

Finally, there was a general willingness on the part of the powers to share in the effort to maintain the peace and the balance. This was true even of Great Britain, whose geographical position and world-wide interests made her connection with Europe more tenuous than that of other powers. In 1852, Lord John Russell could say with both pride and accuracy: "We are connected, and have been for more than a century, with the general system of Europe, and any territorial increase of one power, any aggrandizement which disturbs the general balance of power in Europe ... could not be a matter of indifference to this country...."

It was because other powers, too, could not view with indifference changes in the European system that they had established at Vienna in 1815 that the Concert of Europe was a reality in this period and the general peace was maintained.

Chapter 2 THE EASTERN POWERS: ABSOLUTISM AND ITS LIMITATIONS

ABSOLUTISM AND ITS APOLOGISTS

When the exigencies of foreign policy required it, the members of the Holy Alliance could compromise with liberalism and revolution, at least to the extent of cooperating with the liberal powers, Britain and France, and even of accepting revolutionary *faits accomplis,* as in the case of Belgian independence. But within their own national boundaries, or in areas that they effectively controlled, they tolerated no compromise of any kind. The domestic policies of the Russian and Austrian empires and the kingdom of Prussia were marked by inflexible opposition to revolution; and a good part of the energies of their administrations was devoted to hunting down real or suspected revolutionaries and imprisoning, exiling, or executing them. It was in the eastern empires, for example, that secret police systems attained their fullest development and their greatest influence, with chiefs who stood at the elbows of their sovereigns and participated in the most intimate councils of state.

But fear of revolution went further than persecution of rebels and conspirators. It also involved reverence of existing institutions simply because they existed and reprobation of novelty simply because it was new. It involved opposition to change because change subverted the established order, to speculation because it led to change, and to learning because it led to speculation. "Too much learning kills character," wrote the reactionary Prussian squire Marwitz. It was responsible for

the war of the have-nots against property, of industry against agriculture, of the mobile against stability, of crass materialism against God's estab-

36

lished order, of [illusory] gain against right, of the present against the past and the future, of the individual against the family, of speculators and counting-desks against fields and trades, of science and puffed-up talent against virtue and honorable character.

Here is the true voice of reaction. Gone were the days when monarchs patronized scholars and a Prussian king was proud to be the friend of so completely subversive a writer as Voltaire. To stand in the good graces of the courts and the ruling classes of the eastern empires, a writer had to compose elaborate justifications of what he saw around him or fulsome panegyrics on the past.

The modern reader will find little stimulation in the works of the men who wrote under these conditions, with the possible exception of those of Joseph de Maistre (1753–1821). This talented writer was a Savoyard who served for fourteen years as Sardinian envoy to the court of St. Petersburg. His essays bear the hallmark of the romantic school in their repudiation of reason, their respect for tradition, and their veneration of established religion. But their most arresting characteristic is the passion that animates them, as de Maistre pours vituperation on the presumption of men who seek to lay impious hands on a civil order that he believes to have been sanctioned by God. To de Maistre, opposition to constituted authority was not merely a political crime; it was an act of blasphemy. The high incidence of civil disobedience convinced him that man was too wicked for freedom and absolutism was the only means of holding sinful arrogance in check. He did not hesitate to argue that the public executioner should be honored as the protector of social order and that war should be accepted as a divine institution designed to purge and punish the unregenerate.

In his own time de Maistre was probably admired less than the Swiss theorist Karl Ludwig von Haller (1768–1854), whose *Restoration of Political Science* became a kind of political Bible in the German courts. This dreary treatise had none of the brilliance or fire that one finds in de Maistre, a fact that probably enhanced its merit in the eyes of its readers. It expressed the political ideas of the eastern courts perfectly by holding up as an ideal a state established on the basis of romantic feudalism and Christian piety, with an absolute king as God's vicegerent ruling over subjects who had no rights except those he gave them of his own free will, a state, moreover, in which nothing new ever happened and nothing old was ever changed.

Haller's perfect society, in short, was authoritarian and completely immobile; and this was the goal of the ruling classes of the eastern empires. But, in the long run, *quieta non movere* is not a very practical principle of politics. Censorship, thought control, and police persecution cannot successfully destroy all new ideas; and, in the period from 1815 to 1848, there were lots of new ideas and new forces at work beneath the surface in Russia, Prussia, and Austria.

THE RUSSIAN EMPIRE TO 1848

The Land and the People   Thanks to the persistent policy of territorial expansion followed by every tsar since the days of Ivan the Terrible, the Russian empire in 1815 stretched from Poland, Courland, and Finland in the west to

Siberia and the banks of the Amur in the Far East, and from the Arctic Ocean in the north to the shores of the Black, Caspian, and Aral seas in the south. Even if Finland, annexed after the Russo-Swedish war of 1808–1809, and the kingdom of Poland, as defined at Vienna in 1815, were excluded, this was a vast and potentially powerful realm. Its population, which had remained relatively stable in the first half of the eighteenth century, had begun to grow rapidly thereafter. In 1725, it had stood at about fourteen million; at the turn of the nineteenth century, it had increased to forty million; on the eve of the 1848 revolutions, it was close to seventy million.

Of this population by far the greatest number lived off the land. As late as the middle of the nineteenth century, only 3,500,000 persons were town dwellers. Thus, the Russian economy was primarily agricultural. A thriving export trade was conducted through the Baltic ports, the principal exports being grain, fats, flax, hemp, and furs, and—later in the century—wool and timber; but its scale was not large and, like the import trade, it was carried almost exclusively in foreign bottoms. Moreover, trade was discouraged by the high protective tariffs maintained by the government throughout this whole period. As for industry, according to official statistics, there were 5261 manufacturing enterprises in 1825, with a total of 210,600 workers; but machinery was virtually unknown even in the most important firms, those manufacturing cotton, linen, and woolen cloth; and a large part of what was called industrial production in the official figures went on not in factories but in the homes of workers who were also engaged in agriculture.

The great majority of the population, then, was engaged in agriculture and lived on the land; and this majority was divided into two classes, the landholding nobility and the mass of serfs who worked their estates.

The institution of serfdom dates from the middle of the sixteenth century. Before that time the peasants were free men with the right of transferring their labor from one proprietor to another whenever they wished. After that time, the government began to limit their freedom of movement; and, by the seventeenth century, they were permanently bound to the lords whose lands they occupied. Once this step had been taken, it was not long before they lost other freedoms; serfdom began to be almost indistinguishable from slavery. By the eighteenth century the landholders had received the right to punish their serfs as they saw fit, to exile them to Siberia, even to sell them (although laws at the beginning of the nineteenth century placed limitations on this last right, in order to prevent the division of families by sale).

Serfdom hung like a dead weight over Russian society in the first half of the nineteenth century, stifling its vital energies. If the institution was the mainstay of Russian agriculture, it was also the most important factor in keeping agriculture in a chronic state of inefficiency, for this too plentiful supply of manual labor discouraged efforts to find the capital that might have enabled landowners to buy machinery and introduce scientific farming methods. At the same time, the execrable conditions in which many serfs had to live and the oppressive treatment they received led to sporadic and bloody risings; between 1825 and 1854 there were hundreds of agrarian revolts, all of them violent, and some of them on such a scale that considerable force had to be exerted to suppress them. Fear

EUROPEAN RUSSIA
IN THE FIRST HALF
OF THE 19TH CENTURY

0   300
Miles

of a large-scale rising was never far from the minds of the ruling classes of Russia, but only the most enlightened believed that the way to banish this shadow was to emancipate the serfs. The nobility felt that their livelihood depended on serfdom; the government had come to rely on the institution for recruits for the army and for labor for those industries, like the metallurgical and clothing industries, in which, for military reasons, it had an interest. Emancipation seeming impossible, repression appeared to be the only safeguard against revolt; and thus the continued existence of serfdom helped fasten a brutal authoritarianism on the country.

The political and social pyramids were identical in Russia. At the apex stood the tsar, his ministers, and his military staff, and, immediately below them, the nobility, which comprised the aristocratic landholders on their estates and all those who had been ennobled for military or civil service. This was the ruling class. It was often divided within itself, for in a country whose history had been marked by frequent palace revolutions there was inevitably tension between the tsar and the great nobles, and the landed nobility was jealous of its traditional privileges and fearful lest they be curtailed. But tsar and nobility generally presented a common front against the classes below them and against dissident aristocrats and intellectuals who wanted to change the existing order.

At the bottom of the triangle was the great mass of the peasantry; and between it and the ruling class was the bourgeoisie, still hardly numerous enough to warrant attention.

Last Years of Alexander I   When Alexander I came to the throne in 1801, there had been some expectation that he would institute liberal political and social changes. These hopes were disappointed. Alexander talked a good deal about reform; he surrounded himself with enlightened advisers; and, in his first years, he actually promulgated laws that seemed to herald the coming of a new age. But, in most cases, nothing came of all these gestures. The constitutional reforms of 1801 and 1809, which were supposed to temper tsarist absolutism, were wholly ineffective; the law of February 1803, which provided for the emancipation of serfs by voluntary agreement with their masters, resulted in the liberation of only 37,000 serfs in the next twenty years; the ambitious educational statute of 1803 broke down because of lack of funds and local interest.

It is of course true that the exertions required by the wars against France made it difficult for Alexander to concentrate on internal policy; but this is only a partial explanation. More important was his volatile nature, which caused him to go haring off after new enthusiasms before his old ones had begun to assume tangible form. By 1815 he was so distracted by his international schemes and his plans for Poland (see p. 15) that he had little time for thoughts of domestic reform. In the years that followed, his concern over the rising tide of revolution in Western Europe made him drift away from the muddled liberalism of his youth. He never broke with it completely—as late as 1820 he was playing again with ideas of constitutional reform—but in general the governmental methods of his last years showed an increasing degree of the kind of arbitrariness he had deprecated earlier. His closest advisers were reactionaries. Arakcheev, the chairman of the department of military affairs in the State Council, a brutal, cynical, dissolute man, whose reprisals against his own serfs at Gruzino when they rebelled and murdered his mistress shocked all Russia, encouraged him to break all contact with progressive circles; and the Archimandrite Photius, a fanatical cleric who was one of Arakcheev's protégés, overcame Alexander's tendency to religious mysticism and brought him back to a narrow and intolerant orthodoxy.

In short, before he fell sick of fever and died at Taganrog in December 1825, Alexander was reverting rapidly to the absolutism of his predecessors. This tendency was to be carried further by the tsar who now came to the throne.

The Decembrist Revolt   Alexander's presumptive successor was his brother, the Grand Duke Constantine, but it had been decided with his permission that he should be passed over and the crown given to the younger brother Nicholas. Alexander's sudden death, however, left the question of succession in confusion, for each of the brothers protested that the other should be tsar. Before the situation had been clarified and Nicholas persuaded to take office, the pathetic incident known as the Decembrist revolt had taken place.

The leaders of this unhappy rising were officers of noble birth, some of them related to the most powerful families in Russia. Many of them had been members of the army that had occupied France after Waterloo and had acquired from the experience political and social ideas somewhat more enlightened than they found in their own country. They were young, romantic, idealistic, and they hated the regime they found when they returned home: the stagnant and corrupt administrative system, the censorship of opinion, the rigid control of the university, the abuses of serfdom, and, worst of all, Arakcheev's "military colonies," instituted after 1815, in which soldiers and their families were ordered to combine soldiering with agricultural labor—men, women, and children wearing uniform and being subjected to brutal discipline. "Is it for this we liberated Europe?" one of them wrote later. "We have bought with our blood the highest place among nations, and at home we are humiliated."

As early as 1816, officers were forming conspiratorial groups. After 1820, there were three principal societies devoted to a change in existing conditions: the Society of the North, led by Prince Trubetskoi and the poet Ryleev; the Southern Society, led by Serge Murav'ev-Apostol, Bestuzhev-Riumin, and Colonel Paul Pestel; and a smaller group known as the United Slavs. Among these groups there was little coordination; within any one of them there was agreement only on the idea that things must be changed. Some of the members were moved more by religious than political motives; only Pestel had taken the trouble to draw up a detailed program. Pestel was a radical republican who knew what he wanted; most of the others had no clear idea of either their immediate or their ultimate objectives.

Nevertheless, when the succession crisis came, they began feverishly to plan an insurrection, and, when the troops were summoned to take the oath of loyalty to the new emperor, the leaders of the Northern Society spread the word among the garrisons in St. Petersburg that Nicholas was a usurper and raised the cry, "Long live Constantine! Long live the Constitution!" Some of the men doubtless believed that the Constitution was Constantine's wife; others, the fabricated story that Nicholas had suppressed a decree of Alexander's shortening the term of service. In any case, on December 14, 1825, three thousand troops, including part of the Moscow Regiment, the Life Guards, and the Marines, mutinied and marched to the Senate Square.

It was at this point that the lack of planning made itself felt. For four hours the troops stood shivering in the square, while the leaders harangued them and each other—and did nothing. As darkness fell, government cavalry charged the rebel lines and were thrown back. Four field pieces were then brought into the square and fired point-blank at the mutineers. After the third volley they fled, and the revolt in the capital was over.

The Southern Society had not moved on the 14th, perhaps because Pestel and others had been arrested by General Diebitch the day before. But on December 30, Murav'ev-Apostol and Bestuzhev incited troops of the Chernigov Regiment to mutiny and —after a ceremony in which they solemnly proclaimed Jesus Christ

Tsar Nicholas I, 1825–1855
(Culver Pictures)

King of the Universe—advanced on Kiev. This "Christian army," however, was defeated in its first brush with government troops and its officers taken.

After the collapse, most of the leaders of the Decembrist revolt surrendered; and, in the investigation that followed, they showed an enthusiasm about telling all that reminds one of Russian trials in more recent years. Only Pestel was immune to this epidemic of repentance. The confessions were not answered with clemency. Although the death penalty had been abolished by Empress Elizabeth in the middle of the eighteenth century, Nicholas sentenced five of the ringleaders—Pestel, Ryleev, Murav'ev, Bestuzhev, and Kakhovsky—to death by hanging and handed over a hundred others to penal servitude and exile in Siberia.[1]

The Decembrist revolt created a legend that inspired future revolutionaries. Immediately, however, it encouraged a deepening of government repression.

Repression under Nicholas I   Until his accession to the throne Nicholas I had commanded a brigade of guards and, according to one critic, was hated by them because of "his cold cruelty, his petty fussiness, and his vindictiveness." He was the kind of soldier who put a higher valuation on discipline and drill than on initiative; and, as emperor, he soon showed that his ideal was a dis-

---

[1] The executions are to be explained by the gravity of the offense. For the rest of his reign Nicholas took pride in the fact that the death penalty did not exist in Russia. This did not prevent him from sentencing soldiers, as he did in one case in 1827, to run the gauntlet four times through a thousand men, which meant almost certain death.

ciplined state in which all subjects recognized that their first duty was to obey authority. Like Metternich, Nicholas believed that change was reprehensible in itself; therefore he opposed the reform even of institutions which he personally regarded as evil, like serfdom. He feared the masses; he feared the Russian nobility (so much, indeed, that he preferred to rely on German administrators); he feared intellectuals. His anxieties were constantly heightened—by the Decembrist revolt, by the revolutions in Western Europe, and in 1831 by the rising in his own kingdom of Poland (see pp. 30–31)—and they gradually narrowed his view and encouraged the dictatorial strain in his character.

The symbol of Nicholas' reign is the secret police—that notorious Third Section of the Imperial Chancery which was directed, from 1826 until 1844, by Count Benckendorff, who, in the words of Alexander Herzen, stood "outside the law and above the law, having a right to meddle in everything." The Third Section operated through a uniformed *gendarmerie* and a vast network of secret agents of every walk of life; its aim was to prevent another 14th of December; its accomplishment was to make a whole generation live in fear of informers and arbitrary police procedure. The intelligentsia of writers, journalists, and teachers were the principle objects of scrutiny, as they were also the targets of government decrees that forbade travel abroad without permission, prohibited the entry of subversive literature or dangerous radicals, and censored newspapers, journals, and university lectures.

The effects of all this were bitterly described by Alexander Herzen, himself an intellectual who suffered five years detention at Perm because of his political views and who finally, in 1848, succeeded in escaping to London. Herzen accused Nicholas of "the moral destruction of a generation" and the "spiritual depraving" of Russian youth, of having frustrated their best impulses and made them "sick, deranged ... inoculated with a sort of spiritlessness, a sense of impotence, of fatigue before beginning work." Herzen wrote this in his private diary and did not have to pay for it. It was different in the case of Peter Chaadayev, whose reflections on the existing system in the first of his *Philosophical Letters* were published in the Moscow monthly *Teleskop* in 1836. Chaadayev wrote:

> The experience of time is nothing to us; the ages and the generations have passed without any profit for us. To look at us one might say that the general law of humanity had been repealed. Alone in the world, we have given nothing to it and have taught it nothing; we have not given a single idea to the total of human intelligence; we have contributed nothing to the progress of the human spirit, and everything that has come to us from that progress we have disfigured. We have an indefinable something in our blood that repulses all true progress.... Russia's past is empty, her present insufferable, and there is no future at all, a terrible lesson given to the nations of the plight to which a people can be brought by isolation and slavery.

Nicholas' reaction was swift and brutal. He ordered the philosopher to be declared insane and forbidden to write anything else.

Domestic Policy and Territorial Growth   Given Nicholas' suspicion of ideas and those who possessed them, it is understandable that his reign was barren of domestic reforms. Indeed, the only notable innovations before 1848 were the successful codification of Russian laws, completed under the supervision of Speransky in 1833, and the stabilization of the currency and the elimination of depreciated paper money by the finance minister Kankrin, a capable civil servant of Hessian extraction. Both reforms were long overdue; unfortunately, Kankrin's achievement was of temporary duration, for, after his retirement in 1844, his successors departed from his cautious policies and encouraged inflation and depreciation by issuing new money whenever they suffered financial embarrassment.

In other areas there was no sign of reform or improvement. The only change in governmental structure was a steady growth of the executive department (His Majesty's Own Chancery), which, as Nicholas' autocratic tendencies developed, continually absorbed new functions and, by doing so, made the whole government dangerously top-heavy. With respect to serfdom, the tsar deferred to the wishes of the great landowners and studiously avoided anything that resembled reform. In education—another field where improvement was badly needed—conditions worsened, if anything, as a result of the policies of Count S. S. Uvarov, minister of education from 1833 to 1849. Uvarov believed that Russia's educational system must be based on the principles of "orthodoxy, autocracy, and nationality"—in other words, on piety, respect for the tsar, and patriotism—and that it should serve to freeze the existing social system by discouraging members of the lower classes from seeking higher education and, in the case of those who refused to be discouraged, by making it impossible for them to acquire it. He was so intent on these objectives that he paid rather too little attention to educational standards, which, especially in the secondary schools, declined sharply.

If Nicholas' domestic accomplishments were unimpressive, he did achieve success in his foreign policy. Russia's international prestige was enhanced by the assistance given to the Greeks, although this was somewhat dimmed by the excesses resorted to in Poland and by Nicholas' role in the two Egyptian crises of the 1830s. Russia's territorial gains under Nicholas were sufficiently great to indicate that the empire was not yet a sated power. A shortsighted attack on Russia by Persian troops in 1826 led to a brief campaign that left the provinces of Nakhichevan and Erivan in northern Persia in Russian hands along with naval rights on the Caspian Sea; and, as we have already seen (pp. 26–27), the war against Turkey in 1827 brought more of the Caucasus and the Black Sea coast into Russia's possession, while strengthening its position in Rumania. Attempts to extend Russian influence in Afghanistan were less successful, and an expedition against Khiva in 1839 was a failure.

PRUSSIA TO 1848

The Land and the People   The settlement at Vienna had wrought significant changes in the nature of the Prussian state. When Prussia ceded most of its former Polish possessions to Russia and received compensation in Saxony and in Rhineland-Westphalia, its center of interest shifted from eastern Europe to central Europe and its population, hitherto predominantly German, now became overwhelmingly so.

Prussia was destined, before the century was over, to unite all Germany under its control, but few would have guessed that in 1815. Of the Eastern Powers it was easily the weakest, even in population, which stood at eleven million in 1815 and did not exceed sixteen million in 1848. Moreover, although it had acquired new territories, they did not form a solid mass, for Prussia's Rhenish provinces were separated from the older ones—and from the nation's capital at Berlin—by the independent territories of Hanover, Brunswick, and Hesse-Cassel. The fact that so much of the population was composed of new subjects was also a source of weakness. The inhabitants of the Polish districts had always been recalcitrant and hard to manage. Now, to what remained of them were added many resentful Saxons and thousands of Rhinelanders who differed in religion, historical background, and temperament from their new overlords.

Economically, Prussia was still predominantly agricultural, although not to the same extent as Russia and without Russia's system of servile labor. During the period of basic reform that followed Prussia's defeat by France in 1807, the government abolished serfdom by the emancipation edict of 1807, supplemented by later decrees. The serfs who were affected by these laws had, however, to pay for their liberation by surrendering much of their land to their former masters or by incurring heavy debts in order to acquire ownership. The terms of emancipation helped the owners of the large estates (the so-called *Junker*) to increase their holdings and transformed the mass of the peasantry into landless agricultural workers who were so dependent on the landlords that their freedom sometimes seemed illusory.

The acquisition of the Rhineland made Prussia potentially the strongest industrial power in Germany, for the rich mineral resources of that area, so happily wedded to coal deposits and water power, were now added to those of Upper Silesia. The importance of this was not widely appreciated in 1815, for industrial enterprise was still hardly existent. Yet notable steps forward were taken in the next thirty years. The efforts of the Westphalian manufacturer Friedrich Harkort to introduce English methods into textile and iron production, to mechanize these industries, and to combine under one control all the processes necessary for the transformation of the raw material into the finished product were the first significant steps in building up German industry. Under Harkort's influence, old small-scale family concerns—like the Stumm iron works and the Hoesch puddling works (famous names in the later history of German industry)—revolutionized their methods and entered the export trade. In the 1820s the Borsig machine works were founded, and the Haniel engineering works began to build steamboats for the river trade; in the 1840s the Krupp concern was established at Essen. In the same years the transformation of the textile industry began, with the mechanization of the Mevissen linen mills at Krefeld and the woolen mills of David Hansemann, another notable Rhineland manufacturer. Too much should not be made of these developments, of course. The industrial development of Prussia was still far behind that of her western neighbors; and, despite the richness of the Silesian and Westphalian coal deposits, the coal production of all Germany still lagged behind that of Belgium in 1846. But these developments were pledges of future progress.

Prussian trade was handicapped by the fact that the country had no direct access to the North Sea and did not control the mouths of the Elbe, the Weser, and the Rhine rivers. Moreover, it has been estimated that, until 1818, Prussia had sixty-seven different tariff areas within its borders, a fact that made the transit of goods from one part of the realm to another complicated and costly. In that year, however, in order to make customs duties uniform throughout the kingdom, to discourage smuggling, and to raise a reasonable amount of revenue, the government introduced a new tariff law that abolished all internal tolls, while imposing a moderate tariff on goods coming in from outside. This law was so successful in achieving its purposes that it was emulated by other German states. Moreover, since the latter wished to avoid having to pay heavy tolls for the privilege of shipping goods across Prussian territory, they began to negotiate economic agreements with the Prussian government. This led to the formation in 1834 of the Prussian Customs Union (*Zollverein*), which included all German states except Hanover, the Hanse towns, Mecklenburg, Oldenburg, Holstein, and Austria. The political importance of this union is obvious; it made the member states increasingly dependent upon Prussia, gradually undermined Austrian influence in Germany, and thus paved the way for the hegemony Prussia achieved by force of arms in 1866 (see pp. 210–215). Immediately the tariff of 1818 and the trade agreements between that date and 1834 enormously stimulated Prussian trade, which was encouraged also in these years by new road building, the beginning of railroad construction (1000 miles of new lines were laid on Prussian territory between 1844 and 1848 alone), and a treaty with Holland in 1831 which opened the lower Rhine to Prussian goods.

Prussia's political and social hierarchy was, in its broadest outlines, similar to that of Russia. The tie between the crown and the nobility was perhaps more intimate than in that country; for, since the seventeenth century, Prussian kings had protected the economic privileges of their landed nobles while the nobles had recognized their obligation to send their sons into the service of the state. In the military establishment, although the war against Napoleon had necessitated the commissioning of members of the middle class, their advancement was not encouraged after 1815 and they were isolated, for the most part, in the technical branches of the service. The nobility maintained its virtual monopoly in the officer corps, and its influence was paramount also in the highest councils of state.

Because of Prussia's more advanced economic development, the system of social stratification differed from the Russian in two respects. The industrial working class was larger and growing faster than its Russian counterpart and, by the end of the period, was already introducing an element of violence into the Prussian class system. In the second place, the bourgeoisie was more numerous, wealthy, and self-confident than the Russian merchant class. The Mevissens and Hansemanns of the Rhineland, seeking to imitate their models in England and France, looked upon themselves as the progressive force that would make the Germany of the future. They were both contemptuous of the stiff, uncultivated, and sometimes penurious East Elbian squires and resentful of their social and political power. This attitude was strengthened by the political events of the postwar period.

The Return to Reaction   In the melancholy years that followed the Prussian defeat at Jena in 1806, when the country lay under the heel of Napoleon and its status as a Great Power was in question, a remarkable group of new leaders had come to the fore in Prussian politics. These men, among whom Stein, Scharnhorst, Gneisenau, and Humboldt were outstanding, wanted to arouse the patriotic spirit of the nation so that French rule could be thrown off; and they believed that the best way to accomplish this was—in Gneisenau's words—to make all Prussian subjects "free, noble, and independent so that they believe that they are part of the whole." In pursuit of these objects they persuaded the king, between 1807 and 1813, to approve a series of edicts abolishing serfdom, broadening the powers of local government, increasing educational opportunity, opening the officer corps to the bourgeoisie and making merit the test of promotion, reforming the disciplinary code of the army, and making other fundamental changes in the structure of the state and society. By 1815 it appeared also that Prussia was on its way to becoming a state with liberal representative institutions; for on May 22, Frederick William III promised to repay his subjects for their successful efforts in expelling the French by granting them a written constitution.

All of this was misleading. Frederick William was an honorable man but not a resolute one; timidity and vacillation were the keys to his character, and he distrusted innovation. Because of the hard necessities of war, he had allowed himself to be pushed along the road to reform, but he had not liked the process or the men who did the pushing. He had never got on with Stein, whom he had once accused of being "refractory, insolent, obstinate, and disobedient"; by 1815 he was grumbling that Gneisenau, Prussia's most gifted military strategist and a passionate advocate of a constitution, was too clever for his own good; and his sympathy for the ideas of other members of the reform group who were still in government service was wearing thin.

The king was influenced in his attitude toward the reformers by the opinions of his fellow monarchs in eastern Europe and by the criticism of his own nobility. Alexander of Russia, Francis of Austria, and Prince Metternich made no secret of the fact that they believed Frederick William had embarked on a dangerous course when he began to patronize the reformers; and a group of the most influential nobles in Prussia, led by Duke Karl von Mecklenburg and the minister of police, Prince Wittgenstein, used every opportunity to insinuate into the king's mind the idea that Stein and his colleagues had "brought revolution into the country" and that it was only a question of time before the destruction of the monarchy and the war of the propertyless against the propertied got under way.

Under the twofold pressure the king turned against his ministers and their ideas. In 1819 Frederick William dismissed War Minister von Boyen because that official had resisted what appeared to be a royal attempt to undo the military reforms. At the same time, he dropped Humboldt and Finance Minister Beyme because they had objected to Prussia's adherence to the Carlsbad Decrees (see p. 56). Since Gneisenau had already gone into retirement, this virtually destroyed the influence of the reform group and left the field free for reaction.

The government functioned effectively enough in the years that followed. In 1817 Frederick William had created a Council of State, composed of princes of the royal house, leaders of the provincial nobility, and high officials; this body improved the government of the dispersed provinces and gradually developed a centralized administration. Ever since the seventeenth century, Prussia had had an efficient bureaucracy, and it worked well now and improved the public services.

Nevertheless, there were many in Prussia after 1819 who felt as the great archaeologist Winckelmann had felt when he fled the rule of Frederick the Great, that it was "better to be a circumcised Turk than a Prussian." All the hopes of the reform era were now disappointed. When the citizens of the Rhineland sent a petition to the king in 1818 reminding him of his promise of a constitution, they were abruptly informed that by "wantonly casting doubts on the inviolability of the sovereign's word" they were committing the crime of *lèse majesté*. The only concession that the king made to the demand for representative institutions was the reform of the old provincial estates and the establishment, in 1823, of provincial diets. Since these were permitted to meet only infrequently and to possess only advisory powers and since, in addition, they were dominated by the landed aristocracy, there was little danger that they would advocate progressive ideas.

Those reforms that were on the books were seriously watered down in the subsequent period. Every decree designed to supplement the emancipation edict of 1807 seemed to benefit the landlords and hurt the former serfs. The local government ordinance was revised in a conservative direction, and the merit principle was quietly dropped as the test of army promotions. The liberal spirit that had inspired the educational reforms of Humboldt was absent from the administration of Altenstein, minister of education from 1817 to 1838; and both universities and schools fell under rigid bureaucratic control.

In Prussian education the influence of Georg Friedrich Hegel (1770–1831) now reached its height. Both Altenstein and his supervisor of secondary schools, Johannes Schulze, were ardent Hegelians; and it was not therefore accidental that so many of Hegel's students began to fill teaching positions in the gymnasia and university chairs in philosophy, education, and political economy. Through their efforts the more extreme Hegelian doctrines—the personification of the state, the insistence that the life of the individual attained meaning only when he was absorbed in the state, the belief that the essence and the justification of the state was its power and that "what is rational is actual, and what is actual is rational"—were drilled into students in the hope of persuading them of the merits of the existing regime. This endeavor was not without success. If the system of Haller had been the official philosophy of Prussian authoritarianism in the first years after 1815, it was replaced in Frederick William III's last years by this kind of Hegelianism; and it gave a cast to Prussian political thinking that was to last a long time, since, as Hajo Holborn has written, it "fitted exactly the situation of a people who were deeply convinced of the power of reason over reality but wanted [once the hopes of the reform period had been disappointed] to be persuaded that progress toward freedom was possible within an authoritarian order."

The reaction under Frederick William III had its ludicrous aspects. An incredible amount of effort was expended in keeping members of the reform party under surveillance in the hope of discovering plots against the government. Newspapers were suppressed for reasons that were neither logical nor consistent; and journalists were apt, on the slightest pretext, to be hauled into court and charged with disrespect for the royal person, like the hapless publisher who had placed an advertisement for herring too close to the court calendar. But even the incidents that aroused ridicule were depressing when seen in the total context of press and university censorship, thought control, persecution of "demagogues," and what appeared to be an attempt to destroy the independence of the Catholic Church (see pp. 59–60). Prussia, which in the years between 1807 and 1813 had seemed to be in the vanguard of German liberalism, was now apparently what it had always been in the past—an autocratic, militaristic state whose efficient administration did not redeem the absence of freedom within its borders.

Nor was the picture relieved when the king died in 1840 and was succeeded by his son, under the title Frederick William IV. This ruler was a man of great personal charm and intellectual power, although these gifts were offset by a tendency to abstruse thought and devious methods and a habit of indecision in moments of crisis. But his greatest weakness was his ability to arouse in others mistaken ideas concerning his intentions. Because of this, his first years were filled with misunderstandings.

The new king began his reign with a coronation address in which he talked of the intimate relation that should exist between a monarch and his subjects. He then issued a series of decrees, freeing political prisoners, moderating the censorship of the press, and restoring former liberals to honor and to office. Not unnaturally, this led to widespread expectation that Prussia, with a liberal monarch on the throne, was now going to receive representative institutions and a written constitution.

But Frederick William was not a liberal; he was a romantic. In the new world of industrialism, he was probably the last sovereign who really believed in the theory of divine right of kings. He expected allegiance from his subjects as a matter of course. He was willing to make certain voluntary concessions to them because he wanted to appear as a wise and magnanimous ruler; but for them to demand something from him was, in his opinion, presumptuous.

The king had no intention of satisfying the hopes of his people. He did, after much hesitation, convoke a joint meeting of the provincial diets in 1847 to discuss financial matters and raise new taxes. But when that body met, he made it clear that this was the limit of his concessions and, at the same time, gave his opinion of constitutions:

> No power on earth will ever force me to transform the natural relationship ... between prince and people into a conventional constitutional one; neither now nor ever will I permit a written piece of paper to force itself, like some second providence, between our Lord God in heaven and this land, to rule us with its paragraphs and, through them, to replace the ancient sacred loyalty.

In the face of this intransigent defense of the authoritarian principle, there was no hope of constitutional progress or social reform; and Prussia remained a center of reaction until the storm of 1848 swept over the land.

THE AUSTRIAN EMPIRE TO 1848

The Land and the People   After 1815 the Austrian empire comprised Austria proper, Bohemia, Galicia, the kingdom of Hungary, Illyria on the Dalmatian coast, and the northern Italian provinces of Lombardy and Venetia. The Vienna settlement had made it more compact than it had been before the Napoleonic period, but this compactness did not make for internal unity. The thirty million people who inhabited the Habsburg lands differed in racial origins, historical background, language, and customs. The Austrian duchies were peopled for the most part by Germans; but Bohemia was inhabited by Czechs and Slovaks, Galicia by Poles and Ruthenians, Hungary by the Magyars but also by Croats, Ruthenians, Rumanians, and Slovaks, Illyria by Croats, Serbs, and Slovenes, and Lombardy and Venetia by Italians. These peoples had little in common except the bond of the imperial house and the Catholic Church.

Within the empire the Germans were the dominant people. The ruling house was German; German was the official language, the language of commerce, and the language of the towns (not only of Vienna, but also of Budapest and Prague); and Germans filled most of the positions in the imperial bureaucracy. But this position was to be challenged in time by the strongest of the subject nationalities. Even in the first years after 1815 the Magyars were restive, and they did not become any less so as time passed. In general, Austria's greatest problem, which became one of life or death, was that of adjusting and balancing the desires of its diverse peoples in such a way as to preserve the bond of empire.

The Austrian economy was largely agricultural. There were some signs of industrial development in the western towns, and in the "hungry forties" this had gone far enough for there to be riots by factory workers in Prague. In Lombardy also factory organization was getting under way at the end of this period in the cotton, silk, and linen industries. But this was still on a very small scale. The government sought to increase export trade by building the port of Trieste as an outlet to the Mediterranean, and it also made some gestures in the direction of railway promotion, although its efforts in this latter respect were neither as consistent nor as successful as those of the Prussian government. This was true also of tariff policy, which was certainly less imaginative than the policy that led to the formation of the Prussian *Zollverein,* as was shown by the continued existence throughout these years of a customs barrier between Austria and Hungary. Austrian trade policy was enlightened only in fits and starts, and there was no appreciable commercial growth. In any event, the backbone of the economy was agriculture, which engaged the great majority of the population.

As in the case of Russia, the nature of the economy was reflected in the social and political hierarchy. The nobility owned most of the land, dispensed local justice, administered local affairs, and provided the imperial government with officers for its army, diplomats for its foreign service, and department heads

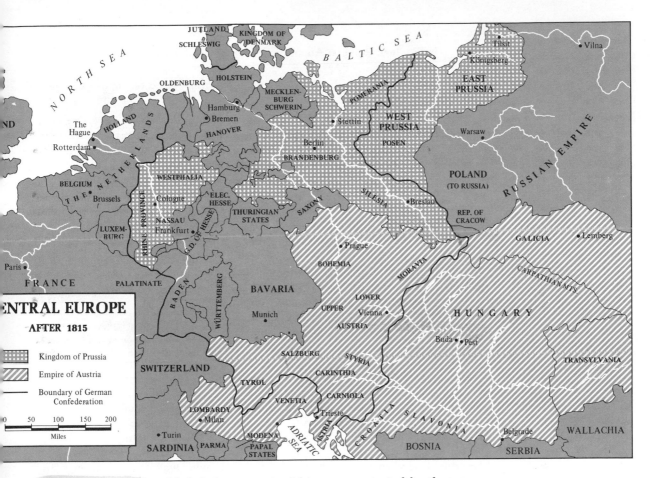

CENTRAL EUROPE

AFTER 1815

Kingdom of Prussia

Empire of Austria

Boundary of German Confederation

0   50   100   150   200

Miles

for its ministries. Provided their economic rights were protected by the crown, they supported it, although they were jealous of any infringement of their inherited feudal privileges. Within their ranks there were gradations, especially in Hungary, where there was a considerable economic gap between the magnates, who might own estates covering as much as 40,000 acres of land, and the small squires, who often had more pride than possessions. This division had some political importance, but it did not affect the attitude of the nobility, great and small, toward the class that supported it.

The peasants lived in conditions similar to those of the serfs in Russia. They were subject to the legal jurisdiction of the local lord and forced to pay dues and labor services, and this burden was heavy. It has been estimated that, in Bohemia, peasants owed half of their time and two thirds of their crops to their lords, and conditions were no different in other parts of the empire. This meant that the great mass of the population was oppressed and miserable and that the conditions of their life excluded them from political affairs.

Special mention should perhaps be made of the imperial bureaucracy, which, while not a class in the economic sense, was an important factor in the political and social life of the empire. Although this service included Hungarian and Czech aristocrats and, indeed, men of every nationality, most of its members were Germans, generally of the lesser nobility. They were held together by a tradition inherited from the days of Emperor Joseph II, who had tried to impose German culture and customs on the whole empire; and they believed that their mission was to fight the forces of decentralization, local patriotism, and aristocratic privilege. The labors of the bureaucracy kept the empire functioning but, at the same time, invited conflict with the local magnates and the different national groups.

The Course of Domestic Policy   Until his death in 1835, Austria was ruled by Emperor Francis I. This monarch is sometimes dismissed as childish or frivolous, and Sir Harold Nicolson has written that he was happiest when he was in his workshop stamping seals on sealing wax or making toffee on the stove. But this does not do Francis justice. He may have been indolent, but he was very far from being a cipher in imperial affairs. As Metternich wrote in 1820, the emperor knew exactly what he wanted, and he was autocrat enough to see that he got it. His real weakness was narrowness of view. In an empire held together by bureaucrats, he was the bureaucrat par excellence: fond of red tape and protocol, suspicious of ideas and methods that did not conform to inherited practice and of people who were too obviously brilliant, averse to novelty, and bitterly hostile to reform—a man whose motto might well have been "Govern and change nothing."

Francis succeeded in remaining true to this principle in the face of the dictates of common sense and the arguments of his ministers. There can be little doubt that the imperial administration would have been greatly improved if the welter of redundant chancelleries, courts, directories, and councils that made up the machinery of state could either have been abolished completely or, at least, coordinated by the creation of some kind of council for the whole empire. Metternich, who was certainly no reformer but who was sensible enough to see that even autocracies should be run efficiently, repeatedly suggested such a reorganization. Not only were his proposals never acted upon but after 1826 they were never seriously considered. In that year Count Kolowrat became minister of state, and the Czech aristocrat hated Metternich and succeeded in undermining his position sufficiently so that he had to restrict himself henceforward to foreign affairs. Kolowrat himself was not unaware of the need of administrative reform, but he was not a strong enough man to overcome the emperor's inertia.

The result was that there were no essential changes in any branch of the imperial administration and, in some cases, notably the army, programs of modernization that had been started before 1815 were sharply curtailed. Despite the pressing need for financial reform, the imperial debt was allowed to go on mounting; despite the example of effective tariff reform shown by Prussia, the old restrictions on trade remained; and so forth. "I won't have any innovations," Francis said in 1831. "Let the laws be justly applied; they are good and adequate."

People who persisted in advocating change Francis hounded down mercilessly. It is fair to say that in internal affairs Metternich and Kolowrat were both less influential than the man who was minister of police after 1817, Count Sedlnitzky. His agents opened even Metternich's letters and had little respect for less important persons. Espionage, denunciation, secret trials, and arbitrary punishment were as much a part of life in Austria as they were in Russia in the heyday of Benckendorff. The Austrian press was censored even more rigorously than the Prussian. Professors and schoolteachers were under constant surveillance, never knowing who in their audiences might be a police spy, and school authorities were strictly enjoined to report the expression of any sentiments that might be considered subversive. Students were forbidden to study in foreign universities and were forced to content themselves with an educational system in which everything that they and their professors read had to be approved by the government. It is no wonder that so many of them came to regard their country as one large, and very dull, prison.

Francis died in February 1835. He was succeeded by his eldest son, Ferdinand, who was, unfortunately, of such feeble intelligence that it was said that his only sensible remark after his accession was, "I'm the emperor and I want noodles!" However that may be, the direction of the government for the next thirteen years was in the hands of a "council of state" of three men: Archduke Ludwig, the least gifted of the brothers of Francis I, Metternich, and Kolowrat. Ludwig, like his dead brother, wanted nothing changed; Metternich and Kolowrat were engaged in such involved intrigues against each other that they had no time to think of reforms; so the empire lumbered on in its usual way.

Developments in Hungary before 1848   There were signs of life, however, in Hungary. Despite attempts at Germanization and centralization, the Magyars had preserved their medieval local assemblies, which were sounding boards for the grievances of the nobility. Strong resistance on the part of these bodies to certain tax and recruiting decrees of imperial authorities induced the Vienna government to try to propitiate the Hungarian magnates by convoking a Central Hungarian Diet in 1825. The meeting was so stormy and so critical of the regime that the emperor was forced to agree to raise no taxes in the future without the consent of this body, which was to be reconvened periodically.

It was at the Diet of 1825 that a remarkable leader appeared in the person of Stephan Széchenyi. A former officer and one of the richest men in Hungary, Széchenyi wished to lift his country out of the torpor in which it had lived so long by awakening a sense of responsibility among his fellows in the upper nobility. He dreamed of a Hungary in which the nobility would give up such privileges as its freedom from the land tax and would cooperate in efforts to ameliorate the lot of the peasantry—a Hungary, moreover, in which an economic transformation would be effected by means of technical assistance to improve agriculture, the creation of capital resources to stimulate industry, the improvement of communications, the abolition of the tariff wall separating Hungary from Austria, and the inclusion of Hungary in the Austrian railroad system. Although disappointed in his hopes that he might receive encouragement and assistance from Vienna, Széchenyi was able to induce his fellow magnates, between 1825 and 1832, to carry through some economic improvements, including the construction of a bridge between Buda and Pest (until then unconnected) and the inauguration of steam navigation on the Danube. Under his influence, the Hungarian Diet of 1832 actually began to consider a reform of the condition of the peasantry.

But Széchenyi could not win the support of the lesser nobility, whose reduced circumstances made them cling to the very privileges that he wanted to abolish; and in 1832 they found a leader in Louis Kossuth. This romantic figure, a journalist by trade, attained tremendous popularity by appealing to the hostility with which the lesser nobles viewed the magnates and by urging not closer union with Austria, which was the gist of Széchenyi's economic program, but a greater degree of Hungarian independence. Kossuth used the arguments of the German protectionist Friedrich List to urge the necessity of a national economy for Hungary with separate tariff and communications systems and autonomous institutions. The fervor with which he pleaded this case and his increasingly radical views and violent language divided the Hungarian nobility into two camps, while at the same time creating a turbulence that could not help but affect the peasant masses as well. By the late 1840s, Hungary was in a dangerous state of unrest.

The Austrian Mission   One of Metternich's foreign colleagues said on one occasion that Austria was Europe's House of Lords, meaning, no doubt, that its function was to restrain the passions and undo the mistakes of the common run of petty states in Europe. Austria's geographical position made it the logical power to maintain order in central Europe; there is no doubt that Metternich regarded that as the mission of his country after 1815. Some mention has been made (pp. 22, 30) of the vigilance with which he watched over Italian affairs and the promptness with which he intervened to snuff out revolutionary movements. It is now time to review his activities in Germany.

GERMANY TO 1848

The German States and the Confederation   One of the great services that Napoleon Bonaparte performed for Germany was to simplify its political structure. Before his time the area we think of as Germany was a crazy quilt of conflicting sovereignties; it comprised over three hundred separate political units, each with its own laws and regulations. The French emperor had followed a policy of amalgamation and, in the end, had reduced the number to less than fifty. The Congress of Vienna carried Napoleon's work further; when it was finished, Germany was composed of thirty-eight states, ranging in size and importance from the five kingdoms of Prussia, Hanover, Bavaria, Württemberg, and Saxony to such miniscule states as Lippe and the free cities of the north.

All of these states, plus the German part of the Austrian empire, were members of the Germanic Confederation, which had been created at Vienna. The central body of this organization was the Diet, which met periodically at Frankfurt on the Main and was composed of representatives chosen by the rulers of the various member states. The Diet was not, in other words, an elective assembly or parliament but a diplomatic organization which, in some respects, resembled the United Nations of our time. It had a complicated procedure and a very involved voting system on which it is unnecessary to dilate, except to note that on all matters of importance two thirds of the members had to agree before a decision was taken and on some matters unanimous agreement was required. This made action of any kind difficult. Aside from this, the Congress of Vienna had not defined the competence and jurisdiction of the Diet; and, true to the age-old German tradition of particularism, the member states were not inclined to admit that it had, or should have, any substantial authority.

Article XIII of the Federal Constitution, which was incorporated in the Final Act of the Congress of Vienna, stipulated that all member states should have constitutions that would provide for assemblies of the estates. Such a constitution was granted by the Grand Duke of Saxe-Weimar, and he was followed by the rulers of Bavaria, Württemburg, Baden, and Hesse-Darmstadt. But, as we have seen above, Prussia did not follow suit, despite the solemn promise of her king, and other rulers did not even bother to make empty promises. A ruler like the elector of Hesse—who, when he returned to Cassel after seven years of French rule, proceeded to invalidate all laws passed and even all military and bureaucratic promotions made during his absence[2]—was obviously not interested in issuing a charter of liberties to his subjects. As for the ruling groups in the free cities of Hamburg and Lübeck, they outdid the Hessian prince by returning to their charters of 1669 and 1528, respectively. This obviously flouted the sense of Article XIII of the Federal Act, but the Diet proved powerless to do anything about it. Nor was it able to carry out certain other assigned tasks, like the establishment of a competent federal army or of a central court to adjudicate disputes between member states.

It is obvious that if the Confederation could not impose its will on member states in small matters, it would be incapable of giving Germany any real bond of unity. It seemed more likely that—in the words of the Prussian general Clausewitz—"Germany can achieve political unity only in one way, by the sword, by one of its states subjugating all the others." The only states capable of such an act of conquest were Austria and Prussia. The Austrians, who had been invested with the permament presidency of the Confederation, wanted no change; the Prussians not only agreed with this view but seemed perfectly happy to play second fiddle to the Austrians. The closeness of Austro-Prussian collaboration in these years gave no hint of the future struggle for supremacy between the two great German powers.

Liberalism and Nationalism in Germany   The historian Sybel wrote of the German Confederation that it was "received by the German nation at large partly with cold indifference and partly with patriotic indignation." The first reaction was probably the one felt by most persons. It is always a mistake to think that the majority of any people are interested in politics; and in Germany these years formed the so-called *Biedermeier* period, a time of relative stability and peace in which the ordinary people did not look far beyond their family circle or the affairs of their village and in which they accepted both the political and the social facts of life as they were presented to them.

But there were forces of movement in the German states, and they were to

---

[2] When it was announced, in 1813, that this prince was returning to his capital, a former servant of his donned his old uniform and went to the residence. As the elector drove up, he shouted proudly, "Here I am, Your Highness! At my post!" The prince replied, "Good heavens, the old chap's been standing there since 1806!"

be found in the commercial and industrial towns and in the universities. It was among the latter that the first real movement of protest against the status quo got under way. Students who had fought in the war of liberation came back to the universities to found a new kind of organization, unlike the old beer-swilling, dueling corporations, and devoted instead to the moral and political regeneration of Germany and the cause of national unity. These societies were called *Burschenschaften* and, by 1816, they were organized into a national federation with branches in sixteen universities.

In 1817, in celebration of the fourth anniversary of the Battle of Leipzig (turning point in Germany's struggle against Napoleon) and also of the three hundredth anniversary of Martin Luther's defiance of authority, the *Burschenschaft* of the University of Jena convoked a national assembly and held a dramatic meeting at the Wartburg Castle. Here speeches were made about unity and freedom and the disappointment of the high hopes of the liberation period; the princes who had not granted constitutions to their peoples were held up to execration; and a bonfire was kindled into which were thrown such things as a Prussian corporal's cane, Haller's book on political philosophy, some regulations of the Prussian ministry of education, and other symbols of institutions detested by the *Burschen*.

Sporadic agitations of this nature continued for the next two years, to the growing annoyance of the authorities and of Prince Metternich. But in 1819 the protest movement took a turn that played into the hands of the Austrian chancellor. A young student named Karl Sand, of disturbed mind and muddled purpose, stabbed to death a playwright named Kotzebue who was supposed to be a spy in the pay of the tsar of Russia. When he heard of this pointless crime, Metternich struck immediately. He summoned a meeting of the principal German states and, at Carlsbad in August 1819, they drew up a series of decrees—later approved by the Federal Diet—providing for the dissolution of the *Burschenschaften* and the imposition of strict censorship over the press and universities in all German states. Moreover, a commission was to be established at Mainz to study the discontent in Germany and to institute proceedings against subversive individuals and organizations.

Metternich now had the weapons for imposing the same kind of control over Germany that the secret police exercised in the Austrian empire. Yet they failed to prevent new incidents and agitations. When revolution erupted in France in 1830, for instance, it aroused enthusiasm in Germany too; and liberal movements in Brunswick, Hanover, Saxony, and Hesse-Cassel succeeded in forcing constitutional concessions from the rulers of those states. Two years later, at Hambach in Rhenish Bavaria, at least 30,000 people, drawn from every social class, assembled and listened with enthusiasm to a series of speeches extolling national unity and popular freedom. This meeting was even more radical than the Wartburg festival of 1817; one of the speakers not only demanded the destruction of absolutism in Austria and Prussia but the liberation of Poland, Hungary, and Italy as well; he called down a "lasting curse upon kings, the betrayers of their peoples and all mankind," and proposed the establishment of a European republic. This language was alarming enough to make the Diet strike back with more repressive legislation; in June 1832 it passed a series of articles intended to make all existing representative assemblies powerless to limit the sovereignty

Moritz von Schwind, "The Wedding Trip," 1862. No artist conveys the atmosphere of the Biedermeier period as perfectly as Schwind, unless perhaps his contemporary, the composer Albert Lortzing (1801–1851), whose operas, especially *Zar und Zimmermann,* have the same feeling as this painting. (Bayerische Staatsgemäldesammlungen, Munich)

of their princes or to use whatever financial powers they might possess to exact other concessions. But these attempts to prop up the authority of German princes by decree were no more successful than earlier ones.

Proof of this was given in 1837 when the new king of Hanover dissolved his assembly and absolved all of his civil servants from the oath they had taken to the constitution that his predecessor had granted. Seven distinguished professors at the University of Göttingen, including the historians Dahlmann and Gervinus and the philologists and folklorists Jakob and Wilhelm Grimm, refused to comply. Jakob Grimm pointed out that the universities were the conscience of the nation and university professors must have a jealous regard for their word, lest students, seeing them waver on one issue, think them capable of compromising in their teaching. The Göttingen Seven defied their prince and were expelled from Hanover; but they became heroes in the eyes of the middle and intellectual classes of Germany.

But the excitement aroused by these incidents was exceeded by that caused by the sudden war scare of 1840, when it appeared for a time that the French might seek revenge for their isolation in Near Eastern affairs (see pp. 33–34) by striking across the Rhine. The menacing sounds that came from Paris caused a patriotic response so intense that the historian Treitschke wrote later that here, for the first time, the Germans were one, despite the political fragmentation of their country. All over Germany men were singing the new songs brought forth by the crisis: Nikolaus Becker's *Song of the Rhine,* with its challenging opening words

> They shall not have our free German Rhine
> Though they scream after it like greedy ravens;

the now better-known *Watch on the Rhine* by Max Schneckenburger; and, a little later, Hoffmann von Fallersleben's *Deutschland, Deutschland über alles.*

The last of these songs, which was to become the national anthem of the united Germany of the future, has a final verse which calls for

> Unity and Law and Freedom
> For the German Fatherland.

At the time those words were written, there is no doubt that the desired objects went together. The young patriots of 1840, the members of the *Burschenschaften,* the progressive businessmen, the champions of railroad building and tariff reform, in short, all the workers for change and progress saw no reason why they should choose between Unity and Law and Freedom; they took it for granted that attaining one would mean attaining all.

Yet there was already, even among the most sincere believers in constitutional freedom, a tendency to become impatient over the delay in attaining German unity; and impatience led some of them to wonder whether it might not be necessary, temporarily, to give unity the priority over liberal objectives and material considerations priority over high ideals. Even before 1848 German patriots were more conscious of the factor of power than their cloudy rhetoric would seem to indicate. The Hegelians had done their work well; and it is interesting to note in the writings of that fervent advocate of unity, the economist Friedrich List, how the author, in defining the requirements of nationhood, placed increasing emphasis on things like "extensive territory," railroads, protective tariffs, colonies, and "adequate power on land and sea" rather than on matters of law and the spirit.

Nor was this tendency confined to northern Germany. The period before 1848 was the heyday of South German liberalism, for all of the southern states had constitutions and representative assemblies, and their parliamentary orators, like Karl Theodor Welcker and Karl von Rotteck, received a national hearing. Compared with the English and French parliaments of this period, these assemblies had little real power; but the middle classes of South Germany were proud of them and took pleasure in comparing their enlightened institutions with the repressive system of Austria and—more contemptuously—with the reactionary military kingdom of Prussia.

Yet one of the most interesting of the South German political thinkers, Paul Pfizer, believed that if Germany were ever to be unified, Prussia must lead the way, and he was not put off by his recognition of Prussia's illiberal character:

> Germany is not greatly aided by the mere axioms of civil liberty, however
> meritorious and necessary their propagation may be. Despite the urge for
> liberty on the part of individuals, the Germans will always play a sorry
> role ... until they desire freedom as a nation. ... It is, of course, foolish
> to demand that Germans wholly forget about freedom within until they
> have secured independence from without; but it is just as wrong, if not
> more so, to wish to sacrifice the latter to the former.

Pfizer, like List, was not entirely representative of his time; few German
intellectuals before 1848 had attained this kind of realism. To most of them
nationalism and liberalism went hand in hand; and, since they saw Metternich
opposing both, they turned all their efforts to the task of undermining the system
he was trying to maintain. They were heartened equally by the example of the
Göttingen Seven and by the patriotic enthusiasm of 1840; and, as the world
neared the great year 1848, they were confident that time was on their side.

RELIGION AND THE ARTS UNDER ABSOLUTISM

Throne and Altar   Whatever disagreements there were between the established churches and the governments of the Eastern Powers, they did not arise
from any difference in political attitude. The churches, which had suffered much
during the Enlightenment and the French Revolution, were even more inflexible
in their opposition to liberal movements than the political authorities; and this
supplied a basis for that intimate cooperation between throne and altar that
was characteristic of this period.

It should not be assumed, however, that perfect harmony reigned between
the two institutions, except perhaps in Russia. In that country the Orthodox
Church was completely under governmental control, for its ecclesiastical ruling
body, the Holy Synod, had little authority and all real power was in the hands
of the chief procurator, who was a government official. Between 1836 and 1855
that office was filled by N. A. Protasov, a colonel of hussars who ran church
administration as if he were commanding a cavalry division. This may have
been irritating, but there were no essential differences between the government
and the religious hierarchy. High church officials gladly cooperated with the
state in its opposition to political dissidents, while the government assisted them
in the persecution of members of unorthodox religious sects.

The situation in Prussia was more complex. The Protestant majority in that
country had been sharply diminished by the acquisition of the predominantly
Catholic Rhine provinces, and this fact led Frederick William III into policies
that filled his last years with religious controversy. To offset Catholic strength
and also, perhaps, to make the Protestant faith a stronger bulwark against
liberalism, the king in 1817 ordered the union of the Lutheran and Reformed
churches and, after a long dispute and a few concessions on his part, had his
way, although his victory was doubtless won at the expense of the independent
spirit of the Protestant churches. The king then became involved in a long struggle

with the Catholic Church, going so far in 1837 as to imprison the archbishops of Cologne and Posen in order to force them to comply with government decrees in matters of public education and mixed marriages. Here he was less successful, and the quarrel had to be patched up by his successor, after which the government and the Catholic Church, in political matters especially, saw eye to eye.

Frederick William III's attitude toward Catholicism was doubtless influenced by the spread of ultramontanism after 1815. This movement, the religious counterpart to secular absolutism, was designed to enhance the authority of the papacy. It found its most eloquent literary justification in Joseph de Maistre's *Du Pape* (1819), as well as in Lamennais' *Essay on Indifference in Religious Matters* (1817)[3]; it was symbolized also by the return of the Jesuits, those doughty champions of papal authority, to Rome in 1814 and to other countries in the course of the next decade. The intensity with which ultramontanism was pushed by some of its advocates alarmed most secular governments, and the Prussians were not alone in their opposition to it. The Austrian government, for instance, showed a decided coolness in its official relations with the Catholic Church, refusing to conclude a concordat with the Vatican or to permit the Society of Jesus to re-establish itself in the empire.

On the other hand, Metternich raised no objections to the growth of ultramontanism in southern Germany, where it seemed to him to be a useful counterbalance to liberalism; and he placed no difficulties in the way of the San Fedist Society and other Catholic laymen's societies in Italy which, with the support of the Jesuits, combated the influence of the liberals. These societies, indeed, helped to supplement the activities of the Austrian secret police and, because they did so, received the chancellor's blessing.

Within both the Catholic and Protestant churches there were some more progressive tendencies than the ones described here; but the men who represented them were less influential than those who shared the reactionary views of the governments.

Literature and the Arts   Enough has been said above about the general nature of the absolutist regimes to indicate that creative artists who tried to say anything about the society in which they lived encountered difficulties. The heavy hand of the censor hung over everything they did, and their creations were always in danger of disfigurement or complete suppression. The fact that, despite this handicap, this was a remarkably productive period leads one to wonder what might not have been produced if its writers had been completely free.

In Russia, for instance, these were the years in which a truly national literature first came into existence with the appearance of Krylov's fables, Griboedov's fine comedy *The Misfortune of Being Wise* (1823), the lyric and dramatic works of Russia's greatest poet Alexander Pushkin (1799-1837), the poetry and novels of Michael Lermontov (1814-1841), and the novels and dramas of Nicholas Gogol (1809-1852). Yet Griboedov did not live to see a complete version of his satire on Moscow society performed, because parts of it offended the censor. Pushkin,

[3] On Lamennais, see Chapter 3, page 85.

suspected of association with the Decembrists, had to protect himself by taking a position at court and submitting to the patronage of Nicholas and Benckendorff, a situation he found insupportable and which involved him in emotional problems that led to his early death. Five months before that tragic event, the poet wrote:

> No hands have wrought my monument; no weeds
> Will hide the nation's footpath to its site.
> Tsar Alexander's column it exceeds
> In splendid insubmissive height.

Nevertheless, he seems to have abandoned plans to write a history of Peter the Great and a novel on contemporary life in Russia because he knew that these works would not meet with official approval. Similarly, Lermontov's great poem *The Demon* (1829) could not be published during his lifetime, and Gogol, despite his impeccably conservative political views, was strongly criticized for his satire on impoverished landlords in *Dead Souls* (1842).

Examples of the same kind can be given for the German states. In Austria even the works of the dead Schiller had to be cut before they were performed in the theaters of Vienna; and writers like the German-Hungarian poet Lenau and Anastasius Grün (Count Auersperg), whose *Promenades of a Viennese Poet* openly attacked the Metternich system, were in constant trouble with the censor. The life of Austria's greatest dramatist, Franz Grillparzer (1791–1872), was made a torment by official interference. Although his drama *King Ottokar's Fortune and Death* (1823) was a patriotic tribute to the House of Hapsburg, its production was delayed for two years by the censor; and, in the case of all his subsequent plays, Grillparzer had to fight for the right of publication. After 1838 he buried his dramatic creations in the drawer of his writing table. "Despotism," he said, "has destroyed my literary life."[4]

In Germany the romantic movement reached its height and began its decline in this period. Novalis and Kleist were dead before the end of the wars; the great names of the first years of peace were the brothers Schlegel, Ludwig Tieck, Clemens Brentano, and E. T. A. Hoffmann, a writer of fantastic tales which are still justly admired for their ironical twists and their grotesque humor. They were succeeded by the superb lyricist Eduard Mörike, the Franconian poet Friedrich Rückert, and Joseph von Eichendorff, author of, among other things, the delightful short novel *The Life of a Good-for-nothing* (1826). There was little in the works of these writers to bother the censor, since their themes were generally taken from the remote past or nature or the world of fantasy or dealt with love and romantic longing. Nor was the work of the greatest German writer of this and the previous age, Johann Wolfgang von Goethe (1749–1832), subject to interference, for the political instinct had never been highly developed in

---

[4] In his autobiography Grillparzer wrote that he once met an official in the censor's bureau who admitted pleasantly that he had been responsible for holding up *King Ottokar*. "But, Herr Hofrat," the poet asked, "what did you find in the piece that was dangerous?" "Not a thing," was the answer, "but I thought to myself, 'One never can tell!' "

him, even during the fight against Napoleon. In his last years Goethe wrote his memoirs, composed the remarkable cycle called the *Westöstlicher Divan,* and finished the second part of his masterpiece *Faust,* which has been called an electrocardiogram of the German character. From the events of his day he preserved an Olympian detachment and, during the revolution of 1830, was more interested in a debate between Cuvier and Geoffrey Saint-Hilaire over the development of the earth's crust than he was in the expulsion of Charles X from the throne of France (see pp. 72–73).

This attitude made Goethe the target of criticism and even contempt for a group of younger writers who, in the first years after 1830, formed the movement called Young Germany, whose most distinguished representatives were Heinrich Heine (1797–1856), renowned equally for the lyrical passion of his poetry and his satirical genius, and Ludwig Börne, whose *Letters from Paris* (1830–1834) helped stimulate the beginning of critical journalism in Germany. The members of this movement shared the conviction that writers have a responsibility to society and must play a political role, but most of them had no clear idea about how to implement this philosophy and lost themselves in an incoherent welter of projects ranging from the liberation of Poland to the emancipation of women. It is a sign of absolutism's fundamental lack of perspective that the works of Young Germany should have been taken so seriously that they were banned by formal decision of the German Confederation in 1835. The persecution of Heine and Börne, who had by this time dissociated themselves from the movement, is more understandable. They were formidable opponents—Börne's *Menzel, the Gobbler-up of Frenchmen* and other attacks upon philistinism, servility, and narrow nationalism made a deep impression upon the young Friedrich Engels, and Heine's wicked pen delighted Karl Marx—and one is not surprised to learn that they died in exile in Paris. Exile was also the fate of the most original genius of his day, Georg Büchner, the author of two dramas that were to find appreciative audiences only in the twentieth century, *Danton's Death* and *Woyzek.* Because of revolutionary activity among the Hessian peasantry, Büchner was sought by the police and had to flee to Strassburg and later to Zürich, where he died of a fever in February 1837 at the age of twenty-four.

Painting, sculpture, and music had greater freedom to develop because their subject matter was less obviously political and their message, if they had one, harder to communicate; and for music in particular this was a rich period. In Russia Michael Glinka (1804–1867) wrote his two operas, *A Life for the Tsar* (1836) and *Ruslan and Liudmila* (1842), and the orchestral works, *Kamarinskaia* and the so-called Spanish overtures, that were to have such a marked influence upon the technique of his successors, Tchaikovsky and Rimski-Korsakov. In Germany, Beethoven's last work showed the transition from classicism to romanticism, as did the songs of Schubert and the work of Weber, whose *Der Freischütz* had a sensational premiere in Berlin in 1821 and marked the birth of modern German opera. Meyerbeer's *Robert the Devil* (1831) and the young Richard Wagner's first operas, *Rienzi* and *The Flying Dutchman* (1841), were also in the romantic manner, discoursing, like *Der Freischütz,* on passion and virtue, on the beneficent and diabolical aspects of nature, on the responsibility and the corruptibility of power, on servitude and freedom, in music that was

Georg Büchner's *Woyzek,* the story of a common soldier who is brutalized by poverty and driven to madness and murder by ill-treatment, was not published in its entirety until 1879. It is probably best known in the operatic version of Alban Berg (1921), which follows the text closely and whose music heightens its somber revolutionary intensity. One of the greatest modern interpreters of the role of Marie, Woyzek's mistress and victim, is the American soprano Evelyn Lear, a leading member of the Metropolitan Opera and the Deutsche Oper Berlin, seen here with the famous German baritone Dietrich Fischer-Dieskau as Woyzek. (Deutsche Grammophon/Jacoby)

alternately mystical, sensuous, and melancholy and always filled with dramatic intensity.

The absolutist regimes, which deformed and crushed so much that lay within their control, left these expressions of the creative spirit, for the most part, alone. One of the king of Saxony's ministers, however, on learning that Weber had composed the music for some songs of the dead soldier poet Theodor Körner, grumbled, "We didn't know that Weber composed that demagogic rubbish or we would never have engaged him to come to Dresden."

Chapter 3 FRANCE: THE RESTORATION AND THE JULY MONARCHY

THE ECONOMIC AND SOCIAL ORGANIZATION OF THE COUNTRY

The Effects of the Revolution   The period of French history that opened in 1814 is usually called the Restoration; but, as has often been pointed out, very little was in fact restored, except the Bourbon dynasty. France had had twenty-five years of revolutionary change since 1789, and it was so obviously impossible to re-establish the institutions and laws of the old regime that the first French ruler of this period resisted the advice of those councillors who wanted him to turn back the clock. Louis XVIII was wise enough to see that very few people in France had any desire to see the past recaptured.

Thanks to the Revolution and to Napoleon, the feudal customs and the privileges of the nobility had been swept away, the old administrative system with its plethora of provincial agencies and local boundaries had been replaced by a centralized, logical system that really worked, and the ancient judicial system, with its many conflicting sovereignties and law codes, had given way to a uniform system of courts and by-laws that were codified and binding on all parts of the country. The majority of Frenchmen put too high a valuation on efficiency to want to see outworn institutions restored merely for the sake of tradition.

There were more persons, perhaps, who were sympathetic to the idea of restoring clerical influence in education; but, even here, the merits of Napoleon's centralization of the whole educational system under the Université de France were too obvious to permit its abolition, and most people were content to argue that neither the state nor the church should be allowed to monopolize education.

Finally, in the case of the most profound changes effected by the revolution, those in the economic and social organization of the country, there were too many people who had benefited directly from the transformation of the last twenty-five years to permit efforts to restore the old system.

The changes, then, were permanent; and the economic and social changes in particular made France profoundly different from the countries discussed above, despite occasional superficial similarities.

Economic Organization   In 1815 France had a population of twenty-eight million people, and, by 1850, this had risen to almost thirty-five million. At the latter date there were eight million more Frenchmen than inhabitants of the British Isles, and, among the Great Powers, France was second only to Russia in number of subjects.

The great majority of Frenchmen still lived off the land. As late as 1850 there were only five French cities with 100,000 inhabitants or more: Paris, with 1,420,000; Marseille, with 195,000; Lyon, with 177,000; Bordeaux, with 131,000; and Rouen, with 100,000. The fact that Paris increased its numbers by 300,000 between 1830 and 1850 indicates that a shift to the cities was getting under way; but this was still on a small scale, and France was a predominantly rural country.

The state of agriculture was potentially healthy. Thanks to the abolition of feudalism, France was now a nation of free farmers, and the division and sale of church properties and of some of the large estates belonging to the nobility had greatly favored the intensive cultivation of the soil. The most important crops were grain (which was protected against foreign competition by an adjustable tariff), grapes, garden products, olives, and—introduced most recently—sugar beets. There was a slow but steady expansion of all crops during this period; and, by 1835, the yield of wine grapes was double what it had been in 1815, while there was generally a surplus of cereals for export.

Both the government and private agricultural societies took an active interest in scientific methods; a Ministry of Agriculture was founded in 1836; and there was widespread dissemination of agricultural studies. The effect of this was diminished, however, by the high degree of illiteracy in the rural districts and the extreme conservatism of the French peasant, who looked with suspicion upon novelty and resisted even such useful innovations as selective breeding and artificial fertilization. The fact that primogeniture had been abolished during the Revolution also has a bearing here, for the distribution of land among all members of the family meant that allotments tended to be small, so that—even when they were used—scientific methods had less striking effects than they might have had on more extensive farms. As a result of this, French agriculture remained highly vulnerable to natural disasters. The effects of poor harvests, for instance, tended to be widespread and, because the peasants were free citizens, to have violent political results.

France's industrial progress was more advanced than that of its eastern neighbors. It had been stimulated by government assistance during the war and by the necessity of producing goods normally imported but at that time cut off by the blockade. Thus, the cotton industry at Rouen, Lille, and Saint-Quentin was in a flourishing condition when peace was restored. Both it and the linen industry were protected by tariffs and produced for the internal market, rather than the external, where the British were supreme. In both these industries the putting-out system of household production was still the rule, although concentration of manufacture in factories was beginning, especially in the silk industry, which had its center at Lyon. It was in silk also that mechanization was most pronounced, both Jacquard and power looms being widely used in this period.

Aside from textiles, the most important industries were the metallurgical and machine-making industries. France was handicapped by the lack of good coking coal, and, until the mid-forties, most of its pig iron was smelted in small charcoal furnaces. Even so, the beginnings of concentration and mechanization were made, and such firms as Schneider-Creuzot and Wendel were producing iron in modern puddling and rolling mills in the middle 1820s. In this period also, machine industry became firmly established in Alsace, Lille, Marseille, and the vicinity of Paris. Power for manufacturing was still produced by water; but by 1846 France had a total of 5000 steam engines with a combined horsepower of 60,000.

Domestic commerce was encouraged by the improvement of roads and canals and by the creation in 1831 of a special Ministry of Public Works charged with their construction and upkeep. Some measure of French success here is indicated by the fact that one could travel by highway from Paris to Bordeaux in thirty-six hours in 1848, whereas the same trip had taken eighty-six hours in 1814. In the same period the canal network was tripled in length, and all of France's major rivers were fitted into it. Railroad development was relatively slow. The first regular railway was started at the industrial town of Saint-Etienne on the Loire in 1827 and was extended as far as Lyon by 1832. In 1842, a railroad law was passed, providing for the construction of a national network by private companies with government aid and supervision. By 1848 about 1000 miles of railway were in operation and another 1500 being constructed.

France's foreign commerce had been pretty well ruined by the wars and, at the beginning of this period, the older ports were in decline. Marseille was revived by the conquest of Algeria in 1830 and Bordeaux by the growth of French industry, which also stimulated the rise of the newest and fastest growing port, Le Havre. Probably the greatest barrier to the resuscitation of foreign trade was the generally protectionist character of European tariff policy. After 1846, when Great Britain went in for free trade, there was growing interest in France in the possible advantages of following suit.

Social Organization   The social system of the *ancien régime* had been completely smashed by the revolution. In the new France the king and the court played a much diminished role, and were generally unpopular in Paris, to which they had removed from Versailles. As for the nobility, they found it impossible to regain their former monopoly of political and social power. Even in the first years after their return, their position was contested by the wealthy bourgeoisie and, after 1830, it was captured by the great bankers, merchants, speculators, and industrialists, who formed that class. There was a tendency, as time went on, for the nobility and the upper bourgeoisie to cooperate, if not to combine, as there was also for the sons of the bourgeoisie to turn from the business world of their fathers to the professions, government service, and the army. Thus, in

Stendhal's penetrating analysis of French society in this period, *Lucien Leuwen,* we find the hero, the son of a great Paris banker, first serving as a lieutenant in a regiment in the provinces and then seeking a post as secretary in one of the ministries.

Beneath the nobility and the upper bourgeoisie was the lower bourgeoisie, that solid, respectable, unadventurous class of urban tradesmen, wealthy peasants, *rentiers,* and pensioners described so well in the pages of Balzac and Flaubert. Their outlook was restricted, for the most part, to the events of their own small world; they were not widely read; and, in politics, they were interested only in actions that affected their financial well-being. But they comprised the class with which any government had to reckon, for their support was necessary if it was to retain power.

At the bottom of the scale were the poorer peasantry and the working class. The majority of French peasants now owned some land of their own, but a large part of what they held was mortgaged and they had to pay ruinous interest rates to the speculators who had sold it to them, a situation also well described by that percipient observer Balzac, particularly in *Les Paysans* (1844), in which a radical agitator warns the peasants against the village usurer who has "been sucking the marrow from your bones for the last thirty years, and you still don't see that the *bourgeois* will be worse than the *seigneur.* A peasant will always be a peasant!" The lot of the French peasantry was, of course, far superior to that of their Austrian, Prussian, and Russian counterparts but their standard of living was often not far above the subsistence level, their housing conditions were often wretched, and their lives were ones of unremitting toil. They were mostly illiterate and conservative in their views, although prone to violent action in time of economic distress.

Finally, the working class in the urban centers included craftsmen in small shops, factory workers, construction workers, day laborers, and beggars. Even those who were steadily employed were more vulnerable economically than they would have been under the old guild system, which had now been abolished. They were forbidden to organize and hence had no means of protection against depreciation of wages or abominable working conditions. All the evidence indicates that their existence became steadily more wretched from 1815 to 1848, as their numbers were swollen by new arrivals from the countryside, and they became increasingly rebellious. Although strikes were illegal and were followed by heavy jail sentences for their instigators, they were numerous and violent in these years. The German poet Heine, who visited some of the factories in the Faubourg Saint-Marceau in 1842 and saw the kind of reading matter that was being circulated among the workers and read to them, wrote: "The harvest that will sooner or later come from this sowing in France threatens to be a republican outbreak."

Thanks to the revolution, then, and to the advance of industry, the old and relatively static division of society had been replaced by one that was much more complicated. It was also more fluid, partly because the revolutionary doctrine of equality was taken seriously by Frenchmen and led them to be less inclined to accept the station into which they were born and readier, when other methods failed, to take violent action to improve it.

THE LAST OF THE BOURBONS, 1814–1830

The King and the Charter   Louis XVIII has generally been treated with respect by French historians, probably because of the sober good sense he showed in the first years of his reign, when it would have been easy to act emotionally. He demonstrated his intelligence at the very outset by admitting that the Allied Powers were right in insisting that France be ruled in a constitutional manner; one of his first acts was to grant to his subjects the Constitutional Charter that was to remain in force until the February days of 1848.

This document began with a preamble that sought to justify the divine right of kings in general and to list the great services of the French monarchs of the past, and then added:

> While We recognized that a free monarchical constitution should fulfill the expectations of an enlightened Europe, We had also to remember that Our first duty toward Our people was, in their own interest, to preserve the rights and prerogatives of the Crown.

It then claimed for the king the right to make treaties, to declare war and make peace, to command the military forces, and to make appointments; and it went on to state that legislative power would be shared between the king and the two houses of parliament, the king alone having the right to introduce or amend laws and the parliament the right to accept or reject them. Parliament was to consist of a Chamber of Peers, composed of hereditary peers and members appointed by the king for life, and a Chamber of Deputies, composed of members elected for a term of five years, unless the king decided to dissolve the Chamber and call for new elections. To be eligible for election as a deputy one had to be at least forty years old and to own enough property to necessitate the annual payment of 1000 francs in direct taxes. To vote in elections one had to be at least thirty years old and to pay taxes amounting to 300 francs a year. What this meant was that only about 100,000 men could vote and only 12,000 stand for election out of a population of twenty-eight million.

The Charter, therefore, did not provide for anything resembling democratic participation in government. On the other hand, it enabled a higher proportion of the population to have some share in politics than was true at this time in countries further to the east. It was relatively enlightened in another way: it declared the equality of all Frenchmen before the law, their eligibility for all civil and military positions, their freedom from arbitrary arrest and from imprisonment without legal process, their freedom to worship as they saw fit and to have a free press. Moreover, in an announcement made a month before the Charter was issued, the king had made it clear that his subjects need have no fear of expropriation in case they had acquired land formerly belonging to the church or the *émigrés;* and he had added:

> The guaranteed government debt, pensions, distinctions, and military honors will be maintained, as well as the old and the new [the Napoleonic] nobility. The Legion of Honor will be preserved, and We will decide upon the nominations.

Taken all together, this was a charter of liberties the like of which was unknown in eastern Europe. It was, in effect, a recognition of the principal changes wrought by the Revolution.

The Charter itself was regarded with aversion by some people in France. Speaking generally, one can distinguish four main political groupings in the country: the Ultra-Royalists, the Doctrinaires, the Liberals, and the Radicals. The first and the last of these groups opposed the constitutional grant and everything it stood for.

In his great novel about Restoration France, *Les Misérables,* Victor Hugo described the attitude of the Ultra-Royalists. He wrote:

> To be Ultra is to quarrel with the stake as to the degree of cooking heretics should undergo; it is to reproach the idol for its want of idolatry; it is to find in the Pope insufficient papism, in the king too little royalty, and too much light in the night.

The Ultras lived in the world of Bouvines and Fontenoy; and, not unnaturally, they regarded the Charter as an abomination. They were, indeed, so completely reactionary that Louis XVIII once grumbled, "If these gentlemen had their way, they would end by purging me."

At the other end of the political spectrum were the Radicals, a confused group of varying views, united only in their desire to destroy the existing regime so that either the empire could be restored or a republic established. They opposed the Charter for obvious reasons, but they had little strength or importance before 1830.

The two middle groups accepted the Charter but differed in their attitude toward it. To the Doctrinaires it seemed as reasonable a balance between government power and individual freedom as could be devised; therefore, it should not be tampered with. The Liberals, on the other hand, felt that it was inadequate and must be amended in such a way as to extend civil liberties and strengthen the powers of the Chamber of Deputies by making the king's ministers responsible to it. In other things these groups were in general agreement. Neither favored any real widening of the suffrage; both opposed democracy as steadfastly as they did absolutism; both believed that France should be run by the well-to-do and educated middle class. If they had been able to cooperate in a political system run according to well-defined and mutually satisfactory rules, in which they could have alternated in power, both the Charter and the monarchy might have survived. Instead, as a result of events that could not have been foreseen, the Doctrinaires were driven into the arms of the Ultras, while the Liberals drifted toward the Radical position.

Domestic Politics under Louis XVIII   The political history of this period began with the unedifying spectacle of royalist-inspired riots, plundering forays, and political murders, especially in the southern departments. This White Terror, which the government proved incompetent or disinclined to suppress, had the effect of intimidating liberal-minded electors when the first election of deputies took place in 1815; and the Chamber that resulted from these elections was so reactionary in its complexion that the king called it a *Chambre introuvable,* "a chamber the like of which will never be found again." This body further encouraged rightist excesses by demanding the execution of Marshal Ney and other soldiers who had rallied to the cause of Napoleon during the Hundred Days. A foreign observer was moved by this blood bath to remark: "The French are behaving as if there were no such thing as history or the future." The Chamber's insistence on repressive measures was so patently vindictive that the other Great Powers became alarmed. The Russian Foreign Minister Nesselrode warned the Count of Artois, the darling of the Ultras, that they were not occupying France in order "to sustain his foolishness," and the Duke of Wellington wrote Louis XVIII that this crude provincial royalism might very well cost him his crown. The king was not opposed to this kind of encouragement. In September 1816 he dissolved the Chamber, forcing new elections that brought a more moderate-minded assembly into existence.

This action ushered in the most constructive period of Louis XVIII's reign. In the next four years the ministers Decazes and Richelieu, supported by a Chamber in which the majority was composed of Doctrinaires and Liberals, passed the laws that were necessary to elaborate the suffrage and press provisions of the Charter. They also restored France's fiscal sovereignty and raised the money needed to pay off the war indemnity, which not only freed French soil of foreign troops but restored France to the family of nations, as was demonstrated by her admission to the consultations at Aix-la-Chapelle in 1818. In the same year, the famous law drafted by Gouvion St. Cyr was passed, providing for the reorganization of the army and laying down the principles—voluntary enlistment, equality of opportunity, promotion by merit—which were to guide military training and recruitment policy until 1868. These and other constructive measures infuriated the Ultras, who found the press law too liberal and the army law prejudicial to the nobility and who accused the king's chief minister, Decazes, of encouraging the growth of liberalism.

Their criticism might have been ineffective if it had not been for an unforeseen calamity. On February 13, 1820, a fanatic named Louvel stabbed and killed the Duke of Berry as he was helping his wife into a carriage at the Opera. The duke was the youngest son of the Count of Artois and he was considered the only member of the Bourbon family likely to have a son who would assure the line of succession. The murderer admitted that his motive was to remove this possibility, although events were to show that his attempt had been belated, the Duchess of Berry being already with child.

The importance of the Berry murder was that it introduced a new period of reaction. As Chateaubriand wrote, "Decazes' foot slipped in the blood and he fell." The ministry that replaced his was Ultra in its views and, in being so, now received the support of many Doctrinaires who seem to have believed that the murder was a sign that their past policies had been too liberal to be safe. As a result, the government was able to ram through laws that suspended the liberty of the subject, reconstituted a rigorous censorship of the press, and, finally, rewrote electoral procedure in such a way as to give virtual control of the elections to the Chamber of Deputies to the large landlords and the old nobility. This new law worked so effectively, from the Ultra point of view, that the elections of 1820 reduced the Liberals to a group of 80 in a Chamber of

450 members, leaving the Ultras and their Doctrinaire allies in complete control.

Louis XVIII made little attempt now to resist their demands. He had been genuinely shocked by the Berry assassination, and this inclined him to the Ultras, as did the fact that his new mistress, Mme. du Cayla, was an uncompromising Ultra in her opinions. Moreover, the king's tendency toward indolence had grown with the years, and he was now willing to leave the initiative in most things to his heir, the Count of Artois. Villèle, the minister who came to exercise greatest influence over him after Decazes' fall, was also of the extreme royalist persuasion. It was Villèle who persuaded the hesitant king to authorize the expedition into Spain in 1823 (see pp. 22–23), which published to all Europe France's apparently inflexible opposition to liberalism. Apart from this, the last years of Louis XVIII were marked, on the one hand, by a deepening of repressive legislation and a growth of religious influence in education and, on the other, by a number of attempts on the part of frustrated Liberals and Radicals to escape from their impotence by secret conspiracies and *coups de main*. The failure of these further discredited the left; and, in 1823, there were only fifteen Liberals left in the Chamber.

It is little wonder that, by September 1824, when Louis XVIII died and was succeeded by the Count of Artois, the Ultras felt that the satisfaction of their wildest hopes was at hand.

The Reign of Charles X   The new king was a kindly and charming man, but one with limited intelligence in political matters, a reputation for cowardice, and an ostentatious piety that exasperated his subjects, who were soon repeating the story that he was a Jesuit and bound by the rules of the order. This charge was not true, but it seemed plausible at a time when the government was passing a law punishing certain kinds of sacrilege with death, when the church was conducting a clamant campaign against civil marriage, and when the University of Paris was being submitted to the control of the archbishop of Paris and having certain of its courses suspended by that authority as dangerous to morals.

The favors shown the church were not, however, as unpopular as the persistent attempts to restore the power of the nobility. One of the first actions of Charles X's reign was a clever bit of financial jugglery with the national debt which saved the state a billion francs, which the government promptly handed over to the *émigrés* to indemnify them for their losses during the Revolution. Not only did this seriously hurt the great bankers—the holders of the bonds whose interest rate had been lowered in order to effect the saving—but it infuriated a lot of other people who saw it for what it was: a piece of special legislation for the advantage of a class whose members had not only left France during the Revolution but who had actually fought against their country.

This was followed by an attempt to restore a measure of primogeniture, by allowing fathers to leave a double portion of their estates to their eldest sons—a modest enough proposal on the surface but, quite plainly, a first step in a planned return to the feudal economy. One deputy said indignantly, "This is no law. It is a manifesto against existing society. It is a forerunner of twenty other laws which ... will break in on us and leave no rest to the society of France...." The bill was passed by the Ultra-dominated Chamber of Deputies but rejected by the Peers, enough of whom still regarded the abolition of primogeniture as one of the great achievements of the Revolution.

But it is really unnecessary to dwell in detail on the events of the reign of Charles X. History is doubtless filled with examples of political folly, but surely there are few that are so unrelieved as the one afforded by the last Bourbon ruler of France. His most marked quality was stubbornness, and it was this that lost him his crown, for it prevented him from learning anything from his defeats. His dogged pursuit of objectives in which only the nobility and the conservative clergy would find any advantage soon united all of the other groups that possessed any political influence against the regime. It alienated the lesser bourgeoisie as well as the great bankers, converted even moderate Liberals into antimonarchists for the time being, and thus effected a fusion between Liberals and Radicals that was ominous for the dynasty. It is significant that the king's successes in the field of foreign affairs—the participation in the Allied fleet action against the Turkish navy at Navarino in 1827 (see p. 27), and, in 1829–1830, the preparation and successful launching of the expedition that was to conquer Algeria and mark the beginning of the establishment of France's new colonial empire—went virtually unnoticed in France, where all attention was focused on the reactionary policies of the king's ministers.

Some kind of crisis was inevitable; and the way for it was prepared at the end of 1829 when Charles reconstructed his ministry, filling it almost completely with extreme royalists, including such men as General Bourmont, who had betrayed Napoleon, and Labourdonnaye, who had been active in the White Terror of 1815. The head of this new combination was Count Polignac, a former émigré, an embittered opponent of the charter, a fanatical churchman who had visions and who claimed to have frequent conversations with the Virgin Mary. Polignac was politically so incompetent that he did not know enough to disguise his real intentions. His object, he admitted openly, was "to reorganize society, to restore to the clergy its former preponderance in the state, and to create a powerful aristocracy and surround it with privileges."

This was to confirm the worst suspicions of the middle class, and that part of it which possessed political power now met Polignac's challenge. In the elections of 1827, Liberal strength in the Chamber of Deputies had revived markedly, and, in March 1830, it was sufficient to pass an Address to the Throne which, in effect, asked for the dismissal of the ministry. The king responded by dissolving the Chamber and calling for new elections, doubtless expecting the support of the electors. In this he was disappointed, for the voters elected a Chamber that was overwhelmingly antigovernment.

It was apparently at this point that those shrewder reactionaries, Nicholas I and Metternich, advised Charles to yield. But he was too insistent on his royal prerogatives to consider that. He tried, instead, to break the opposition by issuing, on July 26, 1830, four ordinances. These suspended the liberty of the press, dissolved the Chamber again on the grounds that misdemeanors had occurred during the recent elections, altered the electoral law in such a way as to reduce the electorate by about three fourths and to exclude the whole of the bourgeoisie from it, and, finally, set a date for new elections.

Once he had authorized these decrees, Charles went off to Rambouillet to hunt; when he came back, he was no longer king. A protest against the edicts was started by the Liberal editors of Paris, led by Adolphe Thiers (1797–1877) of *Le National;* it was taken up by the printers, unemployed because of the new press law, and by other workers, students, intellectuals, and the like. On July 28 Rouget de Lisle, now seventy years old, burst into a friend's house and quavered, "Things look bad. They are singing *La Marseillaise!*" Outside in the narrow, twisting streets, the great barricades for which Paris was famous began to be erected, barriers fifty to eighty feet high, made of paving-stones, boxes, furniture, trees, wagons, and anything else that came to hand.

On the same day General Marmont brought troops into the city and sent them against the barricades, but with indifferent success. The soldiers were neither trained nor properly armed for street fighting; they did not know the unconventional terrain in which they were engaged, whereas the insurgents knew every short cut and alleyway; and their hearts were not in the fight anyway. Marmont was later to claim that he would have had better results if he had been allowed to surround and bombard the city, but this was a favorite excuse of commanders in the midcentury who had the uncomfortable experience of having their troops worsted by untrained students and workers. In any case, after three days of hard fighting, it was clear even to the king that he was not going to be able to put down the revolt. He decided, therefore, to withdraw the edicts, but now it was too late.

Indeed, the only real question now was what was going to take the place of Charles' discredited and defeated regime, and who, if anyone, was to have his throne. The weary and powder-stained fighters on the barricades would probably have voted for a republic; but the initiative was now taken by the Liberal editors and businessmen and deputies, again led by Thiers. After some involved maneuvering, they persuaded a rump Chamber of Deputies to invite Louis Philippe, the Duc d'Orleans, to come to Paris as lieutenant-governor of the kingdom, and when he did so, managed to get Lafayette, the nominal leader of the small republican party, to throw his support to him. Finally, on August 3, 1830, the full Chamber invited Louis Philippe to take the throne, and he accepted.

A week later, Charles X sailed off to exile in Scotland. He was not destined to return to his country, nor was any of his line ever again to sit upon the throne of France.

THE JULY MONARCHY

Government by the Middle Class   One of the shrewdest political observers of the nineteenth century was Alexis de Tocqueville (1805–1859), who won a European reputation when he published the first part of his *Democracy in America* in 1835. At the time of its publication this book infuriated many Ameri-

---

[1] Rouget de Lisle was the author of *La Marseillaise,* having composed it when he was a young lieutenant in 1792. Now an old man living in obscurity, he was before long reassured and flattered by the revival of his work, which was given a new and splendidly dramatic setting by Berlioz.

cans because of de Tocqueville's criticism of certain institutions and customs in this country. They would probably have been less annoyed if they had known that de Tocqueville was an infinitely more scathing critic of his own nation. Indeed, it is in his posthumously published memoirs that we find the most trenchant indictment of the regime established after the July revolution.

That revolution, de Tocqueville wrote, marked the definitive conquest of political power by the middle class, and they proceeded now, in exercising it, to exclude the other classes from any share in it.

> The particular spirit of the middle class became the general spirit of the government; it ruled the latter's foreign policy as well as affairs at home: an active, industrious spirit, often dishonorable, generally orderly, occasionally reckless through vanity or egoism, but timid by temperament, moderate in all things except in its love of ease and comfort, and, last but not least, mediocre. It was a spirit which, mingled with that of the people or of the aristocracy, can do wonders; but which, by itself, will never produce more than a government shorn of both virtue and greatness.... The middle class, when called upon to assume the government, took it up as an industrial enterprise.

It was not merely aristocratic disdain that prompted these sentiments. De Tocqueville saw clearly what a great many Frenchmen sensed after 1830: the pettiness, the narrowness of view, and what might be called the lack of political style of their new rulers. His charge that the bourgeoisie sought to monopolize power and exercise it in their own interest is a fair one. Before the triumphant Liberals offered the crown to Louis Philippe, they had amended the Charter in such a way as to weaken the position of other classes or institutions that might threaten their own position. They deleted the preamble, thus repudiating the whole idea of divine right of kings (although they substituted no alternative theory to give a logical basis for the institution of monarchy, which they retained). They did away with the paragraph that made Roman Catholicism the official religion of France, thus undermining the position of the clergy. In subsequent years, they greatly weakened the prerogatives of members of the House of Peers and deprived them of their hereditary character. On the other hand, by the law of 1831, they widened the suffrage slightly by reducing the property qualification from 300 to 200 francs in annual taxes and by also giving the vote to professional men, like lawyers, doctors, and professors, who paid at least 100 francs in taxes. This, and the lowering of the voting age to twenty-five years, doubled the electorate; but still only about 200,000 people could vote out of a population that was getting close to thirty-two million; and, if most of the bourgeoisie were now enfranchised, all of the working class was excluded from power. Finally, by a law that is entirely characteristic of the class character of the new regime, the National Guard—the force designed to protect the Charter and maintain law and order—was reorganized so that service in it was obligatory only for citizens who paid direct taxes and could afford to buy their own uniforms and equipment.

To the bourgeoisie it seemed perfectly reasonable that power should be theirs and theirs alone. The most eloquent spokesman of this class and, in the last stages of the July monarchy, its leading statesman, was François Guizot (1787–1874), university professor, historian of the English revolution, member of the Doctrinaire party. Guizot argued that political power should be exercised by *la classe moyenne* because it alone possessed "not only the necessary fortune [to devote itself to political work] but also the intelligence and the independence without which that work cannot be accomplished." He was not moved by arguments that the middle class was dominated by the commercial and financial oligarchy of the country, although he did not deny that this was true. The political system of the July Monarchy was admirable, he said, because, "at the same time that it sets limits to political rights by a property qualification, it works to remove that limit by allowing men to become wealthy and to extend it."

In general, the new ruling class took a typically middle class attitude toward government: they regarded it as a necessary evil, whose functions should be kept to the bare minimum. Aside from protecting property from civil disorder, government was not supposed to *do* things. Above all, it was not supposed to

"The Napoleon of Peace: Louis Philippe." From an impression by the famous cartoonist, Dicky Doyle, in *Punch,* October 23, 1847.

become involved in foreign adventures, because nothing was more detrimental to business. Guizot, who had additional motives for this feeling (he hated the cheap chauvinism which became so pronounced in the 1840s and which was encouraged by his antagonist Thiers), once said, "Let us not talk about our country having to conquer territory, to wage great wars, to undertake bold deeds of vengeance. If France is prosperous, if she remains free, rich, peaceful, and wise, we need not complain if we exercise only a small influence in the world abroad."

These attitudes of the bourgeoisie were shared by the new king. Louis Philippe was the son of that Duke of Orleans called Philippe Égalité who had supported, and then been executed by, the Revolution. He himself had fought for his country at Valmy and Jemappes and had then gone into exile, traveling extensively and actually visiting the United States. This romantic background did not alter the fact that he was not a man of wide interests or with a temperament calculated to inspire his people. Fifty-seven years old at the time of his accession to the throne, he showed himself a knowing, garrulous, but cautious man, who distrusted talent unless it had proven itself in the business world and who had a reverence for industry and finance that bordered on the ridiculous. He was personally brave, as he was to show on numerous occasions during his reign when he was the target of assassins, but his foreign policy especially seemed the reverse of courageous to many Frenchmen. Victor Hugo, who had a high opinion of the king's qualities, wrote in *Les Misérables* that "his great fault was that he was modest in the name of France. . . . [His reign was marked by] excessive timidity, which is offensive to a nation that has July 14 in its civil traditions and Austerlitz in its military annals."

The political principles shared by Louis Philippe and the bourgeoisie could not help but alienate important sections of the population. The supporters of the Bourbons rejected Louis Philippe for obvious reasons; but there was also a marked growth of republicanism in this period and a revival of the democratic spirit of 1793. At the same time, the working classes regarded the existing system as oppressive; the patriots agreed with General Lamarque's bitter description of the July monarchy as a "halt in the mud"; and the intellectuals and the romantically minded youth of the country felt, like Stendhal, that this was a regime of "charlatanism without talent."

Some Insurrections   This opposition took violent forms, and the first years of Louis Philippe's reign were filled with conspiracies, insurrections, and attempts at assassination. The Duchess of Berry, for instance, attempted a legitimist counterrevolution in 1832. This charming, courageous, but giddy-minded woman, scorning the sober doubts of her friends, landed in France in April 1832, with her head a muddle of improbable schemes and unwise expectations. When the city of Marseille failed to rise in revolution as she had hoped, she made her way by a series of hairbreadth escapes to the Vendée, only to find that her plans had been anticipated by the government. Escaping once more, she went into hiding in Nantes but was betrayed to the police and put in prison, where she astonished both her captors and her supporters by giving birth to a daughter, a fitting end to an episode that resembled sensational fiction rather than fact.

Even before this, there had been disorders in Paris, and in June 1832 there was a bloody republican insurrection in the capital. Since 1830, a radical republican movement had taken form, centered in two societies called *Les amis du peuple* and *La société de l'homme et du citoyen,* the latter of which had branches in the provinces. The 1832 affair, however, was more a spontaneous action by the republican rank and file than a deliberately planned revolt. The occasion for it was the funeral of General Lamarque, a popular and avowedly republican commander. As his funeral procession reached the Place de la Bastille, it was joined by groups of men shouting, "Long live the republic!" The temper of the crowd was inflamed by speeches by several republican notables; cries of "Lamarque to the Pantheon!" began to be heard; attempts were made to divert the procession, hearse and all, for an assault upon the Hôtel de Ville; and dragoons charged the crowd. The disorders spread; barricades were built; and there was open warfare in the streets of Paris for two days before order was restored.

The government struck back by passing a series of measures submitting all political associations to government surveillance and tightening restrictions on the republican press. These, and the prosecution of the ringleaders of the rising, had the effect of discouraging the growth of republicanism for a time; but it is nevertheless true that, in the insurrection of June 1832—so stirringly commemorated in Hugo's *Les Misérables*—French republicanism had found another symbol to hearten its followers.

In addition to these large-scale movements, there were several actions against the constituted authorities by individuals, including a number of attempts to assassinate the king. The most shocking of these was the work of a Corsican named Fieschi, who rigged up a kind of machine gun made of linked rifle barrels and fired it off as Louis Philippe, his three sons, and his suite were passing in parade in Paris in July 1835. The king and the princes escaped unhurt, but Fieschi's machine killed eighteen people and wounded many more. The incident inspired a revulsion of feeling in favor of the monarch but did not prevent new plots against him. All told, more than eighty attempts were made on Louis Philippe's life, a striking commentary both upon his indestructibility and the violence of his reign.

Workers' Revolts and the Beginnings of Socialism   More serious, and historically more significant, than these incidents were those that gave evidence of an increasingly rebellious temper among the working classes. In November 1831, the silk weavers of Lyon, who had to work eighteen hours a day for a pittance, rose in desperation and seized the town, controlling it for some days until their revolt was crushed by a military force under Marshal Soult. Three years later the weavers rose again, this time holding on for five days before their resistance was broken; and this time their effort touched off sympathetic disorders among workers in Paris and other cities. The indifference of the bourgeoisie to the plight of the workers and their antagonism to social legislation in these days when industry was expanding rapidly and dislocating the old economic order were forcing the workers to strike out blindly in the hope of securing some kind of relief.

It was in these circumstances that socialism began to grow in France. Among the more progressive bourgeoisie, who were worried by the disaffection of the

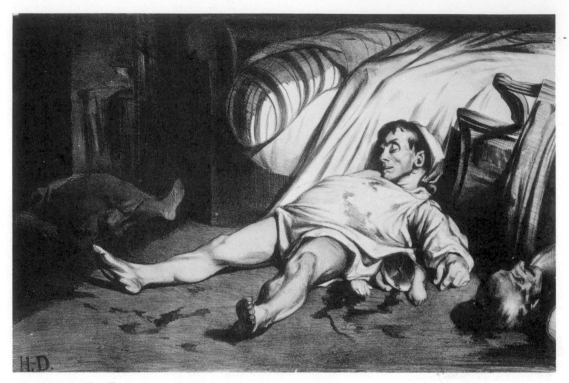

"Murder in the Rue Transnonain," 1834, by Honoré Daumier. This drawing is a biting comment on an incident that occurred during republican disturbances in Paris during April 1834. Government troops, claiming that they had been fired upon from the window of a house in the Rue Transnonain, where workers suspected of being active in the revolt lived, indulged in an indiscriminate massacre of its tenants. (Metropolitan Museum of Art, Rogers Fund, 1920)

working class, and among intellectuals in general, serious attention began to be paid to the work of thinkers like Henri de Saint-Simon (1760–1825). This is not the place to elaborate on the various writings of this profound and original thinker, but it can at least be said that Saint-Simon and his followers Bazard and Enfantin demonstrated to their contemporaries that the age of industrialism could be understood only by analyzing its economic foundations and that the future peace of society would depend on the success with which relations between the different classes were adjusted. Enfantin wrote:

Charles X thought that a few soldiers would silence inopportune voices, and the bourgeoisie are almost as blind as he; recent events have helped us to show them up. . . . This is the crux of the whole political problem, that it is no longer a question of priests and noblemen as in '89, or even as in 1829, but one of the people and the bourgeoisie or better of workers and nonworkers; one has gone a long way when the question is known, also how it should be put.

The Saint-Simonians hoped that moral reform and education would in the long run promote better understanding among classes and bring a gradual improvement of the economic conditions of the working class. They were not, however, egalitarians but social engineers, who believed that a society based on a hierarchy of talent and function would be more efficient than one that stressed equality, and they were more interested in efficiency than in political freedom. This was true also of Charles Fourier (1772–1837), who believed that the way to regenerate modern society was to decentralize it by encouraging its members to form themselves into small agricultural communities or phalansteries in which they would find it possible to develop all their faculties in fruitful cooperation with their fellows. Convinced that the success of only one such utopian experiment would be enough to convince mankind that this was the way of the future, Fourier announced that he would be at home every day at noon in case some benevolent patron might wish to give him the funds for the establishment of a society that would prove the feasibility of his plans. Although he waited for twelve years, no generous stranger ever appeared.

There were also more revolutionary socialists in France in this period. Philippe Buonarroti (1767–1837) had been a member of the Babeuf conspiracy in 1796[2] and now carried on that tradition by preaching the necessity of political revolution as a means of winning social reform. More extreme in his views was Auguste Blanqui (1805–1881), the perpetual conspirator, with his frock coat buttoned up to his chin, his flashing eyes, and that sallow skin that made Herzen think that he must live in the sewers or catacombs. Blanqui talked of "the duel to death between dividends and wages" and called upon the new worker, "the mechanized man," to wage unremitting war against the bourgeoisie, since there could be no community of interest between the classes. In his emphasis on underground activity and on a clear and systematic revolutionary strategy, Blanqui was a forerunner of those professional revolutionaries whom Lenin was to consider indispensable for a successful overthrow of bourgeois society. But the enthusiasm with which he supported even the most hopeless of conspiracies and émeutes makes one suspect that he believed in violence for the sake of violence and that it would not be illogical to class him with the early anarchists. Anarchist in essence also was the work of Pierre-Joseph Proudhon (1809–1865), whose famous book *What Is Property?* appeared in 1840, with its bold assertion that property was theft and its exposition of the theory that the measure of value is the labor that goes into the product evaluated.

But the most influential of all the French socialists of this period was Louis Blanc (1811–1882). In a sympathetic portrait in her novel *Le Piccinino*, George Sand described Blanc as possessing "great ambition lodged in a small body; a soft, insinuating voice; and a will of iron." Born in poverty, he made his way in life with the aid of these qualities and his great literary gifts. He first attracted attention in 1840, when his *History of Ten Years* gave a striking analysis of

[2] Gracchus Babeuf, sometimes called the first truly class-conscious leader of the European working class, organized a Society of the Pantheon which planned an insurrection against the Directory. Betrayed by informers, he was arrested, tried, and executed in the spring of 1796.

the social forces at work in France in the Restoration period. But the effect of this was nothing to that of his book *L'Organisation du Travail,* which appeared in the same year and immediately became one of the most discussed books of the whole period.

This work was a frontal attack upon the competitive system that was held in such reverence by capitalists of the early nineteenth century. Blanc set out to prove that competition was ruinous, not only for the common people but also for the bourgeoisie, since it was always wasteful and was productive of continual crises. All classes, therefore, had an interest in abolishing it; and, in this respect, "there exists a solidarity between all interests, and . . . social reform is for all members of . . . society, without exception, a means of salvation." Blanc wished to replace the competitive system of free enterprise with a national economy. He dreamed of a democratic republic in which the government would organize national workshops, or communal plants, in the most important industries. In each of these organizations the regulation of production and the allocation of function would be designed to alleviate the miserable plight of the working class in a country that was slowly adjusting to industrialism, in which unemployment was heavy because of the decline of the older trades, and in which wages were low and working conditions execrable.

Both the misery of the workers and the socialist theories it inspired were to have consequences in 1848.

Nationalism and the Revival of Bonapartism   To these opponents of the regime must be added all those who believed that the defeat of 1815 must be avenged and that France must demonstrate to Europe that it was still what it had been under Napoleon. In the cautious foreign policy of Louis Philippe's first decade, these people found little to admire. It is true that French arms were engaged in Algeria, where they were trying to finish the campaign begun by Charles X. But the African fighting gave little cause for national pride, since it was waged against a native people, and one, moreover, for whom the French came to have a good deal of sympathy, especially after Abd-el-Kader, the emir of Mascara, became the leader of the forces opposing France. A handsome and audacious commander, the emir was able to harry French columns and to burn isolated French forts for over ten years; and it was only in the midforties, after the government had committed about 100,000 men, that the French were able to win mastery over all of Algeria.

Meanwhile, patriots had been infuriated by the diplomatic defeat imposed on France during the Egyptian crisis of 1840 (pp. 33–34), which seemed to indicate that the other powers believed that it was worth no more consideration than it had been immediately after Waterloo. One of the republican leaders of this period, Edgar Quinet, said in 1840: "We thought that the Revolution was going to pick up her sword again in 1830, but her mighty wounded body could only raise itself on one knee. . . . For five and twenty years we have been bowed beneath the Caudine Forks, endeavoring to put a cheerful face on things and to gild our chain."

It is perhaps not surprising that, in these circumstances, the memory of Napo-

leon should have occurred to many people and that the glories of his reign should
have begun to be contrasted with the drabness of Louis Philippe's regime.

The growth of the Napoleonic cult during the July Monarchy was aided by
the work of men like Pierre Jean de Béranger, Victor Hugo, Emile de Girardin,
and Adolphe Thiers. Béranger (1780–1857) was a versifier with the common touch,
who had tremendous success with songs about the homelier aspects of Napoleon's
career and with sentimental tributes like the famous *Memories of the People,*
which described the love in which the common people held the emperor. Hugo
(1802–1885), an infinitely greater poet, invoked the emperor's memory in his
splendid *Ode à la Colonne,* written in 1831, and his *Napoléon II,* written after
the death of the emperor's son. Girardin edited the enormously popular newspaper *La Presse,* which was one of the most effective channels of Napoleonic
propaganda, while Thiers (1797–1877) wrote a twenty-volume history of the
Consulate and the Empire which breathed admiration of Napoleon's political
and military genius in every line. It was Thiers also who, as a minister of Louis
Philippe, completed the Arc de Triomphe, which had been left unfinished by
Napoleon, named streets and bridges after Napoleon's victories, and finally, in
a reverent ceremony in 1840, brought the emperor's bones back from St. Helena.

But it would be unwise to give too much credit to individuals for the revival
of Bonapartism. It was only natural that, sooner or later, there would be a
revulsion of feeling in Napoleon's favor. France was filled with young men who,
as Alfred de Musset wrote in his *Confessions of a Child of the Age,* had been
"dreaming for fifteen years of the snows of Moscow and the sun of the Pyramids"
and who—like Julien Sorel in Stendhal's *The Red and the Black*—were bored
with "the kind of eloquence that had replaced the Empire's rapidity of action."
They made a private cult of the Corsican. The dullness and the timidity of Louis
Philippe's government encouraged this to spread further, and it is significant
that it did so among the common people. It has been said that every popular
almanac published between 1840 and 1848 contributed to the apotheosis of
Napoleon; it might be added that the tremendous numbers of pipes, handker-
chiefs, jam jars, and beer mugs bearing his image, which were sold in village
shops or hawked by itinerant pedlars, did the same.

The beneficiary of all this was Louis Napoleon Bonaparte, the son of the
emperor's brother Louis and, after the death of the emperor's son, the Bonaparte
pretender. He had been educated in Germany (and never, in fact, overcame a
slight German accent) and had gone to Italy in 1831. Here he and his older brother
had become involved in the secret revolutionary movement known as the *Carbonari* (or Charcoal Burners), and here his brother had died of an illness con-
tracted during flight from the police. Louis Napoleon was a man of energy,
ambition, and will; he was determined to win his uncle's throne; and, in 1836,
he tried to do so. He appeared with a few companions at the fortress in Strasbourg
and called upon the garrison to follow him in an attempt to seize power. He
was arrested by an alert commander and taken off to Paris, where the king
had to decide what to do with him. Louis Philippe thought it wise in the end
to let the prince go and allowed him to sail off to the New World, doubtless
hoping he would remain there. But, after a brief visit to the United States, Louis
Napoleon returned to Europe and, in August 1840, with sixty companions, he

Honoré Daumier: "Victor Hugo and Emile Girardin Elevating Louis Napoleon." From *Le Charivari,* December 11, 1848. (New York Public Library, Print Division)

landed at Boulogne, declared the deposition of the House of Orleans, appealed once more for support, and was again arrested.

This time the authorities were not so lenient. The prince was tried before the Chamber of Peers, where he was condemned to imprisonment for life in the fortress of Ham. But the trial gave him an opportunity to make a ringing speech, in which he cried: "I represent before you a principle, a cause, a defeat. The principle is the sovereignty of the people; the cause is that of the Empire; the defeat is Waterloo." Eloquence was not the strong suit of the French bourgeoisie, and Louis Napoleon was doubtless dismissed as a crackbrained young man by some of the soberest minds in France. But his words were heard far beyond the walls of the Chamber that condemned him; and that was not unimportant, for although he remained at Ham for some years, writing brochures on such subjects as "The Extinction of Poverty," he eventually tired of this comfortable detention. One morning in the spring of 1846, while a doctor friend, pretending that the prince was ill, hovered around his empty bed, Louis Napoleon, dressed in workman's clothes, put a short pipe in his mouth and a plank on his shoulder and walked out the front gates of the fortress; a day later, he was safe in England. There he remained for two years, happy in the knowledge that his own name was now inextricably tied up with the Napoleonic legend and confident that every failure of Louis Philippe's government brought closer the day when he would be able to restore the Empire in France.

The Guizot System   At the height of the Egyptian crisis the government of France had been headed by Adolphe Thiers, but his inflammatory tactics, his apparent willingness to run the risk of war, and his tendency to pander to the Paris mob led the king to force his resignation. He was replaced by François Guizot, who was to remain in power from 1840 to 1848.

In foreign affairs, the Guizot period was marked by a greater degree of personal intervention by the king. It was largely under his influence that relations with England became cooler, and feelers were put out to Vienna in the hope of encouraging an Austro-French alliance (see p. 34). On the domestic front, the course followed might aptly be described as one of massive immobility. The advance of the years had strengthened Guizot's conservatism, and he was convinced that neither the Charter nor the basic laws of the realm stood in need of change. He had little understanding of social questions—like some other Calvinists before and since, he tended to regard poverty as a result of moral failings—and he possessed an excessive fear of offending groups he considered important. Thus, an advantageous conversion of interest rates on government bonds was avoided in order not to alienate the bondholders; a much-needed scaling-down of tariffs because it would be opposed by the big industrialists; the abolition of slavery in the colonies for fear of offending the planters; and so forth. Guizot's direction of policy invited the famous gibe of the poet-politician Lamartine, who said: "If that were all the genius required of a statesman charged with the direction of affairs, there would be no need of statesmen—a post would do as well."

Guizot's greatest failing was self-righteousness, and he was so convinced of the excellence of his policies that he was willing to commit ignoble actions in order to see that they were supported. Thus, he resorted increasingly to bribery and corruption on a large scale. With only a very limited electorate to worry about and with a highly centralized administrative system at his disposal, he was able to use the carrot and the stick in local electoral colleges, so as to secure the election of loyal deputies, and his shrewd distribution of patronage within the Chamber won him the comfortable majorities he desired.

There can be little doubt that his very success with these methods was self-defeating, for it brought discredit upon the regime as a whole. If the Chamber of Deputies was capable of doing only what Guizot commanded, then, people reasoned, something must be wrong with the Chamber. As de Tocqueville wrote later:

France grew unconsciously accustomed to look upon the debates in the Chamber as exercises of the intellect rather than as serious discussions and upon all the differences between the various parliamentary parties ... as domestic quarrels between children of one family trying to trick one another. A few glaring instances of corruption, discovered by accident, led the country to presuppose a number of hidden cases and convinced it that the whole of the governing class was corrupt.

More and more people began to think that radical change in the electoral system was needed; and, by the end of the 1840s, a campaign was under way to effect this.

Meanwhile, France's economic problems were increasing. The harvest of 1846 was a poor one, and agricultural distress was great. An international financial crisis in the same year forced manufacturers to cut back their production by about one third, and this caused a sharp increase in unemployment figures, which were already high. As a consequence, about a third of the working population of Paris was starving or being supported by charity in 1847. The government had no machinery for meeting this crisis and was opposed to devising any; and it is not therefore surprising that Louis Blanc's call for a democratic and social republic was heard by an increasing number of the town dwellers. In a speech in the Chamber of Deputies in January 1848, de Tocqueville warned his fellows of the rising discontent of the working class and pointed out that their "passions, instead of being political, [had] become social" and were more and more directed toward the destruction of the whole existing system. "I believe," he said ominously, "we are at this moment sleeping on a volcano.... In God's name, change the spirit of the government; for ... that spirit will lead you to the abyss."

RELIGION AND THE ARTS, 1815–1848

Church, Bourgeoisie, and Working Class   The two most notable religious developments in this period were the reconciliation between the bourgeoisie and the Roman Catholic Church and the parallel decline of the church's influence over the masses.

During the first postwar years, anticlericalism was still strong among the middle classes. Suspicion of the church was encouraged by the activities of the Jesuits, who returned to France after the restoration of the monarchy and whose special missions to the common people assumed the tone of antirevolutionary demonstrations, by the ultramontanism of people like de Maistre (see p. 37), by the growing political influence of the powerful Catholic laymen's society, the *Congrégation,* by the success of the church in infiltrating the commissions of the Université de France, and by the subsequent censorship of university teaching and the dismissal or suspension of liberal professors like the historian Guizot and the philosopher Cousin.

The cumulative effect of these things was to arouse the hostility of the literate classes of society. There was a sudden boom in the books of antireligious writers, and between 1814 and 1824 one and a half million copies of various works by Voltaire were sold. Simultaneously, jokes and songs directed against the clergy circulated, like Béranger's song:

Hommes noirs, d'où sortez-vous?
Nous sortons de dessous terre.
Moitié renards, moitié loups,
Notre règle est un mystère . . .
Nous rentrons, songez à vous taire,
Et que vos enfants suivent nos leçons.[3]

This antagonism grew steadily during Villèle's ministry and increased so sharply after Charles X came to the throne that the revolution of 1830 can be considered almost as much an attack against the church as it was against the monarchy.

In the subsequent period, however, there was a change. The new rulers of France, the bourgeoisie, came to regard religion as a useful protection against the social theories of republicanism and the more radical philosophies that threatened their position. All of a sudden it became unfashionable to be irreligious, and the formerly anticlerical bourgeoisie began to troop into the cathedral of Notre Dame where they could listen to preachers like Lacordaire and Montalembert explaining gravely that property was "one of the fundamental bases of society . . . the guardian of liberty and the dignity of man" and that poverty was the result of the improvidence of the masses. These were comforting doctrines, and the wealthy middle class abandoned its old antagonism to the church as it listened to them.

But the church acquired enemies to replace old-fashioned middle class anticlericalism. The advance of industrialism, by changing old ways of life, destroying traditional trades, and forcing people to leave their homes and drift toward the towns in search of employment, weakened the hold of the churches on the masses. This had not gone as far as it was to go later in the century; but Proudhon noted in 1844 that some workers in Lyon had lost contact with the church and were no longer baptized, married, or buried by the priest. There was enough evidence of this sort to stimulate attempts to check the religious decline by more missions. When clerics like Félicité Robert de Lamennais (1782–1854) tried to alleviate the misery of the working class by advocating social legislation, however, they received little sympathy from their fellows. Lamennais himself—later described by Sainte-Beuve as one of the great cornerstones of French socialism and philanthropy[4]—ended as an outcast from his own church. The church as a whole paid rather too little attention to the ills of the masses; and this was the reason why, among parts of the working class and even of the peasantry, there was, as Lacordaire noted, "an almost total absence of faith . . . and an immense scorn for the priest."

Other Churches   During the early Restoration some of the more fanatical churchmen had hoped for a new crusade against heresy—that is, against Protes-

[3] "Black men, where do you come from?" / "We come from under the ground / Half foxes, half wolves / Our discipline is a mystery . . . / We'll be back, so see that you keep quiet / And that your children follow our teaching."
The view of the Jesuit order as a gigantic conspiracy bent on conquering the world was one of the major themes in Eugène Sue's popular novel *The Wandering Jew* (1844–1845).
[4] The others, he said, were Béranger, George Sand, and Eugène Sue.

tantism; but the government discouraged this and protected the rights of the non-Catholic believers. In the first part of this period, the Reformed Church was weakened by internal disorganization and doctrinal disputes; but after 1830, when the *Réveil* or awakening came to France from Geneva, there was a strong movement toward unity, consolidation, and a return to the basic doctrines of the Reformation, and, under this inspiration, membership was greatly strengthened. Within Judaism there were also some doctrinal differences, as modernists sought to modify certain ritual practices; but these had no effect on the orthodoxy of the majority. Aside from this, for France's 60,000 Jews, this was a period in which many of the disabilities from which they had formerly suffered disappeared.

A word might be said here of attempts to provide new religions to replace the established ones. The followers of Saint-Simon, for instance, undertook to found a "church" with dogma, rites, and a priesthood, which was designed to deify science and humanity. A more elaborate attempt of this kind was made by Auguste Comte (1798–1857), who wished to transform modern society into an authoritarian state in which the scientists and the leaders of industry would be priests and rulers alike, and the great benefactors of society would be venerated as saints. Both Saint-Simon and Comte will be remembered for other things than these grandiose schemes—Saint-Simon for his pioneer analysis of industrial society, Comte because he was the father of modern sociology—and it is enough to say here that their churches did not attract many followers.

Literature and the Arts   In literature and the arts this was a period in which romanticism reached its finest flowering and began its decline. The general characteristics of romanticism have been described above (pp. 7–8); but it might be added that, precisely because it was a movement that broke with the standards of the past, it had a verve and a spirit that have rarely been matched since. Its representatives took a belligerent pride in their iconoclasm. A play in the romantic style was not just a play but a kind of military assault on the entrenched positions of classicism; and its presentation was likely to be the scene of stormy altercation and tumultuous demonstration, as was true of the production of Hugo's *Hernani* in February 1830. Because the movement broke also with the polished urbanity of the eighteenth century and with its cultivated and ironical rationalism, the romantics were apt, on the one hand, to deal with life in the raw—the delights of nature and the adventures of primitive and exotic peoples—and, on the other, to be highly emotional in the content and style of their works. George Sand, probably the most popular romantic novelist, wrote once to Gustave Flaubert, "My style has its ups and downs, its sounding harmonies and its failures. I do not fundamentally much mind, as long as the *emotion* comes through!"

Perhaps the truest representatives of romanticism were François-René de Chateaubriand (1768–1848), whose popular "epics of nature," *Atala* and *René,* were written before our period begins; Alphonse de Lamartine (1790–1869), whose *Méditations* (1820), with their haunting melodies, their extreme simplicity, and their intense emotion, took France by storm and, incidentally, kept Talleyrand awake all night; the young Hugo, the preface of whose play *Cromwell* (1827) was the manifesto of romanticism in the drama and whose *Hernani* was a kind

George Sand, 1804–1876.
(Culver Pictures)

Alexis de Tocqueville, 1805–1859.
(Culver Pictures)

of July revolution in literature; Alfred de Vigny (1797–1863), whose play *Chatterton* presented the ideal romantic hero, the proud egoist who is "a being apart," and whose somber poetry remains one of the great achievements of this period; Alfred de Musset (1810–1857), who carried emotionalism to the point of morbidity, but whose plays, with their wonderful blend of fantasy and reality, are the most successful products of the romantic drama; and, finally, George Sand (1804–1876), who used the novel as a means of expressing her own remarkable individuality and as a vehicle not only for sentiment but also for socialist and humanitarian ideals.

After 1830, romanticism began to lose its vitality, and by 1840 the public was beginning to demand of its writers less sensibility and more realism. In the work of Stendhal (Henri Beyle, 1785–1842), they had realism at its most superb; but, although *The Red and the Black* had appeared in 1831 and *The Charterhouse of Parma* in 1839, these works were not yet widely understood or appreciated, and Stendhal's satirical chronicle of the July Monarchy, *Lucien Leuwen,* was not to be known until years after his death. The other early master of the realistic novel, Honoré de Balzac (1799–1850), was writing his *Comédie humaine* in these years, that vast picture of French society under the Empire, the Restoration, and the July Monarchy. But Balzac's great fame was to come later also, and he can hardly be called a representative writer of this period. Perhaps the man who comes closest to representing the spirit of the last years of the July Monarchy was, as Louise Varèse has suggested, that "spiritual brother of the political and financial go-getters, that old charlatan, Alexandre Dumas, with his factory of ghostwriters, his shameless plagiarism and quite un-romantic love of money—the one-man Hollywood of his day."

"Berlioz Conducting," a nineteenth-century caricature by Gustave Doré.

Just as romanticism had broken the restrictive mold of the past and breathed new life into literature, so did it perform that service in painting and music. Jean Louis Géricault, whose realistic painting *The Raft of the Medusa* outraged the classicists in 1819, probably deserves credit for starting the revolt against the tyranny of the David school in painting, but the man who carried the romantics to victory, and certainly the greatest painter of this period, was Eugène Delacroix.

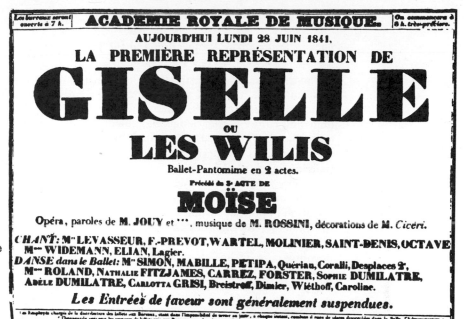

The original playbill for the ballet *Giselle*, 1841.

The revolution in sculpture was less violent and the break with classicism less pronounced, as is evident from the works of such men as David d'Angers and François Rude, the author of the splendid stone relief *The Departure of the Volunteers of 1792*, which stands on one side of the Arc de Triomphe. French music had in Hector Berlioz (1803–1869) a composer of outstanding virtuosity who has rightly been called the founder of musical romanticism, both because of his choice of theme—as in the *Fantastic Symphony* (1830), with its witches' sabbath and execution scenes, and the Byronic *Harold in Italy* (1834)—and because of his exuberant rejection of classical ideals of order and restraint. Berlioz was a link between Beethoven, whom he sought to make French audiences understand, and Wagner, whose opera *Tristan and Isolde* (1859) was, as Wagner himself admitted, strongly influenced by the new world of tonal color that had opened to him when he had listened to Berlioz's dramatic symphony *Romeo and Juliet* twenty years earlier. On opera in his own day, Berlioz had little influence, the most popular composers being less original minds like Auber, whose *Dumb Girl of Portici* (*Masaniello*) helped stimulate the revolutionary spirit in Brussels in August 1830 (see p. 29), a tribute to its political content rather than its musical power, and Meyerbeer, who found Paris more congenial than Berlin.

Nor was he alone in regarding Paris as the natural habitat of the muses. Since 1831 the great Polish pianist and composer Frédéric Chopin (1810–1849) had lived in the French capital, writing the lovely nocturnes and études that were the happiest expression of his genius, while George Sand watched over him and nursed his failing health. And Paris was the home in these years also of Franz Liszt (1811–1886), who gave pianoforte lessons, attended meetings of the Saint-Simonians, became a disciple of Enfantin and then of Lamennais, and dazzled audiences with his virtuosity at the keyboard until 1848, when he gave up public performances. Finally, it was during the July Monarchy that Paris became the center of European ballet, where the great ballerinas Carlotta Grisi, Marie Taglioni, and Fanny Elssler delighted audiences in performances of *Robert le Diable* (1831), *La Sylphide* (1832), and Adolphe Adam's still popular *Giselle* (1841).[5]

The artists of this period were not untouched by the political and social questions of the day, and one of the striking features of the last years of the July Monarchy was the way in which even the most illustrious of them took an active part in the public life of the nation. Victor Hugo turned practically all of his attention to politics for ten years after 1841; and Lamartine, after he had entered the Chamber of Deputies in 1834, became so well known as a politician that he gave up poetry almost entirely. As for George Sand, by the 1840s she was devoting most of her abundant energies to relieving the misery of the working class, and, in January 1848, it was she who supplied Alexis de Tocqueville with that information about their state of mind with which he tried in vain to impress the Chamber.

[5] Most of the great ballerinas of the period were Italian. Fanny Elssler, however, came from Vienna, where she had been an intimate friend of Friedrich von Gentz in 1830–1831. The former secretary of the Congress of Vienna, a notorious hypochondriac, claimed that her love had saved his life. He died, however, in 1832.

Chapter 4 GREAT BRITAIN: SOCIAL UNREST AND SOCIAL COMPROMISE, 1815–1848

ECONOMIC AND SOCIAL CONDITIONS AFTER 1815

Tides of Change   Compared with any of the countries discussed so far, Great Britain, in the first half of the nineteenth century, possessed undeniable material advantages. English wealth was a byword on the Continent, and English industrial and commercial supremacy was patent to every eye. Foreign visitors to England were often so carried away by the evidences of economic power that they drew hasty and unsound conclusions from them. Thus, in the last stages of the war against Napoleon, one traveler wrote:

> I have found the great mass of the people richer, happier and more respectable than any other with which I am acquainted. I have seen prevailing among all ranks of people that emulation of industry and independence which characterises a state of advancing civilisation properly directed. The manners and the whole deportment of superiors to inferiors are marked with that just regard and circumspection which announce the presence of laws equal for all. By such signs, I know this to be the best government that ever existed.[1]

One might suppose from this exuberant endorsement that Great Britain was immune to all the agitations and disturbances that infected her continental neighbors. This was far from being true. The very circumstances that led to England's economic growth and her commercial and industrial supremacy gave

---

[1] L. Simond, cited in E.L. Woodward, *The Age of Reform* (Oxford, 1938), p. 28.

rise to social and political problems that were incapable of easy solution but which, while unsolved, posed the gravest possible threat to the established order.

At the basis of all social change in Great Britain was the marked demographic growth of this period. Between 1700 and 1801, the population had doubled; it stood at ten and a half million in the latter year; and in the course of the next one hundred years this figure was to increase threefold. This tremendous upsurge was made possible by improved medical services, the first glimmerings of an understanding of public sanitation, and, among other things, certain economic developments that promoted health (the manufacture of cheap washable clothing, for instance). As in the case of other countries where population was rising steeply, the increase had profound and continuing repercussions.

Above all, it doomed the old agricultural system of England—the open-field system of farming, which was characterized by a multiplicity of small holdings and by the possession, by the poorer tenant farmers and the agricultural laborers, of grazing and other rights on waste land and village commons. In the latter half of the eighteenth century, the already significant rise in population increased the demand for food and forced prices upward. High grain prices encouraged landowners to consolidate small individually held plots into large farms capable of meeting the demands of the expanded market; and it induced them also to seek, by legal and other means, to enclose former common lands and turn them into cultivation. These tendencies were heightened during the war against Napoleon, when the need for an increase in the supply of food became so pressing that enclosures seemed almost a patriotic necessity.

The enclosure movement eliminated much of the inefficiency that had been inherent in the old system; it permitted full use of new farming methods; it improved the soil; and it achieved its major purpose by expanding production. But these gains were accompanied by a considerable amount of social dislocation and human suffering. In general, the English agricultural scene came to be dominated by the great landowners and the wealthier tenant farmers (those who held long-term leases on farms of from 100 to 500 acres of land). The less wealthy leaseholders became fewer in number, while the poorest tenants were apt to be squeezed out, either by eviction or by an inability to compete with their more efficient neighbors. This last was true also of many in the so-called yeoman class of small independent proprietors, who were ruined by the erratic harvests and the wild price fluctuations of the war years and were, like the most vulnerable tenant farmers, reduced to the status of agricultural laborers or forced to leave the land.

As long as the war with France continued, there were means of absorbing the shock of these changes. Although it did not keep pace with the increase in rural population, the demand for agricultural labor rose steadily from 1793 to 1815. Most of those who left the soil, moreover, found other occupations. The war years were boom years for England's rapidly expanding industry; its new urban centers—Manchester, Birmingham, Leeds, Sheffield, Bristol—were growing feverishly; and, while English firms were supplying the armies of England, Russia, Prussia, and Sweden with guns and greatcoats and blankets, there were lots of jobs in the foundries and the mills. Even the hordes of Irish immigrants who began to pour into Glasgow and Liverpool in the last years of the war could be absorbed by the expanding economic system.

The Postwar Depression   But all this changed after the wars had ceased, for peace brought with it a general economic slump; and, in the decade that followed—while export trade to Europe and America fell by a third—agriculture, the heavy industries, and textiles alike suffered from severe depression. In 1815, wheat prices fell catastrophically from 126s. 6d. a quarter to 65s. 7d., and, although Parliament immediately passed a Corn Law which imposed heavy duties upon foreign grains, domestic prices recovered very slowly and never completely. In rural areas this brought hardship to all classes and ruin to tenant farmers and yeomen who had overextended their operations. As for the agricultural laborer, deprived by enclosures of the means of having a plot of his own or even of keeping a pig or some geese on the village commons, he now saw his wages forced down implacably and found himself confronted with the choice between misery on the land or flight from it.

Not that the latter course had much to offer. The postwar price slump was general and affected industry as well as agriculture. In the mines and the mills, workers were being dismissed by the thousands after 1815, and those who were kept on were forced to work long hours under appalling conditions for wretched wages. To the prevailing misery, two other factors made a contribution. The first was the disbandment of the militia and the reduction of the regular forces, which added hundreds of thousands of men to an already glutted labor market. The second was the struggle of the old household industries, like handloom weaving and the stocking trades, to hold their own against the advancing factory system—a fight that was doomed to failure and was already throwing many out of employment or subjecting them to the excesses of sweated labor. With the population curve still rising and Irish immigration showing no signs of abatement, the industrial towns of England in the first years of the peace became centers of squalor and want, while the countryside was filled with able-bodied paupers and unemployed handicraftsmen.

All those who were, directly or indirectly, affected by these conditions looked to the government for measures to correct them. For a number of reasons, the government was ill-prepared to supply them. Dominated as it still was by the landed magnates of the east and south, it had difficulty even in understanding, let alone solving, problems that had their roots in the new industrial society of Manchester and Sheffield. In an age in which statistical information was meager and no civil service existed to collect it, it had, moreover, a very imperfect knowledge of the extent of social misery and was often made aware of it only when it took violent forms.

Years of Violence, 1815–1819   Writing of the government that ruled England in the first years after Waterloo, the historians J.L. and B. Hammond once asserted that "probably no English government has ever been quite so near, in spirit and licence, to the atmosphere that we used to associate with the tsar's government in Russia."

These are strong words, but, one suspects, singularly inappropriate ones. There was no Alexander or Nicholas, no Arakcheev or Benckendorff in England after 1815. The monarchy was at a low ebb in its fortunes, the king, George III, being sunk in hopeless mania, while his son, the prince regent, was a cypher interested only in painting, architecture, fashion, and women. Effective power lay in the houses of Parliament and was wielded, with their consent, by the cabinet. The prime minister was Lord Liverpool, a patient and phlegmatic man who had been in ministerial posts since 1793. His most important colleagues were the lord chancellor Eldon, the foreign secretary Castlereagh, the home secretary Sidmouth, and the leader of the Tories in the House of Lords, the Duke of Wellington—all men of conservative views. It was said of Liverpool that, if he had been present on the day of creation, he would have said, "Let us conserve chaos!"; while Eldon, a kindly enough man in his personal relations, was an inflexible supporter of the most severe aspects of the criminal code, apparently on the grounds that social stability depended upon strict observance of the letter of the law. Even so, these men were not heartless tyrants, as they have sometimes been portrayed. They had worked long years to overcome the armies of Napoleon and were, even now, engaged in an effort to establish a European system that would prevent new outbursts of revolutionary agitation on the continent. They could not but be sensitive to the possibility of revolution at home. They were responsible to Parliament, which represented the wealthiest classes of society and was prone to panic whenever social misery led to social disorder. Even before 1789, the well-to-do classes of England had learned to fear mob violence—as well they might in a land that possessed no regular police force—and their fears had been enhanced by what had happened in France during the Terror. After 1815, whenever there were signs of popular unrest, they exaggerated the danger and called for extreme measures to avert it. The government, unfortunately, was usually responsive to their wishes and, all too often, met demands for relief of misery not with reform but with repression.

It should not be supposed, however, that the threat to the established order was imaginary. As the depression deepened, sporadic rioting began in the eastern counties, and there was a considerable amount of machine-breaking in Nottinghamshire. Strikes were widespread, and deputations from the Wolverhampton colliers began to travel about the country to recruit aid. Even more frightening for the wealthy classes was the appearance of a number of popular tribunes and agitators. Some of these were responsible men of moderate opinions who sympathized with the lot of the poor and believed that it could be improved by legal means, usually by a reform that would make Parliament more representative of the country as a whole. These included the indomitable and eloquent William Cobbett, perhaps the most powerful pamphleteer of his time, Sir Francis Burdett, member of Parliament for the borough of Westminster, and the so-called "father of reform," the seventy-five-year-old Major John Cartwright. Some were flamboyant *poseurs,* like the fiery "Orator" Hunt, whose doubtless sincere efforts in behalf of the poor were made ineffective by his personal vanity. Some were harmless fanatics, who advocated primitive communism and other panaceas. But there were also more dangerous agitators, like the perennial conspirator Arthur Thistlewood, who talked of overthrowing the monarchy by force and ruling England by a Committee of Public Safety on the French model.

The extremists, unfortunately, assumed an importance out of proportion to their numbers. In December 1816, for instance, Thistlewood and his associates invaded a reform meeting at Spa Fields in London, led part of the crowd away, broke into a gunshop, and made an attack upon the City of London. This foolish

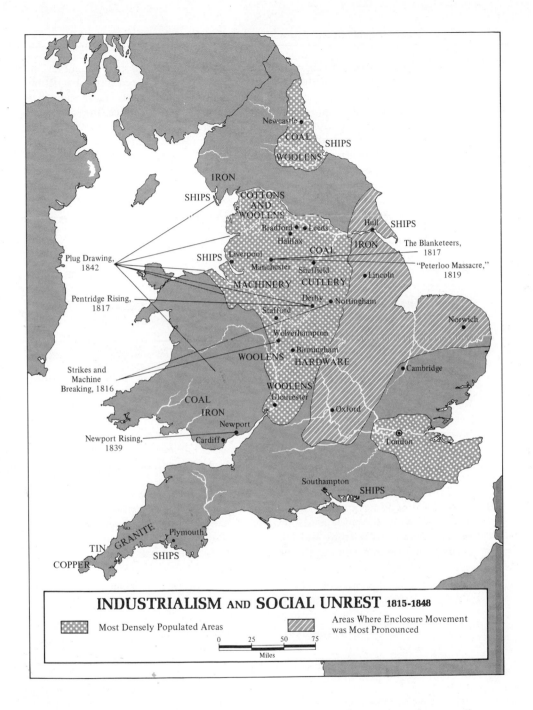

INDUSTRIALISM AND SOCIAL UNREST 1815-1848

Most Densely Populated Areas

Areas Where Enclosure Movement was Most Pronounced

0   25   50   75

Miles

Newcastle

COAL

SHIPS

WOOLENS

IRON

SHIPS

COTTONS
AND
WOOLENS

Bradford • • Leeds

Halifax

Hull   SHIPS

Liverpool   COAL   IRON

Manchester   Sheffield

The Blanketeers,
1817

"Peterloo Massacre,"
1819

MACHINERY   CUTLERY

Lincoln

Derby • • Nottingham

Plug Drawing,
1842

Pentridge Rising,
1817

Stafford

Norwich

Wolverhampton

Strikes and
Machine
Breaking, 1816

WOOLENS   • Birmingham

HARDWARE

Cambridge

WOOLENS

Gloucester

Oxford

COAL
IRON

Newport

London

Newport Rising,
1839

Cardiff •

Southampton   SHIPS

TIN   GRANITE   Plymouth

COPPER   SHIPS

affair—which landed its authors in prison—and a supposed attempt on the regent's life a few days later caused such excitement in ruling circles that the cabinet, after listening to the evidence of hired informers who claimed to have evidence of widespread conspiracy against the government,[2] secured Parliamentary approval of the suspension of the Habeas Corpus Act and the banning of seditious meetings. This was not popular in the country and may have encouraged new incidents that increased the uneasiness of the propertied classes: the attempted march of a band of petitioners (the Blanketeers) from Manchester to London; and, in June 1817 at Pentridge in Derbyshire, a muddled rising of the poor under the leadership of an unemployed stockinger named Jeremiah Brandreth. In the latter case, the insurrectionaries seemed to have believed that their action would touch off a general rising against the government; and a historian of their movement has said that its spirit and objectives could be summed up in the words of a song heard in those days in Belper in Derbyshire:

> The Levelution is begun.
> So I'll go home and get my gun,
> And shoot the Duke of Wellington.

But the government struck out quickly and brutally: the Blanketeers' progress was broken up by troops; Brandreth and his associates were arrested, given speedy trial, and hanged.

This unhappy state of affairs reached its height in August 1819, when about 50,000 people assembled in St. Peter's Fields, Manchester, to hear Hunt and others talk about the need for government reform. Although some of the banners displayed bore revolutionary slogans, the crowd was an orderly one, made up of respectable artisans and laborers and their families. The local magistrates, however, alarmed by the size and the remarkable (and to them doubtless menacing) discipline of the gathering, ordered the Manchester and Salford yeomanry to advance into the crowd and arrest the speakers. The yeomanry was a badly trained troop of local notables. In attempting to carry out their orders, they became hopelessly stuck in the middle of the now angry crowd. The magistrates then lost their heads completely and ordered six troops of the 15th Hussars, who were standing by, to extricate the militia; and these professional troops advanced with drawn sabers and cleared the field—killing eleven people and injuring hundreds as they did so. Samuel Bamford, who was present at this scene of horror, recorded in his *Passages in the Life of a Radical* that

> In ten minutes the field was an open and almost deserted place. . . . The hustings remained, with a few broken and hewed flag-staves erect, and a torn and gashed banner or two drooping; whilst over the whole field were strewed caps, bonnets, hats, shawls and shoes, and other parts of male and female dress, trampled, torn and bloody. The yeomanry had dismounted—some were easing their horses' girths, other adjusting their accoutrements, and some were wiping their sabres.

[2] This evidence came from paid informers and spies upon whom the government had to rely since it had no regular police force. Since these informers were paid only as long as they supplied information, it can be imagined that at least some of the conspiracies they reported were completely imaginary.

The 15th had fought last at Waterloo. Their employment against their own countrymen shocked men of all classes and led them to speak bitterly of this incident as the Massacre of Peterloo. But the government was unmoved by this reaction. The prince regent and the home secretary expressed their satisfaction with the behavior of the authorities at Manchester; and, in the fall of 1819, Parliament passed the so-called Six Acts. Two of these dealt quite sensibly with the procedure for bringing cases to trial and the issue of warrants for search for arms. The other four prohibited meetings for military exercises, restricted gatherings for the purpose of drawing up and signing petitions to residents of the parishes in which the meetings were held (a serious restriction of the right of public assembly), gave magistrates the right to seize literature that they considered blasphemous or seditious, and hampered the circulation of papers and pamphlets by extending the incidence of the stamp tax.

This sort of thing threatened to drive political dissension underground and to make it assume secret and conspiratorial forms, as it had on the continent; in fact, only two months after the passing of the Six Acts, there was some indication that this might be happening. Arthur Thistlewood, once again at liberty, spent the last months of 1819 devising a plot to murder the whole of the cabinet and to establish a Britannic Republic. The plotters were betrayed by a spy and arrested in a loft in Cato Street as they were arming for their effort; but the affair seemed ominous.

Fortunately, the Cato Street conspiracy was not imitated, and the period of violence and counterviolence came to an end. An improvement of economic conditions sensibly modified the misery that had been the principal motive for the machine-breaking, the disorder, and the abortive risings of these years; and Pentridge and Peterloo gradually faded into the past. They had not, however, been without effect. On the one hand, the failure of violence to achieve positive results convinced a great many people that Cobbett and Cartwright were correct in arguing that the best way of achieving improvement of social conditions was by reforming Parliament. On the other hand, the Tory party itself seemed dissatisfied with the policy it had followed since Waterloo and willing to consider remedial and progressive legislation.

THE REFORM MOVEMENT, 1820–1832

Tory Reforms   The Tory party, which commanded the allegiance of most of the great landed families as well as the country gentry, the universities, and the services, had held power almost uninterruptedly since 1793, thanks largely to the persistent disunity of its opponents, the Whigs. Its uninspiring record in the first years of the peace seemed to indicate the onset of the fatal inertia with which long tenure of office often affects political bodies. After 1820, however, the party showed its inherent vitality by throwing up a group of young and energetic leaders to replace those who had directed affairs since the war. Liverpool continued as prime minister, but his principal colleagues were now George Canning (1770–1827) at the Foreign Office, F.J. Robinson (1782–1859) at the Exchequer, William Huskisson (1770–1830) at the Board of Trade, and Robert Peel (1788–1850) at the Home Office. While Canning (see pp. 23, 25–26) was investing foreign policy with new vigor, his associates addressed themselves to the problems of the home front with spirit and determination, and, for a few years at least, Tory policy became progressive enough to win the approval even of followers of Jeremy Bentham (1748–1832.)

Bentham, the eccentric and inspired analyst of the British political system, had long preached that political and social institutions must constantly be measured by the yardstick of utility, that their continued existence should be approved only if they worked efficiently, and that all antiquated institutions and feudal anomalies must be ruthlessly extirpated. It was very much in accordance with this philosophy that the new Tory group went to work.

All the efforts of Robinson and Huskisson, for example, were animated by the desire to free the country from the restrictions of an outworn fiscal and commercial system. While the former overhauled the tax structure and reformed the national debt, Huskisson attacked the mass of duties and rebates with which English trade was encumbered. Pointing out that the Navigation Acts, which required imports into the country to be carried in British ships or ships of the country of origin, were inviting retaliatory legislation on the part of the United States and other countries, Huskisson succeeded in replacing them by a series of reciprocal trade agreements which increased British shipping by 50 percent within the decade. He alleviated the rigidity of the Corn Law of 1815 by placing grain duties on a sliding scale, and he persuaded Parliament to reduce duties on a whole range of products from pig iron to raw silk. "National prosperity," Huskisson said in 1825, "would be most effectually promoted by an unrestrained competition"; and, although he did not live to see the coming of free trade, his success in removing commercial regulations that had outlived their usefulness was the first real step toward the free-trade economy.

Meanwhile, Huskisson's colleague Peel was attacking the mass of antiquated procedures and inhuman penalties that passed for criminal law in England. He drafted a simplified criminal code that abolished the death penalty in almost 200 cases and simultaneously reduced the number of offenses punishable by transportation. He reformed judicial procedure and abolished the use of spies and paid informers in criminal cases; and he made a beginning to the difficult but necessary job of reforming prison conditions. Finally, in what is probably his best remembered reform, he established a trained police force in the national capital. The organization of these "peelers'" or "bobbies," which was soon copied by other cities, was an enormously important contribution to the cause of public order and, by reducing the dependence of local authorities, in time of popular unrest, upon the militia or the regular army, it prevented the repetition of incidents like Peterloo. Its effectiveness was demonstrated also by the almost immediate reduction of crime, which had hitherto been regarded as an unfortunate but unavoidable feature of society.

Even before this last reform was accomplished, the influence of the reformers in the cabinet had been greatly reduced. After Liverpool's retirement from public life in the spring of 1827, Canning had become prime minister. But his death in August and the failure of Robinson (now Lord Goderich) to fill his place adequately brought the Duke of Wellington to the head of the government, and the mood of the cabinet was immediately less favorable to change of any kind.

Sir Robert Peel, 1788–1850. From *Illustrated London News,* January 31, 1846.

Nevertheless, the government was forced against its will to tolerate additional reforms. For one thing, the removal of the disabilities from which nonmembers of the established church had to suffer was long overdue. Whereas Englishmen could worship as they pleased, the Test and Corporation acts prevented them from holding public office unless they were willing to take communion according to the rite of the Church of England. In the case of Protestant dissenters, these laws had for years been bypassed by various expedients, but their continued existence was an affront to non-Anglicans; and, in 1828, under opposition pressure, the government agreed to the repeal of the offending acts.

Inevitably, this raised the much more difficult question of Catholic emancipation. The repeal of the Test and Corporation acts opened most public offices to Roman Catholics, but they were still effectively barred from Parliament by an act of 1679, which required all members of Parliament to declare themselves opposed to the doctrine of transsubstantiation and the adoration of the Virgin Mary. This situation was especially anomalous in Ireland, where the great bulk of the voting public was Catholic but was forced to vote for Protestants in order to make their votes effective.

The patience of the Irish now seemed to have been exhausted. In 1823 Daniel O'Connell (1775–1847), a Dublin barrister with a talent for leadership and remarkable gifts of oratory, had founded a body known as the Catholic Association in order to fight for the removal of Catholic disabilities. The mass meetings organized by O'Connell inflamed all Ireland and greatly alarmed the government, which tried in vain to obstruct and even to dissolve the association. This alarm increased in 1828, when O'Connell decided to stand as a candidate in a Parliamentary by-election in County Clare and was, in defiance of the existing law, triumphantly elected. It was obvious that, unless something was done, Catholics would be elected for every constituency in Ireland in the next general election and that attempts to deny them the right to sit in Parliament might, given the country's present temper, lead to something very like civil war. Wellington and Peel were both opposed to emancipation, but they were realists enough to see that they could not meet O'Connell's challenge. Therefore, they brought in a bill to remove the last restrictions upon the political activities of the Catholics and, in March 1829, it was passed by Parliament. The young John Stuart Mill, with that gift of generalization that made him the most interesting if not the most profound political thinker of the midcentury, hailed this vote as "one of those great events, which periodically occur, by which the institutions of a country are brought into harmony with the better part of the mind of that country—by which that which previously existed in the minds of the more intelligent portion only of the community becomes the law of the land and by consequence raises the whole of the community to its own level."

The passage of this law marked the end of the long period of Tory political domination. This end had been prepared by the activities of Canning, Huskisson, and their associates, whose zeal for change had worried the majority of the party even while it acquiesced in their reforms. It has been brought closer by the reluctant decision to emancipate the Catholics, which many Tories regarded as a betrayal of principle. And it was made inevitable now by the revival of the agitation for Parliamentary reform, which was much too explosive a question to be handled by a badly split party.

The Great Reform Bill   Perhaps the best way of describing what the reformers wanted to change in the parliamentary system is to quote from a speech made by Lord John Russell during the reform debate:

> A stranger who was told that this country is unparalleled in wealth and industry, that it is a country that prides itself on its freedom and that once in every seven years it elects representatives from its population to act as the guardians and preservers of that freedom, would be anxious and curious to see how . . . the people choose their representatives. . . . Such a person would be very much astonished if he were taken to a ruined mound and told that that mound sent two representatives to Parliament; if he were taken to a stone wall and told that three niches in it sent two representatives to Parliament; if he were taken to a park where no houses were to be seen, and told that that park sent two representatives to Parliament. But if he were told all this, and were astonished at hearing it, he

would be still more astonished if he were to see large and opulent towns
. . . and were then told that these towns sent no representatives to Parliament.

England's system of representative government had simply not changed with
the times and with the new social and economic facts of life; and this was
painfully obvious when one looked—as Russell was looking—at the way in which
men were elected to the House of Commons. That body was composed of some
660 members, of whom 489 came from English constituencies, 100 from Irish,
45 from Scottish, and 24 from Welsh. Those who represented county constituencies (190 of the total) were elected by the so-called forty-shilling freeholders
of their country—that is, by the men who owned land which brought them an
income of at least forty shillings a year. But, as we have seen, economic developments since the middle of the eighteenth century and especially during the war
years had led to a steady reduction of the number of independent proprietors,
and this meant that the county electorate was dwindling and that the control
of the county seats was falling into the hands of the wealthy few.

The county suffrage was at least uniform. This was far from being the case
in the boroughs, which sent 465 members to the House of Commons. In one
borough the electorate might comprise all the taxpayers, in another, only the
inhabitants of certain houses; in a third, only the mayor and his corporation.

"The Election at Eatanswill,"
1836, by Phiz. (The Pierpont
Morgan Library, New York)

In most cases, the number of voters was small enough to be influenced easily by the government or, more generally, by local magnates; and there were some cases, like those described by Russell, in which election was a legal fiction, the members simply being appointed by peers into whose control the borough had fallen. There were members of the House of Lords who controlled as many as nine boroughs at a time and could either fill or sell the seats as they saw fit. In 1827 it was estimated that 276 seats were controlled by landed proprietors and that eight peers alone controlled 51 seats. This was another illustration of the predominantly aristocratic nature of the political system before 1832.

What struck critics as being quite as reprehensible as these features of the system was the obvious inequality of the representation. Scotland, with eight times the population of Cornwall, had fewer members in Parliament than that county. The ten southern counties of England had almost as many members as the thirty others, although their population was only a third as large. The plight of the industrial towns was even more striking. In 1828, when Mr. Pickwick went on his famous but unsuccessful mission to Birmingham to soften the heart of Mr. Winkle's father, he was impressed by the vigor of the town and the way in which

> the sights and sounds of earnest occupation struck . . . forcibly on the senses. The streets were thronged with working-people. The hum of labor resounded from every house, lights gleamed from the long casement windows in the attic stories, and the whirl of wheels and noise of machinery shook the trembling walls. The fires, whose lurid sullen light had been visible for miles, blazed fiercely up, in the great works and factories of the town. The din of hammers, the rushing of steam, and the dead heavy clanking of engines, was the harsh music which arose from every quarter.

Yet this hive of activity had no parliamentary representation whatsoever, and the same was true of Bradford, Halifax, Leeds, Manchester, and Sheffield.

All of these things had been pointed out for years by popular agitators like Cobbett, by followers of Bentham, and by spokesmen for the industrial interest. The defenders of the status quo always answered with a variety of arguments: that the existing system enabled men of talent who could not have been elected to Parliament to be appointed to it; that every member of Parliament represented all parts of the country, that this "virtual representation" was preferable to a system in which members regarded themselves as representing individual constituencies, and that, therefore, it was unnecessary and unwise to give representation to all localities; and that any change would destroy the balance of the constitution, diminish the influence of the crown, and give rise to a host of unspecified dangers.

By 1830, however, these last arguments were having a diminishing effect upon the educated classes, who recognized that there were other things in England that needed to be reformed (the spoils system in government, for instance, and the control of municipal government by closed corporations) but which would not be reformed as long as the composition of Parliament remained unchanged. And they had no effect at all upon the common people, who seemed to entertain unreasonable expectations concerning reform and were now clamoring for action.

If the passage of the bill for Catholic emancipation had contributed to this agitation, two other events gave it additional impetus: the fall of the Bourbon monarchy in France, which inspired English reformers as much as it frightened their opponents, and the combination of a sudden trade recession and a disastrous crop failure in 1830, which led to a new wave of rioting, machine-breaking, and rick-burning and made a number of people feel that the time had come for political concession. All events, in short, were conspiring in favor of reform, and when the Tory government refused to see this it was swept away. In the fall of 1830, Wellington—whose Parliamentary majority was dangerously slim in any case—had the bad judgment to praise the English government as the acme of perfection and to declare that he was "not only not prepared to bring forward any measure of [parliamentary reform]" but that "as long as he held any station in the Government of the country, he should always feel it his duty to resist such measures when proposed by others." The government was immediately attacked from every quarter, and the duke was compelled to resign.

The new government, which was headed by Lord Grey and was predominantly Whig in composition, although it included some of Canning's former followers, was pledged to reform and got down to it immediately. In March 1831 Lord John Russell introduced a reform bill in the House of Commons. When it was defeated on a technicality, Grey took the issue to the country and, in new elections, won a majority of 100 seats. He then reintroduced the bill; and, after a debate that lasted months and in which the opposition used every possible delaying tactic, it was passed by a majority of 106 votes. This was an illusory victory, for the bill was immediately killed by the House of Lords, then as later a center of hidebound conservatism.

This caused widespread indignation, which was expressed in riots and demonstrations throughout the land. The atmosphere was not unlike that of Paris in July 1830, and this mood deepened when the bill was introduced for a third time and again passed by Commons in March 1832, for it was recognized as virtually certain that the Lords would again thwart the popular desire for reform. This result was, indeed, plainly forecast in May, when Grey became discouraged and handed in his resignation. It was immediately known throughout the country that the king was trying to persuade Wellington to take office; and this brought popular feeling to a whiter heat and increased the dangers of the situation in general.

The constitutional deadlock was, however, overcome. Wellington could not form a cabinet, and his failure may have been due in part to a run on the banks and a tax strike organized by certain middle class agitators, notably the Benthamite Francis Place. As the price of returning to office, Grey secured what had been denied him earlier, a royal promise to create a sufficient number of new peers to secure the passage of the reform bill by the upper house. They did not have to be created; the threat was enough to break the resistance of the Lords. On June 4, 1832, the Great Reform Bill passed its final hurdle and became the law of the land.

The bill did not do everything that its supporters had expected, nor did it remove all the abuses that had led to its introduction. There were rotten boroughs after 1832 as before; there were boroughs in which fifty votes could decide the election of a member; and there were still startling inequalities of representation. But there were many fewer abuses of this kind. One hundred and forty-three seats were redistributed in such a way as to take representation away from centers of no population, to add to the representation of the larger counties and of Scotland and Ireland, and to allow the industrial towns to send members to Commons.

At the same time, the suffrage was widened. The county suffrage was no longer restricted to people who owned their land, but was given to long-term tenant farmers whose land yielded ten pounds of value annually and to tenants-at-will whose land was worth fifty pounds a year. In the boroughs, all special franchises were abolished, and the vote was given to all men who owned or rented a building whose annual rental value was ten pounds. Throughout England and Wales one man in five now had the vote; in Scotland, one man in eight; in Ireland, one man in twenty. This was not democracy—a fact that becomes clearer when we recall that members of Parliament still received no pay and that there was a property qualification for election—but it was the first hopeful step in that direction.

In the history of English political organization, the reform campaign has great importance. In it we can discern the first beginning of the kind of propaganda and pressure tactics that have become commonplace in our own age. At critical junctures in the campaign, the London Radical Reform Association, in which Francis Place was active, and Joseph Attwood's Birmingham Political Union showed a virtuosity in mobilizing public feeling that would be admired by contemporary professional politicians.

At the same time, the passing of the Reform Act marked the real beginning of modern party organization in England. The Tory and Whig parties of the pre-1832 period were very loose associations of interest, without formal machinery, consultative organs, or internal discipline. After 1832 the transformation of the old groups into the modern Conservative and Liberal parties began. During the reform campaign the Carlton Club was formed with the specific purpose of giving some unity to Tory policy inside and outside Parliament; and a few years later the Reform Club was founded to facilitate unity of view and tactics between the Whigs and their Benthamite allies, the so-called Radicals. These political clubs gave the parties their first machinery, which was developed further as a result of the provisions of the Reform Act itself. For the act made legal enrollment of voters a preliminary condition of voting, and this provision was a stimulus to such things as the formation of party associations in the local constituencies (to promote enrollment in the party interest), the creation of central registration committees, the growth of election agents and party managers, and other features of the modern political party. In a real sense, the present political system of England dates from 1832.

THE POLITICS OF THE PEOPLE

Popular Dissatisfaction with the Reform Act   The passing of the Reform Act had enfranchised virtually the whole of the middle class. It brought fewer obvious advantages to the working class, who had helped secure its passage but had not been granted the vote by it; and the reaction of the articulate sections of the working class was one of disappointment and resentment.

This deepened when the first reformed Parliament met. In the new House of Commons the Whigs and Radicals were in a commanding position. They soon showed, however, by the limited use they made of their power, that they were no real friends of their former working-class supporters and had no intention of doing anything to satisfy their political aspirations. Neither the Whig aristocrats nor the new representatives of the middle class who were allied with them had any sympathy for democracy. In their view—and this was to become doctrine in the Liberal party that emerged from the Whig-Radical fusion—social stability required that the suffrage be restricted to those who had an economic stake in society and were sufficiently educated to use the vote intelligently. The Reform Act represented a limit beyond which they did not wish to go, and Lord John Russell now earned the name Finality Jack by making this clear.

The Whigs and the Radicals did not merely rest on their laurels after 1832. They passed some enormously important legislation: the act of 1833 abolishing slavery throughout the British colonies, for instance, and the Municipal Corporations Act of 1835, which removed the government of towns from the hands of self-elected bodies and vested it in corporations elected by all taxpaying residents. But, while they were ready to remove palpable abuses and to take steps to increase efficiency and economy in the government, according to the Benthamite prescription, their attitude toward the economic and social needs of the working class was almost entirely negative. The Factory Act of 1833, which reduced and regulated the labor of children and young people in the textile mills, owed its passage less to them than to the strenuous efforts of Tory reformers like Lord Ashley; and it was opposed by many Whigs and Radicals because it seemed an unwarranted interference with the freedom of trade.

The representatives of the industrial interest were, indeed, all too ready to cite the population studies of Thomas Malthus (1766–1834) and the economic analyses of David Ricardo (1772–1823) in support of the view that the mass of the population would always live on the barest subsistence level and that their lot could not be improved by government action but only by self-help, continence, and personal discipline. When they supported legislation in the social field, therefore, it was apt to take severe forms, like the new Poor Law of 1834. This act, which was Benthamite in inspiration, sought to lighten the burden which the relief of poverty imposed upon local taxpayers by ending outdoor relief to the able-bodied and forcing all recipients of relief to enter workhouses, in which they were denied the privilege of living with their families (lest they breed) and were forced to lead the most primitive and degrading kind of existence. The new system was doubtless more economical than the old, and it was administered by men who in other respects had progressive and even enlightened views—Edwin Chadwick, the greatest sanitary reformer of the century, and Dr. John Kay (later Kay-Shuttleworth), a zealous worker for a national system of education. But one has only to read Charles Dickens's description of workhouse conditions in *Oliver Twist*, published in 1837, to understand how high the cost was in human suffering. Thirty years later Dickens could still write: "I believe there has been in England since the days of the Stuarts no law so often infamously administered."

The spirit and the policies of the post-1832 government alienated the working classes and, at the same time, forced them to realize that improvement of their lot would depend on their own efforts. Out of this realization came two movements: trade unionism and chartism.

The Trade-Union Movement   In the first years after the war the development of a strong union movement had been impossible because of the existence of the Combination Acts of 1790 and 1800 and other legislation that forbade all working class combinations, except purely benevolent societies, as criminal conspiracies in restraint of trade. In 1824, however, in the period of the Canningite reforms, Parliament had repealed the Combination Acts and permitted the organization of working men for peaceful bargaining about wages and hours, provided such organization did not encourage breach of contract or lead to "molestation" or "obstruction" of employers. The terms of the new act, as amended in 1825, still made it difficult for workers to strike, and the courts were very zealous in finding evidence of obstructionism; but at least trade unions could now pursue their activities openly without disguising themselves as benevolent societies.

Between 1825 and 1832 there was a steady growth of union membership and the beginning of systematic efforts to form national unions out of local ones. In 1829, for example, John Doherty succeeded in forming a single union for the whole cotton trade. Doherty hoped to carry this tendency further and to establish a union of all trades; and, in June 1830, he founded the National Association for the Protection of Labor with this end in view. This organization faded away

"Thrusters and Trapper." Children who worked in the English mines were also called "hurriers." An illustration from the book, *The White Slaves of England,* 1853. (New York Public Library)

almost as quickly as it had grown, but in its short existence it did encourage the establishment of new unions among the miners, the colliers, the clothiers, the potters, and other trades.

The disillusionment that affected the working classes after the passing of the Reform Act seems to have encouraged the growth of unionism and added to its militancy. In the latter half of 1832 union membership in general began to grow, strike activity began to increase, and there was a renewal of the earlier effort to unite all the trades. What Doherty had attempted was now tried again with the formation, in October 1833, of the Grand National Consolidated Trades Union which, in a very short space of time, had an estimated membership of half a million skilled and unskilled workers, including agricultural workers, gas workers, miners, tailors, bonnetmakers, bakers, and shearers, and had branches all over England and in Scotland and Ireland as well.

The leading spirit in this movement was Robert Owen (1771–1858). A self-made man, who at the age of twenty was the head of one of Lancashire's greatest cotton mills, Owen was a born social reformer. He had made his New Lanark mills a model establishment in which wages were good and employment regular, and in which sanitary housing and recreational facilities were available to workers and full-time education was provided for their children. His success here encouraged him to think of the possibility of founding model communities in other parts of the world and, in 1824, he actually went to America to try out his gospel there. New Harmony, the Owenite community founded in the United States, was not a success; but it helped attract the attention of the workers to Owen's schemes and to stimulate what was perhaps the most permanent of his experiments, the establishment of self-governing, nonprofit cooperative shops and producers' societies catering to the needs of the workers. As early as 1830, there were already more than 300 of these cooperative societies in existence.

Owen's thought had progressed from simple philanthropy to a rather unsystematic socialism, and he had come to oppose the whole capitalistic profit system and to support all causes that promised to reduce the exploitation of the workers. It was natural, therefore, that he should be drawn to the trade-union movement. He was heart and soul behind the Grand National and seems to have believed that, within five years, it would enable the organized workers to gain control of the economic machinery of the country, to replace capitalism with a cooperative system, and to supersede both Parliament and all existing bodies of local government. With this dream of a socialist commonwealth before his eyes, Owen threw himself into the effort to spread the principle of unionism and cooperation in the unorganized trades.

The tremendous enthusiasm that attended his efforts made the trade-union movement appear much stronger than it was. In reality, when their strength was tested, the unions collapsed with remarkable celerity. In 1833, alarmed employers began to unite and to refuse employment to union members. Disregarding Owen's advice, the unions responded with strikes, forgetting that it was unwise to attempt to combine expensive cooperative experiments with even more costly strike payments. Before long, they were in serious financial embarrassment. At the same time, the government's attitude toward them hardened. Early in 1834, in the Dorsetshire village of Tolpuddle, six farm laborers were arrested for swearing men into a union that planned to join the Grand National and were subsequently tried and sentenced to seven years' transportation to a penal colony overseas for administering illegal oaths. It was clear from this that the government intended to strain the interpretation of the law if necessary in order to hamper the effectiveness of the union movement; and the fate of the "Tolpuddle martyrs" had a depressing effect upon union organization.

Financial mismanagement, an unwise strike policy, concerted opposition by employers, government persecution, and, finally, personal differences between Owen and his chief collaborators destroyed the militant trade-union movement of the 1830s. By 1835 the Grand National had fallen to pieces, and its member unions were in retreat. Those that survived in the next period were for the most part unions in the highly skilled trades, which resisted all ambitious schemes of organization and concentrated on their own problems and benevolent activities. The extension of union organization among the unskilled came to a halt and made little new progress for the next half century.

The failure of the Owenite union movement had one more positive result, however. It made working class leaders realize that they could not win measures of social reform unless the workers had the vote. Abandoning the economic weapon, they now turned to political pressure in the hope that they could force the new ruling class to share its power with the workers. This attempt was made in the agitation for the People's Charter.

Chartism   In 1836 a group of working class leaders in London, headed by William Lovett, a former storekeeper in London's first Owenite cooperative, founded the London Working Men's Association, in order "to draw into one bond of unity the intelligent and influential portion of the working classes in town and country, and to seek by every legal means to place all classes of society in possession of equal political and social rights." To attain this happy state of affairs, six things, it was felt, were necessary, and these were spelled out in the People's Charter, which was published in May 1838. They were annual Parliaments, universal male suffrage, equal electoral districts, the removal of the property qualification for membership in Commons, the secret ballot, and payment of members of Parliament. Under the influence of the Birmingham Political Union, which had played an important part in the reform campaign of 1831–1832 and which was now revived, the charter was embodied in a national petition and the nation-wide collection of signatures was begun, in the hope that Parliament might be impressed by the number of declared supporters of the program.

The London and Birmingham leaders doubtless wished to carry on this new campaign in a systematic, respectable, and peaceful fashion. But the Charter made a direct appeal to men who were indignant about the provisions of the new Poor Law, who were cast down by the failure of Owen's movement, who were unemployed as a result of the extension of machine industry, or who for more obscure reasons were resentful and disinclined to act moderately. Moreover, the leadership of Lovett and his associates was soon challenged by more violent spirits: the former Wesleyan minister J.R. Stephens, who wanted to establish a new theocracy with the charter as its Bible and did not hesitate to call for the free employment of the pike and the firebrand to attain that end; G.J. Harney, who thought of himself as the English Marat; James Bronterre O'Brien, an assiduous preacher of class hatred; and Feargus O'Connor, a violent, unprincipled bully who had once been a follower of O'Connell and was now editing a radical newspaper in Leeds called the *Northern Star*.

It was O'Connor and O'Brien who overcame the influence of the moderates at a Convention of the Industrious Classes held in London in February 1839 and persuaded it not only to accept the charter but to recognize the right of the people to arm themselves and to agree to a general strike in the event that Parliament should reject their claims. This had the effect of arousing a dangerous degree of excitement, and it is not surprising, therefore, that when the petition and the charter, with 1,200,000 signatures, were in fact rejected by the House of Commons in July, there were a number of ugly incidents. Although the general strike never materialized, there was actually an attempt at an armed rebellion at Newport in Monmouthshire, in which fourteen men were killed and ten died of wounds. This tragic affair—which was followed by the arrest and imprisonment of a number of Chartist leaders—brought the first phase of Chartism to an end.

The hope of success was never again as bright as it had been in this first period, but Chartism remained alive for another ten years, becoming active in periods of economic hardship, subsiding in better times. It flared up strongly, for instance, in the winter of 1841–1842 when, as a result of bad harvests and a slump in domestic and foreign trade, nearly one tenth of the nation was unemployed and one fifth of the population of Birmingham, to cite one example, was on relief rolls. Under O'Connor's leadership, a new national petition was circulated and in May 1842, bearing 3,317,752 signatures, it was submitted to the House of Commons.

On this occasion the charter was actually debated, but both political parties opposed the key change proposed by it, universal suffrage, which was described by that epitome of middle class liberalism, Thomas Babington Macaulay (1800–1859), as "fatal to all the purposes for which government exists and utterly incompatible with the very existence of civilization." The House rejected the petition by 287 to 49. This had the same effect as the earlier rejection: it touched off disorders throughout the country. A strike movement began in Staffordshire and spread rapidly over Lancashire, Yorkshire, Cheshire, Warwickshire, and into Wales and Scotland, the strikers marching from town to town, drawing the plugs from factory boilers in order to stop all work. O'Connor and his associates openly encouraged these disorders, a political mistake that made them appear responsible for the eventual, and inevitable, failure of the strike.

By this time it was clear that the supplanting of the moderate Chartist leaders by O'Connor had fatally weakened the movement's hope of success. It was virtually impossible for the Chartists to find any support in Parliament, because even members who sympathized with working class demands regarded O'Connor—in the words of one of them—as "a foolish, malignant, cowardly demagogue" and wanted nothing to do with a movement that he led. Moreover, under O'Connor's leadership. Chartism had become an anti-industrial movement. O'Connor himself hated factories and towns and had a vague dream of restoring England to the small landholder. This creed appealed to thousands who still dreamed of a return to the past, but it was in conflict with all the realities of the age. It gradually destroyed the originally strong following that Chartism had had in the trade unions and, at the same time, made impossible any kind of cooperation with the middle class movement that might have been an effective ally: namely, the Anti-Corn Law League. For this reason, Chartism declined steadily after 1842, and the objectives that it sought had to be achieved later and by other forces.

THE ROAD TO COMPROMISE

Queen Victoria   During the tumultuous years of trade-union and Chartist agitation, a new sovereign had ascended the throne. William IV, who had become king in the days when Lord Grey was forming his first ministry, died in 1837 and was succeeded by his niece Victoria. A girl of eighteen at the time of her accession, with little knowledge of court ways, the new monarch had energy and determination as well as the intelligence to see that politics is an art that must be learned like anything else. Under the guidance of the Whig leader

Queen Victoria, the Prince Consort, and Prince Arthur, with the prince's godfather, the Duke of Wellington, from the painting by F. Winterhalter. (Victoria and Albert Museum, London)

Melbourne and, after her marriage in 1840, of her husband, Prince Albert of Saxe-Coburg, she became a well-informed and conscientious ruler, aware of the limitations of her constitutional role but insistent upon the proper observance of her prerogatives. Her reign (1837–1901) was to be the longest in English history and, from the standpoint of material prosperity, political power, scientific progress, and cultural attainment, the richest as well.

The first years of Victoria's reign were years of economic distress and social disorder. But they were also years in which a profoundly important political change was completed: the transference of political leadership in the country from the aristocracy to the middle class. This change began, as we have seen, with the passing of the Reform Act, five years before Victoria's accession, but the event that consolidated middle class predominance was the repeal of the Corn Laws in 1846.

The Repeal of the Corn Laws   The agitation for the repeal of the Corn Laws began during the same years of agricultural and economic depression that saw the rise of Chartism; it received organized form with the establishment of the Anti-Corn Law League in 1839, the most effective propaganda machine that Britain had ever seen, with local branches throughout the country and a war chest made up of donations from the capitalist class that enabled it to publish and distribute newspapers and pamphlets, arrange innumerable meetings, and bring various kinds of pressure to bear upon Parliament. The leaders of the League were Richard Cobden (1804–1865) and John Bright (1811–1889), both manufacturers and free traders, sincerely convinced that the existing protective tariff system jeopardized the development of English manufactures, by making it difficult for the commodities of other countries to come into England and inviting reprisals from the countries denied. The Corn Laws were the key to the protective system, and their removal, the free traders believed, would cause the whole system to fall, ushering in a period of unexampled industrial and commercial expansion.

The arguments of the free traders were a curious mixture of economic hardheadedness, social benevolence, cosmopolitan idealism, and class prejudice. Many manufacturers supported the league because they believed that repeal of the Corn Laws would in the long run enable them to decrease wages; but it is probably equally true that just as many sincerely believed that, by lowering the price of bread, repeal would bring direct advantage to the working class and mitigate some of the rigors of industrialism. In some of the speeches for repeal there was evangelistic fervor and a conviction that free trade would bring interdependence of nations and international peace. In others, one can detect a desire to smash the political power of the aristocracy by removing their economic privileges. In 1845, Cobden said: "The sooner the power in this country is transferred from the landed oligarchy, which has so misused it, and is placed absolutely—mind, I say absolutely—in the hands of the intelligent middle and industrious classes, the better for the condition and destinies of this country." In the heat of public meetings, members of the league were often less temperate in their expression and were wont to refer jeeringly to "bread stealers," "footpad aristocrats," and "titled felons."

The League's arguments could not be lightly disregarded by the government in power. In 1841, the Whigs were replaced by a Tory cabinet under Sir Robert Peel, and that able man of business recognized from the outset that the economic structure of the country was in need of reform. "We must," he wrote a friend, "make this country a *cheap* country for living." He sought to make it so by reducing import duties in the hope of stimulating trade, making good the loss in revenue by an income tax, by strengthening the monetary system and the credit facilities of the country (by the Bank Charter Act of 1844), and by other financial measures. But Peel was the head of a party that represented the agricultural interest, and this prevented him from touching the Corn Laws.

At least, it would have done so if times had remained good. But, in August 1845 the potato blight appeared in Ireland, and that overpopulated island, dependent almost entirely on that crop, was faced with starvation. The English harvest had been poor, so little help could be expected from that quarter. The Anti-Corn Law League was quick to seize this opportunity to renew its attack upon the protective system; its campaign had been so effective over the years that there

Richard Cobden, 1804–1865. From *Illustrated London News*, February 28, 1846.

was evidence now that the country was behind it; and Peel was courageous enough to face realities and to decide that the Corn Laws must go. In May 1846, after a long and bitter debate, he managed, with opposition aid, to carry repeal in Commons, and in June the Duke of Wellington, out of loyalty to the Prime Minister, steered it through the Lords.

The immediate economic results of repeal were not as dramatic as had been expected. The nominal price of grain did not fall appreciably and, for the next two decades, it remained stable. Since these were years of rising world prices, on the other hand, it can be argued that there was a real and significant lowering of the price of grain in the English market. To the extent that this was so, repeal contributed to the improvement of the lot of the poor and to the buttressing of social peace.

The agricultural interest suffered no immediate loss. It was not until a quarter of a century later, when improved transportation facilities brought American grains into the domestic market, that British agriculture was seriously threatened. Its vulnerability then, however, can be traced back to the repeal of 1846, the long-range economic effects of which were to weaken agriculture and to transform Great Britain into a country with a predominantly industrial and commercial economy.

By destroying the preferred economic position of the landholding aristocracy, the repeal of the Corn Laws demonstrated the political supremacy of the class that had been enfranchised in 1832. The aristocracy continued to possess great social power, to monopolize the House of Lords, and to control the armed services, diplomacy, and the established church. But at the center of power, the House of Commons, the middle class was in command.

As far as party politics was concerned, the result of repeal was the splitting of the Tory party. Under the lead of Lord George Bentinck and a young and ambitious politician named Benjamin Disraeli, the majority of the party repudiated their greatest statesman, charging him with betrayal. The withdrawal of the Peelites added a new element of confusion to English politics, for, by adding one more to the political groups in the House of Commons, it increased the difficulty of forming a stable majority in that chamber. It was not until the 1860s that this situation was clarified and something like a two-party system was able to emerge.

Toward Social Peace   The *laissez-faire* philosophy that had animated the drive to repeal the Corn Laws was not, as we have seen, sympathetic to the idea of positive social reform. Measures to ameliorate the conditions of the poor seemed to represent an unwarranted interference with economic laws and one that could have dangerous results. Yet the very men who repeated the shibboleths of Manchesterian liberalism most fervently could not entirely still the voice of their own consciences. In the 1840s a series of reports of royal commissions bared, to all who could read, some of the results of the unregulated extension of industrialism: the deplorable conditions in factory towns, many of which had no sewage systems, no adequate water supply, and no housing for the working classes except the most flimsy and unsanitary hovels; the shameful situation in the mines, where women and children were found working like animals; the

"An Outline of Society in Our Own Times," by George Cruikshank. (New York Public Library, Print Division)

wretched state of many of the factories, in which *laissez-faire* often meant irresponsibility and callousness on the part of employers.

The effect of these admirable reports was to stimulate a demand for basic reform that cut across party lines and led to effective remedies for the most obvious abuses. The most inveterate Manchesterians held out to the last, but they could not prevent the passage of a series of acts improving the working conditions of the poor: Ashley's Act of 1842, excluding all women, girls, and boys under ten from the mines; Graham's Factory Act of 1844, limiting child labor and providing for inspection to assure the observance of safety measures; and, finally, Fielden's Act of 1847, which established a normal working day of ten and a half hours for all women and young people in the factories and, by implication, for the male operatives as well. These acts were important as a first recognition of the responsibility government has for the well-being of its citizens; and they could not help but have the effect of alleviating much of the social resentment that had marked the early part of our period.

To this alleviation the general improvement of economic conditions in the late 1840s also made a contribution. Employment figures were rising steadily; coal production was on the increase, and pig-iron tonnage was three times what it had been in 1832; and the export trade had doubled since that year. These

"Dr. Church's Steam Locomotive," 1833. (New York Public Library, Print Division)

were the years, among other things, of the great development of railways; and, between 1843 and 1849, two hundred thousand laborers, drawn from the depressed classes, laid 5000 miles of track and began the construction of 7000 more. Their labors opened up the interior of the country to heavy as well as light industry, facilitated the transportation of goods and the movement of labor, and had other effects too numerous to mention here. In 1850 there were 6621 miles of railway in operation and they carried seventy-three million travelers before the year was over. In these figures we can sense the social and economic revolution that had taken place since 1815.

The economy, thanks in part to Peel's reforms but also to its own expansion, now possessed a strength and balance that made it less sensitive to crop failures and sudden market fluctuations. It is perhaps for this reason that, although the years 1847 and 1848 were years of some economic unsteadiness and considerable unemployment, there was no serious attempt in England to imitate the risings that were taking place on the Continent. The Chartists, it is true, tried to exploit the situation by preparing a third national petition, which embodied their original demands, and by organizing a monster parade to carry it to Parliament. The government responded by concentrating troops on the capital and forbidding the procession; and the Chartists, discovering on the chosen day that they had much less public support than they had bargained on, caved in. The petition was taken to Parliament in three cabs and, upon examination, was found to contain many obviously forged signatures, including those of the queen and the Duke of Wellington. After this fiasco, Chartism disappeared from the English scene. Its cause was far from being a failure, since most of its political objectives were later attained, in no small part because of its agitations.

Once the petition was disposed of, the social order seemed secure for the first time since 1815, and Thomas Babington Macaulay, finishing the second volume of his *History of England* in the midst of alarming news of revolution on the continent, could write with satisfaction:

> All around us the world is convulsed by the agonies of great nations. Governments which lately seemed likely to stand during ages have been on a sudden shaken and overthrown.... Meanwhile, in our island the regular course of government has never been for a day interrupted.... We have order in the midst of anarchy.

RELIGION, EDUCATION, AND THE ARTS

The Churches   England was still a churchgoing country, and the churches were powerful bodies with large memberships. The Church of England was supported by the majority of the upper classes and by the mass of the rural population. There was a large minority of Protestant dissenters or Nonconformists, especially in Wales, and in Scotland where there were more Presbyterians than members of the established church. Roman Catholics were, of course, predominant in Ireland and, thanks to immigration, were increasing in towns like Glasgow and Liverpool. In general, as far as England was concerned, the established church, the dissenters, and the Catholics were in the ratio of 120, 80, and 4.

Despite its numerical strength, organized religion was weakened by the tendencies of the time and by the attitude of the churches to social problems. As we have seen in the case of France (see above, pp 84–85), the advance of industrialism, by drawing rural laborers to the factory towns, often severed their religious connections permanently. The industrial town that is the scene of Dickens's *Hard Times* (written in the early 1850s) is described as having eighteen churches and chapels. But, asks the author,

> Who belonged to the eighteen denominations? Whoever did, the labouring people did not. It was very strange to walk through the streets on a Sunday morning and note how few of *them* the barbarous jangling of bells ... called away from their own quarter, from their own close rooms, from the corners of their own streets, where they lounged listlessly, gazing at all the church and chapel going as at a thing with which they had no manner of concern.

Factory life was not conducive to religious reflection or observance.

Apart from this, the churches took an almost entirely negative view of the political and social problems that affected the mass of the population. The almost solid resistance of the bishops of the Church of England to parliamentary reform before 1832 was hardly calculated to inspire popular respect, and the blank indifference of the church to factory abuses tended to alienate the masses. Especially after 1832, the Church of England was the center of vigorous intellectual activity, but none of it seemed to be related to problems of the day. Of the two parties within the church, the evangelicals did much to raise the moral standards of the age by the strict piety of their behavior, but they had no conception of the social responsibility incumbent on a church that was, after all, supported by state funds. The high church party, on the other hand, was given over to the kind of absorption in doctrinal speculation that led, in the 1840s, to the Oxford Movement. This movement—perhaps best remembered because it led to the dramatic decision of John Henry Newman (1801–1890) and his followers to join the Roman Catholic church—stimulated internal reform and encouraged, within a body that had not always been scrupulous about its appointments, a deeper conception of the clerical office. But it also had the disadvantage of involving the Church of England in controversy about ritual and dogma at a time when it would have been well advised to give some thought to trade unionism and Chartism.

The strongest of the dissenting sects in England was Wesleyanism, which numbered half a million members in 1840. Wesleyanism was less remote from the actualities of contemporary existence. It was usually on the side of authority; the response of the Methodist Committee of Privileges to the events of 1819, for instance, was a condemnation of "tumultuous assemblies" like the one at Manchester, "calculated, both from the infidel principles, the wild and delusive political theories and the violent and inflammatory declamations ... to bring all government into contempt, and to introduce universal discontent, insubordination and anarchy." But Radicalism and Chartism did not leave its members untouched, and it, in turn, made its contribution to popular movements. Many of the more responsible leaders of the trade unions and other working class movements, at this time and later in the century, received their first training in administration, government, and public speaking in Wesleyan chapels and the churches of other dissenting sects.

The Schools   Both the established church and the Nonconformists were interested in education, and what primary education there was for the masses was provided by societies established by them: the National Society ("for promoting the education of the poor in the principles of the established church") and the British and Foreign School Society (which was nondenominational). For very low fees, students received training in the Bible and catechism and some acquaintance with the three R's. How slight this acquaintance was likely to be was shown by a survey made in the 1830s which revealed that, of 5000 children in Hull who had been to school, 800 could not read and 1800 could not write, and that, in Leeds, 15,000 children were receiving no schooling whatsoever. It is clear that the general level of education was not high.

The first government grant in aid of education was made in 1833, when a sum of £20,000 was divided between the two voluntary societies mentioned above and was expended for new schools. This sum, which was less than was being currently spent for education in the state of Massachusetts, had little effect in altering the existing state of affairs. One might have imagined that an industrial society, which had a need for educated operatives, clerks, supervisors, and salesmen, would insist upon a more massive effort in the direction of free and compulsory elementary education; and in time, of course, this happened. But in the period under review the suspicion of government intervention in new spheres, which was characteristic of Manchester liberalism, combined with sectarian animosity to block all efforts at large-scale educational reform; and it was not until 1870 that anything constructive was done. The result was that England entered the fierce economic rivalry of the post-1870 period with her artisan class less well trained and her business managers less well educated than many of her competitors.

Secondary education was restricted, for obvious reasons, to the upper and middle classes, who sent their sons to private schools of various types. The period before 1848 was one of basic reform in these schools. Between 1818 and 1848, Thomas Arnold, the headmaster at Rugby, modernized and expanded the curriculum and replaced rote learning with a greater degree of free enquiry. These ideas, and others about school government, athletics, and character training, were carried by Arnold's disciples to other schools, with generally beneficial results.

For the universities this was not a distinguished period. Both Oxford and Cambridge were still clerical in character and governed by outworn statutes (dissenters were not yet allowed to graduate) and the reform of studies was badly needed; yet new ideas were blocked by clerical opposition or by the conservative governing boards of the member colleges. It is possible, of course, that this imperviousness to change was not wholly bad. At least, by resisting the tendency to make all learning "useful," the older universities managed to survive as centers of liberal education in an increasingly materialistic society.

In general, university education was expanding. The University of London—radical in origin, secular, and with a wider curriculum than either Oxford or Cambridge—got its start in the late 1820s. The University of Durham was established in 1832; colleges and technical schools were founded in Leeds, Birmingham, and Sheffield in the same decade; and the universities of St. Andrews, Glasgow, Aberdeen, and Edinburgh grew in size.

Mention should be made also of the earnest attempts to bring education to adult members of the working class through organizations like the Society for the Diffusion of Useful Knowledge (1827), which published cheap technical handbooks and textbooks on a wide range of subjects, and the mechanics' institutes, which were designed to be libraries and discussion centers for the intelligent and ambitious members of the laboring class.

The Arts   These years of economic expansion and social disorder were also years of remarkable literary activity and achievement. In 1815 the romantics were still at the height of their power, and the great figures in letters were Wordsworth, Coleridge, Keats, Byron, Shelley, Southey, Lamb, Jane Austen, Hazlitt, Landor, Blake, and Scott. By 1832, these had passed away or had written their best work, and a new period opened in which—as perhaps was natural in an age that was becoming more matter of fact—the accent was on prose rather than poetry. It is true that Tennyson and Browning began to write in the 1830s, but they received no very wide following until later. The most respected writers of the post-Reform Act period were prose writers, and by no means all writers of imaginative literature: Dickens, whose *Sketches by Boz* appeared in 1834–1835 and who scored his first great success with *The Posthumous Papers of the Pickwick Club* in 1836–1837; J.H. Newman and Thomas Carlyle; Macaulay, whose *History of England*, the first two volumes of which appeared in 1848, was a runaway best seller; John Stuart Mill, whose *System of Logic* (1843) had a tremendous vogue; and—at the very end of the period—Thackeray and the Brontës, although most of their work was later.

It was a sign of the vitality of English literature that most of even the purely literary figures in these lists concerned themselves with the problems of their time. The liberalism of Byron and Shelley did not, perhaps, produce their best poetry, and Coleridge's political writings are often too Germanic to be intelligible, but it is hard to deny that Blake at the beginning of the period and Dickens at the end were eloquent and persuasive social critics.

This period was enlivened by the development of a vigorous press—in 1815 there were already 252 papers circulating in England—and by a number of excellent critical journals, including the *Edinburgh Review*, of Whig persuasion, the Tory *Quarterly Review*, and the Radical *Westminster Review*, which was founded in 1824 and edited by John Stuart Mill.

Although the theater and the concert hall were popular, England produced no great dramatists or composers in these years. In art, the early part of the

The Crystal Palace Exhibition of 1851 provided a somewhat garish summation of the artistic as well as the industrial achievements of the previous decade. The view of the gallery above suggests that engineering talent was somewhat stronger than that in the plastic arts. (Brown Brothers)

period saw the last work of Lawrence, Raeburn, Constable, and Turner. After their passing there was no one to replace them but conventional painters like Landseer and Maclise.

THE EMPIRE

Emigration and Colonial Expansion   The pressure of population and economic misery during the period before 1848 persuaded an increasing number of Englishmen to try their fortunes abroad, in the United States and the Canadian provinces primarily, but in other areas as well. At the beginning of the period only about 30,000 men and women were leaving England annually; by 1832 this figure was in excess of 100,000, and the troubles of the 1840s doubled this number. The practice of using Australia as a dumping ground for convicts was terminated in 1840, and the white population increased rapidly from 130,000 in that year to well over a million twenty years later. To the south, the first English settlers began to move into New Zealand in 1837; and on the other side of the world, in South Africa, there were 5000 English settlers at the Cape as early as 1820.

There was astonishingly little interest in the colonies on the part of the people who stayed home. This was not an age in which Englishmen took pride in their empire; and those who gave any thought to the colonies were likely to regard them as useless encumbrances. This was an article of faith with the followers of Cobden and Bright. Interested in the benefits of trade rather than the problems of overseas administration, these people could perhaps view with equanimity the high-handed tactics used by Palmerston in his dispute with the Chinese government in 1839–1841, because—at the cost of a small war—they won access for Britain to Shanghai, Canton, and three other ports and acquired the valuable entrepôt of Hong Kong. But they were not disposed to address themselves seriously to the problems of colonial policy. Because they were not, the government was not; and this meant that Great Britain had no colonial policy except what was improvised from day to day by men on the spot. In both South Africa and India, advances were made and commitments taken without the full knowledge or approval of the government. In South Africa, the unremitting pressure of English settlers upon the Dutch farmers already settled there and upon the native tribes was pregnant with future trouble; in India, where British expansion went forward steadily, inconsistency of purpose led to more than one setback, like the humiliating defeat in the Afghan wars of 1842.

The Abolition of Slavery and the Durham Report   Despite the prevailing negativism of British thinking about colonial affairs, two positive and imaginative steps were taken by the British government in this period. The abolition of slavery in the colonies in 1833 has already been mentioned, and all that need be added here is that this action, while setting the world an example that it eventually followed, made it certain that the future colonial empire would be one of free men.

A little later a precedent-making solution was found for difficulties that had arisen in Canada. These were the result of friction that had developed between the elected representative assemblies of the two provinces of Upper and Lower Canada (which controlled legislation and taxation) and their governors (who were responsible to the British crown), and they were complicated further by bad feeling between the British and French populations of the provinces.

In 1838 Lord Durham (1792–1840) and the noted critic of British colonial policy Gibbon Wakefield (1796–1862) went to Canada to study the problem and in the following year they drew up the so-called Durham Report. This urged, first, that Upper and Lower Canada be reunited and, second, that the Canadian executive be made responsible not to the crown but to the local parliament. Anything less, they felt, would lead eventually to the violent severance of the ties between Canada and the home country, as had happened in the case of the United States. Responsible government, on the other hand, would forge a tie of imperial unity between them.

The Durham proposals were not immediately accepted. But in 1840 the provinces were united, and, seven years later, when Lord Elgin became governor-general of Canada, the attempt to apply the principle of responsible government began. It succeeded, and its success led to its being copied in New Zealand (1854), Australia (1856), and the Cape Colony (1872). The direction was already set for the road that would lead to the establishment of the British Commonwealth of Nations in 1931 (see p. 624).

Chapter 5 THE REVOLUTIONS OF 1848

When the year 1848 opened, significant sections of the populations of all the continental countries lying between the English Channel and the borders of Russia had reasons for dissatisfaction with their governments. With varying degrees of intensity, the middle classes desired either to acquire civil and political rights denied them or to extend rights already acquired; and, in Germany and Italy, these desires were accompanied by a growing fervor for national unity and independence. The vanguard of the middle class reform movement were merchants and industrialists, professors and journalists, lawyers and intellectuals and university students, all of whom had become alienated from governments that were wedded to the status quo and showed no sympathy for their ideas.

At the same time, the mass of the ordinary people of most countries was suffering from economic distress. The period since 1815 had been one of great industrial expansion, but it had been accompanied by the ills attendant upon the replacement of the old handicraft system by new methods of production and also by periodic dislocations caused by overexpansion and unwise speculation. After the prosperity of the early forties, for instance, the seaports and industrial towns of Europe suffered from the repercussions of a sudden and severe economic crash in England, and the subsequent forced retrenchment hurt the old guild trades more severely than it did factory industry and threw thousands of artisans and journeymen out of work. Simultaneously, the failure of the potato crop in 1845 and of both the potato and grain crops in 1846 was felt in all countries from Ireland to Poland and was reflected in a sharp rise in the cost of food—an increase that, in the German states, averaged 50 percent

123

between 1844 and 1847. By the latter year, the linen industry of Belgium was in a pitiable state; the weavers of Silesia were on the verge of starvation; one out of every three families in Solingen in the Rhineland was destitute; and crime, prostitution, and lawlessness were increasing everywhere.

All these conditions were to take a sharp turn for the better in mid-1848, when a new industrial boom got under way. But that could not be foreseen at the beginning of the year. In January and February, economic distress was supplementing political discontent in most continental countries, and the middle class reformers and the rebellious artisans were drifting together into an uneasy alliance. Conditions in the various countries were so much alike, moreover, that it was likely that a revolutionary explosion in one center would touch off explosions elsewhere.

That is precisely what happened in March.

The Revolution in France   The center from which all the disorders of 1848 spread was Paris; yet revolution succeeded there less because of the strength of the revolutionary forces than because of the weakness and procrastination of the government of the July Monarchy.

We have already noted that, in the late 1840s, there was growing opposition in France to the policies of the Guizot government (see pp. 83–84). In 1847, indeed, the middle class reforming groups sought to dramatize this and give it greater force by organizing a series of "reform banquets" at which oratory would be the chief item on the bill of fare and antigovernment speeches would be delivered and antigovernment resolutions passed. The government might have drawn the teeth of this movement by some timely reforms. Instead, it did nothing until these windy feasts had attracted widespread attention and then compounded its error by seeking to prevent further banquets. This attitude advertised the movement it was meant to destroy. As excitement mounted, the opposition planned a monster banquet in Paris, to be held on February 22, 1848; and, when the government first refused to authorize it and then sought to denature it by laying down the conditions under which it could be held, groups of students and workingmen assembled in the streets, there were brushes with the police, and an ugly temper began to reign in the capital. Suddenly alarmed at the pass to which his inactivity had brought him, Louis Philippe turned upon his chief minister, Guizot, who had long been the target of popular hatred, and dismissed him from office.

Taken six months previously, this action might have prevented further trouble; now it inspired it. On the evening of February 23, a noisy but good-tempered crowd, some of whose members were republican agitators but most of whom were persons drawn together by the excitement in the air, set off to Guizot's official residence, doubtless intending to hold a demonstration in front of it. On the way they ran into a file of soldiers drawn up across a street called the Rue des Capucines and were informed by the commanding officer that they could not pass. The crowd was indignant; there was some shoving and hauling; someone seized a torch and thrust it into the officer's face; a shot was fired— probably by a soldier seeking to protect his commander, possibly by someone in the crowd, perhaps the result of an accidental discharge caused by jostling.

"Death on the Barricades," From the famous series of woodcuts, "A New Dance of Death," by the German artist Alfred Rethel.

It was followed by a volley from the troops which killed some forty persons—and brought the July Monarchy to an end.

The news of the "massacre" in the Rue des Capucines spread swiftly through the city; before night was out 1500 barricades had been built in main thoroughfares and across narrow streets, and groups of excited students were attacking police stations to procure arms; and by morning the cry "Long Live the Republic!" could be heard on all sides. If Louis Philippe wished to save his throne, it was clear that he would have to act now with decision. This was something of which he no longer seemed capable. He shied away from the idea of using all-out force to restore order and actually ordered his regular troops to evacuate the city; and he counted on the support of the National Guard long after it was clear that the citizen force was fraternizing with the rebels. Throughout the morning and afternoon of February 24, the king held interminable conferences with politicians, soldiers, and members of his own family while the situation got increasingly out of hand. Finally, despite the urgent pleas of his wife and daughter-in-law, he signed a note of abdication and fled to England.

Having seen an apparently stable regime overthrown in a matter of hours with a minimum of bloodshed, a stupefied Europe now watched while power in France was assumed by a provisional government whose members were selected in the offices of two radical newspapers (*Le National* and *La Réforme*) and which included a poet (Alphonse Lamartine), an astronomer (Francois Arago), a socialist theorist (Louis Blanc), and a common workingman whose full name no one seemed to remember and who was referred to simply by his given name, Albert.[1] Despite its unorthodox appearance, however, this group got down to

[1] His name was, in fact, Alexandre Martin, and he was a buttonmaker. He contributed nothing to the work of the government and, because of this, was criticized for killing the chances of future worker representation.

work with dispatch. Its first action, taken doubtless to appease the mobs surging in the streets of Paris, was to proclaim the republic. It then announced that elections for a new Parliament would be held in April and, to prepare the way for them, set about restoring order and consolidating the authority of the government. To guard against the possibility of foreign intervention, the armed forces were strengthened and African troops were recalled to France, while within the army and navy long-needed improvements of rations and pay and reforms of the disciplinary code were introduced. To reduce the possibility of new mob violence, service in the National Guard—formerly a middle class force—was made compulsory for all adult males, and a new mobile guard of 15,000 men was set up in Paris. Strenuous efforts were made to extend the ministry's authority to the provinces by the appointment of commissioners whose first duty was—as the new minister of interior said— "to reassure the public." In Paris itself this process of reassurance included efficient measures to reduce street disorders and crime and to improve the city's food supplies.

The most pressing obstacle to social peace was the continued economic distress. This had worsened as a result of the February rising, which had frightened some employers into leaving the city, had forced some concerns to close by cutting off their sources of credit, and had brought the luxury trades to a virtual standstill. Throughout the early months of 1848, unemployment mounted steadily in Paris, and demands for government relief action increased.

On February 25, the new ministry had proclaimed its belief in the right of all citizens to work. The problem was how to implement this. One man in the ministry, Louis Blanc, had long ago formulated a socialist blueprint for national prosperity; but the majority of the ministers, led by Lamartine, were staunch defenders of property and wanted no part of Blanc's program for the nationalization and decentralization of industry. They could not very well ignore their uncomfortable colleague, but they managed to sidetrack him into a position where his energies were expended on theoretical studies of labor problems and questions of negotiation between labor and management. Meanwhile, they tried to meet the unemployment crisis with what can only be called a caricature of Blanc's old idea of national workshops (see p. 80).

As authorized by the cabinet and administered by a young engineer named Emile Thomas, the national workshops of 1848 were simply semimilitary organizations of unemployed that undertook to find work for their members and to pay them at a rate of two francs a day when employed and one franc a day when not. This assurance of pay was enough to make them popular, and thousands of unemployed workers streamed into Paris to enroll, thus greatly increasing the difficulty of finding jobs for workshop members. The end result was that, while the workshops did some useful work (replanting trees, leveling the Champ de Mars, and other public works), the great majority of their members received wages for doing nothing and gave the impression to the country at large that Paris was filled with idlers living at public expense.

The irritation that this caused among the conservative and frugal peasantry of the country was reflected in the election returns when France went to the polls in April. The National Constituent Assembly that was elected by universal manhood suffrage at that time and assembled in Paris on May 4 was republican in political attitude but predominantly conservative in social philosophy. The election results were received with suspicion on the part of the working classes of Paris and with indignation by the radical clubs of the city, where men like Blanqui were agitating for a more thoroughgoing reform than that carried out so far by Lamartine and his colleagues. It was clear that new disorders were imminent.

The Revolution in the Austrian Empire   While these events were taking place, other parts of the continent were in the throes of revolution. Even before the February rising in Paris, a revolt in Palermo in Sicily had forced the reactionary King Ferdinand II of Naples to grant a constitution to his people. This rising was largely the result of Sicilian particularism and would probably, by itself, have had no further consequences. What started the revolutionary tide rolling in central Europe was the news of Louis Philippe's expulsion from the throne of France, and before long the exiled monarch was saying with dour satisfaction, "Europe is giving me splendid obsequies."

PRINCIPAL CENTERS OF REVOLUTION

1848-1849

0   100   200   300

Miles

The news of this event reached the city of Vienna on February 29 and aroused great excitement, which increased as word came of demonstrations in Stuttgart, Mannheim, and other German cities. Crowds began to gather in the cafés of the Austrian capital to hear the latest news from abroad; nervousness led to a run on the banks; food prices began to rise steeply; and, as they did, criticism of the government became vocal. Then, on March 3, came reports of a speech delivered in Budapest by Kossuth (see p. 54), in which that gifted agitator had denounced the abuses of the absolutist system and called for the immediate introduction of constitutional government in Hungary. This would be impossible, Kossuth admitted, as long as "a corrupting puff of wind that benumbs our senses and paralyzes the flight of our spirit comes to us from the charnel house of the cabinet in Vienna"; therefore, basic reform must be introduced in every branch of the imperial government. Translated immediately into German, this speech was circulated in thousands of copies in the western half of the empire, where its very violence appealed to the middle class businessmen who felt handicapped by the economic backwardness of the government, the artisans who—despite their lack of employment—had to pay a sales tax on the necessities of life, the peasants who were still bound by the feudal restrictions of an outworn agricultural system, and the intellectuals who had long chafed at police supervision of all literary and artistic activity. Petitions began to circulate demanding administrative changes, enlargement of the system of estates and immediate convocation of a diet, abolition of censorship, and economic reform.

In face of this ground swell of opposition, the government in Vienna showed a remarkable lack of imagination, rejecting all petitions and refusing all concessions. This standpat attitude proved to be the immediate cause of an all-out revolution against the regime. On March 13 demonstrations began among the students of the university, a group made rebellious by their long experience of uninspired instruction, police despotism, and unmentionable living conditions. A throng marched to the *Landhaus,* where the Estates of Lower Austria were meeting and, after some preliminary harangues, stormed the building. By midafternoon fighting had started in the inner city between detachments of the local garrison and the students, who had now been joined by workingmen from the suburbs.

The first reaction of the court was stupefaction; and the Emperor Ferdinand is reported to have gasped, when news of the fighting arrived, *"Ja, derfn s'denn das?"* ("But are they allowed to do that?"). As the situation deteriorated, this mood was replaced by one of panic; and, at nine in the evening, fearing that the mob might actually break into the imperial palace, the royal family abandoned Metternich as abruptly as Louis Philippe had dropped Guizot, announcing that the man who had held office uninterruptedly for thirty-nine years had resigned. Metternich, who had argued vigorously that capitulation of this kind might be fatal to the monarchy, accepted his fate philosophically and made a dignified departure to London, the end station for all dismissed monarchs and oligarchs, leaving behind him a Vienna enraptured by the thought that the very symbol of despotism had been overthrown.

If Kossuth's speech had played an important part in precipitating these events in Vienna, the fall of the chancellor now gave new impetus to the revolutionary currents running in Hungary. On March 15, the Hungarian Diet gave a precise and dramatic formulation to ambitions held by Magyar patriots for a generation. It promulgated a new Hungarian constitution, which provided for a national diet to be elected by all Hungarians owning property worth one hundred and fifty dollars, established civil and religious liberty for all subjects and freedom for the press, and abolished the traditional privileges of the feudal nobility. Hungary was to remain within the empire but to have its own ministries of war, finance, and foreign affairs; and, to all intents and purposes, the Hungarians would henceforth enjoy complete autonomy.

On March 31, the government in Vienna was forced to agree to these sweeping reforms, which had been gained without loss of blood or even the exertion of physical force.

Where the Hungarians led, the leaders of the Czech national movement followed. In March they sent deputations to Vienna to demand the convocation of a Bohemian diet elected by democratic franchise, basic civil and religious freedoms, and, especially, the equality of the Czech and German languages in schools and government services. On April 8 the emperor granted most of these demands, thus giving Bohemia the same degree of local autonomy as that already won by Hungary.

It is said of Emperor Ferdinand that, on one occasion when his doctor forbade him certain foods because "Your Majesty's constitution will not tolerate them," he said firmly, *"I hob halt ka Konstitution und i mag halt ka Konstitution!"*[2] Yet he was now compelled not only to accept the Hungarian and Czech demands but to repudiate his principles in Austria proper, by consenting to the formation of a National Guard, which was to include a separate Academic Legion of students, and by summoning a united diet for the purpose of drawing up a new constitution—because he had no armed force capable of controlling the situation. This weakness was caused by the development of affairs in the Austrian provinces of Italy. In a violent insurrection that lasted for five days, the city of Milan arose and expelled the Austrian troops; and on March 22, Daniele Manin, a lawyer and politician of Jewish heritage, led a swift and entirely successful revolt in Venice and proclaimed the republic. Taking advantage of this situation, Charles Albert of Piedmont, an ambitious if emotionally unbalanced ruler, threw in his lot with the rebels of Lombardy and Venetia and sent his armies to help them forge Italian freedom. These sudden blows sent the Austrian forces commanded by Radetzky reeling back into the so-called Quadrilateral, four strong fortresses on the Adige and Mincio. The eighty-two-year-old field marshal, who, despite his years, had lost neither his interest in women nor his vigor in war, was not alarmed by these setbacks; but he saw that, unless put right, they might lead to the total collapse of the Hapsburg Empire. He insisted, therefore, that—even at the cost of temporary concessions at home—reinforcements be sent to him, and he had his way.

This meant, however, that the emperor had to accept the reforms in Hungary and Bohemia, and, in Austria itself, to dismiss other unpopular ministers (like the police chief Sedlnitzky) and to agree to a whole series of further reforms.

[2] "I have no constitution and I don't want a constitution!"

These included a reduction of the sales tax on food, the abolition of the censorship, and a general political amnesty; but the most notable of them was the imperial manifesto of April 11, which promised to free the peasants from all services and duties incumbent on the land. This new freedom was to be inaugurated on January 1, 1849, after the Diet had framed the necessary legislation, but it could be effected earlier by private arrangement, provided proprietors received suitable compensation.

The April decree was probably the most important positive action of the whole Austrian revolution, and, even before it was confirmed by the Austrian parliament in September, it was exercising a moderating influence upon the course of events. It was greeted with enthusiasm by the peasants and had the almost immediate effect of transforming them into a conservative force, more interested in law and order than in revolutionary agitation. As in France, the peasantry now grew critical of continued disorders in the capital. Their attitude was shared by the wealthier middle class in Vienna, who were satisfied with the gains already made and were increasingly fearful of the excesses of the students and the workers, and by some of the intellectuals. Austria's greatest novelist in this period, Adalbert Stifter, wrote gloomily during 1848: "God grant that people begin to see that only good sense and moderation can lead to constructive work. What we have to do is to build, not just to tear down. I am a man of moderation *and* of freedom, but both are now unfortunately jeopardized. . . ."

Thus, as early as April, the unity of the revolutionary movement was beginning to split. Nor was this caused only by economic and social differences. Nationality also played a part, as Austrian Germans came to resent the gains made by the Czechs and Hungarians, and Magyars to fear the growing ambitions of their Slav neighbors, who aspired to the same kind of privileges won by the followers of Kossuth. The imperial house, still impotent in April and May, was going to win its ultimate victory over the revolution by exploiting those widening social and national divisions.

The Revolution in Prussia and the German States   The Russian exile Alexander Herzen, who made a lifetime career of revolutionary agitation, was bitterly scornful of the risings in Germany in 1848. The Germans were not, he wrote in his memoirs, serious about revolution at all; they were merely enjoying themselves by imitating France in the days of the Terror.

> There was not a town . . . where . . . there was not an attempt at a "committee of public safety" with all its principal characters: with a frigid youth as Saint-Just, with gloomy terrorists, and a military genius representing Carnot. I knew two or three Robespierres personally; they always put on clean shirts, washed their hands and had clean nails. . . . If there happened to be a man . . . fonder of beer than the rest and more openly given to dangling after *Stubenmädchen*—he was the Danton.

This was written after the collapse of the revolution and reflects the bitterness induced by that failure (if not by the additional fact that, in his retreat in

London, Herzen had to put up with the eccentricities of German exiles for years after 1848—and actually lost the affections of his wife to one of them). But this statement hardly does justice to the idealistic drive of the German revolution or to the force that enabled it to humble the monarchy of the most militaristic power in Europe, the kingdom of Prussia. The mood of the German revolution is better described by the distinguished emigrant to the United States, Carl Schurz, who tells in his memoirs of how the news of the fall of Louis Philippe came to him when he was a student at Bonn and how it affected the academic youth of the day, who saw suddenly opening before them the chance not only to attain the civil liberties and the constituional form of government so long denied them but also to realize the dream of German unity. "The word democracy," he writes, "was on all tongues and many thought it a matter of course that, if the princes should try to withhold from the people the rights and liberties demanded, force would take the place of mere petition."

In general, the petty princes did not relish the latter possibility and tumbled over themselves in an effort to grant concessions to their subjects before it was too late. In Baden and Württemberg, in Hesse-Darmstadt and Bavaria, in Saxony and Hanover, the rulers called to their side moderate liberals whom they would formerly have ignored or persecuted and made promises of constitutional charters and other reforms.

In Prussia, however, the concessions came too late. Frederick William IV's attitude toward constitutional reform had not softened since 1847; and, now, with economic depression gripping much of the country, with artisans' riots breaking out in provincial cities like Cologne and Breslau, and with agitators beginning to address excited crowds in the Berlin Tiergarten, he still stubbornly refused to consider concessions and relied upon his troops to break up demonstrations, with a not inconsiderable number of resultant casualties. It was not until he heard the shattering news of Metternich's fall that the king turned from his military to his civilian advisers and, at their bidding, on the night of March 17, drafted a manifesto to his people in which he promised to convoke the Prussian Diet at the beginning of April, to grant a constitution and sponsor a program of internal reform, and to use Prussian influence to promote a constitutional reorganization of the Germanic Confederation.

These promises, which, despite their lateness, appealed to moderate reformers and to advocates of national unity, were announced to the people of Berlin on the morning of the 18th. There then followed one of those unhappy accidents that always seem to occur in revolutionary situations. At noon a large throng, composed of both well-to-do citizens and common working people, crowded into the palace square, presumably to cheer the king for his concessions. Fearing for the king's safety, the commander of the royal cavalry guard sent a detachment to clear the area. Remembering the bloodshed of recent days, the crowd was first stubborn and then angry. More troops had to be put in to support their fellows; and in the resultant scuffling—much as in Paris—someone fired two shots, and the troops responded with a volley into the crowd. With a cry of treason, the demonstrators fled from the palace; and, within an hour, barricades had been built across all the thoroughfares leading to the *Schloß*, and fighting was in progress.

The Prussian army had not been engaged in battle since Waterloo, and it had never fought in cobbled streets against adversaries who sniped from rooftops or dropped chimney pots or boiling water from attic windows. When it took a barricade by frontal assault, it was apt to find that its defenders had escaped down side lanes or through corner houses, and new barricades were constantly springing up behind it. It was discouraging work; by nightfall the troops were spent; by morning they were demoralized, and their commander was urging the king to authorize their withdrawal from the city so that they could encircle and bombard it from outside. The king was aghast at the idea of his city being leveled by artillery and rejected the idea. But he ordered the troops to leave Berlin, although refusing to go with them, preferring to put his trust in his "dear Berliners."

This was a gallant action and, from the long-range point of view, probably a wise one, but for the time being it left Frederick William a captive of the revolution—a "king of the pavement," as the tsar of Russia said savagely at this time. Like his brother sovereigns in Vienna and the lesser German capitals, he had to call liberal business and professional men to office and to promise speedy convocation of a National Prussian Assembly. Later in his life, he was ashamed of the speed with which his regime had capitulated, and said ruefully, "At that time we were all on our bellies."

The Frankfurt Parliament   The events in Prussia seemed to complete and make definitive the collapse of absolutism; and the time appeared to have come now to exploit this opportunity to satisfy the yearnings of generations of Germans and to transform the rickety old Germanic Confederation into an effective organization of national unity. Since the first days of March, leaders of the constitutional movement in southern Germany had been consulting among themselves about the tasks of national reconstruction. At the end of the month, they joined with liberal leaders from other states to draw up a tentative program of action and persuaded the Diet to invite the governments of all German states, including Austria and Prussia, to elect delegates to a National Parliament that would then proceed to transform Germany into a federal union with a liberal constitution. The individual states, now under liberal ministries, accepted the invitations; elections were held in the course of April; and on May 18, the first National Parliament in German history was solemnly convened in St. Paul's Church in Frankfurt on the Main.

The Frankfurt parliament has often been described as a gathering of impractical intellectuals who debated theoretical questions to the exclusion of the issues that demanded immediate attention. It is true that the percentage of highly educated people among its members was very large; out of a total of 586 members there were 95 lawyers, 104 professors, 124 bureaucrats, and 100 judicial officials. Moreover, from May until December, they did spend a lot of time talking about abstract questions, for this was the period in which they drafted the Fundamental Rights of the German People. Yet surely, after a past of unrelieved absolutism, it was important to have such things clearly defined. When it was completed, the Declaration of Fundamental Rights was an eloquent expression of middle-class liberal philosophy, which established freedom of speech and religion and equality before the law as basic rights of all Germans, asserted the sanctity of private property, and laid down rules for representative government and ministerial responsibility in the individual states.

It was hoped that this constitution would be put into effect in a Germany that was a federal union, presided over by a hereditary emperor, but with a strong parliament representing the educated and propertied classes and a ministry that was responsible to it. The exact composition of the empire and the role of Austria in it was the subject of long debate between two schools of thought. The Great German (*Großdeutsch*) party believed that the empire must embrace all German states, including the German provinces of Austria, a solution that implied that there would be a Hapsburg emperor; whereas the Small German (*Kleindeutsch*) party insisted that all of Austria must be excluded. Eventually, the majority agreed on the latter solution, while advocating a close future connection between the new Germany and the Hapsburg realm; and they concluded also—as we shall see—that the king of Prussia must be invited to preside over the new German Reich.

Before the time-consuming debates on these matters were finished, events had taken a turn that made it unlikely that the conclusions reached in them would be accepted by the German states. This was not, as is sometimes argued, the fault of the longwindedness of the Frankfurt parliamentarians. Considering the complicated issues with which they had to deal, they did their job with dispatch. But, while their deliberations continued, the unity of purpose that had made the March revolution successful began to break down, and suspicion and ill feeling began to arise among the different classes and nationalities. The forces of reaction now showed an ability to exploit these divisions in such a way as to nullify the work accomplished at Frankfurt and the gains of the revolution in general.

It was not only in Germany that this reaction occurred. Like the revolution, it was European in scope; and, like the revolution, it had its first significant success in France.

THE FAILURE OF THE REVOLUTION

The June Days in France   The majority of the members of the newly elected French National Assembly came to Paris at the beginning of May 1848 with a strong desire to prevent new revolutionary experiments or disorders. They revealed the nature of their thinking by refusing to give Lamartine's ministry a vote of confidence until he had dropped from it not only the workingman Albert but also Louis Blanc, who was distrusted in the provinces because of his socialist views. Their attitude hardened when an excited mob broke into the Assembly on May 15, in a pointless demonstration which working class leaders like Blanqui had vainly sought to stop because they feared it would invite reprisals. It did exactly that, by encouraging the Assembly to strike out at what they considered the root of all the disorder in Paris, the national workshops.

On May 24, an executive commission of the Assembly ordered Emile Thomas to begin the dissolution of the workshops by enlisting its younger members in the army, paying its rural members to return to their homes, and forcing others

"The Judgment of Paris." A British comment on the French presidential elections. The figures are Lamartine, Cavaignac, and Louis Napoleon. From *Punch,* October 28, 1848.

either to enter private industry or to undertake public works outside of Paris. Thomas tried to delay, recognizing that the members would resent being forced into private employment at reduced wages or into tasks for which they had no stomach; but he had no success, and by mid-June it was clear that the Assembly would soon act to dissolve the workshops completely. This prompted counteraction on the part of national workshop leaders and other workers' groups; on June 18, some of them issued a call for a democratic and social republic; and on June 23, the day army enlistments were supposed to start in the workshops, a great throng of workers met at the Place de la Bastille, pledged themselves to fight for their rights, and began to build barricades.

With the issue thus forced, the Assembly acted with merciless efficiency. The National Guard was mobilized immediately, and its majority rallied to the Assembly's cause. Calls were sent out to other towns for reinforcements and were answered promptly, 3000 National Guards from Amiens arriving in Paris on June 23, and 1500 traveling 200 miles from Brittany some days later. Provincial France seemed all too ready to settle with radical Paris.

Even before the 23d was over, the Assembly had enough troops to proceed against the barricades and, in General Cavaignac, the new minister of war, it had a commander who was ruthless and uncompromising. In the circumstances, despite the valor shown by the workers and the ingenuity they displayed in the construction of defensive works, they had no chance. It took four days for Cavaignac's forces to put down the insurrection. Before the fighting ended, some 1460 lives had been lost, and after it was over 3000 insurgents were hunted down and killed and 12,000 additional persons arrested. The government's victory was definitive and left the working class with no will to further resistance, but the cost of this bloody restoration of order was a legacy of class hatred that was to become a permanent feature of French life in the second half of the century.

After the June Days, the desire for order and stability was unmistakable and encouraged the Assembly to push ahead its plans for a new constitution. This was completed and accepted in October and provided that the Republic would have a president to be elected for a four-year term by universal manhood suffrage. When the presidential elections were held in December, the real beneficiary of the June Days was revealed. He was Prince Louis Napoleon, who had returned to France after the March revolution and been elected to the Assembly in June, and who now appealed equally to the wealthy bourgeoisie, the conservative peasants, the Catholic Church, the nationalists, and even some workers and socialists who found him preferable to his opponents, Cavaignac and Lamartine. Napoleon's election, by 5,434,266 votes to 1,448,107 for Cavaignac and a mere 17,910 for Lamartine, was the end of the French revolution of 1848 and the prelude to the establishment of a new authoritarian regime.

The Recovery of Royal Power in Prussia   The failure of the revolution in Prussia can be attributed, like the corresponding failure in France, to increasing disunity and suspicion among the different classes of society; but two other factors played a part. The first was the stubbornness with which the king opposed basic reform of the Prussian state, and the second was the failure of the Prussian Assembly to fathom his intentions and to impose its will upon him. After his apparent submission to the people in March, Frederick William IV showed remarkable resilience. Once the first shock of revolution had passed, he persisted in acting as if his powers were, and would remain, undiminished; and, although he acquiesced in the appointment of a new liberal ministry, he steadfastly resisted their efforts to do what they wanted to do—namely, to arrogate to themselves the kinds of powers possessed by cabinet ministers in England.

The king's opposition might have been fruitless if parliamentary action had been effective. A National Assembly, the first in Prussia's history, was elected by universal manhood suffrage in May 1848 and settled down to the task of writing a new constitution for the Prussian kingdom. But it showed no urgency in its work; it failed to assure its control over the real sources of power in Prussia, the army and the police; and it exhausted time and energy in interminable debates between liberal reformers, who wanted to devise constitutional restrictions for royal power while retaining monarchical institutions, and radicals, who were hoping to establish a republic. The incessant wrangling prevented any direct attack upon the royal prerogative, irritated moderate opinion, and tended to arouse sympathy for the sovereign. This last tendency was strengthened by the new government's inability to prevent disorders in Berlin, where a sudden out-break of mob violence on June 14, during which the armory was attacked and its stores of weapons and ammunition plundered, struck fear into the hearts of respectable burghers.

All of this played directly into the king's hands and, before the year was over, he calculated that the Assembly had been so discredited that he could risk a blow against it. Consequently, in November, he announced that its meetings would be suspended pending its removal to another place of meeting outside of Berlin and, simultaneously, he ordered the army under General von Wrangel to return to the barracks in the capital that they had been forced to evacuate in March. The king's order caused a momentary flare-up of revolution-ary zeal. Attempts were made to raise a defensive force in the city, and one group of diehards captured Wrangel's wife and sent a message to the general, warning that they would hang her unless he stopped his advance toward the city. Wrangel did not allow himself to be influenced by this. As he led his grenadiers toward the capital he was heard to mutter, "I wonder if they have really hanged her? I hardly believe so!"; and the event proved him right.

The army's entrance into Berlin brought an end to the revolution in Prussia; but it did not usher in a period of black reaction, as some people had feared it might. To the dismay of his most conservative advisers, the king—unpredictable as ever—now decided to grant a constitution to his people of his own accord. The document that was issued by royal decree at the end of 1848, and was revised in 1850, laid down safeguards for the liberties of Prussian subjects and assured the country of a bicameral legislature that would meet annually. There was, to be sure, little likelihood that the new parliament would ever become a radical body. Its upper house was to be composed of hereditary members (princes of the royal house and the heads of certain noble families) and a smaller number of persons appointed by the king for life. The lower house was elected by uni-versal manhood suffrage, but in a curiously complicated way. In each electoral district throughout the land, voters were divided into three groups, according to the amount of taxes they paid; and each group, voting separately, elected an equal number of delegates to a district convention, which then proceeded to elect the district's parliamentary deputies. In practice, this meant that the two wealthier groups, comprising at most about 15 percent of the population, effec-tively controlled two thirds of the seats in the lower house of parliament. It is not difficult to see that this system, which was to last until 1918, would serve as a barrier to democratic reform and social legislation in behalf of the masses. On the other hand, it was better than what had preceded it. Prussia could at least be described now as a constitutional parliamentary state.

The restoration of royal power in Prussia had marked effects throughout Ger-many, especially in Frankfurt. In that capital, the National Assembly had now completed drafting its Fundamental Rights (which, incidentally, went further than Frederick William's *charte* in guaranteeing basic liberties) and had defined the geographical limits of the united German empire that they had their hearts set on. It remained now to choose a hereditary ruler for their creation and, in March 1849, they did so, by sending a delegation to Berlin to offer the crown to Frederick William IV.

Once more secure in his power, the Prussian king turned the offer aside with contumely. He may have been influenced by the knowledge that to accept a crown that had been worn by the Hapsburgs would be to invite certain Austrian hostility. He may also have been alienated by claims by Frankfurt parliamentarians that, in their new Reich, Prussia would lose its separate identity and be "merged" with the rest of Germany; and it is not unlikely that he had dreams of Prussia's uniting Germany by conquest. However that may be, in public he argued that a Prussian king could not take a crown from the hands of intellectuals and tradesmen who claimed to be representatives of the people. "If the thousand-year-old crown of the German nation, in abeyance now these forty-two years,[3] is again to be given away," he said proudly, "it is I and my likes who will give it." He was deaf to all appeals made by the delegation, whose members had to return dejectedly to Frankfurt.

The disappointing news they took with them had the effect of dividing the Frankfurt parliament hopelessly into factions. While some of the delegates, in discouragement, wanted to give up the fight for unity and freedom, and others hoped, by diplomacy and patience, to persuade the Prussian ruler to change his mind, a group of extremists advocated resort to armed insurrection as the most effective way of gaining the parliament's objectives. These hotheads were encouraged by the effect of the king's refusal throughout Germany, and especially in Saxony, the Rhine Palatinate, and Baden, where outbreaks of mob violence paralyzed government and seemed to presage a new wave of revolutionary action.

But Frederick William IV, having restored order in his own realm, was in no mood to tolerate agitation in the territory of his neighbors. In May 1849, Prussian troops were dispatched to Dresden where they suppressed the rebellion and restored the King of Saxony to his throne. The troubles in Baden and the Palatinate were more serious, for a revolutionary army of thirty to forty thousand men had been raised under the command of the Polish refugee Mieroslawski and an exotic group of poets, publicists, professional revolutionaries, and foreign adventurers. Before this "people's army" was routed and order restored, two Prussian army corps, under the command of the king's brother, the future king-emperor William I, had to be put into the field, and the fortress of Rastadt had to be bombarded into submission. Later generations of Germans were to recall this fighting with pride—as did the first president of the Federal Republic of Germany, Theodor Heuss, whose grandfather led a company of volunteers against the Prussians—and to argue that it proved that a genuine democratic spirit was strong in 1849, especially in southern Germany. In its own time, it is likely that the rising in Baden further alarmed middle class opinion and made it welcome both the Prussian victory and, a few months later, the dissolution of the Frankfurt parliament which that victory made inevitable.

Even after the failure of the Frankfurt parliament, the desire for unification of the long-fragmented German lands was still strong enough to persuade the king of Prussia to try, in his own way, to make some progress toward that goal. His scheme, which was devised under the influence of Josef Maria von Radowitz,

[3]That is, since Napoleon Bonaparte had abolished the Holy Roman Empire in 1806.

a Catholic nobleman who had become the king's closest confidant, called for an agreement by the German princes to join their territories in a union that would be led by Prussia and would exclude Austria, although, for purposes of foreign and economic affairs, it would be bound in perpetual alliance with the Hapsburg state. This was obviously a plan that could be effected, if at all, only by lengthy and laborious negotiations; and such negotiations did, indeed, fill the rest of 1849 and the first months of the new year. But these consultations never gave much reality to the Prussian union; and, before it was much more than an idea, the Austrians completed their recovery from the revolution and intervened to break up Frederick William's ambitious plans.

The Recovery of Austria   The Austrian crown took longer than either the French or the Prussians to put its house in order because it could not concentrate upon the situation in the imperial capital but had to think also of the revolutionary movements that had taken place in Bohemia, Hungary, and Italy. Yet it did master the situation in time, thanks to the social and national prejudices that came to divide the rebels and the vigor of the Austrian army and its commanders Radetzky, Windischgrätz, and Jellachich.

The tide began to turn in June 1848 in Bohemia, where the German and Czech wings of the revolutionary movement had become hopelessly estranged after their common victory in March. Led by men like Frantísek Palacký (1798–1876), the author of the great *History of the Czech People* (1836–1848), the Czechs had begun to dream of a nation of their own. They opposed sending a delegation to the Frankfurt Assembly and took a leading part in the calling of a Pan-Slav Congress, which met in Prague early in June, and which issued a ringing call for the conversion of the Hapsburg empire into "a federation of nations all enjoying equal rights." This inflamed the feelings of the German population; brawling between Czechs and Germans led to more serious disorders; and, by mid-June, barricades were being built and mobs of Czech students were marching through the streets, smashing store fronts as they searched for arms. This violence, engendered by nationalistic passions, had a bloody sequel, for—after some days of negotiation for the purpose of restoring order—the imperial military commandant of Prague, General Windischgrätz, withdrew his troops from the city and then proceeded to bombard it with artillery with a ruthlessness that was perhaps influenced by the fact that his wife had been fatally wounded by a stray bullet a few days before. Helpless before this kind of force, the Czech students capitulated on June 17; the political liberties won in March were abrogated; and supporters of royal authority all over the empire had reason to feel that the situation was not as hopeless as it had seemed earlier.

This feeling was strengthened by events in Italy. In the first victories against the Austrians, the rebels of Lombardy had been supported by the army of the king of Piedmont and by detachments from Rome, Tuscany, and Naples. But by the middle of the year these last units were recalled to deal with troubles in their own states; and a waning of enthusiasm had begun to affect the Piedmontese and the Lombards. It was in these circumstances that Radetzky emerged from the Quadrilateral and overwhelmed the Piedmontese at Custoza on July 24. Within two weeks Lombardy had been rewon. The restoration of order in

Tuscany had to wait until the spring of 1849 (as did that in Rome, where French troops put down a republic and restored papal authority in June); and Radetzky was not able to subdue Venice until August 1849.[4] But Custoza was, in a sense, a promise that those things were coming. Thousands of people now quoted Grillparzer's ode to Radetzky:

> Glück auf, mein Feldherr, führe den Streich!
> Nicht bloß um des Ruhmes Schimmer,
> In deinem Lager ist Oesterreich,
> Wir andern sind einzelne Trümmer.
>
> Aus Thorheit und aus Eitelkeit
> Sind wir in uns zerfallen;
> In denen, die du führst zum Streit,
> Lebt noch Ein Geist in Allen.[5]

The Italian victories produced a degree of enthusiasm for army and emperor that boded ill for the cause of revolution.

The next victory was in Vienna itself, although it was made possible by the course of events in Hungary. In that country, the victory won for autonomy by the Magyars in March was now challenged by the non-Magyar elements—notably the Croats, the Serbs, and the Rumanians, who demanded recognition of their separate identity and their right to conduct their affairs in their own language and under leaders of their own choice. These demands the Magyars, intent on a policy of centralization and cultural uniformity, refused; and this uncompromising attitude led to an explosion of indignation on the part of the other national groups. The Vienna government aggravated these passions by appointing an inveterate anti-Magyar, Colonel Jellachich, as governor of Croatia, from which position he did everything possible to defy the Magyar authorities. Jellachich's policy culminated finally in open revolution against the Hungarian government, an action that in its turn brought the radical anti-Slav, anti-Austrian party of Kossuth to power in Budapest and made any political compromise impossible. That the Austrian crown welcomed this situation was indicated by the alacrity with which the emperor now dissolved the Hungarian Diet and gave Jellachich command of all imperial forces in Hungary.

These provocative actions were almost disastrous, for they inspired a wave of sympathy for the Magyars that touched off a new and bloody rising in Vienna, during which the minister of war, Count Latour, was murdered by the mob. Powerless to preserve order, the court and the government fled the city on October 7, leaving it in the hands of the students, the artisans and shopkeepers, and the proletarian masses. It was, however, a rising doomed to failure; for

---

[4] For a fuller account of events in Italy in 1848–1849, see pages 190–192.
[5] Here's to my general! Now strike home; / Not only fame for thy fee! / Thy camp encloses Austria, / Her separate members are we. / By foolishness and vanity / Came our collapse and fall. / But when thou leadest men to war / The old fire glows in all.

its leaders were bereft of political talent and their violence alienated not only
the bulk of the middle class but also the peasants, who refused to give any
support to the rebels in the capital, arrested emissaries sent out to appeal to
them, and took advantage of the plight of the democrats in Vienna to exact
exorbitant prices for the food they supplied. Meanwhile, the government showed
that it had not forgotten the lesson of Prague. On October 15, at Olmütz, the
emperor gave full powers to Windischgrätz to end "the reign of terror" in Vienna;
on October 23, the "bombardment prince," as he was called by the Viennese
democrats, gave the city forty-eight hours to surrender; on October 28, after
an artillery barrage, his troops began the assault on the city. Recognizing his
debt to the Viennese rebels, Kossuth sent a Hungarian force of 25,000 men to
their aid, but they were beaten off by Jellachich's Croats on October 30. Windischgrätz overcame the resistance of the last extremists on the following day
and imposed martial law over the city.

The capture of the capital brought a significant change in the government.
Earlier in the month, Windischgrätz's brother-in-law, Prince Felix Schwarzenberg
(1800–1852) had been authorized to form a government. He did so now, filling
it with men who, like himself, were opposed to all reforms except those granted
from above and whose first objective was the restoration of the imperial power.
At the beginning of December, they persuaded the foolish and ineffective sovereign Ferdinand to abdicate in favor of his nephew Francis Joseph. This eighteen-
year-old boy, who accepted his office with the rueful words "Farewell youth!"
had a strong sense of responsibility and a willingness to work hard; but the
circumstances of his accession to the throne and the tutelage of Schwarzenberg
prejudiced him against the desires of his subject nationalities and the very idea
of liberal reform, gave him an exaggerated regard for his own prerogatives, and
induced in him an excessive reliance upon soldiers and bureaucrats. This was
hardly the best preparation for a reign that was to last until 1916.

The eyes of the new emperor and his ministers turned naturally, in the first
months of their power, to the situation in Hungary. Not for a moment did they
contemplate a compromise with the Magyars. The concessions that had been
made to them in March by Ferdinand were now abrogated, and war was declared.
It was not a glorious war for the Austrians, whose commanders showed greater
success against open cities and peasant villages than against the Hungarian forces.
These last had been molded into a spirited and effective army by Arthur Görgey.
an almost unknown officer who had so distinguished himself in fighting against
Jellachich's Croats that Kossuth had made him a general. In the first months of
1849, in an astonishing series of victories, Görgey drove the Austrian forces of
Windischgrätz back to the frontiers of their own country. Inspired by these
victories, the Hungarian Diet formally declared its independence of Austria, and
Kossuth became the president of the new state.

But Francis Joseph and Schwarzenberg were willing to go to any length to
suppress the rebels. They appealed now to the tsar of Russia for aid, and Nicholas,
who prided himself on being the archfoe of revolution, responded by sending
140,000 troops against the Hungarians. Even Görgey's undoubted strategical gifts
were not enough to overcome this addition to his enemy's strength; and on August
13, at Világos, his armies surrendered to the Russians. Kossuth and his cabinet

fled, with several thousand soldiers, to Turkish soil, thus avoiding the fate of many of their companions, who died in the wave of hangings, shootings, and public floggings with which the Austrians celebrated their victory, to the accompaniment of shocked protests from the British and American governments and even the Russian field commanders.

Schwarzenberg, the real director of Austrian policy in these years, was impervious to these complaints. A cold and ruthless nature, scornful of the idealism that had motivated many of the forty-eighters, regarding power as the only thing that deserved respect, provided it was energetically employed ("Bayonets" he had warned Francis Joseph, "are good for everything except sitting upon"), he was determined to show the world that Austria's recovery from the revolution was complete. Simultaneously with the destruction of Hungarian liberties, Radetzky's armies had completed the reconquest of northern Italy. The only remaining threat to Austria's position was in the German states, which Frederick William IV had been seeking to form into a union under Prussian leadership. Schwarzenberg was now prepared to deal with that.

Since the middle of 1849, he had done everything possible to sabotage Prussian efforts by diplomatic means. Now, he resorted to menaces, and, in the course of 1850, made it clear to the Prussians that they would have to choose between abandonment of their project and war. As tension mounted between the two great German powers and Austrian troops were put in readiness. Prussian conservatives urged their king to give in, arguing that Russia would certainly support Austria and that the resultant conflict would help no one but the advocates of revolution. The king's friend Radowitz and his brother Prince William pleaded that Prussian honor forbade capitulation, but they were overborne. In November 1850, at Olmütz, Prussian ministers signed a convention—later called "the humiliation of Olmütz" by nationalists—by which they gave up the king's plan for the reorganization of Germany and agreed to the re-establishment of the old German Confederation, which had been superseded by the Frankfurt parliament two years before.

This action completed Austria's recovery from the revolution that had come upon her in March 1848. While Schwarzenberg had been dealing with the Hungarian, Italian, and Prussian challenges to imperial authority, he had summarily disposed of one other source of irritation. This was the Austrian Constitutional Assembly, which was first elected in 1848 and, after the rising in Vienna in October, had removed to Kremsier in Bohemia, where its members had been patiently working on a constitution for the whole empire. At the beginning of 1849, they had actually put the finishing touches to a document that later generations of Austrians were to feel might have spared the empire many troubles. For the so-called Kremsier constitution sought to solve the nationalities problem by providing for extensive provincial autonomy, while at the same time granting local self-government to towns and villages, so that a German village in Bohemia, for example, would be assured of minority rights. This was certainly a more rational arrangement than any tried in the subsequent period; but Schwarzenberg, who was opposed to decentralization of any kind, would have none of it. In March 1849, he confiscated all copies of the draft constitution and dissolved the Assembly. Some time later the emperor himself granted a charter to his subjects, which had none of the liberal features of the Kremsier constitution and was in any case abrogated in 1852.

CONCLUSION

By 1850, the fires of revolution had burned themselves out, and the victories of March 1848 seemed a remote and unreal memory. After all the rhetoric and the resolutions and the bravery on the barricades and in the field, the continent of Europe seemed to be, on the whole, unchanged. The attempt to liberalize and federalize the Hapsburg empire had failed as ignominiously as the movement to unify Germany; both Kremsier and Frankfurt were might-have-beens. The Bourbons were back in Naples and the pope was back in Rome. Austria was supreme in northern Italy; her influence in Germany was restored; and, if her serfs had been freed, her other subjects had not. The governmental methods of the Hapsburg state were still as autocratic as those of Russia, and this could almost be said of Prussia too, for despite their new constitutional system, the Prussians returned after Olmütz to their old association with the Eastern Powers and aped their ways. The only nation whose governmental structure had undergone marked change was France, but there was little reason in 1850 to put much faith in the durability of her republican institutions in view of the tactics of her president.

The psychological effects of the collapse of all the high hopes of March were profound and affected every aspect of European thought and activity after 1850. This was most immediately evident in the field of foreign affairs, where the principles and the tactics of those who guided the fortunes of the Great Powers were determined by their memory of the revolutions and where the nature of their objectives soon destroyed the European system that still seemed intact in 1850. These psychological and diplomatic effects of the revolutionary years are the subject of the pages that follow.

PART TWO
1850-1871

GENERAL
OBSERVATIONS

The climate of opinion that prevailed after 1850 was marked by disillusionment with the values and methods of the past, distaste for ideals and abstractions, and exaggerated veneration of concreteness and tangibility. The new generation prided itself on its realism.

This was encouraged and reinforced by the contrast between the failure of political idealism in 1848 and the triumphs of science and industry in the years that followed. The European public could hardly fail to be impressed by scientific progress, because they saw its utility demonstrated daily in fields like metallurgy, where chemists discovered how to remove phosphorus from iron ore, and medicine, where Lister's germ theory decreased the incidence of death by blood poisoning, or embodied in such convenient by-products of scientific investigation as linoleum (1860), celluloid (1863), cement (1850), and vulcanized rubber (1869).

Their respect for these achievements tended to make them receptive to the generalizations that scientists now began to offer about human life and the universe. To a disillusioned generation seeking comfort in tangible things, the concept of the indestructibility of matter made a direct appeal; it was easy to be so impressed by it that one began to regard it as the ultimate reality, in terms of which all things had to be explained. Similarly, the formulation by Charles Darwin (1809-1882) of the theory of the origin of the species, with its emphasis upon the survival of those species that are selected by nature because of their ability to adjust themselves to the conditions of the continuing struggle for existence, was so seductive that those who accepted it were apt to apply it not only to the sphere of biology but also to sociology and politics, economic activity, and international diplomacy. One of the outstanding characteristics of this period and the one that succeeded it was, thus, a deepening materialism, which, as we shall see, assumed some dangerous forms.

This materialism was encouraged by the almost uninterrupted economic expansion of the period, as the indices of production, trade, and finance showed steady acceleration. In agriculture, the increase of yield was largely due to the use of artificial fertilizers, made possible by the chemical researches of Liebig, Chevreul, and Dumas, by the importation of Chilean nitrates and guano, which increased rapidly in the 1850s, and by the discovery of European deposits of phosphates. All of this made possible intensive cultivation, which increased grain production in Great Britain by 20 percent in ten years and in France by 10 percent in the same period and which, together with the beginning of the importation of American and Australian grains, freed Europe from the threat of famine which had been constantly present in the past. The growth of truck farming and cattle breeding was equally impressive, while the studies of fermentation made at the end of the 1850s by Louis Pasteur (1822–1895) facilitated the improvement and the profitable expansion of dairy farming, wine culture, and the brewing of beer.

More spectacular was the progress of industrial production, as can be seen from even the briefest consideration of progress in textiles and the heavy industries. The textile industry in these years was characterized by increasing mechanization; and the introduction of such devices as the sewing machine (first used successfully in the United States in the 1840s but widely adopted in Europe in the following decade) enabled the production of cotton goods to increase by 25 percent between 1850 and 1860. Simultaneously, the application of machinery to coal mining, in the form of improved drills, water and ventilation pumps, and hydraulic extraction devices, doubled French coal production and tripled that of Germany in the ten years after the revolution, and similar gains were registered in other industrial countries. This expansion in turn had an immediate effect upon metallurgy, which, by the end of the period, had become almost exclusively dependent upon coal and coke rather than on wood. The superiority of the new furnaces and the general introduction of the Bessemer process (1856), which removed carbon and other impurities by blowing air through the molten iron, and the Siemens-Martin open-hearth process (1865), which did this more effectively and made possible the use of scrap iron and low-grade ores, was reflected in the doubling of European iron and steel production in the twenty years after 1860.

These advances were facilitated by the changes that were taking place in this period in the field of transportation. Oceanic transport was revolutionized by the increased use of steel and steam, by the introduction of the screw propeller in the 1850s and the compound engine in the 1860s, and by the shortening of well-traveled routes by such notable achievements as the opening of the Suez Canal in 1869; and the new British, French, German, and American lines founded in the 1840s and 1850s carried a mounting volume of trade. The world freight total in 1840 was about 10 million tons; in 1870 it was 25 million tons. The progress of railway transportation was no less remarkable, the European network alone growing from about 14,000 miles of track in 1850 to about 32,000 miles in 1860 and 78,000 miles in 1870. As a

Charles Darwin (1809–1882). (Culver Pictures)

result of improvements in rolling stock, standardization of the gauge in all European countries except Russia and Spain, the growing adoption of the steel rail and the introduction of new signaling and braking devices, the safety, speed, and volume of railway travel grew throughout the period. The part this played in stimulating industrial and agricultural production is obvious.

Two other factors helped this ballooning production and exchange of goods: the expansion of the money economy resulting from the discovery of deposits in California and Australia, which doubled the stock of monetary gold during this twenty-year period, and the introduction of credit devices and new legislation that lent more flexibility to the fiscal system. No single innovation or reform was more important in this latter respect than the general adoption of the principle of limited liability. Employed first in the charters of railway companies, this principle made it safe for individuals to invest

without risking the loss of their total resources in case the company failed; and its extension to other forms of legitimate speculation enormously expanded corporate investment. This in turn encouraged the establishment of investment banks, like the French Crédit Mobilier (1852) and the Berliner Handelsgesellschaft (1856), which sold stock to private investors and used the proceeds to found new companies by the extension of long-term loans. Short-term credit was simultaneously expanded by the founding of new deposit and discount banks, which helped the movement of raw materials, the expansion of plant facilities, and the increase of variety and volume of production.

In face of all of this activity and the undeniable achievements of technical and economic progress, it is not surprising that the new generation should have been impressed and that its goals and its values should have been changed. Werner Sombart once wrote

Charles Dickens (1812–1870) as a young man of 27. (New York Public Library)

that after the disappointment of 1848, young Germans turned more readily to business than to politics when they chose their careers, for the adventure promised to be as exciting and the rewards more sure. Nor was German youth alone in this. In all countries young men read, and were stirred by, the international best-seller *Self Help* (1859), in which Samuel Smiles held before their eyes dozens of examples of men who had risen from rags to riches by making the most of their talents in the exciting and opportunity-laden world of business enterprise.[1] In an earlier period they might, like Stendhal's heroes, have dreamed of emulating Napoleon; now, like the protagonist of Gustav Freytag's novel *Debit and Credit* (1855), they were more likely to think of mercantile triumphs.

The Freytag book, with its detailed descriptions of commercial activity, il-lustrates the pronounced change that was taking place in literature and the arts in these years. If romanticism was not dead, it was no longer fashionable. The emphasis was now on the kind of realism that portrayed life not as it might or should be but as it was. In the novels of Gustave Flaubert, the fidelity to detail in description and characterization is impressive; and the characters who fail to recognize the facts of life, or who revolt against them, either undergo a painful conversion to reality, as did Frédéric Moreau in *The Sentimental Education* (1870), or are broken by it, like Emma in *Madame Bovary* (1856). The new realism char-acterized the works of Turgenev, George Eliot, and Émile Zola, whose first masterpieces, *Thérèse Raquin* and *Les Rougon-Macquart*, appeared in the closing years of our period; in the last novels of George Sand, it eclipsed

[1] So, apparently, did their sons. The protagonist in George Orwell's *Coming Up for Air* (1939) says: "Father had never read a book in his life, except the Bible and Smiles' *Self Help.*"

the buoyant idealism of her earlier works and was combined with social criticism and reforming zeal; and this was also true of Charles Dickens's last great novels: *Bleak House, Hard Times, Little Dorrit, Great Expectations,* and *Our Mutual Friend,* all written between 1852 and 1865. In the works of the Russian novelists Dostoevsky and Tolstoy, some of the older themes of romanticism persisted—the problem of the isolation of the individual from society, for instance, and the tendency to idealize the rebel—and, indeed, in the later works of both authors, the emphasis on the irrational was to be heightened; but few would question the mastery of realistic detail shown in *War and Peace* (1869) or deny that Dostoevsky, particularly in *Crime and Punishment* (1866), ranks with Dickens and Balzac in ability to give a truly naturalistic representation of the modern metropolis.

The transition from romanticism to realism was less pronounced in drama, poetry, and music, although it should be noted that the plays ground out by the enormously popular French dramatists Dumas and Augier proclaimed the optimism and materialism of the middle classes, who flocked to see them, and emphasized the values and the institutions that made for the kind of social stability desired by the bourgeoisie. Among the poets, Tennyson and Heine might take an occasional cut at the prevailing materialism, but they—and poets like Swinburne, Baudelaire, Verlaine, Mallarmé, Möricke, and Conrad Ferdinand Meyer—generally cultivated detachment from contemporary problems and remained true to an older lyrical tradition. Something of the sort was true also in music, where the brilliant harmonies of Berlioz and the tumultuous crescendos of Rossini continued to resound throughout the 1860s; where

essentially romantic themes appealed both to Gounod (*Faust,* 1859; *Romeo et Juliette,* 1867) and to Verdi (*Aida,* 1869); and where Wagner's poetic dramas (*Tristan und Isolde,* 1859; *Die Meistersinger von Nürnberg,* 1868; *Das Rheingold,* 1869; *Die Walküre,* 1870) shocked and entranced audiences. In the visual arts, however, the changed mode was made apparent by the almost brutal directness of Gustave Courbet (whose *Burial at Ornans,* 1850, first prompted the use of the word realism to describe a style of painting) and by its refinement and illumination in the works of the impressionist school, which had its beginnings in the 1860s with such paint-

"The Music of the Future." Cartoon of Wagner by Spy in *Vanity Fair,* 1877.

ings as Manet's *Dejeuner champêtre* (1863) and *Olympia* (1865), which scandalized the public of their time but are accepted today as among the finest achievements of modern art.

In three fields of human activity—religion, social relations, and international politics—the deepening materialism and increasing emphasis upon realism had pronounced, and generally unhappy, effects. These were years in which the established churches lost strength and prestige. This was due in part to the increasing drift of the working population toward the cities, where living and working conditions were hardly conducive to the retention or practice of faith; but it was attributable also to the fact that the literate classes of society were affected by the rationalism that marked the works of contemporary philosophers, historians, and popularizers of science. The scientific writers, in particular, showed a delight in making frontal assaults upon religious dogma, claiming that discoveries in astronomy, geology, physics, and biology invalidated theological explanations of human existence. The very intemperance of these attacks might have been self-defeating had it not been for the correspondingly passionate reaction of leading churchmen. All too often prominent divines elected to plunge into controversy for which they were inadequately prepared and to reveal publicly what appeared to be a stubborn resistance not only to change but even to common sense. There was no reason why the emendation and new interpretations proposed by the scientific biblical critics of the 1860s could not have been accepted in the spirit with which they have since been accepted. Instead, Protestant leaders often fought bitterly against any but the most literal interpretation of the sacred writ-

ings; and this attitude explains the astonishing vehemence of their resistance to Darwin's theory of evolution, which hurt rather than helped the cause they served.

Simultaneously, the hold of the Roman Church upon the intelligent sections of society was jeopardized by Pope Pius IX's systematic attack upon the major intellectual tendencies of the age in the encyclical *Quanta cura* of September 1864 and its accompanying *Syllabus,* in which such things as rationalism, indifferentism in religion, the idea that salvation was attainable outside the Roman faith, the principle of lay education, separation of church and state, political liberalism, and the idea of progress were castigated as errors to be shunned by the faithful. Liberal Catholic theologians like Bishops Döllinger and Ketteler in Germany were disturbed by the radical comprehensiveness of this condemnation, as they were six years later by the proclamation of the doctrine of papal infallibility, which claimed that, when speaking on matters of faith and doctrine, the pope's word was final. The resistance of these critics was, on the whole, ineffective, but their instinct was sound, for the papal policy seemed to many to be a vain attempt to resist the march of the intellect, and, because it did so, it alienated the European intelligentsia.

These controversies and internal storms absorbed most of the energies of the established churches and weakened their ability to play a reforming or mediatory role in the social life of the times. This was regrettable, since relations among classes were increasingly affected by materialistic and evolutionary theories that promised to subvert social peace. Classical economists like John Stuart Mill (1806–1873), venerators of science like Herbert

Spencer (1820–1903), and followers of Karl Marx were all materialists at heart, believing that the phenomena they studied were subject to natural laws (supply and demand, struggle for existence, the inevitable movement from capitalism to proletarian society) that were not amenable to human control. With these leaders to supply them with arguments, it was not difficult for the middle class that dominated Western society to disclaim social responsibility, for the mill owner to act toward his laborers with the callousness of Mr. Bounderby in Dickens's *Hard Times,* and for organizers of working class movements to think in terms of inevitable class struggle. Both the capitalist and the socialist theorists of this period assumed that man was motivated primarily by the acquisitive instinct, an idea that would in other times have been rejected as ignoble and as a denial of history; and this kind of thinking led to an acceptance of the legitimacy of the use of violence in the solution of social and economic problems that was to find frightening expression in the last years of the century.

The stratification of most European societies in this period was different in marked respects from the period preceding it. Whereas the nobility might still occupy the social positions of greatest prestige, some of their prerogatives had been swept away by the revolution of 1848. East of the Elbe, in Hungary and in Russia, they still combined the possession of great landed estates with judicial and other rights over the workers of those lands (although the emancipation of the serfs in Russia in 1861 sensibly diminished noble privileges); and in other countries as well aristocrats had a virtual monopoly of positions in certain branches of the army. In general, however, poli-

tics fell increasingly under the control of those who dominated the economic life of Europe, the wealthier middle class; and political philosophy and state policy came increasingly to mirror their views. A striking characteristic of this period was the growing distinction between the upper and lower middle class, first made dramatically clear in the collapse of the 1848 revolutions, and the expansion in size of the latter. The petty bourgeoisie, composed of lesser officials, small business men, and what we have come to call white collar workers, benefited from the democratic reforms in Great Britain in the 1860s; but in other countries it became a volatile and disorganized class, craving security and leadership, an important and potentially dangerous political force. At the base of the social pyramid were the agricultural and industrial workers, the former of whom were decreasing in number throughout this period (60 percent of the population of Europe in 1860, they were to comprise less than half twenty years later). To the swelling numbers of industrial workers, trade unionism and socialism promised protection against the wrongs they felt implicit in capitalism; and the working class movement made its first significant advances in this period.

The period that opened with hopes of international solidarity and harmony and that, indeed, through the mouths of apostles of free trade like Richard Cobden, preached that the extension of the *laissez-faire* principle in international economics could not help but promote universal peace, ended nevertheless in a series of violent conflicts. These were prepared by statesmen who brought into international politics the same values that impregnated so many other aspects of European society at this time: realism, willingness to consider morals as irrelevant, refusal to consider any criterion for judging action except expediency, insistence that politics was an unremitting struggle in which only the facts of power counted. In these years also nationalism lost the idealism of the ingenuous pre-March days and often degenerated into jingoism, while the relation between national aspiration and liberal ambition tended to change. The Mazzinian nationalists had fought for the unity and greatness of their country in order that it might be in the van of constitutional progress, human rights, and universal freedom; the liberal of the 1860s, especially in Italy and Germany, was not disinclined to jettison his constitutional and humanitarian ambitions so that his country might be able to demonstrate its greatness to others.

It is easy for us, looking back to the period 1850–1871, to see tendencies at work within the system that were to cause disaster and suffering later on. The gift of prescience was not given to contemporaries, and they did not believe that the realism of which they were so proud and the material progress that was so obvious could produce other than good. They can hardly be blamed for being impressed by the tremendous triumphs of their day: by engineering feats like the building of the Suez Canal and the piercing of the Alps by tunnel and the laying of the transatlantic cable; by the penetration of European trade into every port of the known world, and the establishment of European entrepôts in the Far East; and by the carrying of European ideas and institutions to the United States, Canada, Australia, New Zealand, and Latin America by the 200,000–300,000 emigrants who left Europe yearly in this period. European culture appeared to be attaining its finest flower, and there seemed every reason to believe that, by trade and emigration, the benefits of that culture would be shared to the universal advantage.

Chapter 6 THE BREAKDOWN
OF THE CONCERT AND
THE CRIMEAN WAR

The Revolutionary Period   One of the most remarkable aspects of the revolutions of 1848 was the fact that the disorders they caused precipitated no war between major powers. That no great state was led by ambition or fear to take action that invited retaliation by another was a tribute in the first place to the habits of cooperation and restraint that had grown up between the powers in the years since 1815. But the maintenance of international peace during these difficult times was due also to the careful diplomacy of the two powers not affected by revolution at home, Great Britain and Russia.

At the very beginning of the disorders in Vienna and Berlin, Tsar Nicholas had written to the British queen and urged that an intimate union between their countries would be advisable if general disaster was to be averted; and, although Lord Palmerston was not willing to admit the necessity of a formal tie between the two countries, he wrote: "Our feelings and sentiments towards Russia are exactly similar to those [they express] towards England. We are at present the only two Powers in Europe . . . that remain standing upright, and we ought to look with confidence to each other." The basis of this mutual confidence was the desire of the two countries to prevent local disorders from leading to anything that might upset the arrangements of 1815; and, while it cannot be said that they worked together intimately in averting such situations, at least they understood and trusted each other's intentions and exercised mutual forbearance as they took the action they considered necessary.

The British were primarily concerned, at the beginning of the revolutionary disturbances, with two possibilities: namely, that the French republicans might

153

be inspired by the traditions of 1792 to attempt to support the cause of revolution in Italy; and that the Prussian liberals, flushed with their initial victory in Berlin, might seek to liberate Poland, deliberately courting a war with Russia in order to arouse national sentiment and hasten the unification of Germany. In March 1848 the latter scheme was within the realm of practical politics, and Prussian envoys were actually seeking French support for a blow in behalf of the Poles. Nothing came of this, probably because of a stern dispatch from Lord Palmerston to the Prussian government, urging it "to abstain from any proceeding which could be considered by Russia as aggressive"—a warning that stiffened Frederick William IV's resistance to his ministers' designs and doubtless had a restraining effect in Paris also.

The danger of large-scale French intervention in Italy, either in 1848 or in 1849, was also averted in large part by Palmerston's diplomacy. In the first phase of the Italian disorders, when Radetzky lost Venetia and Lombardy, the British foreign secretary sought to remove the temptation to intervene by persuading the Austrians to acquiesce in the loss of those provinces. When the Austrians refused, and when the tide turned in their favor with their victories over the Piedmontese at Custoza in July 1848, and at Novara when the war was renewed in the spring of 1849, Palmerston restrained the French by the simple expedient of asking them to associate with him in urging the Austrians to show a decent leniency toward their rebellious subjects. Although the French came dangerously close to intervening by force of arms in support of Piedmont, they never quite did so; and major war was avoided in the Italian peninsula.[1]

In pursuing his policy, Palmerston was concerned solely with the requirements of the balance of power and had scant regard for the aspirations of Italian nationalists. This was true also of his attitude in Hungarian affairs, where, despite his private sympathies for the rebels, he took the line that he had "no knowledge of Hungary except as one of the component parts of the Austrian Empire." He rejected all the requests for aid that came to him from Kossuth's supporters; and when the Russians intervened to suppress the Hungarian revolution, he told the Russian ambassador that he approved of the step but hoped they would "finish as quickly as possible." With this encouragement, the tsar assumed the role of guardian of the balance of power in eastern and central Europe, a part he also played, as we have seen (see p. 141), by assuming a threatening position behind the scenes in the days when the Austro-Prussian conflict came to a head in 1850. One of the most important causes of Frederick William's collapse before Olmütz and his willingness to give up his cherished plan of Prussian union was a blunt warning from the tsar that he would consider changes in European treaties that were made without the approval of the co-signatories as acts of aggression.

The British played no part in that affair, although they doubtless approved of the Russian attitude. Certainly they copied it in their intervention in one final dispute during the revolutionary years. This was the situation created by the revolt of the duchies of Schleswig and Holstein against the Danish crown,

---

[1] The French did intervene in Rome in 1849 on behalf of the papacy and suppressed the republic. But this was the kind of intervention of which the Austrians would approve. See Chapters 7 and 8.

and the intervention of troops from Prussia and the German states in their behalf. With the tacit support of the Russians, Palmerston sought to have the status quo restored, lest the balance in the Baltic Sea be disturbed and friction created between Russia and Prussia; and, after two years of effort, he succeeded in arranging a settlement in that sense, which, in 1852, was approved by all the Great Powers sitting in concert.

If the revolutions of 1848 did not lead to international war, it was largely because the efforts of Britain and Russia and the acquiescence of the other powers maintained the diplomatic principles of the previous period.

After the Revolution   But those principles were not to remain unchallenged much longer, nor was the territorial settlement they protected. As has been indicated above, the revolutions had the effect of shaking the validity of all of the values of the past, and this was as true in the field of diplomacy as in any other.

For one thing, the revolutions marked the entrance into politics of a generation of European statesmen who were much less responsive to arguments in favor of restraint and compromise than their predecessors and who were more ruthless in their methods. If the new diplomatic style was created by Schwarzenberg, with his preference for solutions by force and his contemptuous disregard for the rules of private morality in the conduct of politics, he had many followers. The most gifted of them were Count Camillo di Cavour of Piedmont (1810–1861) and Otto von Bismarck of Prussia (1815–1898), who entered politics during the years of revolution and rose to prominence in the decade that followed. Their single-minded devotion to the interest of their countries and their willingness to use any means, including violent and cynical repudiation of the public law, in order to advance it came to be known as *Realpolitik*. Cavour once unconsciously defined this when he said; "If we did for ourselves what we do for Italy, we would be great rascals." The rise of these men was a clear threat to the existing treaty structure, for the simple reason that existing treaties blocked the attainment of their desire to increase the power and territory of their countries. This was true also of the man who made himself emperor of the French in 1852, Louis Napoleon, whose very name was a challenge to the territorial balance arranged in 1815.

In addition to this, the revolutions had left a legacy of distrust and suspicion between the powers that was to make it much harder for them to act in concert than it had been in the past. Tsar Nicholas of Russia could hardly be expected to put much confidence in a France that seemed to be repeating the pattern of the years 1789–1815; and Great Britain was also disturbed by the French transition from republic to empire. The Austrians resented the fact that they had had to rely upon Russian aid in the liquidation of their Hungarian troubles; and Schwarzenberg was reported to have said, "We shall astonish the world with our ingratitude." Prussian conservatives, for the most part, accepted the setback at Olmütz and favored cooperation with Austria (see p. 205), but this was made difficult by the imperious manner with which the Austrians treated them in the Diet of the Germanic Confederation in the years that followed. Before 1848, Austria and Prussia had tacitly agreed to submit no issue to the Diet to which either took exception; in amicable consultation, they always decided what should and should not be placed before the representatives of the lesser German states. After the Confederation was re-established in 1850, this cooperation disappeared. Increasingly, the Austrians sought to isolate the Prussians or overrule them by majority votes; increasingly, the Prussians resorted to sabotage and other blocking tactics in self-defense. This imposed a continued strain upon Austro-Prussian relations and convinced the Prussian delegate to the Diet, Otto von Bismarck, that war with Austria was, sooner or later, inevitable.

The new international atmosphere affected even the two powers who had managed to escape revolution in 1848 and whose long-distance collaboration had prevented the outbreak of major war between that date and 1850. It was the deterioration of relations between Great Britain and Russia that led to the Crimean War, the first conflict between major powers since 1815; and the war, in its turn, further increased tension among the powers and opened up new opportunities for the *Realpolitiker*.

THE CRIMEAN WAR

The Causes of the War   The Crimean War had its immediate origins in what will appear to modern readers to be a trifling dispute between Christians of different sects over their rights in the Holy Land. Its essential causes, however, were two in number: the tactics employed by Russia in the dispute, which were high-handed and adopted without a clear appreciation of the effect they would have in the West; and the inability of the British government, as the dispute reached a critical stage, to follow a consistent course or to withstand the pressure of an excited public opinion.

In 1852, under French pressure, the Turkish government gave privileges in certain sanctuaries in the Holy Land to Roman Catholic religious orders. The grant seemed to infringe rights previously recognized as belonging to Greek Orthodox orders, and the Russian government intervened in their behalf. In doing so, however, it demanded not only that the Turkish government revise its earlier decision with respect to the sanctuaries but that it give formal recognition to Russia's right to protect Greek Orthodox believers throughout the length and breadth of Turkish dominions. This demand seemed as potentially menacing as it was vague in its formulation; and the Turkish government refused to comply with it. Feeling that his personal prestige was at stake, the tsar, in June 1853, ordered Russian troops to cross the Pruth River into the Danubian principalities, with the intention of holding this Turkish territory as a pledge until the Turks gave in.

In taking this injudicious step, Tsar Nicholas seems to have been convinced that he was doing nothing more than protecting rights that had been properly his since the eighteenth century. He failed to see that his bullying intervention in the Holy Land dispute would be interpreted in the West as the first move in an attempt to destroy and dominate the Turkish empire. He made the mistake of believing that the men whom he had visited during his English tour in 1844 would understand that, however much he might favor the breakup of the Turkish empire, he would never seek to effect it unilaterally, but only in collaboration with the other powers. He unwisely believed that his friend Lord Aberdeen, now prime minister of England, would not only appreciate this but would be able to persuade the other members of the government that this was true.

But Lord Aberdeen was in no position to do this. As a consequence of the confusion introduced into British politics by the split of the Tory party over the Corn Law issue in 1846 (see pp. 111–113), the British cabinet in 1853 was a coalition ministry with no unified leadership. With respect to foreign affairs, two schools of thought were represented in it. One of them, led by Aberdeen and his foreign secretary Lord Clarendon, believed in secret diplomacy, collaboration with other powers, and the settlement of disputes as quickly and quietly as possible. The other was led by the former foreign secretary, now home secretary, Lord Palmerston, always an impulsive man and now increasingly given to irresponsibility, a believer in a forceful foreign policy, and always more inclined to bully than to parley. Aberdeen wanted to solve the Eastern dispute by having the European concert of powers arrange a settlement and impose it on the Turks, for whom he had no great regard. Palmerston apparently suspected Russian intentions and believed that the tsar would observe the integrity of the Turkish empire only when convinced by a forceful demonstration that he must. He wished, therefore, to solve the dispute by giving open and undeviating support to Constantinople.[2]

If either course had been followed consistently, war might have been avoided. As it was, a badly split cabinet vacillated between the two. In addition, Aberdeen and Clarendon were not happy with their ambassador at Constantinople, Stratford Canning (Lord Stratford de Redcliffe). Stratford had served a total of twenty-five years in Turkey; he was admired by the Turks and liked them in return; in contrast, he distrusted the Russians and had a personal animus against Nicholas I, who had refused to accept him as ambassador to St. Petersburg in 1831. Clarendon and the prime minister suspected that he was not acting in the sense of the instructions they sent to him, and the foreign secretary wrote to a friend:

> It is a misfortune and a complication that we cannot feel sure of Stratford acting with us for a peaceful solution. He pretends to do so . . . and appears to carry out his instructions; but it is impossible to believe, if he put his heart into it and set about work *as he knows how to do there,* that everything should fail as it does. . . . He is *bent on war,* and on playing the first part in settling the great Eastern Question. . . . He seems just as wild as the Turks themselves, and together they may and will defeat every combination coming from the west, however well devised it may be.

But Clarendon made no attempt to withdraw Stratford, perhaps because Aberdeen and he feared that the ambassador might form an alliance with Palmerston and stampede the country into war. The result of this temporizing was to obscure British intentions. The tsar was encouraged by the diplomatic behavior of Aber-

---

[2] The Soviet historian Tarlé has argued that Aberdeen's pacific attitude was fraudulent and that both he and Palmerston were seeking to maneuver the tsar into a ruinous war. The evidence he adduces to support this view is not impressive.

deen and Clarendon to believe that they sympathized with him; whereas the Turks were led, by Stratford's attitude and by British fleet movements in the vicinity of the Dardanelles, to assume that the British (and the French, who had dispatched a fleet to Salamis even before the Russians crossed the Pruth) were on their side.

Attempts were made by representatives of the Great Powers sitting at Vienna to find a formula that would guarantee the tsar's interests in the Turkish empire and his right to protect his co-religionists, while at the same time safeguarding the actual and potential integrity of the Turkish realm. The solutions that the diplomats devised always failed because of the inflexible opposition of the Turks or because of declarations in St. Petersburg that cast doubt on Russian good faith. Thus, affairs were allowed to drift until October 1853, when the Turks demanded the immediate withdrawal of Russian troops from the Danubian principalities and, receiving no reply, declared war upon the tsar. A month later they opened hostilities by sending a fleet of seven frigates, three corvettes, and two steam gunboats into the Black Sea to shell the Russian coast. Off Sinope, this force was intercepted by a Russian squadron of equal strength under Admiral Nakhimov. In four hours of fighting, the Russians sank all but one of the Turkish naval units, with a loss to the Turks of 4000 men.

The tsar seemed sobered, rather than exhilarated, by this victory over Turkey; for he now proposed that he try to draft the terms of settlement of the Russo-Turkish dispute, which could then be amended by the other powers. Once they had persuaded the Turkish government to agree to it, he would withdraw his army from the principalities, and the British and French would withdraw their fleets from the straits. This seems, in retrospect, to have been a not unreasonable proposal. Yet when, in February 1854, the tsar submitted his draft settlement to the representatives of the powers at Vienna, it was rejected without having been given careful consideration; and Great Britain and France immediately declared war on Russia.

The French, who had displayed little initiative since the first phase of the long dispute, apparently took this step because the British were bent on action, and they did not want to be left out. Alliance with England was always Louis Napoleon's dearest wish. It is more difficult to explain the British declaration of war. There were neither convincing strategic nor plausible economic reasons for it, and one is led to the conclusion that the government was swept into war by the pressure of public opinion.

Ever since 1848, the English public had been in an exalted frame of mind. The revolutions that had toppled so many thrones in Europe increased their pride in their own institutions and their contempt for the foreigner. Believing in the natural superiority of the British nation, they found it easy to feel that Britain had a moral duty to interfere in all European disputes. Combined with this superiority complex and this distorted sense of moral responsibility, there was a curious kind of romantic nationalism at work in England in 1853. This was perhaps a form of protest against the dull and pacific decorum of mid-century liberalism which did little to satisfy what seemed to be a new craving for excitement. Tennyson expressed this amalgam of confused feeling excellently when he wrote, as the war approached:

> it lighten'd my despair
> When I thought that a war would rise in defence
>   of the right,
> That an iron tyranny now should bend or cease,
> The glory of mankind stand on his ancient height,
> Nor Britain's one sole God be the millionaire:
> No more shall commerce be all in all, and Peace
> Pipe on her pastoral hillock a languid note ...
> For the peace, that I deem'd no peace, is over and
>   done
> And now by the side of the Black and Baltic deep,
> And deathful-grinning mouths of the fortress, flames
> The blood-red blossom of war with a heart of fire.

The quarrel in the Holy Land had meant little to the English people until Russian troops marched into the Danubian principalities; after that, the vast majority were pro-Turk and anti-Russian. The spontaneous affection for Turkey was remarkable. Richard Cobden, one of the few men in public life who had some knowledge of the Near East, tried to tell audiences some of the less palatable truths about the Turkish empire—about its inefficiency, the corruption of its government, and its imperviousness to reform. He was howled down by people who preferred to regard Turkey as a weak liberal nation being attacked by a strong autocratic one.

These feelings were encouraged by the newspaper press, which was predominantly anti-Russian and which vilified all attempts at moderation and sane diplomacy. The more sensational papers portrayed Palmerston as fighting a lone fight against colleagues who wanted to cede Constantinople to the tsar, while even ordinarily respectable journals wrote of "the senile hesitations" of Aberdeen and Clarendon. After the Turks declared war on Russia, pro-Turkish sentiment was transformed into pro-war sentiment; and, when the Russians won their victory at Sinope, this perfectly legitimate act of war was labeled "the massacre of Sinope." By this time public opinion was so rabid that people could seriously believe that the prince consort was working in the Russian interest and could applaud newspaper statements like the one that said: "Better that a few drops of guilty blood be shed on a scaffold on Tower Hill than that the country should be balked of its desire for war."

The Crimean War came as a result of Turkish intransigence and inept diplomacy and incautious military moves on the part of Russia and the Western Powers. It would appear also, however, that there is much justification for the diary notation made by Thomas Carlyle after the outbreak of war: "It is the idle population of editors etc. that have done all this in England. One perceives clearly that the Ministers go forward in it against their will. . . . Poor Souls! What could the Ministry *do* after all?"

The Conduct of the War   The two things that are most frequently remembered about the Crimean War are, first, that a heroic British nurse named Florence Nightingale organized field hospitals for cholera-stricken British troops and, second (and this because of Lord Tennyson's poem), that a brigade of British light cavalry was sent, because of a badly drafted and wrongly interpreted order, against impregnable Russian gun positions and was almost completely destroyed. It is understandable that popular recollection goes no further. Disease bulked larger in the war than military action, which was on the whole undistinguished; no belligerent emerged from the conflict with laurels; and the military reputation of the Russians and the British in particular was seriously diminished.

It is significant of the failure of the Western allies to make careful plans for war before precipitating it that, although Britain and France declared war on Russia in March 1854, their troops made no contact with the enemy until late September. The intervening six months was filled with negotiations designed to persuade Austria to join their alliance. The presence of Russian troops in the principalities, where they threatened Austrian economic interests on the Danube, gave a plausible pretext for Austrian intervention in the eyes of some civilian statesmen in Vienna; but the soldiers firmly opposed the idea, fearing that it would bring the whole weight of the war against the Austrian borders. In any case, the Russians, in August, withdrew the pretext by evacuating the principalities, and the Austrians decided, for the time being, to remain neutral.

The Prussians chose neutrality for reasons much like the Austrian; and the Swedes refused to be tempted into coming into the war by promises of the acquisition of Finland. The allies were finding it difficult to come to grips with their foe and were embarrassed at having to cheat their public of the promised victories. They decided, therefore, to strike at the most important Russian naval base on the Black Sea, the port of Sebastopol; and in mid-September they landed 50,000 troops on the Crimean peninsula. Except for some confused and unrewarding naval maneuvers far to the north in the Aaland islands, the military action of the war was confined to the Crimea.

Direct and determined action immediately after the landing would probably have enabled the allies to take Sebastopol at once, for they broke the initial Russian resistance at the battle of the Alma River and should have learned from their success that they were confronted with an army that had steadily deteriorated during the reign of Nicholas I and possessed neither sound tactical doctrine, efficient leadership, nor adequate infantry firepower. But they preferred to rely on elaborate maneuvers, and this gave their opponent time to fortify the base and forced the Western armies into siege warfare that lasted until June 1855. The Russians, on their side, tried to mount a counteroffensive that would clear the peninsula, but they failed at Balaklava (where the unfortunate charge of the Light Brigade took place) in October 1854 and again at Inkerman in November. After that, the conflict degenerated into a weary war of attrition broken by sporadic raids, while the troops suffered fearfully from cold, dysentery, and cholera.

In the accounts written of the war by *The Times's* correspondent W. H. Russell, one can sense the gradual dissipation of the romantic aura that surrounded its opening campaigns and the dawning of a sense of the pointless brutality of the last battles. During the allied advance toward the Russian positions overlooking the Alma River, Russell was impressed by the gallantry and color of the battle array; he wrote gaily:

The troops steadily advanced in grand lines like the waves of the ocean, with our left frittered away as it were into a foam of skirmishers under Colonel Lawrence and Major Norcott, of the Rifle Brigade, 2nd battalion, covered by squadrons of the 11th and 8th Hussars, and portions of the 4th, 13th Light Dragoons, and 17th Lancers. This was a sight of inexpressible grandeur, and for the first time one was struck with the splendid appearance of our Infantry in line. Red is the colour, after all, and the white slashings of the breast of the coat and the cross belts, though rendering a man conspicuous enough, give him an appearance of size which other uniforms do not produce. The dark French columns on our right looked very small compared to our battalions, though we knew they were quite as strong; but the marching of our allies, laden as they were with all their packs, &, was wonderful—the pace at which they went was really "killing." It was observable, too, that our staff was more conspicuous and more numerous than the staff of our brave friends. Nothing strikes the eye like a cocked hat and a bunch of white cock's feathers. . . .

Russell's account of the dogged seesaw fighting at Inkerman, on the other hand, was in a different vein, emphasizing the fortuitousness and the planlessness of the struggle.

Who was in command whilst the battle—a continuous series of detached combats and isolated engagements—was consuming the weary, dismal, anxious hours? No one in particular, I think! No one could judge of the progress of the fight, least of all those who were in the midst of it, and perhaps it was as well that "giving orders" was not much indulged in. Every one was fighting for his own hand where he stood. Wherever a grey cloud of Russians emerged in whirling columns from the mist, and became visible to any body of our infantry in valley, ravine, or hill, it was assailed by fire—fiercely resisted!—aye! charged with the bayonet! Every foot of ground was disputed by handfuls of men led by the officer of the moment, the accidental chief who became master of some vital spot, unknown perhaps to him in its relation to the safety of our whole position, but which was held with bulldog tenacity till death or numbers asserted their power. And so it was that mere subordinate personalities, inspiring the obdurate and resolute handfuls with their own power and resolution, without orders of general direction, carried out the great purposes of resistance, and as rocks meet the onset of the angry sea, broke the rush of the waves of Muscovites as they rolled on from the void.

As in later wars, the Russians seemed to have inexhaustible supplies of manpower, and it began to dawn upon the weary allies that even the capture of Sebastopol might not induce them to surrender. This consideration, and increasing criticism at home of the way in which they were conducting the war, convinced the Western governments that something must be done to impress the tsar and to induce him to yield. One possible way of doing this was by widening their coalition. In January 1855, they had made a start toward this by winning the alliance of Piedmont, whose chief minister Cavour hoped that intervention might safeguard his country's interests in Italy by winning the sympathy of Britain and France. But this meant an addition of only 17,000 troops to the allied war effort, and it did not and could not open another front against Russia. It was clear that only Austrian intervention would contribute significantly to Western strength.

In December 1854, under strong Western pressure, the Austrian government signed an engagement that seemed to assure such intervention. The basis of this was a statement of war aims called the Four Points of Vienna, which called for the renunciation by Russia of her preponderant influence in the principalities, a similar renunciation of her claim to protect Turkish subjects of Greek Orthodox faith, an international guarantee of free navigation at the mouth of the Danube, and a revision of the Straits Convention of 1841 "in the interests of the balance of power in Europe." If Russia did not agree to these points within two months, Austria agreed to enter the war, and the Western Powers agreed to guarantee her against any revolutionary troubles in Italy while the fighting continued.

The agreement of December 1854, which caused premature rejoicing in the West, remained a dead letter. In negotiating it, Britain and France had yielded to the Austrian argument that the Hapsburg empire could raise the necessary troops only if supported by the German Confederation; and this had been made

The siege of Sebastopol, 1854. This contemporary drawing shows the allied sea blockade of the Russian port and in the foreground, the allied positions for the bombardment of the base. From *Illustrated London News,* November 18, 1854.

a condition of the alliance. But the smaller German states had no stomach for dangerous adventures, and Bismarck, the Prussian envoy to the Confederation, had no desire to help the Austrians drag all Germany into a war from which the Hapsburgs would derive whatever benefits accrued from victory. Bismarck's arguments and their own fears persuaded the members of the Diet to turn down the Austrian request for support.

The Western governments were infuriated by this check, which meant further prolongation of the miserable campaign in the Crimea. They went on trying to win Austria's help; but it was not until Sebastopol had fallen in September 1855 and they had resorted to naked blackmail that they broke down her neutrality. Declarations to Cavour that they were now prepared to offer their "good offices" in Italian affairs, and threatening intimations to Vienna that continued neutrality might lead them to support a new Piedmontese drive, persuaded the Vienna cabinet, in December 1855, to send an ultimatum to St. Petersburg. This would probably merely have stiffened the resistance of Tsar Nicholas I, who bitterly resented Francis Joseph's failure to repay the service he had done him in 1849. But Nicholas had died in March (in that month, in London, Alexander Herzen, who had fled from the tsar's secret police, heard newsboys laughing and shouting: "Impernickle is dead!") and his successor Alexander II was ready for peace. On receipt of the Austrian ultimatum he declared his willingness to accept the Four Points; and the war was effectively over, having cost the lives of half a million men (a figure larger than that for any European war between 1815 and 1914), two thirds of whom died not of wounds but of disease.

THE AFTERMATH

The Peace of Paris   The settlement of the issues that had caused war was already forecast in the Four Points and was now made more precise in the peace negotiations that took place in Paris between February and April 1856. For the Russians, the price of defeat was not exorbitant, but it was certainly humiliating. The tsar was now formally deprived of the rights for which he had contested so stubbornly. The treaty placed the Danubian principalities of Moldavia and Wallachia outside the Russian sphere of influence; and it also denied Russian claims to a protectorate over the sultan's Greek Orthodox subjects by affirming the complete independence of the Ottoman empire. In addition, the tsar was forced to agree to leave the Aaland Islands, in the Gulf of Finland, unfortified, to return the fortress of Kars, which his armies had captured from Turkey in the last months of the war, to give up control of the mouths of the Danube by ceding the Bessarabian territory on both sides of the river to Turkey, and to acknowledge the authority of two international commissions which were appointed to deal with navigation rights on the important waterway.

At the same time, the Straits Convention of 1841 was revised. The sultan of Turkey undertook "to maintain the principle invariably established as the ancient rule of the Empire," prohibiting the entrance of war vessels into the Dardanelles and the Bosphorus, and the powers agreed to observe this rule. The Black Sea was neutralized; all arsenals and fortifications on its shores were forbidden; and freedom of trade was established in its waters. These provisions affected the

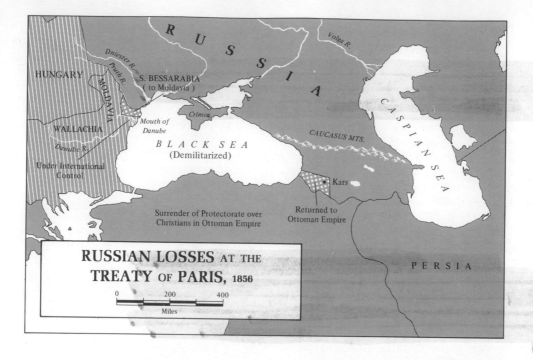

RUSSIAN LOSSES AT THE TREATY OF PARIS, 1856

0   200   400
Miles

Turks as much as the Russians, but they were clearly directed against the latter and designed to erect a barrier to Russian expansion to the south and west.

Probably the most important single action of the delegates to the Paris Conference was their regulation of the situation of the Danubian principalities. By abrogating the rights of interference that the tsar had possessed since the treaty of Adrianople in 1829 (see p. 27), they took the first step toward creating a new European state, that of Rumania. Although the principalities were left under Turkish sovereignty, they really became wards of the powers, who promised them an "independent and national administration" within the Turkish realm. Before the decade was over, that promise had been more than realized, and the principalities were united under a ruler of their own choice and had begun a career of political independence that was to last until 1941.

Another result of the conference's work was to be remembered by future generations, and especially by neutral nations in time of war. This was the so-called Declaration of Paris, by which the powers sought to codify the rules governing commerce during maritime wars. It laid down the principle that free ships make free goods and that noncontraband neutral property must be respected even on enemy ships. It forbade neutrals to issue letters of marque to privateers in wartime. It denied the validity of "paper blockades" by stating that the right to impose a blockade could be claimed only if it were established with adequate force to make it respected.

Finally, the conference brought Turkey into the Concert of Europe, and the signatory powers guaranteed the independence and territorial integrity of the Ottoman empire and promised to settle individual disputes with the Turkish government by consultation with each other. The treaty specifically mentioned a recent Turkish announcement of prospective concessions to the empire's Christian subjects and commended it. If this was an indication that the powers hoped, by exerting delicate pressure and encouragement, to lead the Turks into the paths of progressive internal reform, it failed in the result. Until the end of the century. Turkish reforms were largely on paper, and their insensitivity to the grievances of their subject peoples was the cause of much trouble for the powers.

The Future of the Concert   The conference in Paris seemed to be an impressive reaffirmation of the principle of collective responsibility and action by the Great Powers, and the delegates acted as if they fully believed that the European Concert would be effective in the years that followed. They showed this by the solemnity with which they declared that the Ottoman empire would henceforth "participate in the benefits of the public law of Europe and of the European Concert"; and they showed it also by the specific rights and responsibilities they claimed for "Europe." The peace treaty gave to the powers acting in concert a general right of intervention in international disputes and a number of specific mandates: to mediate when necessary between the Turkish empire and any other state, to protect the privileges of the Danubian principalities and to watch over the autonomous rights of Serbia, to guarantee the Ionian Isles, and to define and regulate the free navigation of the Danube River. Moreover, by permitting Cavour to bring the Italian question before the conference in its last sessions, to criticize conditions in Naples and the papal states, and to attack Austrian policy in the peninsula, the conferees seemed to imply that the future of Italy—and, indeed, all problems of similar international scope and importance—would have to be solved by the Concert of Europe and by it alone.

These apparent signs of a hopeful future for the principle of collective action in the interest of peace were misleading. The Italian question was not going to be solved by collaborative effort on the part of the powers; and the Concert was to prove generally ineffective in the next twenty years.

This was almost inevitable, for the war had strengthened the suspicions and resentments that the revolutions of 1848 had sown among the powers, while at the same time it gravely weakened their commitment to the existing territorial and legal organization of Europe. Napoleon III had been in favor of thoroughgoing revision of the Vienna settlement even before he went to war in the Crimea, and his desire to advance that end, and to win glory and perhaps territory for his country, had been heightened by his military success. Nor was he alone in preferring change to the sanctity of the written law. There were signs that the Prussians were discontented with their present condition. The Prussian government had been angered and frightened by what had appeared to be an Austrian attempt to drag them into the war; and the reluctance with which the other powers extended an invitation to them to participate in the peace conference made Prussian statesmen fear that the Great Power status of their country was endangered. That fear soon led to the reorganization and strengthening of the Prussian army and the inauguration of an aggressive and expansionist foreign policy. Finally, Russia was transformed by the war from the strongest supporter of the treaty structure to a bitterly revisionist power. It could no longer be counted on to come to the defense of the European balance when it was threatened. This was partly because the damage wrought by the war necessitated a temporary withdrawal from the sphere of foreign politics (as Prince Gorchakov, the new Russian foreign minister, said at this time: "*La Russie ne boude pas; la Russie se recueille*"), but more because of resentment over the territorial losses suffered at Paris and the policy of containment adopted by the other powers. The peace treaty, in Palmerston's words, represented "a long line of circumvallation to confine the future extension of Russia ... at any rate to her present circumference." The Russians were resolved to defy that containment, and the first step in that direction would be to regain their military rights on the Black Sea. It did not take long for Russian statesmen to realize that this objective might be advanced if trouble rather than order prevailed in other parts of Europe. This is what Gorchakov meant in May 1856 when he wrote to his ambassador in Paris: "I am looking for a man who will annul the clauses of the treaty of Paris.... I am looking for him and I shall find him."

Austria and Great Britain could, it is true, still be described as supporters of the existing balance, but was it likely that they could, or would, withstand adventures by ambitious powers? Although it had not become an active belligerent in the war, Austria had been weakened by heavy expenditures for weapons that were never used, and it had lost even more heavily in reputation. Prussia resented its wartime behavior for reasons already discussed; Russia, because it smacked of rank ingratitude; Britain and France, because it had consisted of military commitments and promises never fulfilled. Isolated by this general dislike, and threatened in Italy, Austria hardly promised to be an effective bulwark of peace and the existing order.

As for Great Britain, doubt was thrown on its ability to withstand attacks on the public law by the disappointing performance of its forces in the Crimea. Its army had gone into the war without a field commissariat, an effective system of supply, a corps of service troops, or an ambulance corps or medical service (after the battle of the Alma it was discovered that there were no splints or bandages on hand), without any experience in the combined use of cavalry, infantry, and artillery, and without any generals who knew the duties of their rank. The military talents of the supreme commander, Lord Raglan, were exiguous; those of his chief subordinates, Lords Lucan and Cardigan, nonexistent. A junior officer wrote of this pair: "Without mincing matters, two such fools could hardly be picked out of the British Army. And they take command. But they are Earls!" The effect of all this on Britain's military reputation was shattering. When the war was over, Alexis de Tocqueville wrote to an English friend:

> The heroic courage of your soldiers was everywhere and unreservedly praised, but I found also a general belief that the importance of England as a military power had been greatly exaggerated, that she is utterly devoid of military talent, which is shown as much in administration as in fighting, and that, even in the most pressing circumstances, she cannot raise a large army.

Apart from this, it became increasingly clear in the years after 1856 that the British people wanted to be involved in no new European troubles. The war had had a sobering effect in England and had bred a desire for peace and a reluctance to make any commitments that might jeopardize it. This was known on the Continent; and subsequently, whenever British statesmen and diplomats talked about the possibility of active intervention in European disputes, the other powers were less impressed than they might have been if the popular mood in England (and her military reputation) had been what they were before the fighting in the Crimea. Indeed, in 1864, Benjamin Disraeli was to say angrily in the House of Commons: "Within twelve months we have been twice repulsed at St. Petersburg. Twice we have supplicated in vain at Paris. We have menaced Austria, and Austria has allowed our menaces to pass her like the idle wind. We have threatened Prussia, and Prussia has defied us."

Because of the mutual distrust of the powers, the new ambitions of certain of their number, and the new weakness of others, the future of Europe was to be determined not by the Concert of Europe but by the actions of individual adventurers. Of these, the one who seemed most impressive and formidable in 1856 was Louis Napoleon, emperor of the French.

Chapter 7 FRANCE: THE SECOND EMPIRE

FROM REPUBLIC TO EMPIRE

In January 1853, in one of his many savage attacks upon Louis Napoleon, the poet Victor Hugo wrote:

> *O deuil! par un bandit féroce*
> *L'avenir est mort poignardé!*[1]

Hugo was thinking of the coup d'état by which the prince president had overcome the republic, stealing power by an act of violence that caused considerable loss of life. Yet even in the light of that event, it is hard to think of Louis Napoleon as a "ferocious bandit," just as it is difficult to agree with those more recent writers who have described him as the prototype of modern totalitarianism, the forerunner of the Mussolinis and Hitlers of the twentieth century. That he was a political adventurer, bent on securing power and willing to resort to force to attain it, is perfectly obvious; but he was no lover of violence and no believer in power for power's sake. On the contrary, at the height of his influence he showed himself capable of sacrificing his personal prerogatives in the interest of liberal political reform, and in both domestic and foreign policy his egotism was offset by genuinely humanitarian aspirations. It is the tragedy of his career that the deviousness that characterized his methods, and was perhaps derived from his conspiratorial past, often made even his most enlightened ideas suspect, while his desire to placate public opinion involved him in fatal contradictions in foreign affairs. But the debacle that ended his regime should not make us forget that he governed France well; and, far from killing

[1] O sorrow! By a ferocious bandit/The future has been stabbed to death!

168

her future, as Hugo thought he had done, he left her stronger, economically at least, than he found her.

The Prince President and the Assembly

The man who had been carried to political prominence by the revival of the Napoleonic legend in the 1840s (see p. 80) and elected, on the strength of his name, to the position of president of the French Republic in December 1848 (see p. 135) was not, at first sight, a commanding figure. Short in stature and already given to corpulence, he had a sallow complexion and a somewhat melancholy cast of features that led the governor-general of Paris, General Changarnier, to describe him, in an irreverent moment, as a "depressed parrot." When the Prussian soldier Moltke met him for the first time, he was struck by the immobility of his features and "the almost extinct look of his eyes," as well as his "friendly and good-natured smile which has nothing Napoleonic about it. He mostly sits quietly with his head on one side."

The appearance was misleading. Behind the pleasant, if enigmatic, mask, a keen political intelligence was making an estimate of the balance of political forces in France. Although his first action was to take an oath "to remain faithful to the democratic republic," and although he had declared that he would "regard as enemies of the country all those who endeavor to change by illegal means that which France has established," Louis Napoleon did not regard himself as committed to the republic. He seems, indeed, to have regarded the tremendous vote that elected him to the presidency as a sign of general dissatisfaction with the existing regime; and he might have acted immediately to overthrow it, as some of his intimates wished him to do, if he had not considered it wiser to wait until he was sure of the strength of his popular support.

In May 1849, elections were held for the Legislative Assembly, and the results showed a serious diminution of national support for the republic. Out of 750 deputies, only a third could be described as republicans: 75 followers of Lamartine and 180 democrats and socialists. Moreover, even this remnant seemed determined to destroy itself, and, only a month after the elections, came pretty close to doing so in an ill-considered gesture against the prince president.

This came as a result of certain events that were transpiring in Rome, where the pope had been forced to flee from the city during the revolutionary disturbances of 1848, and a Roman republic had been established under Giuseppe Mazzini. A French military expedition led by General Oudinot had been dispatched to Italy with the vague mission of effecting a reconciliation between the pope and his people; but at the end of April 1849 it had become involved in fighting around Rome, and Louis Napoleon ordered Oudinot to begin an all-out offensive against the rebels in the city (see pp. 191–192). In France, the republican leaders in the Assembly immediately accused the president of exceeding his authority and violating the constitution of 1848, which stipulated that France "should never turn her arms against the liberty of any nation." Their declaration that they would defend the constitution, if necessary, "by force of arms" touched off demonstrations and riots in Paris on June 13 and in Toulouse, Perpignan, Strasbourg, and Lyon in the days that followed. Except in Lyon, however, where barricades had to be reduced by artillery bombardment, these émeutes were at best halfhearted and were easily suppressed. Their real importance was that they made it easy for the French right to take positive action against republicanism.

Thus, the Assembly, whose majority was now strongly monarchist, ordered the arrest of thirty-three republican deputies, enacted legislation closing the political clubs that had been their centers of agitation and propaganda, and passed a new press law against "the spirit of revolt and disorder." Having dispersed the leaders of the opposition and silenced their newspapers, they pushed their advantage further; and, in the months that followed, they revised the franchise by introducing property and residence requirements, and thus deprived three million workingmen of the vote. Finally, striking out at republican influence in the schools, they passed the so-called Falloux Law, which largely subjected the educational system of the country to church control, while reserving supervisory rights to the state.

While the monarchists in the Assembly were thus destroying the republican movement and earning the hatred of the working classes and the intellectuals in the process, Louis Napoleon held himself aloof. He sensed that, sooner or later, conflict would arise between the Assembly and himself, and he concentrated his efforts upon strengthening his own position in preparation for that. His first step in this direction was to secure unchallenged control of the executive branch of the government. The members of his first cabinet of ministers were elder statesmen who seemed to regard their duty as consisting mainly of curbing his independence and preventing indiscretions on his part. In October 1849, Louis Napoleon abruptly dismissed them, informing the Assembly that he had decided that the ministers should be of his own choosing and should, in general, share his views. As for the policy of the new cabinet, he said blandly:

> The name of Napoleon is in itself a whole program. It means order, authority, religion, popular welfare at home, national dignity abroad. This policy, inaugurated by my election, I hope to make triumph with the support of the Assembly and that of the people.

The Assembly responded to this gesture of independence with irritation and with some petty reprisals in the form of limitations on the president's official expenditures. This did not worry him. He had embarked now on a campaign to appeal directly to the people of France; and, wherever bridges were to be opened or new railroad spurs dedicated or harvest festivals held, Louis Napoleon was almost certain to appear. In these continual junketings, he made himself known to millions of Frenchmen and developed a knack of saying precisely what they wanted to hear—telling businessmen about the necessity of civil peace and commercial prosperity, discussing agricultural problems with peasants, showing an interest in local problems, appealing to local patriotism. Before long, people were shouting "*Vive Napoléon!*" and "*Vive l'Empereur!*" at his meetings.

Meanwhile, he was also taking care to ingratiate himself with the army. His name commended him to the rank and file; his office gave him the right of appointment, enabling him to place his supporters in the upper echelons of the command; and he had long made a point of getting to know younger officers, especially those who had commanded troops in Algeria and were, in consequence, men of action rather than desk officers. Many of these *beaux sabreurs* distrusted politicians in principle and were, therefore, ideal allies against the Assembly.

On the other hand, there were senior officers who disapproved of, and sought to check, the increasingly frequent army demonstrations that took place when Louis Napoleon appeared at parades. One of these was Changarnier, the governor general of Paris, who was regarded by the members of the Assembly as their protector against the president's ambitions. But, in January 1851, Louis Napoleon—long wearied by Changarnier's vanity and his ill-concealed lack of respect for his own person—compelled his ministers to concur in the dismissal of the general, a stroke that deprived the Assembly of its hope of retaining the support of the Paris garrison in the case of a serious dispute with the prince president.

That was now not very far away. The road was prepared for it by a quarrel over Article 45 of the constitution, which forbade the re-election of the president after the expiration of his four-year term. Louis Napoleon had no desire to retire in 1852, and he could claim that the country did not want this either, since 79 out of 86 departments had petitioned for revision. When the Assembly refused to consider changing the constitution, the president resolved to destroy its power by force, and, to lay the basis for this, he began a systematic attack upon the Assembly's franchise law, insisting that France must return to universal suffrage. Meanwhile, with his half-brother, the Duke of Morny, a daring and steel-nerved gambler, whether in the Bourse or in the world of politics, and with men like Persigny, the companion of his Strasbourg and Boulogne expeditions, Maupas, the chief of police, and Saint-Arnaud, the most dashing of "the Africans," who had become minister of war in August 1851, Louis Napoleon drew up a precise plan of action.

The Coup d'État and After   During the night of December 1–2, 1851, Paris was silently occupied by troops;[2] and police agents quietly and efficiently arrested

---

[2] In his poem "Cette nuit-là," Hugo described the operation:

Paris dormait, hélas! et bientôt, sur les places,
Sur les quais, les soldats, dociles populaces,
Janissaires conduits par Raybell et Sauboul,
Payés comme à Byzance, ivres comme à Stamboul,
Ceux de Dulac, et ceux de Kort et d'Espinasse,
La cartouchière au flanc et dans l'oeil la menace,
Vinrent, le régiment après le régiment,
Et le long des maisons ils passaient lentement,
A pas sourds, comme on voit les tigres dans les jongles
Qui rampent sur le ventre en allongeant leurs ongles;
Et la nuit était morne, et Paris sommeillait
Comme un aigle endormi pris sous un noir filet.
Les chefs attendaient l'aube en fumant leurs cigares.

[Paris, alas!, was sleeping; and soon, across the squares / and along the quays, came the soldiers, an obedient breed— / the janissaries of Raybell and Sauboul, / mercenaries like those of Byzantium, drunk like those of Istanbul— / the troops of Dulac and Kort and d'Espinasse, / with their cartridge cases on their hips and their menacing eyes. / Regiment after regiment they came, / passing quietly beside the houses, / with silent tread like the tigers one sees in the jungle, / creeping on their bellies and extending their claws. / And the night was gloomy, and Paris slumbered, / like a sleeping eagle caught in a black snare. / Their commanders waited for the dawn, smoking their cigars.]

seventy-eight persons, including most of the leaders of the Assembly and such opposition-minded notables as Cavaignac and Thiers. In the gray hours before dawn, placards were plastered on walls and kiosks announcing, in the name of the president, that the Assembly had been dissolved and that the franchise law was abrogated and universal suffrage restored. The people of France, it was stated, would be asked to vote on a new constitution, which would give the country a bicameral legislature, a council of state to frame necessary legislation, and a chief who would rule for ten years. In proposing this return to the pattern of his uncle's Consulate, Louis Napoleon nevertheless claimed to be the savior of the republic and called upon the army to respect "the first law of the land—the sovereignty of the people."

Morny, who had planned the details of the coup, had said that "intelligent arrests may prevent civil war." They almost did. Deprived of their leaders, the deputies of the Assembly lacked plan and determination. A group of them assembled at the *mairie* of the Tenth *arrondissement* at noon on December 2, but they were arrested by troops before they could decide on a course of action (and then released singly). Meanwhile, the president installed Morny, Saint-Arnaud, Persigny, and others as ministers, with apparent confidence that there would be no further resistance.

He was wrong. On December 3, deputies of the left republican faction succeeded in organizing disorders in the working class district in the Faubourg Saint-Antoine, and, when local troop detachments failed to put these down, the troubles spread. With icy self-control, Morny proclaimed a state of siege but ordered General Magnan, commander of the troops in Paris, to withhold action until the rebellion had come to a head. This was done; and there was no interference as the insurrectionists erected their barricades and concentrated their operations. It was not until the afternoon of the 4th that Magnan made a three-pronged attack upon the center of these activities. A column under General Canrobert was blocked by a small barricade across the Boulevard de Montmartre near the Saint-Denis Gate and, under the insults of the mob, gave way to panic or rage and opened indiscriminate fire with small arms and guns upon the fleeing citizens and the shops and cafés in the vicinity. Some two hundred people lost their lives in this senseless melee; and Louis Napoleon, who had wanted to take power without the shedding of blood, was never to be wholly forgiven for the massacre of December 4. Years later his wife Eugénie was to say to a friend: "A coup d'état is like a convict's ball and chain. You drag it along and eventually it paralyzes your leg."

The shooting, nevertheless, assured the success of the coup. Terrified by the brutal efficiency of the army, Paris was not to rise again until 1871, and then in quite different circumstances. Apart from this, the troop action in Paris strengthened Louis Napoleon's support outside the capital, for the provinces regarded the insurrectionists as foes of order and property who ought to be put down ruthlessly. On December 21, 1851, the country was asked to vote yes or no on the motion: "The French people desire the maintenance of the authority of Louis Napoleon Bonaparte and delegate to him the powers necessary for the establishment of the constitution on the foundation proposed by the proclamation." In Paris, out of 300,000 registered voters, only 133,000 voted for the motion, 80,000 voting no and the same number abstaining. But in the country at large, the president's majority was overwhelming—7,500,000 voting yes to 640,000 voting no.

In the months that followed, the new constitution was proclaimed and elaborated. The president's tenure of power was now extended to ten years, and he was given very extensive powers: to declare war and command the armies of France, to make treaties, to appoint ministers and ambassadors, to initiate all legislation and frame all laws, and, in the execution of all this, to be responsible "to the French people." In the machinery of government he was the motive force, for, although France was to have a bicameral legislature, composed of a Senate of life members appointed by the president and a Legislative Body (*Corps Législatif*) of 250 members elected for terms of six years by universal manhood suffrage, its operation always depended on impulse from above. The president proposed the laws, and they were then drawn up by a Council of State appointed by him, and sent on to a commission of the *Corps Législatif*, where they were explained and defended, if necessary, by members of the council. Any amendments proposed had to be approved by the Council of State before the law was presented to the *Corps Législatif* as a whole. That body, whose presiding officers were appointed by the government, had virtually no powers of debate and was expected to pass what was submitted to it. As for the Senate, it merely examined what the Legislative Body approved, to see that it was not unconstitutional or prejudicial to religion or morality, although it might occasionally promulgate *senatus consulta* or constitutional rulings, which had to be approved by the president.

An important feature of the new system was the use of the plebiscite. Since the people were sovereign, the president reserved the right to appeal directly to them over the heads of their representatives. This was a practice that he intended to use only sparingly, for, as he said on one occasion, "I don't mind being baptised with the water of universal suffrage, but I refuse to live with my feet in it." Nevertheless, the plebiscite was conceived of, and used, as a means of supporting the president's authority.

His power was maintained also by the administrative system imposed upon the country as a whole. The government extended its appointive powers into the smallest communes of the nation, making the mayors appointive servants of the national government. At the same time, in the departments, measures were taken to root out oppositional officials and, especially, to see to it that the prefects performed their duties with undeviating obedience to the policies the government laid down for them.

This was the system of government by which France was to be governed until 1860. The only significant change in it before then was one that had been forecast by the vote of December 1851. Increasingly after that time—sometimes spontaneously, sometimes by careful arrangement —crowds greeted the president with cries of "*Vive Napoléon III!*"; and, although Louis Napoleon hesitated for almost a year, he finally took the plunge in November 1852. In that month, the French people were asked whether they desired "the restoration of the imperial dignity" and answered affirmatively by 7,800,000 votes to 250,000. On December 2, 1852, Louis Napoleon was proclaimed emperor of the French.

THE DOMESTIC POLITICS OF THE SECOND EMPIRE

In a famous speech at Bordeaux on September 2, 1852, Louis Napoleon had said:

> We have immense territories to cultivate, roads to open, canals to dig, rivers to render navigable, railways to complete.... That is how I interpret the Empire, if the Empire is to be restored. Such are the conquests I contemplate; and you, all of you who surround me, you who wish our country's good, you are my soldiers.

This was not mere platform rhetoric. Ever since his imprisonment in the fortress at Ham, where he had passed the time by writing pamphlets on such themes as the extinction of poverty, the cultivation of the sugar beet, and the benefits to be derived from a trans-Isthmian canal in Central America, Napoleon's mind had teemed with schemes for the material betterment of his country. Those who have called him a Saint-Simon on horseback have been close to the mark, for, like the Saint-Simonians (see p. 79), he believed that society ought to organize all its resources scientifically for the benefit of all its members. Once he had consolidated his power, he turned his mind from politics to his plans for society; and France's economy was soon showing the beneficial effects of his enthusiasm.

Economic Policies   Napoleon wanted to make France a prosperous country by encouraging industry, building railroads, expanding commerce, supporting agriculture, and inaugurating an expansive program of public works to reduce unemployment. The key to this comprehensive program lay in the expansion of credit; and from the beginning the emperor did everything possible to stimulate new investment.

Up to this time, the credit resources of the country had been controlled by a few great bankers who profited from their monopoly. One of the emperor's greatest personal contributions to the economic boom that was to begin during his regime was his use of public bond issues for the sake of raising funds that could be used for business expansion. Always oversubscribed, these bond issues helped the state to intervene in every sector of the economy, priming the pump in such a way as to encourage private investment. The combined use of public patronage and private investment under the guarantee of the state had particularly striking results in railroad construction. In 1848, there were only about 2000 miles of track in all France; in 1864, the historian Taine noted that 2000 miles of rail had been laid in the previous year alone; in 1870, France had 11,000 miles of railroad open to traffic, in a well-articulated network with Paris as its hub and with connections with the rail systems of Italy, Germany, and the Low Countries.

The government further promoted economic expansion by authorizing the establishment of a number of semipublic banking corporations, the most important of which were the Crédit Mobilier and the Crédit Foncier. The first of these was designed to promote industrial joint-stock enterprises and to open up new fields of business. Founded in 1852, it was particularly successful in financing railroad and harbor construction, public utilities, and shipping companies; and, although it failed in 1867, it did a great deal to demonstrate the advantages that accrued from the close association of industry and banking. The Crédit Foncier, also founded in 1852, was a national mortgage bank, advancing funds to peasants and town dwellers on the security of their property. It has survived to our own time, as have other organizations like it which were established later in the Second Empire to encourage industry and commerce.

The emperor was an enthusiastic advocate of free trade and lost no time in attacking the protective tariffs left over from the July Monarchy. There is no doubt that he was motivated in part by political considerations, hoping to ingratiate his regime with the greatest free-trading nation of this time, Great Britain. But free trade also accorded with his vision of a Europe of free nationalities living in interdependence; and, apart from that, he hoped it would bring solid advantages to the French people: cheaper food for the poor, cheaper thread for the textile firms, cheaper rails for the railroads, and wider markets for French wines, silks, and articles de Paris. Even established industries would benefit, despite the loss of protection, if they adjusted their methods and products to the change. Between 1853 and 1855, therefore, Napoleon effected reductions in the duties on iron, steel, coal, and certain other raw materials and food stuffs; and in 1860, after much secret negotiation, he approved the so-called Cobden-Chevalier Treaty, which appreciably lowered duties on English goods entering France and opened the English market to French manufactures and wines and spirits. This Anglo-French treaty had, indeed, a wider importance, for it supplied a model that encouraged the general tendency of Europe toward a free-trade economy. From a strictly national point of view, there is no doubt that French commerce benefited from this treaty (as it did from the treaties concluded between 1860 and 1866 with Belgium, Turkey, the Zollverein, Italy, Sweden, the Low Countries, and Austria); and the industries that suffered were helped by subventions from the state.

The emperor was always more interested in industry than in agriculture, but he did not neglect a way of life that still claimed the energies of most Frenchmen. He encouraged scientific farming and selective breeding; he organized agricultural societies, fairs, and model farms; he personally authorized projects that reclaimed waste land, drained swamps, preserved forests, and otherwise aided rural districts. Public works of this kind served the double purpose of improving the land and supporting the rural and the urban unemployed; and the importance that Napoleon attributed to the social good performed by public works gave substance to his claim that he was not a Bonapartist ("Only Persigny is a Bonapartist," he said once, "and he's crazy!") but a socialist.

The most impressive of Napoleon's public works were those performed in the cities. Albert Guérard has written that Marseille "owes more to the eighteen years of Napoleon III than to the preceding twenty-five hundred," and something of the same sort might be said of Paris. The imagination and daring of Napoleon and his prefect of the Seine, Baron Haussmann, completely transformed the capital, destroying the narrow winding streets of the medieval city and constructing wide boulevards and broad places with radiating avenues, like the Place de l'Étoile and the Place de la République, rebuilding the central markets (accord-

The reconstruction of Paris by Napoleon III: The new opera house. Designed by a young architect named Charles Garnier, who was selected after a public competition, the house took more than a decade to build. Work began in 1861 and the south front was finished in time for the Universal Exposition of 1867. The other façades were not uncovered until 1869, and the interior was not completed until 1874. This contemporary drawing shows the house from the Rue Meyerbeer. Adolph Hitler, who at one time dreamed of becoming an architect, admired this building and knew its plans by heart, as he demonstrated when he visited it with Albert Speer in 1940, after the surrender of the French forces. From *L'Illustration,* October 7, 1871.

ing to a design inspired by Napoleon himself), constructing a new opera house, and giving the city a modern water supply, a new sewage system, and several new parks. The vigor with which the emperor pushed the reconstruction of Paris has often been ascribed to a desire to make barricade-building difficult and give imperial troops a clear field of fire in case of a repetition of December 4, 1851. Napoleon was always a man of mixed motives, and it would be idle to deny that strategical considerations played their part here. But certainly he was equally moved by the desire to provide for the increasing traffic of Paris, to improve the living conditions and recreational opportunities of the poor, and to make his capital a more beautiful city. All of these objectives he attained, while at the same time giving employment to thousands of skilled and unskilled laborers while the city was remade.

During the Second Empire, France had her moments of economic distress, especially in the 1850s, when the country suffered crop failures, a cholera epidemic, floods, and diseases of the silkworm and the vines, and during the American Civil War, when the interruption of shipments of raw cotton hurt the textile industry of Normandy and other departments. The losses occasioned by these events, however, were made good; and, when Napoleon fell from power, France was basically prosperous and healthy. This she owed to Napoleon III, who had the imagination to see how the financial resources of the state could be used to stimulate private enterprise and lead it in new directions, while at the same time ameliorating the lot of the poor.

Toward Political Liberalism   During the 1850s the French people were almost completely deprived of the kind of political discussion and controversy that was so much a part of their past. The constitution of 1852 gave parliament virtually no power of debate; and, in any case, the electoral procedure, which was manipulated by the prefects so as to give maximum advantage to government-approved candidates, and the almost complete disappearance of organized political parties made the formation of an opposition in the *Corps Législatif* difficult, if not impossible. Newspapers were kept under constant surveillance, and political criticism was answered with suspension or loss of license, a situation that led to the almost complete disappearance of the provincial political press and the survival only of the hardiest Parisian journals, most of which found it expedient to be noncommittal if they did not support the regime. Even the universities were quiet, perhaps because their boards of direction were closely supervised by the state.

It cannot be said that during this decade there were many apparent signs of discontent with this authoritarian and bureaucratic regime. Most Frenchmen seemed perfectly content to let the emperor rule France and to turn their attention to economic or other activities. In the parliamentary elections of June 1857, the first held since 1852, government candidates polled 5,500,000 votes, opposition candidates only 665,000; and these figures seemed to indicate the general satisfaction of the country. It was not until 1860 that this mood began to change and, when it did, the emperor seemed to be ready to change with it.

By a decree of November 24, 1860, Napoleon granted both to the *Corps Législatif* and the Senate the right to respond to the speech from the throne, which meant, in effect, the right to hold an annual debate on the state of the nation. It has often been said that this step was prompted by the desire to strengthen the popularity of his regime with the middle classes at a time when industrialists were criticizing the Cobden-Chevalier Treaty and the clerical vote was hostile to France's policy in Italy (see pp. 195–200); and this was probably true. But there is some indication that Napoleon, who had written in his youth of the strong hand that would dare bring liberty out of order, would have experimented with the relaxation of authority in any case.

As it turned out, the decree of November 1860 was the first step in a progressive liberalization of the regime. Publication of parliamentary discussion was authorized in 1860; and restrictions on press and public debate were slowly relaxed in the years that followed. The surveillance and intimidation that characterized elections in the early years were lightened, and the last elections of the empire were generally admitted to be free. Moreover, parliament's power was widened step by step. In November 1861, the *Corps Législatif* received broader rights over the imperial budget; in January 1862, it was announced that henceforth three ministers without portfolio would represent the government and defend its policies before the two legislative bodies. This first step toward ministerial responsibility was followed in 1863 by the decision to have the president of the Council of State, Rouher, sit regularly in the *Corps Législatif* and the Senate.

Napoleon's relaxation of controls was not confined solely to the political sphere. In 1865–1866, he instituted a comprehensive educational reform based upon recommendations by his minister of public instruction, Victor Duruy (1811–1894), historian, liberal, anticleric, and one of the most farsighted educational reformers in the nineteenth century. Duruy's vision of an educational system—providing a free compulsory primary education for the masses and a secondary school curriculum that recognized the increasing complexity of life in industrial society as well as the compromises necessary in mass education (for example, that many students need vocational training more than they do the elements of classical education)—was not perfectly realized. However, the first steps were taken toward these objectives and toward the expansion of educational facilities for girls, and at the same time clerical control over secondary education was reduced, which pleased people of liberal persuasion. In all of this, the emperor loyally supported his minister against attacks from the right. On another front also, Napoleon demonstrated his liberality of view. In May 1864, he allowed his long-held sympathy for the working classes to overcome his suspicion of combinations of workers by legalizing trade unions and the right to strike.

This whole line of imperial policy culminated in the years 1867–1869 when, in order to divert popular attention from setbacks abroad, freedom of the press and assembly was confirmed in law, parliament's power further widened, and Rouher and other unpopular ministers sacrificed to the now sizable opposition in the *Corps Législatif*. When, finally, in January 1870, Émile Ollivier, one of the famous Five, the leaders of the republican opposition since 1857, was asked to form a cabinet that would be (except for its military and naval members) independent of the emperor, the liberalization of the empire seemed to be complete and a new period of genuine parliamentary government about to dawn.

As has been indicated, the emperor's course along the liberal road had been accelerated by growing criticism of his policies, especially with respect to foreign affairs. This was reflected in election returns. If only 600,000 opposition votes were cast in the parliamentary elections of 1852 and only 665,000 in 1857, the parliamentary elections of 1863 saw the negative ballots mount to 2,000,000; in the elections of 1869, all the large cities voted against government candidates, and the regime triumphed only by a vote of 4,438,000 to 3,355,000. It should be remembered, however, that these were parliamentary elections in which the emperor was not himself a candidate. There is every reason to believe that he was always more popular than his candidates and that he remained so, with the great majority of Frenchmen, until his defeat in battle.

This would seem to be proved by the great plebiscite of May 1870 when the

French people were asked whether they wished to approve "the liberal reforms introduced by the Emperor since 1860." Every Frenchman knew that he was really being asked whether he wanted Napoleon III to remain on the throne, and he voted accordingly. When the votes were counted, the emperor had been endorsed by 7,336,000 citizens, with 1,572,000 against him. After twenty-one years of power, this was an impressive vote of confidence.

The Arts under the Empire Even in the most authoritarian period of the empire, it does not appear that arts and letters suffered seriously from government policy. France's most distinguished literary figure, Victor Hugo, was, it is true, in exile on the island of Jersey, whence he launched bitter verse attacks upon the man he called *Napoléon le petit*. The historian Michelet lost his professorship in 1851; Renan lost his in 1863 after his *Vie de Jésus* had earned the implacable hostility of the clergy; Flaubert was prosecuted in 1857 for publishing *Madame Bovary*; and there were other cases of injustice to individuals. But there was no systematic policy of repression and nothing faintly resembling persecution of literature (the court censured Flaubert, but noted the literary excellence of his work and acquitted him and his publishers, and the attendant publicity increased his sales). Sainte-Beuve could write sincerely in 1865: "I owe

The pleasures of life under the empire, for those of comfortable income, are admirably portrayed in the paintings of Eugène Boudin. Here is his "Beach At Villerville," 1864. (National Gallery of Art, Washington, D.C., Chester Dale Collection, 1962)

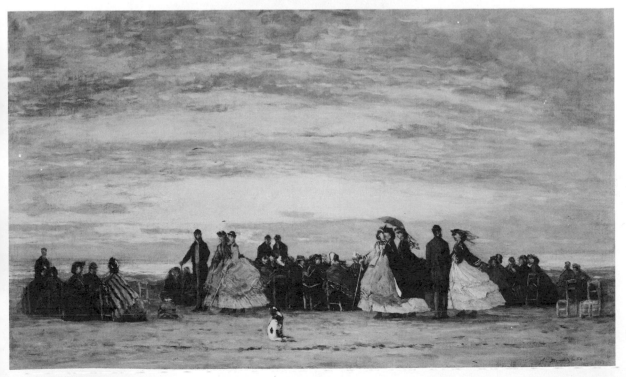

"The Dance," Façade of the Paris opera house, 1868–1869, Jean-Baptiste Carpeaux. (Giraudon)

it to the Emperor that I have been able to work for fifteen years in peace and security under a regime that allows everyone to exercise his talents and spend his leisure on whatever work he finds useful or congenial."

The artistic achievement of the period was impressive, although this cannot in any way be credited to imperial patronage, since the literary tastes of Napoleon and the Empress Eugénie were pedestrian (as is shown by their preferring Mérimée to Flaubert). The luster of this period rests rather on the fact that, during it, Flaubert and Baudelaire did their major work and Zola and Verlaine had their beginnings, while such secondary figures as the brothers Goncourt (*Germinie Lacerteux, Renée Máuperin*), Alphonse Daudet, Théophile Gautier, Leconte de Lisle, and Stéphane Mallarmé contributed to the variety and excitement of the literary scene.

The allied arts were scarcely less distinguished. The musical style of the empire was, without doubt, that of Offenbach. The greatest achievements of the French theater were his operettas, *Orpheus in the Underworld* (1858), *Fair Helen* (1865), and *The Grand Duchess of Gerolstein,* in which Hortense Schneider bewitched audiences during the exposition year 1867; and Augier's and Dumas's plays on moral conflict and family problems. The French ballet, which had been in decline since the 1840s, now had a brilliant revival, which began with the debut of the enchanting Emma Livry in 1858[3] and ended (for nothing new or remarkable occurred in the ballet until the advent of the Russians at the end of the century) with the production of Delibes's *Coppélia* in 1870. The pictorial arts saw both the realism of Courbet and Daumier and the beginnings of impressionism; Manet, Renoir, Degas, and Cézanne all began their careers under Napoleon; and the great sculptor Carpeaux demonstrated his talent in busts of all the great figures of the imperial court. As for architecture, it was almost an official art, patronized by the emperor and Baron Haussmann; and its achievements can still be judged by any visitor to Paris.

COLONIAL AND FOREIGN POLICY

French Activities beyond the Seas   During the years of the empire, France was remarkably active in many areas outside the Continent, and the *tricouleur* was planted in farflung places whose names must have mystified French peasants when they heard them for the first time. In these activities, as in so many others that took place in his reign, the emperor took a leading part.

He took a personal interest, for instance, in the affairs of Algeria, a French colony since the crushing of Abd-el-Kader in the 1840s (see pp. 72, 80); and it was largely under his inspiration that a remarkable program of public works, port and railroad construction, and sanitary engineering was carried through in that colony. He was less successful with his plans to make an equitable land settlement between the natives and the French settlers (*colons*), to bring all the tribes within the same legal system, and to extend the rights of French citizenship to them. His famous decree of 1865, which declared full equality of rights between the Arabs and the *colons,* remained largely a dead letter; and the administrative and social problems of Algeria remained alive to vex Napoleon's successors.

At the other end of the Mediterranean, Napoleon intervened, as we have seen, to protect the rights of Roman Christians in the Holy Places (see pp. 156ff.)—a dispute that helped bring on the Crimean War—and in 1860 he acted, for much the same reason, in Syria. With this Turkish province, France had historical and sentimental ties—Napoleon III's own mother had written a song, *"Partant pour la Syrie,"* which was a kind of unofficial anthem during the Second Empire—and the French church had a close association with the Maronite sect of Christians in Lebanon. In the spring of 1860, the warlike tribe of Druses attacked and massacred thousands of the Maronites and some Jesuits working among them. The French government immediately notified the other powers of its intention to intervene to restore order and, despite momentary opposition on the part of the British, received their approval and landed six thousand troops in Lebanon, where they remained for a year.

An infinitely more significant example of French initiative was provided in this same decade in Egypt. Since the 1830s, French engineers and traders had

---

[3] A pupil of the great Marie Taglioni. Emma Livry died in 1864 from burns suffered when her dress caught fire during a rehearsal of Auber's *The Dumb Girl of Portici* (see p. 89).

been interested in the possibility of constructing a canal across the isthmus of Suez between the Mediterranean and the Red Sea. In 1854, Ferdinand de Lesseps, a former vice-consul of France at Alexandria, persuaded the khedive of Egypt to grant him a concession to build one. Strictly speaking, the construction of the canal was a private undertaking; but, if it had not been for pressure by the French government at Constantinople, the sultan would probably have refused to approve the khedive's concession (as the British were seeking to make him do), and, if it had not been for French investors, who supplied the greater part of the capital needed, the canal could not have been built. When the first ship passed through this vital waterway in November 1869, it was wholly fitting, therefore, that the empress should have been her most honored passenger (and it is not uninteresting that among her companions were such lesser lights as Ibsen, Gautier, Zola, and the painter and art critic Fromentin).

In other parts of the world also French influence was felt. Settlements were established on the west coast of Africa, and, between 1854 and 1864, General Faidherbe created the port of Dakar and laid the basis for the flourishing colony of Senegal. In Somaliland, Obok became a French base in 1862; and in the same year the naval captain Dupré negotiated a treaty of friendship and commerce with the king of Madagascar. In the Far East, the French government cooperated with the British in 1858–1860 to wrest concessions for European traders from the Chinese government (see p. 223), and in 1864, French troops aided those of the Chinese government in putting down the Taiping Rebellion. In China proper French influence remained greatly inferior to that of Britain; but in Southeast Asia it grew rapidly. In 1859 Napoleon authorized a naval demonstration and landing at Saigon; the following year he sent the troops that had been cooperating with the British in the north into Cochin China. By the end of the decade all Indochina was under French control, the emperor was protector of Cambodia, and French traders were opening up the routes into South China.

To balance these not inconsiderable successes, there was one very considerable failure. In 1861, Napoleon decided to take advantage of the American Civil War to send a military expedition into Mexico to overthrow the revolutionary government of Benito Juarez (1806–1872) and establish a monarchy, in the person of the Archduke Maximilian of Austria. His motivation in transforming what had started as a joint Anglo-Franco-Spanish diplomatic campaign to force the Mexicans to respect foreign property rights into a unilateral imperialist adventure is somewhat obscure. He probably wished to persuade zealous Catholics to forgive his Italian policy by attacking a Mexican regime that was notorious for its anticlericalism; and he may have wished to win favor in Vienna by giving a throne to Maximilian. The part played by financiers with Mexican interests in shaping his decisions was probably less than it appeared to some contemporaries; but certainly economic considerations played a large part in this venture, for Napoleon had been interested in the economic potential of central America since the 1840s. Whatever his reasons, he set out to win Mexico, and suffered a spectacular defeat.

Considerable time passed before this became apparent. French troops took Puebla and Mexico City in the middle of 1863; an assembly of notables was convoked; and this body offered the crown to Maximilian, who accepted it with the sincere belief that it was his duty to do so and the hope that he could bring good government and prosperity to the Mexican people. For two years, Maximilian tried to rule the country. But he developed no popular backing (as early as July 1862 a French officer had written home, "The Emperor has been shamefully misled . . . we are supporting a cause that neither has, nor can have, any partisans"). The *Juaristas* remained in control of the northern and southern districts of the country; and it was clear that only the French garrison prevented them from overthrowing the new ruler. That bulwark was not to last, for, when the American Civil War came to an end, the United States government invoked the Monroe Doctrine and demanded the withdrawal of the French troops. Not wishing war with the United States, Napoleon complied; and the completion of the evacuation in 1867 was followed swiftly by the execution of Maximilian by a firing squad at Queretaro. Napoleon's most daring overseas adventure had been a fiasco which seriously impaired the emperor's personal prestige; at the same time, by tying up a large body of French troops in Mexico, it weakened France's position in Europe.

The Dilemmas of Continental Policy   The main reason for the failure of the July Monarchy, Napoleon III was convinced, was the ineffectiveness of its foreign policy. Louis Philippe had done nothing to restore France to her rightful position of continental leadership and, by maladroitness and lack of energy, had allowed her to be isolated and humiliated by the other powers. Napoleon was determined that the French people would not one day make the same reproaches of his own conduct of foreign affairs, and he set out deliberately to make France's voice heard in the councils of Europe.

As he did ·so, however, he was conscious of the suspicions aroused by his name and by his assumption of the imperial title and of the danger of diplomatic isolation. In his first years, therefore, he sought the friendship of Great Britain; and his desire for the British alliance was probably the chief reason for his violating his own promise that *"l'Empire c'est la paix"* by taking·France into the Crimean War.

The war achieved Napoleon's original foreign policy objectives. It demonstrated that France was a considerable military power (at least, in comparison with the British and Russian commands, the French showed something resembling military talent); it wiped out the memory of the setback in Egypt in 1840–1841; and, in the disorganized situation created by the war, it left France in an apparently dominant position. Certainly Paris now became the diplomatic capital of Europe; both the Russians and the British found French friendship valuable, and the emperor's advice was sought by lesser powers.

He could now look ahead toward the realization of greater ambitions. He had long believed that the most striking demonstration of France's recovery, and the most gratifying to French esteem, would be a thorough-going revision of the settlement that had been imposed on France at Vienna in 1815. In thinking of this, he does not seem to have envisaged any significant acquisitions of territory for France; it would be enough for Frenchmen to know that the new order came into being under her aegis. For the new Europe would be one based on "completed nationalities and satisfied general interests"; and the drawing of boundaries

The attempted assassination of the Emperor Napoleon III and Empress Eugénie by Felice Orsini, January 14, 1858. This artist's reconstruction shows the scene in front of the old opera house on Rue Le Peletier as the bombs exploded, killing or wounding several members of the imperial escort and injuring many in the crowd. From *L'Illustration,* January 23, 1858.

according to the principle of national self-determination would bring such harmony and prosperity to the continent that the country that inspired the transformation would be held in universal respect. This noble dream of international amity Napoleon had nurtured since his youth, when he had written that if "the nationalities [were granted] the institutions they demand, . . . then all nations [would] be brothers, and they [would] embrace one another in the presence of tyranny dethroned, of a world refreshed and consoled, and of a contented humanity." Like the most fervent Mazzinian or Saint-Simonian, he still believed in it and thought it might be realized. Indeed, in 1858 when the principalities of Moldavia and Wallachia, with Napoleon's encouragement, united under one ruler and under common institutions and thus laid the foundations of modern Rumania, it appeared that the process of transformation might be beginning.

But there were dilemmas to be faced. Was it reasonable to suppose that Russia's new friendship with France, which began in 1856, would withstand the strain of an attempt to apply the principle of national self-determination to Poland, or that Prussia and Austria, who also had Polish provinces, would tolerate any such proposal? Or—to bring things closer to home—was it reasonable to suppose that the French people themselves would favor a transformation of Europe that would create a united Italy and a united Germany of France's flanks? Even if they acquiesced in the destruction of the pope's temporal power, which would follow Italian unification, would they accept the shift in the balance of power caused by the creation of two new and vigorous rivals without demanding territorial compensation for France; and, if Napoleon yielded to such demands, would he not confirm the old suspicions of the British, destroy the tie with London, compromise his principles, and become involved in a maze of contradictions?

Questions like these might have made another man hesitate. But in foreign policy Napoleon was always less responsive to doubts than to appeals to his faith in his grand design; and he was given a reminder of this kind in 1858. On the evening of January 14, as the imperial carriage drew up before the old opera house, bringing Napoleon and Empress Eugénie to hear a performance of *William Tell*, there were three loud explosions; and the windows and gas lamps in the entrance way were shattered to bits, wounding 150 persons with flying glass and killing eight persons. The imperial carriage was virtually demolished, but Napoleon and his wife escaped serious harm and insisted upon entering the theater and showing themselves to the audience. Before the night was over, the police had rounded up the perpetrators of the attempted assassination. They were four Italian patriots who had been living in exile in London and had planned the *attentat* to call attention to the plight of their country. Their leader, Felice Orsini, who had spent his life fighting for Italian freedom and had made a dramatic escape some years before from the dreadful Austrian prison called the Spielberg, was condemned to death after a dramatic trial, in the course of which his counsel read a letter from him to the emperor. Orsini wrote,

> Upon your will hangs the fate of my country for good or ill. I adjure your Majesty to return to Italy the independence her children lost in 1849 through the fault of France. . . . As long as Italy is not independent, the peace of Europe and of Your Majesty will be but a will o' the wisp. Let not Your Majesty deny the last prayer of a patriot on the steps of the scaffold, but deliver my country, and the blessings of five-and-twenty millions of citizens will follow you down the ages.

This appeal could not but affect a man who had himself conspired against Austria in Italy and whose dream was of a Europe of free nationalities. Before the year was out, Napoleon's plans for Italy had taken shape and, with their execution in 1859, he became involved in the foreign complications that were in the end to bring his downfall.

Chapter 8 THE UNIFICATION OF ITALY

In 1858, when Orsini and his accomplices threw their homemade bombs at Napoleon's carriage, their own country was still what Metternich had once called it, "a geographical expression." Politically, there was no Italy, for the peninsula that bore that name was divided into a number of separate states: the Bourbon kingdom of Naples and Sicily in the south; the papal states, which straddled the Apennine range and extended from the Roman Campagna north through Umbria and the Romagna to the Adriatic coast; the Grand Duchy of Tuscany, with its capital of Florence, and its two small neighbors to the north, the duchies of Modena and Parma, all three under rulers who were members of the Hapsburg family; Lombardy and Venetia, provinces directly under Austrian administration and legally part of the Austrian Empire; and, in the northwest corner, bordering on France, the state of Piedmont, ruled by the house of Savoy, which also had title to the island of Sardinia. Between these separate states there were only the most tenuous connections. The condition of transportation was still so primitive that there was no real economic bond between north and south; and, in a country where a native of the Romagna could understand the language neither of a peasant of Sicily nor of townsmen of Milan or Turin, it was impossible to talk of even cultural unity.

The economic and cultural divisions of Italy were to continue and to present problems for a long time; indeed, they have not yet been entirely overcome. This was not true of the political divisions, most of which were swept aside by the dramatic events that filled the three years that followed Orsini's *attentat*.

THE NATIONAL MOVEMENT TO 1859

The Growth of National Feeling   Among the intelligentsia and the progressive middle class there was, after 1815, a growing interest in the prospects of national unification. This feeling was inspired and strengthened by a number of things. The fact that northern Italy had been under French control in the days of the great Napoleon was of particular significance, for memories of the efficiency of French administration and the liberalism of French legal codes made men dissatisfied with the feudal and reactionary practices that were restored in most Italian states in 1815 and made them believe that unification would sweep these away and bring an enlightened and efficient regime. At the same time, the mercantile classes became increasingly interested in unification because it promised to bring solid economic advantages: the removal of customs barriers between the Italian states; a wider Italian market; the construction of an Italian rail net; and improvement of port facilities so that Italy could play a major role in the expansion of the Mediterranean trade promised by the advent of steam. There were visionaries who thought of Italy as the future main route between England and India, once a canal had been built at Suez and there was a railroad from Turin or Milan to the heel of the Italian boot.

The interest in and desire for unity was inspired also by a growing hatred of Austria, whose armies, based on the four great fortresses of Verona, Mantua, Peschiera, and Legnano (the Quadrilateral), not only secured Austrian possession of Lombardy and Venetia but dominated the whole peninsula and supported reactionary regimes in all states. The presence of the Austrians was in itself enough to be a perpetual reminder to a historically minded people of the reduced state to which they had fallen; and this sense of humiliation rings through many of the odes of the greatest Italian poet of this period, Giacomo Leopardi (1798–1837).

> O patria mia, vedo le muri et gli archi
> E le colonne e i simulacri et l'erme
> Torri degli avi nostri,
> Ma la gloria non vedo.[1]

Moreover, the ruthlessness with which the Austrians suppressed liberal movements like the risings of 1820 and 1821 and the brutal persecution they visited upon everyone suspected of subversive activity made the term *tedeschi* one of opprobrium throughout Italy and led thousands of young Italians to regard the expulsion of Austria as a mission calling for the full expenditure of their talents. This feeling was fed by books like Silvio Pellico's *My Prisons* (*Le Mie Prigioni*, 1832), a meticulous description of the author's ten years in the Austrian prison of the Spielberg in Moravia, where political prisoners were kept in close confinement, chained to their benches or the walls of their cells when they were not working, and where they often died of fatigue, ill-treatment, scurvy, or plain

---

[1] *O my country, I see the walls and the arches / And the columns and the images and the solitary / Towers of our Roman forbears— / But I do not see the glory. To Italy.*

starvation. The tremendous popularity of Alessandro Manzoni's *The Betrothed* (*I Promessi Sposi*, 1827) was also partly due to anti-Austrian feeling, for this sentimental novel of life in the seventeenth century, when the Duchy of Milan was under Spanish rule, was filled with sketches of Spanish officialdom which could be interpreted as hidden attacks upon Austrian bureaucracy.[2]

Mazzini and Young Italy   For twenty years after the Congress of Vienna had confirmed Austrian domination in Italy, the most significant movement of resistance was the *Carboneria* or Society of Charcoal Burners. A secret revolutionary society devoted to the expulsion of Austria from Italy, it had been active in the revolutions in Naples and Piedmont in 1820 and 1821 (see p. 22) and in Modena and the Papal States in 1831. The failure of those risings demonstrated the weaknesses of the *Carboneria:* its loose regional organization tended to break down in times of crisis, while its failure to define its aims clearly meant that its membership was heterogeneous and incapable of uniting on tactics.

In 1831, a young Genoan, Giuseppe Mazzini (1805–1872), founded a new society that was intended to avoid the mistakes of the Charcoal Burners. It was called Young Italy; and it was designed as a national rather than a regional movement and one that, while necessarily secret with respect to its plans and tactics, was

[2] The popularity of this novel, and the fact that the author, in the second edition, corrected the style to conform to the Tuscan dialect, helped confirm the primacy of Tuscan as the language of literature and to this extent also contributed to the unity movement.

Giuseppe Mazzini, 1805–1872. (Bettmann Archive)

open with respect to its aims. Whereas the *Carbonari* had sought on occasion to win the sympathy and support of local rulers, Young Italy was opposed to cooperation with them. It was to be a people's movement, guided by a national directorate under Mazzini's leadership and dedicated to the establishment of a free, independent, and republican Italian nation.

An English contemporary once described Mazzini as having the greatest fascination of manner he had ever encountered; and this feeling was shared by the great majority of those Italians who came to know him. The attractiveness of his personality was the result of his striking physical beauty, his indomitable courage, his infectious enthusiasm, his complete optimism, and, not least important, the essential idealism of his thinking about Italy's future. If Mazzini worked for national unity, it was not because he thought in terms of potential material or military strength or because he wanted his country to have the prestige of other great powers. His patriotism had none of the narrowness that was to characterize the nationalism of Bismarck, or even of Cavour, to say nothing of that of the patrioteers of the 1870s and 1880s. It was rather a genuinely cosmopolitan philosophy. As Mazzini said in his essay on "The Duties of Man":

> In laboring according to true principles for our Country we are laboring for Humanity; our Country is the fulcrum of the lever which we have to wield for the common good.... Humanity is a great army moving to the conquest of unknown lands, against powerful and wary enemies. The peoples are the different corps and divisions of that army. Each has a post entrusted to it; each a special operation to perform; and the common victory depends on the exactness with which the different operations are carried out.... Your Country is the token of the mission which God has given you to fulfil in Humanity.... [It is] a fellowship of free and equal men bound together in a brotherly concord of labor towards a single end.

Italy must, in short, be united so that she could play an effective part in leading the world to a better future, which—as Mazzini made clear elsewhere—would be one of mutual interdependence of nations, universal peace, and republican freedom.

This noble dream, which Mazzini believed could be achieved by democratic revolution against all existing authorities, was bound to have only a limited appeal. The rural masses were generally unmoved by it, bound as they were for the most part by old institutions and ways of thought; the middle classes, even when sympathetic to the idea of unity, were too property-conscious to welcome the kind of revolution that threatened to overthrow the social as well as the political structure. The philosophy of Young Italy had its greatest effect upon the radical intelligentsia and upon inexperienced youth; and, as the years passed and Mazzini's faith in armed insurrection proved as barren of practical results as the tactics of the *Carbonari* before him, the movement lost strength even among these groups.

It would nevertheless be difficult to overestimate the importance of Mazzini's role in forging Italian unity. He was without doubt the most eloquent and effective prophet of the *Risorgimento;* and the generation that succeeded in uniting

Italy was one that had been inspired, in its youth, by the articles, manifestoes, and pamphlets that poured from his pen. Even after his influence had begun to wane, it was strong enough, as we shall see, to act as a goad to Cavour, whose policy in the 1850s might have developed more slowly had he not been afraid of losing the initiative to the leader of Young Italy; and the Mazzinian faith in liberation by popular insurrection had its greatest triumph in southern Italy in 1860. For the unification of Italy, therefore, Mazzini must be given much of the credit, despite the fact that, when he died in 1872, he died a disappointed man who regarded the new Italian nation as a betrayal of his principles of republicanism and humanitarian nationalism.

The Neo-Guelf Movement   A second school of unitarian thought was the Neo-Guelf movement, which took its name from that of the medieval papal party. The idea that the papacy was the best instrument for uniting the Italian states and modernizing political institutions had always had supporters in Italy; and the belief in organized religion as the regenerating force in Italian life had been one of the themes in Manzoni's famous novel. In 1843 it was given new strength by the publication of a 700-page volume by V. Gioberti (1801–1852), *The Civil and Moral Primacy of the Italians,* in which the author called for a federation of all Italian states under the papacy, with executive power being wielded by a college of princes.

This work was widely read and loudly praised, although there were skeptics who pointed out that for two problems Gioberti's treatise had no answer. It neither offered a program for freeing Italy from the Austrians nor explained how an Italy federated under the papacy would escape the corruption and reactionary methods that characterized the administration of the Papal States. But these embarrassing questions did not immediately slow the momentum of the Neo-Guelf movement, for in 1846 a new pope was elected whose talents seemed admirably suited to the task of national leadership.

Giovanni Mastai Ferretti (1792–1878), who became Pope Pius IX in 1846, began his long tenure of office with the reputation of being a liberal and seemed bent upon proving that it was genuine. In his first two years, he issued political amnesties, allowed exiles to come back to Rome in freedom, granted limited freedom of speech and the press, and—at the beginning of 1848—agreed to the establishment of a council of elected deputies to share in the government of Rome. There was nothing very radical about any of these measures. The most that can be said of them was that they were more progressive than anything that had been experienced in the Papal States since 1815. But they annoyed the Austrians, who actually occupied the town of Ferrara with troops in August 1847 in protest against the direction of papal policy.

This in itself was enough to encourage many people who were devoted to the cause of unity, but were too moderate to follow Mazzini, to put their faith in Pius IX.

The Roman Republic and Garibaldi   The Neo-Guelf movement was not, however, to retain this initial strength, for in 1848 Italy was caught up in the tide of revolution; and, before it had ebbed, faith in papal leadership of the unity movement had been weakened even more seriously than confidence in the efficacy of Mazzinian methods.

The revolution in Palermo in January 1848, the granting of constitutional charters in Sardinia and Tuscany in the same month, and the rising of Milan against Austrian rule caused tremendous excitement in Rome; and the Neo-Guelfs were confident that Pius IX would lend his support to the revolutionary cause. When the war in Lombardy began, papal troops were actually dispatched to the north, presumably to cooperate with the armies of Sardinia. But the enthusiasm engendered by this action disappeared completely on April 29, 1848, when the pope announced that he was opposed to an offensive war against Austria and would not permit his troops to fight against fellow Catholics. With that statement Pius IX lost the support of all liberals.

He also lost control of his capital city, for his action discredited the moderates in Rome and stimulated a radical republican movement which grew rapidly during the summer months. By autumn, disorders were so great that the papal bureaucracy was helpless to control them. The Austrian victory in Lombardy in August merely aggravated the pope's troubles, for many of the soldiers of the defeated armies flocked to Rome to take up the fight there. On November 15, the Pope's chief minister, Pellegrino Rossi, was stabbed to death by Lombard Volunteers as he was entering the Palazzo dell Cantelliera for the new session of the Council of Deputies; and on the following day the mob demonstrated before the Quirinal and fired upon the pope's Swiss Guards. After trying vainly to ride out the storm, Pius IX fled the city on November 24, disguised as a simple priest. This action handed Rome over to the republicans. A provisional government governed the city until a constituent assembly could be elected, and in February 1849, this latter body proclaimed Rome a republic and called Mazzini to the capital to head its first government.

The expulsion of the pope aroused the whole of the Catholic world; and the governments of Spain, Naples, and Austria indicated their intention of coming to his aid. As we have seen (see p. 169), they were anticipated by France. In Paris, the Constituent Assembly voted funds in March 1849 for a military expedition whose mission would be to effect a reconciliation between the pope and his rebellious subjects. A French army of eight to ten thousand troops commanded by General Oudinot was, therefore, landed at Città Vecchia in April. When its first advances toward Rome were repulsed by the rebels, however, Oudinot—acting on orders from the prince president, Louis Napoleon—abandoned his ill-defined mission of mediation and began operations that were designed to force the surrender of the republican government inside the city.

The defense of Rome was conducted by Giuseppe Garibaldi (1807–1882), whose life from this moment onward was inextricably entwined with the history of Italian unification. Born in Nice, Garibaldi spent his early years as a sailor, winning his master's certificate in 1832. In 1833 he met Mazzini and became a member of Young Italy, taking a solemn oath (to which he remained true) to fight against injustice, oppression, and tyranny and to make Italy a united nation. In 1834 he was expelled from the kingdom of Sardinia for revolutionary activity and, for the next thirteen years, lived as an exile and a soldier of fortune in Latin America, where he fought vainly against Brazil for the independence of the province of Rio Grande and, later, commanded the Uruguayan fleet and an Italian Legion in the service of Uruguay in war against Argentina. Thanks to this apprenticeship, he became a soldier of great talent, particularly skilled in the leadership of irregular forces and the conduct of guerrilla warfare. His political gifts were less noticeable, for he was an essentially simple man who thought in stereotypes and was irritated by those whose approach to the complications of Italian politics was more sophisticated. But his candor and forthrightness added to the impression made by the nobility of his bearing and the leonine cast of his features. Tennyson was not sneering when he wrote that Garibaldi had "the divine stupidity of a hero." His heroic qualities he certainly displayed in 1848, when he sped back to Italy at the first news of the revolution and led a legion of volunteers in the fight against Radetzky's troops in Lombardy. When the fortunes of war turned against Piedmont, he recruited another force, hoping to make his way to Venice to fight for the republic established by Manin in March (see p. 129): but the news of the murder of Rossi made him turn instead to Rome, where he placed his troops at Mazzini's disposal.

There was little likelihood that this motley group of adventurers, clad in red shirts and Calabrian hats and indifferently armed, and the other volunteers raised by Mazzini, could successfully withstand an assault upon Rome by a force of French professionals. Garibaldi would have preferred to remain in the mountains, conducting guerrilla operations and keeping the revolution alive. Mazzini, however, resolved on a defense of the capital, knowing that it would probably fail, in order, as he said, "to attract the eyes and reverence of my country towards [Rome] . . . to place her again at the summit, so that the Italians might again learn to regard her as the temple of their common country." His decision probably did have the long-term result of making the European powers realize that Rome would sooner or later have to belong to a united Italy; but, immediately, it doomed the city to a protracted siege in which prodigies of valor were performed by Garibaldi's legion but at the cost of great destruction and loss of life.

Garibaldi defended Rome against the pounding of Oudinot's army from the end of April to the end of June. When further resistance was hopeless, he was given permission to break out of the city and make his way north. He did so, hoping to arouse the countryside to new efforts; but the Italian people were unresponsive to his appeals, and his volunteers melted away. Hounded by Austrian detachments, he managed to reach San Marino, where he disbanded his army and with his wife Anita and a small number of followers, slipped through the Austrian lines to the Adriatic Sea. Here his wife, who had been his loyal comrade in arms since he had wooed her in Brazil in 1839, died of exhaustion; and, crushed by this final disaster, Garibaldi went once more into exile.

Piedmont and the Policy of Cavour   When the revolution was finally liquidated in Rome and the rest of Italy, it was clear that the Neo-Guelf movement was dead, while the failure of any truly popular unitary movement to materialize had seriously weakened confidence in Mazzinian tactics. In the circumstances, those who continued to work for Italian unity turned increasingly for leadership to the kingdom of Piedmont-Sardinia.

This was understandable. Of all the established regimes in Italy, the House of Savoy had been the only one to fight wholeheartedly for freedom from Austria. In March 1848, King Charles Albert had brought his army into the war in Lombardy, and, although his conduct of the campaign was ineffective and had led to his crushing defeat at Custoza and his withdrawal from the war in August, he had reopened hostilities in the spring of 1849. This time his defeat had been even more disastrous (Novara, March 23, 1849), and the unfortunate king abdicated in favor of his son and went into exile, where he shortly died. When he did so, however, he was regarded by many as a martyr to the cause of Italian unity, and these same people looked to his successor to complete his work.

The new ruler, Victor Emmanuel II, was indeed to become the first king of united Italy. This was not, to be sure, because of any conspicuous political talent of his own. A rude, almost primitive man, Victor Emmanuel preferred the joys of the chase and the ballet to the labors of politics. His greatest contribution to the cause of Italian unity was the popularity he won for himself and the dynasty by his bluff manners and his almost excessive virility. But it may be noted, in addition, that he possessed a native shrewdness that also served Italy well, for it prevented him from indulging his own political preferences and made him accept the advice of a minister whom he personally detested, Count Camillo di Cavour (1810–1861).

Cavour became a member of the Piedmontese cabinet in 1850, after years of experience as a soldier, farmer, industrialist, and banker. Starting as minister for agriculture, industry, and commerce, he soon took over the portfolio for naval affairs as well and, by the time of the Crimean War, dominated the council of ministers. A round-faced, rather rumpled man, he bore a vague resemblance to Mr. Pickwick, but was considerably less ingenuous than that gentleman. The

Count Camillo di Cavour, 1810–
1861 (Bettmann Archive)

basic ingredient of his political genius was a strong sense of practicality—the ability to recognize the prerequisites of political success and the will to set about acquiring them before committing himself to a dangerous course of action.

It is this pragmatic approach to politics that explains Cavour's views on the national question. He was a Piedmontese patriot, whose greatest ambition was to increase the material and political strength of his country. As for unification in a wider sense, he was willing to consider it as a possibility but not to regard it as an end to which everything else must be sacrificed. After 1848, Cavour had no illusions about Italy "making herself" by a spontaneous mass movement of the kind imagined by the Mazzinians, and he was convinced that further attempts at popular insurrection would only delay Italian unity. If Italy were ever to be one, this would come only after Piedmont had expelled the Austrians from northern Italy and absorbed Lombardy and Venetia; and Custoza and Novara had shown that even this first step could not be achieved by Italians alone. The aid of a foreign power would be essential.

And how was one to win such aid? Surely the first step must be to dispel the idea that the Italians were a volatile and irresponsible people, given to pointless political frenzies but incapable of considered action. What Italy needed was a period of domestic peace and progress that might help her accumulate political credit abroad; and Piedmont must set the example.

It was thoughts like these that determined Cavour's domestic policy in his own country in the 1850s. A convinced believer in the principles of English liberalism, he sought to make over Piedmont on the English model, and he came close to doing so. By a skillful amalgamation of the middle of the road political groups (the so-called *connubio* or "marriage"), he forged a cohesive liberal-conservative alliance that was capable of controlling the parliamentary situation and of keeping the extremists to the left and right powerless. It was this bloc that carried through the great program of domestic reform that made Piedmont easily the most progressive of the states of southern Europe—a program that included the stabilization of the currency, a reformation of the tax and tariff structure, the funding of the national debt, the improvement of the railway net and the establishment of a transatlantic steamship system, the encouragement of new private enterprise, and numerous other projects that aroused interest throughout Italy and Europe.

If the *connubio* and the domestic program helped win the approval of the powers, and particularly of Great Britain and France, Piedmont's intervention in the Crimean War won their friendship. As has been pointed out, Cavour's action in this respect was planned at a time when it seemed certain that Austria would be an active ally of the West against Russia and was conceived of as a defensive measure. But Austria's failure in the end to enter the war enhanced the value of Piedmont's contribution; and the British and French governments showed their gratitude by allowing Cavour to deliver a scathing indictment of Austria's Italian policy during the peace negotiations in Paris.

Cavour believed that this gesture was an indication that Britain and France would support his country in the event that it went to war again against Austria. This was not immediately true; and, in discussions in London and Paris after the Peace Conference, he was advised not to force the pace in Italy and warned that he would have to pay the penalty for any irresponsible action. In other circumstances, Cavour might have accepted that advice; he could not now. The sentiment for national unity had received new impetus from Piedmont's role in the war and at the Paris conference, and it would not be denied. As Cavour wrote later:

> If we had dropped the flag that we waved at Paris, Mazzinianism would have recovered and the moral influence of the revolutionary party would have reached complete ascendancy.

If that happened, all his work would be undone. Realizing this, Cavour saw that he had to push ahead with his anti-Austrian program, while simultaneously seeking foreign support for the inevitable conflict.

To maintain Piedmont's ascendancy in the national movement, Cavour followed a deliberately provocative, and well-advertised, program of anti-Austrian speeches in the Chamber, contrived diplomatic incidents, and various types of subversion. Simultaneously, he gave secret support to the National Society, an organization founded in 1856 by Daniele Manin, Giorgio Pallavicino, and the Sicilian La Farina for the purpose of uniting monarchists, federalists, and even republicans behind a movement to make Victor Emmanuel king of Italy. Cavour thought the ends of this society somewhat utopian, but he found it useful in spreading anti-Austrian propaganda and encouraging disaffection in Lombardy and Venetia.

For foreign support he turned back to Paris and, in the end, found Napoleon III—perhaps partly because of the shock caused by Orsini's bombs—willing to give him a sympathetic hearing.

THE FIRST STEPS TOWARD UNITY

The Plombières Agreement　　On July 20, 1858, Cavour and Napoleon met and talked for five hours at Plombières les Bains. The meeting had been preceded by an elaborate correspondence during which the emperor's readiness to do something for Italy had become clear; and the details were now worked out without great difficulty. The emperor agreed that, if Piedmont found herself at war with Austria, she would receive the support of the armies of France. In the event of victory, Piedmont would be allowed to annex Lombardy and Venetia, Parma and Modena, and part of the Papal States. Italy, as a whole, would be constituted as a federation under the presidency of the pope, which would include this new Piedmontese kingdom, as well as a Tuscan state enlarged by the acquisition of papal Umbria and the Marches, a greatly reduced Roman state, and an unchanged Naples. France would receive Nice and Savoy, and the bargain would be sealed by the marriage of Victor Emmanuel's fifteen-year-old daughter Clotilde to Napoleon's cousin Jerome, a man rich in years and bad habits.

In the history of international affairs in the nineteenth century, Plombières represented a new departure. It was less a concerting of defensive measures against an expected attack than a deliberate attempt to manufacture a war.

However one may judge the motives of the participants, their agreement was clearly aggressive in nature. In a letter to Victor Emmanuel, Cavour described the way in which Napoleon and he spent the latter part of their conference poring over a map in a search for a place where an incident might be created that would provoke the Austrians to action and how, in the end, they decided that troubles deliberately incited in the Duchy of Modena might serve that purpose.

Yet, if Plombières stands as a classic example of the new *Realpolitik,* it must nevertheless be noted that the subsequent course of events was far different from what Cavour imagined it would be. Indeed, Cavour would probably not have gotten the war he wanted at all if it had not been for the unparalleled ineptitude of the Austrians. In the first place, they supplied him with a much better opportunity for spreading anti-Austrian sentiment than he would have found in Modena. This they did at the end of 1858 by imposing military conscription upon Lombardy and Venetia, which proved to be so unpopular that hundreds of draft-evaders fled to Piedmont, and Austrian demands for their extradition and Piedmontese refusals to comply led to mutual recrimination and mounting tension, especially in the frontier areas. This gave Cavour an excuse for beginning military preparations, which he did by floating an issue of war bonds in February, securing legislation for the creation of a body of volunteers, and persuading the king in March to call up the army reserves.

Cavour's road to war might still have been blocked by the Great Powers if it had not been for a second Austrian blunder. In March and April 1859, it appeared likely that international pressure upon Napoleon III was going to force him to withdraw from the engagement he had taken at Plombières. On April 18, indeed, the French emperor actually asked Cavour to agree to the beginning of demobilization in order to prepare the way for an international conference on Italian and related problems. But, at the very moment when Cavour was yielding, with a heavy heart and a feeling that all his cleverness had been to no purpose, the Austrian government saved the day for him. The emperor's chief minister, Buol-Schauenstein, had persistently ignored the warnings of his more cautious colleagues, including some of the soldiers, to avoid precipitate action unless the French position were clarified or alliances with the German states secured. With what can only be described as levity, he now despatched an ultimatum to the Piedmontese government, offering it the choice between immediate disarmament and war. Victor Emmanuel's government could not give way in face of threats, and war followed between the Hapsburg monarchy and the partners of Plombières.

Even so, the pattern of subsequent events bore little resemblance to the expectations that Cavour and Napoleon had when they made their pact.

The War of 1859 and the Armistice of Villafranca   The war began in late April and was conducted with a lack of decisiveness on both sides. The Austrian army marched into Italy without an adequate supply system or accurate intelligence of enemy strength and capabilities or even reliable maps to guide its movements. Although it possessed able commanders, like Benedek, and competent strategists, like Hess, who had planned the campaigns of 1848 and 1849, it made no good use of them. Emperor Francis Joseph preferred to rely for military advice upon his adjutant general, Count Grünne, a courtier-soldier who had no combat experience; and Grünne's choice for supreme command in Italy was a general named Gyulai, whose only talent was the ability to appreciate his own deficiencies. Gyulai sought so strenuously to avoid being appointed that Grünne had to write to him: "What is the matter with you? What an old ass like Radetzky could manage at the age of eighty you will surely be able to pull off." Grünne was wrong. Gyulai's timid conduct of operations allowed the French to make a juncture with the armies of their ally, and this led to the serious Austrian defeats at Magenta (June 4) and Solferino (June 24), the conquest of all Lombardy by the allies, and the occupation of Milan.

Determined action on the part of Napoleon III might at this point have led to the liberation of Venetia as well. But the French emperor, who had taken to the field with his armies, was shaken by the heavy losses at Solferino; he was discovering that the war was not popular at home, especially among loyal Catholics; and he was afraid that the Prussian army, already in the first stages of mobilization, might enter the war at any moment. Without consulting his ally, then, Napoleon began secret negotiations with the emperor of Austria and, finding him as eager to abandon the war as he had been to bolt into it, concluded an armistice with him at Villafranca on July 11. The terms agreed upon provided for the transfer of Lombardy to Piedmont; but, for the rest, they foresaw the restoration of the Grand Duke of Tuscany and the Duke of Modena to the thrones from which they had been driven during the war, and the establishment, under papal leadership, of an Italian confederation in which Austria, by virtue of her retention of Venetia, would be a member. These last provisions seemed to negate the purposes of the war and to confirm Austrian domination of Italy.

When Cavour heard of Villafranca from his king, he raved like a maniac, becoming so violent that Victor Emmanuel had to leave the room. Rather than approve this termination of the war he had planned, the Piedmontese statesman resigned his office. He might have spared himself the trouble, for here again the actual course of events defied his expectations.

Villafranca was, in fact, unenforceable. In Tuscany and Modena, and in Parma and the Romagna, where the governing authorities had been expelled during the fighting, it proved impossible to turn back the clock. Thanks to skillful propaganda and leadership by agents of the National Society, revolutionary assemblies in these states met in August 1859 and voted in favor of union with Piedmont; and, in the months that followed, it was clear that only the use of military force could make them change their decision. It was most unlikely that Napoleon would condone this, and, if he did, it was clear that he would arouse the opposition of Great Britain, where a strong liberal government had come into power and was openly sympathetic to the aspirations of the people of central Italy. In January 1860, indeed, the British government let it be known that it favored "freedom from foreign interference by force of arms in the internal concerns of the people of Italy."

The return of Cavour to power in the same month facilitated a solution of this problem, for he now bluntly asked Napoleon's price for assent to the union. The emperor answered by giving him a choice. He would agree to Piedmont's annexation of Parma and Modena provided Tuscany and the Romagna were given separate administrations, with nominal papal authority retained in the latter; and for this he would ask no compensation. If, however, Piedmont insisted on the annexation of Tuscany and the Romagna as well, thus creating a powerful state on France's flank, he would have to be compensated by the cession of Nice and Savoy. Cavour and his king did not hesitate. They chose the latter alternative; and later, when he defended the cession of Nice and Savoy to France before the Piedmontese parliament, Cavour never even mentioned that it had not been strictly necessary.

In March 1860, plebiscites in the four areas of central Italy confirmed the popular desire for annexation to Piedmont; and in April they passed under Victor Emmanuel's rule. Cavour had won rather more than he had bargained for at Plombières. His accomplice, Napoleon III, had not been so fortunate. He had performed undeniable services for Italy, but Villafranca had diminished the gratitude he might have expected in return. The papal losses of territory had alienated the French Catholics, and the acquisition of Nice and Savoy had seriously weakened his good relations with the British government, which regarded it as the opening gun in a new program of imperialism, without having the compensating effect of allaying the misgivings of nationalists in his own country.

Garibaldi's Conquest of Naples   The momentum of the revolution was still by no means spent. The success of the national movement in central Italy was an encouragement to its supporters in the south; and, in the spring of 1860, disorders began to occur on the island of Sicily. These gave Garibaldi an opportunity to come again to the center of the political stage.

He had not, to be sure, been far from it during the past year. The outbreak of hostilities in 1859 had brought him back from his solitary home on the island of Caprera, and he had commanded a body of irregulars in the Lombard hills in the neighborhood of Como and Varese. Later, when the revolutionary governments of central Italy formed a military league, he commanded part of their forces. He proved to be a temperamental and unreliable subordinate, for he was impatient with the delays imposed by diplomacy, wanted to invade the other papal provinces without delay, and resented the refusal of the political authorities to permit this. In the spring of 1860, he began to build up a personal army of his own, and there were fears in Piedmont that he might use this to attack Venetia or Rome, with unforseen results. Instead, the Sicilian disorders, and the news that the people of that island were expecting his support, drew him to the south. In May, with a tiny force of 1000 red-shirted volunteers packed aboard two leaky steamers, he slipped through a screen of Neapolitan gunboats, landed at Marsala, and declared himself dictator of Sicily.

The king of Naples had 20,000 troops on the island of Sicily, which should have been more than enough to defeat Garibaldi's collection of poets, students, and soldiers of fortune. But the Neapolitans were divided among the coastal garrisons and allowed themselves to be outmaneuvered and defeated piecemeal. After an initial victory over 3000 Neapolitan troops at Calatafimi, Garibaldi's army won thousands of local recruits; a rising in Palermo helped open the road to that city; and within six weeks Garibaldi was living in the royal palace there. By mid-July the rest of the island was under his control, and his army—now 10,000 strong—was poised for the leap to the mainland.

Cavour had watched Garibaldi's actions with suspicion and misgivings. The whole expedition of the Thousand he regarded as a Mazzinian enterprise, and he had no faith in Garibaldi's strong monarchical feelings and his sincere desire to unite Italy under Victor Emmanuel. He had done everything in his power to prevent Garibaldi's going to Sicily (although he tried to pretend later that he had aided the expedition), for he was sure that the adventure would either fail miserably or succeed so well that Garibaldi would be encouraged to try an assault on Rome, and, in either case, there would be international complications. A gradualist and a believer in diplomacy, Cavour had no sympathy for Garibaldi's precipitate tactics and, even when Sicily had fallen, he was opposed to a Garibaldian attempt against Naples itself. He was, indeed, actually in diplomatic communication with the Bourbon government of Naples, doubtless feeling that circumstances might arise that would make a deal between Piedmont and Naples expedient.

"The Right Leg in the Boot at Last!" Garibaldi: "If it won't go on, Sire, try a little more powder." From *Punch,* November 17, 1860.

Garibaldi had now, however, aroused such a tide of popular enthusiasm that neither warnings nor diplomatic considerations could influence him. During the night of August 18 he crossed the Strait of Messina with a small advance force of 3500 men and within two days had forced the capitulation of the Neapolitan garrison at Reggio. Panic now affected the Bourbon armies, and they dispersed or capitulated at the very appearance of detachments of red shirts. Their resistance was so negligible that Garibaldi threw caution to the winds and, outpacing his own army, raced ahead to the city of Naples, which he entered with half a dozen companions on September 7.

To have conquered a country of eleven million people in less than five months was a remarkable achievement, but Garibaldi was never one to rest on his laurels, and he did not allow the rapturous acclamations of the citizens of Naples to divert him from his most cherished objective. He remembered his Mazzinian oath to devote his life to freeing all of Italy, and he doubtless also remembered his own defeat in the Holy City in 1849; and he began to plan an invasion of the Papal Marches. He was apparently being encouraged secretly by King Victor Emmanuel, who seems to have felt that Garibaldi might free him from his dependence upon Cavour and that he had nothing to lose in urging Garibaldi forward, since he could always disavow him in case of failure.

Cavour may not have known of the irresponsible conduct of his sovereign (although he doubtless suspected it), but he was fully conscious of Garibaldi's military preparations and aware that an attack on the Marches would almost certainly lead to trouble at Rome, where—as he never forgot—there was still a French garrison protecting the pope. He therefore decided to forestall this danger by action of his own. After preparing the way by convincing Napoleon III that it was necessary to block the further progress of Garibaldi's adventurers and after assuring him also that the position of Rome itself need not be affected, he threw the bulk of the Piedmontese army into the Papal States. On September 18 they overwhelmed the pope's forces at Castelfidardo; they then crossed into the state of Naples, defeated the Neapolitans at Capua, and bottled up the last of the Bourbon forces in the fortress of Gaeta.

This forthright military action was not, in fact, necessary to block Garibaldi, for in his northward drive he had become involved in a series of dogged engagements with a large enemy force posted along the Volturno River; and it was not until October that he had eked out a victory. But the Piedmontese invasion restored the initiative in the campaign for national unity to Cavour's hands, and he made the most of this. Even before the military issue had been decided, he had secured parliamentary consent for the annexation of southern Italy, provided it was approved by plebiscite in the districts concerned; and in October plebiscites in Naples, Sicily, the Marches, and Umbria voted overwhelmingly for union with Piedmont. In the face of this, Garibaldi surrendered his conquests to Victor Emmanuel and sailed off alone to his obscure island home. In February, after the end of Neapolitan resistance at Gaeta, the city of Turin witnessed the assembling of a new Italian parliament, representing the whole of the peninsula except Rome and Venetia, and Victor Emmanuel II was declared king of Italy. Shortly thereafter, the national government took up new headquarters in Florence, which was to be Italy's capital city until 1870.

THE COMPLETION OF ITALIAN UNITY, 1860–1871

Cavour's Work in Retrospect   The crowning of the achievements of 1859 and 1860 by the addition of Venetia and Rome to the united realm was to take another decade, and Cavour did not live to see it realized. Worn out by the pressures and anxieties of the period that opened at Plombières, he fell seriously ill in the spring of 1861 and died, at the age of fifty-one, in June of that year. In his relatively short career in public life he had displayed political gifts of the highest order and diplomatic adroitness unequaled by any other statesman in the long history of the Italian states. Even so, while granting this and his other great talents—his foresight in economic matters, for instance, and his contribution to the strengthening of parliamentary institutions in Italy—it is worth noting that, seen from the vantage point of the twentieth century, Cavour's contribution to the territorial and administrative unification of Italy seems somewhat less impressive, and his diplomatic methods seem considerably more questionable, than they were to contemporaries.

With respect to the latter point, it need only be said that Cavour's diplomacy was founded upon calculated duplicity and flagrant disregard for inherited values and the stipulations of the public law, and that its very success had the unfortunate effect of encouraging imitation. With respect to the former, it should be noted that, once the plebiscites had been held, the Piedmontese government showed scant respect for the wishes or the traditional usages of their southern provinces, preferring to impose a rigidly centralized administrative system on the country as a whole. Had Cavour taken the trouble to visit the south in 1860, he might have sensed the opposition that centralization would surely arouse; but he refused even to go to Naples at the time of Victor Emmanuel's triumphal entry into that city, writing to a friend: "I am ready to sacrifice for the King my life and everything I own; but as a man I ask of him but one favor, to remain as far away from his person as possible."

This pettiness made impossible the accumulation of information that would have avoided trouble. As a result, the Piedmontese treated the kingdom of Naples almost as if it were an African colony; local customs and codes were ruthlessly stamped out; there were numerous and flagrant incidents of economic spoliation and exploitation by northern administrators; and, as a result, the popularity that Victor Emmanuel possessed when he rode into Naples in November had almost completely evaporated by January. Pro-Bourbon agitation was common in the 1860s; there were open brushes between Piedmontese troops and peasant bands; and the south started off its new life in the united Italy with a feeling of resentment against the foreigners of the north that is not entirely dead even today.

Venetia and Rome   The primary objective of the new Italy's policy in the 1860s was the acquisition of Venetia; and Cavour's successors took a leaf out of the master's book in pursuing this, for they relied entirely upon the expedients of diplomacy. Since even the most skillful diplomacy in the world could not persuade the Austrians voluntarily to abandon their last Italian possession, the Italian government had to take advantage of the growing friction between Prussia and Austria and to sell their services to the former before Venetia was acquired.

THE UNIFICATION OF ITALY

Italy in 1860

Gained in 1866

Gained in 1870

0   50   100   150
Miles

Italy's participation in the German war of 1866 was inglorious. Her armies were soundly defeated by the Austrians, and her fleet was destroyed in the disastrous battle off Lissa; but Venetia was nevertheless granted to Italy when the Austrians surrendered to their German rival.

Rome was a more difficult problem. Thanks to Mazzini's decision in 1848 to fight for the city, and thanks to Cavour's last political act, the securing of a parliamentary declaration that Rome should be the capital of Italy, most Italians regarded unification incomplete as long as the city remained independent. Yet Pope Pius IX steadfastly refused to compromise in any way with the new Italy, protesting formally against Victor Emmanuel's assumption of the Italian crown; and the Pope was still protected by a French garrison. There was reason to believe that Napoleon III was willing to terminate the military situation he had created in sending Oudinot's army to Rome in 1849—and as the emperor's political troubles multiplied in the late 1860s he became more so—but he was always restrained by the fear of alienating Catholic votes at home. On two occasions, in 1862 and in 1867, Garibaldi, with oddly assorted and ill-equipped bands, tried to reach the Holy City. In the first attempt he was stopped by royal troops; and in 1867 his forces came under the merciless fire of the new French rifle—the chassepot—and ran away, in Garibaldi's own words, "like cowardly rabbits." This latter expedition had been secretly encouraged by Victor Emmanuel, although he denied it. Its only result was to cause parliamentary storms in Piedmont and to confirm French protection of Rome.

In the end, Rome was occupied by royal troops when there was no one to challenge their entrance into the city—during the Franco-Prussian war, when French armies were otherwise engaged. The royal government immediately transferred its capital to the Holy City, while the pope, withdrawing behind the walls of the Vatican, continued his steadfast opposition to the regime that now controlled the whole peninsula.

Chapter 9 THE GERMAN QUESTION, 1850–1866

The events that had taken place in Italy in 1859 and 1860 had their counterpart in Germany in the decade that followed. There too the leadership in the movement toward national unification was taken by the strongest and economically most progressive of the interested states. There too the process was achieved by war and by the subsequent absorption of some of the lesser states by the victor and the imposition of his control over the others. And there too the victim was Austria, whose position in Germany was destroyed as completely as her place in Italy had been, with serious resultant repercussions on the internal structure of the Hapsburg empire.

THE EVOLUTION OF PRUSSIAN POLICY

Prussia after 1850   To the ordinary observer of German affairs in 1850, it would not have appeared likely that Prussia would extend her hegemony over Germany in the foreseeable future. It was true that the Prussian government had shown more imagination in economic affairs than other governments and had maintained the primacy Prussia had won in commercial matters when the *Zollverein* was founded earlier in the century (see pp. 46, 50); and it was true that great economic progress had been made in the Prussian kingdom. Berlin had grown in two decades from a provincial capital to a thriving commercial center of 450,000 inhabitants, and Cologne, Magdeburg, and Breslau were growing fast. By 1860 the kingdom would have 3750 miles of all-season roads, a ninefold increase since 1815, and a railway net that was developing as quickly as any in Europe. Industrial production was expanding rapidly and becoming increasingly mechanized, the number of steam engines employed growing almost six times in the decade following the revolutions of 1848. The textile and clothing industry was still the most important single industry, but the iron, steel, and machine works of the Rhineland and Silesia were now beginning a period of marked growth, and smaller industries—brick kilns, breweries, saw mills, distilleries, refineries, and the like—were moving out into the rural areas and changing the predominantly agricultural character of the kingdom. All of this vitality and development was in sharp contrast to conditions in other German states and particularly in Austria, where industrial growth was slow, communication backward, and government encouragement of economic progress virtually nonexistent.

Leaving economic progress aside, however, there were few other obvious indications of progress in the Prussia of the 1850s and none of the kind of political enlightenment that would, presumably, be required if Prussia was to become the acknowledged leader of the movement for national unification.

For a decade after the revolutions of 1848, Prussian policy, both domestic and foreign, was completely negative in character. Despite Prussia's transformation into a constitutional state, and despite the marked growth of the middle class as a result of the economic growth of the country, political power was still in the hands of the aristocracy and the large landholders, who were entrenched in key positions at court, in the state administration and the army command, and in the upper house of parliament. This ruling caste devoted its energies to guarding against the possibility of any recurrence of revolutionary agitation by persecuting persons who were suspected of harboring democratic or socialist ideas and by suppressing newspapers, books, and plays that expressed progressive sentiments. In foreign affairs it had no interest and made no attempt to pursue an independent policy, preferring rather to follow the advice of Austria and, whenever possible, Russia. In effect, this meant acquiescing in the dominance in German affairs that Austria had won at Olmütz. Not all Prussians, to be sure, liked this policy of playing second fiddle to Vienna, and some argued that Prussia should take advantage of Austria's foreign difficulties to extend her influence and territory in Germany; but even in 1859, when Austria was at war with France and Piedmont, the Prussian government made no attempt to experiment with this kind of realism and, if the war had lasted a few weeks longer, Prussia would probably have intervened on Austria's side.

The possibility of Prussia's playing an independent hand in German affairs and making any significant contribution to the cause of national unification seemed to be even further reduced after Frederick William IV yielded the throne to his brother William, who became regent in 1858 and king in January 1861. The accession of this ruler was hailed as the beginning of a "new era"; but William was already sixty-one years old when he became regent and was, if anything, more conservative than his brother. In any case, his coming to power was followed by a domestic conflict that threatened to make Prussia a complete nullity in foreign and German affairs.

The Constitutional Conflict   The reasons for this were rooted in the character of William I. A soldier by profession, he had long been critical of certain aspects of Prussian military organization and particularly of two things: the restriction of the term of active service, in most cases, to two years, and the heavy reliance placed upon a civilian militia (*Landwehr*) that elected its own officers and was largely independent of the regular army. In February 1860, on the basis of plans drawn up by his war minister Albrecht von Roon (1803–1879), William laid an army reorganization bill before the Prussian parliament. It called for a marked increase in the annual number of conscripts in order to provide for a regular army double its present size; it lengthened the term of service to three years, with corresponding adjustments for special services and the reserve; it sharply diminished the role and the independence of the *Landwehr;* and it asked for a greatly expanded military budget to pay for the new regiments envisaged, as well as for barracks, schools, and training grounds.

This bill aroused the immediate opposition of the Prussian middle class, which was generally liberal in its views and suspicious of the military establishment on economic and political grounds; and its representatives—who, thanks to the franchise provisions of the constitution (see p. 136), now controlled the majority of seats in the Prussian Chamber of Deputies—attacked the proposed reform. Some of them objected to the cost of the reorganization. Others, mindful of the role played by the *Landwehr* in the fight against Napoleon, protested that the reform would destroy the "citizen-soldier" tradition. Some suggested that the lengthening of the term of service was designed to "militarize" the conscripts and turn them against liberal and civilian values. Finally, many noted that since Prussia had no foreign policy, she had no need of a larger military force; and they went on to charge that the new units would be employed only as a police force to subvert popular liberties. When the bill went to committee, so many amendments were proposed that the government withdrew the proposed legislation from consideration.

In doing so, it asked for the extraordinary sum of 9,000,000 thaler to strengthen existing units of the army; and this the Chamber of Deputies granted on the understanding that the sum would not be used to make departures from the existing law. Once he had this money in his possession, however, William proceeded to use it to effect the changes for which he had not been able to win approval. Not unnaturally the liberal majority protested, and throughout 1861 they demanded that their ruler submit a comprehensive military reform bill for their approval. When the king did so at the beginning of 1862, laying before them proposals virtually identical with those of 1860, they defeated them out of hand and refused to make any further grant of funds to the government unless the recent military innovations were withdrawn, the two-year service term restored, the *Landwehr's* position protected, and the military budget completely itemized. The king's answer was to dissolve the Chamber. When new elections were held in May, however, the liberal majority was strengthened, rather than weakened, as he had hoped.

What followed was a complete and dangerous deadlock. Emboldened by their electoral success and led now by the new Progressive party, which had emerged in 1861, the liberal opposition became more ambitious, seeing in the crisis an opportunity to gain control not only over the army but over all aspects of the state administration, and, more intransigent, abandoning their earlier willingness to compromise. On the other hand, the conservative forces, confronted by what seemed to them to be a revival of the spirit of 1848, became equally inflexible and increasingly inclined to listen to those reactionaries who argued that force alone would solve the parliamentary problem. In the immediate entourage of the king, men like Edwin von Manteuffel, chief of William's military cabinet, actually urged that the crisis be exploited in such a way as to force a liberal insurrection, or agitations that could be described as such, which could then be put down by military means and punished by the revocation of the constitution and a return to absolute government. One shrewd observer wrote at the time: "The military are panting after riots like the hart after the waterbrooks."

The king resisted the advice of his more reactionary advisers, for he had sworn to uphold the constitution and he took his oath seriously. But he resented the pretensions of the parliamentarians and refused either to yield to their desires or to undo the military reforms already instituted. Since the Chamber simultaneously held to its refusal to vote any funds for the conduct of state affairs unless it had its way, Prussian government was threatened with complete paralysis, and the king, in despair, seriously considered giving up his throne. When he had got to the point of drafting an abdication note, however, his war minister urged him to see whether a new chief minister might not be able to break the impasse and persuaded him, in September 1862, to appoint Otto von Bismarck (1815–1898) as his minister president.

Bismarck's Political Ideas   Because it was known that he had been an outspoken foe of the revolution of March 1848 and had violently opposed all royal concessions made at that time, Bismarck was generally considered to be a reactionary; and his appointment was greeted with satisfaction by those who hoped to crush liberalism once and for all. In reality, although he was himself an East Elbian landholder, the new minister president had none of the provincialism of his fellow *Junker*, nor was he, like them, preoccupied only with the domestic issues involved in the constitutional conflict. Since 1850, he had been serving his country as a diplomat, first in the Diet of the Germanic Confederation at Frankfurt, later in St. Petersburg and Paris; and this experience had broadened his vision and his ambitions for Prussia. Far from sharing the sentimental attachment to Austria that Prussian conservatives generally favored, he had become convinced that it was Prussia's destiny to extend her power in Germany, and that this could be accomplished only at the expense of Austria. As early as 1856 Bismarck had written: "Germany is clearly too small for us both. . . . In the not too distant future, we shall have to fight for our existence against Austria . . . since the course of events in Germany has no other solution."

Bismarck's views on the German question necessarily influenced his attitude toward the conflict with parliament. He fully agreed with the king's desire to reform the army, which would, after all, be the instrument that assured Prussian growth; and, as a supporter of the monarchical principle, he was opposed to any increase in parliamentary powers. On the other hand, he knew that in the eventual struggle with Austria, Prussia would need the intelligence and industry of the middle classes just as much as the valor of the army and that the liberal opposition, for economic and other reasons, would be more sympathetic to his German plans than the conservatives. He had no desire to turn the clock back

Bismarck at the time of the Prussian constitutional conflict. From *Illustrated London News,* September 29, 1866.

by smashing the constitutional regime, for this would merely confirm Prussia's servitude to Austria.

After an initial attempt to persuade the parliamentary opposition to compromise was unsuccessful, Bismarck did not therefore go over to the camp of the extreme absolutists but struck out on a completely novel line. He decided to ignore the Chamber's failure to support the government's policy. If the Chamber of Deputies would not vote the budget, he said, "we will take the money where we find it." He ordered the civil service to carry out their duties—including those of recruiting troops and collecting the taxes needed to support government activities—with no regard for the speeches in parliament; and he punished or dismissed national, provincial, or city officials who had any qualms about this or who associated with the Progressive party in any way.

These tactics kept the government going. They did not weaken the parliamentary opposition, which increased its strength in the elections of 1863; but this was an illusory gain. Bismarck was by now looking beyond the walls of parliament to the world of foreign affairs. It was his belief that an active and successful foreign policy, which demonstrated the need for an effective army, would break the opposition and swing many of the liberals to his side; and he was determined to act upon this principle.

His first sally into foreign politics did not justify his hopes, although it was successful to a degree not realized at the time. At the end of 1862 the Russian government promulgated a decree calling for the conscription of young Poles into the Russian army and, in doing so, gave the patriotic party of Polish students and army officers the kind of issue they had long been waiting for. They hastily improvised a network of cells to sabotage the conscription process and drew up plans for an insurrection, which ultimately broke out in January 1863. The Polish cause aroused sympathy in western Europe, particularly in France, and Napoleon III, always sensitive to public opinion, mounted a diplomatic campaign to force the tsar to restore to the Poles the autonomous position they had lost in 1831 (see p. 31). To the disgust of German liberals, Bismarck took a contrary line and concluded a secret convention with the Russian government providing for collaboration in suppressing the revolt. He did this out of fear that the tsar might otherwise defer to the pressure of the Western Powers and free Poland, in which case Prussia could expect serious trouble in her own Polish districts. Bismarck's action paid unexpected dividends. It not only encouraged the tsar to stand firm (so that Napoleon's efforts on behalf of the Poles came to nothing, to the clamant dissatisfaction of his own subjects) but it helped persuade him to reorient his foreign policy, breaking off the cordial relations that he had had since the Crimean War with France and inaugurating a friendship with Prussia that was to last for almost thirty years.

Bismarck's convention with Russia was not of any immediate use in solving his domestic troubles, for it was roundly attacked by the liberals. Their opposition was to be far less united, however, to the minister president's next move in the foreign field.

FROM DÜPPEL TO KÖNIGGRÄTZ

Schleswig and Holstein   In the last months of 1863 a new chapter opened in the tangled history of Schleswig and Holstein.[1] Those provinces, thanks to the historical accident that one of their dukes had become king of Denmark, had for years been among the personal possessions of the Danish sovereign, without actually being part of the Danish kingdom. A further complication arose from the fact that Holstein, whose population was almost entirely German, was a member of the Germanic Confederation, while Schleswig was not, although its German citizens, comprising two thirds of its population, wished it to become so. This last wish was violently opposed by the Danish minority, which wanted Schleswig to be absorbed by Denmark; and, in November 1863, the wishes of these nationalists were gratified by the promulgation of a new Danish consti-tution, which declared Schleswig an integral part of the kingdom.

This action was resisted in both Schleswig and Holstein, and it aroused a wave of nationalistic indignation in Germany, where the Federal Diet immedi-ately protested and, when this was unavailing, ordered a federal army to pre-vent the execution of the terms of Denmark's new constitution. Throughout Germany there was a vocal desire for the severance of all ties between Denmark and the two duchies, and the establishment of the latter as independent members of the Confederation.

Bismarck's conduct in the subsequent course of this dispute was so devious that one cannot, with any confidence, say what his thoughts and intentions were at any given moment. It seems clear, however, that he was always opposed to a solution that would have turned the duchies, which were of great potential

---

[1] Lord Palmerston once said that only three men had ever fully understood the complications of the Schleswig-Holstein question and that unfortunately one (the prince consort) was dead, one (a former Foreign Office clerk) had gone mad, and he himself, the third, had forgotten them.

strategic importance to Prussia, into independent federal states; and he probably thought from the beginning in terms of eventual Prussian annexation. He did not, in any case, publish his true views but instead—when the crisis broke out—stood forward as a defender of the treaty of 1852, by which the European Concert had assured the king of Denmark possession of the duchies, provided their autonomous position was left unchanged (see p. 154). He urged the Austrian government to join Prussia in upholding international law, and the Vienna government, doubtless feeling that it might be awkward to do anything else, agreed. Disregarding the action of the Germanic Confederation, therefore, the two powers sent an ultimatum to the Danes, demanding that the new constitution be revoked; and, when the Danes refused (as Bismarck had calculated they would), they declared war.

The Danish war is important for several reasons. It provided a baptism of fire, and a completely gratifying one, for the new Prussian army. It was in the campaign in Jutland that the field commanders who were later to defeat Austrian and French armies were tested, and it was here that the architect of those later victories, Chief of the General Staff Helmuth von Moltke (1800–1891), won the confidence of the king. And it was in this war, and particularly in the successful assault of the formidable Danish strongpoint of Düppel, that the army as a whole called itself to the attention of Europe. The victory at Düppel was described by the historian Droysen as "one of the events that mark an epoch in a nation's history"; and this is just, for it aroused a degree of patriotic pride that simultaneously weakened liberal opposition to the much-contested army reform and strengthened the tendency of German nationalists to look to Prussia for leadership.

Aside from this, the Danish war demonstrated the inadequacy of the European Concert in this new age, for, when the European powers, midway in the war, held a conference on the Schleswig-Holstein question, they were unable to agree on a settlement that would satisfy all parties and were powerless to prevent the resumption of hostilities, which continued until Denmark was defeated by the German powers and deprived of the duchies.

Austro-Prussian Friction   The comradeship in arms against the Danes had temporarily relieved a deterioration of Austro-Prussian relations that had continued since 1859 and had been marked, on each side, by economic maneuvering and attempts to reform the machinery of the Germanic Confederation to its own advantage. The rapprochement effected by the war was, however, quickly broken down by the failure of the allies to agree on the disposition of the spoils. Denmark, in defeat, had been forced to hand Schleswig and Holstein over to the victors; and it was up to them to decide their future. The Austrian government advocated the establishment of a separate Schleswig-Holstein state; Bismarck, with annexation in the back of his mind, took the position that this could be permitted only on condition that far-reaching military and commercial rights be granted to Prussia—that Kiel, for instance, be made a Prussian naval base. To this the Austrians, not unnaturally, refused to agree.

This Austrian opposition had the effect of causing a fundamental change in the attitude of the Prussian court, and of Prussian conservatives in general,

toward the Hapsburg monarchy. The king, who was proud of his army's performance in the recent war, gradually, unconsciously, but nonetheless firmly, began
to regard the duchies as having been won by Prussia alone and to view Austria's
policy as an attempt to deprive Prussian troops of their legitmate reward; and,
like him, the traditionally pro-Austrian conservative circles showed increasing
irritation over Austrian tactics. It is significant that, in May 1865, a Prussian
crown council could actually discuss the advisability of making war upon Austria
if her government did not change its position.

The Prussian government did not force the issue in 1865, primarily because
it realized that the power that took the initiative in precipitating a territorial
dispute would find German public opinion solidly against it. Instead, after much
involved haggling, the two disputants concluded the so-called Convention of
Gastein (August 1865), by which they divided the duchies between them—Austria
taking over the administration of Holstein and Prussia that of Schleswig. It is
difficult to understand why the Austrians agreed to this arrangement, or why
they insisted it be a provisional rather than a definitive one, for this meant that
Prussia reserved her rights in Holstein and could protest against anything that
happened there that was not to her liking. This blunder played into Bismarck's
hands and enabled him to create incidents that, he hoped, would further alienate
his sovereign's sympathies from Vienna and might even goad the Austrians into
injudicious action that would give Prussia an excuse for war.

Meanwhile, the minister president took the political steps that he felt would
assure success if the Austrians were persuaded to force the issue. In the first
place, he made his diplomatic preparations for war. He was reasonably sure
that neither Great Britain nor Russia would intervene; but France's attitude was
doubtful and, like Cavour before him, Bismarck found it expedient to have
discussions with Napoleon III. These took place at Biarritz in October 1865, and,
while no written agreement was made, there seems to have been an understanding that France would remain neutral in the case of a German war, although she
might receive some territorial compensation along the Rhine if a successful
Prussia felt called upon to make extensive annexations in Germany. The vague-
ness of this agreement, if it may be called that, was probably due to Napoleon's
belief that a German war would be a protracted struggle with results far different
from those imagined by Bismarck and that his own role and compensation would
be best determined during the hostilities. But the Biarritz meeting gave Bismarck
a reasonable assurance against interference by France; and he strengthened it,
and created military complications for his opponents, by concluding an alliance
with the government of Italy in April 1866, by which Italy agreed to fight on
Prussia's side if war came within the next three months, and Prussia agreed
to reward her with the province of Venetia. This pact with Italy was a violation
of Prussia's obligation to the Germanic Confederation, which bound her not
to make alliances against fellow members; but Bismarck was too much the *Realpolitiker* to be deterred by that.

Simultaneously, Bismarck made his bid for the support of German public
opinion by proposing a thoroughgoing reform of the Germanic Confederation,
to be effected by adding to that body a national assembly elected by universal
suffrage in all the member states. This revolutionary proposal, which summoned

up memories of the Frankfurt Assembly and which could not, by any stretch of the imagination, be accepted by the Austrian government, bewildered but impressed liberal opinion throughout Germany, which had long been drawn to Prussia by her economic and political vigor but repelled by her reputation for reactionary government and militarism. To the extent that it did so, it prepared the way for the radical revision of the tenets of German liberalism that was soon to come.

Bismarck's tactics in Holstein and in the Diet at Frankfurt were in the end successful. As early as April 1866, the Austrians had convinced themselves that war was inevitable— "How can one avoid war," Francis Joseph was reported to have said, "when the other side wants it?"—and, after that, they neither tried very hard to avoid it nor guarded against measures that might seem to indicate that they were responsible for causing it. They actually resigned themselves to the loss of Venetia, promising Napoleon III (who was by now negotiating with both sides) that they would cede it to him for transfer to Italy if he would maintain a benevolent neutrality in case of war. One might have thought that the knowledge that Venetia was lost to them regardless of the fortunes of war would have persuaded the Vienna cabinet to grasp at any straw to avoid a conflict. Instead, it was Austria that first began the mobilization of troops; and, when Napoleon III suggested an international conference of the powers to consider the whole German question, it was Austria's objections and conditions that made the meeting impossible.

After that events moved swiftly. On June 1, 1866, Austria brought the Schleswig-Holstein question before the Diet of the Germanic Confederation, a move of questionable legality which Bismarck promptly described as a violation of the Gastein Convention. The Prussians immediately moved into Holstein. The Austrian government countered with a demand for military action by the Confederation against Prussia, and the Diet voted in favor of this on June 14. The Prussian government had warned that this would be considered a declaration of war. They now declared the Confederation dissolved and threw their armies into the field.

The Seven Weeks' War   The war between Austria and Prussia lasted a scant seven weeks and ended with the overwhelming defeat of Austria. The Austrian debacle was the result of a number of factors. The army, for one thing, had not kept abreast of the latest military advances. Its administration and its intelligence and staff work were lamentably deficient in comparison with the Prussian army's general staff system, which was unrivaled for efficiency in Europe. Its commanding generals, including Benedek, the commander-in-chief on the Bohemian front, lacked confidence and—thanks to the role played by imperial favoritism in the upper echelons of the army—had insufficient control over their subordinates. The troops were willing and brave, but they were trained in outmoded shock tactics in a day when battles were won by superior firepower; and they found it virtually impossible to come to grips with the Prussian infantry, who were armed with the new Dreyse "needle-gun," a breech-loading rifle that fired farther and more rapidly than their own.

In addition, Italy's intervention in the war forced Austria to fight on two fronts and made impossible a concentration of all forces against Prussia. This need

The advance of the army of the crown prince of Prussia at the battle of Königgrätz. (*Illustrated London News,* 1866)

not have been as serious as it turned out to be, for, as early as June 24, the Austrians virtually knocked Italy out of the war by a crushing victory at Custoza, which should have freed troops for transfer to the Bohemian front.

But the truly decisive factor in the war proved to be Austria's deficiency in railroads. This not only made the movement of troops from the Italian front difficult but reduced Austrian mobility and paralyzed Austrian energies generally. The fact that there was only one main line running north from Vienna to Olmütz meant that the route to the main theater of war was clogged. It was this that prevented Austrian toops, despite a head start in mobilization, from effecting a juncture with their German allies and deprived Benedek of the reinforcements he wanted when he took his stand on the Bohemian plain.

In contrast, the Prussians had a highly developed rail net that enabled the chief of staff, Moltke, to deploy his troops along an arc 600 miles wide, from the Elbe to the Neisse, to overrun the middle states and defeat the army of Hanover, and then to concentrate his forces against Benedek. After a series of clashes between isolated units in places where the armies of Frederick the Great had maneuvered against the Austrians a century earlier, the decisive battle of the war was fought on July 3, 1866, in the hilly terrain between the Bohemian towns of Sadowa and Königgrätz. One of the greatest battles of the modern era (between 440,000 and 460,000 men were engaged), this encounter was also an almost perfect illustration of the way in which Moltke's principle of "dispersed advance but concentration on the battlefield" could be applied to encircle and defeat an enemy. The trap did not quite close, and Benedek, thanks to skillful use of his artillery and the spirited rearguard action of the superb Austrian cavalry, extricated 180,000 men from the stricken field. The defeat was, nonetheless, a shattering one (the Austrians and their Saxon allies had 44,313 casualties at Königgrätz, compared with 9153 Prussian); and it decided the result of the war.

For the student of the political aspects of military affairs the war between Austria and Prussia has a special interest, for it illustrates the sharp conflict between civilian and military authority that became commonplace as techniques of warfare expanded in scope and in technical complexity. After Königgrätz Bismarck had serious difficulties with the Prussian high command which, now that it smelled victory, wished to make it as big as possible, with heavy annexations of Austrian territory and a triumphal march into the Austrian capital. Bismarck opposed this plan because it would needlessly protract the war, thus increasing the risk of intervention by the other powers. During July, through his ambassador in Paris, he was carrying on delicate negotiations with Napoleon III, seeking to win his permission to organize all north Germany into a new confederation under Prussian leadership and, simultaneously, to make very extensive annexations. He was afraid that the policy favored by the soldiers and the king would make those negotiations fail and bring Napoleon to Austria's side. Moreover, he saw no point in inflicting needless punishment upon Austria, for this would only serve as a barrier to future friendship.

After the great victory in Bohemia, then, Bismarck boldly opposed all military plans for new advances to the southeast, and by doing so he earned the dislike of Moltke and the circle of young general staff officers, "the demigods," who resented a civilian intervening in what they considered a strictly military sphere. Four years later, during the war against France, they showed that their resentment was still alive by seeking to exclude Bismarck from all strategical conferences, even when political issues were at stake. In 1870 as in 1866, however, Bismarck had his way, pointing out that as long as he was responsible for policy, he could not cede his powers to soldiers simply because there happened to be a war on, and that, in any case, wars were fought for political objectives and should stop when those objectives were achieved. In 1866, he was aided in winning his point by Napoleon III's agreement that Prussia could have the annexations she desired in north Germany and could organize Germany north of the Main into a confederation, provided the southern states of Baden, Württemberg, and Bavaria remained independent and Saxony was not wholly destroyed. Even so, to make King William, who was more belligerent than his most belligerent soldiers, agree to peace on these handsome terms was not easy; and before William was won over Bismarck had to enlist the support of the crown prince and to threaten resignation.

Peace terms were drawn up at Nikolsburg in July and confirmed and completed by the Peace of Prague a month later. Austria was forced to recognize its permanent separation from Germany, to pay a small indemnity, and to cede Venetia to Italy. Otherwise it lost nothing. Its German allies were less fortunate. The kingdom of Hanover, the duchies of Nassau and Hesse-Cassel, and the free city of Frankfurt were annexed by Prussia, whose territory was now united by the absorption of all the states between her eastern and western provinces and increased by 1300 square miles and four and a half million new subjects. All north Germany was under Prussian control, and even the independence of the southern states, upon which Napoleon III had insisted, was compromised, for, immediately after the re-establishment of peace, Bismarck negotiated offensive and defensive military alliances with all of them.

THE CONSEQUENCES OF THE WAR

Dualism in the Austrian Empire   Austria's defeat and its subsequent exclusion from Germany made it imperative for the Hapsburg monarchy to hasten the execution of plans that transformed the internal structure of the empire but which, as events were to prove, aggravated rather than alleviated its most pressing internal problems. To understand this change it is necessary to return, very briefly, to the events of 1848–1849.

The revolutions of those years had shaken the empire to its foundations and had revealed grave dissatisfaction, on the part of Austria's subject nationalities, with a form of government that did not recognize their historical rights or give scope to their cultural differences. They seemed to indicate further that a federal structure—similar to that proposed in the constitution drawn up at Kremsier (see pp. 141–142)—would have the best chance of holding the multinational empire together. These things, however, were completely disregarded by Francis Joseph and the Schwarzenberg government, who, after the revolutions had been suppressed, made absolutism and centralization their guiding principles. In the ten years that followed, local diets were abolished and the ancient constitution of Hungary was declared in abeyance; and the empire was ruled by an elaborately bureaucratic machine. This was directed by the minister of the interior, Alexander Bach, who sent his civil servants (the so-called Bach Hussars) into every nook and cranny of the empire to supervise recruiting, collect taxes, and exercise judicial and administrative functions, and it was supported, whenever local disaffection occurred, by the secret police and the army.

This system was unpopular throughout the empire, and most of all in Hungary, where resentment over the suppression of ancient rights took active forms and was one of the reasons for the uncertainty and vacillation of Francis Joseph's foreign policy during the Crimean War. But it was not until 1859, when the defeat in Italy shook the prestige of the monarchy, that the government became seriously concerned about the opposition to the Bach system and began to consider reforms.

In 1860 and 1861 the provincial diets were revived; the competence of the Imperial Council (*Reichsrat*) was broadened to give it the appearance of a consultative chamber; and a whole series of imperial declarations were issued, asserting the government's intention of recognizing the rights of all its subject peoples and of moving toward a constitutional system. To give a detailed description of these plans and declarations, and the subsequent ones that filled the years before 1866, would be otiose. The important thing about them all is that they were vitiated by the emperor's reluctance to countenance anything resembling genuine federalism or to abandon the bureaucratic methods to which he was accustomed. Thus, in 1860, while claiming to re-establish Hungary's political institutions in their full vigor, Francis Joseph sought to restrict the competence of the Hungarian Diet by reserving certain important matters for the exclusive deliberation of the *Reichsrat,* which was dominated by aristocratic and German elements who could be expected to follow the imperial desires. Thus again, in 1861, when a two-chamber parliament was established for the whole empire, the electoral procedure was such as to assure German majorities in the delegations sent to this parliament from the various regions of the realm.

These practices not only caused protests, and sometimes boycott of the imperial parliament by the provincial diets, but also had the effect of stimulating cultural movements that emphasized resistance to German domination. The establishment of a national theater in Prague and the organization throughout Bohemia of gymnastic and patriotic societies called *sokols,* the foundation of a society for the propagation of national culture by the Rumanians of Transylvania, and the beginning of a national political press in Croatia were all symptoms of growing dissatisfaction with the governmental principles of the Hapsburg monarchy.

Most implacable in their resistance were the Magyars of Hungary, who found a leader in Francis Déak (1803–1876), a superb tactician who exploited all the weaknesses of the imperial government. Déak was no extremist; he set his face against the ambitions of exiles like Kossuth, who dreamed of Hungarian independence, because he did not believe that Hungary could stand alone. But he insisted that agreement with the Vienna government was possible only on the basis of the restoration to Hungary of all the liberties she had won in 1848 (see p. 129); and, until these were granted, he advocated a policy of noncollaboration on Hungary's part—which meant refusal to participate in meetings of the Imperial Diet or to pay taxes or to participate in other imperial activities.

The opposition of the subject nationalities made the efficient operation of the imperial system impossible, and, as Francis Joseph's ministers became convinced that war with Prussia was unavoidable, they were oppressed with visions of strikes and military desertions like those that had occurred during the war of 1859. They decided, therefore, to temporize and entered into negotiations with the most formidable of the dissidents, the Magyars. These discussions were interrupted by the outbreak of the war with Prussia, and it is impossible to say what their result would have been had that war been won. The fact that it was not won, however, made it inevitable that an arrangement would be reached on Hungary's terms, for her cooperation was needed, if not to prevent the complete dissolution of the empire, then at least to make Austria's recovery as a Great Power possible.

The negotiations terminated in 1867 with the conclusion of the so-called *Ausgleich* or Compromise, which transformed the Hapsburg empire into a dual monarchy, comprising two independent and equal states with one ruler (who would be emperor of Austria and king of Hungary), one imperial and royal Army, and a joint ministry with responsibility for foreign policy, military affairs and financial matters. Each half of this new Austria-Hungary, as it was henceforth to be called, would have its own parliament, its separate cabinet of ministers, and its own civil service and administrative system. To supervise the work of the joint departments of foreign affairs, war, and finance, the two national parliaments chose committees of "delegations," which met in Vienna and Budapest, communicating with each other in writing and, very rarely, by means of joint sessions.

The Compromise restored reasonable efficiency to the governmental operations of the empire, permitted the Hapsburg monarchy to play an important role in international affairs, and even had beneficial economic results by making possible an effective customs union and creating a great market in which the industrial and agricultural districts complemented each other to mutual advantage. But it did nothing to solve the nationalities problem, and did not try to do so. It may truly be described as a "deal" between the German minority in the western half of the empire and the Magyar minority in the eastern at the expense of all of the other peoples—the Czechs, the Slovaks, the Croats, the Serbs, the Poles, and the Rumanians. The true character of the arrangement was shown by the laws that implemented it in the two halves of the empire. By a series of decrees in the latter part of 1867, parliamentary government was established in Austria with a bicameral legislature chosen by the diets of the seventeen provinces west of the Leitha River; but the realm was gerrymandered so that German domination was assured and the system was run by bureaucrats in such a way as to make any truly liberal development impossible. In Hungary the constitution of 1848 was restored, but the suffrage was so limited that three fourths of the adult male population had no political power, a fact that facilitated the policy of Magyarization followed by the government.

The Compromise had the long-run effect of transforming the desire of the subject nationalities for autonomy within the empire into a desire for independence from the empire. As early as 1867, for instance, Czech leaders went to Moscow to attend a Pan-Slav congress; and in July 1868 the celebration in Prague of the anniversary of the birth of John Huss was so obviously an anti-Hapsburg demonstration that the city had to be placed under martial law. This was a sign of things to come. In short, the defeat in Germany, which might have led to the kind of reform of the imperial structure that would encourage internal harmony and peaceful development, brought instead an exacerbation of the national differences that were to pull the empire to pieces.

The Surrender of Prussian Liberalism   When the Prussian army smashed Benedek's forces at Königgrätz, it simultaneously inflicted a decisive defeat upon the liberal opposition in the Chamber of Deputies. The vigor and enthusiasm with which the liberals had opposed the royal military reforms in 1862 and 1863 had begun to wane during the campaign against Denmark and had been further attenuated when Bismarck announced, in April 1866, that he favored a basic reform of the Germanic Confederation and the creation of a national assembly elected by universal manhood suffrage. It disappeared almost completely as the war with Austria approached, for even the diehards of the Progressive party began to see that their opposition was losing them the support not only of the masses, who were filled with patriotic spirit, but also of the middle classes, who had formerly supported them in their fight against Bismarck but who were now becoming convinced that his policies promised to create the national unity that they had always advocated.

This belated realization of the popularity of the government's policy was confirmed by the elections to the Chamber of Deputies which were held after the war had started, for these were an unmistakable defeat for the liberal forces. While the conservatives increased their representation from 38 to 142 deputies, the Progressive party received the smallest vote it had had since the beginning of its existence and was left so weak that even in combination with the moderates, it was still in the minority in the Chamber.

In viewing these results, Bismarck remained true to the ideas that had guided him in 1862. He was gratified by the liberals' defeat but was not anxious to see it go further, for he felt that he would need their support in the further elaboration of his German program. Therefore, he took advantage of the electoral victory to give the liberals a chance to end their opposition without completely losing face. He let it be known that the government was prepared to admit that it had acted in violation of the constitution by operating without a budget since 1862, if, in return, the Chamber would legitimize all past expenditures by an act of indemnity. The liberals seized this opportunity to escape from their predicament—indeed, it was easier to persuade them to agree to the arrangement than it was to win the approval of the king—and, in September 1866, after listening to a royal address that admitted the unconstitutionality but emphasized the necessity of the government's actions, the Chamber voted the indemnity bill by a large majority.

It cannot be denied that this was a capitulation on the part of the Prussian liberals. The socialist leader Wilhelm Liebknecht said scornfully: "Blood appears to be a special elixir, for the angel of darkness [Bismarck] has become the angel of light.... The stigma of violation of the constitution has been washed from his brow, and in its place the halo of glory rings his laurelled head." The liberals' change of front, their acceptance of the actions they had once condemned, and their significant silence about the military reforms during the indemnity debate could not be explained on the grounds of political expediency alone; for many of them had voted for the indemnity with enthusiasm and now showed a distressing eagerness to declare themselves followers of Bismarck and believers in his principles and methods.

Thus, in October 1866, the Progressive party split in two. One group announced their complete acceptance of Bismarck's foreign policy, adding, almost as an afterthought, that in domestic affairs they would carry out "the duties of a vigilant and loyal oppositon." This marked the birth of the National Liberal party, which was to be the chief spokesman of the middle classes in the next generation; but the gulf that separated its principles from those of the liberalism of 1848 and 1862 may be seen in the words of one of its members, who said: "The time of ideals is past.... Politicians must ask themselves today less what is desirable than what is attainable." Middle class liberals had become somewhat ashamed of their earlier history and seemed determined to demonstrate that they were as realistic and as capable of appreciating the importance of facts as anyone else. All of this showed how effective Bismarck has been in debauching the values of his opponents so that they could now forget their former desire for freedom in face of the seductive attractions of force and its achievements.

Two other points may be made in this connection. In the first place, the Prussian victory over Austria, soon to be followed by an even more glorious victory over France, weakened the self-confidence of the middle classes when they compared themselves to the aristocracy. There had been a time when their own economic triumphs and their virtual monopoly of both wealth and culture had made them think of themselves as the future ruling class of Germany and encouraged them to regard the aristocracy with condescension, as a class of titled boobies, penniless backwoodsmen, and boorish brass hats. But the victories on the battlefield, and their own political failure, had transformed this picture. The prestige of the officer corps, and the nobility that supplied it with candidates, rose to an all-time high, and their social and political position was made virtually impregnable. The upper middle class tended henceforth to accept this situation, while at the same time seeking to associate themselves with this now respected and glamorous upper social stratum by a sedulous aping of its manners, its pastimes, and even its vices. Thus, one of the long-term results of the wars of unification was a kind of feudalization of the upper middle class.

Another result, which stemmed from the sharp contrast between military and diplomatic success on the one hand and parliamentary ineffectiveness on the other, was to confirm many Germans in the belief, already widespread after 1848, that nothing much could be expected from parliaments and politicians. This was to impede Germany's progress toward democracy.

The North German Confederation   The war with Austria had destroyed the old Germanic Confederation, and Prussia now gave to the part of the nation that she controlled a new one. In July 1867, after months of planning, drafting, and debate, the constitution of this new body came into effect. The North German Confederation comprised the twenty-two German states that lay north of the Main River. Its president was the king of Prussia, and it had a bicameral legislature: a parliament (*Reichstag*) elected by universal manhood suffrage and possessing budgetary powers and the right to debate and approve or disapprove of all laws, but with no rights of legislative initiative and no effective control over ministers or over foreign and military policy, which were under the king's direction; and a Federal Council (*Bundesrat*) of delegates appointed by the princes of the separate federal states, which could veto laws passed by the Reichstag and had to approve amendments proposed there. Prussian preponderance was assured by the king's right to choose his ministers, by their immunity to Reichstag control, by Prussian control of the army, and by the fact that Prussia had 17 of the 43 seats in the Bundestag, which made it easy for her, by a minimum of negotiation, to get enough additional votes for a majority.

There was nothing about this organization to prevent its being widened to include other states, and it was, of course, the hope of those who voted for it that it would in fact be expanded soon to include Baden, Württemberg, Bavaria, and the part of Hesse-Darmstadt that lay south of the Main. It was true that the governing classes of those southern states did not look forward to union with enthusiasm, and that the Catholic clergy and many Catholic believers as well as democrats, socialists, and professional antimilitarists opposed it bitterly; but it was also undeniable that strong segments of the populations of all these states were eager to join the northern confederation. The National Society (*Nationalverein*), which had been working for a united Germany under Prussian leadership since 1859, had branches in all these states and found no difficulty

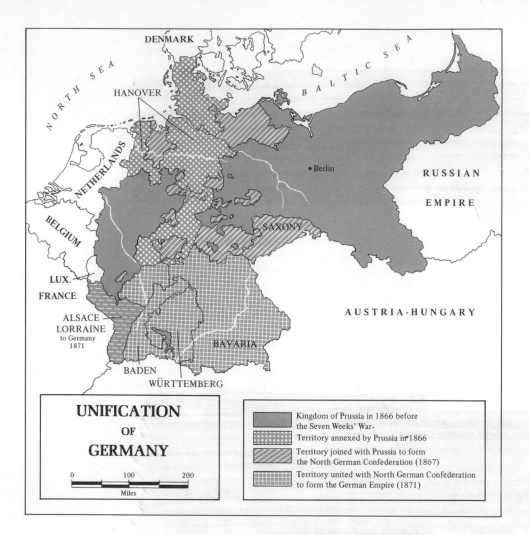

UNIFICATION

OF

GERMANY

0   100   200

Miles

Kingdom of Prussia in 1866 before
the Seven Weeks' War.

Territory annexed by Prussia in 1866

Territory joined with Prussia to form
the North German Confederation (1867)

Territory united with North German Confederation
to form the German Empire (1871)

in making converts. Even people who hated the thought of being under Prussian
leadership had to admit that there was no very attractive alternative. The southern states could not join Austria, for she was permanently excluded from Germany; if they formed a union of their own, it would be dominated by Bavaria,
a prospect that did not seem desirable to the citizens of Baden and Württemberg;
and, if they remained as they were, their economic and political position in
a troubled Europe would be precarious. Slowly, therefore, the sentiment for
fusion with the north grew.

The state of southern opinion was one of Bismarck's main concerns after 1866,
for, although he was determined to complete the unification of the German
nation, he did not want to move in this direction until he was reasonably sure
that a majority of the populations of the southern states would support him.
But this was not, of course, his only concern. France was also interested in
the fate of southern Germany, and Bismarck's policy had to be determined with
Napoleon III in mind.

Chapter 10 THE REORGANIZATION OF EUROPE, 1866–1871

While these tremendous events were taking place in central Europe, the rest of the continent and its neighboring islands remained uninvolved. Only the French government seriously considered intervening in the armed rivalry of the German powers, and, in the end, Napoleon III decided that neutrality offered more tangible advantages—an expectation that was not, as we shall see, fulfilled in the sequel. The attention of the other Great Powers was absorbed by pressing domestic problems, and the lesser states had neither the interest nor the power to be other than neutral.

GREAT BRITAIN FROM PALMERSTON TO GLADSTONE

Nonintervention and Colonial Problems The English appetite for foreign involvements had been thoroughly sated by the unhappy experience of the Crimean War. In the years that followed that conflict, Britain was considerably less active in continental affairs than she had been at any time since 1815. The desire for peace was so strong in both political parties that, when British governments wished to take a stand or express an opinion on foreign problems, they could never be sure of parliamentary or popular support. During the Polish revolt of 1863, the Palmerston-Russell government made statements that came close to being promises of assistance to the rebels; and, during the early stages of the dispute over Schleswig and Holstein, the same government warned the German powers that an attack on Denmark might have serious consequences. But when the tsar refused to be cowed in the first case and Austria and Prussia disregarded the veiled threat in the second, the British government acquiesced in the result, sensing that the country would condone no positive resistance. The *Pall Mall Gazette* was probably speaking for most Englishmen when it said, rather brutally, in 1863: "Englishmen know that most of the Poles they have seen are dirty and that a good many that they have not seen are oppressed; but to go to war for a distant race of unwashed martyrs seems a desperate remedy." If the government was criticized, it was because it had been interested enough in continental events to express any opinion on them at all; and, in a debate in Commons in July 1864, speakers on both sides of the House called for an end of the "policy of meddle and muddle" and a return to the principle of nonintervention—by which was meant, apparently, a policy of leaving Europe strictly alone. In any case, that is the policy that was followed by all parties after 1864; and Britain had nothing to say about the great decisions of 1866 and 1870.

It was, of course, not only the reaction to the debacle in the Crimea that produced this result. Unlike the states in central Europe, Britain possessed important territories and interest overseas, and these were constantly demanding attention. In the years of European transformation, problems arose in India, in the Far East, in the southwestern Pacific, and in North America; and these absorbed some of the interest and energy that might in other times have been turned across the Channel.

The year that followed the end of hostilities in the Crimea, for instance, witnessed a bloody rising against British power in India. Changes in the conditions of service in the Bengal army had for some time been causing discontent among the native troops of the British East India Company; and this was fanned by Indian civilians whose position had been weakened by British reforms and by Brahmin priests who objected to certain administrative decrees that affected religious practices and Hindu custom. Disorders were touched off when the rumor spread among sepoy regiments that the cartridges used in the new Enfield rifle, which had to be bitten before they were inserted in the breech, were greased with the fat of cows and swine and, thus, would pollute Hindus and Moslems who used them. British officers were dilatory in taking measures to reassure the troops and, when three regiments near Calcutta mutinied in January 1857, showed insufficient energy in their attempts to restore order. After killing their officers, the mutineers advanced on Delhi and took and sacked the citadel and the European quarters. These successes inspired risings and the murder of European men, women, and children elsewhere, until about a third of India's total area was under the control of the rebels.

The mutiny, however, had no clearly formulated aims, no central direction, and few talented leaders; and, after the initial shock had passed, the British put down the disorders with firmness and speed, repeatedly demonstrating, as they did so, that numbers were of no avail against good organization and modern weapons. In the last stages of the fighting, for instance, Sir Hugh Rose, with 3000 European troops and somewhat fewer native auxiliaries, captured the town of Jhansi, which had a garrison of 12,000, losing only 345 men in doing so, as against enemy casualties in the thousands; and, during the siege, he detached 2000 of his troops and with them defeated another native army of 22,000.

British authority in India was restored by January 1858, although mopping-up operations continued for some months. The most important result of the mutiny was a deepening of the gulf between the British and their native subjects, which was—as Sir Llewellyn Woodward has written—shown in a tendency on the part of the former to rely more on efficient administration than on the hope that India could be "Westernized" and freed of superstition and prejudice by the introduction of social or political reforms. In the interest of efficiency, the last remnants of the authority of the East India Company were now assumed by the British crown, which took over the company's property and troops and henceforth governed India through a secretary of state and a council of fifteen members.

During the same years, British troops were engaged in the Far East, where Lord Palmerston, as a result of a series of brushes with Chinese authorities, demanded clear recognition of European diplomatic and commercial rights in China and, in conjunction with the French, resorted to force in order to secure compliance with his demands. In 1858, a joint force captured the Taku forts at the mouth of the Peiho River. When the Chinese continued to equivocate, another expedition advanced to Peking, capturing it in 1860 and burning down the emperor's summer palace in retaliation for a Chinese breach of truce. Under this pressure, the imperial government had to yield to the desires of the Western nations and opened Tientsin and a number of other ports to their trade, simultaneously granting residence in Peking to their diplomatic representatives.

Far to the south in the Pacific, both Australia and New Zealand were in these years demanding attention from British legislators. Thanks to the discovery of gold in Victoria and New South Wales in the early 1850s, the population of Australia increased almost threefold between 1850 and 1860, and this growth brought political and administrative problems in its wake. These were solved, for the most part, by the willingness of the home government to grant a large degree of self-government to the colonists, approving locally drafted constitutions for the separate areas until such time as the country should be sufficiently developed for federation. In New Zealand, which had been a crown colony since 1840, the rapid increase of European population in this period (it doubled between 1847 and 1860) led to difficulties with the indigenous Maori people. Disputes over land titles and a general fear on the part of the Maoris that their civilization and tribal organization were threatened by European encroachments led to the outbreak of a war in 1860 that lasted for ten years. The fact that the expenses of the conflict had to be borne, for the most part, by the home government enabled it to bring pressure to bear upon colonial authorities to ameliorate their native policies, particularly with respect to land ownership. Eventually this led to a reconciliation and, by the middle of the 1870s, to Maori participation in the government of the country.

Finally, through much of this period, British attention was diverted from Europe to North America, especially after the outbreak of the Civil War in the United States. This conflict aroused much deeper passions in the British Isles than any of the wars that took place in Europe, partly because it had a direct impact upon the British economy by sharply reducing the imports of raw cotton to the mills of Lancashire and Yorkshire and thus affecting the livelihood of mill operatives in those districts, and partly because it raised political, ideological, and moral issues of the gravest importance. The question of the advisability of recognizing the Confederacy as a nation divided the government and the country. A man's stand upon it was apt to be determined as much by his views on the relative merits of aristocratic and democratic forms of government or the moral justification of slavery as it was by his calculation of the political results of recognition.

In the end, the government followed what it believed to be the will of the people, which was predominately pro-Northern in sympathy, particularly (and this defied all theories of economic determinism) in those areas hit hardest by the cotton shortage. Even so, there were sharp crises between Great Britain and the Union government—over the boarding of a British ship by a Union commander (the famous Trent affair of 1861), over the depredations of commerce raiders built in British yards and sold to the Confederacy, and over other issues—and sometimes war between the two countries seemed not very far away. The British government was well aware that such a conflict would almost certainly lead to an American attack upon Canada. Concern for Canada continued, indeed, even after the American Civil War came to an end. In May 1866 a band of Irish nationalists, most of whom had fought in the Union army and were now organized in a society known as the Fenian Brotherhood, attempted a raid across the Canadian border. It was easily broken up, but it appeared to indicate that Canadian security could not simply be taken for granted.

All of these events across the seas are important in helping to explain Britain's relative abstention from European complications after 1856. But they do not stand alone. There was much going on in England itself in these years.

Party Politics   In the field of politics the most important single event, and the one that aroused the greatest amount of popular passion, was the passage of the second Reform Bill of 1867. But this was preceded, and in an important sense made possible, by a change in the nature and leadership of the political parties.

For some years after the end of the Crimean War, the confusion that had been introduced into British politics by the debate over the repeal of the Corn Laws in the 1840s was perpetuated. The parties had become loose coalitions without internal cohesion and with a continually shifting membership. On the one side, the aristocratic Whigs and the Manchester radicals made very strange bedfellows; on the other, the Tories had not made up their quarrel with the followers of Peel, who wavered between the two groupings. It has been said that it was impossible until the first Parliamentary vote after a general election to tell what the exact state of the parties was. In the circumstances, it is apparent that they would not have sharply differentiated programs. Indeed, one can almost say that they had no programs at all and did not feel any need for them. Constant legislative activity was not yet considered a necessary or desirable aspect of governing the country. The leader of the Tories, Lord Derby, was more interested in racing and Homer than in political issues; and Lord Palmerston, the Whig chieftain, devoted himself to foreign policy almost to the exclusion of everything else.

This situation began to change in the 1860s, largely as a result of the rise

Caricature of Disraeli by Ape (Carlo Pellegrini) in *Vanity Fair,* 1878.

and acceptance of new leaders. The emergence of a modern Conservative party that would appeal to urban voters as well as to the agricultural interest became possible only after the Tory party had accepted Benjamin Disraeli (1804–1881) as Derby's successor. This brilliant but flamboyant figure, the descendant of Spanish Jews who had come to England in 1748, had first made his mark in politics by leading the attack on Peel in 1846; but he was long viewed with suspicion by his colleagues as opportunistic, un-English, and unreliable. Yet, as his political novels show, Disraeli had reflected more deeply than any of his critics on the nature of parties and the character and traditions of British conservatism. Since the early 1850s he had urged Derby to turn his mind to issues that would win the support of the country and had founded a newspaper to spread party ideas; and his effective leadership of the party in the House of Commons gradually overcame opposition and led to his acceptance as Derby's successor in 1868. It was not, however, until the next decade that he was able to show the country what his idea of a Conservative program was.

The transformation of the old Whig-Liberal coalition into the modern Liberal party was largely the result of the efforts of two men, John Bright and William Ewart Gladstone (1809–1898). Bright, a cotton manufacturer and a Quaker, had, with Cobden, led the fight for the repeal of the Corn Laws. After 1847, he was a member of Parliament for Manchester and the foremost leader of the so-called

Manchester School, which stood for the extension of the principle of free trade, the reduction of taxation, a cheaper foreign policy, and the extension of the suffrage to give greater representation to the populous districts of the country as opposed to the rural areas. One of England's greatest orators, he distinguished himself by his opposition to the Crimean War and his spirited advocacy of the Union cause during the American Civil War, which did much to assure Britain's neutrality. Perhaps his greatest service to modern British liberalism was the way in which he combatted Palmerston's prejudice against adding to the statute book by arguing the moral necessity of political and social reform and transforming an essentially negative *laissez-faire* philosophy into a positive creed of improvement.

For all his great gifts, Bright was not the man to lead a modern political party; he held extreme views on too many subjects for that, and his doctrinaire pacifism alone made him seem, to many people, to be impractical. The man who became the first leader of the new Liberal party and who continued in that position until almost the end of the century was Gladstone, who possessed as much eloquence as Bright on the hustings and in Parliament and as highly developed a sense of responsibility and passion for improvement, but was generally considered to be steadier and more reliable. The son of a Liverpool merchant, Gladstone, after a brilliant scholastic record at Oxford, had considered taking holy orders but had turned instead to politics, where he became a follower of Sir Robert Peel and served in that statesman's last ministry as president of the Board of Trade and, later, as secretary for war and the colonies. In the governments of Aberdeen (1852–1855) and Palmerston and Russell (1859–1866), he was appointed chancellor of the exchequer and distinguished himself by carrying forward the free-trade policy, by abolishing the excise on paper—which helped increase the size of the reading public by reducing the price of books and newspapers—by devising an effective postal savings and insurance system that was much used by the working class, and by systematically reducing both direct and indirect taxation. His prestige and popularity were so great by this time that there was little question that he would become leader of the party after Palmerston and Russell had passed from the scene.

The Reform Act of 1867   The new spirit that Gladstone and Bright brought to the Liberal coalition was shown in the campaign that culminated in the passing of the Reform Act of 1867. That there was need for a new law governing the franchise and the allocation of parliamentary seats had been painfully clear for years. In the 1860s, only one adult male out of six had the vote and, although population distribution had profoundly altered since 1832, seats in Parliament had not been redistributed, leaving the metropolitan areas greatly underrepresented. On several occasions proposals for reform had been introduced in Parliament but had died there because of the lack of interest of the older party leaders and their deference to the fear on both sides of the House that to widen the suffrage appreciably would be to invite mob rule and raids on the treasury by an uncultivated and irresponsible electorate.

By the middle of the 1860s the country was in no mood to tolerate this situation any longer. It is probably true that the victory of the North in the American

The disorders in Hyde Park, London, in July 1866, during the agitation for parliamentary reform. The interest these outbreaks aroused in Europe is shown by this French drawing from *L'Illustration,* July 1866.

Civil War contributed to the growth of reform sentiment, for it was widely interpreted as a demonstration of the strength and effectiveness of democratic government. But even without this, it is unlikely that the limited suffrage could have been maintained. Gladstone seems to have realized this in May 1864 when, in a famous speech in Commons, he expressed the belief that "every man who is not presumably incapacitated by some consideration of personal unfitness or of political danger is morally entitled to come within the pale of the constitution." Bright had always favored the wider distribution of political power, and he now became the most impassioned pleader for change, calling upon the English people to repudiate those politicians "who, in every speech they utter, insult the workingmen, describing them as a multitude given up to ignorance and vice," and encouraging them to demonstrate actively for parliamentary action.

The issue was joined in June 1866 when Gladstone, as leader in the House of Commons in the Russell cabinet, introduced a reform bill that was promptly defeated by the combined efforts of the Conservatives and dissident Liberals led by Robert Lowe, who believed that suffrage extension would be a national disaster. This setback caused the fall of the Russell government but actually made the victory of the reform movement inevitable. It angered the Liberal reformers and increased their fervor; and it led to popular disturbances, like one in July 1866, when a reform demonstration that was barred from Hyde Park got out of hand and tore down 1400 yards of park railings. The effective leader of the Conservative government that had replaced the Liberals was Disraeli, and that wily politician decided that it was better to accede to the popular demand, and gain whatever political credit was to be derived from doing so, than to oppose it fruitlessly. It was Disraeli, therefore, who, in a masterly demonstration of parliamentary skill, introduced the Reform Bill of 1867 and secured its passage.

But the real authors of the bill—which started Britain on the road to democracy by doubling the electorate[1]—were Gladstone and Bright. Their efforts inspired the popular demonstrations that persuaded Parliament that further delay would be unwise; and the details of the bill passed were based on features of Gladstone's earlier schemes. The new electorate seemed to realize this, for, in the elections of 1868, it returned the Liberals to power with a commanding majority; and Gladstone, for the first time, became prime minister.

Gladstone's Reforms   Gladstone's first term of office, the so-called Great Ministry, lasted from 1868 to 1874 and was characterized by a burst of legislative activity. This was least notable in the area of factory regulation and labor relations, for government intervention in this field was contrary to liberal principles and working class organizations were not, in any case, actively pushing for reform in these years.[2] But elsewhere the government tried earnestly to supply needs and correct grievances. It passed basic reforms in the fields of civil administration, education, and Irish affairs; it finally satisfied the old Chartist demand for the secret ballot with the Ballot Act of 1872; and it made the first basic changes in the administration of the army since Waterloo (see p. 296).

Two measures that were typical of the Liberal spirit of reform were the civil service reform of 1870 and the Education Act of the same year. The first of these made appointments to most positions in the civil service dependent upon open competitive examinations. The second gave a tremendous stimulus to popular education, although it did not provide the kind of free, compulsory elementary education already available in some continental countries. The voluntary principle was so strong and the fear of state dictation so much a part of the liberal tradition that the Education Act was a tissue of ingenious compromises. It divided the country into school districts, which were treated according to their nature and needs. In those in which adequate elementary school facilities existed, no change was made, except that existing schools had to submit to government inspection and could apply for parliamentary aid. Districts without

[1] The Reform Act of 1867 gave the vote in the boroughs to all householders, whatever the value of their houses, and to all lodgers who occupied quarters for which they paid at least £10 a year. In counties ·it gave the vote to everyone owning property that yielded £5 income a year and to all tenants paying £12 a year. It added 938,000 voters to the existing English and Welsh electorate of 1,056,000. It was followed by an act redistributing parliamentary representation.

[2] For labor conditions and trade-union activities in these years, see pages 268–271.

schools were provided with local school boards, which organized and supervised new schools and levied local taxes to support them. In districts where there was exceptional poverty, the school boards could set up free schools or pay fees for poor students; but, in general, it was expected that parents would pay for their children's tuition. Elementary education was not to become free until 1891.

If the Education Act of 1870 showed the old Liberal faith in private enterprise and the traditional distrust of extending government power, it was also characterized by the suspicion of established religion that was a part of the philosophy of liberalism. Although religious instruction was to be permitted in both voluntary and board schools, in the latter it was to be undenominational; and, in either case, parents could request that their children be excused from religious instruction on grounds of conscience. Another victory over denominationalism was recorded in 1870, when the English universities were made truly national for the first time by the abolition of the religious tests that had reserved them for members of the Church of England.

Gladstone and Ireland   The energies of the first Gladstone ministry were concentrated primarily, however, on the problems of Ireland. That unhappy country's grievances against England were religious, political, and economic. Predominantly Catholic, the Irish objected to having to pay tithes to the Anglican Church in Ireland and resented the fact that there was no Catholic university in the country that was qualified to grant degrees. Politically, they opposed the Act of Union of 1800 and were not at all grateful for the belated Act of Emancipation of 1829 which had given Ireland parliamentary representation by permitting Catholics to sit in the House of Commons. Economically, they were the victims of a situation in which there was not enough land to support a rapidly growing population and no appreciable industrial development to absorb excess population. Those Irish who did not seek escape by emigration subsisted on the yield of miniscule subdivisions leased to them by tenants of English landlords. Most of them lived on one crop, the potato; and, when that failed, as it did in 1845 and 1846, their plight was pitiful in the extreme and deaths from starvation staggering in number. These economic ills could not fairly be laid at the doors of the English, but they were, simply because the English held most of the land; and these grievances were aggravated by others, such as the fact that most tenants had no security of tenure and could be evicted at a moment's notice without any compensation for improvements made during their possession. From the landlord's point of view, the right of eviction without compensation protected him from seeing his land subdivided indefinitely and covered with hovels for which he had to assume ultimate responsibility; but the Irish could not be expected to see things in the same way.

When Gladstone came to office in 1868, he had said, "My mission is to pacify Ireland!" and his first step in this direction was to call for the disestablishment and disendowment of the Anglican Church in Ireland. In winning support for this, the widening of the franchise in 1867 was important, for a good proportion of the new electorate was Nonconformist and not disinclined to measures calculated to weaken the established church. The supporters of the church were wise enough to realize this and, although they fought for generous compensation for the property lost by the Irish church, they permitted the passage of the Disestablishment Act in 1869.

The prime minister turned immediately to the more difficult question of land tenure and, in 1870, secured parliamentary approval for an act designed to give justice to the Irish tenants. The Land Act of 1870 protected them from arbitrary eviction by providing for payment of damages to the tenant in all cases of eviction except when it was the result of nonpayment of rent and by stipulating that compensation must be paid for all improvements. This effected some amelioration of the Irish situation, although loopholes and inequities were soon discovered in the working of the act. At the same time, the act did not go to the root of the Irish difficulty. The tenants wanted security of tenure and fair rents. Gladstone did not satisfy these demands and could not have done so without interfering with the rights of property, which the Liberal party would not have condoned.

Neither these reforms nor Gladstone's avowed intention of giving adequate facilities to Ireland for higher education,[3] therefore, appeased the Irish people; and their agitations continued to be a source of concern to British governments until World War I.

RUSSIA UNDER ALEXANDER II

Nonintervention and Imperial Expansion   The course of Russian history in these years bore a marked similarity to that of British history. Russia's abstention from European affairs was also determined by reaction to the Crimean adventure, by colonial concerns, and by the urgency of domestic affairs. As we have noted (see p. 165), both her losses in the war and her resentment over the Black Sea clauses of the Treaty of Paris inclined Russia to a policy of watchful neutrality as the duel for supremacy in central Europe proceeded.

As in the case of Britain, this abstention was accompanied, and to some extent caused, by a shift of interest to areas far from the European center. Russian governments were discovering the Pacific area in these years and beginning to realize the potential significance of expansion in that direction. Even before the Crimean War, Russian traders had begun to make inroads into Chinese territory in the valley of the Amur River; in 1854 an expedition led by Nicholas Muravëv, the governor-general of Eastern Siberia, founded the city of Khabarovsk on that river. During the Chinese difficulties with the British and French in the late 1850s (see p. 223), Muravëv extended his holdings; other expeditions established coastal settlements and founded the city of Vladivostok in 1860; and the Russian government forced the Chinese government to recognize these acquisitions and to accord to Russia the privileges given the other powers in the treaties of Tientsin and Peking. In the decade that followed, the Russians also occupied the province of Kuldja in Chinese Turkestan and began their settlement of Sakhalin Island, which was confirmed by treaty with Japan in 1875.

[3] A bill for this purpose was introduced by Gladstone in February 1873 and was defeated by Parliament.

As this new interest in expansion in the Chinese mainland was pursued, the Russian government, for economic and political reasons, decided to liquidate its holdings in North America. Thus, in March 1867, Russian rights and properties in what is now Alaska were transferred by treaty to the United States for a sum of $7,200,000. In the light of Alaska's present strategic and economic importance, it is interesting to note that the purchase was unpopular in the United States and the sale unregretted in Russia.

Along the southern borders of the Russian empire, the outward thrust continued in these years also. By 1864, Russian troops had put down the stout resistance of the Caucasian and Circassian tribes and made good their claim to all of the western shore of the Caspian Sea north of Persia. In the same year a major drive was begun against the Moslem khanates of Kokand, Khiva, and Bokhara; and forces led by Generals Cherniaev, Kaufman, and Skobelev finally subjugated and annexed them, although the process was not complete until the middle 1870s.

The economic promises sometimes made to justify this expansion were never fully realized. Even so, expansion in central Asia, like that in the Far East, was popular in court circles, among the military (for obvious reasons) and among the informed public, to many of whom it appeared to offset the humiliation caused by the Crimean defeat. Its very popularity reinforced the tendency of the country to remain aloof from European affairs.

The Great Reforms   While these important territorial conquests were being made, the social and political structure of Russia was being profoundly affected by a series of reforms even more comprehensive than those introduced in England. After the Crimean War, Russia seemed—as the anarchist Prince Kropotkin was to write in his memoirs—to "awaken from the heavy slumber and the terrible nightmare of Nicholas I's reign." The new ruler, Alexander II (1855–1881), could hardly be described as a liberal or a believer in reform for reform's sake, but he was shrewd enough to realize that there are times when change is imperative. He knew that the imperial regime had lost prestige as a result of the recent military defeat; and he feared that this might encourage groups with grievances to think that the time had come for them to take matters into their own hands and seek redress by revolutionary means. In particular, he seems to have feared that this might be the attitude of the peasants, and it was his hope that action by them might be forestalled if the government took the initiative in reforming the conditions of their life.

The great mass of the Russian peasantry were still, to all intents and purposes, slaves. They belonged to landowners who could dictate the most intimate details of their personal life, inflict corporal punishment upon them, even sell them or raise money by mortgaging them (in ways described in detail in Gogol's masterpiece *Dead Souls*). The peasants worked the landlord's soil for him with their own tools and performed other services in return for a living that was never much more than bare subsistence; and they had no authority to whom they could appeal against the landlord's decrees. Their resentment against these conditions flared up sporadically in the form of peasant riots; and the increasing frequency of these gave some substance to Alexander's fears. During the Crimean

War, for instance, when militia units were raised all over Russia, peasant disorders became so serious that in some places whole regiments of troops, with artillery, had to be sent to quell them. Apart from this, serfdom as an institution could hardly be defended on moral grounds, and there was increasing reason to suppose that it was not even defensible on economic ones. At a time when conditions abroad favored Russia's developing an export trade in wheat, the transition to large-scale grain farming was held back by a system in which the majority of the landlords knew nothing themselves about farming and the majority of the serfs employed traditional and uneconomic methods.

In March 1856 Alexander announced to an assembly of nobles in Moscow that "the existing order of ruling over living souls cannot remain unchanged." "It is better," he continued, "to abolish bondage from above than to wait for the time when it will begin to abolish itself from below." These words inaugurated five years of investigation, negotiation, and formulation, during which the nobility, predominantly opposed to the projected change, slowly yielded to imperial pressure while at the same time fighting for the highest possible compensation for the rights they were going to relinquish. Plans were worked out on the local level and filtered through an elaborate committee framework until finally, in March 1861, the coordinated plan, which one writer has called the greatest single piece of state-directed social engineering in modern European history before the twentieth century, was promulgated by decree.

The emancipation edicts ended the personal dependence of the serf upon the landlord and made him, legally at least, a person who could move about freely, enter contractual relations, change his occupation, and enjoy other freedoms. These liberties, however, were restricted by the fact that the greatest number of serfs, after 1861 as before, lived in village communes which exercised considerable power over them. What land they received they held through the commune, which assumed a collective responsibility for seeing that redemption payments were made to the nobility and taxes paid to the government. The commune carefully supervised the activities of the individual householder, restricting not only his freedom to dispose of the produce of his land as he saw fit but even his personal mobility. In comparison with other members of society, therefore, the peasant remained subject to significant disabilities for some years.

A basic assumption of the reform was that the liberated peasants (with the exception of those who had been household servants) would be given land to support them, but that, in order not to impoverish the nobility, they should pay for it over a period of years. In general, the nobility received more equitable treatment than the peasants. Kropotkin wrote later:

> For many landlords, the liberation of the serfs was an excellent money transaction. Thus, land which my father, in anticipation of the emancipation, sold in parcels at the rate of eleven roubles, was now estimated at forty roubles in the peasants' allotments—that is three and a half times above its market value—and this was the rule in all our neighborhood; while in my father's Tambòv estate, on the prairies, the *mir*—that is the village community—rented all his land for twelve years, at a price which represented twice as much as he used to get from that land by cultivating it with servile labor.

It is true that peasants who lived on estates of the imperial family or on state domains received generous allotments with moderate charges. Elsewhere, however, it has been estimated that close to half of the peasant allotments were too small to provide subsistence living, and in many cases the loss of the use of woods and pastures caused additional hardships. It should also be noted that most of the peasants regarded the necessity of making any payment for their allotments unjust; and it is indicative of the disillusionment that followed promulgation of the decrees that peasant disturbances were resumed within a very short period.

It should not be assumed that all or even most of the landlords were as fortunate as Kropotkin's father. Thousands of middling gentry—those who had between a hundred and a hundred and fifty serfs—had been in debt before the emancipation. They now lost their free labor supply and their debts were paid out of their redemption fees before they received them. This meant that they had inadequate capital for adjustment to the new conditions; and this was soon reflected in hardship and resentments that were not without political significance.

The emancipation of the peasants brought other reforms in its train, although these did not live up to the desires of the liberal nobles and the intellectuals, who dreamed of a national assembly like those in Western countries. The tsar had no intention of establishing anything of the kind (he was alarmed by the very thought that the emancipation decree should have aroused political expectations), but in January 1864, although with some reluctance, he did issue a statute instituting measures of regional self-government. This established assemblies called *zemstvos* in all counties and provinces of the empire. Country zemstvos were elected by property holders of three categories: proprietors, townsmen, and peasants; provincial zemstvos were elected by county zemstvos. The amount of peasant participation, because of the ignorance of the peasant mass and the elaborateness of the electoral procedure, was not great.

The zemstvos were supposed to concern themselves with local affairs like the upkeep of roads and bridges, health and sanitation, maintenance of public institutions, promotion of trade and agriculture, education and relief of poverty, and the like. They were always kept on a very tight financial rein by the imperial government and could not, therefore, fulfill all of their assigned functions adequately. But, in a country in which centralized and bureaucratic methods had long been normal government procedure, the institution of these local and provincial assemblies was a first step toward representative government; the zemstvos built up public services to a height previously unknown in Russia; and, despite their inadequacies, they were popular.

The third significant reform carried through in the early years of Alexander II affected the judicial system of the country. The disorder, inefficiency, and corruption of Russia's courts had long been known and, during the reign of Nicholas I, a committee had been set up to study the need for reform and draft appropriate legislation. New impetus was given to this committee's efforts by Alexander II; in 1862 its basic ideas were widely publicized and discussed; and in November 1864 they were incorporated into statute form.

The principles underlying the reform were those long honored in Western countries: equality before the law, trial by jury, uniformity of procedure, irremovability of judges (except for misconduct in office), and the like. These were announced in ringing tones to a country long used to executive trials and star-chamber methods. At the same time, a rigorous and systematic simplification of the court system was announced, with minor cases to be tried by justices of the peace and more important ones in a hierarchy of courts.

The promise inherent in all this was never fully kept. For one thing, the simplification of the court system was handicapped by the continued existence of military, ecclesiastical, and (for peasant affairs) township courts. For another, the individual legal rights so proudly announced were vitiated to some extent by the crown's retention of the right not only to pardon but to increase sentences and to take executive action to prevent crime or illegal activities. Finally, the system was operated by ministers of justice who were opposed to the spirit that animated the reform and who had no great respect for the principle of independence of judges. Despite these faults, however, the new system was superior to the old.

THE SHOWDOWN BETWEEN FRANCE AND GERMANY

Napoleon III and the German Question   While the two great powers on the periphery of Europe busied themselves with domestic reforms and the Austrian empire underwent a fundamental reorganization as a result of the defeat suffered in 1866, relations between France and Prussia deteriorated rapidly. This was understandable. The Prussian victory over Austria and the subsequent establishment of the North German Confederation had simultaneously electrified advocates of German unification and dismayed French patriots, who regarded a united Germany as contrary to the interest of their country. It was unlikely that Prussia would refrain from attempting, sooner or later, to complete the process so far advanced in 1866; it was inevitable that French public opinion would oppose further increases of Prussian strength.

In the years after 1866, Napoleon III seems to have tried to appease French patriots without seriously violating his professed faith in the principle of nationalities. He attempted to do this by seeking to persuade the Prussians to promise him compensation for any advance beyond the Main River, in the form of territorial grants in areas to which France had some historical claims, such as the Saarland, the Grand Duchy of Luxembourg, and even Belgium. These efforts were productive of nothing but bad feeling. In April 1867, for instance, after elaborate and protracted negotiations, Bismarck informed the French government that German public opinion would not tolerate France's acquisition of Luxembourg, and there was an ugly crisis in which serious consequences were averted only by an international conference that neutralized the disputed area.

After this rude blow, Napoleon's opposition to further Prussian growth hardened, and he sought to devise effective barriers to check it. His diplomats redoubled their activities at the courts of the German states south of the Main, seeking to inflame the traditional southern prejudice against Prussia. Simultaneously, conversations were begun with the Austrian and Italian governments with the intention of creating a triple alliance that might restrain Prussia's ambition or, failing that, defeat her in war.

Like so many of the schemes of Napoleon's declining years, these came to nothing. The emperor was a sick man, suffering from kidney trouble. Lord Acton, a contemporary, wrote that he "made his preparations languidly, like a man in whom pain has extinguished resolution and activity and hopefulness, and he took so much time that he never concluded." Yet, even if he had been in excellent health, it is not likely that his schemes would have succeeded. Some antipathy to Prussia still existed in Baden, Württemberg, and especially Bavaria, but it was not strong enough to serve French interests and, in 1870, it was to be swept away by patriotic enthusiasm. As for the negotiations in Vienna and Florence, they were—despite the sympathy for France that existed in those capitals—doomed from the start. Even if the Austrian Germans were willing to contemplate a new war against Prussia to regain the position lost in 1866 (and this was doubtful), the Hungarians were inflexibly opposed to it, for the simple reason that, if successful, it might lead to the loss of the powers gained by the Magyars by the Compromise of 1867 (see p. 216). And even though many Italians were grateful to Napoleon for his services to their country, they were unwilling to commit themselves to go to war for a government whose troops still denied them the possession of Rome. Since Napoleon dared not alienate Catholic opinion in France by withdrawing the garrison that had protected the pope since 1849, the Italian alliance, like the Austrian one, went aglimmering.

Meanwhile, in Prussia, Bismarck had watched the French negotiations and had insured himself against the unlikely chance of their succeeding by making a secret agreement with Russia. In return for a promise of Prussian support in the event of any Austro-Hungarian threat to Russian interests in southeastern Europe, the Russian government promised, in March 1868, to concentrate enough troops in Galicia to keep the Austrians neutral in a Franco-Prussian war.

This does not mean that Bismarck was planning either a move south or a war against France at this time. For one thing, he was still too uncertain of the state of South German opinion to force the pace of German unification. For another, he had some hopes, as he saw the French government being liberalized, that the new ministers in Paris would eventually reconcile themselves to the inevitable and greet German unification with no more than verbal protests—again, provided he did not force the pace unduly.

Bismarck's willingness to wait, however, was shaken by the French plebiscite of May 1870 (p. 179). This gave the emperor such a resounding majority that the North German chancellor feared the results might encourage the imperial regime to be more, rather than less, intransigent. If this were so, nothing was to be gained by a policy of patience. Bismarck decided to go on the offensive.

The Hohenzollern Candidature   Since 1868, when a revolution in Spain had deposed Queen Isabella II, a provisional government in Madrid had been searching for a successor to the throne. The candidate most favored by the government was Prince Leopold of Hohenzollern, a distant relative of King William I of Prussia; but Bismarck, out of deference to French feeling, had discouraged the first offers to the prince, and he continued to oppose the project as long as he thought there was a possibility of a conciliatory French attitude in German affairs. When the results of the French plebiscite of May 1870 made this appear unlikely, the chancellor revived the succession question; and, on July 2, 1870, it was announced that Prince Leopold had accepted the Spanish throne.

Firm but prudent diplomacy on the part of France might have turned this stroke of the chancellor's against him, and for a moment it looked as if this was going to be the result. The French foreign minister, the Duke of Gramont, announced to the Chamber on July 6 that the presence of a German prince "on the throne of Charles V" would constitute an intolerable derangement of the European balance; and a few days later Benedetti, the French ambassador to Prussia, talked with the Prussian king at Ems and remonstrated so eloquently that William insisted that Leopold renounce the intention of going to Spain as king. But Gramont was not content with this substantial success: he wanted—as he admitted to the Austrian ambassador—"a political triumph that will efface the memory of previous retreats"; he now insisted that King William give assurances that Leopold's candidacy would not be renewed in the future.

In a further interview with Benedetti at Ems, the king refused courteously, but firmly, to give such promises. He then telegraphed a description of the conversation to Bismarck, who released the telegram to the press, after first abbreviating its text in such a way as to make his monarch's language much curter and the rebuff to Benedetti much sharper than they had, in fact, been. The publication of this Ems dispatch and the resultant elaboration upon it in sensational newspapers on both sides of the border created an atmosphere in which reason and compromise were impossible. Under the pressure of inflamed Parisian mobs and a belligerent Chamber, the French government declared war on Prussia on July 19.

The Franco-Prussian War   In his memoirs Bismarck claims that he had always believed "that a Franco-German war must take place before the construction of a united Germany could be realized." If he had in fact believed this—and one cannot always trust the veracity of Bismarck's recollections—he was proved right even before the firing began, for the first result of the French declaration was the decision of the South German states to throw their lot in with Prussia and to send troops against France.

Thanks to this and to superior efficiency in mobilization, the German armies at the outset of the war outnumbered the French nearly two to one. They also had the advantage of a better supply system, which provided the troops with the means to fight, which was not always true on the French side, as well as a superior staff system, and a high command whose war plan had long been in readiness and was now put into effect with speed and efficiency. Napoleon, in the last week before the fighting began, improvised a plan for diversionary amphibious operations in the Baltic and an offensive of massed armies against southern Germany. Before the widely dispersed French reserves could be concentrated for any such operations, however, the Prussians rammed their way through the Lorraine gap and, after some hard-fought battles in which they suffered greater casualties than the French, got between Paris and the two main French armies, those of Marshals Bazaine and MacMahon. Bazaine was forced back eastward and bottled up in the fortress of Metz. When MacMahon's army, which had now been joined by the emperor, tried to come to his aid, it was surrounded at Sedan on the Belgian frontier and hammered by artillery fire until it surrendered.

The news that Napoleon III and over 100,000 troops were in Prussian hands brought the imperial regime crashing to the ground. In Paris a republican regime was organized with General Trochu as president; and, through the exertions of Léon Gambetta (1838–1882), who made his way from Paris to the provinces by balloon, new armies were raised along the Loire and an attempt was made to prosecute the war. These raw levies fought valiantly throughout the autumn and early winter months, but the heart of their resistance was broken when Bazaine surrendered his still very substantial forces at Metz in October. When Paris, besieged since September, finally capitulated in January—after every scrap of food in the city, including the animals in the zoo and the rats in the garrets, had been eaten, and the trees in the Champs Élysées and the Bois de Boulogne had been cut down for fuel—the armies in the provinces gave up too.

Before peace could be concluded, the Germans insisted that France be represented by a government that could speak for the whole nation; and, in February 1871, elections were held for a National Assembly, which then elected Adolphe Thiers as chief of the executive power and authorized him to negotiate with the enemy. Thiers discovered that the Germans were in no mood for bargaining. He was forced to promise the payment within three years of a war indemnity of five billion francs and to accept a German army of occupation until the sum was paid. In addition, his country had to cede to the victor all of Alsace and most of Lorraine with their potentially rich deposits of iron ore and their flourishing textile industry. Thiers' diplomatic skill was able to ameliorate these terms

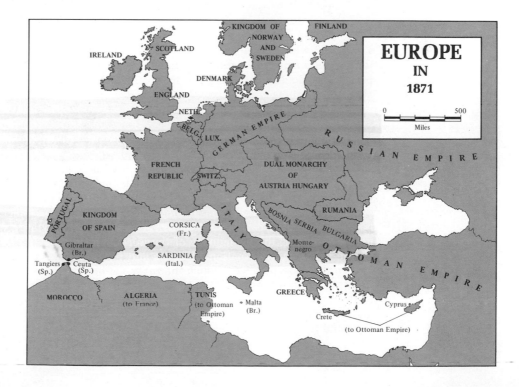

in some details—he saved the fortress of Belfort for France—but the Treaty of Frankfurt of May 1871 was, even so, a heavy burden on France and one whose memory was to plague the peace of Europe for two generations.

The Reorganization of Central Europe   The battles in France settled more than the fate of the Bonaparte dynasty; they completed the unification of both Germany and Italy. The fellowship in arms between the northern and southern German states was given political substance in January 1871 when the king of Bavaria was persuaded by Bismarck to urge the king of Prussia to revive the German empire and assume its crown. King William, Prussian to the very marrow, acted as if he resented the suggestion and was conspicuously cool for some time toward its real author; but he gave way and, on January 18 in the Hall of Mirrors in the Palace of Versailles, was proclaimed emperor of a Germany that now stretched from the Baltic to the Inn.

Meanwhile, the Italian government had taken advantage of the war to send their troops into Rome. It was not the most impressive way to secure a national capital; and the poet Carducci was later to write a scornful poem in which the geese on Capitoline Hill were heard to say

> Hush! Hush! Who goes there in the light
>   of the moon?

and were answered

> Geese of the Capitol, be silent!
> It is I, Italy, the grand and united!

The pope, who retired behind the walls of the Vatican, refused to recognize the pretensions of the Italian government, which meant that in the subsequent period Italy had to contend with the hostility of ardent Catholics at home and abroad as well as with all its other problems.

Back in the days when he first came to power, Napoleon III had dreamed of redrawing the map of Europe on national lines. That had now been done; but, although he had contributed strongly to the final result, he had gained none of the profit he thought would accrue from this accomplishment and had, instead, lost his throne. The new Europe was in any case different from the one he had imagined. Its reorganization on national lines had not increased the interdependence and harmony of nations, as Mazzini and other nationalists of an earlier age had believed. The methods used to effect the changes in the map had left a heritage of bitterness between the continental states, while simultaneously showing the inadequacy of the European Concert and throwing doubt on the validity of international treaties and public law. Nothing better demonstrated the disrespect with which international obligations were now held than the unilateral abrogation of the Black Sea clauses of the Treaty of 1856 by the Russian government, an action taken in the middle of the Franco-Prussian war and accepted by the other powers because they were powerless, or disinclined, to forbid it.

PART THREE
1871-1914

GENERAL
OBSERVATIONS

Perhaps the most striking aspect of the period that opened in 1871 was that, at its beginning, liberalism was in the ascendancy whereas, at its end, it was in full retreat. In the 1870s the most widely accepted economic and political ideas were those that had been elaborated by champions of the middle class like Richard Cobden, John Stuart Mill, Benjamin Constant, Wilhelm von Humboldt. The prevailing economic philosophy was that of free trade, and, since 1860, most countries had been following the British and French example and scaling down their tariff schedules. The strongest political parties in Great Britain, Germany, Belgium, Italy, Switzerland, and Spain and strong ones in the Netherlands, Denmark, and Sweden either called themselves Liberal or held to such traditionally liberal tenets as constitutional parliamentary government based on limited suffrage, freedom of opportunity and protection of individual liberties against arbitrary power, religious toleration, *laissez-faire* economics, national self-determination, and, in general, the solution of problems by rational and orderly means. Even in France, which had a republican government based on universal suffrage, the largest organized political grouping was a moderate middle class party that held to most of these same beliefs; and we have already seen that tsarist Russia was by no means impervious to their influence either.

By the end of the period, this situation was greatly changed. Nations that had subscribed to the free-trade policy in the 1850s and 1860s reversed themselves in the 1880s and 1890s, and tariff protectionism had once more become the order of the day. The great liberal parties had either fallen to pieces—as was true in Germany—or lost strength in comparison to the conservative and the new working class parties. And, most important, liberalism as a philosophy had lost its cohesiveness and much of its relevance to the problems of the age.

This last point requires some elucidation. Back in the 1850s, and even in the 1870s, it was possible for an intelligent man to subscribe to all the creeds of liberalism—individualism, competition, *laissez faire,* suspicion of big government, and the like—without feeling any inconsistency. By the 1880s this was no longer easy. The prevailing economic tendencies seemed to favor not individualism and competition but combination, for this was the age of trusts, monopolies, and cartels. Industrialists who in an earlier age would have insisted that the government stay out of business now argued that it was the duty of government to support it by tariffs, subventions, convenient corporation laws, the acquisition of new markets in colonial areas, and the like. They frequently sought political support for their new ideas from parties of the right, which, because they had traditionally believed in a strong active government, were more open to these ideas than the liberal parties; and this explains both the transformation of the conservative parties into parties of big business (or, as in Germany, into allies of heavy industry) and the waning strength of liberal parties.

Simultaneously, men whose liberalism centered around a sincere belief in the necessity of protecting the individual from arbitrary power and who, for that very reason, believed in *laissez faire* and opposed the growth of government functions began to suspect that the real threat to the individual was the tendency toward combination in business and that only the government could protect the individual, by regulating the operations of the great eco-

nomic combines. These men, when their new belief proved unpopular with their former political associates, were apt to turn to the new labor parties which *did* believe in government regulation, with another resultant loss to the liberal center. This latter tendency is shown clearly in the career of John Stuart Mill; in his classic *Essay on Liberty* (1859), he still regarded strong government as a threat to the free individual, but by the end of his life he was drifting rapidly in the direction of socialism.

The economic tendencies of the time, then, by forcing men to revise their views on the role of government, inevitably weakened the persuasiveness of the creeds of liberalism and the strength of liberal parties. This in turn encouraged two things: on the one hand, a polarization of politics, a division into extremes, which was the inevitable result of the decline of the moderate parties of the middle, and was to reach its most dangerous form in the twentieth century; and, on the other, a growing acceptance of big government, the welfare state, and collectivism in general.

Another development that should be noted in this period was the weakening of the liberal attitude in politics, which may be defined as a belief in the efficacy of human reason to solve all of man's problems. In contrast to this faith, all of the prevailing intellectual tendencies seemed either to deify violence or to emphasize the irrational factors in human motivation. This was true of Social Darwinism, which attempted to justify international war, colonial competition, and domestic strife as natural manifestations of the struggle for existence, as well as of Marxism and anarchism, which emphasized class struggle and (in the case of the latter) the use of violence for its own sake. It was largely true also of the newly developed behavioral sciences (sociology, anthropology, and the like), which tended to regard man as a statistic[1] or as a being capable only of acting as a member of a class or group or other category, and, at the end of the period, of both Bergsonian philosophy, with its emphasis upon the *élan vital,* and Freudian psychology, with its insistence that man is moved not by reason but by instinctual forces that he finds it difficult to control. The wide acceptance of the assumptions of these movements wore away the old liberal conviction, expressed in the writings of both Mill and Samuel Smiles, that man is a responsible being capable of improving himself by his own efforts and solving his difficulties with his own mind.

At a time when difficult new social problems were being created by the ballooning of European population (which increased by more than 30 percent between 1870 and 1900), by the continued drift to the cities (the majority of the British nation were born in cities after 1871 and the number of German cities with more than 100,000 inhabitants increased from eight in 1870 to forty-one in 1900), and by not infrequent crises of unemployment resulting from business depressions, the weakening of reliance upon reason was not a hopeful sign. For if reason could not be applied to these problems, how could they be solved? The answer that was given in more than one country was violence, applied either at those points where social distress led to agitation or at more remote points, outside the country or in distant colonial areas, where it might divert the attention of the masses from the troubles that beset them.

In these circumstances, the domestic politics of the European nations came to be marked by an increasing amount of class conflict and the relations among them by a degree of insecurity unknown in the past. In international affairs, these were, for the most part, years that were free from war, but they could hardly be described as years of peace. The mutual suspicions left over from the wars of the 1860s were heightened now by the increased interstate friction that resulted from the return from free trade to protection and from the resultant tariff wars and competition for markets overseas. They could hardly help but be increased further by the tendency just alluded to, that of seeking to solve domestic discontent by a search for impressive triumphs in the foreign field.

Other characteristic features of this period contributed to the uneasiness of the powers in their relations with each other. The new custom of forming permanent alliances in peacetime—a practice begun in the 1870s—had the effect, in the end, of splitting Europe up into two great leagues held in an uneasy balance that was always threatening to, and finally did, break down. And equally important in increasing tension and insecurity were the important changes in military administration that occurred in this period.

With the exception of Great Britain, all of the major European states

---

[1] Benjamin Jowett, the famous Master of Balliol College, Oxford, once said: "I have always felt a certain horror of political economists since I heard one of them say that he feared the famine in Ireland would not kill more than a million people, and that would scarcely be enough to do much good".

adopted universal military service after 1871, and military expenditures and the numbers in the standing army and reserves soon dwarfed the figures of the earlier period. In the conditions of competition that ensued, the lengthening by one nation of its term of service, with an implied increase in its number of effectives, became a matter of international importance, and the addition of a battalion to each regiment in Germany could cause consternation and debate in France. Moreover, all nations now copied the German general staff system, which had proven its worth in 1870–1871, and the continent was soon crowded with pseudo-Moltkes and latter-day Scharnhorsts. The chief occupation of such staffs was the scientific preparation of war plans for all possible eventualities, a task that required the combined efforts of thousands of specialists in intelligence, topography, communications, ordnance, transportation, and logistics, to say nothing of the labors of the military attachés abroad and the agents they employed to detect the plans of other powers. Once these formidable machines were put in motion, it was inevitable that they would arrogate to themselves policy-making functions. In all countries, the leaders of the armed forces were consulted when difficult decisions of foreign policy had to be made; in some countries, they tended to make decisions themselves of which the foreign office and government were only dimly aware but which had the effect of destroying their freedom of action in moments of crisis. Questions of peace or war tended thus to be settled on the basis of military expediency.

None of this would have mattered if there had existed other means or other organizations to check the destructive forces of the age, but there were not. The liberal parties were not alone in losing strength in these years; no political or social or religious organization proved capable in 1914 of asserting the claims of reason against the drift into chaos. For that matter, the most important religion of this age—stronger than liberalism, stronger than the varieties of socialism that will be described below, stronger even than organized Christianity—was nationalism, a blatant, uncritical, assertive nationalism that was propagated in the public schools, in the yellow journals, which invented jingoism for the new and credulous reading public produced by those schools, and even in the lectures of university professors. Popular tribunes like Heinrich von Treitschke, Maurice Barrès, and Charles Maurras preached that the end of all state action should be "the exclusive pursuit of national policies, the absolute maintenance of national integrity, and the steady increase of national power"; and their eloquence persuaded countless numbers of otherwise reasonable people to regard foreigners as dangerous and untrustworthy enemies against whom stringent action was necessary and commendable. The existence of a new literate but gullible reading public, capable of being played upon by the apostles of integral nationalism, was one of the complications of the age. Statesmen who sincerely wanted to preserve peace had to spend unceasing effort to inform and direct this impressionable public opinion. Politicians interested only in holding their jobs were tempted to tickle the ears of the groundlings, thus aiding and abetting the ugly nationalism of the age.

That the period which extended from 1871 to 1914 was one filled with impressive achievements in many fields cannot be denied. One need only think of the tremendous improvement in the material conditions of living, the achievement in most countries of systems of free compulsory elementary education, the steady progress of science, which was marked by such notable triumphs as the promulgation of the electron theory and the discovery of radioactivity, or the great increases in medical knowledge, which found immediate reflection in longer life and the decline of infant mortality.

In the field of the arts, the accomplishments of this period were hardly less distinguished. The least cultivated elements of the vastly expanded reading public doubtless found their artistic tastes satisfied by the popular newspapers (like *Le Petit Journal* of Paris and *The Daily Mail* of London, which consistently sold more than a million copies daily by providing a varied literary fare for its subscribers) or by family journals with names like *Tit Bits* and *Die Gartenlaube*. But more serious readers could choose from a literature varied enough to suit every taste. This included the work of such masters of psychological realism as Tolstoy, Zola, Thomas Hardy, the Berlin novelist Theodor Fontane, and the Norwegian Björnson; the historical romances of Robert Louis Stevenson, Conrad Ferdinand Meyer, and Henryk Sienkiewicz, and tales of adventure in exotic lands by Rudyard Kipling, H. Rider Haggard, and Pierre Loti; H. G. Wells's stories of science and future worlds and A. Conan Doyle's reports on the exploits of Sherlock Holmes (who became a European figure in the 1880s); the elaborately styled novels of George Meredith, Henry James, and George Moore; and the first works of such writers of the postwar period as John Galsworthy, Thomas Mann, and Marcel Proust. In the field of the drama, the most popular productions continued to be of the type made fashionable by Dumas, but at the beginning of the 1880s naturalism began to conquer the stage. The most profound influence in this respect was that wielded by the Norwegian Henrick Ibsen, whose attacks upon the conventions of the romantic drama affected the work of a whole generation and were reflected in the plays of Hauptmann and Sudermann in Germany, Chekhov in Russia, Schnitzler in Austria, and, above all, Ibsen's truest follower, George Bernard Shaw, whose assaults upon bourgeois morality, romantic idealism, and the heroic and the sublime equaled those of his master in vigor.

In painting and in poetry the most significant movement was that of impressionism, which Arnold Hauser has suggested was an artistic reflection of the new dynamism and new feeling for speed and change that were introduced into European life by modern technology. In painting impressionism was characterized by an attempt to portray reality not as something existing but as something in the process of becoming or ceasing to be; and every impressionistic picture, whether it was painted by Degas or by Toulouse-Lautrec, was the portrayal of a moment in time in such a way that it enabled the observer to sense the unceasing processes of growth and decline. In the age of rapid urbanization, impressionism was art for the city dweller, who lived amidst impermanence and sensation. The poets of impressionism sought equally to express reality in terms of fleeting sensations, momentary moods, and vague perceptions; and this made it more difficult for the general reader to understand the poetry of Verlaine and Mallarmé, or Detlev von Liliencron and Rilke, than it had been to understand that of Lamartine or Eichendorff.

Impressionism affected the philosophy as well as the art of the last years of this period. Both Freud's psycho-

"Bar at the Folies Bèrgeres," 1881–1882, by Edouard Manet. (Courtauld Institute, London)

analysis and Bergson's philosophy of vitalism are intimately connected with it, for the Viennese doctor's notions would be incomprehensible without impressionism's view of reality as composed of constantly changing moods, impressions, and ideas, and Bergson's emphasis upon the spiritual as opposed to the mechanical forces in life was informed by impressionism's implicit denial of materialism as a philosophy. With respect to this last point, it may be noted that, in the years immediately preceding the outbreak of World War I, Bergson's philosophy had great influence not only upon introspective novelists and poets like Alain-Fournier, Francis Jammes, André Gide and Stefan George but upon others, like Charles

Péguy, Romain Rolland, Jules Romains and Gabriele d'Annunzio, who abandoned the passive art for art's sake attitude of earlier impressionist writers and turned to a new activism that sought to change society.

In music the giants of the period were still Wagner, Gounod, and Verdi, whose work had begun before 1870. The last of these was to grow in stature as a result of his inspired collaboration with Arrigo Boito, which was to produce *Otello* in 1887 and *Falstaff* in 1893. But there were new names also. Tchaikovsky, Moussorgsky, Rimski-Korsakov, Smetana, Dvorak, and, in the last years before the war, Enescu made the folk music of eastern Europe known to the whole continent, while Grieg and

Sibelius accustomed audiences to novel Nordic strains. Italy gave the world the music of Leoncavallo, Mascagni, Respighi, and that master of operatic writing Puccini, whose *Manon Lescaut* (1893) and *La Bohême* (1896) aroused lachrymose enthusiasm all over the Western world. For French music this was a golden age, introduced by the premiere of Bizet's *Carmen* in 1875 (an event that led Nietzsche to cry delightedly, "We must Mediterranean-ize music!"); marked in the years that followed by the great achievements of Saint-Saëns and Gabriel Fauré and Jules Massenet, whose *Manon* (1884) is the most French of all operas; and reaching a new height in the year 1902 with the first presentation of Maurice Ravel's *Pavane pour une enfante défunte* and of Claude Debussy's opera *Pelléas et Mélisande,* a work which, in the words of Ernest Walker, is "the summit of musical impressionism, catching every faint nuance of the words, always suggesting rather than saying, but always tense and direct and full of throbbing beauty." In Austria and Germany the majestic blending of the classical and romantic symphonic styles that had begun with Beethoven was continued by Brahms in the first years of the period and by Gustav Mahler in the last; while in opera Wagner's penchant for the grandiose and sensational was carried further by Richard Strauß, whose first operas, *Salome* (1905) and *Elektra* (1909), outraged or baffled critics. The British were less productive; but no one would deny that the Savoy Operas of Gilbert and Sullivan, which had their first performances between 1871 and 1889, were a valuable contribution to the gaiety of nations.

These triumphs were so notable that one wonders what might have been achieved in Europe had not so much of the energy of these years been devoted to activities that were essentially destructive.

Maurice Ravel, 1875–1937.
(Brown Brothers)

Claude Debussy, 1862–1918.
(Brown Brothers)

Chapter 11 THE GREAT POWERS AND THE BALANCE OF POWER, 1871–1890

After a great storm, the sea is likely to work for some time. So, after all the conflicts of the 1860s and the culminating war of 1870, it was not surprising that the international climate should have been turbulent for a period. What was alarming, however, was that the atmosphere did not improve with the passing of time.

The Great Powers of Europe, in their dealings with each other, were never after 1871 able to re-establish that sense of interdependence and mutual confidence that had enabled the European Concert to work so effectively and with so little formal machinery in the first part of the nineteenth century. The Concert of Europe was, on occasion, called into existence, and on one notable occasion, at Berlin in 1878, it acted with the authority and efficiency of an earlier age. For the rest, however, its infrequent meetings were for the purpose of dealing with matters that were not of vital interest to the powers, such as colonial affairs, rights of international navigation, and the like. For the protection of their essential interests, on the other hand, the powers preferred to rely on their own resources and efforts or—increasingly in the years after 1880—to find security in long-term secret alliances with states they felt they could trust against others whom they were sure they could not. Once this latter tendency had set in, it inevitably came to embrace all the large states of Europe so that they were arrayed against each other in armed coalitions. To be sure, this created a kind of balance of power, but one that had none of the free play that characterized the equilibrium of forces that had maintained the peace in the first half of the century. Woodrow Wilson once said that the secret alliances were the principal cause of World War I. To the extent that they increased the distrust of the powers while at the same time limiting their freedom of maneuver, he was right.

Insecurity after 1871   The overwhelming German victory over France and the resultant reorganization of Europe left all states feeling insecure and distrustful of their neighbors. Even the ordinarily phlegmatic British were dismayed by the completeness of the German victory. Gladstone felt that it would "lead from bad to worse and . . . be the beginning of a new series of European complications"; and, speaking in the House of Commons, Sir Robert Peel (the younger) said, "I must say that I look on the unification of Germany as a great peril to Europe. . . . It cannot be for the good of Europe that there should be a great military despotism in Germany built on the ruin and destruction of France." Other British leaders foresaw the possibility of German attacks upon the Low Countries; and there were some who actually feared a German invasion of England at a convenient moment.

This particular English fear was alleviated to some extent in the years that followed, for Bismarck's Germany took care not to threaten any of England's vital interests. But the marked increase in German population and power continued to worry the British and probably had something to do with their affirmative response to Disraeli's insistence, in a speech of 1872, that they must stop thinking in continental and begin to think in world terms, building up their imperial strength lest they suffer the fate of those whose horizons were limited to Europe (doubtless an oblique reference to Germany's recent victims). And, when the British people began to put a higher valuation upon their empire than they had formerly done, they began to be suspicious of all powers that could jeopardize their lines of communication with the empire, especially the Russians, whose activities in the Middle East, the Persian Gulf, and central Asia began seriously to worry Whitehall in the middle 1870s.

The Russians reciprocated these feelings, for the British were the main obstacle to their ambitions at Constantinople and along the northwestern frontier of India. But they were even more apprehensive of the Austrians who, barred from Germany in 1866, had, under Hungarian influence, become increasingly interested in the opportunities for the economic exploitation of the Balkans. That great agglomeration of Slavic peoples the Russians regarded as an area to be liberated from Turkish rule by Russian initiative when the right occasion arose, and the thought of being anticipated by the Austrians was insupportable. Unless the proper countermeasures were taken it might well be—as one Russian diplomat said in the 1890s,—that "Austria [would] girdle the Balkan Peninsula with railways, encircle Montenegro with fortresses, subject the Serbs and Bulgarians economically, and flood Bulgaria, Serbia, and Macedonia with Jesuit missions, with educational institutions, with Catholic propaganda, and finally, with German colonists."

Austria's ambitions were not, perhaps, as extensive as the Russians thought, but there was no doubt that the Austro-Hungarian government was interested in the Balkans in general and was opposed to any pronounced extension of Russian influence there, or any liberation movement inspired by Russia that might affect the security of its own Slavic provinces. Thus, even in the early 1870s, it was possible to discern the outlines of future Austro-Russian conflict in this important area. Nor was the Austro-Hungarian government concerned only with the potential Russian threat to imperial unity. The newly united Italy also represented a danger, since the most ardent Italian patriots regarded the Austrian Brenner provinces (the so-called Trentino) and the port of Trieste as legitimate territorial objectives, because they were peopled largely by Italian-speaking inhabitants. The question of this "unredeemed Italy" was therefore a barrier to complete understanding between Austria and its southern neighbor.

Italy was the most recently recognized great power and the one whose status was most in question as a result of her unhappy military past. The desire to make other peoples forget that record often seemed to be a determinant of Italian policy, giving it an active character that aroused the irritation and suspicion of other powers. The sporadic agitations for the Trentino and Trieste are to be explained by this; and so are the repeated campaigns against the papacy, which had lost its temporal power as a result of Italy's unification but had steadfastly refused to recognize the government that had dispossessed it. The anti-Vatican demonstrations, which were as often as not supported by the Italian government, made Italy's relations with other Catholic countries difficult and, in the first years after 1871, this was especially true with respect to France.

As the one republican government in Europe, France was regarded with wariness by all the powers. In return, its government treated Great Britain, Austria-Hungary, and Russia with formal correctness, Italy with irritated condescension, and Germany with cold hostility. The results of the war of 1870 would have made relations between France and its eastern neighbor difficult in any case; but the necessity of ceding Alsace and Lorraine to Germany made them doubly so. "The surrender of Alsace-Lorraine," one French deputy wrote, "means an endless war behind the mask of peace."

In such conditions of insecurity the possibility of war was never absent from the minds of European statesmen in the decade after 1870.

The War Scare of 1875   Momentarily, in the year 1875, it seemed as if their worst fears might be realized. Franco-German relations deteriorated steadily in the first years after the restoration of peace. This was partly due, as we have already seen, to the nature of the peace terms, but there were other reasons as well. The chief of them was the remarkable speed with which the French nation recovered from its defeat. The German terms had been conceived as a means of delaying the material and political recovery of France until its traditional rival had attained a position of unassailable superiority; and it had been assumed that the French would be unable to pay off the war indemnity on the date set in the treaty, March 2, 1874, and that in consequence German troops would continue to occupy France for perhaps a decade. To everyone's surprise, the French government fulfilled its obligations six months before the legal date. Moreover, in a gesture apparently designed to advertise France's return to great-power status, the government proceeded with the reconstitution of the French army. A law of 1872 made military service obligatory for all males (although with liberal provision for exemptions) and set the term of service at five years in the line army, and a cadre law of 1875 increased the number of battalions and indicated an intention of expanding the officer and noncommissioned officer corps.

All of this was profoundly disturbing to the Germans, who were under no illusion about French feelings. Among German soldiers the argument began to be heard that it was better to deal with France now, before she became too strong; and this preventive-war psychology seems to have affected even the chief of the general staff, Helmuth von Moltke, despite the fact or, perhaps because of the fact, that the recent war had imbued him with considerable respect for French military prowess. Nor was this feeling confined to the soldiers. A high-ranking German diplomat admitted in the presence of his French counterpart that a preventive war would be considered justifiable by Germans; and a part of the German press took the position that war was inevitable.

It is still impossible to say with complete certainty what Bismarck's views were in this situation. He always claimed that he was opposed to preventive war on religious as well as political grounds, and once said that such a war was like committing suicide because you were afraid to die. Believing that Germany was now, in Metternich's phrase, a "saturated power," he was aware that the advantages which even successful war could bring to it were not very tangible and the dangers involved in resorting to such conflict almost overwhelming. He was nevertheless alarmed by the speed with which France was recovering and was irritated by the protests made by French churchmen against recent measures that the Prussian government had taken against the Catholic Church.[1] He seems to have encouraged both the equivocal statements made by his diplomats and the menacing tone of the German press; and one may conclude from this that, at the very least, he was intent on intimidating the French government, perhaps in the hope of making it renounce its recent military legislation.

If this was his intention, he made the mistake of giving too much encouragement to the advocates of war. This had the effect of alarming other powers besides France, and the French government was able to play upon this fear. In response to its solicitation, both the British government and the Russian government intervened in Berlin; and the tsar of Russia paid a special visit to the German capital, presumably to remonstrate with his brother sovereign. Bismarck found it expedient to protest that Germany's intentions were entirely peaceful and that the crisis was an imaginary one; but there were many who agreed with Disraeli's foreign secretary, Lord Derby, who said tartly: "It is really imposing on our supposed credulity to tell us now that our ears have deceived us and that nothing was said or meant against France."

For France this affair of 1875 was a minor triumph, proving that she could, in certain circumstances, count upon the sympathy of other powers. For Bismarck it was a decided setback, not only because he was powerless now to impede French rearmament but because his tactics had weakened Germany's position in other ways. Certainly all the powers who had earlier regarded Germany's acquisition of Alsace-Lorraine as a violation of the principle of nationalities and a sign that Germany might have wider territorial ambitions had been given additional reason for their suspicions. Moreover, even Germany's friends had shown no disposition to support her in this affair. In 1873 Germany, Austria-Hungary, and Russia had concluded a loose agreement calling for mutual consultation and support in matters of international importance. This so-called Three Emper-

---

[1] On these measures, which were part of the so-called *Kulturkampf*, see pages 344–346.

ors' League had now proved to be without real meaning, for the Russians had seen fit to support France in the crisis of 1875. All in all, Bismarck was led to believe that his country was in a state bordering on isolation and this, unless corrected, might be dangerous.

Balkan Troubles, 1875–1877   While the German chancellor was reflecting on these things, a new series of Balkan complications began. In August 1875, in Bosnia and Herzegovina, an area lying to the northwest of Serbia, an insurrection began against Turkish rule. The causes of this were mixed. The provinces in question were Southern Slav in nationality and predominantly Christian in religion and, for both reasons, were unhappy about their political condition. Their national self-consciousness had been encouraged by Serbian propaganda, for the Serbs had dreams of acquiring this sizable territory; and it had been influenced further by crop failures, which reduced much of the peasantry to penury, and by unemployment among the artisan class, which seems to have been caused by Turkish trade practices.

Once agitation began in Bosnia and Herzegovina, it spread rapidly to other Turkish parts of the Balkans. This was particularly true of Bulgaria, where the ground had been carefully prepared by the Bulgarian church (which had been given a large measure of autonomy by the sultan in 1870 and had immediately become a focal point of nationalistic agitation), by schoolteachers and intellectuals, and, not least, by Russian agents, who were beginning to show great interest in Bulgaria.

If proof were needed of the inadequacy of the European Concert in the period after 1870 it would be easy to find it in the long series of Balkan crises. In this one, there can be no doubt that peace could have been restored if Russia, Great Britain, and Austria-Hungary had worked together to that end. But the Disraeli government in England was suspicious of Russian intentions at the Straits and was consequently reluctant to join in any pressure upon the Turkish government that might lead to territorial losses by that government. Simultaneously, the Russian government was split between those who favored working with the other powers for the maintenance of the status quo in the Balkans and the influential Pan-Slav group, who believed that Russia must take advantage of the Balkan troubles to free the Slavic peoples from the yoke of foreign bondage and mold them into a great federation under Russian patronage. At the onset of the Balkan risings, Prince Gorchakov worked energetically for Austro-Russian collaboration; by 1876, as the agitations continued and as the principalities of Serbia and Montenegro declared war against the Turks, Russian foreign policy fell increasingly under the influence of the Pan-Slavs, who argued that Russia must go her own way.

The disharmony of the powers was seen most clearly at the end of 1876. Despite the inefficiency of Turkish government in general, the sultan was fortunate in possessing able military commanders, and one of these, Osman Pasha, imposed such crushing defeats upon the Serbian forces in September and October that they appealed to the powers for protection. Under international pressure, the Turkish government was forced to agree to a conference which met at Constantinople in December and drafted a general settlement. But the British govern-

In the Russian trenches during the siege of Plevna, 1877. From *Illustrated London News,* November 10, 1877.

ment—deluded perhaps by the promulgation of a new and supposedly "liberal" constitution by the new sultan, Abdul Hamid II—secretly encouraged that unscrupulous ruler to defy the conference, which he proceeded to do in January 1877.

This action exhausted Russian patience. In April 1877, when its military preparations were complete, the Russian government announced that it could no longer tolerate Turkish atrocities against its fellow religionists; and, in June, Russian forces crossed the Danube and began to move swiftly toward Constantinople, with every prospect of reaching it within a month. What the future history of Europe might have been like if they had succeeded, it is impossible to guess; it is difficult to see how the Russians could have been dislodged from the Straits if they had once been permitted to capture them. But it never came to that. In the middle of July a Turkish force of 12,000 men under Osman Pasha moved into the Bulgarian town of Plevna on the Russian flank and began swiftly to entrench themselves and to build redoubts for reinforcements that were on their way. The Russians did not dare proceed without removing this threat to their line of communications, and they turned their forces against Plevna. Despite prodigies of heroism and incredible losses, they were, however, unable to break the Turkish resistance until December 1877.

The battle of Plevna proved that, after the swift wars of movement of the 1860s, the power of the defense in warfare had revived and that—although professional soldiers were slow to realize this—the vast improvement in fire power made possible by the magazine rifle (and, in the not-too-distant future, the machine gun) would call into question all plans based on shock tactics alone. The political results of the battle were more immediate. The protracted Turkish defense at Plevna transformed the anti-Turkish sentiment in the West into something bordering on sympathy, if not enthusiasm, while at the same time allowing suspicion of Russia's intentions to grow and preparations to block its ambitions to take form. When the Russians resumed their push toward the Straits, they found the international climate had cooled significantly; and, when Turkish resistance collapsed and the Russian government imposed terms, they discovered that Great Britain and Austria-Hungary were prepared to oppose them.

This is understandable, for the Peace of San Stefano of March 1878, negotiated by the Russian ambassador at Constantinople, an ardent Pan-Slav named Ignatiev, threatened to make Russian influence paramount from the Straits to the Adriatic. It called for the cession to Russia of Kars, Ardahan, and Bayazid, and of Batum on the eastern shores of the Black Sea, as well as the area known as the Dobrudja. More significantly, it provided for the creation of a large Bulgarian state, which would stretch from Macedonia to Salonika on the Aegean and which would be occupied by Russian troops for a period of two years. The additional provisions of the treaty, for an increase of Serbian and Montenegrin territory and for the creation of an autonomous Bosnia-Herzegovina under Austro-Russian supervision, were hardly calculated to allay Austro-Hungarian fears (the more so because the Russians conveniently forgot that they had previously promised that, in the event of Balkan changes, they would support the Austrian acquisition of Bosnia); and the treaty as a whole was considered completely inadmissible by Great Britain. Indeed, even before its signature, the British government had ordered the fleet to proceed to the Straits, and British public opinion was in an excitable state. The modern term jingoism, meaning belligerence, stems from those tense moments of 1878, when British music hall audiences were chanting

> We don't want to fight
> But, by jingo!, if we do
> We've got the ships, we've got the men,
> We've got the money too!

Throughout these complications, Prince Bismarck, to the irritation of those powers that wanted his advice or support, had remained elaborately disinterested; it was, indeed, during this tangled affair that he made his famous remark about the Balkans not being worth the bones of a Pomeranian musketeer. The German chancellor was, however, aware that he would be in an awkward position if war actually broke out, especially if Austria-Hungary and Russia were on opposite sides, for each would expect Germany's support, and refusal to give it might have unhappy political results (as Austria had proved during the Crimean War). Aside from this, any major war would have incalculable consequences in the present state of Europe. Bismarck, therefore, assumed the task of mediation and offered the hospitality of Berlin for an international congress that might draw up a general settlement for eastern affairs.

The Congress of Berlin   The Russians accepted the offer primarily because their armies were exhausted by the unexpected rigors of the Turkish war and were not enthusiastic about a test against Great Britain, aided perhaps by Austria. The other powers fell in line, and the congress assembled in the German capital in June 1878. Including among its delegates such ornaments of the diplomatic art as Bismarck himself, Disraeli and Salisbury of Great Britain, Gorchakov and Shuvalov of Russia, Andrassy of Hungary, Waddington of France, and Corti of Italy, in addition to the representatives of Turkey and the observers of the Balkan states, the Congress of Berlin was easily the most distinguished diplomatic gathering between the Vienna Congress of 1814–1815 and the Paris Peace Conference of 1919. The results of its labors were not, however, as brilliant as its cast of characters.

It was probably inevitable that more people would be disappointed than pleased by a settlement of any kind, for almost all the Balkan peoples had been led by the events of the previous three years to entertain unreasonable expectations. Some of their aspirations were certainly realized. Rumania now completed

"The Congress of Berlin, 1878," by Anton von Werner, a contemporary artist. In the left foreground, Count Karolyi (Austria-Hungary), Prince Gorchakov, seated (Russia), and the Earl of Beaconsfield (Disraeli). In the center foreground, Count Andrassy (Austria-Hungary), Bismarck, and Count Shuvalov (Russia). In the right rear, with the bald head, Lord Sailsbury (Great Britain). (Ullstein-Bilderdienst)

the process begun in 1856 by becoming an independent sovereign state, as did Serbia and Montenegro; and Bulgaria was made an autonomous principality that was, to all intents and purposes, free from any further Turkish interference. On the other hand, when the terms of the Berlin Treaty were complete, in July 1878, the Serbs, who had hoped to acquire Bosnia and Herzegovina, found that these provinces were to pass under Austrian administration. The Rumanians were asked, in return for the Dobrudja, to cede to Russia those Bessarabian provinces that they had gained in 1856, although this meant that many of their co-nationals must now live under alien rule. The Bulgars, after all the high hopes of 1877, found that their country was going to be much smaller than they had expected and that the Serbs were to be compensated with districts they felt should rightly belong to them. The Greeks, who had expected a complete Turkish collapse that would bring them Epirus and Crete, received neither and were further outraged to see a restored and guaranteed Turkey cede Cyprus to Great Britain. Almost every territorial decision made at Berlin contained disappointment and the seeds of future Balkan revisionism and war.

Of the hopes of the Russian Pan-Slavs, very little was left; and because of this Russia was probably the most aggrieved member of the Congress (except Turkey, which lost half of its European territory and population). Despite their heavy expenditure of money and men in the recent hostilities, the Russians had little to show. The Bulgaria that was to have been the springboard of further Russian expansion was a mere shadow of what had been hoped for; and Russian acquisition of Bessarabia, Kars, Batum, and Ardahan was hardly impressive, especially when one considered that, without the loss of a man, Great Britain had acquired Cyprus and strengthened its position at the Straits, Austria-Hungary had gained Bosnia, and the French had been encouraged to move into Tunis whenever they saw fit. The Russians were mortified with these results, and they tended to blame them on the man who, in their opinion, had refused to repay the services they had done him in 1866 and 1870 and had invited them to Berlin only to despoil them—Prince Bismarck.

Bismarck's Alliance System   The German chancellor was fully aware of Russian feelings and sufficiently impressed by them to feel that some urgent action on his part was necessary. Russian resentment might conceivably lead, he feared, to a rapprochement between St. Petersburg and Paris, which would place the German empire in a dangerously exposed position. In the past Bismarck had been willing to pursue his policies unencumbered by any but the most casual of engagements with other powers. Now, however, he felt it expedient to have some more formal assurances of aid in the event of trouble; and, in 1879, he turned to Vienna and concluded the famous Dual Alliance with the Hapsburg empire.

Because of his emperor's strong predilection for Russia, Bismarck hoped to make this a general treaty, calling for mutual assistance if either partner were attacked by a third power. The Austro-Hungarian foreign minister, Count Andrassy, felt that this might be interpreted as anti-French and, his own relations with Paris being good, insisted that the new treaty mention Russia explicitly. It is a measure of Bismarck's feeling of insecurity that he gave way, agreeing to a treaty which called for mutual assistance if either signatory were attacked by Russia and for benevolent neutrality if either were attacked by another power. The completed treaty (which Bismarck persuaded his sovereign to ratify only by threatening to resign if he refused to do so) was a landmark in European history. While previous treaties had usually been concluded during or on the eve of wars, or for specific purposes and restricted duration, this was a peacetime treaty and, as it turned out, a permanent one, for it did not lapse until 1918. It was, moreover, the first of the secret treaties, whose contents were never fully known but always suspected and which encouraged other powers to negotiate similar treaties in self-defense, until all Europe was divided into league and counterleague.

With these long-term results Bismarck could not be expected to be concerned. He had sought this treaty in order to attain a greater degree of security than he had felt since 1871, and it more than fulfilled his expectations. The Russian government proved to be less interested in the friendship of France than Bismarck had feared in 1878; and the treaty of 1879, far from driving them toward Paris, brought them back to Berlin. Doubtless calculating that Austro-German collaboration might be turned against Russia in the Balkans, the Russians in 1880 asked for what amounted to a renewal of the Three Emperors' League of 1872 and, although the Austrians were less enthusiastic about this than Bismarck was, an alliance was signed in June 1881 that pledged the three partners to neutrality in the event of a war between one of their number and a fourth European power and provided for mutual consultation in Balkan affairs.

The renewal of the *Dreikaiserbündnis* gave Bismarck reason to hope that he might be able to avoid future troubles between Austria and Russia in southeast Europe. From a more general point of view, it gratified him because it gave him a measure of control over all European politics. As he said on one occasion, one must not lose sight of

> the importance of being one of three on the European chess-board. That is the invariable objective of all cabinets and of mine above all others. Nobody wishes to be in a minority. All politics reduce themselves to this formula: to try to be one of three, so long as the world is governed by an unstable equilibrium of five Great Powers.

Aside from this, the alliance of 1881 effectively isolated France. There was always a possibility, of course, that it might become allied either with Italy or with Great Britain, but this was unlikely. The French seizure of Tunis in 1881—a belated consequence of the deliberations at Berlin in 1878—made the Italians fearful that this was the beginning of a policy that would eventuate in French control of all North Africa. To secure some assurance that they would not be excluded from an area where their economic interests were slowly growing, they consulted Bismarck about the possibility of an alliance but were told by him that they must first negotiate with the Austrians. This meant an end to any immediate hope of winning the Trentino or Trieste, but the Italians felt they had no choice. In May 1882 they joined with Germany and Austria in the so-called Triple Alliance, which assured them of aid in the event of a French attack on

Italy but obliged them to go to war if Germany were attacked by France or if either Germany or Austria were attacked by two or more powers.

The Italian gains from this engagement were illusory, and France's resentment at Italy's association with her enemy eventually took the form of a tariff war that had ruinous effects in Italy (see p. 313). For Bismarck the Triple Alliance had the advantage of eliminating one more potential ally of France. Almost simultaneously, the chances of any Anglo-French agreement became negligible. In July 1882 a British fleet bombarded Alexandria and British forces occupied Egypt, and this action, in a country in which France had been active for almost a century, aroused a hostility against Britain that prevented any real understanding until the beginning of the new century.

Thanks to his decision to turn to Austria in 1879, to his subsequent negotiations, to the apprehensions of other powers, and to several unforeseen and unforeseeable occurrences, Bismarck had been able to improve Germany's position immeasurably by 1882. But even at this date the system he had elaborated to give Germany security was a very complicated one, and in its complications were the germs of future trouble.

The Bulgarian Crisis   In the middle 1880s, Bismarck's security system was strained to the utmost by new Balkan complications, this time in the state of Bulgaria. These arose from the fact that Russia, having fought for Bulgarian freedom and, in the first years after the Congress of Berlin, helped the fledgling state organize its political and military institutions, expected Bulgaria to repay these services, not only with gratitude, but with deference to Russian advice. The majority of literate Bulgarians, however, were imbued with national pride and had no desire to be particularly deferential to anyone. This difference of view was given specific point by the politics of Prince Alexander of Battenberg, a nephew of the tsar who had been elected to the Bulgarian throne in 1879 with Russian approval. An energetic but ambitious ruler, without judgment or balance, Alexander first annoyed the Russians by becoming involved in disputes with Russian officials who occupied high positions in his administration; he then infuriated them by giving preference to Austrian groups who wished to construct a Bulgarian link that would complete the projected Orient Railways, designed to run from Austria across Serbia and Bulgaria to Adrianople and Constantinople. To the Russians, already alarmed by Austrian political and commercial treaties with Serbia (1881) and Rumania (1883), it seemed essential to block the construction of the Bulgarian part of this rail system; Alexander's refusal to fall in with their plans was intolerable.

The prince's open brushes with the Russians nevertheless made him popular with the Bulgarian assembly and with those sections of the population who had learned to hate the highhandedness of Russian officials; and this made it impossible for him to change his course. His self-assurance was increased, moreover, by two events in 1885: his successful annexation of the Turkish province of Eastern Rumelia, after a revolution in its capital Philippopolis; and a brilliant military campaign against the Serbs, who were ill-advised enough to seek compensation for the Rumelian annexation by military means and were soundly beaten within four weeks.

After this had happened, the Russians were afraid that they might lose all control over the Bulgarian state. To prevent this, they fomented a conspiracy within the Bulgarian army that succeeded, in August 1886, in deposing Alexander and forcing him to leave the country. This patently contrived affair aroused and alarmed the other Great Powers, and so did the Russian government's high-handed attempts in subsequent months to reduce the Bulgarian state to the position of a satellite with a ruler chosen by itself. Against these tactics the Bulgarian assembly stood firm, eventually (in July 1887) choosing a new prince, Ferdinand of Saxe-Coburg, whose views were even more pronouncedly Austrian than his predecessor's. Before this had happened, however, Bulgarian affairs had embroiled all the Great Powers and come close to destroying Bismarck's alliance system.

Certainly the reconstituted Three Emperors' League of 1881 was brought to the verge of collapse by these events, for the Russians, even in 1886, seemed on the point of employing force to subdue Bulgaria, and the Austrians had begun to make military preparations to counter Russian moves. If a military clash came between his two allies, Bismarck knew that he would have to support Austria-Hungary. He dared not suggest this to the Russians, however, because he feared that, even if such a warning prevented a Balkan war, it might prepare the way for a bigger conflict by driving the Russians into the arms of France. The Pan-Slav press was already openly discussing the possibility of a Franco-Russian alliance. Such an alliance was of special concern to the German chancellor at this moment because of an ugly turn in French politics. In the fall of 1886, there seemed to be a strong possibility that the Third Republic would be replaced by a dictatorship of the war minister General Boulanger, who was currently the idol of French nationalists and who had made some menacing speeches about the necessity of regaining the lost provinces.[2] An alliance between a Boulangist France and a Pan-Slav Russia might confront Germany with a two-front war in the near future.

Or so Bismarck thought. And because he felt this way he believed it necessary, ostensibly at least, to support the tsar's Bulgarian ambitions. On the other hand, since their fulfillment might force Austria to go to war, he had, at the same time, to see that they were not realized. This was a difficult assignment, requiring skill and guile if it were to be effected.

These were qualities, however, with which the chancellor had always been richly endowed. To meet the French threat, he called for an increase in the German standing army from 427,000 to 468,000 men and, when the Reichstag refused to approve it, dissolved that assembly and conducted a tub-thumping electoral campaign that got him the majority he needed for the new appropriations. This dramatized Germany's armed might and her willingness to use it, and had a sensibly sobering effect in Paris. So did the news, in February 1887, that Germany had renewed the Triple Alliance with Austria and Italy. This announcement led the French government to suspect that plans for concerted action against France may have been worked out in the secret discussions.[3]

[2] On the Boulanger crisis, see pages 330–331.

[3] In order to win Italy's renewal, the German government had, in fact, promised to support the Italians if they felt compelled to use military means against any French move in Tripoli or Morocco.

If these events dimmed French ardor for any anti-German action, they did not deter the Russian push toward Bulgaria. But an Italian admission, during the alliance talks, that Italy was interested in the Balkans and would not welcome Russian domination of that area gave Bismarck an opportunity to suggest that Italy might find support for its Balkan views in London and Vienna. In March 1887 this suggestion blossomed into the so-called Mediterranean Agreement among Italy, Austria-Hungary, and Great Britain, which provided for mutual support in the case of differences with a fourth power. The agreement was as much oriented against France as it was against Russia. The Conservative prime minister of Great Britain, Lord Salisbury, hoped that cooperation with the Triple Alliance would provide support for Britain's position in Egypt in case of French or Franco-Russian pressure there. But he was also opposed to the growth of Russian influence in the Balkans and felt, as he said, that "it is well that the tsar should know it." These considerations led him to fall in with Bismarck's plans, and the resultant Mediterranean Agreement helped deter the tsar from aggressive action in Bulgaria without directly involving the German chancellor.

These complicated maneuvers were followed by others even more so. To make quite certain that the tsar would not, even at this date, turn to France, Bismarck negotiated a new alliance with Russia. The Reinsurance Treaty of June 1887 pledged each of the partners to benevolent neutrality in the event that the other was at war, unless the conflict were caused by a Russian attack upon Austria or a German attack upon France. From a strictly legal point of view, it was not incompatible with Germany's alliance of 1879 with Austria, which was, after all, a defensive engagement. From a moral standpoint, it is harder to justify. By its secret clauses Germany promised to support Russian interests in Bulgaria and at the Straits; but, before the year was over, Bismarck was encouraging the three Mediterranean powers to conclude a supplementary agreement. In this second Mediterranean Agreement, signed in December, the British, Austrian, and Italian governments declared themselves defenders of peace and the status quo in the Near East, and more particularly in Bulgaria, Asia Minor, and at the Straits, and agreed to take concerted action in case these were threatened. Before this clear warning the Russian government was forced to abandon its intentions of asserting its control of Bulgaria, not without some bitter reflections about the disadvantages of having an ally who took away with his left hand what he had given with his right. Relative peace now descended on the Balkans.

Economic and Military Influence in Diplomacy   Brief mention may be made here of two interesting aspects of this tangled Bulgarian problem. The first is the importance of economic factors, not only in the inception but also in the solution of the crisis. It had, after all, been economic ambition on the part of Austria and economic fears on the part of Russia that had supplied the context in which Alexander of Battenberg's policies were inaugurated. Moreover, this was only the first of a number of Balkan and Middle Eastern complications in which railroad building played an important part. Finally, among the weapons used by Bismarck to control the Russians at the height of the Bulgarian crisis, financial manipulation was not the least important. The most dramatic instance of this came in November 1887, when the German government forbade the

Reichsbank to accept Russian securities as collateral for loans. This move was regarded by investors as a sign of lack of confidence in Russian credit, and the resultant sales of Russian holdings led to a precipitous fall in prices and seriously handicapped Russian financial operations. The German government's action was, in part, a retaliation against certain discriminatory Russian practices, but there is little doubt that Bismarck's primary motive was to create one more obstacle to effective Russian military action in the Balkans. His stroke doubtless had some effect on the solution of the crisis. It also had a more far-reaching result. It induced the Russian government in subsequent years to turn toward the French financial market and thus helped pave the way for the very Franco-Russian political rapprochement that Bismarck feared.

The Bulgarian crisis also showed a marked increase in the influence of the military in diplomacy. Leaving aside the dangers created by the eruption of General Boulanger in French politics, the most striking manifestation of this came in the development of Austro-German relations in 1887. As the Bulgarian affair reached its most dangerous state, Bismarck learned that the German military attaché in Vienna, apparently with the backing of the Great General Staff in Berlin, was encouraging Emperor Francis Joseph and the Austrian command to believe that Germany would support an Austrian war against Russia. The chancellor reacted swiftly to this recurrence of the preventive-war psychology of 1875. In a masterly instruction to his ambassador in Vienna, he pointed out that, under the Dual Alliance of 1879, Germany was obliged to support its ally only if it were attacked, and he urged him to remind the emperor of this. Simultaneously, Bismarck remonstrated with the military chiefs in Berlin and threatened to wash his hands of responsibility in case of further incursions into foreign policy by the soldiers. This was enough to stop military meddling on this occasion, but there were to be many instances of this sort of thing in the future. In 1909, for instance, another German chief of staff was to assure the Austrians of German support if they felt called upon to take the initiative in a war with Russia and, on that occasion, no German statesman was strong enough to maintain civilian supremacy in the sphere of foreign policy by protesting against this significant expansion of Germany's obligations under the treaty of 1879.

But all that lay far in the future and could not be foreseen in 1888. By the beginning of that year the troublesome Bulgarian crisis had finally been liquidated, and international tension had been relaxed. Bismarck could take satisfaction in the fact that his network of alliances was still in good repair and, indeed, had been strengthened by Great Britain's association with the junior members of the Triple Alliance. There was no immediate prospect of new troubles in Europe. The warmongers in France and the Pan-Slavs in Russia were in eclipse, and the attention of all powers was becoming increasingly absorbed by problems of territorial expansion and colonial exploitation in areas far from the European center.

Chapter 12 THE EVOLUTION OF CAPITALISM AND THE SPREAD OF SOCIALISM, 1871–1914

ECONOMIC DEVELOPMENTS

The Progress of Industrialization   It has become fashionable among economic historians to use the term the take-off to describe that decisive period during which a society abandons its traditional, static, agricultural economy and commits itself to a future of industrialism. When this transformation succeeds, economic growth becomes largely automatic. But in order to be successful, take-off requires, as W. W. Rostow has written, "a massive set of preconditions going to the heart of a society's economic organization and its effective scale of values." The parochialism and regionalism characteristic of an agricultural society must give way to a habit of thinking in national and international terms. A new elite must arise that believes in productive change and formulates methods of attaining it. The income of society above minimum levels of consumption must begin to be invested not in the external adornments of a traditional leisure class but in those things that will make sustained economic growth possible—roads, railways, schools, factories, and other forms of social capital; and the rate of such investment must reach a level at which the increase of output exceeds the increase of population.

In the history of Europe, the precise nature of the psychological and sociological reorientation that preceded take-off and the length of time needed to create the institutions and accumulate the capital necessary for the transition to modern industrialism differed from country to country. Great Britain led the way at the very beginning of the nineteenth century, and she was most closely followed by Belgium, where investment capital and technological skill were supplemented by English loans and assistance. In the years that stretched between 1830 and

262

1870 these trail-blazers were followed by France, whose take-off was presided over by Louis Philippe, and Germany, where the nationalism of the rising middle class and such tangible manifestations of it as the Prussian Customs Union and the railroad building of the 1850s and 1860s were the preconditions for the surge of industrial activity that was to take place after the unification of the country (see pp. 352–354).

The period that began in 1871 and ended with the outbreak of war in 1914 saw the other European nations enter the industrial age. The opening of British and French markets to Swedish timber, after the tariff reductions of the 1860s, stimulated the modernization of the timber industry and the building of railroads, and these, in turn, made possible the capital accumulation that prepared the way for Sweden's take-off in the early 1870s. Denmark and the Low Countries were further behind, largely because of the lack of mineral deposits of their own, but by the middle of the period, with the aid of imported machinery, they were applying modern industrial techniques to the production of glass and porcelain and of comestibles like sugar, cocoa, and alcoholic beverages.

As one moved south or east in Europe, progress was still slower. Italian industry received a pronounced impetus from the completion of national unity, but its initial progress was slowed by the ruinous effects of the tariff war with France in the late 1880s and by the failure to modernize methods of agricultural production in such a way as to increase capital for investment. The traditional agricultural system and the social institutions that went with it had a persistence in Italy that was matched only in Spain in western Europe.

In the Austro-Hungarian Empire, the picture was mixed. Austria itself and Bohemia had become industrial centers of importance even before 1870, but Hungary remained a rural-based traditional society, and, as late as 1914, the empire as a whole still lacked either the kind of social capital mentioned above or a strong class committed to the idea of modernization. In consequence, it still suffered from the growing pains of the pre-take-off stage.

The progress made by Russia was more noticeable than that of her sister empire to the west. The abolition of serfdom was the first definite move away from the traditional system, although it took another generation before its effects in creating a new balance between urban and rural population were felt and a middle class arose that was large enough and energetic enough to have an effect on policy. The railroad building of the 1880s and the efforts of Count Witte, communications and finance minister between 1892 and 1902, to increase investment opportunities and attract capital to industrial ventures were the prelude to Russia's take-off, and the last years before the war saw the creation of an industrial system mature enough to serve as a foundation for the later Soviet five-year plans.

Dynamic Capitalism   The economic growth that took place in the years following take-off tended to be irregular and, in some cases, to disappoint original promise. In France, for example, despite periodic spurts, progress was hampered by the suspicion French businessmen had of mass production and technological experiment. They seemed to remember Baron Rothschild's dictum, "There are three ways to ruin: gambling, women, and engineers. The first two are more agreeable, but the last is more certain." In more adventuresome countries, growth was accompanied by marked fluctuations and periodic crises. Some of the most spectacular of the crashes can be traced to the excessive enthusiasm of investors or lack of experience on the part of company directors; and, in the case of the precipitous fall of English railway stock in the 1860s and the collapse of the German building boom in 1873, the damage could probably have been ameliorated to some extent by private circumspection or government regulation.

It could hardly, however, have been avoided entirely. Schumpeter has written that the outstanding characteristic of mature capitalism is that it is engaged perpetually in a process of creative destruction, in which it uses up and abandons its old forms and creates new ones. This process is effected by recurring surges of productive energy, interspersed with periods of recoil and apparent collapse. Each surge forward is marked by a great increase in activity in certain sectors of the economy. In time, investment in these sectors becomes excessive and leads to some form of setback or depression. This provides an opportunity for a regrouping of the economic resources of society and their allocation, in a renewed burst of creative energy, to new forms or areas of production.

The history of the period after 1871 is rich in examples of this kind of development. Sweden's entrance into the company of the industrial states was, for example, based on the activity of its timber export industry and its railway construction. This first period of productive activity came to an end in the 1890s with a depression that destroyed the country's export markets. Sweden responded by abandoning its former reliance on timber exports in favor of diversified production. There was a greater concentration on wood pulp. Modern extractive methods were employed to exploit local ores, and mining activity led successfully to the production of pig iron and fine steel and the creation and expansion of a modern engineering industry. Simultaneously, the development of hydroelectric sources of power made possible the establishment of an electrical machinery industry that was later to revolutionize methods in all of Sweden's basic industries.

What happened in Sweden happened also among its capitalistic neighbors, as will become apparent in the chapters that follow. The rise and fall of industrial activity that accompanied this recurrent rejuvenation of the productive apparatus was inevitably accompanied by a high degree of social hardship. But the constantly accelerating expansion of industrial production also progressively raised the standard of living of the masses and brought material comforts within their grasp.

Government and Capitalism: Subventions and Tariffs   As industrial capitalism extended its domain in the years after 1871, it began, in certain respects, to change its character. The rugged individualism and the unalloyed competitive spirit that marked the entrepreneurs of the early stages of capitalism disappeared; and their successors relied increasingly on government aid and on forms of combination intended to reduce the rigors and inconveniences of competition.

A much-read spokesman for classical liberalism, the English publicist Herbert Spencer (1820–1903), commenting on the relation of government to business, once wrote: "Perpetually governments have thwarted and deranged growth, but have in no way furthered it, save by partially discharging their proper function and maintaining social order." The most striking thing about this dogmatic utterance is its remoteness from truth. As we have seen, economic growth is dependent in the first instance upon the creation of an efficient transportation system and other forms of social capital. During this phase, the government is generally called upon to play a most important part, since projects that do not promise a quick return on investment often find it difficult to obtain financial support. Students of American history are well aware of the role of federal government subsidies during the construction of the transcontinental railway systems. The same sort of thing occurred in many European countries in the years when they were beginning their economic growth. Napoleon III's use of public bond issues to encourage railroad construction in France has already been mentioned (pp. 174–175), and other forms of pump-priming were noticeable in European countries after 1871.

Indeed, even after the initial fund of social capital (roads, canals, railways) had been accumulated, there were other kinds of aid that the government could give, and soon came to be expected to give, to business. It could facilitate investment by progressive liberalization of laws of incorporation. Thus, one of the important factors in Germany's industrial growth was the general company law of 1870–1872, which ameliorated existing restrictions on corporate growth and extended the principle of limited liability so successfully that joint-stock companies increased in number from 2100 in the early 1880s to 5400 in 1912, and associations with limited liability from 200 to 16,000 in the same period. The government could also open up new opportunities for investment and for the sale of the products of industry by paying the costs and assuming the risks of acquiring overseas colonies, a development whose universality in this period will be discussed below (pp. 400–425). Finally, in time of war, it could protect those industries that were considered vitally important to the war effort from the normal risks of the market, a practice that was common to many European countries during World War I.

One of the most widespread forms of government assistance to private enterprise was the protective tariff. After a period of virtual free trade, which had been inaugurated by the repeal of the British Corn Laws in 1846 (pp. 111–113) and confirmed by the Cobden-Chevalier Treaty of 1860 (p. 175), most European countries turned back to protectionism in the late 1870s. There were a number of reasons for this.

In the first place, in countries where the take-off point was reached after 1871, industrialists were likely to be vulnerable to the competition of those neighbors who had progressed further than they had themselves. German producers, for example, were particularly sensitive to the impact of cheap English imports on the domestic market and were insistent that, without protection, they could not survive. The dumping of English goods at ridiculously low prices in continental markets during the first years of the depression that began in 1873 gave point to these claims, which were made by others besides the Germans.

In the second place, the industrial advocates of protection found supporters among the agricultural interest. Hitherto, European farmers had been reasonably content with the free-trade economy, since prices in the 1850s and 1860s had remained high. But before the latter decade was over, signs of change were apparent. The tremendous growth of railroads in the United States—an increase of 300 percent in the twenty years after 1860—the simultaneous lowering of freight rates, and the improvement of agricultural machinery caused a boom in American grain production at the very moment when the introduction of new marine engines and the decrease of shipping costs made it possible to deliver this grain (and later that of Canada, Argentina, and Australia) cheaply and speedily to European markets. These things (and some others, like the perfection of mechanical refrigeration to a point where frozen meats could be shipped across the ocean as well) caused a crisis in the agriculture of western Europe in the 1870s. Farmers in central Europe were simultaneously feeling the pinch because rail-transported grains from Rumania and Russia were forcing their prices down. It is not surprising that agricultural pressure groups soon came into existence and began to collaborate with others who were seeking government protective action. The alliance between grain and heavy industry became a common phenomenon in European politics.

This coalition was apt to find additional support among groups whose interests were not primarily economic. The wars of the 1860s had, as we have seen, left the European states mutually suspicious and ready to assume that new conflicts were coming soon. After 1871, a good many people were concluding from their reading (or misreading) of the works of Charles Darwin that war was inevitable among the different branches of the human species and that, this being so, reliance on free trade was dangerous, since it encouraged dependence upon imports that might be cut off in time of war. Even at the cost of economic disadvantage, self-sufficiency seemed to these people to be a desirable goal; and they called for tariffs as a means of protecting and promoting the production of critical goods and strategic materials at home.

Under the pressure of these political forces, European governments began to turn away from free trade. Perhaps the decisive push came with the passage of the German tariffs of 1879, although the new direction had already been indicated by upward revision of tariff schedules in Russia, Spain, and Italy in the three preceding years. But the German legislation, which was the result of joint agitation by agricultural and industrial groups, was bound, in view of Germany's leading position on the continent, to have wider effects than action by other countries. The tariff laws of 1879, which placed specific duties on grain, textiles, timber, meat, and iron, were imitated in France, Austria, Sweden, and Switzerland and encouraged Russia, Italy, and other countries to elaborate existing protective systems. When France passed the tariff of 1892, which increased agricultural duties about 25 percent while at the same time giving protection to native industries like silk, Jules Méline, who piloted the bill through the Assembly, cited the successful German and Austrian experience with tariffs in the last decade as an argument for France's following their example. He added:

> If we look over the table of our importations of the last fifteen years we find them perceptibly increasing in proportion as the principal countries of Europe raise their tariff barriers. If we do not give heed to this, we

shall end by becoming the drain of the whole of Europe. Is it right, is it wise, to persist in keeping our doors open when all others are proceeding to close theirs?

His auditors did not think so; nor did legislators in most other countries. As a result, by the middle 1890s, only Great Britain, Belgium, and Holland could still be considered free-trading countries; and they were all countries, it should be noted, in which commerce was more important than agriculture, and industry was so far advanced that protection was difficult to justify.

Some of the results of this swing back to a protectionist economy have already been mentioned (see pp. 241–242). The old liberal idea of international peace based on the economic interdependence of nations seemed, under these new conditions, to lose all hope of realization, for once the administration of commercial relations became a governmental rather than a private matter, the area of potential friction between nations was greatly expanded. Moreover, once governments began to employ tariffs for economic reasons, they discovered that tariffs could be used politically also, and economic pressure became a feature of some of the uglier diplomatic crises of the years before World War I.

For our present purpose, however, it is enough to note that the return to protectionism strengthened the change that had been taking place in the relations between private businessmen and governments. To the extent that tariffs came to be considered indispensable aids to agriculture and industry, the principle of free enterprise—no matter how often invoked in discussion—had been attenuated in practice.

The Movement toward Combination: Trusts and Cartels   The private enterprise system suffered another change as the years passed. Industrial and banking firms that survived the bruising competition of the early stages of capitalism and expanded their operations from a local to a national, and even an international, level seemed to lose their enthusiasm for competition somewhere along the way. As business enterprises got bigger, they tended to collaborate with other large firms in their own field of activity, for the purpose of avoiding duplication of effort, lowering costs of production, dividing markets, or protecting prices from the fluctuations that unrestrained competition might cause.

Various forms of combination were popular. In England and the United States, the preferred arrangements were amalgamation, in which one firm absorbed competitors by purchase or by stock manipulation, and the trust or combine, in which plants that were engaged in the production of the same or allied products united under a joint directorate and pooled their administrative and sales forces. These arrangements made possible a degree of commercial and technical progress that was unlikely in situations where a great number of competing units existed side by side; and it frequently enabled the resulting combination to enjoy monopoly conditions. This was true of such trusts as Standard Oil in the United States and Bryant and May (the match trust) and the Imperial Tobacco Company in England.

The German form of combination, which was also popular in other continental countries, was looser in form but no less effective. This was the cartel, an arrangement among all the enterprises in a given branch of industrial production that regulated their production, purchase of materials, areas of exploitation, sales procedures, and prices. These combinations could cross national frontiers; and, before World War I, there were marketing, production, and price agreements between German cartels and foreign trusts. The *Allgemeine Elektrizitäts-Gesellschaft* (AEG) had such an arrangement with the General Electric Company of the United States, and German manufacturers of steel rails had cartel arrangements with their counterparts in Great Britain, France, Belgium, and the United States and, in collaboration with them, effectively controlled the world market.

Of special interest in this connection was the tendency of banking concerns to combine. In England the last years of the century saw a steady decline in the total number of banking concerns. There had been 600 banking houses in England in 1824. By 1914 there were only fifty-five, and this shrinkage was to continue into the postwar period, so that there were only eleven banking houses in 1937, and five sixths of the country's banking business was handled by the "Big Five": the Midland Bank, the Westminster Bank, Barclay's, Lloyd's, and the National Provincial. In Germany the financial business of the country in the years after 1871 came increasingly under the domination of the four so-called D Banks—the *Disconto Gesellschaft* of Stuttgart (founded in 1851), the *Deutsche Bank* (1870), the *Darmstädter Bank* (1870), and the *Dresdener Bank* (1872). The D Banks were specifically commissioned "to foster commercial relations between Germany and other countries" and were active in the Far East, Latin America, Eastern Europe, and the Middle East. At home, their role in the direction of business was very great, and they generally promoted ever greater degrees of business amalgamation.

In the expansion of the European economy in the last decades of the nineteenth century, these monopolistic practices played a positive role, for they made possible the introduction of new techniques and eliminated much inefficiency and duplicated effort in the productive process. These contributions were not easily perceived by contemporaries. Business combinations were unpopular because they were connected in the national memory with historical cases of exploitation, because the process of amalgamation often caused tragedy in individual cases, and because the misuse of power gained by combination often hurt consumers. Thus, they were a primary target for socialist critics of the capitalistic system.

THE LABOR MOVEMENT: TRADE UNIONS

One of the incidental effects of the large-scale combination of business was the unwitting encouragement it gave to similar combination on the part of labor. During the first part of the century, European businessmen and governments had successfully opposed this, arguing that laboring men should rely on individualism and self-help rather than on collective action. These arguments were still used, but after 1871 they rather lacked conviction; and honest businessmen were forced to agree with the Scottish-American industrialist and philanthropist Andrew Carnegie (1835–1919), who wrote: "The right of the workingman to combine is no less sacred than the right of the manufacturer to enter into associations and conferences with his fellows, and it must sooner or later be conceded."

This change of view, which was shared by national parliaments, gave a new legal standing to trade unions. These bodies, which had existed in England, Belgium, France, and other continental countries since the first decades of the century, had always been subject to crippling restrictions. In England, for example, while given legal status by parliamentary acts of 1824–1825, they were forbidden to "molest" or "obstruct" employers or to do anything that could be construed as encouraging breach of contract and, in the circumstances, found it difficult to bargain effectively for improved wages or working conditions and virtually impossible to strike without being subject to legal action (see p. 107). Conditions in other countries had, if anything, been less favorable for union development. Now they were universally ameliorated. In England, the Gladstone government made a start in 1871 toward regularizing the position of unions; and, in 1875, the Disraeli ministry widened their freedom of action by legalizing peaceful picketing and making it clear that combined action in the furtherance of a trade dispute could not be punished as a conspiracy. In France the rights of unions were progressively widened between 1864 and 1884; in Austria they received legal status in 1870; and in other countries their position received similar clarification.

While these gains were being made, most existing unions were essentially benevolent and protective societies, small in membership and representing only the better-educated, better-paid workers of the skilled trades. They existed primarily for the purpose of extending assistance to their members in the form of unemployment and accident insurance and death benefits. They were cautious with their funds and, because of this, not very aggressive, using the strike weapon rarely. In the late 1880s and the 1890s, however, union membership began to grow significantly, and these characteristics gave way to others. The great increase in membership took place among the unskilled workers and was promoted by labor leaders who believed in more militant tactics than those employed in the past. Dramatic evidence was given of the change in a series of strikes: at Charleroi in Belgium, where there was bitter fighting between glass and mine workers and the police in 1886; at London in 1889, where the dock workers won an increase in wages by an impressive demonstration of discipline and patience; at Hamburg in 1896, where harbor workers sought to duplicate the English success and were stubbornly opposed by employers' associations.

The new unions were often strongly influenced by the doctrines of Marxian socialism and were allied with Marxian parties. This was true in Germany, for instance, where the fortunes of the Independent Unions varied with those of the Social Democratic party, so that they almost disappeared during the years of Bismarck's antisocialist legislation (see p. 348) and revived when it was repealed in 1890. There were other unions in Germany—the Hirsch-Duncker Unions, founded in the 1860s and modeled on the older English craft unions, and the Christian Trade Unions, which came into existence in the 1890s and kept their strength and vitality until 1933. But the Independent Unions always represented the majority of the organized labor force in Germany, and their politics remained socialist. In Austria, Italy, the Scandinavian countries, Holland, and Spain, Marxian socialists also directed the union movement; in England the unions were closely allied with the new Labour party, which, while not Marxian, was socialist in philosophy (see p. 292). France represented a somewhat special case, for the union movement there was strongly influenced by the doctrines of syndicalism (see pp. 281–283).

Despite its association with philosophies that called for the destruction of the existing order, the attitude of the union movement as a whole toward the idea of revolution was always ambiguous. As they grew in strength, unions continued in many cases to pay lip service to it, but they also acquired funds and property that made them feel a certain commitment to the capitalistic system. Moreover, even if their tactics had changed with the rise of industrial as opposed to craft unions, their basic purposes remained what they had always been: to improve the lot of the working classes and to raise their standard of living. When opportunities to do this appeared, they were inclined to grasp them, without troubling their minds too much about whether this would hasten or delay the coming of the revolution. They had no hesitation about making collective bargaining agreements with capitalist employers, and the Independent Unions of Germany were particularly successful in concluding "gentlemen's agreements" with their class enemies. Thus, in general, unions tended to become a moderate force within the socialist movement; and union leaders were apt to be found supporting the revisionist movement, which will be treated below.

The point has often been made that organized labor represented only a fraction

"Workingmen during the noon lunch hour," 1909, by Käthe Kollwitz. (Courtesy Galerie St. Etienne, New York. Collection Mr. and Mrs. William Lincer)

of the total labor force of Europe at this time, and this is undoubtedly true. In the year 1900, total trade-union membership in Great Britain stood at two million, in Germany at 850,000, in France at 250,000; and the numbers in other countries were much smaller. Yet the unions' success in improving the wages and the working conditions of the urban proletariat was felt beyond the confines of their own organizations, and their work in general helped, however slowly, to communicate to the mass of the labor force some idea of their social rights. Oswald Schumann, who first organized the Berlin transport workers' and draymen's union, once wrote of conditions in the German cities in the early days of his work (in the 1890s), when there were thousands of workers who

> had no understanding of what it was that inspired us, but lived the lives of beasts of burden, working fourteen, sixteen, twenty hours a day the whole year round, with the exception of Sunday, when they only had time to sleep off the weekly drunk with which they tried to make themselves forget all the misery, so as to be able to report again with their teams at three o'clock on Monday mornings to offer their *corvée* to the overseers. Among these people the union accomplished cultural work in the most eminent sense of the word.

A PHILOSOPHY FOR LABOR: KARL MARX

His Life and Influence   The second notable kind of labor combination in this period was the formation of working class political parties. The most important of these took their inspiration from the writings of Karl Marx.

Marx was born in 1818 at Trier in the Rhineland. On both sides his parents were Jewish and on both sides descended from rabbis, a fact not without influence on Marx's view of history, which was unrelievedly apocalyptic. He went to local schools and then studied at the universities of Bonn and Berlin, where his original interest shifted, under the influence of the philosopher Hegel, from jurisprudence to philosophy. He received his degree in 1841 and might have embarked on an academic career had a university opening materialized. When it did not, he began to write philosophical articles for a newspaper called the *Rheinische Zeitung* and, in 1843, became its editor. The ferment of the times made it impossible for a mind so energetic to remain wholly sunk in philosophical speculation. The young Marx became interested in questions of the day and, particularly, in the doctrines of French socialism, which he studied critically and with a dawning conviction that, if the times were out of joint, they were not going to be improved by the prescriptions of people like Fourier and Louis Blanc.

Before the year was over, the *Rheinische Zeitung* was banned by the government for being too outspoken on social questions, and Marx moved on to Paris. Here he met Friedrich Engels (1820–1895), the son of a Rhineland industrialist with manufacturing interests in England. The two men became collaborators, and Marx found in Engels not only a lifelong friend who came to his aid at his not infrequent moments of dire want but also an associate with an intimate practical knowledge of the working of the industrial system, which Marx himself

Karl Marx, 1818–1883.
(Culver Pictures)

lacked, as well as other gifts, including a keen insight into military matters, which in later years earned him the party nickname of "the General." Engels, on his side, never stopped admiring Marx's powers of analysis and conceptualization and said on one occasion, "Marx was a genius; we others at best were talented."

Along with others who were suspected of being dangerous radicals, Marx was expelled from France in 1847 and went to Brussels, where he and Engels were asked by a group of German socialists to draw up a program for them. The result was *The Communist Manifesto,* an eloquent and powerful denunciation of the existing social order, written on the very eve of the revolutions of 1848, although it was read only by a relatively small number of people during the next thirty years. During that time, Marx, after being declared *persona non grata* in Belgium, found asylum in Great Britain. He spent the rest of his life working in the British Museum on the researches for his *Critique of Political Economy* (1859) and his monumental work *Capital* (1867), writing analyses of current events for newspapers, and—from the late 1860s until his death in 1883—playing a dominant role in the European socialist movement.

This prominence among socialists was largely the result of the increasing respect felt for *The Communist Manifesto*. As Harold Laski once wrote, this was rather belatedly seen to be the first document of its kind to give a direction and a philosophy to what had before been little more than an inchoate protest against injustice; and in a very real sense it can be said to have created the modern socialist movement, which until now had been run by self-educated cranks. Some sense of why the *Manifesto* was able to do this may emerge from a brief consideration of what it had to say about history, the nature and weaknesses of the capitalistic system, and the role and destiny of the Socialist party.

History, Capitalism, the Party   Marx's views on history were influenced by his study of Hegel, who had believed that history is a logical process in which change is effected by the opposition of antagonistic elements and the resolution of this antagonism in new forms. This idea—sometimes called the dialectic—Marx borrowed; but, whereas Hegel had believed that the key to change was ideological (since all history, to his mind, was a perpetual unfolding of the Absolute Idea), Marx held that the basis of history and the key to historical change was materialistic. In any society, he insisted, "the mode of production in material life determines the general character of the social, political and spiritual processes of life" and, when change takes place, it does so not because of the antagonism of competing ideas but because of the clash of competing economic groupings. As Engels once wrote, "the whole history of mankind . . . has been a history of class struggles, contests between exploiting and exploited, ruling and oppressed classes." The capitalistic society of Marx's day was the net result of a long series of such clashes, ending with the victory of the bourgeoisie over the formerly dominant feudal classes. But this victory was not final. The process of historical change would continue until a great revolutionary event smashed the existing order and ended class conflict by abolishing class differences.

The outlines of that happy event were already looming on the horizon, Marx argued, because the nature of the capitalistic system tended to speed up the process of change by intensifying and simplifying the antagonisms that caused it. In modern capitalistic society, human exploitation had been carried to the most extreme degree, and hatred among classes was greater than ever before. At the same time, the class struggle had been simplified to a sharp confrontation between a small plutocracy and a multiplying and ever more resentful proletariat, which must in time rise and destroy its oppressors and clear the way for the classless society.

Why this was inevitable Marx set out to prove by an analysis of certain features of the capitalistic order. His principal argument was that the labor force was being victimized by what amounted to an organized system of robbery. Like others before him, Marx professed the belief that the value of any commodity is properly measured by the labor expended to produce it; and, upon this law, he erected the proposition that, in an equitable society, workingmen would receive in payment for their labor its equivalent in goods, comforts, and services. Under capitalism this was not true, for the tendency of capitalist employers was to keep wages low and working hours long, with the result that their workers were creating by their daily labor goods whose value greatly exceeded that of what they received in return, and this surplus value was going directly into the pockets of the employers as profits. This was an injustice, and apprehension of this fact by the working classes could not help but feed the flames of revolution.

Revolution was all the more imminent because of another characteristic of capitalism. As the productive process became more complicated, it required techniques and equipment beyond the understanding and the means of smaller entrepreneurs, who were therefore ruined and forced into the wage-earning class. By an inexorable process of concentration, the ownership and control of the economic system fell into fewer and fewer hands. This concentration and the simultaneous ballooning of the proletariat simplified the class struggle, and the social suffering caused by it intensified the resentment of the lower classes.

The proletariat was offered ever more numerous opportunities to express its feelings in revolutionary action, for the capitalists had proved to be incapable of controlling their own system. Marx wrote:

> Modern bourgeois society is like the sorcerer who is no longer able to control the powers of the nether world whom he has called up by his spells.... It is enough to mention the commercial crises that by their periodical return put the existence of the entire bourgeois· society on its trial, each time more threateningly.... And how does the bourgeoisie get over these crises? On the one hand, by the enforced destruction of a mass of productive forces; on the other, by a conquest of new markets and by the more thorough exploitation of old ones. That is to say, by paving the way for more extensive and more destructive crises and by diminishing the means by which crises are prevented.

In short, ruinous economic crises would increase in frequency and scope. Nothing could prevent this, because capitalism was incapable of correcting its own faults. By its very nature, it rested upon contradictions. Its objective was not service or development but gain and accumulation. "Modern society, which soon after its birth pulled Plutus by the hair of his head from the bowels of the earth," Marx wrote in *Capital,* "greets gold as its Holy Grail, as the glittering incarnation of its very principle of life"; and this ideal, far from inspiring attempts to prevent depressions, could only encourage more unbridled competition and more destructive collisions. Again, although capitalistic production, with mechanization, became an increasingly technical effort of collaboration in which the worker played an essential role, the capitalist entrepreneur either was incapable of seeing this truth or pursued his course of selfish exploitation in willful defiance of it. His obtuseness must eventually invite the system's destruction. Finally, however much he might rationalize and coordinate the operations of his own business, the capitalist would not recognize any restraint in his competition for markets with other producers. This state of anarchy encouraged the boom-bust tendencies inherent in the system and hastened the coming of the final debacle.

Marx believed that the destruction of the capitalist system and the ushering in of a new age could be effected only by conscious and violent intervention by the workers themselves. The proletariat must seize the propitious moment for revolution and, until it arrived, must prepare for it. To show it how to do so, to unite working class organizations into a common front, to carry out general tasks of education for effective political action, and to create the organization that would supply leadership when the time came was the first duty of the Socialist party. Its second task was to consolidate the revolution when the existing regime had been toppled. Marx foresaw a violent revolution in which the party-led workers would seize the centers of bourgeois power and the means of production, followed by a transitional period of indefinite duration called "the dictatorship of the proletariat." During this transitional stage, the party would systematically destroy the vestiges of bourgeois institutions and eradicate the remains of class prejudice, and, by educating the masses to their new opportunities and responsibilities, would lay the basis for the classless society of the future in which the state withered away and all men were permitted to live in conditions of justice and liberty.

Marx's picture of that ultimate stage in human development was confessedly vague, for he was more intent upon analyzing the ills of contemporary society and delineating the forces that would overcome them than he was in drawing blueprints for the remote future. But that future *would* come; the logic of history made this a certainty. The question of *when* it would come would depend upon the speed with which the capitalistic system disintegrated and the efficiency of the Socialist party in exploiting its disintegration.

Upon this last point, Marx put considerable emphasis. Both he and Engels were scornful of all socialist movements before their time. This was doubtless due in part to Marx's temperament. He was never kindly disposed to movements or ideas that differed from his own. The German-American writer and statesman Carl Schurz wrote that he had never in his life met a man "of such wounding, intolerable arrogance of behavior" as Marx, adding that he was perpetually denouncing those who dared oppose his views as bourgeois—"that is, as an unmistakeable example of deep spiritual and ethical degradation."

But Marx's feelings about such predecessors as Owen, Fourier, and Saint-Simon were not wholly the result of spleen. He believed that these men were not class-conscious enough and that they had deluded themselves and their followers by believing that socialism could be imposed from above by the disinterested action of benevolent members of the possessing classes. They were blind to history's revelation of the irreconcilable conflict between classes, and their trusting utopianism made them grateful for piddling concessions and surface reforms that left society essentially unchanged.

Marx chose the name communist for his famous manifesto partly to distinguish himself and his brand of socialism from the utopians who had gone before; his followers were to call his socialism scientific socialism for the same reason. Behind the semantic difference was a more essential one. Marx was calling for a socialist movement that would base its theories upon the materialistic view of history and society, upon the inevitability of the class struggle, and upon the clear recognition that the victory of the proletariat must be ushered in by violence.

Scientist or Prophet?   In the strict meaning of the word, Marx's socialism was no more "scientific" than any other social theory. Consider, for instance, his belief that "the mode of production in material life determines the general character of the social, political, and spiritual processes of life." Marx did not, of course, mean by this that economics and economics alone would determine every aspect of our daily life and action, for he always admitted that other factors had a part to play in the drama of history and the life of man. But he did believe that if there were such other factors, they were either themselves rooted in economics or were, in their totality, of less weight in any given situation than the economic factors; and it is precisely here that we must question the realism of his views. One need only think of the interplay of such factors as human ambition and human fallibility, developments in domestic politics, climatic conditions and configurations of geography, economic distress, religious faith, national exaltation or irritation, technological progress or lack of progress, administrative efficiency, military genius, and sheer accident in the events that led to the revolution in Paris in 1848 or the outbreak of the Crimean War to realize that the question of causation is too complicated to permit us to claim that any single factor is always more important than others in determining the course of history. And this is what Marx was inclined to do.

At the same time, it should be noted that Marx's view of history left little or no place for human volition or initiative. Yet the very modes of production to which he gave such emphasis had come into existence not by spontaneous generation but by human decision and action. The system of production in use at any time was not a uniform or monolithic thing, as Marx often seemed to believe, but a composite of many ideas and institutions constantly being changed, corrected, and adapted to new circumstances by human beings. It would appear to be less scientific to talk of man as the tool of the prevailing mode of production than as its author.

In the same way, it is rather less than sound to assume, as Marx did, that individuals will tend to act socially in accordance with their class allegiance, or even that they will always recognize their membership in a given class. History is filled with examples of individuals and groups refusing to act in the way that their economic circumstances would seem to require, because they considered other things—status, social aspiration, tradition, or prestige—more important. An impoverished entrepreneur is likely to resist recognizing himself as a new proletarian and refuse to act like one, as is demonstrated by the fact that throughout recent history such new proletarians have turned more frequently to rightist political parties than to socialist or labor movements. For Marx, moreover, to believe that, as he once said, "the proletarians in all countries [had] one and the same interest, one and the same enemy" and that they were "in the great mass by nature without national prejudice" was to ignore the experience of the revolutionary movements and the impact of nationalistic fervor on all classes in the Europe of his time.

If Marx's historical views were less scientific than his followers were likely to claim, so were his economic theories. His theory of surplus value, for example, had limited application to the realities of the age of high capitalism, for it made no allowance for the hidden costs of production—administration, advertising, interest payments, amortization of new building, and other things—that absorbed much of the profit that Marx claimed went into the employers' pockets; nor did it take account of the special skills of employers or their willingness to assume risks, although these things obviously helped assure employment for workers.

Marx's statements concerning concentration of capital and periodicity of economic depressions bore a closer resemblance to the economic tendencies of his day, as a comparison of his views with the facts stated in the first section of the present chapter will make clear; but, on the other hand, there was evidence, even in Marx's time, that capitalist entrepreneurs were both more enlightened than he was willing to admit and more prepared to make economic sacrifices, if necessary, in order to correct palpable weaknesses in their operations. Recognition of the social character of their enterprises and acquiescence in controls designed to avoid economic trouble did not, in the long run, prove to be impossible for them.

Yet to say all this is in no way to depreciate the importance of Marx's work either as historian or as economist. To historians he brought a necessary corrective to the tendency to give undue weight to purely political factors and to write what has been called "drum and trumpet history"; and historians after his time were persuaded by his influence to devote more thought to the social and economic aspects of human evolution. To economic thought he brought an emphasis upon class structure and attitude that was new and provocative, as well as a more sharply defined conceptualization of capitalist economy that stimulated further study and analysis.

Aside from this, the question as to whether Marx's socialism was scientific or not is probably less important than he himself thought it was. Marx wanted to be thought of as rigorously objective, free from prejudice, completely analytical. He was, of course, nothing of the sort, and he should properly be considered as an angry prophet, denouncing an economic system that he loathed personally and predicting its imminent destruction and the coming of the millennium. It is, perhaps, precisely here that we can see the reason for the remarkable spread and acceptance of his teachings.

Karl Loewith has written that it is no accident that the last great battle between the bourgeoisie and the proletariat of which Marx writes so fervently reminds one of the apocalypses of the Old Testament and of the Book of Revelation. It is not by chance, Loewith continues,

> that the task of the proletariat corresponds to the world-historical mission of the chosen people, that the redemptive and universal function of the most degraded class is conceived on the religious pattern of Cross and Resurrection, that the ultimate transformation of the realm of necessity into a realm of freedom corresponds to the transformation of the *civitas terrena* into a *civitas Dei,* and that the whole process of history as outlined in *The Communist Manifesto* corresponds to the general scheme of the Jewish-Christian interpretation of history as a providential advance toward a final goal which is meaningful. Historical materialism is essentially, though secretly, a history of fulfillment and salvation in terms of social economy.

Marxism was a promise of sure salvation, and it was this aura of inevitability rather than the logic of its propositions that explained its tremendous appeal. The miserable and the underprivileged wanted to be told that they would triumph in the end, and found it easy to turn to a creed that assured them that history was working toward that ultimate objective and could not be stayed. So did the guilty and the insecure. In the continental countries, in particular, bad conscience often led members of the possessing class to embrace Marxism as the surest means of correcting the injustice that they felt their class had caused, while intellectual insecurity and craving after ideological certainty led other representatives of the same class to follow their example.

Nor were the appeals of Marxism restricted to these groups. They were felt also by those whose main motivation was to correct injustices they thought had been done to them—individuals who blamed their loss of economic or social status upon "the system" or who resented the failure of society to appreciate their talents—and those who yearned for personal power and hoped to gain it if the existing system were destroyed.

To the suffering, the deprived, the unappreciated, and the ambitious, Marx held out the promise of a golden age, in which "in place of the old bourgeois society with its classes and class antagonisms [would] come an association in which the free development of each individual [would] be the condition for the free development of all." Yet the means he advocated were hardly likely to produce such millennial freedom. This was because Marx belonged to that group of nineteenth-century thinkers who made a cult out of violence, habituated society to accepting it as a legitimate tool of politics, and, by doing so, weakened the ideas of law, equity, compromise, and adjustment that were the hallmarks of nineteenth-century liberalism and had been in the past the best assurance of progress toward freedom.

THE DEVELOPMENT OF SOCIALISM

Marx and Bakunin: The Challenge of Anarchism   The spread of Marx's influence among the working classes was very slow. The first parties that accepted his doctrines did not come into existence until the end of the 1860s, and their progress was most uncertain for at least another decade. In the first international organization of labor, the International Workingmen's Association, which was founded in London in 1864 and lasted until 1876, Marx played a prominent role—actually delivering the inaugural address and declaration of principles—but hardly a dominant one. Indeed, the short history of the First International was marked by a bitter conflict between his philosophy and the competing doctrine of anarchism.

Anarchism has been called the *reductio ad absurdum* of nineteenth-century romaticism because of its fervent insistence that man was essentially good but had been corrupted by institutions. The anarchist conceived of his goal as one of restoring mankind to its state of primitive virtue by destroying the instruments of corruption—the established churches, the great agglomerations of economic power, and, above all, the modern centralized state. In contrast to Marxists, who wished to take over the existing state and the means of production by revolution, anarchists wished to destroy these things and to reorganize society on a voluntary basis. What, after all, asked Proudhon, the father of modern anarchism, (p. 79) does the individual derive from the government of his country?

To be governed is to be watched over, inspected, spied on, directed, legislated, regulated, docketed, indoctrinated, preached at, controlled, assessed, weighed, censored, ordered about ... noted, registered, taxed, stamped, measured, valued, assayed, patented, licensed, authorized, endorsed, admonished, hampered, reformed, rebuked, arrested. Under pretext of the general interest, it is to be taxed, drilled, held to ransom, exploited, monopolized, extorted, hoaxed, squeezed, robbed; then at least resistance, at the first word of complaint, repressed, fined, abused, annoyed, followed, bullied, beaten, disarmed, garrotted, imprisoned, machine-gunned, judged, condemned, deported, flayed, sold, betrayed, and finally mocked, ridiculed, insulted, dishonored. That's government, that's its justice, that's its morality!

Leaving its rhetorical value aside, Proudhon's thinking was too contradictory—he managed to combine admiration for Louis Napoleon and support of slavery in the United States with his libertarian views—to serve as the basis for an effective political movement. On the other hand, the ideas of Prince Alexander Kropotkin (1842–1921), a Russian nobleman who wrote idealized portraits of voluntary societies in which free men labored for other than financial reward and lived without the necessity of organized government, were perhaps too sophisticated and bloodless. The man who made anarchism an important working class movement and was responsible for its continuing influence in Europe was Michael Bakunin (1814–1876).

Michael Bakunin, 1814–1876, in 1869.
(Brown Brothers)

This remarkable figure had been born, like Kropotkin, a member of the Russian aristocracy. Destined for a military career, he abandoned it in favor of the study of philosophy, became interested in the sufferings of subject nationalities like the Poles and the Italians, and ended by becoming a professional revolutionary. He participated in the February revolution in Paris in 1848 and the rising in Prague later in that year and was arrested by Prussian troops during the fighting in Dresden in 1849. Shipped back to his own country, he spent eight years in prison and four more in enforced exile in Siberia. He then escaped and made his way back to western Europe by way of Yokahama, San Francisco, and New York and plunged immediately into new revolutionary activity. In the 1860s he organized anarchist cells in Switzerland, Spain, and Italy and founded a Social Democratic Alliance with secret statutes and a program calling for "universal revolution." He was an ardent supporter of the Poles during the rising of 1863, was involved in 1869 with Nechaev's Society of the Ax in Russia (see p. 388), and organized a commune in Lyon during the revolutionary disturbances in France in 1871. He died in 1876 at the age of 62, with his body wasted by imprisonment and irregular living but his brain still teeming with revolutionary plans and his heart with hope.

It was during the 1860s, when the national states were taking their modern form and capitalism reaching its full development in the West, that Bakunin formulated his anarchist creed. Echoing Proudhon, he wrote:

> The State was born historically ... of the marriage of violence, rapine, pillage.... It has been from its origin ... the divine sanction of brutal force and triumphant inequality.... Even when it commands what is good, it hinders and spoils it just because it commands it ... because the good, from the moment it is commanded, becomes evil from the point of view of true morality ... and from the point of view of human respect and liberty.

Capitalism was just as bad in its effects upon those whose lives it commanded. So was organized religion, and so was that idol of nineteenth-century intellectuals, modern science, with its presumptuous attempt to regulate life by defining its laws. Bakunin declared war on all institutions, all laws, all abstract principles that regulated—and, by doing so, hampered—human growth.

Bakunin was not a systematic thinker. He was vague about what would replace the things he detested, although he seemed to incline to Proudhon's preference for a society of small voluntary communities in which all decisions would be made by unanimous consent and no one compelled to do anything except by his own will. He did not attempt to spell out the details, preferring to believe that men would solve their own problems once they were free. The act of becoming free would have a regenerating force; and Bakunin went considerably further than Marx in deifying violence as the instrument by which this regeneration would be effected. Alexander Herzen, the dean of the Russian political exiles in London, once described Bakunin's philosophy as "a blind stumbling after the unknown god of destruction," and there is much to be said for this, for Bakunin dreamed of gigantic conflagrations that would accomplish what reason could not define. "Unchain the popular anarchy in country and town," he wrote. "Magnify it, till it rolls like a raging avalanche, devouring and destroying." "The tempest and life, that is what we need. A new world without laws, and consequently free." He called for "a phalanx 40,000 strong of young folk of the educated classes" to lead the masses in daring acts of terrorism and spontaneous risings against authority until the goal of universal revolution had been attained.

The French writer Albert Camus once pointed out that Bakunin's emphasis on the necessity of a revolutionary elite bore some similarity to Marx's insistence on the creation of a disciplined party, and that Lenin, who later elaborated this idea, owed as much to the anarchist as he did to the author of *The Communist Manifesto*. This is probably true but, if so, it is one of the few bonds between Marx and Bakunin, who detested each other personally and disapproved of each other's ideas. Bakunin hated Marx's authoritarianism and saw clearly that a successful Marxist revolution would leave the political and economic institutions that he reprobated untouched, even if they were controlled by other hands. He believed that the dictatorship of the proletariat would be fully as destructive of freedom as the bourgeois order and that, despite Marx's professions, the state would never wither away. Marx, in his turn, was contemptuous of the lack of system and general wooliness of Bakunin's declarations and had a genuine horror of the ill-prepared acts of individual terrorism that the anarchists admired. When Bakunin's eloquence began to win a wide following within the International Workingmen's Association, Marx preferred to force the expulsion of Bakunin's group from that organization in 1873 rather than allow the International to become a sounding board for ideas he considered dangerous, even though the departure of the anarchists so weakened the International that it collapsed three years later.

On the whole, Marx's apprehensions proved to be groundless, and his doctrines, in the long run, won many more converts than those of his rival. Yet Bakunin's influence continued, too. In France it appealed to many who were dissatisfied with the caution and moderation of French socialism after 1871; and there were anarchist-inspired attacks upon church buildings in the Haute-Loire, political assassinations in Paris, Lyon, and other cities (including the murder of the president of the Republic in 1894), a bomb plot inside the Chamber of Deputies, and other acts of terror. In Italy and Spain, where the rural classes were the most depressed and backward in western Europe and were virtually immune to the logical and systematic creed of Marxism, anarchism was particularly successful. Under the influence of Bakunin's follower Malatesta, peasant disorders were fomented in the southern provinces of Italy throughout the last decade of the century, while in Spain anarchism spread rapidly among the landless peasantry of Andalusia and the industrial workers of Catalonia, who were recruited from the most depressed rural areas. By 1882 anarchist organizations in Spain totaled about 50,000 members, and by 1900 anarchism was on its way to becoming the strongest wing of the Spanish working class movement.

Syndicalism   In the period after 1900, an offshoot of anarchism also threatened the position of orthodox socialism. Syndicalism (which took its name from the French word for labor union, *syndicat*) was a protest against the prevailing socialist emphasis upon political action and the growing tendency toward moderation in the European Socialist parties after 1900 (which will be discussed in the section on revisionism that follows). The syndicalists argued that the emancipation of the workers would be won not in parliaments but in the economic field, and not by majority votes but by "direct action." Such action should be exercised through trade union organizations and should take the form of sabotage, "conscious withholding of efficiency," and, above all, the strike. To enhance the effectiveness of such tactics, the syndicalists called for increased effort to unionize the unskilled workers, the organization of new unions for industrial combat rather than benevolent and fraternal purposes, the widest possible federation of such unions, and a general agreement that contractual agreements with employers need not be honored. Direct action would, it was believed, maintain the class consciousness and militancy of the labor movement while weakening the capitalist system and preparing the way for the "general strike" that would one day paralyze it and inaugurate the revolution.

Syndicalism had its most conspicuous success in France, which also produced its most brilliant exponent, Georges Sorel (1847–1922). The *Confédération Générale du Travail* (CGT), which was founded by an anarchist named Fernand Pelloutier, was syndicalist from the beginning. This federation of small aggressive unions set its face against such typical trade-union activities as the accumulation of funds for insurance purposes and devoted its energies to direct action, which it adopted formally as its policy in the so-called Charter of Amiens of 1906. Before World War I, the CGT was active in inspiring strikes among civil servants and railway workers and encouraging disaffection inside the army.

In other countries syndicalist successes were less impressive. The cult of direct action won a not inconsiderable number of recruits in English unions, however, and there was a wave of syndicalist activity in Ireland on the eve of the war. In Italy, Filippo Corridoni was the leader of a strong anarcho-syndicalist movement in the same years. His teachings—and those of Sorel—influenced a young socialist named Benito Mussolini, who wrote in 1909, "Syndicalism restores to its place in history the creative value of man, man who determines and is determined, who can leave the imprint of his force upon things and institutions." After the war, Mussolini's new Fascist party was clearly influenced by the syndicalist emphasis upon applied violence.

In Spain, a federation of syndicalist industrial unions, the *Confederación Nacional del Trabajo* (CNT) was founded in 1910, and a similar agricultural federation, the *Federación Nacional de Agricultores Españoles* (FNAE), in 1913; and, after the war, when the older anarchist organizations called upon their members to enter syndicalist unions, over a million workers of one kind or another could be described as anarcho-syndicalists. As in Italy, the anarcho-syndicalist idealization of violence influenced rightist groups as well as labor organizations. By the 1930s, reactionary army officers were forming *sindicats* for action against the workers, and José Antonio Primo de Rivera had formed an association of ultra conservative groups called the *Juntas de Ofensiva Nacional-Sindicalista* (JONS). It is no exaggeration to say, therefore, that when the Spanish civil war broke out in 1936, there were followers of Bakunin and Sorel on both sides.

But that takes us rather far from the labor movement of the period presently under discussion.

Revisionism   Despite the anarcho-syndicalist preference for direct economic action as opposed to political maneuver, the main tendency in European socialism was political, and, by the 1890s, Socialist parties had been organized in most countries, were vying for popular support in national and local elections, and—as subsequent chapters will show—were having considerable success. Most of these parties were Marxist in inspiration and doctrine, although the English movement looked back to the older socialism of Owen and the Chartists (see p. 107). Even when the Marxist label was present, it did not, of course, mean that the parties bearing it were always united and harmonious, for they often developed splinter groups and dissident minorities and were subject to doctrinal and tactical disagreements. During their lifetimes, Marx and Engels were often able to exert their authority so as to adjudicate these disputes; but even before Engels's death in 1895 a profound division was looming up that would probably have been beyond their powers of conciliation.

This split, which was to have profound and lasting effects wherever socialism developed, came to a head during the so-called revisionist controversy. For some time there had been unease among leading socialist and trade union leaders about the gap between Marx's predictions and the realities of European economic development. Prominent among these was the German Social Democrat Eduard Bernstein (1850–1932), who, after years of study, summed up his views in the terse comment, "Peasants do not sink; middle class does not disappear; crises do not grow ever longer; misery and serfdom do not increase." If this was true—and Bernstein became sure it was as he carried his studies further—then the collapse of the capitalist system was not imminent, and the Socialist parties must change their tactics, if not their goals. Their logical course must be to exploit all the opportunities they could find for gradual reform in the interest of the working classes, even if this meant departing from the aloof, noncooperative attitude they had hitherto maintained toward the bourgeois political parties. They must, in a word, adopt the evolutionary tactics favored by the Fabian Society in Great Britain (see p. 292), with whom Bernstein had worked while in England; they must, as Bernard Shaw once wrote, rescue socialism from the barricades and make it a practical philosophy of social regeneration by democratic rather than revolutionary means.

Bernstein's views, published in articles and book form between 1896 and 1899, had European repercussions. They appealed to those members of Socialist parties who felt that the negative parliamentary tactics of the past doomed socialism to a permanently sterile opposition. They appealed even more directly to the trade-union wing of the socialist movement, whose leaders had long been irritated by the fact that collective-bargaining agreements, union-sponsored unemployment insurance schemes, and other methods of which the union rank and file approved were always opposed by party doctrinaires on the grounds that they would weaken revolutionary fervor or dull the edge of the class struggle. Since Bernstein's strictures on Marx seemed to find verification in the rising level of real wages and the general prosperity of Europe in the years before World War

I, they won wide acceptance in most countries with strong Socialist parties; and even many of the Socialist leaders who stoutly insisted that they were orthodox Marxists began, in fact, in their day-by-day parliamentary work, to act in the spirit of revisionism.

This was true of the great French Socialist leader Jean Jaurès (1859–1914), who—before his career was terminated by an assassin's bullet—had made it quite clear that he found in revisionism nothing alien to the spirit of Marx's teaching, "since Marxism itself contains the means by which it can be supplemented and revised." Like Bernstein, Jaurès rejected both the rigidity of Marx's economic theories and his emphasis on revolution. The victory of the proletariat would certainly come in due course, he believed, but by gradual degrees rather than by a sudden catastrophic event. Socialists should spend less time dwelling on that ultimate goal than on the positive tasks that must and could be carried out in the present. The important thing was "to live always in a socialist state of grace, working each hour, each minute" through the party, the trade unions, consumers' cooperative associations, and whatever other means came to hand to remake the world in accordance with socialist ideals.

The revisionist point of view was bitterly assailed by all those who held to the revolutionary doctrine of the founder of scientific socialism; and in 1902 this group found its most effective spokesman in V. I. Lenin, whose pamphlet, *What Is to Be Done?* castigated the followers of Bernstein for their evident intention of bourgeoisifying the socialist movement. Lenin argued that victory could never be won for the proletariat by gradualist "bread and butter" socialism and that, rather than becoming bodies of parliamentarians and logrollers, the Socialist parties must be disciplined elites of professional revolutionaries, working incessantly to give the workers not what they thought they wanted but what they *should* want, and striving to replace the "trade-union mentality" with a revived faith in the class struggle.

By 1914, revisionism represented the majority view of most of the organized Socialist parties, if we can judge by their stand on major issues; and this result had been achieved by the way in which expanding capitalism had confounded the predictions of Karl Marx. In Lenin's protest against the victory of reformism, however, we can see a program and a rallying cry for all those who, during and after World War I, were to break away and form independent revolutionary parties, thus completing the division of the working class movement into a democratic Socialist wing and a new Communist movement.

The Second International   Despite these doctrinal differences, the various Socialist and labor parties found it possible before 1914 to unite in an international organization that was designed to replace the one that had broken down during the conflict between Marx and Bakunin. In 1889, in Paris, the Second International came into existence, and, at this first meeting delegations were present from France, Germany, Britain, Belgium, Austria, Russia, Holland, Denmark, Sweden, Norway, Switzerland, Poland, Rumania, Italy, Hungary, Spain, Portugal, Bohemia, and Bulgaria, as well as observers from the United States, Argentina, and Finland. The purpose of the new organization was to facilitate contacts and the exchange of information among the various Socialist parties, to provide, whenever possible, for mutual support, and, on great issues, to speak for socialism as a whole. In 1900 the International set up an International Socialist Bureau with headquarters at Brussels, with subcommittees to coordinate the action of national parliamentary parties and to act for the whole International when it was not in session.

One aspect of the work of the International was to create a socialist public opinion on matters affecting the peace of Europe. The constituent parties were antimilitarist and, in the recurrent diplomatic crises of the period 1900–1914, they sought to mobilize world sentiment against the drift to war. The International had no common policy, however, with respect to means of preventing conflict if it should actually materialize; and, when the great crisis of 1914 came, although the International Socialist Bureau sought to coordinate the tactics to be followed by the national parties, its efforts were defeated by the forces of patriotism, which proved as seductive to socialists as to the bourgeoisie. The International did not survive the war that followed.

Chapter 13 FROM LIBERALISM TO DEMOCRACY: POLITICAL PROGRESS IN WESTERN EUROPE, 1871–1914

From what has been said in the previous chapter, it will be easy to guess that the political history of the countries of western Europe was far from placid in the years after 1871. The governing classes were under steady pressure to extend political freedom to the masses and to alleviate the social conditions in which they lived and labored; and in most countries, although sometimes only after protracted political struggles, they acknowledged this and instituted measures of political and economic democracy before 1914. The country that made the most conspicuous progress in this respect was, indubitably, Great Britain; but several of the lesser nations showed an equal ability to adjust their policies and institutions to the changing conditions of the times. Unfortunately, others—and their number included Italy and Spain—showed a greater willingness to imitate the forms than to be inspired by the realities of British parliamentary and social institutions.

GREAT BRITAIN

The Broadening of the Franchise   As a result of the reforms of the 1860s (see pp. 226–229), Great Britain was already far advanced on the road to political democracy, and she now carried this to its logical conclusion. The Reform Act of 1867 had given the franchise to nearly all the male urban population. In 1884 a new act, passed during Gladstone's second ministry (1880–1885), gave similar voting rights to those elements of the rural population who had not been enfranchised in 1867 (farm tenants and agricultural laborers) and made the franchise uniform throughout the United Kingdom. The new act was supplemented a year later by a Redistribution Act that increased the size of the House of Commons to 607 members, who were to be elected, with some exceptions, by single-member constituencies of roughly equal size.

The most important of the demands that the Chartists (see pp. 108–110) had made forty years before this time had now been achieved; and there was little more that an Englishman could ask for in the way of political democracy unless he believed in female suffrage, a cause for which there was already much agitation but which was not to triumph until World War I. Nevertheless, the right to express oneself politically by means of the ballot was meaningless unless the political parties and Parliament itself were responsive to such expression; and some Englishmen in this period, worried by the failure to deal with the problems caused by the great depression, doubted whether those bodies were sufficiently aware of the needs and the desires of the English people.

The Depression, the Parties, and Parliament   Starting in 1873, for reasons already touched upon (see pp. 264–266), the British economy was affected by a series of troubles that were to continue with occasional periods of improvement until the middle of the 1890s. Agriculture was hit particularly hard, as the effects of the revolution in transportation began to be felt in England. Wheat, which had sold for 77 shillings the bushel in 1855, never reached 50 shillings again after 1877 and, in the 1880s, had slipped to below 40. To producers who, unlike their French and German counterparts, were not protected by tariffs, the price drop was ruinous; and their losses were reflected in the abandonment of once-productive grain areas to grazing or dairy and truck farming, the de-population of numerous rural areas, an increased drift of agricultural laborers to the slums of the great cities, and the decline of the wages and working conditions of those who stayed on the soil. English agriculture never completely recovered from the blows of this period. Its troubles were henceforth chronic.

Simultaneously, industry was passing through one of those periods of adjustment which, however much they may contribute in the long run to progress, are apt to involve both employers and laborers in economic distress (see p. 264). The years from 1876 to 1879 were marked by a slump in iron and steel prices that rapidly became general. Although there was some recovery at the end of the decade, prices began to fall again in 1883 and a depression set in that continued until 1886. The late 1880s were once more marked by a cautious recovery, followed by another setback at the beginning of the next decade. Throughout all these fluctuations there never seems to have been any danger of a total collapse; the slumps were linked with the continental speculative crashes of 1873 and 1882, with periodic financial strain, with the effects of continental tariffs and increased foreign competition, and with a retrenchment psychology on the part of business. The wealth of the country as a whole increased during the troubles, as did that of certain individual enterprises; and the fundamental health of the economy was never in doubt. Indeed, the depression encouraged measures which in the long run strengthened England's productive capacity, such as the introduction of new labor-saving devices, electrification, rationalization of processes, and exploitation of new areas of production. (This was not true, unfortunately, of older industries, particularly cotton and coal. They refused to pay the cost of modernization, thus postponing it until it was either too late or beyond the means of private enterprise. But the results of this were not to be felt until after the first World War, nor did the situation become critical until after the second.)

The fact remains, however, that for millions these were hard times. By the 1880s, the word unemployment had attained general currency, as the situation it described became, or appeared to become, a permanent feature of the social order. The continuing decline of agriculture and the industrial slumps reduced thousands to near starvation. In a famous study called *Life and Labour of the People in London,* published in 1892, Charles Booth stated that over 30 percent of the population of England's largest city were living in poverty. A few years before, the economist John Rae had written that government reports showed that "in the wealthiest nation in the world, almost every twentieth inhabitant [was] a pauper," that a fifth of the community was insufficiently fed, that one third or more of the families in rural areas lived in conditions destructive of health and morality, and that the great proportion of the population led "a life of monotonous and incessant toil, with no prospect in old age but penury and parochial support."

Upon the wealthier classes this sort of thing might make little impact. In December 1883, *Punch* pictured a young lady saying breathlessly: "Lord Archibald is going to take us to a dear little slum he had found ... such a fearful place! Fourteen poor things sleeping in one bed!" But Beatrice Webb, one of the founders of Fabianism, was to recall years later that, while working in a clothing factory in London's East End in 1888, she had been appalled to learn how many of her co-workers actually lived in such conditions and what deplorable effects it had.

The major parties made some attempt to correct the most obvious of these ills. But their record of accomplishment was limited, partly because they were distracted by other issues and more, perhaps, because the majority of their members did not agree that the correction of these conditions was a legitimate concern of the government.

The most impressive record of social legislation made by any ministry in the early years of this period was that of Disraeli's Conservative government of 1874–1880. In the single year 1875, existing laws regulating trade-union activities were liberalized (see p. 269), and a Sale of Food and Drugs Act, an Artisans Dwellings Act, and a Public Health Act were passed, the last two of which remained the backbone of government legislation on housing and sanitation until the 1920s. These reforms proved the genuineness of Disraeli's professions about Tory Democracy and his desire to make the Conservative party a party of social progress in the interests of the people. But Disraeli himself, in the last years of his ministry, was forced to devote his declining energies[1] to such things as

[1] Poor health was one of the main reasons for his transference to the House of Lords as the Earl of Beaconsfield in 1876.

Overdoing It. "What? Going already? And in Mackintoshes? Surely you are not going to walk!" "Oh, dear no! Lord Archibald is going to take us to a dear little slum he's found out near the Minories—such a fearful place! Fourteen poor things sleeping in one bed and no window!—and the Mackintoshes are to keep out infection, you know, and hide one's diamonds, and all that!" *Punch,* December 22, 1883.

the crisis in the Near East (see p. 254), the Irish problem (which will be discussed below), and wars against the Zulus in South Africa and the Afghans. After his death in 1881 his party drifted away from Tory Democracy completely.

It is true that, in the 1880s, when the party founded the Primrose League in Disraeli's memory, the famous father of a famous son, Lord Randolph Churchill (1849–1895), declared one of its principal objects to be "the vigorous and earnest promotion of every social reform which can in any degree raise the character and condition of the English people." But Churchill's increasingly radical social views frightened the majority of his party colleagues and—although he had at one time been regarded as a future prime minister—isolated and deprived him of influence. Disraeli's successor as leader of the party, Robert Cecil, third Marquess of Salisbury (1830–1903), was interested almost exclusively in foreign affairs; and the Primrose League, far from becoming a center of reforming activity, developed into an organization largely devoted to attracting the upper middle classes to the Conservative fold, thus helping the party replace the Liberals as the representative of British industrial and commercial interests. This and the

William Ewart Gladstone, 1809–1898. Pen and ink drawing by Harry Furniss. (Courtesy, Museum of Fine Arts, Boston)

party's success in making the cause of imperialism its own (see p. 408) doubtless explains why the Conservative party, in contrast to its rival, continued to grow in strength and why it still thrives as a major party; but these things did not lead to much positive action to improve the conditions caused by the long depression.

In the Liberal party, the majority had never freed themselves from their old faith in the *laissez-faire* principle. Gladstone's own zeal for reform in England seemed to come to an end with the passage of the Education Act of 1870 (p. 229); and, during his ministries of 1880–1885, 1886, and 1892–1895, he concentrated on the problems of Ireland. The Liberals did have a numerous Radical wing which showed an awareness of the need for social reform, and in Joseph Chamberlain

(1836–1914) they possessed an energetic and gifted man who demonstrated what could be done in the way of practical alleviation of the lot of the poor. Chamberlain (another father of famous sons, one of whom was to help negotiate the Locarno treaties of 1925 [p. 509] and another to be prime minister of England from 1937 to 1940 [pp. 611, 643]) made a fortune in business as a young man and then, from the age of 37, devoted most of his time to politics. Elected mayor of Birmingham in 1873, he won an international reputation by his measures to improve housing, public health, and education. But his efforts, after he entered Parliament in 1876, to persuade his party to do similar work on a national scale—and especially his declaration in January 1885 that the main problem of the future was the promotion of the greater happiness of the masses and that Liberal policy should be "to lessen the evils which poverty brings in its train, to increase the rewards of labour, to bring hope to the miserable"—alarmed more people than it convinced. The majority of his colleagues were relieved when differences with Gladstone on Irish policy led him, in 1886, to withdraw and form a group called the Liberal Unionists, which henceforth cooperated with the Conservatives. This loss to the Liberal party was not balanced by any increase in Conservative social conscience as a result of Chamberlain's collaboration, for his energies were soon entirely absorbed by colonial and commercial questions. At the same time, his secession deprived the Liberal party of its strongest advocate of reforming activity, weakened its appeal to the masses, and strengthened a growing feeling that Liberalism was bankrupt.

These remarks about the two parties are not intended to suggest that they did nothing in Parliament. In fact, the amount of legislation passed between 1871 and the turn of the century that regulated business practices dangerous to the health and safety of workers, provided new social services and utilities, facilitated the creation of public parks and libraries, raised the level of literacy (by making elementary education compulsory [1880], making county and borough councils responsible for elementary, secondary, and technical schools, and increasing state subsidies to both private and board schools), and provided for the care of the mentally ill and the seriously disabled would have staggered the generation of 1830. But much of this was done reluctantly, by worried M.P.'s who feared that government intervention was becoming excessive and resisted more thoroughgoing measures to alleviate the continuing economic distress. Even the Radicals, who professed to believe in a redistribution of wealth by taxing the wealthy, shied away from any fundamental criticism of the prevailing economic system and opposed government intervention in the field of wages and prices. When the working classes began in the 1880s to agitate for basic reforms, they got little support from Parliament or the established parties.

Toward a Labour Party   Given the widening of the franchise and the continued economic distress, it was probably inevitable that a new political party would arise to represent the masses. In 1884 revived interest in socialism led to the foundation of the Social Democratic Federation (SDF), the first sizable socialist political body since Owen's day. Marxist in inspiration, it never received the formal blessing of Marx and Engels, largely because its founder, H. M. Hyndman, had not given Marx credit for the ideas he borrowed from him when he wrote his book *England for All* in 1881. Marx's approval would hardly have helped it much, for its emphasis on imminent revolution never attracted the support of the British common people, and by the late 1880s it was already a spent force. The Labour party of the twentieth century sprang not from it but from the Fabian Society, from Keir Hardie's Independent Labour party, and from the new trade unions.

The Fabians were a group of middle class intellectuals who came together in 1883 to discuss social questions and developed into one of the most influential forces in British politics—a point illustrated by the fact that, in 1945, there were 230 Fabians in the House of Commons, most of them associated with the Labour party. In the first years the society included such people as Sidney Webb, its founder and driving force, and his wife Beatrice,[2] the dramatist George Bernard Shaw, Annie Besant (whose organization of the London match girls in the 1880s was one of the first successes of the new unionism in England), the novelist H. G. Wells, the historian of socialism G. D. H. Cole, and the future prime minister Ramsay MacDonald. Claiming as their spiritual predecessors both Robert Owen and John Stuart Mill, they pledged themselves to the ideal of a reconstitution of society and embarked on a systematic study of every phase of the industrial system of their day. In 1889 they presented their first findings and the outlines of their philosophy in a collection called *Fabian Essays*.

The Fabians emphasized the necessity of a fundamental reorganization of British society and stated that this would imply two things: unlimited democracy in the political sphere and socialism in the economic sphere. They made it clear that the socialism they professed was a philosophy of economic equality to be accomplished by democratic means. They were not revolutionaries but gradualists, believing that the country had long been moving in the direction of collectivism, and that the process must now be speeded up and the government induced to abolish the profit motive, nationalize the land and all key industries—public utilities, coal, electricity, railroads and other means of transport, communications, medical services, banks, and the like—grant free higher education to the masses, and otherwise promote a collective life of well-being for all citizens.

This philosophy was summed up succinctly by Bernard Shaw (1856–1950) when he wrote in 1896 that the Fabians aimed

> to persuade the English people to make their political constitution thoroughly democratic and so to socialize their industries as to make the livelihood of the people entirely independent of private Capitalism. . . . Socialism, as understood by the Fabian Society, means the organization and conduct of the necessary industries of the country, and the appropriation of all forms of economic rent of land and capital by the nation as a whole, through the most suitable public authorities, parochial, municipal, provincial or central.

[2] This collaboration, according to Anne Fremantle, inspired the couplet:

The world is so full of a number of plebs
I am sure we should all be as happy as Webbs.

The differences between these doctrines and those of Karl Marx will be obvious. Yet there is some truth in the remark made by Harold Laski, an outstanding twentieth-century Fabian and member of the British Labour party. Speaking of Marxists who had charged him with inadequate comprehension of their master's views, Laski said: "They understand Marx in their way; I understand him in his." It is undeniable that the Fabians appreciated one aspect of Marx's thought more clearly than some of his followers—namely, the strong practical sense that emphasized immediate rather than remote tasks. Fabians like Laski were convinced that if Marx had lived longer, he might have agreed with them, even to the point of relegating the revolution to the remote future and becoming a "gas and water socialist" like themselves.

Fabianism was not originally designed as a working class philosophy. The Fabians hoped to "permeate" the middle classes and the parties and Parliament with the conviction that competitive capitalism had outlived its usefulness and that a careful, gradual transition to socialism was both necessary and practical. Despite their enthusiasm and propagandistic zeal (3339 public lectures were given by their members during 1891–1892 alone), they did not, however, win over the older parties and they turned their attention to organized labor. In 1893, disgusted with the Liberal party's disinclination to follow their advice about necessary reform, the Fabian Society sanctioned the publication in *The Fortnightly Review* of an article by Shaw and Sidney Webb, in which they called upon the working classes "to abandon Liberalism, to form a Trade Union party of their own, to raise £30,000 and finance fifty candidates for Parliament."

In this same year, James Keir Hardie (1856–1915), a miner who had organized one of the first effective unions in Scotland, called a conference of labor leaders at Bradford and founded an organization with the purpose of sponsoring independent candidates for Parliament who would work for "the collective ownership and control of production, distribution and exchange." The establishment of branches of this Independent Labour party (ILP) in other parts of the country was begun with enthusiasm, although their success in their main purpose was delayed by the distrust with which the older unions viewed political activity in general and socialism in particular. But the rapid extension of unionism to the unskilled, encouraged by the success of the dockers' strike of 1889 (see p. 269), soon overcame this obstacle. The militant spirit of the new unions was responsible for a Trades Union Congress resolution in 1899 which authorized a conference to investigate the question of labor's parliamentary representation. In February 1900, union delegations met with representatives of the Fabian Society, the ILP, and the SDF and founded a Labour Representation Committee (soon to be called the Labour party) under the secretaryship of J. Ramsay MacDonald (1866–1937), which would henceforth present a slate of candidates when parliamentary elections were held.

In the decade that followed, the new party won increasing support from the rank and file of labor because of two incidents that seemed to represent government attempts to smash the unions. In 1900 railwaymen working for the Taff Vale Railway Company in South Wales struck for higher pay, without the prior approval of their union. The union nevertheless supported them, but was promptly sued by the company for the losses incurred in the strike and lost the case, having to pay damages in excess of £23,000. The Taff Vale verdict seemed to wipe out all the gains made by Disraeli's legislation of 1875 and to make the strike weapon wholly ineffective; and this made union members believe that it was important to support candidates of the Labour Representation Committee, who might remedy the situation in Parliament. Twenty-nine such candidates won parliamentary seats in the elections of 1906.

The Taff Vale decision was effectively revoked by a new Trade Disputes Act in 1906, but this did not end the threats to the organization of labor. In 1909, the House of Lords, acting as a judicial body, handed down the Osborne Judgment, which declared it illegal for any trade union to spend money in electing members of Parliament or in any other political activities. At a time when members of Parliament were still unpaid, this threatened to make a genuine labor representation impossible, and it was resented by the Labour party and the unions alike. By borrowing and cheese-paring the party managed to get through the two elections of 1910, emerging with 42 seats in the second of them, a growth of 13 since 1906. A year later it was able to win the passage of a law stipulating that members of Parliament would be paid £400 a year; and in 1913 Parliament legalized political action by the unions, although certain annoying restrictions remained. The Liberal party's delay in passing this legislation (it had been in office since 1906) did not ingratiate it with the unions and helped strengthen their tendency to vote for Labour candidates.

On the eve of the war, then, a strong and growing Labour party had come into existence, supported by the new unionism and preaching a native British socialism brought up to date by the Fabian Society, many of whose members were Labour M.P.'s An additional element of its strength lay in the fact that it appealed to religious Nonconformity. Among the leaders of the labor movement in the 1880s and the 1890s, there were a good number of Methodist ministers and chapel members, a fact that may explain something of the moral fervor of the movement and the religious intensity with which its members sang songs like William Blake's moving hymn:

> Bring me my Bow of burning gold:
> Bring me my Arrows of desire:
> Bring me my Spear: O clouds unfold!
> Bring me my Chariot of fire.
>
> I will not cease from Mental Fight,
> Nor shall my Sword sleep in my hand,
> Till we have built Jerusalem
> In England's green and pleasant land.

The Revival and Relapse of Liberalism   Confronted on the one hand with the defection of many of its former supporters to the Conservative party, and with the rise of a labor movement that attracted much of its Radical wing, the Liberal party seemed to face the prospect of a rapid decline. Before anything of the sort set in, however, it had one more great victory and one outburst of reforming activity.

Of the last twenty-five years of the nineteenth century, all but nine were years of Conservative (or Unionist, as the party came to be called at the time) government; and, after the Liberal ministry of 1892–1895, which saw Gladstone's farewell to politics, the Conservatives seemed prepared to govern indefinitely. They presided over the Diamond Jubilee of Queen Victoria in 1897; they survived the disastrous war with the Boers which followed quickly upon that celebration (p. 420); when the old queen died in January 1901, they made the preparations for the coronation of her son Edward VII (1901–1910); and they held on while the Russo-Japanese War and the first Moroccan crisis showed a dangerous deterioration of the international situation (see p. 431). But by 1905 their popularity in the country was beginning to wane rapidly. The Boer War and the new continental troubles ended the appeal of imperialism and inspired demands for an overhaul of the country's foreign policy. The passage of the Education Act of 1902, which provided for state aid to Anglican and Roman Catholic schools as well as to undenominational ones, aroused the Nonconformist churches, led to tax strikes and imprisonments for failures to pay rates, and caused strong defections from the Unionist fold. Finally, in 1903, Joseph Chamberlain began his campaign for imperial preferential tariffs, arguing that this was the only way to prevent disaster to England's already diminished foreign trade; this split the party into warring sects and led to its near collapse. In the elections of January 1906, the Liberals won 377 seats in Commons, a majority of 84 over all other parties combined. The Unionists received only 157; the Irish Nationalists, of whom something will be said below, 83; and the new Labour Party, 29, although they received the additional support of 24 independent trade-union members.

The new Liberal cabinet was headed by Henry Campbell-Bannerman, a wise and unemotional Scot with long parliamentary experience, who was, however, to die after only two years in office. His cabinet included such Liberal veterans as Lord Morley and Lord Bryce, at the India Office and the Irish secretaryship respectively, but its leading luminaries were H. H. Asquith (1852–1928), who became chancellor of the exchequer (and in 1908 prime minister), Sir Edward Grey (1862–1933), at the foreign office, R. B. Haldane (1856–1928), who became minister of war, David Lloyd George (1863–1945), who was at the board of trade, and Winston Churchill (1874–1965), who succeeded him there when he went to the exchequer in 1908.

This combination buckled down to business with an enthusiasm that had been unknown for years. The prime minister's principal accomplishment in his brief term was an honorable and statesmanlike liquidation of the South African situation, which was accomplished by conceding self-government to the Transvaal and laying the basis for the new constitution of the Union of South Africa, which was ratified in 1909. Meanwhile, Lloyd George, who was known to the country only as a Welsh radical and an uncompromising opponent of the Boer War and the Education Act of 1902, showed that he was capable of constructive statesmanship by proposing and securing the passage of the Merchant Shipping Act of 1906, which prescribed standards of food and accommodations designed to stop the deterioration of conditions in the fo'c'sles of British ships, a new Patents Act (1907) to remedy deficiencies in the existing law, and an act setting up a Port of London Authority to amalgamate existing dock authorities and make possible rational development of the port's facilities.

Simultaneously, highly important reforms were carried out in the armed services. There had been some scepticism when R. B. Haldane, a cultivated and urbane gentleman-scholar with a predilection for philosophical speculation, had become minister of war; and Campbell-Bannerman had wondered publicly what Schopenhauer would accomplish in the barracks. But Haldane brought to his task a critical and inquiring mind, fed by reflection upon German and French military theory and he had the good fortune to be supported strongly, in this area where royal influence counted for much, by the king.

Nothing had been done to improve the administration or the organization of the British army since the first Gladstone ministry. At that time, the secretary of war, Edward Cardwell, reformed the army's disciplinary code, reduced the length of service from twelve to six years, placing greater reliance on an able reserve, rearmed the infantry with the Martini-Henry breech-loading rifle, divided Great Britain and Ireland into new regimental districts and fitted existing line regiments to them so as to make an organic link between regular and auxiliary forces, and—most important—abolished the system by which commissions and promotions in the army were secured by purchase. These reforms had corrected important abuses; but, since then, continental armies had moved forward with new techniques and systems of organization, while the British army had been content to rest on Cardwell's work. The Boer War had demonstrated shocking confusion in all units, an awkward dispersal of forces around the globe which made effective union for war difficult, and inefficient administrative practices in the War Office itself.

Haldane corrected this situation and allayed some of the concern caused by disquieting tendencies on the continent by recasting the whole structure of the army. He introduced divisions of the continental type, established an Expeditionary Force of six infantry divisions and one cavalry division with supporting artillery, transport, and medical units and adequate reserves and a Territorial Force that comprised all existing militia units, and devised a speedy and practical mobilization schedule. He established officer training corps at all public and secondary schools, an institution that proved its worth in the war. Finally, he gave the British army its first permanent general staff and saw to it that able men like Sir William Robertson, Henry Wilson, and Douglas Haig were appointed to it. While doing all this, Haldane actually reduced the army budget, thus minimizing the complaints of the Radical wing of the party, which opposed excessive military expenditure.

The Radicals were less happy about the navy reforms that were simultaneously being made by the first sea lord, Admiral Sir John Fisher. This energetic and brilliant sailor advocated the disarming of all superannuted fleet units and the inauguration of a building program that would concentrate on the new dreadnought type of battleship. His arguments were given point by the program of fleet construction currently under way in Germany. Progress in that country was so marked that Fisher, in private conversation with the king, actually suggested the advisability of Copenhagening the German navy before it began to cause real trouble.[3] Edward VII, who always refused to believe that war with

[3] In April 1801, Admiral Lord Nelson sailed into Copenhagen harbor without any declaration of war and destroyed the Danish fleet, thus effectively eliminating the possibility of naval action by the League of Armed Neutrality.

Germany was inevitable, answered indignantly "My God, Fisher, you must be mad!"; but there were many people almost as concerned as Fisher over the German threat. By 1909, public opinion became so aroused that naval estimates had to be revised. This cost money that might otherwise have been expended on social improvements and was resented by many Liberals.

But military expenditures were not the chief obstacle to the most cherished wishes of the more radical Liberals. More serious was the opposition of the House of Lords, which had long been a Conservative stronghold and which now, under the injudicious influence of Conservative leaders like A. J. Balfour and Lord Lansdowne, sought to block what they seemed to consider to be dangerous leveling tendencies on the part of the government.

In 1906 Landsdowne quite properly stated that the House of Lords had the legal right "to arrest the progress of measures whenever they believe they have been insufficiently considered, and are not in accord with the deliberate judgment of the country." The question, however, was how competent this body of hereditary peers was to judge the popular temper. It was not, after all, subject to election, and there was some evidence that it was being rapidly plutocratized by that movement of economic forces which Élie Halévy once described in the words: "While business men were becoming peers, peers were becoming business men, so that when the new rich reached the Upper House they found themselves on familiar ground."

Liberals argued that a hereditary body with large powers was an anomaly in a progressive state, that the House of Lords was a stronghold of privilege, and that it was flagrantly misusing its powers. The first two arguments were perhaps matters of opinion. For the third, there seemed to be substantial grounds. In the years 1888–1892 not a single Conservative measure had been defeated in Lords. In the Liberal ministry of 1892–1895, on the other hand, nearly every measure of social reform proposed had been vetoed and, since the Liberals had returned to power in 1906, this had been happening again. In 1906 Lords vetoed a new education bill and a plural-voting bill; in 1907 they mutilated four land-reform bills; in 1908 they threw out a liquor-licensing bill; and in 1909 they actually rejected the government's budget.

Considering the fact that a civil war had been fought in the seventeenth century to secure the House of Commons's control of the purse, this was a provocative gesture. Those who advocated it took the position that this budget was not a normal money bill but a deliberate attempt to socialize England. It is not hard to understand their position. The author of the budget was David Lloyd George, a curious amalgam of political genius and irresponsibility, now taking the first spectacular steps in a career that would bring him to the most cherished position in British politics. Born in the humblest of circumstances in a mining district of Wales, he had a deep resentment of those with inherited wealth and position and was opportunistic enough to see what could be accomplished by attacking them. "When you find the House of Commons is lifeless and apathetic," he wrote, "you must stir public opinion by violent means, so that the public will react upon legislation." The budget that he drafted upon becoming chancellor of the exchequer in 1908 was designed to do that.

Dubbed by its author the People's Budget, it raised the income tax, especially on unearned incomes, increased death duties, put new taxes on tobacco, spirits,

Rich Fare-The Giant Lloyd-Gorgi-buster: "Fee, fi, fo, fat, I smell the blood of a plutocrat; Be he alive or be he dead, I'll grind his bones to make my bread." From *Punch,* April 28, 1909.

and (now that the motor car had arrived) vehicles and petrol and imposed four new land taxes, the most important of which was a tax on unearned increment—that is, on the increased value of such things as building sites in the vicinity of the Port of London, which had skyrocketed not through the efforts of their owners but because of the growth of the port. There is some evidence that Lloyd George understood only imperfectly the economics of his proposals, and it is also true that his land taxes, in the end, never did produce much revenue. But he was more interested in their propaganda effects than in their economic soundness. He introduced his budget as "a War Budget ... to wage implacable warfare against poverty and squalidness." He hoped the Lords would defeat it, so that he could make them the symbol of the victimization of the poor; and in November 1909 they obliged him.

Neither the defeat of the budget nor the subsequent all-out campaign against the Lords and the landed interest, in which the Heavenly Twins, as Lloyd George and his staunchest supporter Winston Churchill were called, reached new heights of political invective, had quite the political effects expected. In the general elections of January 1910, the Liberal party lost the commanding majority it had enjoyed since 1906 and, when the country went to the polls once more, after the death in May of Edward VII and the accession of George V (1910–1936), it did not improve its strength and henceforth had to depend on Labour votes for a safe margin in the House. But this did not prevent the Liberals from picking up the gauntlet that had been thrown down by the Lords, and they now carried through a constitutional change of the first importance.

In February 1910 the government had introduced in Commons a bill that excluded the House of Lords from interfering with any money bill whatsoever, gave Commons the right to pass any measure into law, despite the Lords' veto, by passing it in three successive parliamentary sessions, provided at least two years had elapsed since its introduction, and reduced the length of Parliaments from seven to five years. The elections and the preparations for the coronation of George V delayed decisive action on this bill until June 1911; but by that time the prime minister, Asquith, was ready to act. A man who is less well remembered today than his more ebullient colleagues, Asquith was nevertheless prime minister for a longer continuous period than anyone since Lord Liverpool at the beginning of the nineteenth century. This achievement was due to his skill in adjudicating the differences of his brilliant but quarrelsome colleagues, the loyalty he inspired in them and in the party rank and file, and his talents as a parliamentary tactician. This last gift he displayed in the struggle with the upper house, pursuing his objective with a sang-froid of which Lloyd George proved incapable and reaching it, in the end, by securing a promise from the new sovereign that, if the Lords refused to pass the Parliament Bill without amendment, he would create enough new peers to secure its passage. Under this threat the opposition collapsed, although only after scenes of unparalleled disorder in both houses of Parliament.

The Parliament Bill of 1911 put an effective limit on the Lords' power of obstruction and, by doing so, cleared the way for that program of basic social reform about which the Liberals had said so much when the government was first formed. Their new freedom seems, however, to have embarrassed them.

Lloyd George once said to a friend, "I don't know exactly what I am, but I'm sure I'm not a Liberal. They have no sympathy with the people. . . . As long as I was settling disputes with their workers . . . these great Business Men said I was the greatest Board President of modern times. When I tried to do something for the welfare of their workmen, they denounced me as a Welsh thief." This is typical George-ian hyperbole. It would be more accurate to say that Lloyd George's colleagues were made restless by the violence of his denunciations of privilege and the sweeping nature of his proclamations of the welfare state; they were willing to be Benthamites but not socialists; and they became increasingly cautious and compromising in spirit after the battle with the Lords was won. The only great measure of social reform passed by them in the years before the war was the National Insurance Act of 1911, which insured workers against accident, sickness, and unemployment. This was an undeniably important piece of legislation, but nevertheless, like Bismarck's social insurance laws of the 1880s (see p. 348), an essentially conservative one, since it was supported not by general taxation but by contributions from employers and employees, with a relatively small additional state subsidy. What other legislation reached the statute books was purely regulatory, like the Coal Mines Regulations Act of 1911, which improved safety provisions in the mines.

In justice to the Liberals, it should be noted that their energies were now diverted to other things and especially to the intricacies of the Irish question. Even so, in their prewar hesitations we can see the reasons for their supersession in the 1920s by the Labour and Conservative parties, which had more resolution and less respect for compromise.

The Irish Question from Gladstone to World War I   The Irish unrest that had marked Gladstone's first ministry was aggravated in the years that followed. The coming of the agricultural depression to Ireland and the precipitous fall of agricultural prices destroyed most of the good effects of Gladstone's Land Act (see p. 230) and led to widespread misery, 2110 families being evicted for failure to pay rent in the year 1880 alone. This led to renewed agitation in favor of comprehensive reform to provide not merely fixed peasant tenure but actual peasant ownership of the land. This was the objective, for instance, of the National Land League, which was founded in 1879 by Michael Davitt, a former peasant himself. Supplied with money by Irish immigrants to the United States and Australia, the Land League inspired and coordinated peasant unrest. Against unpopular landlords, it encouraged the use of those tactics of intimidation, denial of service, property damage, and general ostracism that came to be called boycotting, after a Captain Boycott who, in 1880, was their first victim. Not infrequently, more violent weapons were used by angry tenant farmers: ricks were burned, cattle injured, individuals assaulted.

The activities of the Land League gave added effect to the fight for home rule for Ireland, which was kept up throughout this whole period by the Irish members in the House of Commons. Their leader, Charles Stewart Parnell (1846–1891), was hardly the epitome of those qualities one would expect to find in an Irish nationalist leader, since he was aristocratic in appearance, cold and aloof in manner, and Protestant in religion; but he became the idol of millions in his lifetime, and his name, even after his death, was capable of arousing transports of emotion, like those described in the early chapters of Joyce's *Portrait of the Artist as a Young Man.* A superb orator and a shrewd tactician, Parnell, after his election to the House of Commons in 1875, organized the Irish members into an obstructionist bloc that developed the filibuster to a fine art, kept attention focused on Ireland's grievances, and sought to wear down parliamentary resistance to Irish freedom.

Successive British governments tried to meet these tactics by a combination of reform and coercion. In 1881–1882, the second Gladstone ministry gave Ireland a new Land Reform Act, which assured Irish tenants of fixity of tenure, fair rents, and free sale (the so-called three F's) and also passed an Arrears Act, which helped defaulting tenants regain their land. The good effects of this legislation were offset to a large extent by the coercion employed by the British government in Ireland against boycotters and other agitators. This merely called forth more extreme forms of protest: in 1882 there were twenty-six murders and fifty-eight attempted murders in Ireland, including the slaying in Phoenix Park, Dublin, of the two principal secretaries to the viceroy.

The prevalence of these conditions finally persuaded Gladstone that some form of home rule was inevitable and, when he formed his third ministry in 1886, he brought in a bill that provided for an Irish parliament and executive in Dublin, with authority over all but military, foreign, and fiscal policy and trade, coinage, and customs. It was this conversion of the prime minister that led Joseph Chamberlain to secede from the Liberal party; and it was his opposition, as much as anything else, that defeated the bill. This setback was not decisive, and in the next few years the cause of home rule seemed to be winning new supporters in England. But in 1890, when victory seemed possible, Parnell was named as corespondent in a divorce suit brought by a Captain O'Shea against his wife, and the resultant scandal ruined the Irish leader and his cause. The Conservative party, whose only Irish policy was coercion, gained strength from the disclosure of its enemy as an adulterer; Gladstone, whose private negotiations with Parnell had seemed on the point of success, felt compelled to break with him: and Parnell's own party split, partly because of the position taken by the Irish church.

Despite this disappointment, Gladstone persisted in his efforts—in 1893 his second Home Rule Bill actually passed in Commons, only to be defeated by the House of Lords—and his zeal convinced many people that home rule was inevitable. When his party returned to power in 1906, therefore, it was logical that it should have taken up the issue again. Superficially, conditions now seemed more favorable, for the Gladstone land reforms and the introduction of a degree of self-government in local affairs in Ireland had greatly reduced the violence and terrorism that had necessitated earlier coercion laws. Unfortunately, during this same period the Protestant districts of northeast Ulster had been growing in economic strength and self-consciousness, and they now showed themselves to be inflexibly opposed to any form of home rule that would subordinate them to the Catholic south. When talk of home rule was renewed, indeed, they began to raise volunteer forces to withstand it.

This resistance, which was encouraged by the Conservative party, might have been checked in its early stages, either by a professed willingness to exclude the northern districts from any home rule proposal or by firmness. But the Liberal government could not expect to persuade southern Ireland to accept the idea of partition, while on the other hand, they postponed action against Ulster until the agitation there could no longer be controlled without a major show of force. The upshot of all this was that when a home rule bill modeled on Gladstone's earlier ones was passed by Parliament in 1914, Ulster refused to submit to it, and officers of the British army units that were ordered to Ulster to guard against an explosion declared that they would not obey these orders. The government, with a European war breaking around its ears, decided to postpone the application of home rule until after general peace was restored, a decision that was understandable in the circumstances but that, by frustrating the cause of Irish freedom once more, encouraged a revival of extremism in the south and prepared the way for the Easter revolt of 1916 in Dublin and the time of troubles that followed the world conflict.

British Democracy in 1914   In the years since 1867, Great Britain had moved from the philosophy and institutions of liberalism to an increasingly great degree of political and economic democracy. The extension of the suffrage had made possible a real measure of popular participation in parliamentary elections, and the ability of the House of Lords to balk the popular will as expressed by their representatives had been attenuated. Local government had simultaneously been transformed by the substitution of elected county, district, parish, and borough councils for the older aristocratic system of government by closed corporations or by justices of the peace at quarter sessions. Social services had been expanded, in the form of medical care, health insurance, recreational facilities, sanitation, transportation, and public education, and the government had recognized its duty to protect its citizens by regulating certain aspects of their lives and their employment—all of which forecast the coming of the welfare state proclaimed by the Fabians. To the central government there had been added new Boards of Works (1815), Local Government (1871), Agriculture (1886), and Education (1899); and these agencies permitted the handling of vital problems efficiently and from a truly national point of view. Finally, the liberties and social gains that had been won at home had been extended, through grants of self-government and dominion status, to Canada (1867), Australia (1900), New Zealand (1907), and the Union of South Africa (1909).

These changes, with all their merits, were accompanied by an increase in the size, functions, and cost of government and an acceleration of the tendency toward the bureaucratization of society that would have been deplored by the Liberals of the midcentury. Nor was this their most unfortunate effect. As liberalism gave way to democracy, some of the values for which it had stood fell into disrepute. In the last years before World War I, this was demonstrated by the way in which organized groups in society deliberately abandoned that reliance upon law and reason and compromise that had been the heart of the liberal philosophy. When members of the House of Commons howled down the prime minister as he introduced the Parliament Bill in 1911, when army officers refused to go to Ulster as ordered, when British workers in the years 1912–1914 gave their ears to syndicalist leaders and participated in the bitterest wave of strikes to affect the country since the 1880s, and when the Women's Suffrage Movement indulged in a frenzy of vandalism, personal assault, and exhibitionism in 1913 and 1914 (with their leader remarking that "the broken window pane is the most valuable argument in modern politics" and their most ardent agitator committing suicide by throwing herself under the hooves of the king's horse as it thundered into the stretch in the 1913 Derby), they were all testifying to the decline of the liberal attitude in politics. As Winston Churchill said in 1914, "the civil and parliamentary systems under which [Englishmen] [had] dwelt so long [seemed] to be brought to the rude challenge of force [and] to be exposed to menace and brutality."

Whether this tendency would have continued it is impossible to say, for these manifestations of a new spirit of violence in politics were soon submerged in the greater violence of the World War.

BELGIUM, THE NETHERLANDS, AND SWITZERLAND

The Belgian Democracy   The country whose development most closely paralleled that of Great Britain was Belgium. Like Britain, Belgium was a constitutional monarchy and was fortunate in being ruled by able and conscientious sovereigns whose reigns were long enough to enable them to master their trade and, within the limits of their authority, to contribute to the continuity and stability of national policy, particularly in the area of foreign and colonial affairs.

Belgium's first king, Leopold I (1830–1865), helped consolidate the neutral position in which his country had been placed by the great powers in 1831 (see p. 30), by cultivating good relations with his royal neighbors, and even by giving them the benefit of his advice when they desired it (and sometimes, as the young Queen Victoria had often complained, when they did not). This mentor of Europe was succeeded by Leopold II (1865–1909), who threw his abundant energies into economic enterprise and was the founder of Belgium's rich colonial empire (see p. 409). Albert I (1909–1934), perhaps the best loved of Belgian sovereigns, was the soldier king who tried vainly to stem the German invasion of his country in 1914.

Like Britain, Belgium moved from liberalism to democracy during the period under review. The original constitution of the country had placed political power in the hands of what has been described as a bourgeois oligarchy supported by a very limited franchise based on tax payments. The evolution of the industrial system—until 1870 Belgium was the only continental country to keep pace with the industrial expansion of Great Britain—led to the organization of the working classes for political action. Trade unions and socialists pressed for suffrage reform so successfully that in 1893 the constitution was amended to give the vote to all male citizens who had reached the age of twenty-five, supplementary votes being given to the most highly educated and taxed classes.

Of the two traditional parties, the Catholic party retained its preponderance in the country, but before 1914 the Liberals had become inferior in strength to the rising Socialist party and were able to maintain their position largely because of the introduction of proportional representation. This measure, passed in 1899, was designed to advance the cause of democratic government by assuring the representation of all shades of opinion.

Of democratic intent also was the law of 1898, which gave the Flemish language, widely used in the northern districts, equality with French, which was spoken by the majority of the country.

Finally, as in the case of Great Britain, Belgium experienced the first significant measures of economic democracy with the extension of elementary education to the masses in the 1880s, the beginning of factory regulation after 1890, and the institution of old-age pensions (1900), workmen's compensation for accidents (1903), and improvements in housing and public services for the working classes.

The Dutch Netherlands   Perhaps because its economy remained predominantly agricultural and commercial rather than industrial, as in the case of Belgium, or because, in contrast to Great Britain, its prosperity was more continuous throughout these years, Holland's progress toward democracy was slower than that of the two nations discussed above. The country did not have a constitution until 1849; and, during most of the long reign of William III (1849–1890), the sovereign retained a considerable amount of political power, including the right to veto legislation passed by the parliament. The suffrage was severely limited, and, even after reforms of 1887 and 1896, only 14 percent of the population had the vote. Universal manhood suffrage was legalized only in 1917.

The chief issue in Dutch politics until the end of the nineteenth century was not economic policy or social reform but education. As was true in other countries, the Liberal party advocated a system of free public elementary schooling without religious instruction of any kind. The Protestant Conservative and Catholic parties contended for, and in 1889 secured, state aid for their denominational schools. To contest the predominance of these older parties, which cut across class lines, there was no Labor or Socialist party of any importance before World War I.

Switzerland   At the other political extreme from this essentially conservative state stood the Swiss Federation, a flourishing center of political freedom, proud of its federal form and its institutions of direct democracy, as well as of the refuge it offered to political exiles from other lands.

The great German-Swiss writer and patriot Gottfried Keller (1819–1890) once wrote that, in contrast to other lands whose national self-consciousness was founded on race or language or history, Switzerland based its nationality upon the idea of liberty. He wrote:

> Similar inclinations in a beautiful country, many neighborly contacts, and a common tough determination to maintain independence, have produced in Switzerland a common federal life distinguished from any other national life. This . . . has produced a far-reaching similarity of attitudes and character. In our common nationality we feel protected against the confusion which surrounds us on all sides.

During the first half of the nineteenth century, this independent spirit was so uncompromising as to make it unlikely that the Swiss could form an effective national unit. The federation was a mere collection of independent cantons which differed in language, religion, administrative forms, and educational institutions and even pursued separate commercial policies and entered into private arrangements with foreign powers. Two things, however, corrected this situation. The first was the growth of a strong democratic movement in most cantons in the two decades before 1848, which demanded and secured extension of popular liberties, widening of the franchise, and the reform of local justice. Once entrenched conservatism and parochialism had been weakened by the reforms of this "era of regeneration," as the Swiss call it, it was inevitable that there should be a growing demand for a stronger central government.

This second demand precipitated a conflict between the democratic majority of the cantons, and a league (the *Sonderbund*) which was formed by the Catholic cantons, who resisted the increase of federal power. The issue was settled in 1847 by a short war, which was followed by a dissolution of the Catholic League and a thoroughgoing revision of the national constitution. Henceforward Switzerland was to possess a bicameral legislature similar to that of the United States (one house in which the people were represented on the basis of population, the other in which the cantons had equal representation) and a Federal Tribunal and a Federal Council elected by the legislature. The cantons reserved great powers, especially in regard to education, public health, religion, crime; but the central government controlled foreign and military affairs, commercial policy, post and coinage, and fiscal policy.

Switzerland thus became a strong federal union, and one in which democracy took more advanced forms than in any of the countries of continental Europe. For one thing, the practice of direct democracy—that is, of decisions being taken by the vote of *all* the affected citizens—continued in several of the smaller Swiss cantons. For another, in cantons whose area and population forbade this, laws passed on stipulated subjects by cantonal legislatures had to be referred to the people for their formal assent, and other laws could be referred to them on demand; and there was provision also for the submission of laws to the legislature by the initiative of a certain number of voters.

In 1874, when the federal constitution was revised, enlarging the powers of the central government and authorizing it, among other things, to provide for free elementary education, provision was made for popular referendum on the national as well as the cantonal level and, in 1891, the initiative became part of federal law also. As a kind of corollary to these institutions, which made the Swiss people the absolute masters of their government, the government in 1874 underlined the individual's responsibility for protecting Swiss democracy by introducing a system of compulsory military service. In keeping with the country's neutral position (established as a result of a decision taken by the Great Powers at Vienna in 1815), the military force subsequently raised was a strictly defensive one. But its organization, discipline, and efficiency were favorably commented on abroad, where the Swiss militia was often held up as the model of the kind of army that (in contrast to some of those in larger countries) neither jeopardized domestic liberty nor threatened the general peace by arousing the fear of neighboring countries.

The growth of Swiss industry in the period after 1870 was notable, especially in textiles, watchmaking, luxury goods, and confections; and this led to the establishment of trade unions and the rise of an active socialist movement. This last was encouraged also by the permissiveness of the political climate, which, in the last quarter of the nineteenth century, made Switzerland the refuge for political exiles from other countries. In the 1870s the anarchist movement had headquarters here; later, the German Social Democrats, whose press was destroyed by Bismarck's persecutions (see p. 348), published their newspapers in Basel and smuggled them across the border; and, at the beginning of the new century, a group of left-wing socialists led by Lenin sat at sidewalk cafés in Bern and Geneva and dreamed of the time when they might be able to return to their native Russia.

Besides being a kind of headquarters for refugees, Switzerland, by virtue of its neutral position, was also considered an ideal place for the establishment of organizations like the International Red Cross, the International Postal Union, and the International Telegraph Union.

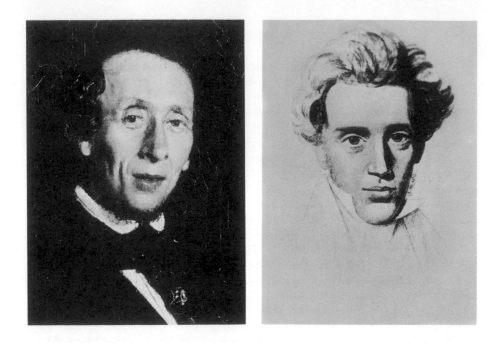

Two Danish writers whose works have exerted continuing influence in their own and other countries: Hans Christian Andersen, 1805–1875, the story teller; Sören Kierkegaard, 1818–1855, the father of existentialism. (Hans Christian Andersen Museum, Odense; Brown Brothers)

NORTHERN EUROPE

Denmark   In the course of the nineteenth century, the kingdom of Denmark had the misfortune to be deprived of much of its territory by action of the Great Powers. At Vienna in 1815, the Danes were punished for their loyalty to Napoleon by being forced to cede Norway to Sweden; and, in 1864, as we have seen (p. 210), they were despoiled by the German powers of the provinces of Schleswig and Holstein. In the reduced realm, progress toward liberalism and democracy was delayed by the fact that the greater part of the population consisted of peasants with little interest in politics and by the resistance of King Christian IX (1863–1906) to anything resembling genuine parliamentary government. During his reign, Denmark was the scene of a constitutional conflict similar to that which took place in Prussia in the 1860s and concerned with the same issues, army reform and control of budget; and, as in Prussia, the king had his way by disregarding the constitutional desires and defying the opposition of the lower house.

By the turn of the century, however, demands for reform were being advanced not only by the urban middle classes but by the Social Democrats, who had been active since the 1870s, the youth movement, inspired and led by Denmark's most distinguished man of letters, Georg Brandes (1842–1927), and the more prosperous farmers. Even so, what appeared to be a victory for responsible parliamentary government in 1901 merely touched off new dissensions, and it was not until 1915 that the reform movement succeeded in winning a new constitution. This provided for an extension of the suffrage to all men and most women, the widening of the competence of the lower house of parliament, and—by measures not unlike those taken in England in 1911—the effective abolition of the veto of the upper house, which had in the past buttressed royal power. Thus, belatedly, Denmark entered a new period of democracy.

Norway and Sweden   In 1814 Sweden had voluntarily relinquished Finland to Russia on the understanding that Norway would be ceded to her. The Swedish regent, Marshal Bernadotte, was forced, however, to take Norway by conquest, for there was strong opposition to union in that country; and, if he was in the end successful, he found it advisable to recognize the Fundamental Law which the Norwegian Storting had accepted in May 1814 and which was based on the liberal Spanish constitution of 1812.

With this beginning, the history of the union of Norway and Sweden was bound to be a stormy one. Norway, already far advanced toward democracy, began her new career with claims that she was "free, indivisible, and independent" even though united with Sweden, and with parliamentary institutions that sought to give actuality to those claims. On the other hand, Sweden was a country whose government was aristocratic and feudal and her rulers showed a stubborn attachment to royal prerogatives. They were particularly insistent on their right to dictate the foreign and military policy of the two countries, and this led to differences, notably in 1864, when the king wished to give aid to the Danes

The Doll's House by the Norwegian dramatist Henrik Ibsen, 1828–1906, leader of the naturalist revolution in the theater. A scene from the original production at the Christiania Theatre in January 1880. (Universitetsbiblioteket, Oslo)

and was opposed by the Norwegian Storting. Apart from this, the two countries had no real community of economic interests, Sweden, as we have seen (p. 263), moving rapidly after 1870 toward industrial maturity and Norway remaining a predominantly agricultural and commercial state. It was indeed this last fact that led to the final rupture of the union, for as the Norwegian carrying trade grew, the Norwegian parliament began to insist on a separate consular service to protect it, and the Swedish government resisted this as destructive of the union. After a dozen years of bitter conflict, in which the Norwegian universities and intellectuals like the poet and dramatist Björnstjerne Björnson (1832–1910) played a prominent part, the Norwegian parliament declared unanimously on June 7, 1905, that the union with Sweden was dissolved, a decision subsequently confirmed by plebiscite. Although there was momentarily some talk of war, the Swedish government acquiesced in the decision; and Norway became an independent constitutional monarchy, inviting the younger son of the king of Denmark to assume the throne with the title Haakon VII. The royal office was largely honorific, and the royal veto, at first provided for, was abolished in 1915.

Norway's democratic tendencies were encouraged by the separation. In 1907 it was the first sovereign state to give the vote to women, and subsequently compulsory education and various forms of social insurance were instituted.

In Sweden itself, the royal absolutism of Bernadotte, who had ruled as Charles XIV from 1818 until 1844, had given way gradually to a moderate liberalism under his successors Oskar I (1844–1859), Charles XV (1859–1872), and Oskar II (1872–1907). The constitutional laws of 1864 abolished the old estates and set up a bicameral legislature with considerable power, although the deputies of the lower house were elected exclusively by the propertied classes. In 1909, during the reign of Gustavus V (1907–1950), universal manhood suffrage was introduced in elections for the lower house and the property qualification for election to the upper house was reduced; and in subsequent years, voting rights were extended to women and proportional representation was introduced in elections for both houses of parliament. This last innovation was of advantage to the socialist movement, which was a natural outgrowth of Sweden's industrial progress.

SOUTHERN EUROPE

In most of the countries discussed in this chapter, substantial progress toward democracy had been registered by 1914 and, even where there was a tendency toward an increased use of violence in politics, it was not so marked as to threaten the existing political regimes, most of which had shown the ability to adjust themselves successfully to changed needs and new problems. None of this was true of the states of southern Europe, where progress toward democracy was minimal, violence uncontrolled, and the stability of established government always in question.

Spain   Gerald Brenan has concisely described the history of Spain in the first seventy years of the nineteenth century by writing: "The glorious national rising against Napoleon had been followed by twenty-six years of savage reaction and civil war: this had been succeeded by the anarchic rule of the generals which under a delightful but scandalously unchaste queen, in a Ruritanian atmosphere of railway speculation and uniforms, had lasted for another twenty-eight." The queen in question was Isabella II, who was deposed in 1868, when her use of the methods that had made her father Ferdinand VII (see p. 21) odious, finally proved too much even for the generals who served her.

Isabella's fall was engineered by General Prim and Marshal Serrano, who also undertook to make arrangements for her successor. Their first attempt, when they offered the vacant throne to Prince Leopold of Hohenzollern, was unsuccessful and had the unforeseen effect, as we have seen (p. 235), of providing the incident that precipitated the outbreak of hostilities between France and Prussia in 1870. Their second was no more fortunate. In November 1870, Serrano's provisional government, with the authorization of the Cortes elected in 1869, invited Amadeo, the second son of the king of Italy, to become king of Spain. When this unhappy prince did so, he found himself opposed by the legitimists, who sought the throne for Isabella's son Alfonso, the Carlists, who were working for the heir of Ferdinand VII's brother, Don Carlos, the Catholic Church, which wanted no king of the dynasty that had robbed the pope of his temporal power, and the republicans, who wanted no king at all. After two years of frustration, while ministries were set up and fell again like ninepins, Amadeo turned his office back on the Cortes with the words: "My good intentions have been in vain. . . . Spain still lives in continual strife, departing day by day more widely from that era of peace and prosperity for which I have so ardently yearned."

There followed a brief republican interval (February 1873–December 1874), but the results were so lamentable that the European powers felt compelled to withhold their recognition of the regime. While monarchists and clericals alike boycotted the new government, the Carlists raised an army of 75,000 men and started operations designed to overthrow it, and in the south other irregular forces burned and looted in the name of federal liberty. Once more the military felt compelled to intervene, and, on Christmas Eve 1874, they declared in favor of Alfonso, the son of Isabella II, and overthrew the republic.

This time at least some superficial stability resulted from the political change. The leading figure in the monarchical restoration and the author of the new constitution was Don Antonio Cánovas del Castillo, a conservative politician, a patriot, and an admirer of the English constitutional system as he understood it (which was, as things turned out, far from perfectly). In the constitution of 1876, Cánovas imitated the forms of English political life, to the extent of establishing a responsible ministry and a parliament of two chambers; and in the deliberations of the lower house in subsequent years members of Cánovas's Conservative party delivered Disraelian philippics and were answered by Gladstonian orotundities from the opposition benches, where the Liberal party of Práxedes Sagasta sat. All of this was artificial. The greatest part of the population was excluded not only from the actual exercise of political power, for only the propertied classes were given the vote, but even from the thoughts of the politicians who were supposed to represent them. No real principles divided the Conservatives and the Liberals; they vied only for power and had no intention of improving the lot of the common people or the general state of law in a country notorious for social injustice. Cánovas gave stability to Spain only by permitting the politicians, the clergy, and the army to enrich themselves at the expense of the nation; and this had the effect of creating a hopeless division between the governed and the governing class. The prime minister was himself a victim of this tragic gulf, for in 1892 he was killed by an Italian anarchist in retaliation for police brutality against the masses.

Alfonso XII died in 1885 and his wife reigned as regent until his son assumed power in 1902. The regency and the first decade of the reign of Alfonso XIII were marked by a series of crises which strained the resources of the regime to the utmost. The first of these had to do with the colonial empire, already greatly reduced in size by the secession of the Latin American colonies in the 1820s (see p. 21). Spain had retained possession of the rich island of Cuba, but persistent maladministration and exploitation had turned that colony into a center of continuous disaffection and caused an insurrection in 1868 that took ten years to liquidate. In 1895, disappointed by the nonfulfillment of promises of self-government, Cuba erupted again, and this time the repressive methods employed by Spanish garrison troops led to intervention by the United States and, in 1898, to a war in which Spain lost both Cuba and the Philippines and was left with a depleted treasury, a shattered military establishment (200,000 Spaniards are said to have died of wounds and disease in Cuba), and, of her once expansive overseas empire, only a few small holdings in Morocco and West Africa.

These events coincided with growing dissatisfaction on the part of the peasantry and the industrial masses, which was shown (as had been indicated, p. 281) by the growth of Marxist socialism and syndicalism in the industrial cities and the spread of anarchism among the peasantry of the south and the working classes of Barcelona. Nor was this all. The ineffectiveness and corruption of the regime led to a resurgence of Carlism and to the growth of separatist feeling among the Basques and Catalans, some of whom supported Carlist reaction while others followed extremists of the Left. As a result of all this, the resort to violence became increasingly marked in Spanish politics: assassinations and terrorism became almost commonplace; there were attempts on the king's life in 1906 and 1912; and in 1909, when the government called up army reserves in Catalonia to avenge an ambush of Spanish troops in Morocco, the city of Barcelona rose in revolt, and there were five days of mob rule during which twenty-two churches and thirty-four convents were burned[4] before the troops restored order by shooting 175 workers in the street and subsequently executing many more.

To bring social peace to the country, the leader of the Liberal party, José Canalejas, tried to form a working coalition with the Republicans and Socialists on the basis of a program of anticlericalism. This traditional Liberal policy may have seemed particularly appropriate in the circumstances, for the Spanish church had persistently chosen to ally itself with the forces of wealth and reaction and to rely upon repression rather than persuasion and understanding to combat

---

[4] The troops had been ambushed on their way to occupy certain iron mines beyond Melilla. Army service had been unpopular since 1898; the conscripts proved receptive to the suggestion that the mines in question were owned by the Jesuits.

the growth of socialism. It has been said that by 1910 Spain was ceasing to be a Catholic country, as anarchism grew among the peasants, skepticism among the middle classes, and naked hostility to church censorship among the intellectuals. Civil marriages were becoming common; church membership was falling off; a large percentage of children born in Barcelona, Valencia, and Madrid were never baptized.

Even so, an anticlerical policy was not enough to weld the atomized forces of the left and center into an effective political bloc. Its only tangible results were the murder of Canalejas himself in 1912 and a deepening of the political confusion of the country.

Portugal The pattern of Portuguese political history was different from that of its neighbor, although the degree of violence that marked it was almost equally great. The first half of the nineteenth century was characterized by continuous wars between rival claimants to the throne and frequent insurrections. During the reigns of Pedro V (1853–1861) and Louis I (1861–1889) the country seemed to be moving toward liberal parliamentary government. This progress was interrupted, however, by the accession of Carlos I (1889–1908), a man whose absolutist temperament and unbridled lust for personal gratification led to financial mismanagement, frequent misuse of the royal prerogative, violation of parliamentary procedure, and, as a result of all these, the growth of internecine strife. On February 1, 1908, this model of self-indulgence and his eldest son were killed in the streets of Lisbon; and when the king's second son took the throne, he was able to hold it only until October 1910, when a revolution in Lisbon proclaimed the republic.

On the outbreak of the war of 1914, Portugal was nominally at least a democratic state. The constitution was modeled on that of the Third French Republic, as was the policy of anticlericalism that the republican government elected to pursue (see p. 336), more successfully, as it turned out, than the short-lived Canalejas government in Spain. Church and state were formally separated in 1911; religious instruction was barred from schools; and church schools were deprived of all state aid. These measures, while popular, did not create the stability the country needed. Like Spain, Portugal continued to suffer from a large debt and an unstable fiscal system, an economy handicapped by a high degree of illiteracy (elementary education was made compulsory only in 1911), a lack of public services, and the usual quota of quarrelsome political parties more intent on planning revolts than on devising constructive policies.

Italy By all odds the most melancholy spectacle presented by the states of southern Europe was that on display in Italy, where all of the high hopes of the *Risorgimento* were confounded and all of the superficial forms of progress belied by the realities behind them.

The Italian political system after 1870 was, like that devised by Cánovas in Spain, modeled on the English and bore just as little real similarity to it. The monarchy was a constitutional one, governing through a ministry responsible to parliament. This was composed of two houses, a Senate of hereditary and life members appointed by the crown and a Chamber of Deputies elected for terms of five years by the propertied and educated classes. Effective power lay in the Chamber, the Senate only rarely exercising its suspensive veto of legislation; and politics in the Chamber was in the hands of two coalitions of parties, the Right (*Destra*) and the Left (*Sinistra*). The flaw in the system was that there was no essential difference between these groupings and no possibility of constructive debate or alternation of power.

This does not mean merely that the vast majority of deputies were middle class in origin and philosophy, rationalist in sentiment, anticlerical in matters touching on religion, and in favor of centralization of government and *laissez-faire* economics, although this is true. It means, rather, that a distressingly large number of them came to be so avid for political office that they avoided issues that might force a clear-cut division of opinion. This tendency, indeed, became so noticeable a characteristic of the system that it was given a name—*trasformismo* or transformism.

Trasformismo was the method by which a chief of ministry could prolong the life of parliament and his own hold on power by disregarding party labels, making bargains with deputies on the left or the right for whatever votes they could command, and thus piecing together parliamentary majorities. In the hands of such gifted practitioners as Agostino Depretis (1813–1887), who dominated Italian politics from 1876 to 1887, and Francesco Crispi (1819–1901), who was supreme in the Chamber from 1887 to 1896, *trasformismo* gradually atomized existing political groups and turned parliament into an amorphous mass of deputies led by a ministry whose members changed so constantly (between 1871 and 1914, Italy had thirty-one different ministers of finance alone) that coherence and continuity of policy were impossible.

This system could be made to work only by an avoidance of the big questions about which differences of opinion were inevitable. There were lots of these. The united nation had inherited, in Naples and Sicily, backward areas that were gravely in need of irrigation and improved communications and were burdened with an inequitable system of land ownership that seemed to cry for rectification. It was seeking to push industrialization without possessing the resources of coal and iron that would make this easily practicable, and this raised some delicate questions of commercial policy. In an age in which economic development depended to an important degree upon the creation of a literate working class, Italy's percentage of literacy was almost the lowest in western Europe. Its rate of population increase, on the other hand, was the highest in Europe, far in excess of job opportunities, and this led to the emigration of the most enterprising elements of the labor force (350,000 emigrated in 1900; 530,000 in 1910) and to a high degree of social distress and unrest among those who remained.

The viability of Italy as a nation depended on the solution of these problems; but they received very little attention while *trasformismo* was the order of the day. When any one of them became so pressing as to cause a dangerous rise in the popular temper, the tendency of the majority-mongers was to divert public opinion to issues capable of producing excitement and distraction. Anticlericalism was such an issue. The refusal of Pope Pius IX to accept the guarantees and the subsidies offered in 1871 by the Italian government in return for recognition, and his insistence on referring to himself as a prisoner and calling upon other governments to rescue him, annoyed Italian patriots. This annoyance could be played upon; and Crispi, for one, had a way of using antipapal demonstrations to bolster his own popularity. Equally useful were attacks on foreign powers, either in the form of irredentism—that is, the demand for the cession by the Austrian government of the predominantly Italian parts of the Hapsburg empire (especially the Trentino and Trieste)—or in the form of attacks upon France, a practice in which Crispi, as a loyal Garibaldian, frequently indulged. Finally, between 1871 and 1914, governments were repeatedly tempted to use colonial adventures to divert thought from domestic problems. Depretis and Crispi both sought glory in Abyssinia (and both failed disastrously to find it), while Giolitti was impelled to find a refuge from domestic complications in Tripoli.

These tactics caused pressing social and economic problems to go unsolved and made them more serious. The attacks on the church angered all Catholic countries and left them disinclined to give any form of assistance to Italy, which sometimes was badly in need of economic or diplomatic aid; and the attacks on France invited French retaliation. When it became known in 1887 that Italy, a member of the Triple Alliance since 1882, had renewed that treaty in circumstances which indicated that its anti-French provisions had been strengthened, the French broke off long-pending commercial negotiations and instituted a tariff war whose effects were felt for almost ten years. As a result of the break, Italian exports dropped 40 percent; the curtailment of French credit caused financial stringency and the stopping of public works projects and railway building; unemployment rose sharply; and the prevalence of social distress led to the rapid increase of emigration.

It was reflected also in widespread popular disaffection. In the south, where the wine trade had been particularly hard hit by the cessation of trade with France and where there had long been strong resentment against absentee ownership, feudal taxes, and other abuses, the year 1893 was marked by attacks on manor houses and police posts, often resulting in bloodshed. In the silk-producing areas of the north, also hurt by the tariff war, similar troubles broke out and continued throughout the decade. If Crispi fell from office in 1896 as a result of the disastrous Italian defeat at Adowa in Abyssinia (see p. 418), the prevalent economic distress of this decade was certainly a contributory factor. In 1898 popular resentment boiled over in a series of bloody riots in all major Italian cities, which culminated in the "Deeds of May" in Milan in which tram cars were upset to form barricades and resultant street battles cost the lives of two policemen and eighty civilians, while 450 were injured. This led to the imposition of martial law and, in the next two years, to a degree of royal and military intervention in politics that threatened the very existence of parliamentary institutions. In June 1899, for instance, General Pelloux, who had been appointed prime minister by the king without any attempt to consult parliament, announced that he would rule by royal decrees that would automatically give his projects the force of law without the necessity of parliamentary discussion or criticism.

This alarming turn of events brought the parliamentarians to their senses, at least momentarily. A new coalition was formed from the so-called Radical Left (a reform party inspired by the doctrines of Auguste Comte, Herbert Spencer, and the Italian sociologist Cesare Lombroso, which put its faith in positivism and experimental science), the Republicans (a small group of devoted Mazzinians), and the new Socialist party founded in 1892 by Filippo Turati (1857–1932).

This union fought Pelloux with the tactics made famous in the House of Commons by the Irish Nationalists, namely, obstructionism and sensation, and, in the end, with the additional support of the more moderate Constitutional Left, forced his resignation in June 1900. This event coincided with the murder of King Humbert by an anarchist in revenge for those who were killed by the police in Milan. The dead ruler had been a ruler of dangerously absolutist tendencies. His successor, Victor Emmanuel III (1900–1946), was supposed to be more sensitive to the needs of the time.

The new era was hailed as the liberal spring of Italy; and, indeed there were some hopeful signs of political regeneration. On the one hand, there was, under the veteran Giuseppe Zanardelli (1826–1903) and the rising star of Italian politics Giovanni Giolitti (1842–1928), an attempt to mold the different sections of the old *Sinistra* into an effective democratic-liberal party. In 1900, Giolitti announced: "The country is sick politically and morally, but the principal cause of its sickness is that the classes in power have been spending enormous sums on themselves and their own interests, and have obtained the money almost entirely from the poorer sections of society." He called for "a policy that is frankly democratic" and talked of a revision of tax schedules, a reform of the law codes, and measures of agricultural reform.

Simultaneously, there was some indication that part of the revolutionary Left might adopt a more constructive policy than it had professed in the past and might even be willing to collaborate in social reform. Anarchism continued to have its effect in rural districts, to be sure, and Sorel's syndicalist doctrines became influential after the publication of the Italian edition of his book in 1903. But revisionism was making inroads among the Marxist socialists, and leaders like Turati, Bissolati, and Bonomi seemed prepared for parliamentary collaboration on key issues.

Finally, the Right seemed not entirely impervious to the new spirit. In 1902, Sidney Sonnino (1847–1922) and Antonio Salandra (1853–1931) began to try to stimulate a new patriotic conservatism, based on the belief in a strong monarchy and a strong centralized government and willing to correct social injustices while opposing the policies of the extreme Left.

Had these three political groups consolidated themselves, there is every likelihood that Italian parliamentary life would have revived, that there would have been a healthy alternation of parties in power, that the most crying of national abuses would have been corrected, and that the country as a whole would have benefited. Instead of this, Italy soon relapsed into the empty acrobatics of *trasformismo*. The three potentially strong coalitions dissolved into quarreling groups, and parliament again became a shapeless mass of deputies, manipulated now by Giolitti. That politician's democratic pretensions were, it is true, given some substance in 1911–1912 by the extension of the suffrage to all males over thirty years of age. But Giolitti proceeded to demonstrate that the new electorate could be manipulated by fraud and violence, a demonstration that was facilitated by the fact that there was no educational qualification for voting.

From 1903 to 1915 Giolitti was the unquestioned master of Italian politics. It may be admitted that he used his power to carry out some measure of necessary reform. The years of his parliamentary dictatorship saw the passage of factory laws, the nationalization of insurance companies and railways, the legalization of trade unions, state aid for agriculture cooperatives, and the encouragement of collective bargaining. The country benefited also from an economic upswing after 1900, although this was due less to the government's economic policy as such than to the end of the tariff war with France.

But, despite all this, Giolitti's unsavory methods in electoral campaigns and in the chamber finally undid the effects of Cavour's *connubio* of the 1850s. They brought the parties of the liberal center into disrepute and dissolved the parliamentary system, while giving a new lease on life to the extremist parties which now—thanks to Giolitti's franchise legislation—had the opportunity to win mass support.

Of the growth of a new extremism, there was lots of evidence in the last years before 1914. At the Socialist Party Congress at Reggio in July 1912, the left wing, led by Costantino Lazzari, Ettore Cicotti, and Benito Mussolini (the last two of whom were later to be Fascists), revolted against the revisionism of Bissolati and Bonomi and declared that democracy was a bourgeois experiment and that socialism must return to the orthodox insistence that it be destroyed. The victory of these extremists was aided by the transformation of the party since 1900 into a mass party; and they were to dominate the party until its dissolution twelve years later.

Among the intellectuals on the extreme right there was a growing interest in the theories of Vilfredo Pareto (1848–1923) and Gaetano Mosca (1858–1941), who mercilessly exposed the inadequacies and the shams of Giolittianism and, in something of the spirit of Sorel, called for a new elite, versed in the ways of power, who would lead society out of its present materialistic swamp. This coincided with the formation, in 1910, of a new Nationalist party which was frankly monarchist, antiparliamentarian, and imperialistic. Its most outspoken leader, Enrico Corradini (1865–1931), announced in his speeches the themes elaborated on by the Fascist movement after the war: the heroic qualities of combat, the insignificance of individual life when the cause of the nation was at stake, modern Italy's legacy from ancient Rome, the necessity of subordinating the concepts of liberty and equality to those of discipline and obedience, and the moral satisfaction that came from living dangerously.

The fact that the youth of Italy in particular should have turned to this kind of thing shows how far Giolitti's cynicism had succeeded in draining the idealism out of Italian politics. This also explains the remarkable vogue of the poet Gabriele d'Annunzio (1863–1938), who in 1900 had forsworn the politics of the extreme right to join the forces fighting General Pelloux, announcing grandiloquently that "as a man of intellect, I shall move toward life." By 1909, in poetry whose content was increasingly empty but whose rhetoric increasingly exhilarating, he was calling on young Italy to seek life, not in politics but in violent action that would make an end of the dullness and mediocrity of the existing regime. On the eve of the war, therefore, the confident voices in Italian politics, and the ones listened to most eagerly by youth, were those of extremists of the right and left, all proclaiming the imminent destruction of a regime that had been unable to make any genuine progress toward a viable democracy and whose political processes seemed now to be affected by creeping paralysis.

Chapter 14 FRANCE: THE DIVIDED REPUBLIC, 1871–1914

If the excesses of Italian political behavior seemed sometimes to be attributable to that nation's having too little history, certain aspects of French politics after 1871 are perhaps to be explained by the circumstance that France had too much. Past glories were always being used to belittle, or past failures to denigrate, the efforts of her ministries; and the fact that since 1789 the country had experienced virtually every possible form of government gave an unhealthy relativism to the French political process. In time of difficulty or crisis, there were always partisans of old regimes ready to call for radical change, and this confirmed a national habit of political instability.

The Third French Republic was to last for seventy years. Had they been told that this would be true, the generation of 1870 would have found it difficult to believe. For the Republic was born in military defeat and civil war, and its adolescence and early maturity were years of almost constant conflict.

THE AFTERMATH OF DEFEAT, 1870–1878

The War's End and the Commune   When it became apparent that victory over the Germans was no longer possible, the French people, as we have seen (p. 237), elected a National Assembly and implicitly authorized it to treat for terms. This Assembly, acting through its elected chief of the executive power, Adolphe Thiers, carried out its assigned duty and then turned to the problem of restoring order in the country and getting its administrative machinery back into operation. Immediately, it came into bitter conflict with Paris.

There were several reasons for this. The people of Paris, who had fought against Germany until they were starved into submission, felt more sensitive about the defeat than they suspected the provinces did, and they were humiliated by the

316

government's accession to the German demand for a triumphal entrance into the city. In the second place, as early as September 1870, Paris had proclaimed the republic; the National Assembly had not done so and, in view of its composition, which was overwhelmingly monarchist, did not seem disposed to do so. The tension caused by this was heightened by other provocative actions on the part of the Assembly. In March 1871 it made its headquarters in Versailles rather than in Paris, a decision that seemed a gratuitous insult to a gallant people, as well as a deliberate blow to their financial interests. Worse were the Assembly's abrupt termination of the moratorium on rents, debts, and promissory notes that had been in force during the siege, its demand that all arrears be made up within forty-eight hours, and its decision to cut off all payments to members of the National Guard. This last stroke was a grievous blow to the majority of workers in Paris who, as a result of the siege and the continuing dislocation of economic activity, had no occupation and depended on their Guard pay for sustenance.

These things encouraged the belief in Paris that the city must itself take the initiative in rallying the nation to the cause of liberty and the republic. This idea was encouraged by activists of various creeds, Jacobins, utopian socialists, and followers of Proudhon, who, working through political clubs organized during the winter of the siege, had become the leaders of the working classes. On March 18, 1871, the Assembly played into their hands by sending a troop of cavalry to remove the guns from the National Guard munitions park on the Butte Montmartre. Violence immediately exploded in Paris; the troops were repulsed and their commanders slain; the National Guard marched on the center of the city and seized the Hôtel de Ville; the government forces left the city; and the tragic episode of the Commune began.

Since Karl Marx, in one of his most brilliant pamphlets (*The Civil War in France*), was to make a legend of the Commune, it is important to note that it had very little in common with the kind of proletarian revolution that he predicted in *The Communist Manifesto*. There was nothing socialistic about its policies or its tactics. Its leaders—a General Council of 90 members, elected on March 26 to direct the Commune's activities—possessed no unifying philosophy and had neither a coherent plan of action nor a sense that one was needed. Bedazzled by their easy acquisition of power, they neglected to take the kind of steps that might have consolidated it, wasting their time instead in paying elaborate obeisance to history. Having taken the name of that Commune of Paris that had overthrown Louis XVI, they seemed to feel it necessary to carry imitation further—adopting the calendar of the Revolution, instituting a regime of virtue *á la* Robespierre (which necessitated raids upon cafés frequented by the higher class *cocottes* and arresting their patrons, who generally turned out to be British journalists) and indulging in floods of neo-Jacobin eloquence. Much of their legislative activity was, in the circumstances in which Paris found itself, plainly irrelevant—laws calling for the separation of church and state, for instance, and for the abolition of the regular army. Their only economic action of any significance was the restoration of the moratorium on rents and debt payments, and their only social legislation was the abolition of night work in bakeries. They never—as Engels regretfully noted later—seemed to have thought of seizing the

Bank of France or to have realized that their very existence depended upon striking Versailles while the National Assembly was still bereft of impressive military power.

Thus, Thiers was given time to rally his shaken forces and to supplement them with prisoners of war released by Bismarck and internees returned from Switzerland. By the beginning of April he had 150,000 men under arms and immediately went over to the offensive. Even this failed to arouse the Commune to effective action. For the next two months, indeed, while government forces closed in around the city, it fell into increasing disarray. The command of its defense forces was entrusted to a series of colorful but irresponsible leaders: Flourens, an adventurer with a great but unconfirmed military reputation who, during a sally against the Versaillese, lost contact with his own forces and was captured and shot; Cluseret, a soldier of fortune who had served with McClellan in the American Civil War, but was so lazy that he made no attempt to improve the city's defenses; Rigault, a doctrinaire anticlerical, probably insane, who was more interested in setting up a revolutionary tribunal to deal with traitors and spies than in the urgent military problem. Thanks to their failures, Thiers's siege operations found no real opposition, and on May 16 his troops stormed into Paris through an undefended section of the city's walls.

Paris in the last days of the Commune: The burning of the General Accounting Office and the Headquarters of the Legion of Honor. From *L'Illustration,* June 3, 1871.

It was at this point, however, that the real resistance began. True to their revolutionary tradition, the workers fell back upon their own quarters, fighting doggedly with gun and torch. In a week of bloody fighting, thousands died on improvised barricades, and the flames took the Porte Saint-Martin, the Church of Saint-Eustache, the Tuileries, the Palais Royal, the Hôtel de Ville, most of the Rue Royale and the Rue de Rivoli, and much else. Not until May 28 did organized resistance end, when the last defiant Communards—having shot their own hostages, including the archbishop of Paris—died under government guns in the cemetery of Père Lachaise.

The revenge of the government was ruthless, despite an earlier promise by Thiers that only the law would punish. Any man wearing a National Guard uniform, or army boots, or a coat with a discolored shoulder was arrested and shot without trial, as were people even faintly resembling Communard leaders. These summary executions were followed by mass trials and deportations. At a conservative estimate, twenty thousand men died in the week following the end of the fighting. Nearly ten thousand more were punished by law, thousands being deported to New Caledonia. It was not until 1879 that an amnesty finally laid the ghost of the Commune and freed those imprisoned for their share in it.

The excesses of the Commune and its liquidation shocked all of Europe. On the whole, middle class opinion tended to believe the theory spread by Thiers's propagandists—that the events in Paris were due to a conspiracy directed by the International Workingmen's Association (see p. 278)—and this helps to explain the virulence of the opposition in many countries to socialism and to other forms of working class organization. In France itself, the development of both trade unionism and an effective socialist party was delayed at least a decade by the Commune, which also left a heritage of distrust between classes that was one of France's weaknesses in years to come.

Thiers as President   In 1871 Thiers was rounding out a varied and controversial career which had begun in the political excitement that preceded the revolution of 1830. He had never been widely liked, and his enemies accused him of excessive ambition and a high degree of disingenuousness; but no one had ever doubted his intelligence and his energy. Now, these qualities were tested to the utmost. As chief of the executive power,[1] he was called on to devise policy for a country shaken by the war and the disorders in Paris, with its economy at a standstill and its institutions in a state of total confusion. In the two years of his power he accomplished much.

Perhaps his greatest service to the country was his avoidance of the issue best calculated to cause new divisions among Frenchmen: the question of a definitive form of government for France. Thiers quite rightly felt that there were more pressing problems, and his prestige was great enough to convince the majority of the Assembly that he was right. Thus, instead of relapsing into new ideological conflict, the nation concentrated upon the task of freeing itself of German occupation troops, who were authorized by treaty to remain in France

---

[1] In August 1871 this title was changed to president of the French Republic.

Adolph Thiers, 1797–1877. After a caricature by the French artist André Gill, in *L'Eclipse,* June 14, 1874.

until the war indemnity of five billion francs had been paid. Thiers paid the entire sum off by September 1873, six months before the final installment was due, by floating two great government bond issues, both of which were over-subscribed by the French people.

The departure of German troops from its soil restored France to a position of equality among the powers, and this had a heartening and unifying effect. Another measure that worked in the same direction was the law of July 1872, which reorganized the military system of the country. This made all French males liable for five years of military service, with partial or total exemptions for university graduates, teachers, priests, ministers, and the like. It also revolutionized the army general staff, adopting certain features of the Prussian system, and in other respects modernized army methods and inspired that quick military recovery that caused so much concern in Berlin in 1874 and 1875 (see p. 250).

While these problems were being dealt with, it became apparent, from certain local elections, that republicanism had not died with the Commune but was on the upswing. To the monarchist majority in the National Assembly, this meant that further postponement of the question of the nature of the regime was inadvisable; and, since Thiers himself was now openly republican in view (believing, as he said, that the republic was the form that divided Frenchmen least), it meant that Thiers must go. In May 1873, the Assembly withdrew its support from the president, and he resigned. As his successor, the Assembly elected Marshal MacMahon, who had contributed to Napoleon III's downfall by losing the battle of Sedan but was apparently expected to atone for this by bringing a new sovereign to France's empty throne.

The Failure of Royalism   French monarchists, however, were confronted with the Ancient Pistol's challenging question: "Under *which* King, Bezonian?" There were three claimants of the throne: the legitimist or Bourbon claimant, the Count of Chambord, grandson of Charles X; the Orleanist candidate, the Count of Paris, grandson of Louis Philippe; and the Bonapartist candidate, the son of the late emperor. Within the Assembly there was no apparent sympathy for the third of these; but the royal claims of the other two claimants had caused protracted and exasperating negotiations ever since peace had been restored. In the course of 1873, an arrangement was finally worked out. The Count of Chambord received the united support of the monarchists and, since he had no heirs, the Count of Paris was promised the succession after his death. There seemed to be no real obstacle now to the accession of the pretender, who let it be known that he would assume the title Henry V.

Unfortunately for the monarchist cause, however, he almost immediately revealed that he had none of his great forbear's ability to adjust to circumstances. Henry of Navarre had been willing to change his religion to assure himself of power; Henry V would not even change his flag. Under his rule, he announced, the banner of France would not be the *tricouleur,* with all its revolutionary associations, but the lily flag of the Bourbon dynasty. The most intransigent royalist could see the folly of this. As MacMahon said at the time, the repudiation of the flag that had waved over the fields of Marengo, Austerlitz, Sebastopol, and Solferino would cause "the chassepots [to] go off by themselves."

The flag issue killed the hopes of a royal restoration in 1873. The pretender was immune to logic and impervious to argument; his supporters were forced to abandon their plans to have him summoned to the throne. The most that they could hope for was that time would bring them to their desired goal; and they decided that it would be wise to keep MacMahon in power, so that he could act when the right moment came—when and if, for instance, the Count of Chambord died, leaving the way clear for his Orleanist rival. Therefore, before the year was over, the Assembly passed the Septennate Law, which, for the first time, set a definite limit to the president's term and assured MacMahon of seven years of power.

In reality, the opportunity lost in 1873 was not to recur. The country was tired of provisional governments and of an Assembly that had been elected to draw up a constitution but had now postponed doing so for five years. Unmistakable signs of popular dissatisfaction in the provinces and the growth of both republican and Bonapartist sentiment finally persuaded the Assembly to complete its work. In the course of the year 1875 it passed a series of basic constitutional laws.

These provided that France would henceforth be governed by a legislature of two houses: a Senate of 300 members, a fourth of whom were to be appointed by the present Assembly for a life term and the rest to be elected by departmental electoral colleges for a period of nine years[2]; and a Chamber of Deputies, elected by universal manhood suffrage for four years. By parliamentary procedure like that of England, the Chamber would control the ministry and, through it, the

---

[2] In 1884 the life term was abolished and all senators came to be elected for nine years.

policy of the country. Joint sessions of Chamber and Senate could be called to amend the constitution when necessary and, at seven-year intervals, would convene in order to elect a president. This official was given the right to initiate legislation and to promulgate laws when they were enacted, to grant pardons, to direct the military establishment, to make appointments to civil and military positions, and, with the consent of the Senate, to dissolve the Chamber and order new elections. These powers were, as it turned out, less real than they appeared.

The only reference in these laws to the republican form of government came in the title of the chief executive, who was called "the president of the Republic," and even this had been opposed by most of the monarchists and accepted by the barest of majorities. Yet whatever the constitutional texts might say, France was now predominantly republican. When the National Assembly finally dissolved itself in December 1875, and elections were held for the new Chamber and Senate, avowed republicans won a large majority in the former and narrowly missed dominating the Senate as well. In the next two years, this partial victory became definitive, although only after a major constitutional crisis, which tested the relative power of the president and the Chamber of Deputies.

This crisis was caused, essentially, by Marshal MacMahon's deepening conviction, in which he was encouraged by the monarchists and the higher clergy, that republicanism would be the ruination of France. His fears in this regard made him amenable in the spring of 1877 to suggestions that he use his power to block the potential republican conquest of the Senate by manipulating the elections of the departmental electoral colleges that selected senators. Since this would be impossible if his present cabinet, a determinedly republican one, was in office, MacMahon, on May 16, 1877, forced it to resign, despite the fact that it had the support of the Chamber. He then appointed a monarchist cabinet under the Duke of Broglie and called upon the Senate to agree to the dissolution of the Chamber, which it did.

MacMahon's intention was, of course, to secure a popular mandate for his assertion of presidential authority over the Chamber; and he was confident that he would secure it. So was Broglie, who undertook to influence election results by the persecution of the republican press, the dismissal of republican mayors, municipal councilors, civil servants, and election officials, the breaking up of republican clubs, and a powerful propaganda campaign in favor of monarchist and clerical candidates. After all this ("The silence of the country is terrifying," Broglie said) MacMahon and he expected victory. They failed, however, to make allowance for the powers of Léon Gambetta.

André Siegfried tells of an old man who said to him, "You see this hand? Gambetta shook it. I have not washed it since." There were many who felt that way about Léon Gambetta, remembering his great services in 1870, when he had been the soul of the resistance to the Germans and, by raising provincial levies, had made possible the renewal of the war and the salvation of France's honor after the defeat of Sedan. Among the working and lower middle classes he was loved for his warm impulsive nature, his splendid gifts of oratory, in which he has been called the equal of Mirabeau and Danton, and his known determination to work implacably for the restoration of the lost provinces.

Léon Gambetta, 1838–1882. From *Illustrated London News,* October 15, 1870.

Gambetta believed in a democratic republic that would be founded on the support of the common people of France, peasants, workers, and lower middle class; and, because of the affection he was able to inspire among them, he generated enough enthusiasm for this ideal to defeat the hopes of the right entirely. He threw himself into the campaign of 1877 with enthusiasm, traveling and speaking incessantly, calling for the creation of one united republican bloc that would embrace the followers of Thiers as well as those of Hugo and Blanc, hurling memorable phrases at his opponents. Some of these were so barbed that he was sentenced to three months' imprisonment for attacks on the president; but this merely spread his message further. When the elections were finally held in October 1877, the results of all this were made clear, for, despite rightist obstructionism, a solid republican majority was returned to the Chamber; and MacMahon had to accept a ministry just as republican as the one he had dismissed.

A year later, the new Senate elections gave the republicans a majority in that Chamber also. This completed MacMahon's discomfiture and rendered his position untenable. For the Chamber now pushed measures that they knew he must oppose, until the president faced the inevitable and, in January 1879, resigned his office. He was succeeded by Jules Grévy, a sincere republican who, it was felt, would indulge in none of the tactics of his predecessor.

THE REPUBLIC: BASIC PROBLEMS

Years of Accomplishment, 1879–1885   Republicanism was now in the ascendant, and its supporters celebrated their triumph by moving the capital back to Paris in 1880 and accepting July 14, the day of the storming of the Bastille, as the national holiday and the *Marseillaise* as the national anthem. These measures were perhaps of a purely symbolical importance; but they were followed by more significant legislation, which safeguarded the civil liberties of the individual, protected the right of assembly, lifted restrictions upon the press, removed local government from the strict control of the central government, and permitted the formation of trade unions.

Like their Liberal colleagues in Belgium and England and Germany, the republicans tended to be strongly anticlerical; and this feeling had been strengthened by the political campaign conducted in behalf of MacMahon by French bishops and priests. In May 1877, Gambetta had cried *"Le cléricalisme, voilá l'ennemi!"* It was in this spirit that the Chamber struck out in two areas in which church control had always seemed to them to be unjustifiable. In 1885 they restored provisions for divorce to the Civil Code, despite outspoken church opposition; and between 1881 and 1885 they carried through a comprehensive reform of education, designed to diminish the influence that the church had enjoyed under Napoleon III.

The man who inspired this legislation and piloted it through the Chamber was Jules Ferry (1832–1893), an able and tenacious statesman who was deeply convinced that the minds of the young, especially of the young bourgeoisie who would be the backbone of the republic in the next years, must be protected from clerical influence. Ferry began his campaign with a gambit that had, through its repeated use in the modern period, become the classic means of initiating anticlerical movements and uniting the Church's enemies: he demanded the expulsion of the Society of Jesus.[3] Having secured this, in 1880, he pressed on with measures that struck at Catholic schools and teaching orders. Henceforth, no teaching order that was unauthorized by the state could maintain a school, and no one could teach in a state school without a state teacher's certificate. This last measure was designed to reduce the large number of nuns and teaching brothers in local schools (some 10,000 brothers and 40,000 nuns in 1877); and it was supplemented by the creation of two new higher normal schools to supply teachers for the departmental normal schools, which, in their turn, trained teachers for elementary education.

The most important of the educational laws were those that made primary education in state schools free (1881) and an elementary education in *some* kind of school compulsory (1882). These laws greatly expanded the school population (and reduced illiteracy to less than 10 percent of the population); they also made it tempting for parents who could afford to pay fees for church schools to send their children to state schools instead. Both tendencies reduced church control of the minds of the literate population.

Laws were passed also which improved standards in state secondary schools and technical schools, and the first steps were taken toward the fundamental reform of university education that was to be carried through in the mid-1890s and was, among other things, to restore to the Sorbonne, after centuries of neglect, the position it had held in the world of learning in the Middle Ages.

[3] For liberals and progressives, the Jesuits were always a convenience. Benjamin Constant once said, "Quand on n'a rien, eh bien! il reste les Jésuites. Je les sonne comme un valet de chambre: ils arrivent toujours."

The Eiffel Tower, built for the International Exposition of 1889. In the drawing, dated October 1888, the tower, viewed from the Trocadero Palace, is shown in the final stages of construction. From *L'Illustration,* November 10, 1888. The structure is a good example of the wedding of art and science, the architect achieving a new relation between inner and outer space by the bold incorporation of light and air into his design. For another example of this, see the Bauhaus Workshop of Gropius, p. 455.

The educational reforms were perhaps the most enduring of the achievements of the first phase of the Republic's history; but they should not be allowed completely to overshadow other constructive activity. In the field of transportation, for instance, the work of Charles de Freycinet deserves brief attention. Freycinet (1828–1893), known as "the white mouse" because of his shy, deferential manner and a general inoffensiveness that won him many cabinet posts in the course of his career, was a brilliant engineer and administrator, who had helped Gambetta raise and organize the army of resistance in 1870. In 1878, as minister of public works, he came forward with a gigantic scheme for what he called the completion of "the national equipment." This involved improvement of existing railways, canals, roads, and harbors, and new building in all categories. Freycinet's comprehensive and systematic program was supported by parliament and, although at the cost of some elaborate financial arrangements between the government and the larger railroad companies, started the process that doubled France's rail net before 1914. It led also the standardization of France's canal system so as to facilitate through communication without transshipment and the improvement of rivers as commercial arteries. These works led to an increase of metric tonnage carried by internal waterways from 21,000,000 in 1886 to 42,000,000 in 1913.

These were years also of Republican triumphs overseas, where the foundations of France's new colonial empire were laid. The guiding spirit in this French imperialism was, again, Jules Ferry. It was he who persuaded the Chamber to grant credits to support a campaign that secured Tunis before the end of 1881. The following year the government had a setback when disorders in Egypt, where French interests had been strong for a century, led the British to intervene unilaterally and to impose what came to be a protectorate over the country (see p. 258). This loss was offset by the gains made under Ferry's leadership in the years 1883–1885, during which France not only penetrated into Indochina, conquering Tonkin and extending a protectorate over Laos and Cambodia, but concluded a treaty with the government of Madagascar, which was the first step toward outright annexation, improved the port of Dakar, and established French Equatorial Africa. These adventures were not universally popular; military setbacks in Tonkin caused the repudiation and fall of Ferry as prime minister in 1885; but, as in the other countries, even the masses became increasingly interested in empire as the years passed; and France's colonial activity was not perceptibly slowed down before the turn of the century.

While these undoubted successes were being registered, the Republic gained in stature and confidence. The new spirit was typified by the condition of Paris, which, in the mid-1880s, left the shadow of the Commune behind it and became, in the eyes of many, the intellectual and artistic capital and the greatest playground of the world. It was in this period that Paris was described as the place to which good Americans went when they died; but thousands were refusing to wait until then, and, with hordes of other tourists, were trooping yearly to the spirited and elegant city on the Seine, to marvel at the newly built Eiffel Tower, to visit the new opera house and hear Gounod's *Faust* or, perhaps, Bizet's *Carmen,* to eat *fraises de bois* in charming restaurants along the Boulevard Montparnasse, to shop on the Rue de Rivoli, to gape at the sinful night life of Montmartre, to watch the racing at Longchamps. More serious visitors came to work at the École des Beaux Arts or to study medicine under Charcot and Becquerel or to hear Henri Bergson lecture at the Collège de France or to learn to write in a city whose literary vitality had never been greater—where French poetry (and that of other countries) was being revolutionized by the influence of Baudelaire's followers Rimbaud, Tristan Corbière, Verlaine, and Mallarmé, where fierce battles raged between naturalists like Zola and de Maupassant and their detractors, and where every year saw a new sensation or a new movement, like the neoromantic decadence that became fashionable with the publication of J. K. Huysmans's À *Rebours* in 1884.

Some Basic Problems   Yet, despite the creative legislative activity of the early 1880s and the vigor of the arts and sciences, all was not well in France. The rate of economic progress was slower than in either Britain or Germany, and the very fact that so high a percentage of French savings (a third to a half) was invested abroad was both a sign of and a reason for a lack of vitality and progress in the economy. France's industrial development was not, after 1870, impressive in relative terms; the average industrial enterprise was small; and there were few great industrial concentrations until the decade before the war, when the output of wrought iron and cast steel shot upward, and the Comité des Forges and the Comptoir Métallurgique de Longwy were established. Some basic industries had been dislocated by the war of 1870 and were hurt in the subsequent period by foreign competition. This was true, for instance, of French cotton spinning, which did not recover until it received a strong measure of protection from the Méline tariffs of the 1890s. The silk industry remained prosperous by changing its basis from home production of silk to importation of raw silk, cocoons, and thrown silk and by introducing power looms; but the linen industry declined steadily after 1870 because of backward techniques and Irish competition. In both chemical and electrical industries France lagged behind her neighbors.

France's economy remained predominantly agricultural throughout most of the period, more than half of the population living in rural areas as late as 1914. The prevalence of small subsistence farms reduced the effects of the agricultural malaise common to all western European countries in these years; but the large grain producers were not immune to foreign competition and falling prices, nor were their laborers. The largest agricultural industry aside from wheat also suffered a grievous blow in this period, when the vines were attacked in the 1870s by phylloxera, a plant louse. Until the turn of the century, when American grafts improved the stock, the French wine industry was fighting for its very existence, not only against the blight that had hit it but against Italian, and (after the beginning of the Franco-Italian tariff war) Spanish, competition.

Economic troubles breed critics of any regime; and France was no exception here. But it was not only in the economic area that the Republic was criticized. The longer the Republic lasted, the less inspired did its political behavior seem to become; and, after the middle 1880s, it betrayed troubling signs of stagnation and lack of direction. French parliamentary life was characterized by a pervasive anarchy in which both forceful leaders and attempts to enforce party discipline were viewed with grave suspicion. It is significant that the two strongest men in the first twenty years of the Republic's life experienced revolts by the Chamber against their authority and were denied the ultimate position for which their talents commended them. The "great ministry" of Gambetta lasted only three months in 1881; and Ferry fell in 1885, ostensibly because of a setback in the Far East but really because there were too many who feared his ability. In the question of the presidency of the Republic, the deputies showed an almost pathological distrust of strong individuals, and, after MacMahon, France's presidents were generally respectable but innocuous men who were considered to be safe.

Meanwhile, the parties proved incapable of exercising control over their members or, indeed, of holding their members, for a steady process of fragmentation of parties continued throughout these years. The republican center, which Gambetta had sought to wield into a permanent bloc, split up into a number of splinter groups; and these fissiparous tendencies were also to be the fate of socialism when it became a political force in the 1880s. More and more, the individual deputy tended to become a law unto himself, which made reasoned political action or systematic attacks upon political and social problems almost as difficult as in Italy.

Aside from this, as has already been indicated, France suffered from history. The artist Forain had once drawn a cartoon entitled "How fine the Republic was—under the Empire." The longer the Republic lasted, the more attractive did other regimes appear, especially to certain more or less organized groups in society.

There was no dearth of critics or, indeed, open enemies of the regime. There were, in the first place, the inveterate antirepublicans: aristocrats, clergy, upper civil service, army. These were generally monarchist in sympathy and opposed to all the prevailing tendencies in the Republic: especially its attacks upon the church, its apparent susceptibility to Jewish and Masonic influence (the Masonry of the Grand Orient did, in fact, have considerable power in French politics, and in the Chamber, in the 1880s), and its failure to give due attention to France's military power. The clerical wing of this group had many spokesmen, including such unregenerate and uncompromising ones as Louis Veuillot, the editor of the Catholic organ L'Univers, who rejected the Republic as both un-Christian and un-French, and Edouard Drumont, who published his La France Juive in 1886 and made anti-Semitism a force to be reckoned with.

The social center of this extreme right wing opposition lay in certain salons in the Faubourg St. Germain. It is doubtful whether the Faubourg by itself could have exercised much influence in French politics; but, by the curious operation of those forces that Proust's Baron Charlus described as "aristocratic prestige and middle-class cowardice," it served as a magnet that attracted socially ambitious members of the upper middle class, as well as those who feared the rise of the working classes. In the long run, that merging of the ideas and the resources of the aristocratic Guermantes and the middle class Verdurins, which is the basic theme of Proust's Remembrance of Things Past, proved dangerous to the Republic.

Allied to the rightist opposition but not entirely enclosed within it was the nationalist opposition, composed of all of those who believed that France's main objective should be revenge for the defeat of 1870 and the loss of Alsace and Lorraine. The most frenetic of the patrioteers—the members of Paul Déroulède's League of Patriots, for instance—took the line that failure to push consistently for revanche, or diversion of the national effort into other lines, was treason to the true France. Déroulède opposed Ferry's policy of imperialism with the words, "I have lost two children and you offer me twenty servants."

Most of the members of Déroulède's society would, of course, have been enemies of the Republic even without the issue of revanche, but not all. There were many in France who were not by political orientation or social inclination enemies of the Republic but who nevertheless felt that what they regarded as lack of patriotic spirit in the government reflected an encroaching materialism and relativism that would be the ruin of France. These people were troubled and moved by Maurice Barrès's fulminations against the decadence of his generation (in his famous novel Les Déracinés in 1897, for instance) and by the appeal to French youth with which Paul Bourget prefaced his novel Le Disciple in 1889.

"Place de l'Europe on a Rainy Day," 1877, by Gustave Caillebotte. A fine representation of bourgeois solidity. (The Art Institute of Chicago)

"Our generation," Bourget wrote, "could never consider that the peace of 1871 was established for all time. How I would like to know if you think as we did! How I would like to be sure that you are not ready to renounce what was the secret dream and the consoling hope of each one of us, even of those who never mentioned it!" The fear that under republicanism France might cease to be herself made potential antirepublicans of many who had no use for the cheap jingoism of Déroulède, the anti-Semitism of Drumont, or the clerical absolutism of Veuillot.

Whether the working classes could be considered enemies or supporters of the middle class Republic was still problematical in the 1880s. But the wounds of the Commune were not yet healed, despite the return of the proscribed Communards in 1880; and dissatisfaction with working conditions, long hours, and low wages was causing an increasing degree of labor unrest. In 1884 there was a violent strike in the Valenciennes coal fields, which inspired Zola to write his best novel, *Germinal;* in 1886 there were others at Decazeville and Vierzon;

and after 1890 the number of work stoppages mounted sharply. Finally, at the end of the 1870s, the influence of Marxist socialism began to spread among the more educated working classes; Marx's son-in-law Paul Laforgue and others encouraged it by translating basic works of Marx and Engels; and in 1879, Jules Guesde, "a Torquemada with a pince-nez," founded a new "Workers party" which proclaimed itself to be Marxist, revolutionary, and self-sufficient (that is, opposed to any cooperation with existing bourgeois parties). If this became an effective political party, it appeared likely that the weight of the organized working class would be thrown against a Republic already harassed by other foes.

THREE CRISES

The Boulanger Case   The last fifteen years of the century saw the Republic tested by three great crises in which the enemies enumerated above sought to overthrow the regime. The first of these was the result of accumulating exasperation with the economic troubles, the lack of leadership in government, the bickering of the parties, and some colonial setbacks that seemed more serious than they actually were. It took the form of a demand for a strong man who would clean up the mess at home and lead France in a victorious war against Germany.

The man who appeared capable of filling this role was General Georges Boulanger (1837–1891), who as minister of war in 1886 won popularity with the army by some improvement of conditions in the barracks and with the Paris mobs by his dashing appearance and the beauty of his black horse Tunis. General Boulanger did not repulse those who began to urge him to overthrow the Republic; and it is possible that, if his intelligence and courage had matched his ambition, and if he had had a sense of political timing, he might have succeeded in doing so. Certainly he was given an opportunity in 1887, when it was discovered that President Grévy's son-in-law, a certain Daniel Wilson, was using his position to influence elections to the Legion of Honor for his private profit, a revelation that forced the president's resignation in December. A coup at any time in the months that followed might have succeeded, but Boulanger seemed to prefer the road Hitler chose years later, the conquest of power by legal means. Throughout 1888, with invariable success, he contested parliamentary vacancies, but this merely gave the republican center time to put an end to its customary dissensions and take action against him. In the spring of 1889, the cabinet summoned Boulanger to appear before the Senate on charges of conspiracy against the state; and the general lost his nerve and fled to Belgium, where he committed suicide two years later. His movement fell to pieces as rapidly as it had formed.

The failure of *Boulangisme* strengthened the Republic by discrediting its enemies and rallying its friends. It also showed that the political parties that claimed to speak for the working classes were not as revolutionary and as opposed to compromise with the bourgeois regime as Guesde claimed. As in other countries, an important section of the socialist movement thought in moderate evolutionary terms rather than in the strictest Marxian ones; and, to many French socialists, heirs of an older tradition, Marxism was too Germanic to be completely palatable and Guesde too authoritarian to be entirely acceptable as a leader. Under the leadership of Paul Brousse, Joffrin, and Benoit Malon, a "Federation of Labor Socialists of France" had been founded to promote practical possible reforms. During the Boulanger agitation, these Possibilists or Opportunists, as they came to be called, formed an alliance with the republican center and declared: "We workers are ready to forget the sixteen years during which the bourgeoisie has betrayed the hopes of the people. We are ready to defend and conserve by all means the weak germ of our republican institutions against military threats. Long live the social Republic!"

Panama   If the Republic seemed to come out of the Boulanger case with renewed strength, its gains were largely dissipated four years later by a scandal worse than the Wilson affair. Since the late 1870s Ferdinand de Lesseps (1805–1894), the builder of the Suez Canal, had been engaged in a project to build a canal across the Isthmus of Panama. The work had been slowed by the unwise choice of a site, by unrealistic engineering, and by the terrible incidence of yellow fever, for which science had as yet found no answer. To prevent loss of faith in the scheme, with resultant drying up of credit and loss of original investment, the canal promoters resorted to bribery of the press and the politicians. But the truth could not be hidden forever, and its disclosure was bound to expose the corrupt attempts to hide it. That is precisely what happened in 1892, when a series of articles called "The Inside Story of Panama" appeared in Edouard Drumont's paper *La Libre Parole*.

The resultant washing of dirty linen could not help but convince many Frenchmen that parliamentary government was rotten to the core and that all politicians were crooks. This and the fact that many of the company manipulators were Jews were exploited to the full by Drumont, and his articles enabled the extreme Right to equate the Republic with corruption, inefficiency, and control by international Jewry. All of this was to affect the war of opinion during the Dreyfus case.

The French people seemed less concerned than many thought they should be by the scandal, and nothing catastrophic happened in the elections of 1893. But Panama perhaps contributed, in an indirect way, to the further development of French socialism in an evolutionary direction. The elections brought an increase in Socialist representation in the Chamber of 50 seats and brought to Parliament two men whose reputations very quickly eclipsed those of Guesde and Brousse. These were Jean Jaurès and Alexandre Millerand, both exponents of social reform by parliamentary means. Under their leadership socialism was to become a potent force in French politics.

The Dreyfus Affair   In October 1894 a cleaning woman working in the office of the German military attaché in Paris extracted a torn and crumpled piece of paper from a wastebasket and sent it to the counter-espionage section (or *Deuxième Bureau*) of the French General Staff. Examined there, it appeared to be a list of items of information about the French army which its unknown author was prepared to sell to the Germans, and it horrified the officers of the *Deuxième Bureau*. They decided that the author of the list (or, as it came to

The kind of resistance to injustice that inspired the supporters of Dreyfus is dramatically represented in Auguste Rodin's famous *Burghers* of *Calais,* 1884–1888. (Rodin Museum, Philadelphia. Courtesy Philadelphia Museum of Art and SPADEM 1970 by French Reproduction Rights Inc.)

be known around the world, the *bordereau*) must be a French General Staff officer, an artillerist, and one who had had a recent opportunity to inspect a number of France's military installations. This description, they further decided, fitted Captain Alfred Dreyfus. They asked Dr. Alphonse Bertillon, the well-known inventor of the fingerprint system and more recently an expert on graphology, to compare this officer's handwriting with that of the *bordereau,* and on the basis of his affirmative findings had the suspect arrested.

There was no apparent reason why Dreyfus should be a spy. A brilliant officer with a good record, the first officer of Jewish faith ever to be admitted to the French General Staff, he was happily married, had independent financial means, and was known to be a fervent patriot. He was nevertheless charged, and, after a trial marked by considerable irregularity in the form of admission of unsupported testimony and reliance on documents the defense was not allowed to see, was found guilty, sentenced to military degradation, loss of rank, and life imprisonment in a fortified place and transported to Devil's Island in French Guiana.

Almost two years later, the *Deuxième Bureau* received a new chief, Colonel Georges Picquart, and Picquart, already puzzled as to why Dreyfus should have betrayed his country, discovered that the sale of secrets to the German embassy was still going on. This led him to embark on an investigation that convinced him that the true author of the *bordereau* was a Commandant Esterhazy, an officer with a known fondness for expensive pleasures and suspicious acquaintances, whose handwriting, moreover, matched that of the *bordereau* much more closely than did that of Dreyfus. Picquart immediately asked his superiors to arrest Esterhazy and make retribution to Dreyfus. To his stupefaction, he was informed that this would be impossible and, when he insisted, was transferred to a post in Algeria.

Before he left, Picquart saw to it that some of his evidence reached the hands of republican deputies of known integrity. Their interest and help gave new hope to the campaign for revision which the Dreyfus family had been doggedly pursuing since 1894. To work for Dreyfus was never easy. At the beginning one had to fight the forces of army evasion, bureaucratic obstructionism, and public indifference; later one had to be prepared to withstand the incredible violence the case released. Luckily for Dreyfus, a small band of deputies, newspapermen, and intellectuals—men like Georges Clemenceau (1841–1929) and the novelist Anatole France (1844–1924)—were prepared to brave these things; and, thanks to their efforts, public interest and concern grew.

The case for revision was given new strength by a series of dramatic events at the beginning of 1898. On January 11, the army, in a gesture that was patently designed to allay any doubts about the merits of the original verdict, arraigned Esterhazy before a packed court martial, swiftly acquitted him of all suspicion, and publicly congratulated him. The next day Picquart was arrested on charges of calumniating Esterhazy's name and was imprisoned. It was these events that led Émile Zola (1840–1902) to release an open letter to the press entitled *J'accuse*, in which the novelist declared Dreyfus innocent and described the army's conduct as corrupt and dangerous to the Republic. The government immediately brought charges against Zola, and he found it expedient to leave the country; but his action had turned the Dreyfus case into an issue of national and international concern.

The resistance of the army hierarchy to a reopening of the case, and their subsequent resort to falsification of documents and forgery of new evidence in order to prevent it, can be explained in part by an unwillingness to admit error and an attempt to rationalize this by arguing that such an admission would be detrimental to the army's prestige in a time of international tension. The republican poet and moralist Charles Péguy (1873–1914), a revisionist himself, put it this way:

> The true position of the people who opposed us was, for a long time, not to say and believe Dreyfus guilty, but to say that innocent or guilty, the life and salvation of a people, the enormous salvation of a people,

could not be troubled, could not be upset, could not be *compromised,* could not be risked for one man, for a single man.... From this point of view it was evident that Dreyfus should be sacrificed for France; not only for the peace of France, but for the salvation itself of France, which he imperilled.

This attitude was inexplicable to anyone who believed in law and morality. Convinced supporters of Dreyfus felt that the acceptance of an injustice of this kind, on any pretext, would not only place the army above the law but would dishonor France by acting—again in Péguy's words—like "a touch of gangrene that corrupts the whole body."

But, apart from this, the supporters of Dreyfus found it significant that the most vociferous defenders of the army's refusal to reopen the case were also those who had shown themselves, during the Boulanger and Panama affairs, to be the most notorious enemies of the Republic: the royalists, the inhabitants of the Faubourg, the upper clergy, the anti-Semites. Oblivious to any reasoned argument, these groups insisted that Dreyfus was a traitor and that his guilt was another sign of the rottenness of the Republic. Within the Chamber of Deputies, their representatives used obstructionist tactics whenever the case was discussed and disrupted proceedings sufficiently to bring new discredit on parliamentary government. Outside parliament, their tactics were even more dangerous. Paul Déroulède, for instance, was openly calling in September 1898 for an army revolt against the Republic.

This apparent threat had one profound political effect, for it persuaded the Socialist wing led by Jaurès and Millerand that an attitude of political neutrality in this crisis would be unwise. In June 1899 this led to an unprecedented example of collaboration, when the parliamentary Socialists declared their support of a new Radical Republican ministry headed by René Waldeck-Rousseau, and when Millerand actually accepted the post of minister of commerce—the first Socialist to serve in a bourgeois government.

This was not immediately successful in securing justice for Dreyfus. When, as a result of the confession and suicide of one of the chief witnesses against him and the subsequent flight of Esterhazy to England, the court of cassation annulled Dreyfus's original court martial and ordered a new trial, the judges again made a travesty of justice by excluding evidence that was clearly in Dreyfus's favor and once more finding him guilty, although this time, wholly illogically, "with extenuating circumstances." The trial and Dreyfus's subsequent sentence to ten years' imprisonment caused a new outburst of passion throughout the country, and this was not allayed when the president of the Republic pardoned the long-maligned officer. His supporters declared that they would be content with nothing less than full exoneration, but this they did not attain until 1906, when the government declared Dreyfus completely innocent, restored him to the army, and made him a member of the Legion of Honor.

The affair has fascinated dozens of great French writers and has received fictional treatment in Anatole France's *Penguin Island,* Proust's *Jean Santeuil* and *Remembrance of Things Past,* and Roger Martin Du Gard's *Jean Barois,* to mention only a few major works. This is not surprising, for it dramatized cleavages in French society and opposition to republican institutions that were to continue long after Dreyfus had been given the right once more to wear the uniform of his country. This division of France continued partly, perhaps, because the violence with which the anti-Dreyfusards had fought against exoneration elicited a violent reaction on the part of Dreyfus's supporters after their cause had won. Perhaps the deeper reason was the one that Charles Péguy saw, namely, that the Dreyfus case had taken the ugly form it did because everyone concerned in it had consciously or unconsciously recognized the weaknesses and corruption of the Republic. However, instead of attacking those faults, they tried to reassure themselves by confirming themselves in the ideological attitudes that had created the situation in the first place.

THE PREWAR YEARS

Army Reform   It was only natural that the aroused republican forces, strengthened by the elections of 1902 and the continued collaboration of the Socialists, should want to strike out at the chief persecutors of Dreyfus, the reactionary officers in the army. Those whose names had figured prominently during the Affair were almost immediately purged, and a known reputation for monarchical or clerical sympathies became a grave handicap for an officer and often cost him his career. Some of the methods used by republican ministers of war were questionable; and it is hard to believe that encouragement of civil authorities in garrison towns to report on the behavior of suspected officers helped the morale of the officer corps or reconciled talented soldiers of rightist views who remained in the service (like the later Marshal Pétain and General Weygand) to the Republic they were supposed to serve.

A more profound military result of the Dreyfus case was a change in the system of recruitment. The law of 1872 had made all Frenchmen liable for five years of active service but had allowed liberal exemptions. A law of 1889 had lowered the length of service to three years and radically reduced the inequalities of the previous law, so that no able male could hope completely to escape service, although, depending on education and career, he might have to serve only one year. Now the republican bloc insisted on further reduction and perfect equality of service; and in 1905 a new recruitment law stipulated two-year service with virtually no exemptions.

This reduction of the period of active training and the simultaneous liberalization of the disciplinary code of the army was intended to diminish the control of the professionals over French youth and prevent the subversion of their values by reactionary officers. One supporter of the law of 1905 actually said that it would open for the army "an era which I will dare to call . . . the era of civilianism." The eruption of the sharp crisis over Morocco in this same year (see p. 431), however, and other signs of mounting international tension threw some doubt on the validity of the basic premise of the new law. At a time when French population was decreasing in relation to that of Germany and when the number of men in annual contingents could be expected to decrease also, was it wise to reduce the length of service? At a time when the German army was known to be basing its plans on a lightning war (*attaque brusque*) by highly trained forces, was it wise to make national security dependent upon a strictly defensive strategy conducted by hastily mobilized reserves? More and more people came to believe that it was not; and as international relations continued to deteriorate after the second Moroccan crisis (see p. 441), the Chamber in 1913 restored the three-year term of service on the grounds that it was necessary to provide the training that would make offensive operations possible. This was far from a unanimous decision, however, and there were many Frenchmen who, thanks to their memories of the Dreyfus case, continued, until the war came, to regard their army with grave suspicion.

Separation of Church and State   At the beginning of the 1890s, Pope Leo XIII had sought to dissociate the Catholic Church from its royalist ties and, through France's most eminent churchman, Cardinal Lavigerie, had called for the acceptance of the Republic by the faithful. This so-called *Ralliement* was wrecked on the shoals of the Dreyfus case; and, in the years that followed it, the church had to pay for the prominent role played by some of its leading dignitaries in the antirevisionist cause. Waldeck-Rousseau, prime minister of the Radical Republican and Socialist coalition in 1899, believed, as firmly as Gambetta had, that clericalism was the Republic's real enemy; and his successor Émile Combes said in 1902, "Clericalism is to be found at the bottom of every agitation and every intrigue from which Republican France has suffered during the last thirty-five years."

These sentiments led to a new spate of anticlerical legislation. In 1901 an Associations Law provided that no religious association could exist in France without specific government authorization. The Assumptionist Order, whose superior had been the most intransigent foe of Dreyfus, was immediately expelled, and others suffered the same fate, so that thousands of nuns and priests had to leave France. More serious was Combes's attempt to give the state a monopoly of education by rigorous execution of a new law of 1904 which stipulated that all teaching by religious orders must be terminated within ten years.

Ever since the Concordat of 1802 between Napoleon and the Vatican, church and state had been intimately associated in France, the state appointing archbishops and bishops with the pope's consent, the bishops appointing the priests with the state's assent, the state paying the salaries of the clergy and permitting it the use of the extensive church property to which it held title. In 1905 the Concordat was abrogated. The state's right to make appointments and its obligation to pay salaries were declared at an end; church property remained at the disposal of the clergy but was to be administered henceforth by elected parish religious corporations (*associations culturelles*). The refusal of Pope Pius X to allow churchmen to obey this legislation or accept the authority of the *associations* did not shake the government's determination to have its way. A new law of 1907 revoked the privileges offered two years before, reduced the amount of property to be used by the clergy, and stipulated that church buildings might be used without charge for purposes of worship on the basis of local arrangements between priests and the civil authorities. In all other respects, the church and the state were now separated.

Politics in the Last Years of Peace   Politically, the Republic was more stable in the decade after 1905 than it had been at any time since 1871. The Dreyfus affair had strengthened the middle-of-the-road republican parties and brought them into fruitful contact with the Socialists. It is true that, officially, this tie was terminated in 1905, when—largely as a result of pressure exerted by the 1904 Congress of the Second International—the different French Socialist parties came together in one, the French Section of the Workers International (or SFIO), and declared themselves to be "a class and revolutionary party" rather than a revisionist one, and specifically repudiated the policy of collaboration with bourgeois governments. Temperamentally, however, the French Socialists remained for the most part revisionists and supporters of the Republic in time of crisis (as the war was to show); and, if Socialists could not sit in bourgeois cabinets, *former* Socialists could. The republican parties were to acquire talented leaders by conversion. It was thus, for example, that Aristide Briand (1862–1932), who started in politics as a revolutionary, made his way to that middle position he was to occupy when he was France's long-term foreign minister after the war.

The new vitality of the republican center was shown by the emergence of other leaders besides those brought over from Socialist ranks. Clemenceau's reputation had grown during the Affair; Joseph Caillaux succeeded Waldeck-Rousseau and Combes as the chief of the Radical Republicans; and the Right Center found a dynamic new leader in Raymond Poincaré (1860–1934), who was to be president of the Republic in 1912 and then, after the war, to go back to the Chamber as leader of the Right.

The strengthening of the Center did not mean that the Republic's enemies had been eliminated. To the left of the Socialists, the Syndicalists carried on their agitations through the smaller and more militant trade unions, and their greatest ideologue, Georges Sorel, preached the uses of direct action. On the extreme Right, the forces of reaction sought a new rallying point and found it in the movement known as the *Action Française,* which had grown out of the Affair and had found its leader in Charles Maurras (1868–1952). A powerful and eloquent publicist, Maurras fulminated against the Republic as a hotbed of freemasonry, Jewry, Protestants, and foreigners (*Métèques*) and called for the restoration of a king who would make France great once more and put an end to the sad comedy of democracy. Maurras drew to his cause all of those foes of the Republic who had been discomfited by the exoneration of Dreyfus; and the *Action Française* held them together until the ills of the 1930s brought them new recruits and new opportunities.

Like Sorel, Maurras placed great emphasis upon action and vitality; and it was probably this, as much as his literary grace, that attracted the youth of France. It has been said that the young intellectuals who did not turn to syndicalism or revolutionary socialism before the war joined the *Action Française.* This is an exaggeration, but there is enough truth in it to show that France was not entirely free of that weakness from which Italy suffered—a tendency of the young to be bored with the system and to want to change it. A good deal of the idealism that had been generated during the fight for Dreyfus, and which had led Péguy in his memoir *Notre Jeunesse* to describe that struggle as a period of heroism and spiritual regeneration, had evaporated during the exploitation of the victory by Waldeck-Rousseau and Combes; and the disillusioned intellectuals who felt that attacks on the church and the army cheapened their fight for abstract justice either withdrew from politics or sought new creeds.

Aside from this, in the popularity of Maurras and Sorel, as in the vogue of Bergsonian philosophy, we can see further evidence of that cult of violence which we have noted in other countries in this period.

Chapter 15 THE GERMAN EMPIRE: PSEUDO-CONSTITUTIONAL ABSOLUTISM, 1871–1914

In a letter to the Munich economist Lujo Brentano, the great historian of Rome, Theodor Mommsen, spoke bitterly of the "pseudo-constitutional absolutism under which we live and which our spineless people has inwardly accepted." As a capsule description of the German empire this could hardly be improved upon. The Reich that Bismarck had created possessed all the trappings of constitutional government and yearly went through the motions of meaningful parliamentary activity. But, in a Europe that was moving toward democracy, Germany remained a state in which decisions affecting the lives and liberties of its citizens remained in the hands of persons and agencies not subject to parliamentary or popular control. Nor did the great majority of the people object to this state of affairs. Until disastrous defeat opened their eyes in 1918, they seemed to prefer the satisfactions that came from being commanded by a regime of material splendor and military might to the labors that political responsibility entailed.

BISMARCKIAN GERMANY, 1871–1890

The Constitutional Structure   By almost any standards, the imperial constitution, promulgated in April 1871, was a clumsy and illogical document. It created an imperial government without sufficient administrative agencies to give it much meaning, a federal state that was prevented from being truly federal by the special position of one of its members, and a parliamentary system based on universal suffrage that was rendered ineffective by limitations placed on its responsibility.

After 1871 the empire embraced Prussia, the kingdoms of Bavaria, Saxony, and Württemberg, eighteen lesser states, three free cities, and the so-called Reichsland, Alsace-Lorraine. Sovereignty was vested by the constitution in the Reich, but most of the matters that affected the daily lives of Germany's citizens were reserved to the individual states. Thus, education, police, the courts, most fiscal affairs, and much else were matters administered by agencies of the separate states, whereas the imperial government had administrative organs only for naval affairs, foreign affairs, posts and telegraphs, customs, and, after the turn of the century, colonies. Even in foreign affairs the South German kingdoms reserved at least a ceremonial independence, and they also had armies of their own, with officers appointed by their kings, although these passed under Prussian command in time of war. There was, it should be noted in this connection, no imperial army; the national army was, and remained, the Prussian one.

Despite the rights reserved to the federal states, there was no equality among them, for they were all, in one way or another, subject to Prussia. The hereditary leadership of the empire was vested in the king of Prussia, with the title German emperor. He appointed the imperial chancellor and other imperial officials; he directed Germany's foreign affairs and, through his chancellor, took the initiative in all domestic legislation; he commanded its armed establishment in time of war; he made war and peace; he convoked and adjourned the two legislative bodies.

It was in the upper of these two chambers, the so-called Bundesrat, that the superiority of Prussia over the other states was most clearly demonstrated. The Bundesrat represented the federal states and was composed of delegates appointed by their governments. The size of the various delegations was determined by their relative extent and power; thus, Prussia had seventeen votes out of a total of fifty-eight,[1] Bavaria six, Saxony and Württemberg four each, and the other states even fewer. From these figures alone it will be clear that, in all of the Bundesrat's business, Prussian influence would be great; and Bundesrat business included all legislation affecting the Reich, which was not legal until its affirmative vote had been secured. But Prussian influence was even more extensive than that, for it was stipulated that no change in military matters or customs and excise duties could be taken without Prussian assent, and no amendment to the constitution could be accepted if fourteen votes were cast against it in the Bundesrat. This meant, in effect, that Prussia alone could block constitutional change.

The lower house of the imperial parliament, the Reichstag, represented the people and was elected by universal manhood suffrage, the legal voting age being twenty-five years. It had far less power than its sister chambers in Britain and France. Its right to initiate legislation was limited, and it acted, for the most part, on matters submitted to it by the government. It had little control over the chancellor and his secretaries of state, for in the German system the chancellor was responsible only to the emperor and the subordinate ministers responsible only to the chancellor, and if he or they were criticized or defeated in the Reichstag they did not lose their positions, as they were apt to do in other countries.

[1] In 1911 Alsace-Lorraine was admitted, raising the total to sixty-one.

The Reichstag was often criticized for these weaknesses, and Hellmut von Gerlach once wrote: "The people call the Reichstag a talk-shop (*Schwatzbude*), because they know that German policy is not made there but in a quite different place." This should not lead us to conclude, however, that it was either an innocuous or an unimportant body. It was a national political body composed of popularly elected representatives and, therefore, was watched with critical interest by the German people. It was an excellent sounding board for ideas and propaganda; and Bismarck found it useful, when he wished to impress foreign opinion, as a place in which to advertise German strength and intentions. It was an indispensable link in the legislative process, and reviewed, debated, and sometimes amended or defeated legislation. And because it possessed powers of obstruction and control of the national purse (it had to vote the budget), it was, theoretically at least, capable of extending its powers, and, indeed, made sporadic attempts to do so. The very fact that reactionaries were constantly agitating for a reduction of the Reichstag's powers shows that its authority was not negligible.

Certainly Bismarck did not believe so. He valued it for its uses in foreign affairs, and he believed also that as a kind of symbol of national unity the Reichstag could be used in domestic affairs as a counterweapon against the forces of particularism in the country. If he had ever heard the statement of Gerlach quoted above, he might have answered that, even if policy was not made in the Reichstag, the details of administrative, economic, and judicial projects were often elaborated and improved in the course of Reichstag debates and committee hearings.

In addition, Bismarck had personal reasons for valuing the Reichstag. Since it had power to obstruct and defeat the government's legislative program, the imperial chancellor had to be someone who could control and manipulate it so as to obtain safe parliamentary majorities. As long as Bismarck could do this better than anyone else, he felt safe from the secret attacks of courtiers and soldiers close to the emperor who wished to displace him. The Reichstag was, thus, a kind of insurance policy for Bismarck. He could use it to demonstrate his indispensability, as he did, for example, during the debate over the military budget in 1874, in which the government's case was presented, during Bismarck's absence from Berlin, by other royal counselors, with results that would have been disastrous if he had not returned at the last moment and pieced together a parliamentary majority.

Bismarck was, of course, opposed to anything approaching a genuine parliamentary system like those of Britain and France, or to the introduction of ministerial responsibility in the chamber, or to an extension of parliamentary powers in the field of foreign or military policy; and, in resisting these things, he and his successors were aided by another peculiarity of the constitutional system, which should be mentioned here. As long as Prussia bulked so large in the empire, through the prerogatives of its king, its weight in the Bundesrat, and the virtual monopoly of force exercised by its army, imperial policy was inevitably determined largely by what Prussia's governing class desired. That class had retained its feudal-conservative character, thanks to the nature of the Prussian constitution of 1850, which was still in force, and of the three-class system of suffrage which was used in elections to the Prussian diet (see p. 136) and which assured a conservative majority. This being so, the imperial chancellor (who was also minister president of Prussia) could resist pressure for liberal constitutional reform from parties in the Reichstag in the sure knowledge that he would be supported by the Prussian diet and the Prussian delegation to the Bundesrat.

Because of this circumstance, the key to all constitutional reform in Germany lay in Prussia; and, before the coming of the war, the democratization of the Prussian franchise had become the primary goal of all German reformers.

The Parties   From the 1870s right down to the outbreak of war, organized political activity in Germany centered in six main political parties, plus a number of splinter groups. It may be convenient here to note their differences in program and social composition.

On the extreme right was the German Conservative party, the party of Prussianism, aristocracy, and landed property, with its main support in the districts east of the Elbe River. This party had its roots in the romantic feudalism of the early nineteenth century. Ideologically it was averse to liberalism and democratic reform, placing a high valuation on loyalty to the monarch and service to the state. Economically, it had no sympathy for, and little understanding of, industry; and although it originally believed in free trade, it came, after the beginning of foreign competition in grain, to be fervently protectionist, taking its economic ideas largely from the Association of Landlords (*Bund der Landwirte*) with which it became closely associated in the 1890s. It was less susceptible to issues affecting the Reich as a whole than other parties, for its horizons tended to be limited to Prussia, and it was in the Prussian Diet, rather than the Reichstag, that the real strength of the party lay. It was a Protestant party that put great emphasis on the necessity of maintaining the Christian foundations of the state. This, at its best, led Conservatives to take a genuine interest in social reform; at its worst, it led to outbursts of anti-Semitism, as in the 1880s when the party supported the Christian Social movement of Adolf Stoecker, whose labors for social reform were marred by virulent attacks upon the Jews who, in his view, were responsible for all the evils of *laissez-faire* capitalism.

An offshoot of the Conservatives was the so-called *Reichspartei* (in Prussia called the Free Conservatives), which, by combining landlords and industrialists in its membership, typified the union of rye and steel that was to be so important in German history. Sometimes called the party of Bismarck *sans phrase,* because of its undeviating support of the chancellor's national policies, the *Reichspartei* sent many of its members into his ministries and his foreign service. The party never attained a mass following and eventually merged once more with the Conservatives, helping as it did so to broaden that party's social and political views.

Infinitely more important was the party that repeatedly, from 1870 until the advent of Adolf Hitler in 1933, played the decisive role at crucial moments in German history. This was the Catholic Center party, which from the date of its founding in 1870 enjoyed mass support, although it was most heavily concentrated in Bavaria and the Rhineland. An avowedly confessional party, the Center always embraced individuals and groups of varied political and social views. This meant that, unless the autonomy of the Catholic Church in Germany, or the question of freedom of religious education, or the defense of states rights was at stake, the party was apt to show a greater freedom of action than others; and it was consequently often accused of opportunism. But there was an inner consistency in its attitude. In general, it was conservative in its defense of tradition, of the prerogatives of the crown, and of the hierarchical structure of society, as well as in all matters affecting the morals of society. On the other hand, it was consistently favorable to constitutional government, in which it saw a means of protecting minority groups against the excessive centralization of state power; and it was progressive in matters of social reform.

With respect to this last point, the party had been profoundly influenced by the doctrines of Adolf Kolping, who in the 1840s had founded Catholic journeymen's associations to give free vocational training to workingmen, and by those of Bishop Wilhem Emmanuel von Ketteler, who from 1850 until his death in 1877 preached the necessity of combating the evils of capitalism by setting up workers' cooperatives, establishing Christian trade unions, and otherwise helping the poor to raise their standards of living. Ketteler, whose work had a profound influence upon Pope Leo XIII and served as a basis for his encyclical *Rerum Novarum* in May 1891, established a tradition of German Social Catholicism that was always strong in the Center party. The Center not only supported and expanded the program of vocational instruction that Kolping had started and encouraged the Catholic union movement, but it also used its influence in behalf of legislation for the improvement of working conditions, the reduction of the working day, factory inspection, child-labor laws, and arbitration between labor and management.

There were two liberal parties. The National Liberals, who had the greatest parliamentary strength in the first decade of the empire, had seceded from the old Progressive party, which had fought against Bismarck in the constitutional conflict of the 1860s (see p. 205), and had given their support to the chancellor. Representing the educated and wealthy middle class and the upper bureaucrats, they shared many of the characteristics of Liberals in other lands, being supporters of centralization, *laissez-faire* economics, secularization of national life, constitutional government, and material progress.

The left liberals, who still called themselves the Progressive party, although the name would change several times before 1914, shared some of these views (*laissez faire* and opposition to socialism, in particular) but were pronouncedly antimilitarist and antistate and were also much more vigorous in their demands for an extension of parliamentary government. Their leader in the early years of the Reich was Eugen Richter, an able critic but an essentially uncreative mind, whose great gift was the ability to infuriate Bismarck. After his death, he was succeeded by Friedrich Naumann, who sought to revitalize liberalism by promoting a merger with socialism. This did not succeed, and the Progressives remained a dwindling party whose strength came predominantly from urban centers and particularly from the lower-middle class and the lesser officials.

Further, starting its remarkable growth in the 1870s and becoming before 1914 the strongest party in Germany and the largest and most disciplined labor party in Europe, there was the Social Democratic party. Its nature and activities will be discussed below.

In addition to these well-organized and relatively stable organizations, there were various splinter groups in the Reichstag. Among these were the Alsatians and the Poles from Posen, who could generally be counted upon to vote against the government but who were too small to be able to cause it much inconvenience. There was also, despite the failure of Stoecker's movement, an anti-Semite party in the Reichstag; and the fact that, after 1890, it sometimes controlled as many as 15 seats was a disturbing augury for the future. Stoecker had reserved his antagonism for Jews who resisted assimilation, and to him a Jew converted to Christianity ceased to be a legitimate target for abuse. To his successors, conversion was a matter of indifference and true assimilation an impossibility. They portrayed the Jew as an alien and subversive force and elaborated fantastic theories of race that impressed a public made credulous by the cult of science. The anti-Semites had no parliamentary or other success before 1914, but their propaganda probably had a not inconsiderable influence upon the German subconscious. The very fact that they could mouth their opinions in the Reichstag gave their cause a spurious respectability.

The National Liberal Period and the Kulturkampf   In the first years of the new empire, Bismarck's objective was to complete the process of unification by giving the Reich the institutions that would make it a homogeneous and effective nation. As far as possible, he wished to reduce institutional diversity and parochialism, at least in so far as they might weaken the political and economic efficiency of the empire. Since this involved legislation, the chancellor found it expedient to work with the party that commanded a majority in the Reichstag and had the greatest sympathy for the principle of centralization. This was the National Liberal party, and it responded to Bismarck's overtures with enthusiasm. In the decade of the 1870s, National Liberal votes were primarily responsible for the great program of constructive legislation that gave Germany its new imperial administrative agencies, a uniform coinage and a commercial code for trade and industry, a national civil and criminal court procedure, an imperial bank, and an imperial bureau of railroads.

Out of the collaboration between the National Liberals and the chancellor there grew, however, an ill-fated campaign against the Catholic Church that disrupted German political life until the mid-1880s. After what has been said above about anticlericalism in other countries, it should not be surprising that the National Liberals were interested in reducing the influence of the Catholic Church in education and in other aspects of German life. European liberals of all shades had been aroused by Pope Pius IX's *Syllabus of Errors* (1864), in which he had condemned "the errors of liberalism"; and German liberals in particular, including many loyal Catholics, had been incensed by the doctrine of papal infallibility in matters of faith and morals, which had been proclaimed in July 1870 during the war against France. Now that that conflict was over they were eager to retaliate.

Bismarck's motives were more complex. He was annoyed by the growth of the Center party, which promised to be less amenable to national appeals than to those that emanated from the Vatican. He seems honestly to have believed that the church was fomenting resistance to the imperial government among

Germany's Polish minority, which was largely Catholic. And, as usual, his views were influenced by considerations of foreign policy. If Germany went on the offensive against the Vatican, it might win the sympathy of other liberal anticlerical powers and seal the isolation of the papacy's strongest supporter, France.[2] This appeared to be doubly necessary, since Bismarck, without much evidence, seems to have believed that the papacy was attempting to inspire a Catholic coalition directed against Germany.

Worn out by the labors of the last ten years and suffering from bad health, Bismarck may not have been thinking very clearly in these years. Certainly he was both intemperate and incautious in his tactics. In 1872 he launched an attack on the church in the imperial Reichstag and the Prussian legislature. As in other countries, the starting gun for the campaign was the expulsion of the Jesuits. There followed, in 1873 and the next two years, a series of laws passed by the Prussian legislature—depriving bishops of their disciplinary powers, placing clerical education under the control of the state, making civil marriage mandatory, abolishing church rights of self-government, dissolving religious orders, and much else.

As was to be expected, the papacy reacted by severing diplomatic relations with Prussia, and German bishops in convocation declared that Catholics could not obey these laws without violating their faith. Subsequently, criticism of the antichurch measures from Belgian and French pulpits led, as we have seen (p. 250), to German threats against France and to a war scare in 1875. But Bismarck's attack on the church—which the Liberals grandiloquently called "the battle for civilization" (*Kulturkampf*)—had two additional results that Bismarck could hardly have foreseen. It aroused Protestants almost as much as it did Catholics and induced the Conservative party to throw its not inconsiderable influence at court against a policy that seemed capable of developing into an attack on all organized religion. At the same time, instead of weakening the Center party, the *Kulturkampf* seemed to strengthen the loyalty of its supporters, so that the Center improved its position in the Reichstag in the elections of 1877.

This last result, after four years of effort, would probably have been enough in itself to convince Bismarck that the anti-Catholic crusade was a mistake. But he had another reason for jettisoning the policy. He had decided to end his collaboration with the National Liberals, which meant that he needed Conservative, and even Center, support.

During the course of 1877, the National Liberals had intimated to Bismarck that their future cooperation would be dependent upon concessions on his part, in the form of ministerial appointments, recognition of the party's voice in policy determination, and other things. This convinced Bismarck that it was necessary for him to find wider parliamentary support than he presently possessed and helped persuade him also to give way to the forces in the country that were demanding the substitution of a protectionist commercial policy in place of free trade. He hoped that if he came out for new tariffs he would ingratiate himself with the landlords of the Conservative party and the industrialists in the Free Conservative party, while simultaneously splitting the National Liberals, some

[2] At this time, the French government was still monarchist and clerical in sympathy.

of whom were losing their zeal for Manchesterian economics. He began secret negotiations with representatives of the two conservative parties with the objective of gaining pledges for the future; and his decision to abandon the fight against the Catholic Church was designed to facilitate collaboration with them.

The death of Pius IX and the accession of Pope Leo XIII in 1878 made it easier for Bismarck to change his direction. The new pope was far less intransigent than his predecessor, and he inaugurated his pontificate by sending a letter to Emperor William I, expressing the hope that an accommodation could be reached. Negotiations were begun; and, in 1879, in return for a promise that the government would receive prior notification of all papal appointments and that the German clergy would desist from attacks on the government, Bismarck began the process of revoking the anticlerical legislation. This took ten years and never completely restored the pre-*Kulturkampf* situation, for civil marriage and state inspection of church schools remained in force; but the great bulk of the legislation of 1873–1875 was suspended and later repealed, and the religious orders, with the exception of the Jesuits, were allowed to return to Germany. Moreover, the new spirit was felt almost at once, and church-state relations could be described as normal again as early as 1881.

Bismarck and Socialism   Once Bismarck had decided to break with the National Liberals, he did everything in his power to reduce that party's representation in the Reichstag. One of the weapons he used was the argument that the National Liberals were protecting the rapidly growing Socialist party, which was, by its own admission, a revolutionary and international party and thus was working against Germany's interests.

The German Social Democratic party had its origins in the activities of Ferdinand Lassalle (1825–1864) in the early 1860s; even after it came to declare itself a Marxian party, it never escaped from his influence. This flamboyant and ambitious tribune of the people, the son of a Jewish merchant in Breslau, had become famous (or notorious, according to one's point of view) by his spectacular efforts in behalf of a Countess von Hatzfeldt, whose attempt to secure a divorce from her husband was blocked by an unjust and antiquated legal system. Lassalle's protracted and eventually successful labors in her behalf, his dramatic court appearances, and his imprisonment for revolutionary agitation before the case was terminated gave him a national reputation, and this led a group of workers in Leipzig, who were founding a political union in 1863, to ask him to help them by giving a systematic exposition of his social views.

His response supplied the new German socialist movement with a working program and made him its leader, although not for long. In the summer of 1864 Lassalle and Fräulein von Dönniges, the daughter of a Bavarian diplomat, decided to marry; but parental pressure broke the match, and Fräulein von Dönniges became affianced, against her will, to a Rumanian nobleman. In a characteristically romantic gesture, Lassalle challenged his rival to a duel and, in August 1864, was fatally wounded.

His legacy to the working class movement was his "Open Answer" to the Leipzig group. In essence, this argued that economic pressure and trade-union activity alone were pointless, that concessions from employers were always vitiated by the operation of the iron law of wages, which kept labor at a bare subsistence level, and that only organized mass political action aimed at the conquest of state power would save the working class from capitalistic exploitation. It would do so because it would assure state aid for producers' cooperatives and other enterprises in the worker's interest. Lassalle's long-run economic objectives were never precisely defined and are not particularly important. His contribution to German socialism was his insistence upon political action.

Lassalle's spirited activities in the last year of his life succeeded, as his critic Karl Marx admitted, in arousing a labor movement that had been asleep since the revolution of 1848. Even so, the German Workingmen's Association that he helped found grew very slowly; and, after 1869, its progress was impeded by the opposition of a new Social Democratic Labor party founded by two followers of Marx, August Bebel (1840–1913) and Wilhelm Liebknecht (1826–1900). It was only after the two parties came together that the growth of German socialism became impressive. This union was effected in 1875 at Gotha, where the participants agreed on a statement of theory and a program of action that combined the two strains of influence, being Marxist in its criticism of capitalist society and its proclamation of the international character of the movement, but Lassallean in its emphasis upon political action to secure such practical objectives as equal and universal manhood suffrage in local and state elections as well as national ones, payment of deputies, abolition of inequalities of class and property, abolition of the standing army, separation of church and state, free compulsory education, progressive income tax, state credit for producers' cooperatives, and the like.

Even before the union, the Socialist vote had begun to grow: 124,000 in the Reichstag elections of 1871, 352,000 in 1874. In 1877, the united party polled 452,000 votes and sent twelve deputies into the Reichstag. This was a matter of concern to Bismarck, who was never able to regard the Socialists as just another political party but thought of them as enemies of his way of life and of the security of his state and, hence, as outlaws against whom the most ruthless of means could be used. In 1877 he began to seek means of taking legal action against them; and, in May of the following year, when a demented tinker named Hödel tried to kill the emperor, he introduced a bill into the Reichstag that embodied a number of anti-Socialist measures. This was heavily defeated, the bulk of the National Liberals remaining true to their avowed belief in political freedom.

A month later, there was a second attempt on the emperor's life, which seriously wounded him. Bismarck immediately dissolved the Reichstag and called for new elections. During the campaign, the government press attributed the assassination attempts to Socialist policy and delivered scathing attacks upon the National Liberals and the Progressives for their failure to vote for a bill that would have prevented the wounding of the emperor. Bismarck was deliberately seeking to turn the middle-class electorate away from the liberal parties and, in particular, to hurt his old ally, the National Liberals. To a large extent, he succeeded. In the elections of 1878, the Progressives lost thirteen seats and the National Liberals twenty-nine. The Progressives did not allow the results to alter their views, but the chastened National Liberals now yielded principle and, when a new anti-

Socialist bill was introduced in October 1878, added their votes to the majority that made it law.

The Anti-Socialist Law forbade all associations and publications that sought to subvert the existing social order or showed "socialist tendencies." It gave the police such large powers of interrogation, arrest, and expulsion that suspected Socialists lost the customary protection of the law, while their party was forced to become a clandestine organization. Simultaneously, the law struck a crippling blow at the Independent Trade Unions, which were closely associated with the Social Democratic party, for unions cannot go underground and remain effective.

In 1866 Bismarck had embraced the cause of universal manhood suffrage in the belief that the masses could always be counted on to be loyal to the throne. The Anti-Socialist Law was a public admission that he no longer felt this way but believed that royal authority must be maintained by restricting freedom of political choice. Every attempt was made to destroy the Socialist party utterly. Many of the party's leaders were forced to leave the country, and others were arrested; the party press was reduced to a few newspapers which were printed abroad and smuggled across the borders; Socialist leaders enjoyed immunity in the Reichstag, but could not speak or campaign in public; party congresses had to be held in Switzerland or Holland.

Bismarck rarely committed himself to a single line of policy in either foreign or domestic affairs; and his offensive against the Socialists was no exception. It has been described as a policy of *Zuckerbrot und Peitsche* (the sugar plum and the whip), for the repressive measures were accompanied by tangible benefits designed to make the working classes forget their resentment over the repression of their organizations. Starting in 1881 the chancellor inaugurated a program of social-insurance legislation that was intended to prove to the unpropertied classes that "the State is not merely a necessary but a benevolent institution." In 1883 the Reichstag passed a Sickness Insurance Law which was to be financed by contributions from the employee and the employer in the ratio of two to one; the following year, another law obliged employers to insure their workers against accident; and in 1889 provision was made for old-age and disability insurance to be supported by contributions from employee, employer, and the government. These laws were revolutionary and aroused interest throughout the Western world. They were the model for Lloyd George's National Insurance Act of 1911 and for similar legislation in other countries.

Bismarck's crusade against socialism was no more successful than his fight against Catholicism. After initial losses, the Social Democratic party adjusted itself to the new conditions in which it had to work and steadily increased its strength. In the period of the Anti-Socialist Law (1878–1890), the party's national vote increased from 437,158 to 1,427,298 and its representation in the Reichstag from nine to thirty-five. And in the next dozen years, it raised its totals to 4,250,401 votes and 110 seats.

It is sometimes argued that, while the whip failed, the sugar plum worked, and there is perhaps some truth in this. In the years of repression, the Social Democratic party seemed to grow increasingly militant. In 1891, at Erfurt, it adopted an unrelievedly Marxist program, which outlined the evils of capitalism and called for its destruction by revolutionary action. Almost immediately, however, as we have seen (p. 283), opposition to these principles grew in the form of revisionism; and, in the first decade of the new century, the powerful Independent Trade Unions, now federated in a General Commission of Trade Unions under the leadership of Carl Legien, threw their influence behind the revisionist opposition, criticizing the Marxist party ideologues as doctrinaire and unrealistic and calling for a policy aimed at tangible objectives. It would be difficult to determine what influence Bismarck's social insurance had in turning the eyes of the working classes to such objectives and convincing them that they had too great a stake in the existing regime to wish to destroy it. Doubtless Bismarck's social policies had some effect, although it is well to remember that revisionism was a European phenomenon and would probably have been felt in Germany even if Bismarck had never existed.

Bismarck's Fall and His Legacy   In 1881, the Berlin novelist and critic, Theodor Fontane, wrote:

> Gradually a storm is brewing in the people against Bismarck.... He deludes himself as to the measure of his popularity. It was once colossal, but this is no longer true.... For his genius everyone still has a tremendous respect, even his enemies.... But the respect for his character is in a marked decline. Men are saying: "He is a great genius but a small man."

As the 1880s proceeded, this appraisal seemed to be true. In the Reichstag, Bismarck had increasing difficulty in constructing parliamentary majorities to support his policies. His break with the National Liberals had split that party, but more of its members were driven into opposition than into dependence on him. The Center was still unreconciled, and its support, sometimes granted, could not be counted on; the Socialists grew steadily in strength and voted against all government measures. In 1887, in order to get necessary legislation passed, Bismarck had to use the scare tactics he had used in 1878—this time seeking a parliamentary majority by exploiting the Boulanger agitation in France and alluding to the possibility of a French attack. This sort of thing could not be repeated often; and, as the Reichstag became more difficult to control, it was perhaps only natural that Bismarck should have dreamed of radical solutions to his problem. In his last years of office, he became increasingly enamored of the possibility of revising the constitution, perhaps by a special convocation of the princes of the realm, and of abolishing universal suffrage, which was proving so unmanageable.

This train of Bismarck's thought certainly played a part in his fall from office in 1890. In 1888, Emperor William I died and was succeeded by his son, who took the title Frederick III. This ruler, who had endeared himself to his subjects by his military exploits in the wars of 1866 and 1870, had been expected to open a new era of liberalism, but at the time of his accession he was suffering from cancer. Within three months he was dead and his son William was on the throne. An inexperienced and impetuous youth who longed to make his mark in the world, William II had little patience with the policies of the past and no desire to be kept on leading strings by Bismarck, of whom he was reported

to have said, "I shall let the old man snuffle on for six months, then I shall rule myself." He became critical of Bismarck's foreign policy, on the grounds that Germany's alliances had become too complicated; and he allowed himself to be persuaded that Bismarck had underestimated the Russian threat to German interests and was keeping information from the emperor's eyes. Moreover, since he wanted to be popular, he wished to abandon the anti-Socialist legislation and inaugurate a program of social reform—factory inspection, guaranteed wages, a shorter working day, and the like. He was appalled to discover that Bismarck not only intended to continue the campaign against Socialism but was thinking in terms of a constitutional coup that might lead to popular resistance and the use of military force. When he heard that the chancellor was negotiating with the parties for support with which to override his own objections, William's patience was exhausted. There was a stormy interview between him and the chancellor on March 15, 1890, and three days later the world learned that Bismarck had been dropped from office.

Under his leadership Germany had become the most powerful of the European states, but he had bequeathed to her some things that militated against that surface strength. His devotion to his country had always been accompanied by the conviction that it could remain great only if the monarchical tradition were protected against the subversive tendencies of the times. In the name of national security he had used parliamentary tactics that contributed to the atomization of the liberal forces in the Reichstag and legal methods that alienated many Germans permanently from the regime. His concern for his country had led him also, in the 1880s, to carry out a purge of progressive elements in the Prussian civil service, which seriously weakened the traditional independence of the Prussian bureaucracy and placed a premium on political conformity.

Bismarck had condoned a similar policy in the military establishment. The officer corps of the Prussian army had long been an aristocratic preserve but, in an age in which the size of armies was increasing rapidly, there were now an insufficient number of aristocrats to man the new units. With Bismarck's encouragement the army followed a deliberate policy of filling its needs exclusively from candidates from the upper middle class who were Christian in religion, conservative in politics, and socially as feudal-minded as the *Junker* themselves. Since membership in the officer corps brought certain desirable social advantages, Bismarck's acceptance of this selection procedure, like his policies with respect to the civil service, encouraged what has been called a "feudalization of the upper middle class," which deprived that class of its independence and its rightful political role, the leadership of the bulk of the middle class. This, in turn, abandoned the lower middle class to a marginal political existence, caught between the organized working class and the new feudal plutocracy, resenting both, and susceptible to the blandishments of demagogues who knew how to exploit resentment. These social tendencies were to be noted in other countries besides Germany, and they should not be attributed to Bismarck alone; but they were aided by his social policies.

Bismarck's greatest achievements were in the field of foreign affairs, where his great diplomatic gifts served his country well and, in the twenty years after 1870, helped preserve the European peace. Even here, however, his legacy to

The gigantic statue of Bismarck at the head of the Reeperbahn in Hamburg. Fashioned from 3350 tons of granite by the sculptor Lederer and the architect Schaudt, it was unveiled in 1906. (© 1968 Beaverbrook Newspapers Ltd.)

his country was an equivocal one. His successors were inclined to overlook the passionate devotion to the nation's interest, the strong sense of responsibility, and the admirable sense of perspective that made Bismarck a great diplomat. Their idea of Bismarckian statecraft was "realism," which they seemed to equate with brutality and bad manners. The very magnitude of Bismarck's achievements made them desire to emulate them and led them to embark on a fateful search for dazzling coups and stupendous triumphs.

WILHELMINE GERMANY, 1890–1914

Material and Intellectual Progress   At the time of Bismarck's fall, Germany was midway in one of the most rapid economic transformations in modern times. Still primarily agrarian in occupation and population distribution in the year 1871, she was to become one of the world's three greatest industrial nations by 1914, with 60 percent of her population living in urban centers.

This remarkable industrial development had been both galvanized and disrupted by the victory over France. On the one hand, the acquisition of Alsace-

The Krupp works at Essen in the Ruhr shortly before World War I.

Lorraine strengthened Germany's textile industry by doubling the number of mechanical looms operating in the country, brought into its possession the Lorraine iron deposits (which became enormously valuable once the Thomas-Gilchrist method of purifying phosphoric ores came into general use), and gave it a virtual monopoly of the European potash industry by bringing it the unexploited Alsatian deposits. On the other hand, the speed with which the French war indemnity was paid touched off an inflationary spiral and a flood of dangerous speculation that contributed to the magnitude of the crash that came to Germany at the time of the world economic crisis in 1873. The years from 1873 to 1877 were years of depression; but the recovery thereafter was steady and, except for slight setbacks in 1900–1901 and 1907, uninterrupted.

This development can be illustrated by a very few examples. Thanks to mineral wealth (supplemented by conquest), rich coal deposits, and a good transportation system, Germany soon possessed the most powerful iron and steel industry in Europe. Pig iron production increased from 1,500,000 tons in 1871 to almost 15,000,000 tons in 1910, while steel production in 1900 stood at 7,000,000 tons and was exceeding that of Great Britain by 1,500,000 tons. The development of heavy industry, in turn, enabled Germany to increase its domestic rail net three and a half times between 1871 and 1914; to build one of the greatest merchant fleets in the world, gross tonnage increasing from 82,000 to 4,500,000 between 1871 and 1913; to expand the machine industry into one of its largest export resources; and to build up that armaments industry which made the name of Krupp of Essen known the world over.

Germany's electrical and chemical industries also ranked among the world leaders in these fields. The Berlin firm of Siemens and Halske, founded by Werner von Siemens in 1847, gave Germany its first telegraph net, its first electric railway, and its extensive trolley system. At the same time, Emil Rathenau, who secured the German rights to Thomas Edison's electric lamps in 1881, established the *Allgemeine Elektrizitäts-Gesellschaft* (AEG) and rapidly built up a mass demand for electrical products. The expansion of the German electrical industry (it employed 26,000 people in 1895 and 107,000 in 1906) is a good illustration of those creative surges in new sectors of the economy that have been mentioned above as characteristic of mature capitalism (p. 264); and it made a large contribution to the prosperity of the prewar years. So did the progress of the chemical industries, which was marked by the greatly increased production of potash, sulphuric acid, potassium salts, and ammonia, and by phenomenal developments in the field of synthetic dyes, photographic supplies, and pharmaceuticals, which made the names Bayer, Agfa, and I. G. Farben as well known as Krupp.

The spectacular increase of foreign trade was perhaps the best indication of Germany's economic power. The value of German exports increased fourfold between 1871 and 1914, from a figure of 2½ billion RM to 10 billion RM; and the value of imports shot up from 3½ billion RM to 11 billion RM. The balance of payments deficit was covered by income from services to foreigners (German ships and railroads were the carriers of many transit goods) and by capital investment abroad, which was increasing as a result of the activities, mentioned above (p. 268), of the so-called D-Banks.

Despite the increase of the proportion of town dwellers to rural inhabitants, the agricultural population remained constant; and, thanks to new techniques of cultivation and the agricultural chemistry introduced by Justus Liebig, production increased by as much as fifty percent in some crops in the twenty-five years following unification. Grain producers, however, could compete with foreign grains only by means of government support in the form of tariffs, and even these could not maintain prices. Since the expectation of high prices had led earlier to an inflation of land values, the result was an unhealthy amount of rural debt. A conversion of acreage from grain to specialized crops or dairy farming might have had better results than continued reliance upon governmental subvention. As it was, German agriculture from now on was dangerously sensitive to movements of the world market.

The vigor of the economy was matched by the intellectual and artistic vitality of Germany in these years. No country in the world matched its prowess in the natural sciences, and these years saw the pioneering researches in chemistry of August Kekulé, the invention of the opthalmoscope by Ludwig Helmholtz and the spectroscope by Gustav Robert Kirchhoff, the discovery of X-rays by Wilhelm Konrad Roentgen and the formulation of the quantum theory by Max Planck, Einstein's first studies on relativity, and the significant medical researches of Robert Koch (tuberculosis, cholera, sleeping sickness), Paul Ehrlich (syphilis), and Rudolph Virchow (pathology). The great achievements of these men drew students from all over the world to German universities, as did the lectures of historians like Theodor Mommsen and Heinrich von Treitschke, philosophers like Wilhelm Dilthey, sociologists like Ferdinand Tönnies, Georg Simmel, and Max Weber, and economists like Adolf Wagner, Lujo Brentano, and Werner Sombart. The work of these scholars and the methods (particularly the seminar) which they used to convey their teaching had great influence on the university life of other countries, perhaps most particularly in the United States.

In the rapidly growing German cities there was a vigorous intellectual atmosphere. This was particularly true of Berlin, whose population grew from 774,498 in 1870 to over two million in 1910. The national capital was, of course, the center of Germany's political activity and of the liveliest and most variegated journalistic life in Germany, some aspects of which were to be described in Heinrich Mann's novel *In the Land of Cockaigne*. But Berlin was also one of the musical centers of Europe; and in the 1880s and 1890s as many as three hundred concerts were presented each year. One might hear Johannes Brahms as soloist with the Meininger Orchestra, under the direction of the great conductor Hans von Bülow, or Richard Strauß conducting his own first works with the Berlin Philharmonic. In the field of literature, it was the city where the major work of the sociological realists Spielhagen, Fontane, and Sudermann was accomplished and where a new era in the theater was inaugurated with the founding, in 1889, of *Die Freie Bühne,* dedicated to the cause of modernity and presenting the works of Ibsen, Strindberg, and Björnson, as well as the new German dramatists—Gerhart Hauptmann, whose *Vor Sonnenaufgang* created a sensation in 1889, and Frank Wedekind, the forerunner of expressionism.

German cultural life was not concentrated in the capital to the same extent as in France. The other large urban centers—Hamburg, with almost a million inhabitants in 1914, Cologne, Leipzig, Frankfurt—had flourishing theaters and opera houses and were proud of their museums and their universities. As for the third city in the empire, Munich, with 650,000 inhabitants in 1914, it was, as Thomas Mann wrote in his story *Gladius Dei,* a radiant city of gay squares and broad avenues, of baroque churches and leaping fountains, a city dedicated to the arts, where line, decoration, and form had become a cult.

Yet these evidences of culture were perhaps less impressive than they seemed. Stefan George, the greatest German poet of this period with the exception of Rilke, called Berlin "the cold city of military and commercial serfs"; and Friedrich Nietzsche wrote scornfully of the culture of the great cities (*Großstadt-Bildung*) and pointed out, with perhaps an ironic allusion to Munich, "how much *beer* there is in the German intelligence!" With the eloquence of an Old Testament prophet, Nietzsche excoriated what he considered to be the true characteristics of the age—mediocrity, vulgarity, materialism, love of power—and was unimpressed by Germany's economic prosperity, which he felt sapped the people's will, or by the achievements of its universities, where what he called "the despiritualizing influence of our current science-industry" prevailed. "Power," he wrote in *The Twilight of the Idols* (1888), "*makes stupid.*"

> Even a rapid estimate shows that it is not only obvious that German culture is declining but that there is sufficient reason for that. In the end, no one can spend more than he has: that is true of the individual, it is true of a people. If one spends oneself for power, for power politics, for economics, world trade, parliamentarianism and military interests—if one spends in this direction the quantum of understanding, seriousness, will, and self-overcoming which one represents, then it will be lacking for the other direction.

In his novel *The Old and the Young* (1889), Conrad Alberti expressed himself even more strongly. "What we need," he wrote, "is a new Sedan in which we are the defeated ones, in order to be torn out of this stinking bed on which the stockbrokers and drill sergeants have thrown us."

If this seemed an unnecessarily harsh judgment of Bismarck's Germany, it was less so of William II's. The prevailing style of the Wilhelmine epoch was one of garish display and vulgar ostentation, manifest equally in such architectural monstrosities as the *Siegesallee* in Berlin, where grandiose statues of the rulers of Brandenburg-Prussia stood in uncomfortable marble attitudes, looking as if they were on their way to a fancy-dress ball; in the inflated and tedious novels of Gustav Frenssen, Hermann Löns, and Hans Friedrich Blunck (infinitely more popular than the social criticism of Fontane, Hauptmann, and Sudermann), which glorified German power and the superiority of the German soul; in the parvenuism and servility of the once self-reliant middle class, which is admirably portrayed in Heinrich Mann's novel *The Patrioteer* (*Der Untertan*); and, finally, in the domestic and foreign politics of the Wilhelmine Reich.

Politics under William II   Typical of the spirit of the age was the emperor himself, of whom a member of one of Prussia's oldest families said icily: "He is and remains a parvenu." William II had attractive qualities and a quick intelligence. But he was ill-educated and fundamentally lacking in culture; his preferred companions were bankers and soldiers and his favorite amusements extensive junkets in luxurious yachts and rowdy parties in which broad practical jokes were considered high art. He cultivated a military bearing and a manly forthrightness of speech, which in practice degenerated into a shrill boasting about Germany's power and an overwhelming arrogance in his dealings with lesser nations. He had a jealous and demanding conception of the prerogatives of his office and sought to assert himself in every aspect of his country's policy, approaching all questions, as a recent biographer has written, with an open mouth. He was the despair of his ministers; and his court chamberlain once said: "We all suffer from the Kaiser; he is the cross laid on us all."

In the first years after Bismarck's fall, William hoped, as we have noted, to check the rise of socialism by a broad program of social legislation. Taking a phrase from Frederick the Great, he saw himself as a *roi des gueux*, a king of the poor, and, in 1891, with that cloudy moralizing about the *Volksgeist* which was so fashionable at the time, he wrote to his old tutor:

> The so-called reformation of the 16th century was nothing more than the first independent step taken by the German spirit in the world of the Idea, the first independent action of the German intellectual will, and it required great energy as well as a high degree of independence of thought and character to break through the strong tradition of centuries in order to take this step. ... Now the solution of the so-called social question, it is my conviction, will be the second action of the German spirit in the world of the Idea. It will require the same high independence of thought and will. I believe that the new German Empire was made for this purpose, only for this and for no other.

The establishment of arbitration boards to help adjudicate labor disputes, the legal provision for health regulations and safety precautions in factories, laws restricting child labor, the establishment of a bureau of labor statistics, and other legislation passed between 1891 and 1894 did not, however, reduce the popular support given to the Socialist party; and the emperor soon became discouraged. Perhaps the Reich had been made for other things after all, he decided, and with some public references to the Socialists as a "treasonable horde" and "a pack of men unworthy to bear the name of Germans," and a good deal of talk, in the late 1890s, about reverting to some form of anti-Socialist legislation, he turned most of his attention permanently to what he now considered the empire's proper concern—the search for more power, to be accomplished by an enhanced armaments program, including the creation of a high-seas fleet, the acquisition of a colonial empire, and a vigorous foreign policy in every part of the globe.

These policies were embarked upon in the 1890s, at a time when Germany's international position was strong and its relations with other powers good. By 1907, all this had changed for the worse, and Germany's new course had aroused the gravest suspicions. This was due partly, as we shall see (p. 428), to the manner in which it was carried out, which was usually a combination of abrupt forcing plays, attempts at blackmail, and the use of threats. It was due also to the essential

One of the many comments on the military posturing of William II which appeared in the pages of the Munich satirical magazine *Simplicissimus.* In this caricature by O. Gulbransson in 1909, the emperor is shown at maneuvers with Prinzregent Luitpold of Bavaria.

inconsistency of the various lines of policy pursued. One would have supposed, for instance, that it was to Germany's interest to retain the friendship of Great Britain, which, thanks to the Mediterranean agreements of Bismarck's last years (see p. 260), had cooperated with the Triple Alliance and whose assistance would be useful if, at this late date, Germany was to acquire a colonial empire. Yet the German government deliberately alienated Great Britain by building a battle fleet that seemed to threaten its interests. Nor was this the only case where love of display and a predilection for the violent gesture militated against German security by turning its neighbors against it.

Absolutism and the Failure of Parliament   All this was much worse than it might have been had there been any effective restraint upon the imperial will. Bismarck had had his difficulties with William I, but he had always in the end kept control of policy in his own hands, thus assuring its consistency and coherence. None of William II's prewar chancellors was capable of this kind of firmness. General Count Leo von Caprivi (1890–1894) tried and failed. The Bavarian Prince Chlodwig zu Hohenlohe-Schillingsfürst (1894–1900) had been in politics since the 1860s and no longer had the energy to control the ebullience of the emperor. Bernhard von Bülow (1900–1909), the ablest of these ministers in terms of natural ability, was as Wilhelmine in style as the emperor himself. To him politics was a continual dramatic performance in which he had a leading role, and he delighted in the bombast and fustian and the artful posturings that imperialism and navalism made possible. His method of handling the emperor was to flatter him, which merely confirmed William in his worst habits. Finally, Theobald von Bethmann Hollweg (1909–1917), a conscientious man with great administrative ability, had too little experience in the field of foreign affairs to feel confident about taking a firm line with the emperor.

One of the gravest difficulties confronting all these ministers was the way in which policy was fragmented, so that vital decisions were sometimes taken by totally irresponsible agencies. The military services, in particular, were able on occasion to make decisions that reversed the policy of the chancellor and the Foreign Office or committed them, without their knowledge, to courses of action that they would ordinarily have rejected. The naval staff consistently opposed Bethmann Hollweg's attempts to reach a naval accommodation with the British and were backed up by the emperor. The general staff of the army not only made plans for the invasion of Belgium in the event of a war with France (leaving the chancellor inadequately informed about them) but also, in 1909, on its own authority, made commitments to Austria that fundamentally changed the defensive character of the Dual Alliance of 1879 (see p. 261) by promising aid in virtually any contingency.

The army and navy staffs were not alone in dabbling in the policy-making process without the perfect knowledge of the responsible minister. The emperor placed much reliance upon his personal adjutants, upon the heads of his civil and military cabinets, upon his traveling companions, and upon other secret camarillas, and they in turn encouraged him to adopt unexpected courses or to change policies agreed upon with his chancellor. It is impossible to give too much weight to the influence of these forces in German politics under William II. One need only remember that Caprivi fell from power in 1894 largely as a result of carefully contrived plots against him and that the dismissal of Bethmann Hollweg in 1917 was prepared in much the same way.

Why then did the parliamentary bodies of the realm not attempt to interfere, especially when it was clear that the policies of William II were to the disadvantage of the state? Part of the answer is that both the Prussian Landtag and the Reichstag had become so accustomed under Bismarck to leaving foreign affairs in the hands of the chancellor that they were incapable of consistent and vigilant criticism of the conduct of this aspect of policy by his successors. It was, moreover, never easy to persuade a majority of the Reichstag to criticize the government's policy of imperialism and navalism, because powerful interests with strong representation in that body had an economic stake in the policy. The same alliance of rye and steel that had secured the passage of the protective tariff of 1879 saw to it that the naval bills of 1898 and 1900 became law. Heavy industry supported these bills for obvious reasons; the agrarians supported them because, in return, they got industrial votes for higher tariffs on foreign grains—which, incidentally, alienated the Russians as completely as the naval bills antagonized the British.

Again, it should be remembered that no representative body finds it easy to oppose public opinion, and popular opinion in Wilhelmine Germany was proud of Germany's power, wholly in favor of expressing it in the building of a fleet and the acquisition of a world empire, and unconscious of the dangers involved in these policies. The Center party, the Progressives, and the Socialists might on occasion unite to vote down a government request for funds to be used in colonial enterprise, as they did in 1906; but the fact of the matter was that in all of these parties, even the Social Democratic party, there was a sizable number of members who supported imperialism and believed it would benefit Germany—as, for example, the revisionist Eduard Bernstein did.

Finally, the assertion of control over the emperor would have required a willingness on the part of parliament to assume future responsibility for all aspects of policy. There is no indication that the members of the Reichstag—even some of those who talked loudly of parliamentary rights and ministerial responsibility—wanted anything of the sort. This at least seems to be the lesson of two incidents that occurred in the last years before the war.

In October 1908, the London *Daily Telegraph* printed an interview which one of its reporters had had with William II, in which the emperor had apparently made some gratuitously offensive statements about foreign powers, as well as claiming credit for devising the war plan used by the British in the Boer War (see p. 420). The storm of protest inside Germany was, for the moment, almost as great as that in England. There were demands for the imposition of restraints upon the emperor's prerogatives in foreign affairs, and one Berlin newspaper declared that to have the operations of government dependent upon the will of a single individual was "unbearable for a self-assured nation." Here, apparently, was an opportunity for the Reichstag to make some progress toward real parliamentary government. Yet nothing was done. As Theodor Eschenburg has written,

> The lack of discipline and solidarity, the uncomprehending indignation and the tendency toward oratorical exaggeration which was characteristic of the whole Wilhelmine era, and the lack of any concrete political objective, caused the debate in the Reichstag . . . to blow itself out without result.

Another opportunity for the Reichstag to demonstrate its determination came in 1913 when troops in the village of Zabern in Alsace became involved in a series of incidents with civilians that led finally to the assumption of police powers by the military authorities and the wholesale arrest of civilians in defiance of normal process of law. When the matter was raised in the Reichstag, the minister of war supported the action taken in Zabern and was in turn backed up by the chancellor, Bethmann Hollweg. The Reichstag immediately passed a vote of no confidence in Bethmann by a vote of 293 to 55. This did not lead to his resignation, however; and, when the Socialists suggested that it should, their view was rejected with indignation by the other parties. Like the *Daily Telegraph* affair, the Zabern case resulted in some rhetorical pyrotechnics and nothing more.

The French socialist Jean Jaurès, addressing the German Socialists at an international conference in 1904, told them: "Even when you attain the majority in the Reichstag you are the only country where you cannot become master. Your parliament is only a demi-parliament." In 1914 Germany was still an absolute state, despite its constitutional forms. It remained so, as the statement by Mommsen quoted at the beginning of this chapter indicates, and as the two incidents just cited would seem to confirm, because the majority of the German people were too satisfied with the *status quo* to have any strong impulsion to change it. It was not until the dangerous tendencies of Wilhelmine policy had helped bring war and defeat to Germany that that mood of self-satisfaction was to change.

Chapter 16 AUSTRIA-HUNGARY, THE BALKAN STATES, AND TURKEY, 1871–1914

THE DUAL MONARCHY

Kakania   In his remarkable book *The Man without Qualities* (1930 ff.), the Austrian writer Robert Musil has painted an affectionate portrait of his country, which he calls Kakania because its ruler was *Kaiser* (emperor) in part of his realm and *König* (king) in the rest and its institutions were all labeled *k.k.* or *k. & k.*

> On paper it called itself the Austro-Hungarian Monarchy; in speaking, however, one referred to it as Austria; that is to say, it was known by a name that it had, as a State, solemnly renounced by oath, while preserving it in all matters of sentiment, as a sign that feelings are just as important as constitutional law. ... The system of government was clerical, but the general attitude to life was liberal. Before the law all citizens were equal, but not everyone, of course, was a citizen. There was a parliament that made such vigorous use of its liberty that it was usually kept shut; but there was also an emergency powers act by means of which it was possible to manage without parliament and whenever everyone was beginning to rejoice in absolutism, the Crown decreed that there must be a return to parliamentary government. Many such things happened in this State, and among them were those national struggles that justifiably aroused Europe's curiosity. ... They were so violent that they several times a year caused the machinery of State to jam and come to a full stop. But between whiles, in breathing-spaces between government and government, everyone got on excellently with everyone else and behaved as if nothing had ever been the matter.

When disastrous things occurred—and they frequently did in Austria—people said:

> Es ist passiert, "it just sort of happened." ... It was a peculiar phrase, not known in this sense to the Germans, and with no equivalent in other languages, the very breath of it transforming facts and the bludgeonings of fate into something light as eiderdown, as thought itself.

Yes, Musil concludes, Kakania was a home for people with a genius for taking things lightly, "and that, probably, was the ruin of it."

This, of course, is satire, but, like all true satire, its core is truth. The Austro-Hungarian empire had many problems. Some of them, at least, might have been solved if it had not also had so many people, especially among the ruling elite, who confronted difficult questions with levity or lack of energy or failure of imagination. One can surely find part of the reason for the decline of the Hapsburg monarchy in the attitude of such members of its governing class as that nameless staff officer who, in 1854, when the Prussian military attaché described to him the Kriegsspiel (war game) that was used in training Prussian commanding officers, asked how one won money at it and lost interest when told that it was not a game of chance; or in the behavior of the foreign minister Berchtold, who, at the height of the crisis of 1914, is reported to have stuck a note from the British government between the pages of his racing program and forgotten all about it. As long as one lives in an organized community, politics is a serious business; and political problems, even when they cannot be solved, must be tackled vigorously and with intelligence. This, all too often, was not true in Austria-Hungary.

In large part, the trouble stemmed from the very center and source of political power. The emperor himself might have inspired and led a constructive attack upon the problems of his realm. But, as another gifted Austrian writer, Karl Kraus, wrote after Francis Joseph's death, it was easier to believe that he was dead than that he had ever really lived. As one of the characters in Kraus's The Last Days of Mankind says, "Never before in world history had a stronger Un-Personality ever placed his stamp on all things and institutions.... Our destiny was decided by a Daemon of mediocrity." In an empire of diverse peoples, the emperor lacked the resources of will and character to embody for them the idea of a united state. He had neither strong convictions about the policy that should be followed nor firmness of will in pursuing what he decided in the end should be done. And, consciously or subconsciously, he avoided strong subordinates, showing—as the distinguished Austrian critic Hermann Bahr once wrote—"an almost touching weakness for untalented people."

This failure of leadership meant that the most serious of the problems confronting the monarchy, the problem of the nationalities, was never really faced. The nature and limitations of the Compromise of 1867, which created the Dual Monarchy by placing Hungary on an equal footing with Austria, have been described above (p. 216). As early as the 1870s, there was much evidence to indicate that, if it remained unchanged, the non-German and non-Magyar majority of the Hapsburg peoples would be progressively alienated from their loyalty to the crown. If the ruling class of the empire was aware of this danger, they made no strenuous attempts to avert it; and, in the last decade before the outbreak of World War I, as we shall see, the emperor himself advertised his lack of interest in any real change by abandoning suffrage reform in Hungary.

Politics and Economics in Austria   The government of the Hapsburg monarchy after 1867 was conducted on three separate levels: the intergovernmental, the Austrian, and the Hungarian. Certain matters of concern to the whole realm—notably foreign affairs, defense matters, and imperial finance—were conducted by a joint ministry appointed by the monarch and supervised in a vague sort of way by Austrian and Hungarian delegates. The internal affairs of Austria and Hungary were in the hands of autonomous and distinct governments, which were so different in structure and practice that they must be discussed separately.

The seventeen provinces that made up the Austrian part of the realm possessed individual diets that administered local affairs and were represented in an imperial parliament that met in Vienna. This latter body had two chambers, an upper one composed of dynastic aristocrats, leading churchmen, and other dignitaries appointed by the emperor and a lower house whose members were originally selected by the local diets but, after 1873, were elected by a clumsy and indirect system that gave preference to property and education. Parliament as a whole had the right to approve or reject important items of state business; the budget and bills fixing the annual contingent for the armed forces had to originate in the lower house, which also had the right to question and to impeach ministers.

Ministers were appointed by the emperor and, although constitutionally responsible to the lower house, were in fact dependent on the monarch for continuance in power. The emperor also had the right to dissolve or suspend the parliament in accordance with rules defined in the constitution and possessed authority, under Article 14 of the constitution, to issue decrees that had the full force of law when parliament was not in session, provided they did not modify fundamental laws and were approved by parliament at its next session. These powers made it possible for the emperor to impose his will upon a refractory parliament, and he was not loath to use them. On the other hand, he preferred to work in harmony with the legislature whenever possible and sought ministers who could create parliamentary majorities. This explains Musil's reference to alternation between absolutism and parliamentarism in Austrian affairs.

In one marked respect, the course of politics in Austria paralleled that in Germany. Throughout the first decade of its new existence, the dominant force was a strong Liberal party which represented the views of the wealthy German middle class that was being created by the rapid industrialization of Austria and Bohemia. Like its German counterpart, this party was strongly in favor of constitutionalism, centralization, and administrative efficiency in the interest of commercial progress, and, in addition, shared the usual Liberal prejudice against clerical influence. During the 1870s, when it was grappling with the problems created by the reorganization of the realm and the economic difficulties caused by the crash of 1873, the crown found it expedient to rely on Liberals for parliamentary support. The legislative results of this collaboration were an improvement of judicial procedure, the liberalization of the press laws, the abolition of laws restricting the rights of the Jews, the revision of the disciplinary code and administrative procedures of the army, and a series of laws designed to promote economic growth and regulate the finances of the state. Simultaneously, the schools were removed from church control and religious instruction became voluntary; all Christian creeds were placed on a footing of equality; and civil marriage was authorized. In 1869, a new law had made elementary education free and compulsory for all children, but its administration was left to the provincial diets, which did little to implement it during the 1870s. Despite this, the amount of progressive legislation passed with the support of the Liberals was impressive to foreign observers.

The Liberal era ended abruptly, however, at about the same time and for much the same reason as it had ended in Germany. The emperor became annoyed at Liberal criticism of the results of the Congress of Berlin of 1878 and, specifically, of the assumption by Austria of administrative control over Bosnia and Herzegovina (see p. 256), which the Liberals believed was an unwise extension of Austrian responsibilities; and he decided to seek a different kind of parliamentary support. Like Bismarck, Francis Joseph seemed to feel that the Liberals were bent on increasing parliamentary rights at the expense of royal power and that it would be wiser to rely upon the support of German conservatives and upon the Slavs.

There was, of course, good reason for the government to turn its attention to the non-German peoples of Austria, who resented German dominance and hoped to win rights similar to those granted to the Magyars in 1867. The Poles of Galicia, the Slovenes and the Serbs in the south all shared this feeling, but it was felt most strongly, perhaps, by the Czechs of Bohemia, who were proud of their long history, of their national heroes from Huss to Palacký, of the achievements of their culture, and of the rapid economic growth of their land.

The relation between the Czech and the German peoples has been called "a neuralgic point of the future of Europe and the maintenance of the peace of the world," a statement that will assume greater meaning when we consider Czechoslovakia's role in the postwar world. It is certainly true that in the history of the Dual Monarchy the Czech problem was crucial; and failure to solve it was one of the most important reasons for the empire's collapse. On only one occasion did Francis Joseph ever come close to grappling with it. In 1871, he promised to elevate Bohemia to the same autonomous position enjoyed by Austria and Hungary, and prepared to go to Prague to be crowned as king of Bohemia. This plan to convert the empire into a triple monarchy was blocked, however, by the intransigence of the Austrian Germans, who feared the loss of their preferred position, and the Magyars, who were afraid that liberation of the Czechs would stimulate a demand for similar rights on the part of their own subject nationalities. The emperor capitulated to German and Hungarian objections; and the Czechs never forgave him. Their immediate response was to boycott the imperial parliament and to pretend that its transactions were of no interest to them.

In 1879, when the emperor broke with the Liberals, he sought simultaneously to appease the Czechs and the other subject nationalities. The man he chose to do this was a friend of his youth, Count Edward Taaffe, a man who hid

NATIONALITIES IN AUSTRIA-HUNGARY

Germans   Slovenes   Slovaks   Ruthenians   Magyars

Czechs   Serbo-Croats   Italians   Rumanians   Poles

0   40   80   120

Miles

behind a veil of levity and cynicism great political gifts, which enabled him
to remain as the emperor's chief minister from 1879 until 1893. The political
combination he created to replace the Liberals was known as the Iron Ring
and was composed of clericals, German Conservatives, Slavs, Poles, and Czechs,
whom Taaffe persuaded to give up their policy of parliamentary abstention.
A deputy from one of the Italian districts once called the Taaffe government
a *luogo di traffico* (a place for making deals), a not inaccurate description, for
the ill-suited partners were kept together by concessions to their special interests.
In Galicia, for example, the Poles were permitted to win special privileges over
the Ruthenians; and in Carniola, the Slovenes were allowed to oppress other
nationalities. As for the Czechs, they were granted a new electoral law that gave
them a majority in the Bohemian diet, as well as stronger representation in the
imperial parliament; the University of Prague was divided into two universities,
one of which was henceforth Czech; and a new ordinance required all civil
servants in Bohemia and Moravia henceforth to render judgments in the language
of the petitioner. This last provision dethroned German as the sole official

language and operated to the disadvantage of German officials, who now had to learn Czech, and it increased the number of Czechs in the civil service.

In the long run, the Taaffe policy of appeasement succeeded only in increasing the opposition of the Slavs and arousing the fury of the Germans, thus exacerbating the nationalities problem almost beyond control. The concessions to Czech nationalism, for instance, failed to cloy the appetite they fed. On the contrary, the moderate Czechs who had cooperated with Taaffe were supplanted by a new Young Czech party, whose spirit was shown by a speech made by one of their leaders, Edward Grégr, in the imperial parliament in 1891:

> Bohemia is being sucked dry by Austria.... The majority of the Czech population is utterly wretched in the midst of this alien empire.... Their nationality is oppressed and persecuted in this Austrian state, which is a state of violence and tyranny to all Slav races. The Bohemian people are made to hate this state—I repeat—hate this state, and mark my words, the day of reckoning will come.

The other Slav peoples of the empire also grew more outspoken in their demands and, at the same time, there was an intensification of the Pan-Slav ideas that had been so prevalent among the subject nationalities in 1848. Indeed, the older idea of the cultural community of all Slavs began now, in some quarters, to be superseded or supplemented by a new political Pan-Slavism that thought in terms of a federation of Slavic peoples free from Austro-Hungarian control. Those who were beginning to think in this way looked to Russia for assistance and were encouraged by the writings of Russian Pan-Slav theorists like R. A. Fadeyev and N. Y. Danilevsky, who talked of a future emancipation of the Slavs by that country.

These tendencies should not, of course, be attributed entirely to Taaffe's appeasement policy, for their origins lay farther back, in the Austrian government's persistent refusal to alter the constitution of the Dual Monarchy. In 1865 the great Czech leader Palacký had said:

> The day that Dualism is proclaimed will become, with irresistible natural necessity, the birthday of Pan-Slavism in its least gladdening form. The leaders of Dualism will be its sponsors. The result can be imagined. We Slavs will await it with justified pain, yet without fear. Before Austria was, we were; and after Austria we shall also be.

Taaffe's policies also aroused the Germans in Bohemia, with resultant disorders that forced the government to place Prague under martial law and, eventually, compelled Taaffe's retirement. German opposition to his policies was reflected also in the rise of a new Pan-German movement, led by Georg von Schönerer, which preached the racial superiority of the Germans over the Slavs and called for a union of Austria's German provinces with the Hohenzollern Reich.

Throughout the Taaffe period, the opposition to his coalition had been the old Liberal party, still the strongest single political grouping in Austria. But the Liberals never recovered the position they had enjoyed before 1879 and, like

Liberal parties in other countries, they now entered a period of decline. In the confused political period that followed Taaffe's fall, their strength was sapped by the movement of economic forces and by the government's decision to attempt to check the agitation of the nationalities by extending the suffrage to classes more interested in social problems than in nationality—a policy that culminated in 1907 in the establishment of universal manhood suffrage in Austria. These factors led to the emergence of two parties that supplanted liberalism and played an important role in Austrian politics until the fall of the independent Austrian republic in 1938.

The first of these was the Christian Socialist party, a curiously ambivalent group that managed to combine within its membership some of the most progressive social thinkers and some of the most fanatical bigots in Austria. A Catholic party, appealing particularly to the urban petty bourgeoisie, the Christian Socialists placed great emphasis upon democracy, social reform, and an enlightened nationalities problem. Under their greatest leader, Karl Lueger, who served as mayor of Vienna from 1897 until his death in 1907, they strongly supported the successful movement to legalize trade unions and to grant accident and sickness insurance to workers (Lueger said in 1886: "A state that has no social insurance laws should be barred from all intercourse with other states!") and, in Vienna itself, carried through a program of municipal socialism that equaled that of Joseph Chamberlain in Birmingham (see p. 291).

But, as was true of the comparable movement led by Adolf Stoecker in Germany (see p. 342)—and of Schönerer's Pan-German movement, many of whose members shifted their allegiance to Lueger's party—the force that gave Christian Socialism its original mass support and always remained an important factor in its policies was anti-Semitism. One of the first effects of industrialism in Austria was the ruin of a number of small concerns and a general depression among the independent artisan class, especially in Vienna where they had to compete with the new factories. It was easy for this class to blame their troubles upon the Jews, especially in view of the important role Jews played in financing Austrian industry, and the conspicuous part they occupied in the professions, the cultural life of the capital, and what Schönerer was pleased, in a parliamentary speech, to call "the corruptible and Judaised Viennese press." Even without that encouragement, they would probably have made the Jews their scapegoat, for in the western parts of the empire migrants from the ghettoes of Galicia and Bukovina had long been objects of suspicion and dislike. Admirers of Karl Lueger have always insisted that he was not an anti-Semite at heart. This is quite possibly true (he certainly had no objection to dining in the mansions of the Jewish *haute bourgeoisie*), but he identified himself so closely with anti-Jewish feeling that, in 1895, when the possibility of his becoming mayor first arose, the Liberal *Neue Freie Presse* lamented that, if this happened, "Vienna will be the only great city in the world whose administration is in the hands of anti-Semitic fanatics."

It may be noted in passing that Lueger's success inspired two men who were to attain an eminence greater than his own. The first was Theodor Herzl, who has been called "the greatest Jewish statesman since the destruction of Jerusalem," who in 1895 wrote a pamphlet which outlined the factors that had made the Jewish problem a universal one and initiated the program soon to be called

Zionism by proposing as a solution the re-establishment of the Jewish people as an independent nation on its own soil. The second was a young man from Linz who also decided to make the Jewish question his ladder to power; his name was Adolf Hitler.

After the suffrage reform of 1907, the Christian Socialist movement turned to the Right, merging with the Conservatives. Meanwhile, the enfranchisement of the working class facilitated the growth of the Social Democratic party which had been organized earlier by Viktor Adler. The Socialists gradually took over the dominant position once held in Vienna by the Christian Socialists, whose strength was now in rural Austria and, while the empire lasted, in Galicia. Marxist in inspiration, the Socialist party maintained close relations with the Socialist parties in neighboring countries. Like them, and perhaps to an even greater degree, it was affected by revisionism and advocated moderate social change to be achieved by parliamentary means. It supported the imperial tie and advocated a liberal policy of concessions to the nationalities.

The introduction of universal manhood suffrage did not check the agitation of the nationality groups in parliament, which continued to be paralyzed periodically by their demonstrations and their tendency to indulge in orgies of fisticuffs and chair-breaking. Parliament's persistent failure to take positive action on any issue forced the government on a number of occasions to resort to rule by emergency powers.

Throughout the whole period, the nationalities problem was exacerbated by difficult economic problems. Since 1850, great progress had been made in the modernization of agriculture and the establishment of new industries, but not enough to make them self-sufficient. Austrian and Czech firms had to be protected from ruinous German and British competition and Hungarian farmers from being swamped by Russian and American surpluses by means of tariffs. These were, on the whole, effective, but Austria-Hungary was a customs union or common market, and what benefited the Austrians and Czechs and Hungarians had to be paid for, in the form of higher prices for consumer goods, by the other nationalities, who were thus given another reason for believing that to be ruled by the Hapsburgs was not to their advantage.

The Kingdom of Hungary   Political life in the Hungarian part of the empire also centered in parliament, which was composed of a House of Magnates and a House of Deputies, the latter of which controlled the ministers and exercised the initiative in legislation. The House of Deputies was in no sense a popular assembly reflecting the wishes of the mass of the population, for the franchise was an extremely restricted one, only about twenty-five percent of the male population possessing the vote.

Out of Hungary's population of fifteen million, the Magyars constituted less than a half, yet they held a monopoly of political power and, through the central parliament and local institutions, not only dominated the subject nationalities but sought to assimilate them. The only exceptions to this were the Croats in the southwestern part of the kingdom, whose services to the Empire in 1848 were remembered and who were permitted to have their own diet, courts, schools, and police and to send a separate bloc of forty members to the central House of Deputies. Yet even the Croats found their rights being whittled away as the years passed; and the other subject nationalities—the Rumanians of Transylvania and the Slovaks and Serbs—were subjected to an unremitting policy of Magyarization. Bismarck once said that all Magyars were either hussars or lawyers. Certainly it was by a blend of force and legalism that the government sought to wipe out national differences and to suppress newspapers, schools, and other agencies that might keep the languages, arts, and customs of the other nationalities alive. Magyar was made compulsory in parliament, the administrative agencies of central and local government, the courts, the schools—even in the railways, where no signs were permitted in any other language. The law of 1868, which had been drafted by the Hungarian liberal Francis Déak and which guaranteed equal rights to all nationalities, was simply ignored.

The right to subjugate the nationalities—which dissolved the bonds of loyalty to the crown and had fateful results during World War I—was implicit in the Compromise of 1867 and may be described as the price paid to the Magyars for their continued support of imperial policies and institutions. As the years passed, however, the Magyars themselves succumbed to chauvinism and actually began to agitate for virtual independence from Austria. The leader of this movement was Francis Kossuth, the son of the hero of 1848, who formed an Independence party and demanded that Hungary be permitted to direct her own tariff and foreign policies and, more immediately, that Magyar become the language used in the Hungarian regiments of the imperial and royal army.

A concession of this nature would, of course, dissolve the unity of the military establishment, and Francis Joseph, who had watched the oppression of the Hungarian minorities with no great concern, reacted swiftly to this threat. The first years of the new century were marked by a series of crises between the crown and the independence movement. The struggle reached its greatest intensity in 1905 when a coalition led by Kossuth won such an overwhelming victory in parliamentary elections that it seemed capable of putting its plans into effect. At this point the emperor appointed an emergency government which threatened to introduce universal manhood suffrage in place of the restricted franchise that was the bulwark of Magyar power.

Had this plan been carried through, the subject nationalities might belatedly have received a measure of justice. But in 1906 the coalition leaders, terrified at the prospect of a new franchise law, agreed to assume office without insisting on the army reform; and Francis Joseph allowed the scheme for universal suffrage to be forgotten. Politics in Hungary became less stormy and, in the election of 1910, a new party founded by Stephen Tisza (1861–1918) and dedicated to maintaining the Compromise of 1867 smashed the Kossuth movement. Tisza, who was to be supreme in Hungarian politics until 1917, put an end to attacks on the emperor's military prerogative, and to the parliamentary obstructionism that accompanied them, by carrying through a radical reform of parliamentary procedure in 1912.

While this was going on, however, the subject nationalities had been forgotten again. By abandoning suffrage reform, the emperor had thrown away his last chance of breaking the power of the Magyar oligarchy, and that failure made the dissolution of his empire inevitable.

Splendor and Decline   This was not immediately perceptible, of course; and the casual observer of Austrian affairs was apt to see not the hidden weaknesses but the surface splendors of the Hapsburg realm. This was particularly true if he visited the imperial capital, for Vienna was never lovelier or more stimulating and gay than it was in the last years before World War I. Since the 1860s, its beauties had been enhanced by the razing of what was left of the medieval wall around the inner city and the construction in its place of the majestic Ringstrasse, one of the most beautiful avenues in the world, by the building of new bridges across the Danube, and by a series of architectural triumphs: the Rathaus, designed by Fredrick Schmidt; the new opera house; Theophil Hansen's Austrian parliament building; Karl Hasenauer's Burgtheater; and many more. Housed so nobly, arts and letters flourished in Vienna: music perhaps most of all, with composers like Anton Bruckner, Gustav Mahler, who became director of the opera in 1898, Brahms (who spent most of his productive years in Vienna), Hugo Wolf, the greatest composer of songs since Schubert, and Richard Strauß, whose opera *Der Rosenkavalier,* with lyrics by Austria's first poet, Hugo von Hofmannsthal, had its triumphant premiere in 1911 and was followed a year later by another charming fruit of this collaboration, *Ariadne auf Naxos.*[1] As for light opera, it was widely considered to be a Viennese specialty, thanks to the achievements of Johann Strauß, Karl Millocker (*The Beggar Student* and *Gasparone*), and Franz Lehar (*The Merry Widow*).

The most popular painters of this period were men like Hans Makart, whose reputations did not long survive their deaths; but the turn of the century saw the emergence of a vigorous new movement called the Vienna Secession, which anticipated some aspects of expressionism and surrealism and whose leadiing representatives (Gustav Klimt, Franz von Stuck, Kolo Moser) had an interesting rebirth in the 1960s.[2] In literature, no prose writer came close to equaling the earlier achievement of Adalbert Stifter (1805–1868), whose novel *Nachsommer* (*Indian Summer*) (1857) was one of the greatest German *Bildungsromane;* but two Viennese dramatists won international reputations: Arthur Schnitzler (1862–1931), who amused audiences with an adroit mixture of irony and sentimentality but was capable also—as his play *Dr. Bernhardi* shows—of incisive thrusts at the social ills of his time;[3] and Strauß's collaborator Hofmannsthal

[1] The "new version" of *Ariadne,* which is the one generally, if not always, played today, did not have its premiere until October 1916.
[2] It was not difficult in 1969 to find inexpensive poster reproductions of works like Klimt's "The Kiss" (see frontispiece) or Stuck's *Sin.* This was not true, on the other hand, of the works of the Berlin Secession (Max Slevogt, Lovis Corinth, Max Liebermann), which may be accounted for by the fact that the Vienna school placed more emphasis on highly abstract decoration, on the one hand, and eroticism on the other.
[3] *Professor Bernhardi* (1912), which deals with the troubles that befall a doctor who refuses to allow a priest to give the last rites to one of his patients because he wishes to spare her the knowledge of her imminent death, was one of Schnitzler's most effective treatments of the problem of anti-Semitism in Austria. He treated this theme more comprehensively in his novel *Der Weg ins Freie* (*The Road into the Open;* 1908).

(1874–1929), whose mystical dramas (*The Fool and Death,* 1893; *Elektra,* 1904; *Everyman,* 1911) were admired for their lyrical beauty, whose comedy *Der Schwierige* (*The Difficult One,* 1921) has been called the most durable monument to the Austria that died in the war, and whose last play, *The Tower* (1925), looked to Europe's future with the same presentiment of doom that characterized the last plays of his great predecessor Grillparzer.

The University of Vienna was renowned the world over, especially for its work in medicine, which was distinguished by Theodor Billroth's pioneer work in antiseptic surgery and Theodor Meynert's in brain surgery. The other faculties were hardly less outstanding, with philosophers of the stature of Ernst Mach, economists like Carl Menger, and the historian of the war of 1866, Heinrich Friedjung. Other Viennese scholars of widespread reputation were Rudolf von Ihering and Joseph Unger in legal studies, Rudolf Pöch in anthropology, and the man who probably had a greater effect upon European thought than any of the others mentioned here, the psychiatrist Sigmund Freud (1856–1939).

Sigmund Freud, 1856–1939. The inscription reads: "There is no cure for death, nor any rule for preventing error.
Sigm Freud, 1925," (Library of Congress)

Emperor Francis Joseph I, 1830–
1916. (Bettmann Archive)

In the middle of this illustrious city stood the Belvedere Palace, where the aging emperor presided over what was still one of the most glittering court societies in Europe and, despite his years, paid meticulous attention to the administration of the higher echelons of the imperial civil service and of the army. It was here, at the heart and motive center of the empire, that realities most clearly belied appearances, for beneath the surface splendor were palpable evidences of declining vitality and efficiency. Sentimental Viennese might attribute to Francis Joseph those qualities of wisdom that are supposed to accompany age. He did not, as his record on the nationalities question showed, possess them; and there was not much evidence that they would be supplied by the dynasty after his death. The emperor's only son, Rudolf, had become involved in an extramarital love affair and had finally killed himself and his mistress at Meyerling in 1889—a tragic event that has been the subject of countless sensational books and several sentimental motion pictures. Rudolf's successor as heir apparent was the emperor's nephew, the Archduke Franz Ferdinand. He was an able soldier, with a good tactical sense and great administrative gifts, but his political capacities were untested. He has often been described as possessing the desire and the will to reform the imperial structure in the interest of the nationalities; but, as his most recent biographer has pointed out, he progressively lost faith in the minority groups and, by 1914, could be considered essentially a defender of the Compromise of 1867. He was, in any case, too ambiguous a figure to restore the confidence of the minorities in the crown; and, even if he had escaped the death that came to him at Sarajevo in 1914, it is unlikely that he could have checked the dissolution of the empire.

Nor were the two services upon which the empire relied for a semblance of unity as healthy as they might appear. The bureaucracy was sometimes called the best bureaucracy in Europe, but—as Robert Musil wrote—"it could not help regarding genius and enterprise of genius in private persons, unless privileged by high birth or State appointment, as ostentation, indeed presumption." As for the army, upon which Francis Joseph had lavished such care and to which he had given so much political latitude—a tendency that had been dangerous in the 1860s when his favorite Count Grünne was alive (see p. 197), and was doubly so after 1906, when Conrad von Hötzendorf, chief of staff of the army, was openly advocating a preventive war against Serbia as a means of solving the South Slav problem—there was some reason to doubt its efficiency and even its reliability. The long dispute over the possible use of the Magyar language in Hungarian regiments had weakened internal unity and morale and given rise to doubts about the loyalty of some of the national contingents in time of war. Much more damaging was the revelation by the newspapers in May 1913 that Colonel Alfred Redl, chief of staff of the Prague corps of the imperial and royal army, and formerly for six years deputy chief of the army's intelligence bureau, had been serving as a spy for the Russians for over ten years. Perhaps more than any single event in the decade before the war, the Redl case shook public confidence in the governmental structure of the Austro-Hungarian Empire, while at the same time weakening its reputation among its allies.

Austria and the Balkans   All of the internal problems of Austria-Hungary were complicated by the relations of the empire with the lesser states of south-eastern Europe, with the Turkish Empire, which still had nominal rights of suzerainty in some of those states, and with imperial Russia. The Hapsburg monarchy was drawn into this area by strategical and economic factors affecting the security and well-being of the whole empire. Its dependence upon the Danube as a trade route meant inevitably that it would be interested in the politics of Serbia, Bulgaria, and Rumania, along whose borders or through whose territory it flowed. Aside from the Danube, the empire's access to the sea depended upon its continued possession of the Istrian Peninsula at the head of the Adriatic, with its three important ports, Trieste, Pola (now Pula), and Fiume (now Ryeka), and of the Dalmatian coast with its ancient port of Ragusa (now Dubrovnik). But these possessions would be natural objectives of any expansionist movement that developed in the kingdom of Serbia, as would the provinces of Bosnia and Herzegovina which—still nominally Turkish—had been under Austrian administration since the Congress of Berlin (see p. 256). Because of this, the Hapsburg monarchy felt compelled to block any Yugoslav movement that would threaten the economic and (given the importance of the Dalmatian coast in a contest with Italy) the strategic interests of the empire.

Until 1903, while Austro-Serbian relations were cordial, there was a school of thought in Austria that held that this could be done by the union of all the Serbs and Croats in Serbia, Montenegro, Dalmatia, Istria, Bosnia, Herzegovina, and the Hungarian province of Croatia-Slavonia in a Yugoslav state *within* the Hapsburg monarchy, a state that would, in every way, be on the same footing as Austria and the kingdom of Hungary. These "trialists" agreed that this would do away with the increasingly dangerous disaffection among the empire's Croats and the growing nationalism of Serbia and would give Austria the dominance of the western Balkans. This plan—like the plan to raise the position of the Czechs in the empire—was bitterly opposed by the Magyars and would probably have foundered on that rock alone, even if a change of dynasty in Belgrade in 1903 had not given rise to a sharp increase in Serbian chauvinism and Serbian intrigues inside Bosnia. As relations between Vienna and Belgrade deteriorated in the years that followed, all thought of winning the Serbs by kindness vanished, and the Hapsburg monarchy sought more aggressive means of solving the South Slav question. This contributed to the coming of that dangerous clash between Austria and Russia in 1908, which will be discussed below (p. 438), and which set in train the events that were to lead to the World War and the collapse of the Austrian-Hungarian empire.

Before proceeding with the story of those events, however, it will be necessary to look briefly at the progress and problems of the Balkan countries since the Congress of Berlin and—in the next chapter—the condition and policies of Austria's great rival in this area, imperial Russia.

THE STATES OF SOUTHEASTERN EUROPE

Rumania   Modern Rumania was largely the creation of the Crimean War, for the Congress of Paris at the end of that conflict had abolished the former Russian protectorate over the Turkish provinces of Moldavia and Wallachia and simultaneously made them virtually independent of the Porte. Within three years, these principalities were united under the leadership of an energetic native prince, Colonel Alexander Cuza, who ruled the new autonomous principality until 1866. In that year Cuza was deposed by the legislative chambers, which then offered the throne to Prince Carol of Hohenzollern-Sigmaringen, a cousin of Emperor William I of Germany. None of the powers objected (not even the French, who were to raise such strong objections to a similar arrangement in Spain four years later); and Carol himself was intrigued enough by the offer to accept. He is reported to have looked into an atlas and, discovering that Bucharest was on a straight line drawn between London and Bombay, to have exclaimed, "That is a country with a future."

During his long reign (1866–1914), Carol strove to lay the basis for that future. At the very outset, he convoked an assembly that drafted a liberal constitution on the Western model, with royal powers limited by ministerial responsibility to the legislature and with a bicameral parliament elected by limited suffrage based upon the Prussian three-class system. Until 1878, the fiction of Turkish overlordship was maintained, but in 1877 Rumania declared herself entirely independent, and the sultan and the other powers acquiesced at the Berlin Congress, on condition that the legal equality of all citizens be recognized by the new state. This provision, designed to protect the Jews, was unfortunately always more honored in the breach than in the observance. In 1881, the Rumanian government proclaimed that the state would henceforth be known as the kingdom of Rumania, and the prince as King Carol I.

A predominantly agricultural country, Rumania suffered from the social troubles incidental to inequitable land distribution, and, in 1907, there was a major peasant revolt that required the use of 140,000 troops to restore order and forced the government to institute a series of reforms. Aside from this, there were many signs of progress. Exports of cereals and oil increased throughout Carol's reign, the first threefold, the second much more than that, since the importance of the Ploesti fields was just beginning to be discovered at the turn of the century. In 1866 Rumania had no railways at all; in 1914 it had almost 2500 miles of railway. Generally speaking, it was the most important of the Balkan countries commercially and, by 1914, was growing rapidly in industry as well.

Much of the revenue that this growth brought to the government was, unfortunately, spent on the army and navy, both of which were excessively large for a country Rumania's size. But Rumania was an ambitious state and one, moreover, with a grievance. Its armies had fought side by side with the Russians in 1877 and had helped break the Turkish resistance at Plevna; but Russia had not seen fit to repay it for this aid by ceding Bessarabia, which Rumanians considered, on ethnic grounds, to be rightfully theirs. Rumania had a vital interest, also, in the future of those Rumanian subjects of the Hapsburg monarchy who lived in Transylvania and Bukovina, and sporadically expressed sympathy for pockets of Rumanians in Macedonia, which Turkey still ruled. The possibility of a territorial dispute with one or more of its neighbors was always present, and, this being so, Rumania maintained a large military establishment, contributing its share to the raising of the general Balkan temperature.

Bulgaria   Because its people had been compelled to free themselves from the rule of the Ottoman empire and, then, almost immediately, to resist being forced into the position of being a mere satellite of Russia, Bulgaria's political history had been a stormy one. The critical events of the years 1885–1888, which saw the rapid growth of anti-Russian feeling in Bulgaria, as well as Prince Alexander of Battenberg's acquisition of Eastern Rumelia, his military victory over the Serbs, and his deposition by a Russian *coup de main,* came close to making Bulgaria the center of a major European war (see p. 258); and, although this was averted, the internal affairs of the country remained confused for some years.

Bulgaria was fortunate, nevertheless, in possessing a statesman of courage and determination in the first years after Alexander's fall. This was Stephen Stambulov, the son of an innkeeper, who had been educated in Russia and returned to his country to enter politics. As president of the national assembly (*Sobranje*), he had played a prominent part in the union with Eastern Rumelia, had headed the provisional government after Alexander's abdication, and had been the leading spirit in the election of Prince Ferdinand of Saxe-Coburg-Gotha as his successor. In the first years of Ferdinand's reign, Stambulov was virtually dictator of Bulgaria. He used his authority to extirpate remnants of Russian and Turkish influence in the country and to encourage railroad building, increase commerce, stimulate the beginnings of industry, modernize the Bulgarian army, and beautify the national capital of Sofia. In a country that lagged far behind the West in educational and other kinds of progress, this program could be achieved only by authoritarian means; Stambulov's lack of scruples and his willingness to resort to brutal compulsion in order to force the pace of reform earned him a host of enemies and cost him his position in 1894 and his life, by assassination, a year later.

The progress made under his direction, however, was so notable that it was recognized by the powers, who finally, in 1896, recognized Prince Ferdinand's title (which they had hesitated to do at the time of his election). Twelve years later, in 1908, they acknowledged his final severance of legal ties to Turkey and his assumption of the title of Tsar of Bulgaria.

Bulgaria's conflict with Russia in the late 1880s threw it, perforce, into the arms of Austria-Hungary, with whom, in any case, it had close economic ties and, after Ferdinand's accession, dynastic ones as well, since the new prince had served in the army of Francis Joseph and felt a bond of loyalty to that ruler. At the same time, Bulgaria's memories of the war with Serbia in 1885 and the fact that its territorial claims in Macedonia conflicted with those of that country made relations between Sofia and Belgrade uncomfortable; and, after 1903, the government of Austria-Hungary recognized this and followed a deliberate plan of playing Bulgaria off against Serbia, encouraging its claims, when occasion arose, to block Serbian growth. This was a dangerous policy and, in the end, involved Bulgaria in a Great Power struggle even more dangerous than that which had threatened it in 1887.

Serbia   An autonomous principality since the first part of the nineteenth century, Serbia had become wholly independent of Turkey at the Congress of Berlin in 1878 and, four years later, proclaimed itself a kingdom. This growth in international stature, if it can be described as such, was not accompanied by any clear evidences of internal strength and vitality. The reign of King Milan Obrenovitch was characterized by domestic disaffection, administrative incompetence, and financial mismanagement, all thrown into greater relief by the personal life of the ruler, who preferred to spend as much time as possible away from his capital, pursuing fashionable vice in Vienna and Abbazia (now Opatija). It was probably to check the swift decline of his popularity, and as a reaction to an attempt on his life, that Milan made the mistake of going to war against the Bulgars in 1885. That short and inglorious campaign completed the bankruptcy of his reputation and, although he held on for four years, he was forced to abdicate in 1889.

This action did not save the dynasty or make for orderly government in Serbia. The new ruler, Alexander I, was only thirteen at the time of his accession and, during the necessary regency, disorder and factionalism increased in the country. They received additional encouragement when Alexander assumed power in his own right in 1893, for he proved to be an impulsive youth with a penchant for authoritarian gestures and with little tact or political judgment. In 1900 he insisted upon marrying one of his mother's ladies-in-waiting, brushing aside as inconsequential the fact that his wife had already divorced one husband and that, for physical reasons, she could not perform the most essential task of queens in countries characterized by dynastic instability: that is, provide Alexander with an heir. The impolitic and unpopular union had a sequel not uncommon in the Balkans. In 1903, Alexander, his wife, and several of her relatives were brutally murdered in Belgrade and their mutilated bodies thrown from the windows of the royal palace.

This action was of revolutionary importance in the history of southeastern Europe. Up till this time, relations between Serbia and the Austro-Hungarian Empire had been friendly, despite certain territorial differences. It had been Austrian intervention that had prevented the utter destruction of the Serbian army after the battle of Slivnitza in 1885; commercial relations between the two countries had been cordial and profitable; the ruling houses had been amicable. Now, however, the murder in Belgrade brought the Karageorgevitch dynasty to the throne in the person of Peter I, and Serbian policy immediately assumed an anti-Austrian character. This was not as clearly attributable to King Peter, whose energies were almost completely absorbed in correcting the internal conditions of his country, to its very great advantage, as to his son, the future King Alexander of Yugoslavia. This able and intelligent young man, a soldier and a patriot, believed that Serbia was destined to be the Piedmont of the Balkans and that her first task was to free Bosnia and Herzegovina from Austrian control and join them to Serbia and her second, to emancipate the Serbs and Croats who were subjects of the Hapsburg monarchy. Although we lack detailed knowledge of the extent of royal complicity in Serbian nationalist agitations in those years, there are strong indications that Prince Alexander gave his support to the secret patriotic societies (the Black Hand and others) that were working for those objectives through agents inside Bosnia and Austria and that he encouraged high-ranking civil servants and army officers to join these organizations. This new policy orientation had results felt throughout Europe in the years 1908–1914 (see p. 445).

In the pursuit of their foreign policy objectives, especially in opposition to Austria, the Serbs could usually count on the support of the tiny kingdom of Montenegro on the Adriatic coast, a country peopled by Serbs of pure blood with a highly developed feeling of Slav nationality, who were destined to become part of Yugoslavia after 1919.

Greece   The southernmost of the Balkan countries, the kingdom of Greece, also presented a picture of internal confusion, discontent, and growing ambition for expansion. After its successful fight for freedom, Greece had been presented with a ruler by the Great Powers (see p. 27). The appointed sovereign, a younger son of the king of Bavaria, ruled Greece as King Otto I from 1832 to 1862. For the first ten years, his reign was marked by an attempt to impose centralized government and Germanic institutions upon a people who were temperamentally democrats and who, even under the Turks, had enjoyed extensive rights of local self-government. They resisted Otto's attempt to bureaucratize the country, eventually showing the seriousness of their protest by resorting, in 1843, to armed insurrection. Brought to his senses, the king authorized an extensive constitutional reform that worked no better than the system it supplanted, since it was elaborately liberal and parliamentary in the Western sense but had no more meaning in a Greek context than the Cánovas constitution had in Spain (see p. 309). It enabled politicians to mimic the procedures of the West but failed utterly to deal with the serious problems of the country: economic backwardness, financial instability, domestic disorder, and brigandage.

In 1833, the Great Powers had drawn the country's borders in such a way as to leave large numbers of Greeks in Thessaly, Epirus, and Macedonia under Turkish rule. Otto's government had no success in securing any amendment of frontiers by negotiation, and an attempt to take advantage of the distraction of the powers during the Crimean War and correct the borders by force was a fiasco. The loss of prestige and the economic repercussions consequent upon this finished what was left of Otto's popularity and, in 1862, confronted with new insurrections, he felt compelled to seek safety abroad.

After some difficulty, a new ruler was found, Prince William George of Denmark, who came to the Greeks bearing gifts, since the British government (perhaps hoping to enhance his chances of survival in an unstable land) decided to accompany his nomination with the cession to Greece of the Ionian Islands (Corfu, Zante, Paxo, Ithaca, Cephalonia, Santa Maura, and Cerigo), which had been under British protection since 1815. The new reign began with a constitutional revision that introduced universal manhood suffrage and made the king's ministers responsible to a single chamber of paid deputies serving for four years. It cannot be said that this shift from a liberal to a democratic constitution made for greater stability. In the reign of George I (1863–1913), there were more than fifty different ministries, a fact that militated against continuity of policy. The state's troubles were enhanced by financial difficulties that were the result of the introduction of new social services (which accomplished a sensible improvement of educational standards), a perhaps too ambitious program of public works (with emphasis upon railroad and canal construction), and the burden of military expenses.

As in the case of other Balkan countries, the military budget was high because Greece's territorial aims were high. The country was not content with the cession of the Ionian Islands or with the acquisition in 1881—as a result of Great Power pressure in Constantinople—of a third of Epirus and the greater part of Thessaly. The rest of those provinces, as well as Macedonia and the island of Crete, were the objectives of all Greek patriots and especially of the *Ethniké Hetaireia* (National Society), a secret society formed in 1894 to encourage the government to break the restraints imposed by the Great Powers, to build up the national military establishment, and to promote union movements in the desired territories.

In 1885 and 1886, when Bulgaria was acquiring Eastern Rumelia and defeating Serbia at war and when great Balkan changes seemed in view, the Greek government mobilized its armed forces and threatened to attack Turkey, but was checked by a Great Power blockade. Ten years later, when the Christians on Crete rose in revolt against Turkish administration and declared their union with Greece, Greek naval forces came to the aid of the insurgents, and Greek irregular forces poured into Thessaly bent on liberating its Turkish districts. In April 1897, the sultan declared war on Greece and, within thirty days, routed its land forces and threatened to take Athens. This debacle led to a precipitous decline of Greece's international reputation, and the hope of winning Crete had to be delayed for another fifteen years and part of Thessaly had to be receded to the victorious sultan.

It cannot be said, however, that this defeat led to any diminution in nationalist agitation in Greece. The *Ethniké Hetaireia* remained alive and the fate of ministries often depended upon their ability to pursue policies favored by it. The Greek cause on Crete was pushed implacably by a gifted lawyer who was to become Greece's greatest modern statesman, Eleutherios Venizelos. And in Macedonia, Greek agents anxiously watched the maneuvers of their rivals, the Bulgars and the Serbs.

Turkey and the Balkans   In the course of the nineteenth century, the Ottoman Empire had been forced, step by step, to yield to the claims of its national minorities and to give up territories that had once made it an unrecognized but very real European power. In the first half of the century Serbia and Montenegro had won their autonomy and Greece its independence; even before the Crimean War Turkish control over Rumania was slight and, after it, it was virtually nonexistent; the Balkan insurrections of the 1870s and the war with Russia had detached Bulgaria from the empire while snapping the last legal ties with Serbia; and the 1880s had been marked by forced cessions to Greece and the loss of Eastern Rumelia to the Bulgarian state. By the end of the century, Turkish possessions in Europe comprised only a belt of territory that extended

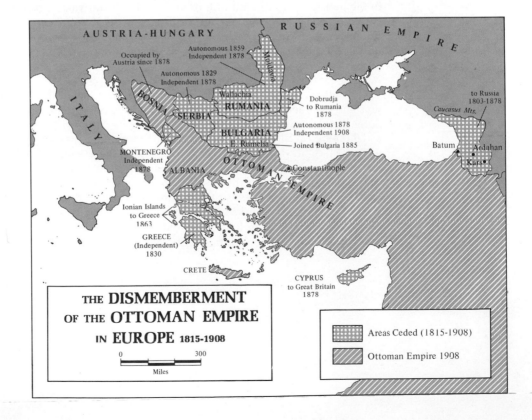

from the Straits of the Bosphorus and the Dardanelles westward, over Thrace, what was left of Rumelia, and Macedonia to Albania and the Epirus and the waters of the Adriatic Sea. In addition, the Turkish government held legal title to the provinces of Bosnia and Herzegovina, which had passed under Austrian administration in 1878.

There was every expectation that these territories would not long remain Turkish. The Turkish government had for generations been characterized by administrative inefficiency and corruption and had been entirely unresponsive to the admonitions of the Great Powers and their insistence upon reform. Even its staunchest supporters among those powers were losing heart; and Lord Salisbury intimated in the 1890s that Great Britain had for years been putting its money on the wrong horse in supporting the Ottoman Empire. On the other hand, the number of those who coveted the Turkish possessions in Europe was uncomfortably large, including not only Greece, Bulgaria, and Serbia but Austria, who had an interest in Macedonian railway routes; and it could not be assumed that Rumania and Russia would remain disinterested in the case of changes either. The knowledge that a partition of Turkey's remaining possessions would be complicated and dangerous, therefore, counseled caution, and most statesmen preferred to play a waiting game.

In 1908, however, to the consternation of Balkan, Hapsburg, and Russian statesmen, there came evidence that Turkey might be on the point of becoming not a declining but a reviving power, not a passive but an active participant in the politics of southeastern Europe. In July of that year, a revolutionary party calling themselves the Young Turks seized control of the government in Constantinople, having first managed to detach the army from the side of the despotic Sultan Abdul Hamid II. The sultan was forced to agree to elections for a national parliament and to constitutional changes that promised to transform Turkey into a liberal state.

The enthusiasm with which this revolution was greeted in the sultan's dominions and the energies it released were in sharp contrast to the spiritless inactivity of the Turkish government in the last quarter of a century. They seemed to herald a tightening up of the administration of the empire, a more vigorous assertion of Turkish rights (in Bosnia, for example), and perhaps even a campaign to recover lost rights and territory. The very possibility of this aroused the apprehension of the Balkan states and those Great Powers with vital interests in southeastern Europe and tempted them to take action to forestall disappointment. Thus, the victory of the Young Turks had effects as revolutionary as the Serbian upheaval of 1903. But the events it precipitated will be discussed appropriately in the context of Great Power politics in the decade before World War I.

Chapter 17 IMPERIAL RUSSIA, 1871–1914

In Anton Chekhov's *The Cherry Orchard,* the "perpetual student" Trofimov has a speech at the end of the second act that must have profoundly moved the audience when the play was first performed in Moscow in January 1904.

> We are at least two hundred years behind, we have really gained nothing yet, we have no definite attitude to the past, we do nothing but theorise or complain of depression or drink vodka. It is clear that to begin to live in the present we must first expiate our past, we must break with it; and we can expiate it only by suffering, by extraordinary unceasing labor.

Ever since the 1860s speeches like this had been made by Russian intellectuals. The fact that Russia lagged behind the major nations of the western world in material progress and in the evolution of its political institutions was obvious to anyone whose view extended beyond the confines of his own country. Awareness of it governed the thinking of the majority of Russians who were politically conscious, making them dissatisfied with the *status quo*. There was no unity of view among them, however, concerning the nature of desirable change or the means of effecting it, although, generally speaking, the advocates of reform divided into three main groupings. The first were those who wanted economic and social improvements granted from above—that is, by imperial ukase or administrative action—without fundamental alteration of the political or social system. This group included Tsar Alexander II in his earlier years and a long line of bureaucratic reformers from Miliutin to Stolypin. The second group, which was composed of university professors, civil servants, members of the professions, and representatives of the growing capitalist class, believed that Russia must seek to emulate the liberal countries of Western Europe, attaining gradual reform by the progressive extension of political rights. The third, and least homogeneous, group was composed of revolutionaries of various types and with various programs, most of whom, however, were agreed that the break with the past must be a violent one.

Opposed to these apostles of change were those members of the governing class, at the court, in the higher civil service and the armed forces, in the church and among the landed gentry, who consciously opposed change for ideological or material reasons, and the inert mass of the population, which was sunk in ignorance and traditionalism. The political influence of organized reaction and the unresponsiveness of the masses helped to defeat or delay the kinds of reform advocated by the first two groups mentioned above and, in the end, to discredit those who favored them; and this meant that, as the years passed, more and more people came to believe in the inevitability of a truly radical reformation of conditions in Russia, including the actual overthrow of the dynasty.

ECONOMIC CONDITIONS

The Agrarian Problem   Nothing better illustrates the backwardness of Russia by Western standards than the lagging pace of Russian agriculture through the period under discussion. Basically, the problem here was one of rural overpopulation, but this was aggravated by other things. The land would have supported many more people than it did if, after the emancipation edict, the traditional communal organization of agriculture had not been maintained (see p. 232). The system of land distribution commonly used by the communes necessitated a reliance upon the three-field system as the only practical method of rotation, and this meant that a third of communal lands were always lying fallow. The productive capacity of the soil was handicapped also by a lack of technical knowledge among the peasantry and by the failure of the government to provide information about methods of intensive cultivation or enough credit to bring machinery and fertilizer within the grasp of the small landholder. While the population increased, therefore, the yield remained stationary. Even so, the pressure upon the soil might have been relieved if the government had not been opposed to having its subjects move about at will. Without papers, which the authorities were reluctant to give, the rural masses had to remain stationary and, in hard years, to starve.

It was possible, of course, for individual peasants to increase their holdings by purchasing or leasing land from noble landlords. To purchase land, however, required funds which very few peasants possessed, and the government was slow to extend credit facilities. Even when a peasants' land bank was founded in 1883, its terms were such that it could be resorted to only by the wealthier peasantry. Leasing took many forms and, for the most vulnerable peasantry, it became a kind of sharecropping that was accompanied by special dues and corvées that were not essentially different from those exacted before the emancipation edict. In whatever form, leasing, too, was an option that was open to a very small minority; the great mass of the peasantry continued to live in the communes in conditions of deepening poverty. It is not surprising that the memory of the exciting promise of the days of emancipation should gradually have been transformed into a legend that the tsar's wishes and the peasants' hopes had been betrayed by evil forces, and that some day justice would be done and another greater sharing out of land, by an expropriation of the proprietors, would take place. In hard times, the willingness to wait wore thin; in 1902, for instance, there were serious peasant uprisings in some parts of European Russia.

The government was always aware of the misery of the rural masses and made sporadic efforts to relieve it, by reduction of land and poll taxes, occasional moratoriums on redemption payments, and the like. But until Stolypin's time, the reforms were palliative rather than basic, partly because the government was afraid of alienating the noble land-owning class by being too generous with the peasantry. The government always seemed to be saying what Alexander II had said in 1861 to a delegation of peasants from Tula: "There will be no emancipation except the one I have granted you. Obey the law and the statutes. Work and toil! Be obedient to the authorities and to noble landowners!"

Industry and Labor   In contrast to agriculture, Russian industry showed decided signs of growth in this period, although it did not reach a magnitude capable of relieving the agricultural overpopulation. The most marked gains were made by the textile and metallurgical industries. The growth of the metal industries received its impetus from the rapid railway building of the 1870s, which continued, although at a slower rate, through the 1880s and accelerated in the next decade, when the government became concerned with the deficiencies of its strategical rail net, and especially of facilities for westward troop movement and the supply of the new defensive works built during the 1890s. Between 1892 and 1902, total rail mileage grew by 46 percent. The demand for steel rails and iron wheels was one of the principal reasons for the development of the great new coal and iron industry in the Donetz basin and the rise of such new industrial centers as Ekaterinoslav and Rostov-on-Don. Another industrial area of growing importance was that around Baku in the oil fields of the Caucasus.

The government was less hesitant in extending assistance to industry than it sometimes seemed to be in dealing with agricultural problems. It promoted the building of railways by subventions of various kinds to private firms (and, at a later date, bought them out on terms favorable to the owners). It aided the metallurgical industry by granting state contracts and imposing heavy duties upon the goods of foreign competitors. From the late 1870s on, Russian tariffs showed a general increase, textiles benefiting from protection as much as the metal goods. Finally, industry in general benefited from the policies of Count S. Y. Witte (1849–1915), who was minister of finance from 1892 to 1903 and thus largely responsible for the second great period of railroad construction mentioned. He was also the moving spirit in the greatest progress in the development of Siberia since the days of Nicholas Muravëv (p. 230). Upon taking office, Witte set out systematically to attract capital to Russia in order to encourage industrial expansion. His method of doing this was to use tariffs to increase state revenues and create a gold reserve sufficiently large to enable Russia to adopt the gold standard, thus enhancing its international fiscal standing. Witte accomplished his primary goal in 1897; and foreign capital began almost immediately to come into the country. By 1900, French and Belgian investors were supporting the development of heavy industries in the Ukraine, and there were 269 foreign firms operating in Russia, helping to exploit her mineral and oil deposits and to stimulate such new industries as electrical and chemical engineering. Thanks to this external aid, at the end of the Witte period, Russia was producing more pig iron than France, standing fourth in world production, and ranked fifth in steel. According to one Soviet calculation (all the more impressive since Soviet writers have been generally critical of his reforms), total industrial production doubled during Witte's term of office; the momentum he had achieved made it increase by 50 percent more in the next decade. Witte's critics claimed that this was achieved at the cost of increasing dependence upon foreign aid and a corresponding loss of freedom. That there was some dependence was true—it was probably inevitable—but without the impetus afforded by foreign capital there would have been virtually no economic progress at all.

This progress was purchased at the cost of new social and political problems. As in other countries, the prevailing tendency in industrial organization was toward large-scale capitalist enterprises, and the appearance of such establishments, armed with all the advantages that mechanization and superior capital resources can bring, made inevitable the decline of craft industries, which also contributed to the complications of the agrarian problem in those areas where handicrafts had supplemented peasant incomes (although in time industrial side, earnings helped, as Theodore von Laue has pointed out, to keep many peasant farmers from starvation).

At the same time, conditions in the new capitalist enterprises resembled those that prevailed in England in the 1820s and France in the 1840s (see p. 113 and 67). Pent up in squalid tenement slums or in miserable company barracks, the factory workers had to work fourteen to sixteen hours a day for wages so trifling that the pay of the head of the family was not sufficient to support its other members, so that women and children also had to labor in the foundries and the mines. Factory inspection, sanitary laws, and safety precautions were, until very late in the century, nonexistent.

Against these conditions and against the steady decline of their real income, the workers had no means of protection. They were caught in an economic squeeze caused by the fact that the growth of industry was not rapid enough to keep pace with the numbers of landless and job-hungry peasants; and, as long as the labor supply exceeded demand, the factory and mine owners could keep their workers at the barest subsistence level. Until the 1880s, the government took only a theoretical interest in labor grievances; and, even when regulation began, its first effect was further to hurt workers' income. The law forbidding the employment of children under 12 (1882), legislation later in the decade prohibiting night work for women and adolescents in certain industries, and the laws of the Witte period, which regulated the working day of all workers, were estimable reforms, long needed; but, at a time when hourly real wages were very low, they must have been regarded as a dubious gain by many workers. The right to form protective organizations of their own was denied to Russian workers. In 1875, while English trade unions were being given a new charter of liberty by the Disraeli government (see p. 288), the Russian penal code laid down a scale of heavy punishments for anyone engaged in organizing societies that were likely to encourage hatred between employers and employees. The definition of such societies was sufficiently broad to include even purely benevolent societies, to say nothing of those that were designed to improve the lot of the workers by exerting economic pressure upon proprietors. Although certain branches of the state service, notably the Ministry of Finance, believed that a more enlightened policy would make for labor peace and greater production, the government in general cooperated with antiunion employers, on the theory that unions represented a political threat to the regime. Troops were often placed at the disposal of employers to put down unrest; and agents were put in factories to spy out attempts at illegal organization or to identify agitators. In 1901, the Ministry of the Interior tried another tack in its fight against unions. It established a workers' society under police patronage, the main purpose of which was to organize patriotic demonstrations, which, it was apparently hoped, would satisfy the workers' desire for direct action. The society was not successful and was disbanded when it was discovered that it supplied a useful cover for the spread of socialist propaganda.

Neither the government's repressive and diversionary tactics nor its cautious reforms prevented labor unrest. Despite the lack of legal organization, strikes were not infrequent from the 1870s on. A serious strike in the Moscow textile industry in 1885 persuaded the government to pass legislation limiting the employers' use of monetary fines for breaches of discipline; and new stoppages in the same industry in 1896 and 1897 prompted Witte's labor legislation. Two years later, Russia entered a general economic depression, which was felt particularly heavily in the metal and oil industries and from which the country had not completely recovered when the war with Japan began. The effect of this was both to increase the number of strikes and to change their character. After 1900, the objectives of the workers always included political demands, and their strikes were often short and designed not to win economic concessions but to serve as demonstrations against the regime. Sympathy strikes also made their appearance. In November 1902, a general strike was declared in Rostov-on-Don and had to be put down by government troops; and in the following years a strike at Baku set off a chain reaction of labor walkouts and demonstrations in other industrial towns.

Foreign Trade   Russia's share in the world's trade did not exceed four percent, which was not markedly higher than it had been in the first half of the nineteenth century. The most striking development in the structure of trade was the steady growth of grain exports, from a yearly average of about 1,120,000 tons in 1860 to about 6,945,000 tons in 1897. Grain represented only fifteen percent of the total value of Russian exports in 1836–1840, but about fifty percent after 1871; and this heavy reliance on the grain trade had effects outside the purely economic sphere, notably in the area of foreign affairs. At the turn of the century, in a period of acute economic depression in Russia, the German government, under pressure from its own agriculturists, passed a tariff law that virtually excluded Russian grain from the German market (see p. 358). This action reinforced anti-German feeling among the Russian governing class (many members of which were hurt financially by the new tariffs) and strengthened the Franco-Russian alliance that had been concluded in 1894 (see p. 427).

POLITICAL DEVELOPMENTS

The Last Years of Alexander II   On April 4, 1866, a young man named D. V. Karakozov tried unsuccessfully to assassinate Alexander II. His shot was a kind of signal for the government to reverse its gears and turn away from the reforming instinct that had guided official policy since the end of the Crimean War and had produced the emancipation edict, the establishment of the zemstvos, and the reorganization of the judicial system (see p. 252). There was still some reforming activity. In the 1870s, the minister of war, D. A. Miliutin, completed a fundamental shake-up of the whole military system that brought a reduction of the top-heavy army bureaucracy, a new regional organization, the appointment for the first time of a chief of the general staff, and, in 1874, the introduction of compulsory military service for all able males. These reforms, which laid the basis for the modern Russian army, were accompanied by disciplinary changes that somewhat reduced the brutal treatment formerly meted out to the ranks; and, generally, they can be described as progressive in temper.

The military reforms, however, were an exception forced on the government by the unmistakable superiority of Western armies in the wars in the Crimea and in central Europe. In matters less obviously vital to the security of the state, an increasingly reactionary tendency was apparent. This was true, for example, in the field of education where, under the inspiration of Count Dimitri Tolstoy, minister of education from 1866 until 1880, academic freedom in the universities was virtually extinguished, the faculties being commanded to make reports to the police about student opinion and all student activities being prohibited. Simultaneously, Tolstoy declared war on natural science, reducing the time allotted to it in secondary school curricula and enforcing a much greater emphasis upon classical and modern languages, literature, history, geography, religion, and other subjects that he appeared to regard as politically and morally innocuous.

These measures were considered an attempt to shelter Russian youth from modern knowledge and were widely resented. From a practical point of view, they neither protected students from subversive influences nor provided a very effective education, since Russia did not have enough competent classicists to make the reforms work. At a time when the country was producing scientists of world reputation—D. I. Mendeleev (1843–1901) in chemistry, I. I. Mechnikov (1845–1916) in biology, I. P. Pavlov (1849–1936) in physiology—they made it difficult for those great scholars to find and train students. In a curious way, this probably aided rather than hurt the future of Russian science, although not without doing a disservice to other disciplines. Hugh Seton-Watson has written that Tolstoy's policy confirmed Russian intellectuals in their ingenuous belief that only scientific education is progressive and in their naive contempt for the humanities and for all disinterested learning. This had far-reaching repercussions, not least of all in the intellectual life of the Soviet Union.

An illustration for Leo Tolstoy's *Resurrection* (1898) by the Russian artist Leonid Pasternak, 1862–1945, the father of Boris Pasternak, who wrote *Dr. Zhivago* (1957). (New York Public Library)

Tolstoy's measures were strongly supported by the tsar, who in his later years fell more and more under the influence of the ultra conservatives. Prominent among those was the Moscow journalist M. N. Katkov (1818–1887), who had the distinction of having first published Leo N. Tolstoy's great novels *War and Peace* (1869) and *Anna Karenina* (1877), but probably considered his work in behalf of a conservative domestic policy and a nationalistic foreign policy as infinitely more important. There is no doubt that Katkov helped convince Alexander II that "destructive notions" were rife among the youth of the land and that a revolutionary movement of real importance threatened the regime.

When one considers the disharmony of opinion and the lack of organization that prevailed among critics of the regime in the 1860s and 1870s, this can be seen to have been an exaggeration. Katkov himself was shocked and revolted by the rise of the attitude that Turgenev, in his famous novel *Fathers and Sons* (1861), called nihilism. This was an exaggerated realism that rejected all traditional values, turned its back on the past, and insisted upon the rights of individuality and the human reason; and its advocates, like the German and French students of the period from 1815 to 1830 and other student rebels since then, assumed (Kropotkin tells us) "a certain external roughness as a protest against the smooth amiability of their fathers." That the progressive intelligentsia did talk a lot about root and branch reform is doubtless true; but nihilism could hardly be considered a force capable of jeopardizing political stability.

More important was the doctrine of populism, which in general held that social revolution was necessary, that it need not wait upon the achievement of a capitalism as mature as that of Western Europe but could be achieved on the basis of Russia's system of communal land tenure, and that the peasantry would be the driving force behind the revolutionary upheaval. Yet there was little agreement among the early populists about tactics and program, and in the 1860s and early 1870s, populism tended to be a formless, idealistic, and highly unrealistic force. In the year 1873, when the remarkable movement "to the people" inspired thousands of young men and women of the educated class to go as missionaries to the peasants to preach the cause of revolution, they found little response, having much the same experience as Bazarov in *Fathers and Sons,* who, as Turgenev tells us, prided himself on being able to talk to the peasants, but never suspected "that in their eyes he was all the while something of the nature of a buffooning-clown." The populist movement of this period made the mistake of idealizing the peasant and expecting wonders from him, ignoring the fact that he was too illiterate and brutalized to comprehend its message.

If the government had let matters take their course, this movement might have died a-borning. But police persecution and mass trials of agitators not only kept it alive but improved its efficiency. After the failure of the movement to the people and the arrests and trials that followed it, populist leaders began to use methods advocated earlier by Serge Nechaev and Peter Tkachëv. Nechaev, a former follower of Bakunin and the leader of a short-lived secret society in the 1860s, had emphasized the uses of terror as a means of promoting revolutionary objectives and had finally given a dramatic demonstration of the meaning of revolutionary discipline by cold-bloodedly murdering an associate suspected of what has come in our own time to be called deviationism. (This murder supplied the theme of Dostoevsky's novel *The Demons.*) Tkachëv, who has been considered a forerunner of Lenin, taught that successful revolutions depended less upon the action of the masses than upon the vision and determination of a revolutionary elite. In the late 1870s, the populists accepted secrecy and terrorism as their methods, and, in particular, advocated the use of political assassination as the effective method of advertising the need for revolution and attracting mass support to the cause. While almost any high-ranking official was considered worth killing, the tsar himself became the most desirable target; and the society The People's Will, led by Andrew Zheliabov and Sophie Perovsky, seems to have made Alexander's death their *raison d' être* and to have organized at least seven attempts on his life. In March 1881, they finally succeeded. As Alexander II was returning from a military review in St. Petersburg, a bomb was thrown at his carriage, wrecking it without harming him. A few moments later, as he stood beside it, a second bomb exploded at his feet, and he died within hours.

Full Reaction, 1881–1905   The perpetrators of this deed were hunted down and hanged; their organizations were smashed; and the revolutionary movement was made ineffective for a generation. The years that followed the death of the tsar-liberator were years of full reaction, in which progressive views of any kind rendered their possessor suspect. In Dostoevsky's *The Demons*, Captain Lebiatkyn says:

> If I were to try to bequeath my skin for a drum to, let us say, the Akmolinsky infantry regiment, in which I had the honor of starting my service, with the proviso that the Russian national anthem might be beaten on it every day in front of the drawn-up regiment, they would consider it a liberal idea and forbid my skin to be used for that purpose.

This, as well as anything, describes the atmosphere that prevailed under Alexander III (1881–1894).

The new tsar was an unsophisticated, conscientious ruler with a firm will and unrelievedly conservative views. His political principles are usually summed up in the words orthodoxy, autocracy, and nationalism. This description is just, for he was personally devout and regarded the Russian Orthodox Church as a bulwark against subversive influences and the spread of free thinking, was uncompromising in his defense of the prerogatives of the crown, and was a firm advocate of a policy of Russification at home, with respect to subject nationalities, and Pan-Slavism abroad.

Of Alexander III's chosen ministers only three need be mentioned. The most important personality in this reign and the first part of the succeeding one was Konstantine Pobedonostsev (1827–1907), procurator of the Holy Synod, that is, lay chairman of the governing body of the Russian Orthodox Church. An opponent of all Western ideas, he was particularly vehement in his belief that a free press was the root of all evil and that parliaments served only the interests of their members. His ideal government was one of rigidly centralized autocracy, and it was largely due to his influence that a plan for a national legislative council with limited powers, which was being considered by Alexander II before his death, was jettisoned, and that the new tsar also curtailed the rights of the zemstvos and the town councils established in the 1860s.

Pobedonostsev's policies were ably seconded by the former minister of education, Tolstoy, who became minister of the interior in 1882 and immediately launched a program that tightened the already formidable censorship of the press, reduced the autonomy of the universities and destroyed the remnants of academic freedom, and placed libraries and reading rooms under stringent observation, removing books that—in official language—did not "correspond to the level of intellectual development and understanding of the simple people." This library policy was merely a reflection of the general educational policy inaugurated in the previous reign by Tolstoy and now administered by Count Delianov, minister of education from 1882 to 1897. The principles guiding elementary education in particular were designed to prevent social mobility and to make the lower orders content with their place in society. How greatly the government feared what education might do to the minds of the working class is perhaps illustrated by how little they accomplished in the field of elementary education. At the end of Alexander III's reign, only twenty-one percent of the population of Russia could read and write; and no appreciable change was to be made here until free compulsory education was instituted in 1908.

When Alexander III died of nephritis in October 1894, his passing brought no alleviation of this atmosphere of persecution and thought control. The new sovereign, Nicholas II (1894–1917), possessed a political philosophy that was not markedly different from that of his father, although it was not accompanied by the steadfastness and resolution characteristic of that ruler. Nicholas was always a tool in the hands of stronger individuals: Pobedonostsev in the first ten years of his reign, as well as certain of his military advisers, active and retired, like Bezobrazov, General Kuropatkin, and Admiral Alekseev, who advocated a dynamic foreign policy and were behind the disastrous adventure in the Far East; in later years, his wife and her favorites, especially the monk Gregory Rasputin, who won royal favor by supposedly saving the heir apparent, a victim of hemophilia, from death by bleeding. It was with Bezobrazov's aid and that of Pobedonostsev that Witte's enemies finally brought him down in 1903. Bezobrazov told the tsar that Witte had pledged the entire mineral wealth of Siberia to the Rothschilds as collateral for a loan, and Pobedonostsev supported the charge that the minister of finance was encouraging all the dissatisfied elements in the country—the Finns, Armenians, Jews, and students—by his reforms. One thing in common all those who exerted influence on Nicholas possessed: the desire that he should do nothing to relax the prevailing absolutism; and the tsar was led by them to try to outdo his father in autocratic inflexibility. Since Nicholas II had no conspicuous talents of his own, it is perhaps not surprising that his reign, which had a tragic beginning, when 1300 people were trampled to death because of police inefficiency during the accession celebration, should have been marked by progressively greater tragedies until its denouement in war, revolution, and the end of the Romanov dynasty.

Reformers and Revolutionaries   The accession of the new tsar brought a revival of political activity not only on the part of advocates of revolution but among moderate liberal groups who had been relatively quiet since the death of Alexander II. In the zemstvos particularly there was an upsurge of hope in liberal reform, and leaders in these organs of local government began to call for a widening of their competence and for the creation of some kind of central zemstvo organization that could play a role in the national government. These proposals received short shrift from the emperor, and when zemstvo leaders tried on their own to establish a continuing national organization, its meetings were forbidden by the police. The zemstvos nevertheless continued to serve as forums for liberal opinion, and the frequent resolutions that they passed on matters beyond their jurisdiction made it clear to the government that such opinion existed.

The revolutionary opposition, which also revived during the first years of

Nicholas's reign, was composed of two main organizations, the first of which was the Russian Social Democratic Labor party. The origins of this party lay back in the 1880s when George Plekhanov (1857–1918), a former populist, emigrated to Switzerland and founded a socialist organization called Liberation of Labor. After his break with populism, Plekhanov adopted the main tenets of Marxism and insisted that Russia must follow the pattern set in the West and pass through capitalism before it could hope for a transition to socialism. He rejected the faith in the peasant masses that had been characteristic of populism and called for the creation of a disciplined working class party. Plekhanov's literary gifts and analytical power contributed to the wide dissemination of Marxist thought in his own country (Lenin once said that he had managed singlehanded to "rear a whole generation of Russian Marxists"), and by the mid-1890s there were twenty Marxist groups in St. Petersburg alone. Since they had to operate clandestinely, they were not very effective. When their first congress convened at Minsk in 1898 to discuss the organization of a nation-wide party, it was poorly attended, and several of the delegates and two members of the central committee elected by the congress were arrested almost immediately by the police. After this, leadership of Russian socialism necessarily shifted to the "League of Russian Social Democrats Abroad," which was located in Switzerland. It was among these exiles that the significant doctrinal developments took place in the next years, and plans were made for the second party congress that met in Brussels (and London) in 1903.

This conference is remembered today primarily because, during its debates, a conflict of view—and one that had important results in the history of world socialism—developed between a group of delegates headed by one of Plekhanov's older associates, Y. O. Martov, and a second led by the most brilliant of the younger leaders, Lenin (1870–1924).

The second son of a school inspector in Simbirsk on the Volga, Lenin, whose real name was Vladimir Ilyich Ulyanov, had become a hardened enemy of the imperial regime in 1887, while still a schoolboy, when his older brother was arrested and hanged for complicity in an assassination plot against the emperor. Participation in a student protest at the University of Kazan a few years later led to the termination of his own formal education, the memory of his brother's crime hardening official minds against him. He nevertheless persisted in his studies and passed his law examinations without benefit of university training. But he then fell under the influence of Plekhanov's writings and turned his attention completely to the study of Marxism and to practical work in a reading circle in St. Petersburg that was intended to indoctrinate the working classes. This eventually led to trouble with the police and to a term of imprisonment and three years of exile in Siberia, which Lenin employed in further theoretical studies. After his release, he managed to make his way abroad; he became one of the first editors of the party newspaper *Iskra* (*The Spark*): and his writings soon won him recognition as a theorist whose stature was comparable with that of Plekhanov himself.

During the dispute with Martov at the 1903 congress, which turned largely on matters of party organization, a momentary voting edge gave Lenin the opportunity to name his faction the Bolsheviks (or majorityites), his opponents automatically becoming the Mensheviks (or minorityites). The names stuck, even during times when Lenin's group was no longer a true majority, and as years passed the momentary differences of 1903 hardened into differences of principle. Both sects continued to hold to the basic tenets of Marxism; both continued to be dedicated to the overthrow of tsardom; and both, following Plekhanov, believed that the fall of the imperial regime would be followed by a period of bourgeois democratic government before socialism could become effective. But, whereas Lenin and the Bolsheviks held that this period of bourgeois rule must be regarded as a purely transitional one during which the party pushed the proletariat and the peasantry on to the final revolutionary effort, the Mensheviks were inclined to regard it as a period that would presumably last a long time and during which genuine cooperation would take place between bourgeois and socialist parties. The Mensheviks were, thus, closer to the revisionist parties of Western Europe than they themselves admitted.

A second important difference had to do with party organization. As he had written in his brilliant pamphlet *What Is To Be Done?* in 1902, Lenin believed that the socialist movement must be led by an elite of professional revolutionaries, since the mass of the workers, without the discipline that such leaders provided, would lose their revolutionary *élan* and sink into the swamp of reformism. Translated into terms of organization, this implied a small party with a centralized and disciplined structure and with no members who did not have definite tasks assigned to them, which they were bound to carry out in accordance with a line determined by the party directorate. At Brussels, Martov protested that he did not want a party whose members "abdicated their right to think"; and the Mensheviks always argued for a more comprehensive party, open not only to professional revolutionaries but to all workers and intellectuals who believed in its goals. But in the long run it was Lenin's view rather than theirs that triumphed, although not without proving that their worst fears were justified.

The victory of Bolshevism was still, however, far in the future; and in the revived revolutionary movement of Nicholas II's first years, Marxism did not have the authority it was to achieve later. It still had a powerful competitor in populism, which won many new converts in Russia and among the exiles in the 1890s and inspired the founding of the Socialist Revolutionary party in the first five years of the new century.

The Socialist Revolutionaries had many beliefs in common with the Social Democrats. Their principal differences lay in the importance they attributed to the peasantry (considered by both Bolsheviks and Mensheviks as a potentially negligible revolutionary force), their readiness to believe that socialism would follow directly upon the fall of the monarchy, and their greater belief in the efficacy of political terrorism. Although Lenin denied that the Social Democrats ever "rejected terror on principle," both he and most of his colleagues felt that its employment distracted revolutionaries from more important tasks of propaganda and organization. The Socialist Revolutionaries, on the other hand, not only approved daring acts of violence but actually had a terroristic organization, which, under orders from the party's central committee, planned and executed political murders.

The Revolution of 1905   As we have noted, Russian industry experienced a protracted slump in the years 1899–1903, in which factory shutdowns caused great suffering among the working classes. Before the country had fully recovered from the effects of the depression, the reckless policy of the government in the Far East had led to war with Japan (see p. 422); this necessitated a calling up of reserves from the rural districts, which disrupted agricultural production and distribution sufficiently to cause serious shortages and new curtailment of industrial employment. The news from the fighting fronts was uniformly bad, a fact that contributed further to general dissatisfaction with the state of affairs, the more so because the government (as if trying to prove the truth of Captain Lebiatkyn's melancholy prophecy) repressed all patriotic movements in support of the war for fear that they might be a front for revolutionary activity. This was the fate, for instance, of a zemstvo organization to aid the wounded, which was made ineffective by restrictions imposed by the minister of the interior V. K. Plehve.

In these years of growing discontent all of the opposition groups became furiously active. This was most spectacularly true of the Socialist Revolutionaries, who carried out a program of terror which, between 1901 and 1904, killed two provincial governors, a minister of education, and two ministers of the interior, the second being the much hated Plehve who was blown to pieces by a bomb in July 1904. The Social Democrats confined themselves, for the most part, to propaganda among factory workers, the effectiveness of which was shown in the St. Petersburg strike of January 1905. As for the liberal movement, which had been centered in the zemstvos, it tended to become broader in membership and acquired a foreign organization, the "League for Liberation," and a journal, edited by P. N. Miliukov and a former Social Democrat named Struve, which boldly called for the end of autocracy and the introduction of a constitutional monarchy. By the fall of 1904, the liberals were holding banquets in St. Petersburg and Moscow similar to those in Paris in February 1848 (see p. 124), and something of the same atmosphere reigned in the country as a whole. "We have been talking and talking for fifty years and reading pamphlets," Chekhov's Uncle Vanya had said in 1899. "It's about time to leave off." This seemed to represent the national mood at the end of 1904.

The accumulated tension exploded at the beginning of the new year. In January 1905 a strike broke out in St. Petersburg and tied up several factories employing thousands of workers; and on Sunday, January 9, many of these joined in a protest march to the Winter Palace. They were organized and led by an Orthodox priest named Gapon, an equivocal figure who had organized the "Assembly of Russian Workers," a patriotic union approved by the police, who was later a Socialist Revolutionary, then once more a police agent (or collaborator), and who was finally "executed" by the Socialist Revolutionaries in 1906. Whatever his ultimate motives, Gapon seems in January to have been sincerely desirous of having the tsar consider the grievances of the workers, and his march was organized with that in view. As usual, the government acted suspiciously and in a spirit of panic. Troops blocked the march and then opened fire on its columns, killing and wounding hundreds of people and causing the day to be commemorated as Bloody Sunday.

Immediately, a general strike gripped the capital and spread rapidly to Moscow, Saratov, Ekaterinoslav, and the principal towns of Poland and the Baltic provinces. A new wave of terrorism cost the life of the tsar's uncle, the Grand Duke Serge. Peasant revolts began in February in the province of Kursk and spread rapidly in subsequent months; and a Peasant Union was founded in June. Both the workers and the urban professional men formed new organizations. The armed services were shaken by reverses in the war (Port Arthur had fallen in December 1904; the Russian army had been routed at Mukden in February; and Admiral Rozhdestvensky's Baltic fleet had been virtually wiped out in the Straits of Tsushima at the end of May) (see p. 424); they also fell under the revolutionary spell. In June the crew of the battleship *Potemkin* mutinied at Odessa—an event that must have sent a thrill of terror through court circles.

With his world apparently falling to pieces around him, the tsar acted hesitantly and without determination, asserting his intention of summoning a consultative assembly "of the most worthy people," but making it clear, by certain decrees of August, that the franchise would be such as to exclude the greater part of the intellectuals and workers. This attitude encouraged new agrarian and urban disturbances, as well as railway and university strikes and another general strike in the capital; and, in October, the first Soviet of Workers Delegates was formed

Soviet poster on the twenty-fifth anniversary of the revolution of 1905. (Hoover Institution)

in St. Petersburg and began to agitate for municipal self-government. In the face of this accumulation of woes, the tsar seriously considered attempting to rule by military dictatorship but was finally persuaded by his advisers to issue the so-called October Manifesto instead. This document provided for a broadening of fundamental liberties (including the guarantee of press freedom and freedom of speech and assembly), announced the calling of a national legislative assembly or Duma, which would be elected by a franchise much wider than that provided for in August, and reorganized the Council of Ministers on Western lines.

With this decree, which apparently marked the transformation of autocratic Russia into a constitutional monarchy, the unity of the revolutionary movement dissolved and its fire subsided. There were some attempts by radical elements in the zemstvo organization and the organized workers' groups to push for greater demands, but the moderates professed to be satisfied, and public opinion was beginning to swing against the radicals. This was shown by the support given by the lower middle class and unskilled workers to the "black hundreds," gangs of hooligans organized by the reactionary agrarian elements and the church and used to attack opponents of the government. When the police dared break up the St. Petersburg Soviet in December, it was a sign that the regime was recovering its confidence. The police action touched off sympathy strikes and large-scale fighting in Rostov and Moscow, but this was the last gasp of the revolution of 1905.

The Constitutional Experiment   Once relative order had been restored, it soon became clear that nothing very much had been won by the revolution after all, and that it was impossible, for the moment at least, to do anything about it. In the years from 1906 to 1914, the great mass of the Russian people seemed to sink back into apathy, while the most sensitive minds, as the poet Alexander Blok wrote in 1908, were conscious of "a constant and wanton feeling of catastrophe." Among the politically active elements in the nation, all the strength and unity of will seemed to lie on the side of reaction rather than on that of progress. The left was hopelessly split. The liberal forces were divided among the Constitutional Democrats or Cadets, who wanted a greater degree of parliamentary power, and the Octobrists, who were content with the tsar's Manifesto. The Social Democrats were embroiled in intestine feuds; and the Socialist Revolutionaries were entirely absorbed in new plots against individuals. On the other side, the nobility, the landlords, the church, the bureaucrats, the soldiers, and the Pan-Slav patriots organized a "Union of the Russian People" to encourage the tsar to resist further concessions and to regain the ground he had ceded in October.

The tsar was readily amenable to this kind of prompting and, within three years, had deprived most of his promises of meaning. Before the first Duma met he had constituted a second parliamentary body by decree—a Council of the Empire that was largely appointive and whose assent was required to all laws before they went to the tsar for approval. When the Duma assembled, with the Cadets in large majority, it was confronted with an imperial announcement excluding certain "organic laws" from its consideration, stipulating that the military prerogatives of the sovereign were inviolate, and even limiting the parliamentary power of the purse by authorizing the government to operate, if necessary, without a budget. After this scarcely encouraging introduction, the Duma engaged in oratorical exercises for two months. The Cadets' attempt to secure a real measure of ministerial responsibility was inflexibly opposed by the tsar, who finally dissolved the Duma and stated that he was "cruelly disappointed" that its members had "strayed into spheres beyond their competence."

A protest signed by 230 members of the Duma was ineffective, leading merely to the unseating of most of the signatories. The tsar's course was set and could no longer be diverted. During the meeting of the second Duma, from March to June 1907, the government actually arrested sixteen members for revolutionary activity, a palpable breach of parliamentary rights. After this inconclusive session, moreover, the franchise was drastically curtailed by decree (although electoral laws were supposed to be invalid without the Duma's assent) and was henceforth based on a system somewhat similar to that used in Prussia, so that the landlord class was given a preponderance of power. Thus, the Duma became a purely consultative body, without any real influence upon the actions of the ministers.

This might not have been disastrous if the tsar had chosen able ministers and given them the authority to remedy the worst of the administrative and economic abuses of the state. But these were precisely the years when the influence of Rasputin over the empress's mind began to grow, and people who could win or purchase the monk's favor were apt to be appointed to high office without regard to their qualifications. This sort of thing, and the tsar's personal lack of resolution when it came to key appointments, weakened the efficiency of all branches of the imperial administration while discouraging attempts at reform. This was true, for example, of the armed services, whose deficiencies had been made obvious by the Japanese war. Their correction, however, was entrusted to General Sukhomlinov, war minister from 1909 to 1914, who spent so much time combating intrigues against himself and conducting intrigues of his own that he found little time to improve the staff and communications system or to raise the level of officer education before Russia became involved in another and greater war.

The ablest of Nicholas's ministers in this period was P. A. Stolypin, prime minister from 1906 until 1911. He owed his position to his suppression of peasant risings in Saratov, where he was provincial governor in 1905, and to his known reputation for nationalism and conservatism; but he was no blind reactionary and showed himself capable of cooperating with liberal elements in the Duma whenever there was an opportunity to do so. Stolypin's first year as a prime minister was largely devoted to hunting down terrorists and breaking up revolutionary cells, an occupation in which he showed a ruthlessness that probably derived from the fact that, in August 1906, Socialist Revolutionaries had blown up his summer residence, killing thirty-two people and wounding twenty-two more, including Stolypin's son and daughter. Thereafter, he devoted his energies to agricultural reform, seeking to improve the efficiency of Russian agriculture by opening the way to modern methods of production. Specifically, he sought, by a series of laws passed in 1906, to reduce the restrictions that the village communes imposed on the individual peasants, which often destroyed their initiative (see p. 232), to help them secede from communes, and to promote communal redistribution of land so as to consolidate scattered holdings. Thanks to this legislation, about one tenth of the holdings in European Russia were consolidated by 1915, with resultant increases in production, and two and a half million households had broken away from the communes to become individual farmers. Russian agriculture was still backward in 1914 from the standpoint of the tenure of the mass of the peasantry and the methods they employed; but Stolypin's reforms had marked the first significant step forward since the emancipation edict.

It was characteristic of the regime that Stolypin suffered the same treatment meted out to Witte earlier, being attacked by reactionaries as a liberal and progressively losing the favor of the tsar as his personal stature grew. It was widely rumored in 1911 that he would soon be dismissed. Instead, while attending a theater performance in Kiev in September of that year, he was shot and killed by Dimitry Bogrov, a man who had been both a Socialist Revolutionary and a police spy, and who possessed a police pass at the time of his attack on the minister.

After this the government made few attempts to alleviate existing abuses. In an atmosphere of unrelieved reaction, Russia once more began to indulge in foreign adventures of the kind that had nearly proved disastrous in 1905 and were to prove so in 1917, when military defeat led to a greater revolution than that of 1905.

THE SUBJECT NATIONALITIES

Russification   Russia had as many subject nationalities as the Austro-Hungarian Empire and treated them no better. Besides those who could call themselves Russians, there were Ukrainians and White Russians, Poles, Germans, Lithuanians, Letts and Estonians, Rumanians, Armenians, various Turkish and Mongol peoples, some five million Jews, who were set apart and treated as an alien people, and Finns, who occupied a somewhat different position than the others.

The prevailing policy with respect to the nationalities, especially after the death of Alexander II, who had shown some respect for their separate cultures and customs, was designed to stamp out differences and impose Russian modes of thought and speech upon them. Under Alexander III, for instance, a deliberate policy of Russification was directed against the Germans in the Baltic provinces, which included the introduction of Russian municipal institutions, the use of Russian as the language of instruction in the schools, the supersession of the German University of Dorpat by a Russian institution, and an attempt to weaken, and even destroy, the Lutheran religion by making the construction of new Lutheran churches dependent upon permission of the Holy Synod of the Orthodox Church. Similar policies were followed in this and the following reign in the case of the Armenians, the Tatars of the Volga, the Georgians, and other nationalities, and—as a general rule—Russification was always intensified in those areas where nationalist or revolutionary parties appeared.

The Jews were the conspicuous exception to this tendency, for every effort was made to make impossible any real assimilation of this people. They had long been kept within a special Jewish pale, comprising Poland and Lithuania, and, although Alexander II issued a series of decrees lightening this restriction and making greater freedom of movement possible for certain categories of Jews, this was reversed by his successor. The death of the tsar-liberator was attributed to them and resulted in fearful pogroms, encouraged by the police, in which thousands died. For the tsarist regime, as for tyrannical regimes elsewhere, victimization of the Jews became a safety valve for popular passions and a means of distracting the masses from other grievances. At the same time, extreme limitation of the number of Jews permitted to attend institutions of higher learning and other humiliating restrictions revealed the government's fixed intention of keeping the Jews in a state of permanent inferiority; this explains the rapid increase in Jewish emigration, especially to the United States, in the 1890s.

Poland   After the suppression of the revolt of 1863 (see pp. 208 and 221), Russian policy in Poland was designed to break up centers of revolution and to weaken potentially dissident groups. Alexander II's government sought to promote these ends by suppressing the University of Warsaw and Russifying the schools, the courts, the railways, and the banks and also by giving a more liberal interpretation of the emancipation edict than was employed in Russia proper in the hope of weakening the nationalist Polish landlord class. The nobility did tend to play a reduced role in Polish affairs in the subsequent period, but the nationalism they had represented was now preached by middle class groups which grew up with the rapid development of Polish industry in this period. The National Democratic party became the most important of these, and in Roman Dmowski it had a leader whose teaching profoundly influenced those who forged Polish liberty in the war years. Nor was nationalism confined to this group. The Polish Socialist party, founded in Paris in 1892, had a strong internationalist wing, headed by Rosa Luxemburg, who considered Polish independence as chimerical; but just as strong were those socialists who took their lead from Joseph Pilsudski (1867-1935), whose socialism was a thin veneer over a burning desire for freedom and who, one day, was to be dictator of a free Polish state (see p. 595).

During the revolution of 1905, there were serious disorders in Poland, and, in the first Russian Duma, Dmowski, who led the Polish delegation, tried to win support for Polish autonomy within the empire. This did not succeed, although the Duma approved some temporary relaxation of the Russification policy in Polish schools. These gains were wiped out in the Stolypin period, for that statesman was an ardent nationalist whose first action with respect to Poland was to withdraw the permission, granted in 1906, to establish private schools in which instruction in Polish would be allowed. Simultaneously, the electoral reform of 1907 greatly reduced Polish representation in the Duma, an action that increased resentment in Poland and encouraged the growth of a desire for a break with Russia.

Finland   Finland had been acquired by Russia in 1809; but until the end of the reign of Alexander II, the connection had been a tenuous one, the state being constituted as a grand duchy with the emperor as grand duke, but having its own constitution and parliament and its own army, currency, and postal service. With the coming of reaction to Russia in 1883 and the growth of specific Russian nationalism, these rights were placed in jeopardy; and Alexander III took the first steps toward the Russification of Finnish institutions. The real turning point in Russo-Finnish relations, however, came in 1899 when an imperial decree stipulated that henceforth laws affecting both Finland and the rest of the empire would be within the jurisdiction of the Russian State Council, and the Finnish Diet would have only advisory powers with respect to them. This was followed by the absorption of the Finnish postal system by the Russian, the disbanding of the Finnish army, and a decree making Finns liable for service in the Russian armed services.

The Finnish people resisted these blows at their autonomy by a highly effective policy of passive resistance; and this, and the troubles attendant on the revolution of 1905, forced the revocation of the offensive decrees. This was only a temporary respite, however. As in the case of Poland, the policy of Russification was resumed under Stolypin, and there was a series of clashes between the Finnish Diet and the tsar's governor-general. By 1914, it was clear that the Russian government intended to wipe out Finnish autonomy, and recognition of this determined Finland's conduct in the last stages of the world war.

The national pride and sturdy independence of the Finns was reflected in the music of Scandinavia's greatest symphonic composer, Jean Sibelius (1865–1957). His work, much of it based on themes from the Finnish epic the *Kalevala*, appealed so directly to the national mood that, in 1897, the Finnish Senate voted him a life pension. His well-known tone poem *Finlandia* was published two years later.

Chapter 18 IMPERIAL EXPANSION, 1871–1914

THE AGE OF IMPERIALISM

The Motive Factors   During the first three quarters of the nineteenth century few of the European states showed much interest in acquiring territory outside of Europe proper; and, in cases where new holdings were established in Africa or Asia (see p. 9), this was not always the result of conscious policy and was rarely accorded much popular support. This was true even in Great Britain, which had emerged from the wars of the eighteenth century and the conflict with Napoleon with the greatest accumulation of dependencies the world had ever seen. Englishmen who gave any thought to these areas were apt to be fretful about the military and administrative costs of possessing them and pessimistic about the possibility of holding them long enough to make good these expenditures. The experience of the American Revolution seemed to prove that colonies could not be made to pay and should not therefore be objectives of government policy. As for the other European states, their energies were for the most part absorbed by domestic problems and friction with their immediate neighbors, and the problem of expansion outside of Europe was too remote to arouse much interest.

All of this began to change in the late 1870s, and the 1880s and 1890s were years in which the European powers not only consolidated their existing non-European possessions but sought feverishly to add to them, with little regard for expense or for the political dangers involved. This was a period of imperialism, if we may use a much-abused word—that is, one in which empire-building became the accepted policy of all major powers and was supported by public opinion with a fervor that cut across class and economic lines.

400

How is one to account for the virtually unanimous pursuit of imperialistic policy by the governments of this period and for the enthusiasm with which it was supported even by those groups in society that received the least tangible advantage from it? The answer seems to lie in the economic and political conditions of this period and in its psychological atmosphere.

There is no doubt that economic factors played an important role in the growth of imperialistic activity. The growing maturity of European industry, the increase in productive capacity, and the accumulation of excess capital created groups of people inside all of the big nations who believed in the necessity of finding new markets, new sources of raw materials, and new areas for capital investment. These groups of individuals were inclined to support colonial policies and, insofar as they had political influence, to promote them, as were other people who, directly or indirectly, derived an economic advantage from national colonial enterprise: professional soldiers, shipping magnates, manufacturers of munitions or solar topees or mosquito netting, and the like. The hard times of the 1870s and 1880s helped to intensify their feelings and to persuade other groups to revise their views about the importance of colonies. In 1870, for instance, a delegation of workingmen presented a petition to Queen Victoria in which they argued that Britain's overseas possessions might help to reduce local distress if the government paid for the emigration of the unemployed; and this idea, which recurred frequently in different forms and under different auspices in the years that followed, indicated a growing belief that colonies need not be a liability after all. Finally, the general return to economic nationalism in the form of protectionism, which has been touched upon (p. 265), aroused the fear, especially in countries that remained committed to free trade, that the area in which they could trade profitably would be steadily diminished unless they protected themselves by something like the British concept of "imperial federation"—which called for the creation, out of Britain's existing dependencies, of a great customs union in which British goods would receive preferential treatment—or by acquiring the richest of the remaining free areas of the world before the protectionist powers did.

The fact that such groups of interested parties existed and such ideas and apprehensions filled the minds of a good many people in most countries does not, of course, prove that economic factors "caused" imperialism. To assert, as the British liberal J. A. Hobson did in a famous study that appeared in 1902, that international finance was the directing force in imperialistic foreign policy, manipulating other influential groups through its control of the press and by more direct pressures, was to oversimplify and distort history, as Hobson himself admitted ruefully years later. To argue, as Lenin did in his brilliant essay *Imperialism, The Highest Stage of Capitalism* (1917), that capitalist states must become imperialistic in their policies simply because they are capitalistic was to give a predominance to the economic factor in policy formulation that was impossible to justify on the basis of concrete evidence. As Louis Fischer has pointed out recently, Lenin's thesis was stood on its head by the liberation of colonies by the imperialists through parliamentary decision after 1945 and by the concentration of capital on development at home (see pp. 717, 718, 782).

If one insists upon thinking in terms of pressure groups, it is probably safe to say that missionary societies often played no less an important role than banking interests. One of the strongest determinants of both British and French policy in tropical Africa, for example, was the antislavery movement. This cause was dramatized by the heroic work of Dr. David Livingstone, who walked the bush tracks of Africa for nearly twenty years accumulating evidence of the activities of Arab slavers, and by the devoted work of small mission communities in Nigeria and Nyasaland, which tried, often with arms in hand, to stem the tide of that shameful trade. It was publicized by eminent church leaders like Cardinal Lavigerie of France (see p. 336), founder of the *Société des missions africaines* in 1873 and the *Société anti-esclavagiste* in 1888, and was strongly supported by both Protestant and Catholic congregations, who often insisted on increased colonial responsibilities and could not be lightly disregarded by their governments.

Even when governments used economic arguments to justify their actions in colonial areas, they sometimes did so only because it seemed easier to win support this way than by speaking frankly of the political and strategical reasons for action. One might suppose, from the elaborate British explanations of their occupation of Egypt in 1882, that economic interests had brought them in. It is probably more accurate to say that their intervention was basically the result of the prevalent unrest in a country that lay athwart Britain's line of communication with India. In the case of the extension of British control over Nyasaland, Lord Salisbury, who had strong political reasons for desiring it, deliberately delayed action until he could arouse the interest of British business circles, which he did by inspiring articles in *The Times* about commercial advantage. Far from exercising a controlling influence over the diplomacy of imperialism, business interests often had to be cajoled or—as in the case of some of the German bankers who invested in the Berlin-Baghdad railway scheme—dragooned into supporting government policy.

Indeed, the more closely one studies the imperialism of this period, the more clearly it appears that the statesmen who directed the policies of the Great Powers embarked on imperialism with only an incidental consideration of economic factors. They were influenced much more directly by mutual suspicion and fear of future disaster, feelings that were encouraged by the psychological atmosphere of the years that followed the Franco-Prussian War. In the wake of that conflict, the significance of power had dawned upon the world, and the idea had taken root that great states possessed the respect of their neighbors only when they acted like great states and gave visible evidence of their power resources. Nations that had lost reputation either by military defeat or by inactivity were anxious now to demonstrate that they were not declining powers; and the most dramatic way of doing this was to increase the overseas territory under their control, Once they had embarked on this course they found it easy to convince themselves that failure to expand beyond the European area was the mark of decadence.

This note was struck first of all by Disraeli who, in a famous speech at the Crystal Palace in 1872, cried:

> I appeal to the sublime instinct of an ancient people.... The issue is not a mean one. It is whether you will be content to be a comfortable England, modelled and moulded upon Continental principles and meeting in due

course an inevitable fate, or whether you will be a great country, an imperial country, a country where your sons, when they rise, rise to paramount positions and obtain not merely the esteem of their countrymen but command the respect of the world.

The same argument, presented with an almost equal grandiloquence, was used by John Ruskin in his lectures at Oxford University.

This is what England must do or perish. She must found colonies as fast and as far as she is able, formed of her most energetic and worthiest men, seizing every piece of fruitful waste ground she can set her foot on, and there teaching her colonists that their chief virtue is to be fidelity to their country, and that their first aim is to be to advance the power of England on land and sea.

In 1883, when Sir John Seeley published his enormously popular book *The Expansion of England,* he pointed to the growth of Russia and the United States and warned that, inside of fifty years, they would have completely dwarfed states like France and Germany and would do the same to Great Britain if its people continued to regard it as "simply a European state." A similar argument had already been made in France by Leroy-Beaulieu, who stated that colonial expansion was for his country "a matter of life and death," and that if France did not become a great African power, it was only a question of time before it was depressed to the position of Greece or Rumania. The same thoughts were expressed in Germany, where advocates of colonial activity pleaded for a German place in the sun and where men like Chief of Staff Schlieffen and the influential foreign office counselor, Holstein, were convinced of the necessity of Germany's breaking out of its continental strait jacket and, in 1905, during the Moroccan crisis, actually desired war against France as the first step toward an effective imperial policy (see p. 432).

These fears for the future were shared by most powers, and this increased the speed and the indiscriminateness of the process of acquisition. Doubts might arise from time to time about the advisability of acquiring territories that seemed to have no great strategic or economic importance and promised to be difficult to defend. Was it to the interest of a maritime nation like Great Britain to acquire tracts of territory which stretched thousands of miles into the interior of Africa or Asia? There were reasons to doubt this, yet the spectacle of other powers vying for those very territories was generally enough to set doubts aside. After all, as the Liberal prime minister Lord Rosebery once asked, who could say how valuable these territories might one day become? The world was not elastic. "We have to consider not what we want now, but what we shall want in the future." Moreover, the governments of Europe could not always control their own agents, who were often, in Lord Salisbury's words, "men of energy and strong will, but probably not distinguished by any great restraint over their feelings . . . trying to establish by means which must constantly degenerate into violence the supremacy of that nation for which they were passionately contending."

These words well describe the breed of men who were the trail blazers of imperialism: men like the German explorer Carl Peters, who in the 1880s, while still in his twenties, explored and acquired, by treaty with native chiefs, a domain of 60,000 square miles in East Africa, or like that strange blend of patriot, visionary, and businessman Cecil Rhodes (1853–1902). A clergyman's son, sent to Africa for his health, Rhodes made a fortune in the Kimberley diamond fields. Returning to England, he studied for a time at Oxford, where he heard and was fascinated by Ruskin's lectures. For the rest of his life he strove to "advance the power of England" in Africa. Like Peters, Rhodes not infrequently believed that he knew better than the British government what his country's interests really were, and he was not disinclined to force its hand. Like Peters also, he was not fastidious in the choice of methods to accomplish his objectives. His services to his country were great, but mixed in nature, and he must bear a large share of the responsibility for the Boer War.

The Popularity of Imperialism   Imperialistic policies were strongly supported by public opinion and were as popular among the working classes as they were among those economic groups that stood to profit more directly from

Cecil J. Rhodes with his secretary "Johnny" Grimmer and his Cape boy Tommy in Rhodesia in 1896. (National Archives of Southern Rhodesia)

them. This may suggest that there is truth in the theory, held by Schumpeter and others, that imperialism had an atavistic power that appealed to hidden instincts within all human beings—to lusts for conflict and domination that survived in the blood. More simply, this mass popularity may have been merely the result of the intrusion of something that was exciting and emotionally satisfying into lives that were confined in the drab ugliness of industrial cities and were yet unable to take advantage of such future anodynes as motion pictures, radio, and television. To read or hear about colonial victories at once relieved the tedium of the daily round and made it possible for the individual to share in the victory and the gained prestige by a simple process of identification.

Aside from that, was it really true, as the critics of imperialism claimed, that the working classes had nothing to gain from imperialism and that the money spent on colonial expeditions might better be devoted to social reform at home? The trade unions apparently did not believe so, inclining rather to the view that imperialism would help trade and industry and, by a trickle-down effect, benefit the whole economy and those employed in it. Taking their key from the unions, the revisionist wing of the Socialist party were generally supporters

A letter from Rhodes to the famous explorer Sir Harry Johnston, who, as agent for the South African Company, collaborated with Rhodes in the acquisition of Rhodesia. (National Archives of Southern Rhodesia)

of imperialism. This was true of Bernstein (see p. 283), for instance, who stressed the humanitarian aspects of colonialism—the material improvements brought to native populations—but also admitted that the proletariat, as the future heirs of the bourgeoisie, "have an interest in a rational geographic expansion of the nation." At the meeting of the International at Stuttgart in 1907, Bernstein argued that even Marx had admitted that possession of colonies was of advantage to the European economy and went on to say: "The colonies are there—one ought to occupy them—and I estimate that a certain tutelage of the civilized peoples over the uncivilized is a necessity."

The acknowledged leader of the German Social Democratic party, August Bebel, while criticizing German tactics during the Moroccan crisis of 1905, added: "It goes without saying that the interests of Germany's foreign trade should be protected"; and, during the second Moroccan crisis of 1911, he was actually heard to say that "the greatest guarantee of peace is the spread of international investments."

The discovery that the masses were emotionally susceptible to the appeals of imperialism and capable of being persuaded that imperialism was of economic advantage to them supplied certain governments with one more motive for embarking on imperialistic policies. In nations in which the possibility of socialist revolution was real, the governing class was inclined to look on a dynamic colonial policy as a possibly effective diversionary tactic. The founder of the modern German navy, Grand Admiral Tirpitz, advocated imperialism because he believed that "in this new national undertaking and the economic gains that will accrue from it lies a strong palliative against trained and potential Social Democrats." In Italy the same motive was at work in the launching of the Tripolitanian War in 1911. Official propaganda took the line that Italy was a proletarian nation that deserved its share of the spoils, and the war was described as an undertaking that would bring new land to the peasants of Italy's southern provinces.

This evidence of popular enthusiasm for imperialism and the fact that the sensational press encouraged it by describing the goriest details of colonial wars worried moralists and made them increasingly critical of governmental colonial policies. In 1906 the Center party bitterly attacked German policy in South West Africa because of the brutality and violation of fundamental decencies that had characterized operations against the Herreros. In England, in 1902, G. P. Gooch claimed that imperialism was debasing the moral currency by spreading the belief that ordinary standards of morality did not apply to the expansion of the dominant races, by narrowing the conception of God to that of a tribal God, by increasing international animosity, by exploiting native populations, and by glorifying war. He wrote:

> When we read on the bills, "Boers sabred by moonlight," we are supplied by a novel and striking image, which for a time relieves the monotony of life. The Romans clamored for *panem et circenses*. We have changed our religion and two thousand years have slipped by; but the cry is the same today.

Imperialism was, indeed, open to many of these criticisms, and in the long run it grievously exacerbated suspicion and friction among the Great Powers. But, while the accusations of promoting brutality and exploitation cannot be dismissed, they must be balanced by the memory of the thousands of devoted missionaries and colonial administrators who strove to combat those abuses and to bring good government, education, material improvement, and the benefits of religion to native masses. The sense of mission that drove these men forward has often been made the object of cynical amusement; but, without it and the benefits it brought, the peoples of Africa and Asia would not have been able to rise, as they have in our day, to the position of self-governing nations.

THE COURSE OF IMPERIALISM

Africa   One of the keys to the understanding of the problems of the new African nations of the twentieth century is the briefness of the period which intervened between the end of their isolation from the modern world and their admission to statehood. As late as the 1880s, most of Africa was still uncharted and free from alien penetration. Then, with a rush that is still astonishing to recall, the white men arrived and within twenty years had carved all of Africa

A typical scene during the great age of Imperialism. A palaver between a tribal leader and an agent of the South African Company. (National Archives of Southern Rhodesia)

into dependencies of their home governments. The traumatic effects of the impact of an advanced industrial civilization upon a primitive tribal society are still having repercussions today—as, indeed, are other aspects of African imperialism: for example, the fine disregard that the empire-builders sometimes showed for tribal boundaries when they drew their own.

At the beginning of the 1870s, knowledge of Africa was largely restricted to the northern fringe, which was still, with the exception of French Algeria, nominally part of the Ottoman Empire, and to the tablelands of what is now the Union of South Africa, where the British had holdings and where communities of Dutch farmers (the Boers) were established in the Transvaal. In addition, there were various coastal settlements, particularly in West Africa where the British and French were established in Senegal and on the Niger River, and where there were also small Spanish holdings; in East Africa and its adjacent islands, where Moslem Arabs had trading settlements under the loose sovereignty of the sultan of Muscat; and in Mozambique and Angola, where Portuguese traders had been active for centuries. Of the interior, however, knowledge was scant and imprecise. The British explorer Speke had discovered Lake Victoria in 1858; Baker, another Englishman, had reached Lake Albert in 1864; and Livingstone, in his wanderings, had traced the course of the Zambezi River and the region around Lakes Nyasa and Tanganyika. But no one had yet reached the sources of the Nile; it was only in 1878 that Henry M. Stanley completed his investigation of the Congo River system; and vast areas of the sub-Sahara Africa were simply *terrae incognitae.*

An increase in the tempo of expansion, however, was already discernible in the 1870s. True to the principles enunciated in his Crystal Palace address, Disraeli advanced Britain's position in Africa during his term as prime minister. In Egypt, whose ruler, the Khedive Ismail, was the fourth successor to that Mehemet Ali who engaged our attention earlier (p. 32) and was as profligate as that sovereign had been energetic, Disraeli succeeded in 1875 in purchasing the khedive's Suez Canal Company shares and also began the negotiations that led in 1879 to Anglo-French supervision of Egyptian finances. These steps were indications of the importance of the Egyptian route to India, and they led inevitably to the action taken reluctantly by Gladstone in 1882, when a native movement under Arabi Pasha and with the slogan "Egypt for Egyptians!" revolted against the khedive and seized Alexandria. The British immediately bombarded that port, landed troops under General Wolseley which defeated Arabi Pasha at Tel-el-Kebir and captured Cairo, and imposed upon the khedive a British adviser, whose "advice" concerning necessary reforms was, as it soon became evident, mandatory.

In South Africa, also, Disraeli was active. Here he fought a war with the Zulus in order to stop the incursions of that proud and energetic nation and its gifted ruler Cetewayo (whose downfall is sympathetically commemorated by one of the most popular fiction writers of the age of imperialism, H. Rider Haggard, in his novels *Marie, Child of Storm,* and *Finished* and his historical study *Cetewayo and His White Neighbours*).[1] Disraeli also announced the formal annexa-

[1] It was during the conflict with Cetewayo in 1879 that the prince imperial, Napoleon III's heir, was killed.

tion of the Republic of the Transvaal (1877), but with less success, for the Boers resisted this decision and, four years later, defeated a British force at Majuba Hill so decisively that Gladstone made peace, with a somewhat ambiguous acknowledgment of the Transvaal's independence.

If the steps that Disraeli took had far-reaching consequences, so did one other event of the 1870s. In 1876 King Leopold II of Belgium convoked a conference of the powers to discuss African problems, with particular reference to "means of opening up the interior of the continent to the commerce, industry, and scientific enterprise of the civilized world." All of the major European powers participated; and the conference established an International African Association that would use funds subscribed by its members to promote the exploration and civilization of Africa. This international association was, to be sure, never very effective, but its establishment served as a signal for the outburst of imperialistic energy that followed on the part of all powers.

The pace was set by the king of Belgium, who now financed a series of expeditions by Henry Stanley into the Congo basin where he began to conclude treaties with native chiefs for the exploitation of their territories. Stanley was allegedly acting for the Association, but he was generally regarded as an agent of Leopold, and his successes stimulated the competition of other powers. The French had already been caught by the imperialist fever and under the vigorous leadership of Jules Ferry (see p. 324) had launched an invasion of Tunis in 1881 (see p. 257). Now they became active also on the north bank of the Congo and in the basin of the Ubangi River, the area soon to be known as French Equatorial Africa. The Italians, impressed by the general activity and bitterly offended by the French action in Tunis, where there were many Italian colonists, occupied Assab on the Red Sea coast in 1882 and Massawa in the same area three years later, thus laying the foundations of Italian East Africa. Finally, in 1884, Germany entered the race for territory and within twelve months proclaimed protectorates over South West Africa, Togoland, and the Cameroons and the territories in East Africa where Carl Peters had been negotiating with local chieftains.

As early as 1884, less than ten years after the assembling of Leopold's conference, the competition among the powers had become so intense that it was considered expedient to call an international conference on African problems. This gathering, which met in Berlin from November 1884 to February 1885, had first to adjudicate the tangle of conflicting claims in the Congo basin, where Stanley's treaties were contested by the Portuguese and the British. In the end, the International Association was given title to the greatest part of the Congo Basin on condition that it be organized as a free and neutral state, which allowed free trade and prohibited slavery. Since Leopold II paid the Association's bills, this made him sovereign of one of the richest areas of the world, for he gave little attention to the international character bestowed on the Congo, regarding it as a personal possession and declaring, in 1889, that, when he died, he intended to will it to the kingdom of Belgium.

The Berlin Congress further stimulated European activity in Africa by facilitating trade on the Congo and Niger rivers, by reducing international law as it applied to Africa to the convenient formula that any power could acquire territory by occupying it and notifying its fellow powers, and most of all, perhaps, by giving further publicity to the opportunities that lay within the continent. As a result, the next ten years saw the almost complete division of Africa among the European powers.

Between 1885 and 1894, the British pushed their control of Nigeria into the interior and simultaneously, from the Cape of Good Hope, advanced northward

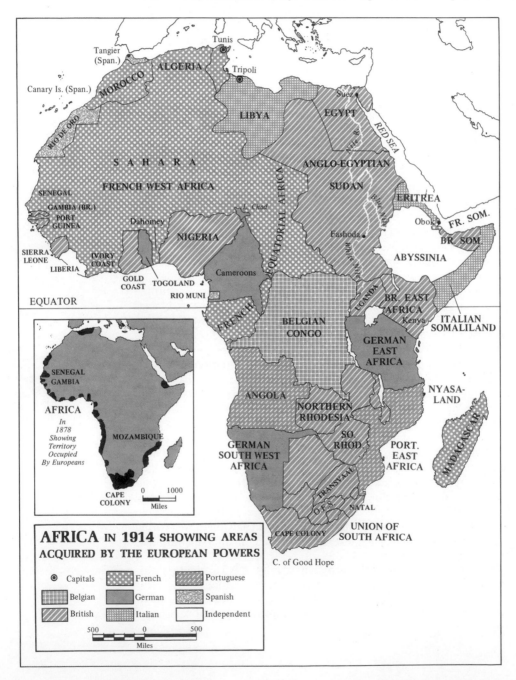

AFRICA IN 1914 SHOWING AREAS
ACQUIRED BY THE EUROPEAN POWERS

- ◉ Capitals
- French
- Portuguese
- Belgian
- German
- Spanish
- British
- Italian
- Independent

over Bechuanaland, Rhodesia, and Nyasaland to the borders of the Congo. In 1890, by treaty with the Caprivi government in Germany, they adjudicated rival claims in East Africa and secured Zanzibar and other territories in return for the cession to Germany of the North Sea island of Helgoland, long coveted by the German navy. Caprivi had no great interest in Africa, being in this respect much like his predecessor Bismarck, who had once complained that the German consul at Zanzibar had written more dispatches and caused more trouble than all the rest of the foreign service combined; but it is indicative of the strength of imperialistic feeling in Germany that the 1890 treaty was bitterly attacked by the press and that Emperor William II soon decided that a more active African policy was necessary.

The hope of the British colonial enthusiasts that their country would one day control a solid strip of territory from the Cape of Good Hope to the mouth of the Nile was, at least momentarily, dashed by the 1890 treaty, which created a common boundary between the Belgian Congo and German East Africa and thus interposed a barrier to further British progress northward. A second obstacle lay in the fact that the British did not control the Sudan. Since the 1880s, that great block of territory, which lay across the headwaters of the Nile, had been in the hands of a native revolutionary army led by a religious prophet who was known as the Mahdi. In 1884, the Gladstone government sent General "Chinese" Gordon, a quixotic and idealistic soldier who had proved in the Far East his knack for winning the confidence of native leaders, into the Sudan to evacuate English garrisons there. Gordon was cut off at Khartoum and, in January 1885, before a relieving column could reach him, was massacred with 11,000 British and Egyptian troops. After that, the region was entirely controlled by the Mahdi, and the British were disinclined to attempt a new push against him. Even so, especially in the minds of soldiers like the future Field Marshal Kitchener and empire-builders like Cecil Rhodes, the hope of an all-red Cape to Cairo route was by no means dead, as the sequel was to show.

Other nations were as energetic as the British. The French pushed up the Ubangi into the region of Lake Chad and simultaneously welded their settlements in Senegal, the Ivory Coast, and Guinea into a great French West African empire, extending as far into the interior as Timbuktu. That fabled town on the upper Niger, which was reputedly founded in the twelfth century, was for three centuries thereafter a center of Moslem culture, and was still an important trading center, visited yearly by great caravans of camels. In 1888, the French founded the town of Djibouti on the Red Sea coast and soon became interested in building rail routes into the independent native kingdom of Abyssinia. If the English direction of expansion was primarily north-south, it was clear by the 1890s that the French was primarily east-west and that they were as interested in the Sudan and the headwaters of the Nile as the English were.

Indeed, by 1894, so much of Africa had been acquired by the European powers that the free and easy rules of the Berlin conference of 1884–1885 were already breaking down. It was no longer possible simply to occupy and notify. The territories that were still not recognized as belonging to one or another of the powers were either subject to conflicting claims (as was true of parts of the Congo) or controlled by native movements that resisted loss of their independence. There had already been many territorial disputes among the powers; and at least three of them had already suffered military setbacks at the hands of nativist movements: the British at Majuba and Khartoum; the Italians, as a result of an ill-conceived sally into Abyssinian politics at Dogali in 1887; and the French in Madagascar, the great island off the southeast coast of Africa, where attempts to subdue the native population proved inadequate and led to a long war which was not completed until 1896. There were to be more serious incidents of this kind in the future.

The Pacific and Asia   Collecting Pacific islands became as favored an occupation of the powers as annexing African colonies. The initiative was taken, as in Africa, sometimes by traders or missionaries and sometimes by governments themselves, for the islands often had more value as coaling stations and strategical strongpoints than as trading posts, as the course of World War II was to show. Of the powers that had Pacific possessions during the first part of the century, Great Britain, Holland, and France showed that their appetites were still good, but Spain showed so little energy that by the end of the century she had lost all of her holdings. The most active of the newcomers were Germany and the United States.

With a sound strategical sense, the British were primarily interested in those areas that were the natural approaches to Australia: New Guinea on the one hand and the Solomon Islands on the other; and they were also interested in the naval possibilities of the Fijis. The acquisition of the latter group of islands was one of Disraeli's first imperialistic coups. New Guinea, on the other hand, proved to be attractive to the Dutch, who wished to add it to their already extensive possessions in Borneo and the Celebes and Molucca islands, as well as to the Germans, who were aggressive competitors of the British all over the southwest Pacific. In 1885 this big island was subjected to a three-way partition: Holland getting the western half; Britain, the territory of Papua in the southeastern corner, which faces Cape York, Australia, across the Torres Strait; and Germany getting the northeastern coast. The Solomons and the Gilberts were taken over by the British somewhat later, as was Sarawak in Northern Borneo, where the British had had settlements since the early 1880s.

French imperialism in the Pacific had begun with Ferry's annexation of Tahiti in 1880, and in subsequent years France occupied the Society Islands, the Marquesas, and the Tuamotu Archipelago. French gains were, however, more spectacular on the Asian mainland. The reverse was true in Germany's case. In addition to her share of New Guinea, Germany acquired the Bismarck Archipelago, which included the islands of New Ireland and New Britain (whose port Rabaul was, as a Japanese base in 1943, to be pounded to helplessness by American planes operating from the Solomons), the Marshall Islands, and later, by purchase from Spain, the Carolines and the Marianas, including Guam, Saipan, and Tinian. Finally, after a dangerous dispute with the United States, Germany divided the Samoan Islands with that power.

These German purchases were largely the result of the disastrous defeat of Spain in 1898 in the war with the United States that resulted from its troubles in Cuba. That defeat was followed also by the annexation by the United States

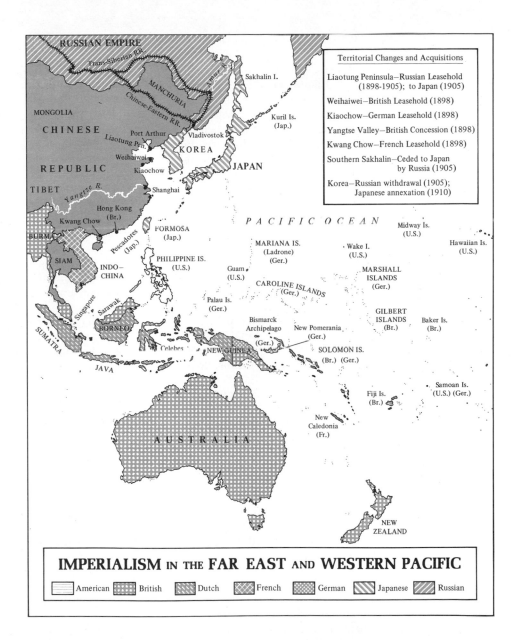

Territorial Changes and Acquisitions

Liaotung Peninsula—Russian Leasehold
(1898-1905); to Japan (1905)

Weihaiwei—British Leasehold (1898)

Kiaochow—German Leasehold (1898)

Yangtse Valley—British Concession (1898)

Kwang Chow—French Leasehold (1898)

Southern Sakhalin—Ceded to Japan
by Russia (1905)

Korea—Russian withdrawal (1905);
Japanese annexation (1910)

IMPERIALISM IN THE FAR EAST AND WESTERN PACIFIC

American   British   Dutch   French   German   Japanese   Russian

of the Philippine Islands. The earlier acquisition of the Hawaiian Islands had already made the United States a Pacific power; this now confirmed it, bringing the once-isolated American nation into the very heart of Asian politics.

The progress of European imperialism on the mainland of Asia was as impetuous and as competitive as it was among the islands, but the stakes were higher and the dangers greater. British policy, for instance, was determined to a large extent by the desire to protect India from possible assault by other powers, notably by Russia, whose swift advances in Turkestan and Baluchistan in the

1860s (see p. 230) aroused fears for the security of India's northwest frontier. The tightening up of India's administrative and military services during Disraeli's government and the passage of the Royal Titles Act of 1876, by which Queen Victoria received the resounding title Empress of India, were partly caused by these apprehensions, although the Titles Act appealed also to Disraeli's romantic nature and his taste for Oriental splendor. A more direct reaction to the fear of Russia was Disraeli's attempt to form a protective *glacis* in front of the supposedly menaced frontier, which he sought to do by using force to impose a protectorate upon the reluctant emir of Afghanistan in 1879. This led to a series of Afghan wars and to a serious crisis in 1884 when Russian horsemen appeared in the Pamirs and on the ridge of Hindukush and, in March 1885, occupied the oasis of Pendjeh, near the pass that leads into the plateau of Afghanistan. Momentarily, an Anglo-Russian war seemed possible, but it was staved off by negotiations, which left Pendjeh in Russian hands while setting a momentary limit to their forward progress. Anglo-Russian rivalry for predominance in Afghan affairs was to continue, however, until 1907 and after (see p. 434).

To the east of India, British expansion was dictated by French advances in what is now Indochina. The French gains in Tonkin and Annam, as a result of their war with China in 1884–1885 (see p. 326), their penetration into what is now Laos, and the consolidation of their control of Cambodia and Cochin-China, where they had been established since the 1860s, were countered by a steady British advance into Burma. Between these two growing blocks of European territory lay the independent kingdom of Siam; and in 1893, the French seemed bent on forcing this state into a subordinate position, actually sending naval units to Bangkok to force concessions along the Mekong River. The British reacted strongly, and the French, while insisting on Siamese recognition of their protectorate over Laos, decided against pushing further. Three years later, an Anglo-French agreement defined the disposition of certain petty principalities on the upper Mekong, drew a common boundary between Burma and Tonkin in that area, and stipulated that nonintervention would be the rule in the valley of the Menam River to the south and in Siamese affairs generally. Simultaneously, British advances north from Singapore to the federated Malay states were halted and the southern boundary of Siam defined.

While these events were taking place, the second stage of Europe's penetration of the sprawling, disorganized, but enormously rich empire of China got under way. During the years between 1830 and 1860, Great Britain had taken the lead in breaking the isolation of China, waging two wars against the imperial government in 1839–1841 and 1857–1858, and forcing the Chinese to pay for defeat by opening their coastal ports to European traders and ceding Hong Kong and part of the Kowloon peninsula to the British crown. In the same years, the Russians had advanced over the Amur River to the Pacific Coast and persuaded the Chinese government in 1860 to cede them the territory that became Russia's maritime province, with its ice-free port of Vladivostok.

For the next thirty years, complications in Europe and the Near East absorbed too much of the attention of the Great Powers to encourage new advances at the expense of China. This period of quiescence came to an end in the mid-

1890s, and the powers that took the initiative in the new wave of imperialism were Russia and Japan.

Until the middle of the nineteenth century, the islands of Japan had been as isolated from the influences of the Western world as the interior of Africa, although their level of culture was infinitely higher. The arrival in Japanese waters of an American fleet under the command of Commodore Perry in 1853 and the subsequent opening of Japanese ports to American ships and traders a year later marked the beginning of Japanese relations with and emulation of the countries of the Western world. Within twenty years the feudal structure of the state had been smashed, a political and social transformation of the country had taken place, and there had been widespread adoption of European institutions. The progress made in this respect was remarkable. Japan was soon endowed with such modern advantages as railroads, public education, modern health standards, popular newspapers, the European calendar, codes of law and judicial procedure, and, in 1889, a constitution modeled on Western charters of liberties and providing for a bicameral legislature. Unfortunately, Japan also copied some less estimable European practices, chief among which were militarism and imperialism. No nation was more profoundly impressed by the Prussian successes of 1866 and 1870 than Japan or quicker to copy the Prussian system of universal military service, the Prussian staff system, and the Prussian tactical organization. The establishment of a modern army was balanced by the development of a modern navy, during whose rapid growth expert British and American aid was solicited.

Imperialism became a prevalent ideology in Japan, perhaps less because it was fashionable in the West (although the writings of Western empire-builders did not go unnoticed in Tokyo) than because Japan was a small country with a very large population. Territorial expansion seemed not only desirable but necessary to Japanese leaders, and this could be effected only on the mainland. The closest desirable area was Korea, a country ridden with factionalism and internal disorder, in which both China and Japan claimed rights of political overlordship.

In 1893 an explosion of internal unrest in Korea prompted a joint Sino-Japanese intervention that degenerated into an interallied conflict and, finally, into a war. In this conflict the Chinese army acted, as the British statesman Curzon said scornfully, "like an undisciplined rabble of tramps." The Japanese invaded Manchuria and the Liaotung peninsula, stormed Port Arthur, captured Weihaiwei, smashed the Chinese fleet in the battle of the Yalu River, and threatened to advance on their capital of Peking. Utterly demoralized, the Chinese surrendered. The terms included a large war indemnity, the cession to Japan of the islands of Formosa and the Pescadores and the Liaotung peninsula, with its strongpoint Port Arthur, and the acknowledgment of the independence of Korea (which was tantamount to opening it to Japanese domination).

It was these terms that brought Russia into the picture and, by doing so, opened the second phase of European imperialism in China. In official circles in St. Petersburg there had always been a school of thought that, in contrast to the Pan-Slavs, felt that Russia's true interest lay in expansion in the Far East. In the 1890s this group was represented by such influential advisers of Nicholas

II as War Minister Kuropatkin and Admiral Alekseev. These men could not be expected to view with equanimity Japan's winning a preponderance in Korea, which was dangerously near Russia's base at Vladivostok, or securing a foothold on the Liaotung peninsula, which would open the way into the province of Manchuria. In 1891, the Russians had begun to construct a trans-Siberian railroad to Vladivostok, and they hoped to persuade the Chinese to grant them permission to cross Manchurian territory, if not to cede the province to them entirely. This would be impossible once Japan was established there.

The Russian government decided, then, to intervene in the negotiations between China and Japan, with a view to reducing Japanese terms. With the backing of their new ally France[2] and of Germany, they insisted that the cession of the Liaotung peninsula to Japan would perpetually menace the peace of China while rendering illusory Korean independence and that it must be set aside. The Japanese, with suppressed indignation, complied.

All of the powers that had intervened now claimed their reward from China, Russia leading the way. By an elaborate series of cessions and financial arrangements in 1895–1896, Russia received the right to build railway lines not only across northern Manchuria to Vladivostok but also from Harbin, on the spur, south into that very Liaotung peninsula from which the Japanese had just been ousted, with the additional privilege of patrolling such lines with troops of its own. In return for underwriting the Chinese war indemnity, the Russians also received supervisory powers with respect to Chinese finances and the right to establish a commission house, the Russo-Chinese Bank, which gave them a preferred position in the economic development of Manchuria.

France was compensated by permission to run a rail line northward from Annam into China and by the cession of valuable mining concessions in the provinces of Yunnan, Kwangsi, and Kwantung. Germany's compensation was delayed, but the murder of two missionaries in Shantung province in 1897 gave William II a pretext for sending naval units into Chinese waters, a show of force that persuaded the Chinese government to grant his subsequent demand for a ninety-nine-year lease of the harbor of Kiaochow and a virtual protectorate over the entire Shantung peninsula. This, in turn, persuaded the Russians to take another step forward, which they did in March 1898, by pressuring the Chinese into leasing Port Arthur to them for a period of twenty-five years. This completed the Russian stranglehold over Manchuria while at the same time placing Korea between Russian pincers at Port Arthur and Vladivostok.

The rapid growth of Russian influence infuriated the Japanese and increased their desire to protect their own interests in Korea before it was too late. It alarmed the British, who saw the Russians encroaching steadily upon what they had considered their own preserve. British apprehension was in no wise relieved by the fact that they themselves were permitted to lease the port of Weihaiwei in 1898. Russian expansion also prompted the United States government to try to defend the fast-weakening independence and integrity of the Chinese Empire by circulating to the powers the so-called Open Door Note, which asked them to admit that they possessed no exclusive rights, economic or other, in the areas

[2] On the Franco-Russian alliance, see page 427.

in which their influence was predominant—a note that was, incidentally, answered evasively by the Russians. And, finally, it stimulated a rising tide of patriotism among Chinese intellectuals, who saw their country being split up into spheres of foreign influence and felt that this process must be resisted by force. In short, everything was shaping up for a major explosion of one kind or another in China as the century reached its close.

The Near East   A word should be said, finally, of imperialism in the Near East, with particular reference to Germany's attempt to secure a predominant economic position in the Turkish Empire and adjoining areas.

Ever since the 1850s and 1860s, German missionaries and teachers had been active in Anatolia and Mesopotamia; and since the 1870s, German banking and commercial interests had also had agents within the Turkish empire. All of these people were impressed by the wealth of Turkey, and some of them were doing their best to tap it. The Deutsche Bank and the Württembergische Vereinsbank of Stuttgart were extending loans to the sultan in the 1880s, and, in the same decade, a syndicate was formed by the Siemens banking group to construct railroads for the more efficient exploitation of the area. This group envisioned the possible linkage of these roads to the Austro-German system across the Bosphorus, so that eventually something in the nature of a Berlin-Constantinople-Baghdad system could be established, with branches running to Aleppo, Damascus, Smyrna, and eventually to Persia, Arabia, and Egypt.

It was not originally believed that this penetration should be exclusively German, and the railroad planners seemed to have hoped to invite the bankers of other countries to participate in their scheme. But all of this changed when William II threw off the restraints of his first chancellors and became an avowed imperialist. In 1898 the emperor paid a visit to the sultan in Constantinople. There he made several speeches which indicated that he believed Germany particularly suited to take the Moslem peoples under its protection. In the period that followed, the government urged German bankers to go on with their railroad planning but to drop their ideas of an international consortium. William, indeed, took to referring to the projected system as "my railroad," and one of his advisers was reported to have said, "With a bow to the British lion and a curtsey to the Russian bear, we will worm our way, little by little, down to the Persian Gulf."

To the British and the Russians, who were rivals for a preferred position in Persia, such avowed intentions were disturbing. So was the rapidity with which the Germans, under government direction, ingratiated themselves with the Turkish government and won a commanding position in Turkish finance, economic life, and even in the development and training of the Turkish military establishment. This concern on the part of the other powers was not without significance. German imperialism in the Near East had profound effects on the diplomatic alignments of Europe.

THE CLIMAX OF IMPERIALISM

European Defeats: Spain   Between 1895 and 1905 enthusiasm for imperialistic expansion reached its climax and began its decline. As the tide of expansion swept forward, it had become increasingly competitive; the clashes among the rival Great Powers had become more frequent and more dangerous; and the imperialistic governments had become incautious and inclined to overreach themselves. Now, within a period of ten years, there came a series of sharp crises, and the European nations that had succumbed to the imperialistic fever suffered setbacks that had sobering effects upon public opinion. Mention has been made above of what happened to Spain 1898—a rather special case, it must be admitted, for Spain's troubles were caused not by policies inaugurated since the 1870s but rather by its inability to give efficient administration to possessions inherited from a more remote past. Even so, the desperate losses inflicted on Spanish garrisons in both Cuba and the Philippines by native insurrectionary movements and the eventual loss of these territories as a result of the war with the United States were hardly designed to support any enthusiasm for imperialism among the Spanish people, as the subsequent liquidation of what was left of Spain's Pacific island empire soon showed. And Spain was not alone in suffering this experience; for similar shocks came to Italy, France, Great Britain, Russia, and Germany.

The Italian Defeat at Adowa   The man who dominated Italian politics for the ten years following 1887 was Francesco Crispi, who set his heart upon avenging the Italian defeat at Dogali in Abyssinia in that year. From the beginning of his period of office, he dabbled in the confused politics of the Abyssinian empire and, when the Negus John was killed by dervishes in 1889, he gave his backing to the successful claimant to the throne, a tribal chieftain called Menelik of Shoa, who had the distinction of having once employed the French poet Rimbaud as a gun runner. The Italians persuaded Menelik to sign the Treaty of Uccialli as a reward for their support, and Crispi subsequently claimed that it gave Italy a protectorate over Abyssinia. He ordered Italian troops to occupy territories inland from Massawa and, in 1890, proclaimed a new Italian Red Sea colony called Eritrea.

Neither Menelik, who soon rejected the Italian interpretation of the treaty, nor the coastal chiefs were willing to tolerate these Italian pretensions. The years 1893–1895 were filled with skirmishes between Italian units and local bands and negotiations between Menelik and the dervishes of the Sudan, who had been aroused by Italian incursions into their domain. On his side, Crispi seems to have concluded that the time had come to conquer all of Ethiopia, and he neither listened to the warnings of his soldiers nor heeded their requests for more men, ammunition, and supplies. When they hesitated to advance into the interior, he accused them of insubordination and cowardice. His irrational behavior finally produced a debacle.

In March 1896, General Baratieri, goaded beyond endurance by Crispi's taunts, marched with four columns of troops, totaling six thousand men, from his base at Massawa into the interior, seeking conquest and glory. The march was badly planned, without proper communications, supplies, or intelligence of the enemy, and with no clear objectives. At a place called Adowa the Italians were surrounded by a much superior force of Abyssinians and dervishes and were literally cut to ribbons, the few survivors being led away into slavery. Thus, Italian imperialism in East Africa came to a shocking denouement with the loss in one day of more men than had died in the wars of 1859 and 1860.

The Anglo-French Showdown   Adowa produced a kind of chain reaction. The Italian defeat left a raging and exultant army of dervishes and Abyssinians in the Sudan, the existence of which seemed infinitely more menacing to the British in Egypt than anything since the' death of General Gordon in 1885. In any event, the Salisbury government resolved to remove this threat, and Sir Herbert Kitchener was ordered to proceed up the Nile with an Anglo-Egyptian force of 20,000 men to smash the dervish power. In a fierce action at the confluence of the Nile and the Atbara, Kitchener destroyed one dervish army and proceeded toward the dervish capital at Khartoum, 200 miles to the south. Before starting, his forces were joined by the 21st Lancers, among whom was a young sublieutenant named Winston Churchill, who later described the march south, the halt at Omdurman where the Mahdi's tomb was located, and the decisive defeat of the dervish army, 60,000 strong, by the crack British units.

Winston Churchill as a lieutenant in the 21st Lancers, shortly after the battle of Omdurman.

The result was not surprising. As the successors of the Saracens descended the long smooth slopes which led to the river and their enemy, they encountered the rifle fire of two and a half divisions of trained infantry, drawn up two deep and in close order and supported by at least 70 guns on the river bank and in the gun boats, all firing with undisturbed efficiency. Under this fire the whole attack withered.

So did a second desperate dervish assault.

Discipline and machinery triumphed over the most desperate valour, and after an enormous carnage, certainly exceeding 20,000 men, who strewed the ground in heaps and swathes "like snowdrifts," the whole mass of the Dervishes dissolved into fragments and into particles and streamed away into the fantastic mirages of the desert.

The British were now, for the first time, able to proceed without fear of native attack toward the headwaters of the Nile. But that objective was one shared with the French, still resentful of the British occupation of Egypt and hopeful that, if they could secure possession of Nilotic Sudan, they might be able to compel their rivals to reopen the Egyptian question. Long before Kitchener had received his orders to liquidate the dervish problem, the French government had ordered an expedition under Captain Marchand to proceed from the French Congo to the upper Nile and another, under Captain Clochette, to march from East Africa and join him there. Clochette died en route and his expedition turned back, but Marchand, with 150 men, reached the Nile and planted the French flag at Fashoda in late September 1898. A few days later Kitchener's victorious columns arrived from the north; and their commander, politely but firmly, requested immediate French evacuation from what was, he claimed, an acknowledged British sphere of influence.

The French had no real alternative to surrender, and this was recognized by their new foreign minister, Théophile Delcassé, a realist who saw that a conflict with Great Britain would serve no useful purpose except to gratify the Germans. He was, Delcassé confessed, "too much of a Gambettist to forget the wound of Strasbourg under the scratch of Fashoda." Even so, Marchand's enforced withdrawal, with its implied recognition of British claims that the French had contested since 1882, was a humiliation. It was bitterly resented in Paris, where anti-British feeling was undiminished in intensity for the next five years.

The Boer War   The Fashoda affair left the British in a bumptious and exalted mood, and, a year later, this led them into difficulties in South Africa that proved, in the end, to be more humiliating than the French experience. To explain the incident, one must recall Britain's attempt to assert control over the Boers in the Transvaal in 1877 and its setback at Majuba Hill. That earlier conflict had been terminated by an agreement that, as was intimated earlier, was ambiguous in wording and meaning, being interpreted by the Boers as a grant of independence but by the British as an understanding that the Transvaal was part of the British empire and subject to British supervision in foreign and other affairs.

"An Attempt at House-breaking." A French view of the British government's responsiblity for the Jameson Raid. The larger figure represents Joseph Chamberlain, Britain's Colonial Secretary at the time of the raid. From *Le Rire,* Paris.

In the late 1880s, gold was discovered in the Transvaal, and it was soon apparent that the deposits were among the richest in the world. The discovery led to a tremendous incursion of foreigners, especially Englishmen from the Cape, and these foreigners, or *Uitlanders,* as the Boers called them, soon outnumbered the Boers themselves. The Boer government, which was led by an energetic and imperious statesman called Paul Kruger, felt compelled to impose political disabilities upon the latecomers, lest they dominate local politics. Simultaneously, they sought to escape economic and financial control by the Cape Colony, which owned all rail outlets from the Transvaal, by constructing railroads of their own to Lorenzo Marques in Portuguese Mozambique and by giving valuable economic concessions to the traders of other European nations, notably Germany.

This was galling to Cape politicians and especially to Cecil Rhodes. To him and others the behavior of the Boer government seemed provocative and its treatment of British subjects in the Transvaal intolerable; and they resolved on reprisals. These took the form of a romantic but badly conceived enterprise led by a Dr. Leander Starr Jameson, who invaded the Transvaal in 1895 with a small band of adventurers based on Bechuanaland. They were quickly surrounded and captured by a superior force of Boer troops.

This affair, promptly disavowed by the British government, caused a world-wide sensation and elicited a personal telegram of encouragement to the Boer government from Emperor William II of Germany. The emperor's message, with its implication that the Transvaal was an independent state with the right to call on other powers for support, was greatly resented in Great Britain, but it confirmed the Boers in their discriminatory policy with respect to the *Uitlanders*. This led to British claims that Kruger was intent on expelling the British from South Africa entirely and establishing a great Boer state. In negotiations in 1899, the British demanded that the grievances of their subjects be satisfied and that the right of suffrage be accorded them. The Boers refused and, after further inconclusive talks and a number of incidents, war broke out in October 1899 between the British on the one hand and the Transvaal and their sister republic, the Orange Free State, on the other.

It was a conflict in which the British won no reputation and which led the British poet Kipling to write later:

> Let us admit it fairly as a business people should.
> We have had no end of a lesson, it will do us no
>   end of good.

To defeat the sixty thousand men whom the Boers put into the field, the British had to employ 350,000 and to fight until 1902, suffering heavy casualties and heavier monetary expenditures. In the end, they were successful and were wise enough to put their victory to good use—treating the defeated with leniency, granting extensive measures of self-government to the Boer governments, and, thus, making possible the act of September 1909 that combined the Transvaal, the Orange Free State, Natal province, and the Cape province into the South African Union. But, in the course of all this, a good many illusions had been dissipated, and the popularity of imperialism in Great Britain had been dimmed.

The Russo-Japanese War   Before the end of the South Africa war, the long-accumulating tension in the Far East exploded into violence. Resentment against European encroachments had led to the growth of certain nationalist societies in China, which came to be known as the Boxers (from their adopted name, which was loosely translated as the Righteous Harmonious Fists). The Boxers were dedicated to the expulsion of foreigners from China and, in the spring and summer of 1900, they inaugurated a program of terrorism directed against European missionaries and their Chinese converts and members of the consulate staffs and trading communities. Scores of Europeans were killed, and the legations at Peking were besieged for two months before a relief expedition of Japanese, Russian, German, French, British, and American troops arrived and restored peace.

During the course of the Boxer Rebellion, thousands of Russian troops had poured into Manchuria, and in the period that followed they showed a stubborn reluctance to leave. Expostulations by the Chinese government were met by evasions that seemed to indicate Russia was intent on transforming Manchuria into another Bokhara, a course that General Kuropatkin had recommended to

The intervention of the powers during the Boxer Rebellion, by the famous French caricaturist, Caran d'Ache. From *Figaro*, Paris.

the tsar as being desirable. This prospect not only worried the Chinese but was also a matter of concern to Great Britain and Japan.

Because of African complications, the British were in no position to take decisive action against Russia in the Far East, but they did wish at least to persuade the Russians (and Russia's ally, France) that any incursions into the British sphere of influence would be resisted. They sought to do this by a diplomatic gesture. In 1902, after a series of involved negotiations, they concluded an alliance with Japan, providing for mutual aid in the event that either partner became involved in a war with two other powers. Significant because it represented a break with Britain's long tradition of freedom from alliances in peacetime, the agreement had a more fateful consequence in Far Eastern politics. It gave the Japanese reasonable assurance that if they went to war against Russia, they would be protected from the intervention of other powers; and this encouraged them to insist that Russia recognize the integrity of China by evacuating Manchuria. Throughout 1903, the request was made repeatedly and as repeatedly declined by the Russians. But the Japanese were, meanwhile, making military preparations and, when these were ready, they struck.

On the night of February 8, 1904, Japanese torpedo boats sank part of the Russian Far Eastern squadron in the harbor of Port Arthur; on the following morning Japanese armies invaded Korea and the Liaotung peninsula. The Russian army, riddled with personal jealousies on the command level and with disaffection among the troops, was in no way prepared for a war against well-equipped and inspired forces. It was rolled back and badly beaten in a series of battles

Naval action at Port Arthur, April 1904. A Japanese impression. (Peabody Museum, Salem, Massachusetts)

around Mukden, in which more troops were engaged and heavier casualties suffered than in any fighting since the Franco-Prussian War. By the beginning of 1905, the Russian armies had been expelled from Manchuria, their fleet had been rendered ineffective, and Port Arthur, after a long siege, had been forced to surrender. A desperate attempt by the Russians to relieve that base by sending another fleet to the Far East failed disastrously; after painfully making its way from Reval around Europe, Africa, and Southeast Asia, this force of superannuated ships, commanded by Admiral Rozhdestvensky, was annihilated by Admiral Togo in a brilliant sea fight in the straits of Tsushima in May 1905.

Tsushima marked an inglorious end to tsarist Russia's imperialistic career in the Far East. In the peace negotiations, held under the good offices of President Theodore Roosevelt of the United States, Russia ceded her lease of Port Arthur and the Liaotung peninsula to Japan, agreed to the evacuation of Manchuria, and admitted the primacy of Japanese influence in Korea.

The Return to Europe   Germany did not experience anything like the stunning setbacks suffered by Great Britain and Russia in these climactic years of European imperialism, but she was far from unscathed, as was demonstrated by her unsuccessful attempt to compete with France in Moroccan affairs in 1905 (see pp. 431–433). Apart from that, the bullying tactics and the not infrequent attempts to blackmail other powers into colonial concessions that had been characteristic of William II's policy in Africa and the Far East aroused the indignation of the other powers and influenced their future diplomatic conduct, to Germany's disadvantage. William II's telegram of encouragement to President Kruger of the Transvaal at the time of the Jameson raid was never wholly forgiven by the British; and German gains in the Near East were resented by the Russians, the more so because they were accomplished while Russia's energies were being fruitlessly expended in the Far East.

By 1905, the great age of imperialism was over. Vast tracts of the world's surface and millions of new subjects had been acquired by the European powers during the years since Disraeli had made his ringing challenge at the Crystal Palace. There were few more great acquisitions to be made. The colonial powers were now to learn how onerous the burdens of empire could be, how hard it was to hold the territories won, and (this was a post-World War II discovery) how many difficulties arose when the decision was made to let them go.

But these discoveries lay in the future. In 1905 the European governments had more immediate problems. During the years of imperialism, and partly because of events in the colonial areas, the great European security system created by Bismarck had broken down, and the balance of power had become so precarious that any diplomatic incident was capable of touching off a major conflagration. Unfortunately for Europe and the world, there was no dearth of such incidents.

Chapter 19 INTERNATIONAL POLITICS AND THE COMING OF WAR, 1890–1914

THE DIPLOMATIC REVOLUTION, 1890–1907

The Franco-Russian Alliance   The fragility of the European balance alluded to at the end of the last chapter was the result of a diplomatic revolution which freed France from the isolation that Bismarck had managed to impose on it and divided the European states into two great coalitions.

This revolution had its origins in Bismarck's dismissal in 1890 and in the dramatic decision of the German government in that same year to repudiate a basic feature of his diplomatic system: the close tie with Russia that had been maintained, except for brief intervals, since 1813, and had been most recently confirmed by the Reinsurance Treaty of June 1887. In 1890, the Russians were told that that treaty could not be renewed.

As in the case of many of the diplomatic decisions of post-Bismarckian German governments, the motives for this move were mixed. The emperor and his new chancellor and foreign minister, Caprivi and Marschall, neither of whom had experience in foreign affairs, were genuinely concerned about the complexity of Bismarck's diplomatic system, desired to clarify Germany's commitments, and wanted to eliminate the apparent incompatibility between their treaty obligations to Austria-Hungary and to Russia. At the same time, 1890 was the high-tide of Anglo-German cooperation—the Zanzibar-Helgoland exchange was effected in July 1890 (see p. 411)—and there were people in the German Foreign Office who felt that the exchange and the future benefits it might bring would be seriously jeopardized if the British government, which was firmly anti-Russian in its views, should learn about the Reinsurance Treaty. Personal motives were doubtless also a part of the decision. The emperor and Baron Holstein, the most influential of the Foreign Office counselors, were clearly anxious to demonstrate their independence from Bismarckian ideas by striking out on a new course. Finally, Holstein's views were influenced by his strong antipathy to Russia and his intimacy with those army circles that had desired war with that country in 1887.

The Russian government was shocked by the German decision and did its best to persuade the Caprivi government to change its mind. When it failed, it took the logical course and turned toward France. The Germans had made the mistake of believing that absolutism and republicanism were irreconcilable; the absolutists and republicans now disproved this. In the summer of 1891, the French and Russian governments exchanged notes in which they decided upon mutual consultation in the event of a threat to the peace and the concerting of measures to deal with it. A year later, upon French insistence, this agreement was supplemented by a military convention that called for common mobilization in the event that either party became involved in a war with a member of the Triple Alliance and mutual aid in the event that either was attacked by Germany. The explosion of the Panama affair in France (see p. 331) delayed ratification of these engagements by strengthening the hand of conservative anti-French circles in Russia. After another year had passed, however, the Russians took up the negotiations again; a Russian naval squadron paid a ceremonial visit to the French port of Toulon, returning an earlier French naval visit to Kronstadt; and, on January 4, 1894, the ratifications were finally completed, and France and Russia became allies.

The alliance was not, of course, necessarily final. In both Germany and Russia there were important groups who believed that the tie between their two countries must be restored. It is probably safe to say that the break was not regarded as definitive until later, after the Germanophils in Russia had been alienated by the exclusive German tariffs against Russian grain (see p. 386), the incursions in the neighborhood of the Persian Gulf (see p. 417), and the ultimatum of 1909 (see p. 440). It is nevertheless significant that, as early as 1892, one important agency seemed to conclude that the Franco-Russian tie was permanent. German war plans had always been based on the assumption that if a major war came, it would probably become a two-front war but that Germany would strike first toward the east. When Count Schlieffen became chief of the German General Staff in 1892, he reversed the order of attack in the German war plans, on the apparent assumption that France was now so closely tied to Russia that any war in eastern Europe must involve France too and must begin with its elimination. To German soldiers after 1892, the Franco-Russian alliance was a fact of life, and their plans to deal with it threatened to turn even minor skirmishes between powers into a major European war.

The End of British Isolation   As we have seen, one of Germany's reasons for abandoning the Reinsurance Treaty had been the desire to avoid weakening what appeared to be a promising Anglo-German entente. In both countries there were influential people who regarded England and Germany as natural allies.

This was the belief of Lord Salisbury, the Conservative prime minister (a realist who saw the advantages of having a continental supporter to deflect French ambitions from Egypt); it was an article of faith of Joseph Chamberlain, and continued to be as long as he lived; and it exercised so powerful an attraction upon Cecil Rhodes that when he set up the Rhodes scholarships, he made it clear that they would be devoted to the idea of training young men in the British colonies, the United States, and Germany to carry on this natural alliance. On the German side, the desire to collaborate with the British was equally strong in many parts of society—some of which are well described in one of Fontane's finest novels, *Der Stechlin*—and in the government and the court. But the German attitude toward Britain was always ambivalent. William II, for instance, who had an English mother and an English grandmother (Queen Victoria), admired the British and was proud to have his portrait painted in the uniform of a British admiral; but, at the same time, he suffered from what appeared to be an uncontrollable inferiority complex that made him want to "show them" that Germany was in no way inferior to them. The emperor's equivocal attitude was reflected in German foreign policy in general and had unfortunate results.

Paul Hatzfeldt, the German ambassador in London in the 1890s, tried to convince his Foreign Ministry that if it was truly the desire of the German government to have a working entente with the British, this would require a certain regard for British interests and desires wherever the two countries came into contact. This was a lesson that the German government never seemed to take to heart. While continuing to profess a desire to convert the British from an associate to an actual member of the Triple Alliance, the German government, in colonial affairs, seemed to believe that it could win territory by a not very subtle policy of blackmail. The British, long accustomed to finding the French in their way, began to discover in the 1890s that, whenever they hoped to extend their possessions in Africa or the Pacific, the Germans were likely to appear and demand compensation. After one such abrupt intervention in 1894, Lord Salisbury commented coldly that the Germans had used language in communicating with Her Majesty's government that they "might properly have used in addressing the State of Monaco," adding that he considered this attitude insufferable.

The gratuitous German intervention into South African affairs at the time of the Jameson raid (see p. 422) was even more impolitic. It appears to have been the result of one of those "incessant hysterical vacillations of William II" that Hatzfeldt predicted in 1901 would destroy Germany; its rationale was murky and its expected results unclear; and it succeeded only in infuriating the British. So did German policy during the Boer War. Their expressions of sympathy with the embattled Boers were so cordial that there seemed reason for Whitehall to believe that the Germans might actually be contemplating some form of intervention. The simultaneous launching of the Baghdad railway scheme was also annoying to London, where the feeling was beginning to grow that Germany was bent on opposing British interests in every part of the globe.

By all odds the most alarming German action and the one most calculated to make a working agreement with the British impossible was the decision to build a battle fleet. In 1896, in a speech delivered before the Colonial Society, William II announced that "the future of Germany [was] on the sea." By laws of April 1898 and June 1900, the government began a program of accelerated construction. Grand Admiral Tirpitz, the moving spirit behind the program, stated that it was necessary to create "a fleet capable of action between Helgoland and the English coast" and made it known that his objective was an armored fleet perhaps two thirds the size of the British fleet and certainly so large that its very existence would, in wartime, make British attempts to destroy it potentially too costly to risk.

There was, of course, no reason why Germany should not build a fleet if it wished to do so. It was unreasonable, however, for the power with the greatest land army in Europe to begin serious competition with Britain on the seas and still, at the same time, to expect Britain to conclude some form of alliance with it. But men like Holstein seem to have believed that Britain was a declining power (and that this was proved by the performance of its troops in the Boer War), that it was confronted with a real possibility of a war with Russia, that it needed allies more than it ever had in its long existence, that its only possible alliance was with Germany, and that if Germany kept the pressure up, it would be willing to pay dearly for an agreement. This explains why British feelers for an alliance, made by Joseph Chamberlain and the Earl of Lansdowne between 1899 and 1902, were always evaded adroitly by the Germans. The chancellor by this time was that monument of superficiality, Prince Bülow, who agreed with Holstein that the longer the British were kept waiting, the more eager they would become. When his ambassador in London suggested in 1903 that the British might try to make an accommodation with the French and the Russians, Bülow waved this aside airily. "In my opinion," he wrote, "we need not worry about such remote possibilities."

The Germans were right in only one respect: the British were concerned about the drift of world events and were prepared to modify their past isolation by diplomatic agreements. The time had come, said Lord Lansdowne in 1902, for the country to stop "being swayed by musty formulae and old fashioned superstitions as to the desirability of pursuing a policy of isolation for this country. . . . *Prima facie,* if there be no countervailing objections, the country that has the good fortune to have allies is more to be envied than the country which is without them." Moreover, the British government had a wider range of choice than was believed in Berlin. After Fashoda had eliminated the Egyptian question as an active issue, there was no insuperable conflict of interest anywhere in the world between France and Great Britain; and, despite the continued antipathy between the two peoples, there were certain issues on which they were beginning to see eye to eye. Although for different reasons, the French were beginning to be as worried about Russia's Far Eastern policy as the British. The British were afraid of Russian encroachments upon their sphere of influence in China. The French had two fears: first, that Russian absorption in Far Eastern affairs would deprive France of Russian support in areas closer to home (where were the Russians, for example, when France was forced to back down at Fashoda?) and, second, that there would be an Anglo-Russian war in the Far East and that Russia would expect French aid there. This latter fear was enhanced by the conclusion, in 1902, of the alliance between Great Britain and Japan (see p. 423).

Delcassé and the Anglo-French Settlement   In Paris the man most awake to the dangers the Russian course held for France was Théophile Delcassé, who had assumed office as foreign minister in 1898. As we have seen (p. 420), Delcassé believed that the principal concern of any French statesman must be France's relations with Germany and that the most desirable objective of French policy was the recovery of Alsace and Lorraine. Delcassé had set himself the task of strengthening France's position vis-à-vis Germany, and he had no intention of diverting the energies of his country into useless wars in far-off places.

In the building up of France's diplomatic position, Delcassé had already had one significant success. When he came to power he had inherited, among other things, a tariff war with Italy that had been going on since 1887 (see p. 313), Delcassé showed himself amenable to the Italian desire for a commercial agreement that would terminate this ruinous conflict. In 1898 he granted it. In return, however, he received an explicit recognition of the primacy of French influence in Morocco (Delcassé assuring his opposite number that France would refrain from meddling in Tripoli, which the Italians coveted), as well as some important assurances with respect to Italy's membership in that obviously anti-French combination, the Triple Alliance. The Italians were anxious to count on the continued support of Paris banking circles, for they were embarking on a complicated refunding of their national debt, and they had no hesitation in giving Delcassé what he wanted. In a series of notes between 1900, when the Triple Alliance was renewed, and 1902, they declared that nothing in the wording of the alliance bound Italy to take any aggressive action against France and that Italy would remain neutral if France became "the object of direct or indirect aggression" or even if France "as the result of direct provocation, should find herself compelled in defense of her honor and security to take the initiative of a declaration of war." If these secret declarations meant anything—and they were made with every evidence of good faith—they indicated that Italy's enthusiasm for the Triple Alliance had reached the vanishing point and that in the event of a war with Germany, France need have no fear of an attack on its flank.

This was heartening to Delcassé, but the threat in the Far East remained. If Russia continued to pursue its dangerous policy there, France might, against its will, find itself involved in the war it had avoided at Fashoda. The best way of avoiding this, he thought, would be to turn directly to Britain. A rapprochement between London and Paris would, Delcassé hoped, not only avoid the danger of French involvement in a Far Eastern war but it might even eliminate the possibility of such a war by promoting agreement between France's ally, Russia, and Britain's new ally, Japan.

In any event, Delcassé made soundings in London and found a cordial response in the government and at court. Indeed, England's new sovereign, King Edward VII, was so enthusiastic over the prospect of Anglo-French reconciliation that he volunteered to go to Paris on an extraordinary state visit designed to prepare public opinion for an agreement. As an example of personal diplomacy, the king's visit in May 1903 was an unparalleled success. Upon his arrival, he was met by hostile crowds who cheered for Marchand, Kruger, and, indeed, anyone but the royal visitor. The king's good-humored acceptance of this treatment, however, soon turned the popular temper in his favor, and when he left the city to return home, the cheers were for him. A subsequent visit to London by the president of the Republic in July went off well; and the diplomats were encouraged to believe that there was no longer any reason to fear public opinion. They accordingly got down to work and, between July 1903 and April 1904, agreed on the details of a comprehensive settlement of differences.

The agreement of 1904 ended certain disputes in Siam and Newfoundland and made boundary adjustments in West Africa, but its most important clauses had to do with Egypt and Morocco. Belatedly, the French government recognized the British protectorate at Cairo and declared that they would not obstruct British work in Egypt "by asking that a time limit be fixed for the British occupation or in any other manner." On their part, the British government recognized Morocco as a French sphere of influence, adding that it was for France alone to provide order in that enormously rich North African province and to suggest reforms to its sultan. The British agreed further, in secret articles, that they would raise no objections to any action that the French might consider appropriate in the event of a collapse of the sultan's authority, provided that northern Morocco with its Atlantic coastline should go not to France but to Spain. This last stipulation was dictated by considerations of strategy.

The broader significance of this agreement was that it marked the beginning of Anglo-French collaboration on other questions and the first step toward the alliance between the two Western powers in World War I.

The First Moroccan Crisis   This was not immediately recognized by the people who were to suffer most from the new entente: namely, the Germans. They were still mesmerized by the vision of an Anglo-Russian war that would involve France also; and, to do them justice, it must be admitted that such a war seemed to be a real possibility in 1904. On a dark October night of that year, when Admiral Rozhdestvensky's Baltic fleet started its long journey toward its sad destiny in the straits of Tsushima (see p. 424), it mistook some British trawlers off the Dogger Bank for Japanese gunboats and blew them out of the water. For some weeks British retaliation seemed probable, but it was averted, partly because of the good offices of the French. As events took their course in the Far East, the possibility of an Anglo-Russian conflict vanished. As it did, the Germans seem to have decided that they would have to give more serious attention to the new Anglo-French combination.

Field Marshall von Moltke once said that the trouble with the Russians as allies in wartime was that they always came too late and then were too strong. The same might be said of Germany's diplomatic tactics in 1905. After having waited a full year, the German government decided to protest against the Anglo-French agreement as it pertained to Morocco, and did so in the most violent way possible. On March 31, 1905, William II landed in Tangier and, riding through enthusiastic native crowds, hailed the sultan as an independent ruler. Simultaneously, complaining that it had not been informed of the Moroccan agreement, the German government demanded, in menacing tones, that it be set aside.

Here again it is difficult to understand what exactly the Germans hoped to gain from intervention; it may well be that they did not know themselves.

Certainly there was no real unity of view among the leading figures in the German government. The chief of the German General Staff, Count Schlieffen, felt that Germany's power position was slowly being altered for the worse, and he would have welcomed an opportunity to stop its decline by a victorious war against France. The year 1905 was ideal for this purpose: Schlieffen had just finished the final revision of his war plan, which now called for a great wheeling move-ment through Belgium and across northeastern France that would encircle Paris and then inexorably drive the French armies south and east toward the Swiss frontier; and Russia, prostrated by her defeat in the Far East, was in no position to come to her ally's aid. In the Foreign Office, Holstein shared Schlieffen's fears for the future and would also have welcomed a trial by arms. He had been an advocate of preventive war in 1887, and there is good evidence that he was thinking along the same lines in 1905, that he planned a forcing play in Morocco, which would either compel the French to give in to the most humil-iating terms (leaving England's faith in France shattered and the new entente useless) or would goad it into a war in which it would be smashed in accordance with Schlieffen's prescription.

If this was Holstein's secret purpose, he either did not wish or did not dare to open his mind to the chancellor, Prince Bülow, who regarded the Moroccan policy as purely a matter of bluff and blackmail for whatever Germany might get out of it, or to the emperor, who was nervous about the whole business, had never wanted to go to Tangier in the first place, and had—as he informed a group of German officers at the height of the crisis—no intention of "fighting a war for Morocco." Given the profound differences of view among Holstein, Bülow, and William II, it is understandable that German policy would be dis-jointed and that at decisive moments it would lack determination. This proved to be true.

At the outset, the vigor of the German intervention shocked and frightened the French government and, although Delcassé pleaded that any willingness to grant concessions under duress would alienate the British, he was unable to convince the majority of his colleagues and, in June 1905, resigned from office. The Germans had long wanted to revenge themselves on the man who had "debauched Italy" in 1902, and Delcassé's fall was a stunning victory for them. It seemed quite possible that the French would now give them anything they asked.

But the lack of coherence in German policy robbed them of their triumph. At the time of the original intervention, the German government had insisted that its object was to have the Moroccan question referred to an international conference. It could not renege on that now. But before a conference met at Algeciras in 1906, the attitude of the French government had stiffened, and a change of British government had brought the Liberals to power and Sir Edward Grey to the Foreign Office. Grey was a man who felt, much more strongly than his predecessor, that the Germans were attempting to dominate Europe and that it was important to prevent this by strengthening the tie with France. Certainly, he insisted, care must be taken not to leave France in the lurch. Thanks to his attitude, therefore, the French and the British went into the Algeciras conference determined to hold to their original Moroccan agreement. The Germans, with much of the steam gone from their drive, ruined what was left of their case by blustering tactics in the conference itself and found, in the first decisive conference vote, that they were virtually isolated, only Austria-Hungary and Morocco voting with them. No essential change was made in the original Moroccan settlement; and what had started out as German diplomatic victory ended as a defeat. It is significant that both Schlieffen and Holstein retired from office at the beginning of 1906. This was just, and underlined the fact that the Anglo-French connection they had hoped to smash had been strengthened by their tactics. It is no coincidence that 1905 marked the beginning of staff talks between British and French soldiers and that these soon led to joint staff planning.

The Formation of the Triple Entente   The Anglo-French entente soon received an accretion of strength by the conclusion of an agreement between Great Britain and Russia. To bring Russia into this company was, as he admitted in 1904, Delcassé's dearest dream; but it had remained a political impossibility until after his fall from office. The event that cleared the way for an Anglo-Russian agreement was Russia's defeat in the Far East, and this was true for a number of reasons. In the first place, Russia wanted to save as much as possible of its Far Eastern position and was anxious for help in negotiations with Japan

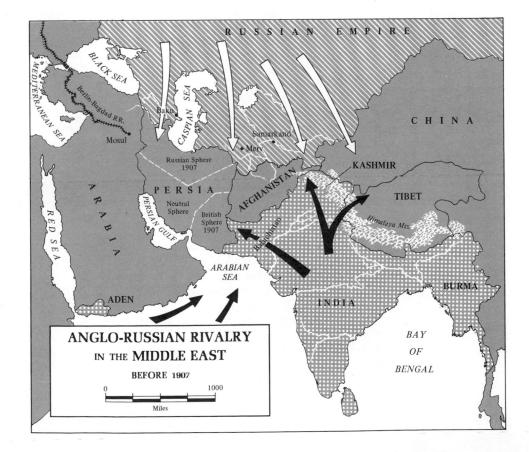

ANGLO-RUSSIAN RIVALRY
IN THE **MIDDLE EAST**

BEFORE 1907

0   1000

Miles

on this point. Britain was Japan's ally, and it seemed logical to suppose that an agreement with it might be advantageous. Britain was also intimate with France, which—at a time when Russia needed French financial aid more than ever before—seemed an additional reason for a new approach to the British. In the third place, the Russian government was already contemplating a renewal of its forward policy in the Balkans in order to divert public opinion from internal grievances; and it had no desire to encounter the kind of opposition it had met in 1887. Finally, the Russians were more anxious than ever before to cooperate with powers bent on balking German ambitions, for they resented the fact that while Russia had been engaged in war with Japan, the Germans had been active in an area dangerously close to Russian interests on the Persian Gulf.

For all these reasons, the Russians were willing and anxious to attain more amicable relations with the British, and this desire was reciprocated. The procedure followed was similar to that used in negotiating the Anglo-French entente. In the course of 1906, the British sent to St. Petersburg one of their most experienced diplomats, Sir Arthur Nicolson. Working directly with the Russian foreign minister Izvolsky, Nicolson applied himself to the three areas of the world where Anglo-Russian friction had been most dangerous: Afghanistan and Tibet, both of which represented threats to British security in India, and Persia, then as now an area of critical strategical importance. Nicolson showed great skill in winning the confidence of the Russian negotiator, but there is no doubt that he was aided in his task by Russian Far Eastern needs and by the fact that the spread of German influence in the vicinity of Persia gave the two powers a common interest.

In August 1907 the agreement was finally ratified. Both powers agreed to stay out of Tibet; and, while Russia agreed to regard Afghanistan as a British sphere of influence, the British in their turn agreed to do nothing to change the existing political situation there. As for Persia, while emphasizing their intention of preserving that country's independence and assuring other nations that their commercial rights would be respected, they proceeded to divide it into three zones. The British were acknowledged to have a virtual protectorate over the southernmost of these, which dominated the entrance to the Persian Gulf and included the province of Seistan, which gave access to Afghanistan and India. The northern zone, which included Ispahan and Teheran, fell to the Russians as their sphere of influence; and a large neutral zone was left between it and the British sphere to the south. Each power agreed not to seek economic concessions in the area allotted to the other; and together they tacitly agreed to bar Germany from Persia as a whole.

The Anglo-Russian agreement was one more example of the high-handedness of the imperialistic powers when dealing with backward countries. Its wider importance was that even though it was popular in neither England nor Russia and by no means ended the mutual suspicion and dislike of the two governments, it did bring advantages to both parties that were important enough to convince them of the necessity of remaining in contact. Even before the ratification of the agreement with Britain, Russia, in a secret agreement with Japan, got a sphere of influence in Manchuria, and its financial requests in Paris were received more cordially than they might have been had the peace with the British not been made. As for the British, they were assured of a diminution of the friction with Russia that had been so constant a preoccupation in the past and could count on Russian cooperation in placing obstacles in front of Germany's Baghdad railway scheme.

Aside from this, the Anglo-Russian agreement laid the foundation for consistent diplomatic cooperation among Britain, France, and Russia. The diplomatic revolution that had begun when the Germans allowed the Reinsurance Treaty to lapse in 1890 was now complete, and the Triple Entente had come into existence to balance the Triple Alliance.

THE ROAD TO WAR, 1907–1914

New Tendencies   The reduction of European politics to this crude dualism was accompanied by three dangerous tendencies.

In the first place, it seemed much more important than it had ever been before to possess allies and much more damaging to lose them. Every government now

"Anxiety," 1896, a lithograph by the Norwegian artist Edvard Munch. (The Museum of Modern Art, New York)

suffered from recurrent nightmares in which it saw itself abandoned by its friends and encircled by a host of enemies; and every government, in its waking moments, strove to strengthen the loyalty of its allies and to avoid even the suggestion of defection. Intent upon this objective, the powers not unnaturally lost some of their freedom of action. Their ability to cooperate in dangerous crises with members of the opposing coalition was limited by their estimate of how their own friends might react, and fear of offending allies was sometimes enough to prevent disinterested action in behalf of the general peace. By the same token, the ability of the coalition to restrain or discipline its own members by withholding support from moves that did not appear to be in the common interest was rendered imperfect by the fear of defection. A premium was placed upon what William II, in an unhappy moment, called *Nibelungen* loyalty; and this meant that, in the long run, both coalitions tended to fall under the control of their most irresponsible members.

In the second place, there was a general increase in armaments, which, of course, merely fed the fears that produced it. Between 1900 and 1910 there had already been a significant rise in the army and naval estimates of the European powers, despite the fact that it was precisely in these years that there was considerable popular interest in arms reduction and two international peace conferences had met at The Hague (1899 and 1907) to discuss the possibility of submitting armaments to international control. These conferences had accomplished some useful work—defining the rules of war, outlawing certain inhumane weapons, extending the Geneva Red Cross Convention to naval warfare, establishing an international prize court and a permanent court of international justice—but they made no progress toward their main objective. Indeed, in the decade that saw these gatherings, the German government increased its army budget by a fifth, Russia by two thirds, Italy by a half, France by a third, Austria-Hungary by a quarter, and Great Britain by a third, while German naval estimates increased threefold and British naval estimates by more than a third. But this was nothing to the increases in the four years between 1910 and 1914, during which German and Austrian army expenditures doubled again and all other countries invested heavily in new ships, new guns, and new battalions. Some idea of this expanding investment in the tools of war is shown in the following table, which presents in approximate figures the per capita expenditure of the Great Powers for armaments in the period we have covered in the last few chapters.

	1870	1880	1890	1900	1910	1914
Great Britain	$3.54	$3.46	$3.84	$12.60*	$7.29	$8.23
France	2.92	4.02	4.66	5.21	6.47	7.07
Russia	1.28	1.50	1.26	1.44	2.32	3.44
Germany	1.28	2.16	2.80	3.48	4.06	8.19
Austria-Hungary	1.08	1.70	1.50	1.46	1.68	3.10
Italy	1.38	1.74	2.52	2.34	3.36	3.16

* This figure represents the cost of the Boer War to the British taxpayer.

A third tendency, closely related to this last one, was the increase of military influence upon policy determination. In all countries military and naval officers were consulted more frequently by the political leadership and listened to more thoughtfully; and sometimes strong military personalities had a tendency to supersede the civilian authorities in certain areas of policy. Austria's policy in the Balkans was always more aggressive when Conrad von Hötzendorf was in office as chief of staff than when he was not; and Grand Admiral Alfred von Tirpitz succeeded in defeating all Foreign Office proposals for a naval accommodation with Great Britain in these critical years.

In the case of both Triple Alliance and Triple Entente, the soldiers of associated states held staff talks, exchanged technical information, and, in some cases, made arrangements of convenience. Theoretically, these had no binding force upon their governments. Yet, after British soldiers had been admitted to the secrets of the French general staff in their continued consultations after 1905, it was difficult to deny that there was at least a presumption that if France were attacked, Britain would help it. (Prime Minister Sir Henry Campbell-Bannerman had been reluctant to authorize the staff talks because he felt that this would constitute an "honourable undertaking." He was won over by Haldane and Grey. The latter argued that the talks were necessary to *preserve* Britain's freedom of action, so that it would be able either to fight or to remain neutral if France were ever attacked, whereas without joint planning it would have no choice but to stand aside. Whether other members of the cabinet would have agreed with this view it is impossible to say, for they were not consulted, and even Asquith, who became prime minister in 1908, did not learn of the military conversations until 1911. A British historian has recently described Grey's behavior as "grossly unconstitutional.")

Between German and Austrian soldiers, commitments were even more explicit. In 1909, Conrad von Hötzendorf asked the German general staff whether he could count on its support if Austria became involved in war as a result of an Austrian attack on Serbia. He was answered in the affirmative, although this reply represented a commitment that, in effect, removed the restrictions placed upon Austrian action by Bismarck's Dual Alliance of 1879 (see p. 256).

Given the mobility of modern war and the vast numbers employed in it, it was necessary for all general staffs to make detailed plans for the wars that might come, and it was only natural that they should have lavished most care upon the plan devised for the war that they considered most likely. In the elaboration of this, the soldiers were apt to allow technical advantage to take precedence over political considerations and to succumb in the end to the belief that any deviation from the projected operations would be disastrous. How destructive of a government's freedom of action this could be is illustrated by the Schlieffen plan. When the world was poised on the brink of war in 1914, a report came to Berlin that Britain might remain neutral if Germany did not attack France. The emperor suggested to his chief of staff that it might be well for Germany, therefore, to strike against Russia. He was informed that such a move was impossible, and that to depart from the plan of an initial assault against France at this late date would be disastrous. Germany's war plan had become so inflexible that the government was virtually incapable of acting in any but the prescribed way. They were even bound by their soldiers to start the war by violating Belgian territory, an act that was sure to alienate neutral sympathy but which the soldiers again said was imperative.

Finally, of course, soldiers who spent their lives studying the shifting power relations of Europe were likely to press for action at moments when they thought their plans and their strength superior to that of any possible enemy combination. Mention has already been made of Schlieffen's fear that Germany's relative strength would decline with the years unless it took radical action against its rivals. He was not alone in this, and similar fears were felt by other soldiers in other countries. One of the most dangerous features of the crises of 1907–1914 was the fact that there were always influential soldiers who believed that this might be the last favorable moment for military action by their country and that it should not be allowed to slip.

The fearful dependence of the powers upon their alliances, their tendency to defer to their more irresponsible partners, the constantly accelerating armaments race, and the excessive military influence in policy determination were doubly dangerous because public opinion was largely unaware of their implications and, even when aware, powerless to do anything about them. Absorbed for the most part in domestic questions and well satisfied with the material comforts created by what appeared to be a century of progress, the great majority of citizens knew little of the way in which their country's foreign policy was made and nothing of the details of the secret agreements that bound it to others. Only when a new series of sharp crises broke out did they become aware that all was not well, and then they were not organized to correct the situation. In the years from 1907 to 1914, as the diplomatic machinery broke down, all of the organized groups of civilized society—churches, trade unions, political parties—proved just as ineffective as the diplomats themselves. The way in which they were overborne by the forces of violence is admirably portrayed in Roger Martin du Gard's great novel, *Summer, 1914.*

The Bosnian Crisis   The series of crises that led inexorably to the world war had its origins in a meeting which took place in a country estate at Buchlau, in Styria, between the Austrian foreign minister Count Aehrenthal and the Russian foreign minister Alexander Izvolsky.

Despite the passage of the years, we still possess no completely reliable account of what these two ambitious and devious statesmen had to say to each other, but it is possible to reconstruct the substance, if not the nuances, of their talk. Izvolsky, who had lately concluded the negotiation of the Anglo-Russian agreement, burned for new triumphs and, in particular, was desirous, as he had told Aehrenthal in 1907, of having the Straits of the Bosphorus and Dardanelles opened to Russian warships so that the Black Sea fleet could enter the Mediterranean. Aehrenthal was, as Izvolsky knew, anxious to annex the Turkish provinces of Bosnia and Herzegovina, which had been administered by Austria since 1878; and he regarded this annexation (although Izvolsky was surely not privy to *this* secret) as the first and necessary step in a policy that would encircle and destroy Serbia. The recent revolution in Turkey (see p. 380), which brought a militant and patriotic Young Turk party to power, served as a goad to both men, for it threatened to balk their designs; this change in the political climate at Constantinople was the principal reason for the Buchlau meeting.

In their talk, the two foreign ministers agreed to support each others' plans, apparently assuming that if their governments announced their intention of changing the status of Bosnia and the Straits, there would be no serious objection by other powers, despite the infringement of treaty obligations such action would entail. They agreed, tacitly, that their announcements should be made at the same time. Yet Izvolsky did not apparently ask when that time was to be; and in that lapse was the seed of much future trouble.

Leaving Buchlau, Izvolsky pursued a leisurely course westward to prepare the other capitals for the impending announcement. When he reached Paris on October 3, however, he was disagreeably surprised to receive a telegram from Aehrenthal saying that circumstances necessitated Austria's acting without further delay, and three days later the annexation of Bosnia was announced in Vienna.

This would not have mattered had Izvolsky been able to make his announcement too. But he was not. The adverse international reaction to the Austrian announcement indicated that there would be strong objection to any new violation of treaty law, which Russia was not prepared to brave. A change at the Straits with the consent of the other powers was also out of the question, as Izvolsky learned when he took the matter up in London. Lord Grey was disgusted with the Austrian action and implacably opposed to any new change that would weaken or offend the Turks, toward whom Grey's Liberal party was strongly sympathetic.

Under the impact of these unpleasant shocks, and the further discovery that Austria's annexation of Bosnia was as bitterly resented in Russia as in Serbia, Izvolsky, who had not informed his colleagues of his actions at Buchlau, lost his head. He denied that he had consented to the annexation, insisting that Buchlau had represented a mere exchange of views; he described Austria's action as a flagrant breach of written engagements; and he asked that an international conference meet to undo its action.

The irrational behavior was the reason for the crisis of 1908. The Serbs, already infuriated by the loss of provinces they had long considered their own, were encouraged by Pan-Slav agitations in Russia and by Izvolsky's lack of moderation to believe that Russia would support them, and they began to prepare for action. The Austrians responded with a partial mobilization and moved troops toward the Serb border. Both Conrad and Aehrenthal seemed delighted with the prospect of a war that would finally eliminate the Serbian irritation, and they were not much worried about what Russia might do. In his airy way, Aehrenthal told the British ambassador in Vienna that he knew Russia "like his own pocket" and was sure that she was in no position to go to war.

For the sake of the internal morale of the Triple Entente, the British decided that they must come to Izvolsky's aid. "It is evident," the permanent under secretary for foreign affairs said, "that we must do our best to support Izvolsky, such as he is." With that genius for devising compromises that is characteristic of British diplomacy, they tried to make an arrangement that would fob off the Serbs with monetary compensation and give Austria what it had taken, after certain ceremonial rituals had been performed to save Izvolsky's face.

This might have worked had not the Germans felt just as strongly about standing by their ally as the British. It was true that they were no more enthusiastic about Aehrenthal than the British about Izvolsky, for the Austrian foreign minister had not consulted them and his annexation of Bosnia had outraged the Turks, whom the Germans were bent on cultivating. Even so, the Germans felt compelled to act, for reasons which Bülow spelled out in words that tell much about the way in which alliance loyalty overruled prudence in the years before 1914:

> Our position would indeed be dangerous if Austria lost confidence in us and turned away. So long as we stand together, we form a bloc which no one will lightly attack. In eastern questions above all, we cannot place ourselves in opposition to Austria, who has nearer and greater interests in the Balkan peninsula than ourselves. A refusal or a grudging attitude in the question of the annexation of Bosnia and Herzegovina would not be forgiven. The old Emperor and official Austria see in the possession of these provinces a compensation for the loss of Italy and Germany.

In March 1909, Bülow proposed a solution of the Bosnian affair that dispensed with any idea of an international conference and supported the Austrian case. When Izvolsky hesitated to give in, Bülow reverted to the brutal directness that characterized so much of the diplomacy of William II. "We expect a precise answer, yes or no," he said. "Any evasive, complicated or ambiguous reply will be regarded as a refusal. In that event we should withdraw and allow matters to take their course." In face of this scarcely veiled threat, Izvolsky caved in, and the crisis came to an end.

It nevertheless had serious consequences. It rendered Austrian policy suspect through all Europe and gave the impression that Germany was more interested in demonstrating its power than in serving the cause of peace. It strengthened the Triple Entente indirectly by making the Russian government more dependent upon it. Most serious of all, it opened the way for an era of Balkan wars. Izvolsky now devoted himself with a molelike persistence to revenging himself on Austria. He encouraged the Serbs to regard the loss of Bosnia as a merely temporary setback, and he provided funds for the continuation of Great-Serb propaganda work in Bosnia and Austria. He carried Delcassé's work in Italy one step further by making a secret agreement with the Italians at Racconigi in October 1909 that provided for consultation in Balkan affairs, for Italian support of Russia's plans at the Straits, and for Russian support of Italy's policy in Tripoli and Cyrenaica, if and when it decided to act in those regions. Finally, Izvolsky bent all his not inconsiderable diplomatic skill to the task of reconciling the long hostile Serbs and Bulgars in the interest of a new Pan-Slav program that would give him the triumph denied him by Aehrenthal. In view of these policies and their results, there was some justification for his boast in 1914: "This is *my* war, *my* war!"

Agadir   It has been argued persuasively that one of the most important contributory causes of the war was the failure of the designated leaders of the German government—that is, the emperor and the chancellor—either to direct or control German policy in the last prewar years. After the *Daily Telegraph* affair in 1908 (see p. 359), the emperor seemed in a chastened and submissive mood, and tended henceforth to defer to his military chiefs. After Bülow's fall in 1909, the chancellorship also seemed to lose some of its authority. In foreign affairs particularly, the new Chancellor, Theobald von Bethmann Hollweg, had no experience and found it difficult to control those who had, or claimed to have: the realist and pro-Austrian school in the foreign office, the military staffs, and the military and naval attachés at foreign posts, all of whom favored a more aggressive policy than he thought safe.

Probably this explains the inexplicable and ill-conceived intervention of Germany in Moroccan affairs in 1911. This was largely the brainchild of the new Foreign Minister Alfred von Kiderlen-Wächter, a self-styled *Kerl* ("tough guy"), who had drafted for Bülow the ultimatum of 1909 to Russia and whose willfulness always terrified the chancellor. In the summer of 1911, he demonstrated just how far he could carry that characteristic. As a result of disorders in Morocco, the French had sent troops into Fez, presumably to protect foreign residents. This exceeded France's legal rights as defined at Algeciras, but the government had argued that the need was great and that even the Germans would see no reason to object, since their economic interests had been protected by a separate Franco-German agreement of 1909. The French were wrong. In July 1911, without warning, Kiderlen dispatched the German gunboat *Panther* to the Moroccan port of Agadir.

This menacing action—it could hardly be regarded as anything else—shocked and puzzled Europe. What exactly did the Germans want? It is likely that the Germans did not know themselves. Kiderlen seems to have believed that a show of truculence would frighten the French into making some kind of offer. When it did not do so, he was embarrassed and perplexed; but, since he had to do something, he demanded that France cede all of the French Congo to Germany as compensation for its real and projected gains in Morocco.

To the Western powers, this claim seemed so fantastic that the French considered it as a mere pretext for military action, while the British concluded that the Germans must really be after something else—perhaps a naval base on Morocco's Atlantic coast. Grey hinted delicately to the German ambassador that, whatever happened from now on, Britain would expect to be consulted. Kiderlen was obtuse enough to try to evade this, which further alarmed the British and finally led to Grey's authorizing a speech by the chancellor of the exchequer, David Lloyd George, which was almost as menacing as the "*Panther's* spring." With all the passion that he could command, Lloyd George accused Germany of seeking to disregard Great Britain in a matter affecting its interests, adding that, if peace could be preserved only

> by the surrender of the great and beneficent position Britain has won by centuries of heroism and achievement, by allowing Britain to be treated, where her interests were vitally affected, as if she were of no account in the Cabinet of Nations, then I say emphatically that peace at that price would be a humiliation intolerable for a great country like ours to endure. National honor is no party question.

The injection of national honor into this muddled dispute raised it to the level of a real threat to the peace. Encouraged by the British attitude, the French hardened to the point of obduracy in the matter of possible concessions; and the Germans were too far committed to back down without something to show for their efforts. In the end, it took all Grey's skill, and some special pleading in Paris by the Russians, to effect a settlement. The French got a free hand in Morocco; the Germans received some thousands of acres of African wastes; and the fragile peace was put together again.

The Consolidation of the Alliances   The narrowness with which war seemed to have been averted in 1911 shocked moderate opinion in both Britain and Germany and led some men of influence to criticize the bases of past policy and to call for a reappraisal. In England there was growing unease over what appeared to be incessant involvement in crises precipitated by French and Russian indiscretions; in Germany, there were increasing complaints over the political effects of the naval program, which Tirpitz now once more wished to expand in scope. Would it not be wise, men in both countries asked, to attempt an Anglo-German accommodation?

It was soon demonstrated that such an arrangement was unlikely. In February 1912, Lord Haldane, the British minister of war, a man who had studied at German universities and loved the country and its people, went to Berlin to discover whether any agreement was possible. The nub of the matter, it was soon apparent, was the projected German naval bill. Tirpitz, who appeared to be the dominant personality in Berlin during Haldane's visit, made it clear that this could not be sacrificed and that even modifications would depend upon Britain's willingness to agree to neutrality in the event of a German war with France. To the British foreign office, quite well aware of the difficulties of defining aggression, a binding promise of neutrality seemed unwise, especially since the more Tirpitz's proposed modifications were studied, the less conciliatory they appeared to be. Fitful negotiations continued for some weeks after Haldane's return to London, but reached no conclusion. Meanwhile, Tirpitz had his way in Berlin; and his bill was passed in its original form by the Reichstag. When this happened, the last chance of an Anglo-German detente was lost.

Instead, both countries turned back to their allies and further strengthened their ties with them—Germany by increasing the intimacy of staff talks with the Austrians, Britain by moving closer to an alliance with France. Lord Grey had always opposed French requests for a formal alliance, for constitutional and political reasons and because he believed Britain must retain as much freedom of action as possible; but he could not avoid taking another step which gave the French a moral right to call for British aid in time of war. In November 1912, in order to persuade the French to move their Atlantic fleet to the Mediterranean to protect British interests there while the British fleet was concentrated in the North Sea, Grey not only specifically authorized a continuation of the Anglo-French staff talks but also gave the French the assurance that "if either Government had grave reason to expect an unprovoked attack by a third Power, it should immediately discuss with the other whether both Governments should act together." This was not the unequivocal pledge that the French would have liked, but it was not far removed from it.

It is safe to say that there was some continued concern in official circles in both Germany and England over these tendencies, but the surge of dangerous events in Eastern Europe now made loyalty to one's allies seem the highest form of political wisdom.

Tripoli and the Balkan Wars   One of the most fateful results of the Agadir crisis was that it aroused the fear in Italy that France might soon, despite all its assurances to the contrary, move into Tripoli, unless it was anticipated there. Before the dust had settled in Morocco, therefore, the Italian government informed the Turkish government that it intended to extend its "protection" over Tripoli and, when the Turks rejected this communication, Italy declared war and invaded Tripoli in September 1911.

The Italian action, in turn, led the Balkan countries to fear that Austria might take advantage of Turkey's embarrassment to seize what was left of its European possessions, and they hastened to complete the work that Izvolsky had projected and which had been promoted by Hartwig and Nekliudov, the Russian ambassadors in Belgrade and Sofia. In March 1912, Bulgaria and Serbia concluded an alliance promising to aid each other in case of attack, to cooperate in repelling attempts by Great Powers to acquire Balkan territory, and to follow a common policy vis-à-vis Turkey, recognizing each other's natural interests if it should become necessary to go to war against her. Within a few months, both Greece and Montenegro had adhered to these articles, and the Balkan League had been formed.

To expect it to remain a league of peace at a time when so many enticing prospects were opening before the eyes of its members would have been unreasonable. In October 1912, the four Balkan powers launched a concerted attack upon Turkish forces in Europe and, within a few months, had swept them back to the Straits. They then turned to the pleasant task of dividing the spoils.

This turned out to be rather more difficult than had been imagined in the talks that preceded the war. For one thing, the two Great Powers most interested in the Balkans intervened: Austria, to prevent the acquisition by Serbia of access to the Adriatic Sea; Russia, to insist that Serbia and Montenegro be granted such access. This and other explosive territorial questions had to be submitted to an international conference at London, which solved the Adriatic problem by creating an independent Albania and compensating Serbia with territory in the interior. Peace was restored in May 1913 and lasted exactly one month, at the end of which time a sudden Bulgarian attack upon Serbia touched off a second war in which the aggressor was despoiled of its recent gains by its late allies, aided by Rumania and Turkey.

In both of these conflicts, peace was maintained among the Great Powers by the cooperation of Great Britain and Germany. Grey and Bethmann Hollweg sponsored the London Conference and devised the Adriatic compromise that was the key to the settlement of the first Balkan war. The English restrained the Russians during both conflicts, and, in the second, when there was a real possibility of Austria intervening by force of arms on the side of Bulgaria, Bethmann persuaded its government not to do so. The success of joint Anglo-German efforts in behalf of peace in 1912 and 1913 seemed to indicate that those who encouraged Haldane to go to Berlin had reason on their side.

Even so, this fruitful cooperation was not destined to continue. At the end of the Balkan wars, the Austrians were critical of Germany's failure to support them and open in their accusations that Germany was responsible for dangerous accretions to Serbian strength. In much the same way, the Russians blamed the British for the creation of Albania, which blocked Serbia from the sea, and were critical of France for having done nothing to defeat this unfortunate arrangement. The bitter complaints of these powers made their diplomatic partners uneasy and unwilling to try their patience with new disappointments. German soldiers, prompted by Conrad's reproaches, warned of the serious consequences of future lack of support. Sir Arthur Nicolson, now permanent under secretary for foreign affairs in Great Britain, confessed that he was haunted by the fear that "Russia should become tired of us and strike a bargain with Germany"; and the French felt even more strongly that Russia must be handled delicately from now on.

This reluctance to continue to restrain the most irresponsible members of the family of nations was doubly ominous in view of two related facts. The first was that both the Austrian and Russian governments were now dominated by men who felt that the moment of decision could not be long delayed—that it must be made clear once and for all whether Austrian or Russian influence was to be predominant in the Balkans. The second was that the Serbian government was not content with its sizable gains during the Balkan wars. Its premier had said bluntly, after the cessation of hostilities in August 1913, "The first round is won; now we must prepare for the second, against Austria."

The Final Crisis   Throughout the spring of 1914 all nations accelerated their military preparations and persuaded their parliaments to vote new funds for expansion. This activity moved Europe one more step toward the brink, for it led to the kind of elaborate calculations which soldiers indulge in and which have not been unknown in our time. The experts of the Central Powers, viewing the projected Russian and French programs, were now more than ever convinced that the balance was turning against them. "For us in the Triple Alliance," Field Marshal Conrad remarked to the German military attaché, "there are only two alternatives, either to strike at once or to strengthen our armaments correspondingly, and of the two the former is by far the more correct from a military point of view." The only thing that seemed to be holding Conrad back was concern over the length of time Austria might have to stand alone against Russia before Germany came to its aid. In May, however, he learned, first, that the German chief of staff, the younger Moltke, was sympathetic to his view that further postponement of a conflict that appeared inevitable would be fatal, and, second, that Moltke's plans, based on those of Schlieffen, called for a thrust westward that would knock France out within six weeks, followed by the diversion of Germany's full strength to the drive against Russia. Moltke apparently believed that Britain would intervene on France's side, but that her intervention would be ineffective and would not disrupt the schedule.

Conrad was heartened by these intimations, and it would be interesting to know how he would have acted upon them if the Serbs had not relieved him of the necessity of action. But on June 28, 1914, in the Bosnian town of Sarajevo, a young Serbian patriot named Gavrilo Princip shot and killed the Austrian heir apparent, Archduke Franz Ferdinand, and his consort; and Conrad and those who thought like him did not have to exercise their powers of invention. There was every reason to suspect that the assassination was not a private act; and, indeed, it was later proved that Princip and his fellow assassins were the idealistic tools of a Colonel Dragutin Dimitrijevic, chief of the intelligence department of the Serbian general staff and leading spirit in the patriotic Black Hand Society, who had coldbloodedly planned the deed. Although this and the degree to which the Serbian government was aware of the planned assassination were not fully known in Vienna, the government there had the excuse it had long wanted for action against Belgrade.

It was not until July 23, however, that Europe learned how drastic that action would be. The initial shock of the coup at Sarajevo had diminished and Europe was beginning to relax again, when on July 23 the Austrian government sent an ultimatum to Belgrade, charging the Serbian government with complicity in the deed and laying down a series of demands which, if fully met, would virtually have deprived Serbia of independence. Lord Grey was shocked when he saw them and told the Austrian ambassador that he had never before seen one government send another "a document of so formidable a character." The Russian foreign minister, Sazonov, who had been counseling the Serbs to do everything in their power to appease the Austrians, was aghast and blurted out to the Austrian ambassador: "This means a European war. You are setting Europe alight!"

Archduke Francis Ferdinand of Austria and his consort in Sarajevo one hour before their assassination. (Bettmann Archive)

The harshness of the Austrian terms was no inadvertence. Both the Austrians and the Germans had come to the conclusion that action against Serbia was imperative, and, on July 5, in a conversation with the Austrian ambassador, William II had promised German support if Austria subsequently found itself at war with Russia, a commitment that Bethmann approved later in the day. Thus, when the Serbian government answered the ultimatum with promises of substantial concessions to its demands, the Austrians declared this unsatisfactory and, on July 28, declared war. The ultimate crisis had arrived.

It is difficult to avoid the conclusion that, when it did so, the diplomats, as if worn out by the long series of crises that had begun in 1908, succumbed

Two views of the responsibility of the great powers for initiating the World War. On the *Simplissimus* cover for 3 August 1914 sole responsibility is attributed to Russia, the sabre-wielding crocodile that is standing over an expiring Peace while Marianne (France) tries to hold it back and England stands by, doing nothing, holding a revolver to give peace the *coup de grace.* The English cartoon by Bernard Partridge reflects the reaction to the German invasion of Belgium.

to defeatism. It is true that they did go through the motions of trying to save the peace, but their hearts were no longer in it. The men of energy and will in August 1914 were the soldiers, and this was particularly true in Berlin and Vienna. The news on July 29 that Germany could not count on British neutrality if it attacked France shocked Bethmann Hollweg, who up to this time had favored a localized war that would increase German and Austrian power, and he tried now, feebly and belatedly, to hold the Austrians back, or at least to slow down the course of events. For the German soldiers, however, there was no turning back: and on July 30, Moltke, having learned that partial Russian mobilization had begun, sent a telegram to Vienna, without informing either the emperor or the chancellor, urging Conrad to start mobilization immediately and to reject compromise solutions that were currently being made by Lord Grey. War, he added, was now a condition of Austria's survival. "Germany will go along with her unconditionally." When Conrad informed Foreign Minister Berchtold of this telegram, Berchtold, who had been listening to Bethmann's pleas, said inelegantly, "That's something! Who's ruling in Berlin?"

The answer was that the soldiers were. On the same day (July 31) that Austria followed their advice and mobilized against Russia, the German government sent an ultimatum to St. Petersburg, demanding that all war measures be halted, and, without giving the Russians time to consider a reply, declared war on August 1. The rigidity of Germany's war plan now required the speediest possible inception of hostilities and in the west of Europe rather than in the Balkans. Dismissing the emperor's suggestion that operations might at least temporarily be confined to the Russian front, Moltke secured the dispatch of an ultimatum to France and a note to Belgium demanding free passage of German troops. When these were refused, the German declaration of war followed automatically on August 3, and the invasion of Belgium began. This action relieved Lord Grey of the necessity of explaining to the House of Commons the extent of his diplomatic commitments to France and allowed him to base his demand for English intervention upon the protection of England's traditional interests. On August 4, Britain and Germany were at war.

Responsibility   If the last few pages have seemed to stress the responsibility of Austria-Hungary and Germany for driving Europe into war, it should not be forgotten that the other powers shared the blame. The incident that brought the final crisis was the result of a crime planned by agents of the Serbian government; the aggressive policy of the Serbs was at least in part the result of Russian encouragement; the foolhardiness of the Russians in promoting a provocative policy on the part of the Serbs was in part the result of the failure of the British and French governments to impose adequate restraints upon them; and this failure was caused by the fact that Britain and France suffered from the same fears that dimmed the judgment of the German and Austrian governments. Whatever one may decide about the relative guilt of the powers—and this is something on which historians still differ widely—it is clear that no power bears the full responsibility for the war and none is completely guiltless.

Seen in a wider setting, the coming of the war may be regarded as a reflection of tendencies that we have noted in the domestic history of the European states in the years after 1871. The division of Europe into two armed camps after 1907 corresponded roughly to the process of polarization that was taking place in internal politics and was dividing country after country into two extreme factions. The erosion of the moderate position, the abandonment of the liberal attitude, the flight from the reasonable solution and, indeed, from the very use of the human reason to reach solutions—these tendencies, which we have noted in the domestic history of Europe, had their counterparts in its diplomatic history. And now in 1914 that idealization of power that characterized so many areas of European thought and activity became complete, and Europe ended its century of progress in an orgy of violence from which it never recovered.

BIBLIOGRAPHY

The lists that follow are intended to be suggestive rather than exhaustive and for that reason have been kept short. They can be supplemented from other sources, notably from the 1961 revision of the *Guide to Historical Literature*, prepared by specialists on various fields under the sponsorship of the American Historical Association, from such useful compilations as Lowell J. Ragatz, *A Bibliography for the Study of European History, 1815–1939* (1942; supplements 1943, 1945) and Alan Bullock and A. J. P. Taylor, *A Select List of Books on European History 1815–1914* (1957), and from the excellent bibliographical essays in the volumes of the series *The Rise of Modern Europe*, edited by William L. Langer.

The selection of titles has been made with an eye to the needs and interests of undergraduate, rather than advanced, students. Emphasis has been placed upon recent historical literature, although not to the exclusion of older works that have stood the test of time. No attempt has been made to list individual works of art and music.

GENERAL WORKS

Among the older single-volume histories of the nineteenth century, Eduard Fueter's *World History, 1815–1920* (1920) and Benedetto Croce's *History of Europe in the Nineteen Century* (1933) are still provocative but are less satisfactory in their treatment of social forces than such recent works as Peter Stearns, *European Society in Upheaval: Social History since 1800* (1967) and Eugene and Pauline Anderson, *Political Institutions and Social Change in Continental Europe in The Nineteenth Century* (1968). Of the general works dealing with shorter periods, the three volumes of the *Cambridge Modern History* (1902–1912) that treat the years since Napoleon are out of date but include chapters on domestic history that have not been superseded. The *New Cambridge Modern History* has four volumes on the nineteenth and twentieth centuries: *War and Peace in an Age of Upheaval, 1793–1830*, edited by C. W. Crawley; *The Zenith of European Power, 1830–1870*, edited by J. P. T. Bury (1960); *Material Progress and World-Wide Problems, 1870–1898*; edited by F. H. Hinsley (1962); and *The Era of Violence, 1898–1945*, edited by David Thomson (1959) (2d ed., *The Shifting Balance of World Forces, 1898–1945*, edited by C. L. Mowat, 1967). These include good chapters on intellectual history, science, and military affairs, in addition to their chapters on politics and economics. In the *Rise of Modern Europe* series, five of the projected volumes on the modern period have been completed: F. B. Artz, *Reaction and Revolution, 1814–1832* (1934); William L. Langer, *Political and Social Upheaval, 1832–1852* (1969); R. C. Binkley, *Realism and Nationalism, 1852–1871* (1935), a brilliantly executed volume; C. J. H. Hayes, *A Generation of Materialism, 1871–1900* (1941); and Gordon Wright's comprehensive and balanced *The Ordeal of Total War, 1939–1945* (1968). A provocative Marxist survey of the first part of the period is E. J. Hobsbawm, *The Age of Revolution: Europe, 1789–1848* (1964).

Among the general histories of economic development, S. H. Clough and C. W. Cole's *An Economic History of Europe* (1941) and Bowden, Karpovich, and Usher's *An Economic History of Europe since 1750* (1937) are outstanding, W. Ashworth, *A Short History of the International Economy, 1850–1950* (1952), is useful; A. Birnie, *An Economic History of Europe, 1760–1939* (rev. ed., 1951), includes good sections on unionism and social legislation; W. A. Lewis, *Economic Survey, 1919–1939* (1949), is an authoritative treatment by a brilliant scholar. Michael Tracy, *Agriculture in Western Europe: Crisis and Adaptation since 1880* (1964) is a solid and authoritative study. On income, population, and technological change, see *The Cambridge Economic History of Europe*, VI: *The Industrial Revolutions and After*, edited by H. J. Habakkuk and M. Postan (1966), particulary for David Landes's essay on technology in Western Europe and Alexander Gershenkron's study of agrarian problems and industrialization in Russia. On the entrepreneurs, see Charles Morazé, *The Triumph of the Middle Classes (Les Bourgeois Conquérants)* (1966).

General accounts of foreign affairs include Sir Charles Petrie, *Diplomatic History, 1713–1933* (1947); R. W. Seton-Watson, *Britain in Europe, 1789–1914* (1937), which is more comprehensive than its title suggests; Lord Strang, *Britain in World Affairs* (1961), an interesting historical survey by a former Permanent Under-Secretary in the Foreign Office; A. J. P. Taylor, *The Struggle for Mastery in Europe, 1848–1918* (1954), sometimes a bit sweeping in its judgments; R. J. Sontag, *European Diplomatic History, 1870–1932* (1933), a fine account whose later chapters are in need of revision; Hajo Holborn, *The Political Collapse of Europe* (1951), brief but illuminating; and L. C. B. Seaman, *From Vienna to Versailles* (1956), slapdash but occasionally rewarding. An extended discussion of internationalist theories and organization, as well as of the evolution of the state system in the nineteenth and twentieth centuries, is to be found in F. H. Hinsley, *Power and the Pursuit of Peace: Theory and Practice in the History of Relations between States* (1963). Broader in scope and essential for an understanding of the general preoccupation with power in this period is *The Responsibility of Power*, edited by Leonard Krieger and Fritz Stern (1967), essays in honor of the late Hajo Holborn. Some provocative essays are to be found in

Studies in Diplomatic History and Historiography in Honour of G. P. Gooch, edited by A. O. Sarkissian (1961) and in Sir Charles Webster, *The Art and Practice of Diplomacy* (1962).

The important part played by war in the history of the period is dealt with in E. L. Woodward, *War and Peace in Europe, 1815–1870* (1931). More detailed and comprehensive are Theodore Ropp, *War in the Modern World* (1959), which has excellent bibliographical notes; Gordon B. Turner, *A History of Military Affairs in Western Society since the Eighteen Century* (1953), a collection of carefully selected readings; J. F. C. Fuller, *A Military History of the Western World,* vol. III (1956), by one of Britain's leading military experts; Viscount Montgomery of Alamein, *A History of Warfare* (1968), a handsome illustrated survey; *Makers of Modern Strategy: Military Thought from Machiavelli to Hitler,* edited by Edward Mead Earle, Gordon A. Craig, and Felix Gilbert (1943); and *The Theory and Practice of War,* edited by Michael Howard (1965). Howard has also edited a volume of essays on civil-military relations, *Soldiers and Governments* (1957). On the same subject, see Alfred Vagts, *A History of Militarism* (1937) and Gordon A. Craig, *War, Politics and Diplomacy: Selected Essays* (1966).

National political histories are listed in the appropriate sections below. *European Political Systems,* edited by Taylor Cole (new ed., 1959) is a useful book which, while emphasizing the recent period, includes historical background on the evolution of institutional forms in the principal European states. Of the general works dealing with political ideas and movements, C. J. H. Hayes, *The Historical Evolution of Modern Nationalism* (1931), treats one of the explosive forces of the age with brevity and authority. J. H. Hallowell's *Main Currents of Modern Political Thought* (1950) is a solid introduction, and M. Oakeshott's *Social and Political Doctrines of Contemporary Europe* (1939) a useful compilation of doctrinal statements. R. Kirk, *The Conservative Mind from Burke to Santayana* (1953), is well written and illuminating. Peter Viereck, *Conservatism Re-Visited: The Revolt against Revolt* (1949), is essentially an attack on the philosophy of liberalism, which finds its classical exposition in Guido Ruggiero, *European Liberalism* (1927), a comparative study. H. Marcuse, *Reason and Revolution: Hegel and the Rise of Social Theory* (1941), and J. L. Talmon, *Political Messianism: The Romantic Phase, 1815–1848* (1960), are learned and original studies. H. W. Laidler, *Social-Economic Movements: An Historical and Comparative Survey of Socialism, Communism, Cooperation, Utopianism and Other Forces of Reform and Reconstruction* (1944), is a valuable reference work which includes succinct summaries of doctrine and of the contents of basic socialist texts.

In the field of intellectual history, George L. Mosse, *The Culture of Western Europe* (1961), is always interesting and perceptive, although occasionally tendentious. Jacques Barzun, *Classic, Romantic, Modern* (new ed., 1961), warmly defends romanticism against its critics. Isaiah Berlin, *The Hedgehog and the Fox* (1953), is a brilliant essay on Tolstoy, which nevertheless manages to range over the whole intellectual history of the nineteenth century. A challenging intellectual history of the recent past is H. Stuart Hughes, *Consciousness and Society: The Re-Orientation of European Social Thought, 1890–1930* (1958).

The whole range of intellectual activity is treated in J. T. Merz, *A History of European Thought in the Nineteenth Century* (4 vols., 1896–1914), which is

Bibliography

particularly important for students interested in the development of science, as are Charles C. Gillispie's *Genesis and Geology* (1951) and *The Edge of Objectivity* (1960). For the spread of Darwin's influence, the most useful works are Loren C. Eiseley's *Darwin's Century* (1958), and Gertrude Himmelfarb, *Darwin and the Darwinian Revolution* (1959); but see also Paul Sears, *Charles Darwin: The Naturalist as a Cultural Force* (1950), and Jacques Barzun, *Darwin, Marx and Wagner* (1941). The work of a great scientific mind is described in Fritz Wittels, *Freud and His Time* (1948), and in the now standard and justly admired work of Ernest Jones, *Sigmund Freud* (3 vols., 1953–1957). The best general works on medicine are Charles Singer, *A Short History of Medicine* (1941), and Richard Shryock, *The Development of Modern Medicine* (1947). James Conant's *On Understanding Science: An Historical Approach* (1947) is illuminating.

William Fleming, *Arts and Ideas* (3d ed., 1967), is an illuminating history of art, music, and literature and their interrelation. Elie Faure, *A History of Art*, vols. IV and V (1937), and Fernand Hazan, ed., *Dictionary of Modern Painting* (1956), are reliable guides. The second volume of Arnold Hauser's stimulating *Social History of Art* (1952) discusses, among other things, the role of the artist in society. Georg Brandes, *Main Currents in Nineteenth Century Literature* (6 vols., 1901–1906), is still an indispensable general guide. Irving Howe, *Politics and the Novel* (1957), examines the relationship between politics and literature with particular reference to Stendhal, Dostoevsky, Malraux, Orwell, and others. Edmund Wilson, *Axel's Castle: A Study in the Imaginative Literature of 1870–1930* (1931), deals with symbolism and its conflict and fusion with naturalism. Studies of national literatures include Harry Levin, *The Gates of Horn* (1962), on the great French realists from Stendhal to Zola; Martin Turnell, *The Novel in France* (1950) and *The Art of French Fiction* (1959); Victor Lange, *Modern German Literature, 1870–1940* (1945); Michael Hamburger, *Reason and Energy: Studies in German Literature* (1957), which includes a good treatment of the expressionists; and Ernest Simmons, *An Outline of Modern Russian Literature, 1880–1940* (1943). Ernst Kohn-Bramstedt's *Aristocracy and the Middle Classes in Germany* (1937) uses literary sources to illustrate problems of social stratification and change. Hugo Leichtentritt, *Music, History and Ideas* (1938), and Jacques Barzun, *Berlioz and His Century: An Introduction to the Age of Romanticism* (1956), place musical activities in their social context. F. Reyna, *A Concise History of Ballet* (1966). and D. J. Grout, *A Short History of Opera* (2d ed., 1966), are informative and highly readable. See also Joseph Kerman, *Opera as Drama* (1966), an exciting and occasionally infuriating study.

The best historical atlases are those of W. R. Shephard (8th ed., 1956), R. R. Palmer (1957), and E. W. Fox (1957).

Chapter 1   The Great Powers and the Balance of Power, 1815–1848

C. K. Webster's *The Congress of Vienna* (1937) and Harold Nicolson's *The Congress of Vienna* (1945) are both sound accounts of the preliminaries and the actual negotiations. The personality and policies of the chief participants in the Congress are analyzed in C. K. Webster, *The Foreign Policy of Castlereagh, 1815–1822* (2d ed., 1937); A. Duff Cooper, *Talleyrand* (1932); Crane Brinton, *The*

Romantic Art: Man and Nature. "Early Morning on the Dam," (1838) by C Købke. (Ny Carlsberg Glyptotek, Copenhagen)

Lives of Talleyrand (1936); G. Ferrero, *The Reconstruction of Europe: Talley-rand and the Congress of Vienna* (1941); A. A. Lobanov-Rostovsky, *Russia and Europe, 1789–1825* (1947), which deals with Alexander I and his advisers; and the biographies of Metternich by Algernon Cecil (1933), which is excessively lauda-tory, H. du Coudray (1935), and G. de Berthier de Sauvigny (Eng. ed., 1962). Paul W. Schroeder, *Metternich's Diplomacy at Its Zenith, 1820–23* (1962), sees Metternich less as a constructive European statesman than as an Austrian diplo-mat dedicating his undoubted talents to the preservation of the status quo. Metternich's approach to foreign affairs is also treated in E. L. Woodward, *Three Studies in European Conservatism* (1930), which includes studies of Guizot and the Roman Catholic Church as well; and, more recently, in Henry Kissinger, *A World Restored: Metternich, Castlereagh and the Problems of Peace, 1812–1822* (new ed., 1964). Indispensable for an understanding of Metter-nich's attitude toward Russia is Enno E. Kraehe, *Metternich's German Policy,* vol. I, *The Contest with Napoleon, 1799–1814* (1963), even though it deals with the period before 1815.

The problems of the Concert are discussed in W. A. Phillips, *The Confedera-tion of Europe* (1914); H. G. Schenk, *The Aftermath of the Napoleonic Wars: The Concert of Europe—An Experiment* (1947); George Romani, *The Neapolitan Rev-olution, 1820–1821* (1950); H. W. V. Temperley, *The Foreign Policy of Canning, 1822–1827* (1925); and P. J. V. Rolo, *George Canning* (1965), which has a careful account of Canning's policy with respect to the Spanish colonies and the Greek revolution. H. C. F. Bell's *Lord Palmerston* (2 vols., 1936) and C. K. Webster's *The Foreign Policy of Palmerston* (2 vols., 1951) have good accounts of Belgian affairs, and the latter contains a sound analysis of the Egyptian crises. On Palmerston's foreign policy, see also Donald Southgate, *The Most English Minister: The Policies and Politics of Palmerston* (1966). Near Eastern problems in general are treated in J. A. R. Marriott, *The Eastern Question* (4th ed., 1940), and W. Miller, *The Ottoman Empire* (4th ed., 1936), and more specifically in C. W. Crawley, *The Question of Greek Independence* (1931), M. L. Harvey, *The Development of Russian Commerce in the Black Sea* (1938), Philip E. Mosely, *Russian Diplomacy and the Opening of the Eastern Question in 1838 and 1839* (1934), V. J. Puryear, *France and the Levant* (1941), and F. S. Rodkey, *The Turco-Egyptian Question in the Relations of England, France and Russia, 1832–1841* (1924).

Chapter 2   The Eastern Powers: Absolutism and Its Critics

Among the many histories of Russia, the most satisfactory are M. T. Florinsky, *Russia: A History and Interpretation* (2 vols., 1953), James Billington, *The Icon and the Axe* (1966), and Hugh Seton-Watson, *The Russian Empire, 1801–1917* (1967), all of which range beyond the purely political aspects. E. M. Almedingen, *The Emperor Alexander I* (1963), has the merit of being brief, comprehensive, accurate, and well written. The Decembrist revolt has been described with psychological overtones in Mikhail Zetlin, *The Decembrists* (1958), and with greater circumstantial detail in A. G. Mazour, *The First Russian Revolution, 1825: The Decembrist Movement* (1937). N. V. Riasanovsky, *Nicholas I and Official Nationality in Russia, 1825–1881* (1959), and Constantin de Grunwald, *Tsar Nicholas I* (1955), are useful in offsetting the passionate denunciations of Nicholas in Alexander Herzen's *My Past and Thoughts* (6 vols., 1924–1928), the remarkable work of the dean of Russian exiles, which has been described as worthy to stand beside the great Russian novels of the nineteenth century. Herzen was also the first real Russian socialist, and his theoretical elaboration of socialism during the reign of Nicholas I is well described in Martin E. Malia, *Alexander Herzen and the Birth of Russian Socialism, 1812–1855* (1961). Sidney Monas, *The Third Section* (1961), based on profound reading, is an absorbing account of the police system under Nicholas. See also the new study of the same subject by P. S. Squire, *The Third Department* (1963). For social and economic development, see the monumental study of Jerome Blum, *Lord and Peasant in Russia* (1961).

Readable texts on German history are Koppel S. Pinson, *Modern Germany: Its History and Civilization* (1954), R. Flenley, *Modern German History* (1953), Veit Valentin, *The German People: Their History and Civilization* (1946), and Hajo Holborn, *A History of Modern Germany, 1648–1840* (1964) and *A History of Modern Germany, 1840–1945* (1969). The economic aspects of the period are treated in the important work of J. H. Clapham, *The Economic Development of France and Germany, 1815–1914* (4th ed., 1936), and in T. S. Hamerow, *Restoration, Revolution, Reaction: Economics and Politics in Germany, 1815–1871* (1958). A book that judges the social ideas and activity of liberals like Camphausen and Mevissen more positively than Hamerow is Donald G. Rohr, *The Origins of Social Liberalism in Germany* (1963). Hans Kohn's *The Mind of Germany* (1960) treats movements of thought, and Leonard Krieger's *The German Idea of Freedom* (1957) the role and dilemma of the intellectuals.

On Prussian history, see Gordon A. Craig, *The Politics of the Prussian Army, 1640–1945* (new ed., 1965), Peter Paret, *Yorck and the Era of Prussian Reform* (1966), Walter Simon, *The Failure of the Prussian Reform Movement, 1807–1819* (1955), and Friedrich Meinecke, "Liberalism and Nationality in Germany," *Cambridge Modern History*, vol. XI. On Austria, see A. J. P. Taylor, *The Habsburg Monarchy, 1809–1819* (new ed., 1948); R. W. Seton-Watson, "Metternich and Internal Austrian Policy," in *The Making of Modern Europe*, edited by H. Ausubel, vol. II (1951); and Jerome Blum, *Noble Landowners and Agriculture in Austria* (1948). On Hungary, see C. A. Macartney, *Hungary, A Short History* (1962), and George Barany, *Stephen Szécheny and the Awakening of Hungarian Nationalism, 1791–1841* (1968). A fine book with interesting information on culture, education, the police system and policies before 1848 and during the revolution is Eric A. Blackall, *Adalbert Stifter: A Critical Study* (1948). Much information is to be found also in Donald E. Emerson, *Metternich and the Political Police* (1968).

Chapter 3   France: The Restoration and the July Monarchy

The liveliest of the good one-volume histories is D. W. Brogan, *The French Nation, 1814–1940* (1957). Less impressionistic are J. P. T. Bury, *France, 1814–1940* (1949), Gordon Wright, *Modern France* (1960), and J. B. Wolf, *A History of France since 1814* (1940), the last work excellent on social organization. Basic to any understanding of socio-economic movements are J. H. Clapham, *The Economic Development of France and Germany* (1936), Shepard H. Clough, *France: A History of National Economics, 1789–1939* (1939), and Rondo E. Cameron, *France and the Economic Development of Europe, 1800–1914: Conquests of Peace and Seeds of War* (1961).

The domestic history of the period is treated in F. B. Artz, *France under the Bourbon Restoration, 1814–1830* (1931); J. Lucas Dubreton, *The Restoration and the July Monarchy* (1929); Gilbert Stenger, *The Return of Louis XVIII* (1909); Daniel Philip Resnick, *The White Terror and the Political Reaction after Waterloo* (1967); Nicholas Richardson, *The French Prefectoral Corps. 1814–1830* (1967). J. M. S. Allison, *Thiers and the French Monarchy* (1926); E. L. Woodward, *Conservatism* (on Guizot); and R. Soltau, *French Political Thought in the Nineteenth Century* (1931). The best general account of the workings of the political system of the July Monarchy is Douglas Johnson, *Guizot: Aspects of French History, 1787–1874* (1963). C. S. Philips, *The Church in France, 1789–1907* (2 vols., 1929, 1936), P. H. Spencer, *The Politics of Belief in Nineteenth Century France* (1954), and Adrian Dansette, *Religious History of Modern France* (2 vols., 1961), throw light on religious developments and controversies. The literature on the political opposition and on reform movements is less rich in English than in French but includes J. Plamenetz, *The Revolutionary Movement in France, 1815–1871* (1952), Alan Spitzer, *The Revolutionary Theories of Louis Auguste Blanqui* (1957), and F. E. Manuel, *The New World of Saint-Simon* (1956) and *The Prophets of Paris* (1962), which has excellent analyses of the thought of Saint-

Simon, Fourier, and Auguste Comte. On Saint-Simonianism, see also the perceptive essay in Élie Halévy, *The Era of Tyrannies*, translated by R. K. Webb (1967). George G. Iggers, *The Cult of Authority: The Political Cult of the Saint-Simonians* (1958), sees the seeds of modern totalitarianism in the movement.

On romanticism, see N. H. Clement, *Romanticism in France* (1939), A. J. George, *The Development of French Romanticism* (1955), and, for its social consequences, D. O. Evans, *Social Romanticism in France, 1830–1848* (1951). On Stendhal, see particularly Victor Brombert, *Stendhal: Fiction and the Themes of Freedom* (1968). André Maurois' *Prometheus: The Life of Balzac* (1965), *Lélia: The Life of George Sand* (1953), and *Olympio: The Life of Victor Hugo* (1956) and Matthew Josephson's *Victor Hugo* (1946) describe the intellectual vigor of the period. César Graña, *Bohemian versus Bourgeois: French Society and the French Man of Letters in the Nineteenth Century* (1964), poses the problem of the intellectual and has some interesting comments. A less effective treatment of the same theme is Malcolm Easton, *Artists and Writers in Paris: The Bohemian Idea, 1803–1867* (1964). Howard P. Vincent, *Daumier and His World* (1969), is the best available biography of the artist. Finally, Alexis de Tocqueville, *Recollections*, edited by J. P. Mayer (1949), should be read by every student of the period, as should *The Memoirs of Hector Berlioz* in the new translation of David Cairns (1969).

Chapter 4   Great Britain: Social Unrest and Social Compromise, 1815–1848

An excellent introduction to British history is R. K. Webb, *Modern England* (1969) which covers the whole period from the eighteenth century to the 1960s. For the first half of the nineteenth century, the most reliable guide is E. L. Woodward, *The Age of Reform* (1938), which includes an account of imperial developments; while the most comprehensive is the magnificent work of Élie Halévy, *A History of the English People in the Nineteenth Century* (vols. I–IV, 1927–1947), equally good on politics and intellectual movements, particularly in the field of religion. Asa Briggs, *The Age of Improvement* (1959), is a gracefully written general survey of political and social history from the 1780s to 1867. Economic developments are discussed in J. H. Clapham, *An Economic History of Modern Britain* (1938), W. H. B. Court, *A Concise Economic History of Britain from 1750 to Recent Times* (1954), and S. G. Checkland, *The Rise of Industrial Society in England, 1815–1885* (1964), an often pedestrian work but with valuable material on technological progress. An important and most readable account is Phyllis Deane, *The First Industrial Revolution* (1965). On agriculture, see Lord Ernle, *English Farming, Past and Present* (1961), and J. D. Chambers and G. E. Mingay, *The Agricultural Revolution, 1750–1880* (1966). Social consequences receive attention in G. D. H. Cole and R. Postgate, *The British Common People, 1748–1938* (1939), J. L. and B. Hammond, *The Village Labourer, 1760–1832* (new ed., 1948) and *The Town Labourer, 1760–1832* (1919), R. J. White, *Waterloo to Peterloo* (1957), and Donald Read, *Peterloo: The Massacre and Its Background* (1958). Particularly good on the conditions of the rural poor in the period between the end of the European war and the agricultural riots of 1830 is E. J. Hobsbawm and George Rudé, *Captain Swing* (1969). Broader in scope is E. P. Thompson, *The Making of the English Working Class* (1963), a "biography of the working class from its adolescence until its early manhood," from the 1780s until about 1832. It is equally good on occupations, organizations, religion, and incidents like Peterloo and the Pentridge rising.

Crane Brinton, *English Political Thought in the Nineteenth Century* (rev. ed., 1950), and S. Maccoby, *English Radicalism, 1786–1832* (1955), are good introductions to the political thinking of the age, while Élie Halévy, *The Growth of Philosophical Radicalism* (one-vol. ed., 1949), is deservedly considered to be the classic analysis of the doctrines of radicalism stimulated by Jeremy Bentham. On these, see also John Bowle, *Politics and Opinion in the Nineteenth Century* (1954), and M. S. J. Packe, *Life of John Stuart Mill* (1954). The movement for political and social reform is described in H. W. C. Davis, *The Age of Grey and Peel* (1929), J. R. M. Butler, *The Passing of the Great Reform Bill* (1914), J. L. Hammond and B. Hammond, *Lord Shaftesbury* (new ed., 1930), Graham Wallas, *The Life of Francis Place* (new ed., 1925), and Norman Gash, *Mr. Secretary Peel: The Life of Sir Robert Peel to 1830* (1961) and *Reaction and Reconstruction in English Politics, 1832–1852* (1964). Early socialism and unionism are treated in Max Beer, *A History of British Socialism* (2 vols., 1920), and the books on Robert Owen by G. D. H. Cole (1930), Rowland H. Harvey (1949), Margaret Cole (1953), and Asa Briggs (1959); and Chartism in M. Hovell, *The Chartist Movement* (2d ed., 1925), still the best account, as well as in Julius West, *The History of the Chartist Movement* (1920), A. R. Schoyen, *The Chartist Challenge: A Portrait of G. J. Harney* (1958), and Asa Briggs, *Chartist Studies* (1959). Illuminating accounts of the consequences of the Reform Bill and the growth of modern political organization are G. Kitson Clark, *Peel and the Conservative Party* (new ed., 1964), Norman Gash, *Politics in the Age of Peel: A Study in the Technique of Parliamentary Representation* (1957), and Norman McCord, *The Anti-Corn Law League* (1968).

A moving account of the famine in Ireland is Cecil Woodham-Smith, *The Great Hunger* (1962). On the life of the greatest Irish leader of this period, see Denis Gwynn, *Daniel O'Connell* (new ed., 1947).

The religious revival of the first half of the century is treated at length in Halévy, but see the useful study of Georgina Battiscombe, *John Keble: A Study in Limitations* (1963). The latest and biggest book on Newman is the two-volume study by Meriol Trevor (1962), but see also C. F. Harrold, *John Henry Newman* (1945), and A. Dwight Culler, *The Imperial Intellect: A Study of Newman's Educational Ideal* (1958). Light is thrown on the state of university education in Geoffrey Faber, *Jowett: A Portrait with Background* (1957).

Edgar Holt, *The Opium Wars in China* (1964), is a readable account of early British imperialism in the Far East.

Chapter 5   The Revolutions of 1848

Priscilla Robertson, *The Revolutions of 1848* (1952), is well written and detailed and covers the whole range of revolutionary disturbances. More entertaining but less thorough is R. Postgate, *The Story of a Year: 1848* (1955). Arnold Whitridge's *Men in Crisis: The Revolution of 1848* (1949) concentrates on the activities of Louis Philippe, Lamartine, Louis Napoleon, Mazzini, Garibaldi, Marx, Széchenyi,

Meeting of the Revolutionary Club, Paris 1848. (Bettmann Archive)

Kossuth, and Metternich. F. Fejtö, ed., *The Opening of an Era: 1848—An Historical Symposium* (1948), is interesting but uneven. Events in Germany are described in Veit Valentin, *1848: Chapters in German History* (1940), J. G. Legge, *Rhyme and Revolution in Germany* (1918), a highly original collection of historical material, and the splendid essay by Sir Lewis Namier, *1848: The Revolution of the Intellectuals* (1945). Events in France are treated in the brilliant impressionistic study of Georges Duveau, *1848: The Making of a Revolution* (1967), R. Arnaud, *The Second Republic and Napoleon III* (1930), and Donald McKay, *The National Workshops: A Study in the French Revolution of 1848* (1933); Italian developments in A. J. P. Taylor, *The Italian Problem in European Diplomacy, 1847–1849* (1934), and G. M. Trevelyan, *Garibaldi and the Defence of the Roman Republic* (1907) and *Manin and the Venetian Revolution of 1848* (1923); and aspects of the revolution in Hungary in C. Sproxton, *Palmerston and the Hungarian Revolution* (1919). Joseph Redlich, *Emperor Francis Joseph* (1929), and R. John Rath, *The Viennese Revolution of 1848* (1957), should be consulted for events in Vienna and for the success of reaction.

A curiously organized but suggestive book is Raymond Aron, *Main Currents in Sociological Thought*, vol. I, *Montesquieu, Comte, Marx, Tocqueville, the Sociologists, and the Revolution of 1848* (1964). See also, for a discussion of the early ideas of its protagonists, Oscar J. Hammen, *The Red '48ers: Karl Marx and Friedrich Engels* (1969).

Bibliography

Chapter 6   The Breakdown of the Concert and the Crimean War

The effects of the revolutions of 1848 on the diplomatic temper of the age are discussed in Binkley's *Realism and Nationalism* and in Gordon A. Craig, "The System of Alliances and the Balance of Power," *New Cambridge Modern History*, vol. X. The background of the Crimean War is dealt with in V. J. Puryear, *International Economics and Diplomacy in the Near East: A Study of British Commercial Policy* (1935) and *England, Russia and the Straits Question, 1844–1856* (1931), and in H. W. V. Temperley's splendid *England and the Near East: The Crimea* (1936). Illuminating essays on the relations between the powers are to be found in G. B. Henderson, *Crimean War Diplomacy* (1947), while the role of public opinion in precipitating the conflict is discussed engagingly in B. Kingsley Martin, *The Triumph of Lord Palmerston* (1924). See also O. Anderson, *Liberal State at War: English Politics and Economics during the Crimean War* (1967). Among the recent works that deal with the course of the war, see especially C. Woodham-Smith, *Florence Nightingale* (1951) and *The Reason Why* (1953), the latter a critical examination of the British performance, and John Shelton Curtiss, *The Russian Army under Nicholas I, 1825–1855* (1965). Peter Gibbs, *The Battle of the Alma* (1963), also gives a good picture of the kind of war fought in the Crimea, while John Hohenberg, *Foreign Correspondence: The Great Reporters and Their Times* (1965), has a section on W. H. Russell, the dean of war correspondents, and his dispute with Lord Raglan. W. E. Mosse, *The Rise and Fall of the Crimean System* (1963), discusses the way in which the Russians were forced to conclude peace, the nature of the settlement, and the progressive breakdown of this attempt to contain Russia. One of the positive results of the war is treated fully in T. W. Riker, *The Making of Rumania* (1931).

Chapter 7   France: The Second Empire

F. A. Simpson, *The Rise of Louis Napoleon* (1909) and *Louis Napoleon and the Recovery of France, 1848–1856* (3d ed., 1951), are rich in detail and balanced in judgment; J. M. Thompson, *Louis Napoleon and the Second Empire* (1954), is less satisfactory on the nonpolitical aspects of the reign; Philip Guedalla, *The Second Empire* (1922), is brilliantly written, entertaining, but often flippant in tone. A. Guérard's *Napoleon III: An Interpretation* (1943) sees Napoleon's "Caesarian democracy" as a forerunner of modern totalitarianism. An interesting and perceptive study is Harold Kurtz, *The Empress Eugenie, 1826–1920* (1964), which effectively destroys the legend that Napoleon's consort was a shrew and a reactionary. T. Zeldin's *The Political System of Napoleon III* (1958) and David Kulstein's *Napoleon III and the Working Class* (1969) are methodical and original studies. F. C. Palm, *England and Napoleon III* (1949), explains the lack of confidence between the Crimean allies. David S. Pinkney's *Napoleon III and the Reconstruction of Paris* (1958) is a fascinating study of how Paris was rebuilt, on which see also J. M. and Brian Chapman, *The Life and Times of Baron Haussman* (1958). Religion, education, the sciences, and the arts are treated in Roger L. Williams, *Gaslight and Shadow: The World of Napoleon III* (1957), an entertaining but occasionally overlooked book. See also Enid Starkie, *Flaubert:*

The Making of the Master (1967), and Victor Brombert, *The Novels of Flaubert* (1967).

Napoleon's Mexican adventure is described in Jack Autrey Dabbs, *The French Army in Mexico, 1816–1867* (1962).

Chapter 8   The Unification of Italy

The most satisfactory general histories are R. Albrecht-Carrié, *Italy from Napoleon to Mussolini* (1950), L. Salvatorelli, *A Concise History of Italy* (1940), A. J. Whyte, *The Evolution of Modern Italy* (1950), and, for economic development, Shepard H. Clough, *The Economic History of Modern Italy* (1964). A brilliant study of the relation between economics and politics is K. Roberts Greenfield, *Economics and Liberalism in the Risorgimento: A Study of Nationalism in Lombardy, 1814–1848* (1934). Bolton King's *A History of Italian Unity* (2 vols., 1899) is still readable and sound, as is William Thayer's *The Life and Times of Cavour* (2 vols., 1914). Cavour's role is treated critically in Denis Mack Smith, *Cavour and Garibaldi in 1860* (1954), and admiringly in M. Paléologue, *Cavour* (1927), and A. J. Whyte, *The Political Life and Letters of Cavour* (1930). An interesting collection of sources will be found in Mack Walker, ed., *Plombières* (1968).

There is no satisfactory life of Mazzini in English, but see Gwilyn O. Griffith, *Mazzini* (1932), and, on doctrine, Gaetano Salvemini, *Mazzini* (1957). Garibaldi's contribution to unification is treated in brief in Denis Mack Smith, *Garibaldi* (1956), and with verve and rich detail in G. M. Trevelyan, *Garibaldi's Defence of the Roman Republic* (1907), *Garibaldi and the Thousand* (1911), and *Garibaldi and the Making of Italy* (1911). Special studies of importance are Raymond Grew, *A Sterner Plan for Italian Unity: The Italian National Society in the Risorgimento* (1963), W. K. Hancock, *Ricasoli and the Risorgimento in Tuscany* (1926), C. S. Forester, *Victor Emmanuel II and the Union of Italy* (1922), and M. S. J. Packe, *Orsini: The Story of a Conspirator* (1957). On the Church, see S. W. Halperin, *The Separation of Church and State in Italian Thought from Cavour to Mussolini* (1937, and C. C. Eckhardt, *The Papacy in World Affairs* (1937).

Silvio Pellico's classical account can now be found in the translation by I. G. Capaldi, Silvio Pellico, *My Prisons* (1963).

Chapter 9   The German Question

The general works cited for Chapter 2 and Craig, *Politics of the Prussian Army,* have sections on Germany's progress toward unification. An original study with much new material is Theodore S. Hamerow. *The Social Foundations of German Unification, 1858–1871: Ideas and Institutions* (1969). On politics and diplomacy, the reader should consult the classical account written in the 1890s by the Austrian historian Heinrich Friedjung, *The Struggle for Supremacy in Germany, 1859–1866* (abridged ed., 1935), and the special studies by C. W. Clark, *Franz Joseph and Bismarck: The Diplomacy of Austria before the War of 1866* (1934), L. Steefel, *The Schleswig-Holstein Question* (1932), and W. E. Mosse, *The European Powers and the German Question* (1958). The best separate account of the Prussian constitutional conflict in English is E. N. Anderson, *The Social and Political Conflict in Prussia, 1858–1864* (1954), which has much new material. The best biographies of Bismarck are those of C. Grant Robertson (1919), A. J. P. Taylor (1955), and Werner Richter (1964). Erich Eyck's *Bismarck and the German Empire* (1950) is an abbreviated version of the author's three-volume biography. W. N. Medlicott, *Bismarck and Modern Germany* (1965), is most perceptive when dealing with the chancellor's foreign policy, which is treated also with authority and detail in Otto Pflanze, *Bismarck and the Development of Germany, vol. I, The Period of Unification, 1815–1871* (1963). Bismarck's own memoirs are printed in English as *Bismarck, the Man and the Statesman* (2 vols., 1899) and *The Kaiser vs. Bismarck: New Chapters of Bismarck's Autobiography* (1921).

The culmination of the Austro-Prussian rivalry is described in Gordon A. Craig, *The Battle of Königgrätz* (1964).

Chapter 10   The Reorganization of Europe, 1866–1871

British imperial developments are described in Woodward's *Age of Reform* and, at greater length, in *The Cambridge History of the British Empire* (8 vols., 1929 ff.). The centenary of the Indian Mutiny brought a rash of books, including J. Leasor's *The Red Fort* (1957) and two Indian accounts, S. N. Sen, *Eighteen Fifty Seven* (1957), and H. Chattopadyaya, *The Sepoy Mutiny* (1957). See also such older accounts as T. R. Holmes, *A History of the Indian Mutiny* (1913), and George Dangerfield, *The Bengal Mutiny* (1933). For the war in China, see W. C. Costin's *Great Britain and China, 1833–1860* (1937), and Edgar Holt, *The Opium Wars* (1964).

G. M. Young's *Victorian England: Portrait of an Age* (2d ed., 1953), and G. Kitson Clark, *The Making of Victorian England* (1962), are books of charm and wisdom. Asa Briggs, *Victorian People: A Reassessment of Persons and Themes, 1851–1867* (1954), includes fine essays on Samuel Smiles, Thomas Hughes, and John Bright and a discussion of Disraeli's role in passing the Second Reform Bill; a companion volume by the same author is *Victorian Cities* (1963). The basic work on Disraeli is still W. F. Monypenny and G. Buckle, *Life of Disraeli, Earl of Beaconsfield* (6 vols., 1913 ff.), but more usable and readable is the excellent biography of Robert Blake, *Disraeli* (1966), which may be supplemented by Paul Smith, *Disraelian Conservatism and Social Reform* (1968). Lord Morley, *Life of Gladstone* (3 vols., 1904), is still essential, despite the excellent qualities of Philip Magnus, *Gladstone: A Biography* (1954). W. D. Jones, *Lord Derby and Victorian Conservatism* (1956), is devoted to the "Rupert of debate" and his part in the reform of 1867, on which see also Maurice Cowling, *Disraeli, Gladstone and Revolution* (1967), and F. B. Smith, *The Making of the Second Reform Bill* (1966). On the court, see Lytton Strachey's *Queen Victoria* (1921), Lady Longford, *Queen Victoria* (1965), and Frank Eyck's *The Prince Consort: A Political Biography* (1959). Among special political studies, H. J. Hanham, *Elections and Party Management: Politics in the Time of Disraeli and Gladstone* (1959), deserves special notice as an admirable supplement to Gash's study of the earlier period.

The reign of the Tsar Liberator is discussed in Stephen Graham, *Tsar of Freedom: The Life and Reign of Alexander II* (1935), and E. M. Almedingen, *The Emperor Alexander II* (1962), although neither gives as thorough a treatment of

Bombardment of Strasbourg, August 1870. (Bettmann Archive)

the reforms and the beginnings of the revolutionary movement as W. E. Mosse, *Alexander II and the Modernization of Russia* (1958), Forest A. Miller, *Dimitri Miliutin and the Reform Era in Russia* (1968) or the fine analysis by Terence Emmons, *The Russian Landed Gentry and the Peasant Emancipation of 1861* (1968). On economic questions, P. I. Liaschenko, *History of the National Economy in Russia* (Eng. trans., 1949), is the work of a distinguished Russian economic historian. On the agrarian problem, see particularly G. T. Robinson, *Rural Russia under the Old Regime* (1932), and G. Pasvolsky, *Agricultural Russia on the Eve of the Revolution* (new ed., 1949).

The Franco-Prussian *dénouement* is treated in several of the works cited under Chapter 9. See also Hermann Oncken, *Napoleon III and the Rhine* (1928), which has a strong anti-French bias, Georges Bonnin, ed., *Bismarck and the Hohenzollern Candidature for the Spanish Throne* (1958), and R. H. Lord, *The Origins of the War of 1870* (1924), still the most satisfactory treatment. Of the many works on the war itself, only one need be cited here, Michael Howard, *The Franco-Prussian War* (1961), a fine book that discusses both the military operations and the civil-military problem in the belligerent countries.

Chapter 11   The Great Powers and the Balance of Power, 1871–1890

The best of the general diplomatic histories of these two decades is W. L. Langer, *European Alliances and Alignments* (rev. ed., 1950), which includes very thorough bibliographical sections at the end of the chapters. The Near Eastern crisis is treated in several of the works cited in Chapter 6; the Russo-Turkish war in an interesting short book by Rupert Furneaux, *The Breakfast War* (1958); and the Congress of Berlin in W. N. Medlicott, *The Congress of Berlin and After* (1938), and M. D. Stojanović, *The Great Powers and the Balkans, 1875–1878* (1939). German policy is surveyed in Malcolm Carroll, *Germany and the Great Powers* (1938). J. V. Fuller's *Bismarck's Diplomacy at Its Zenith* (1922) is a detailed account of the chancellor's handling of the Bulgarian crisis, while Gordon A. Craig's *From Bismark to Adenauer* (rev. ed., 1965) has chapters on the principles guiding Bismarck's statecraft and his methods of foreign policy administration. R. J. Sontag, *Germany and England: The Background of Conflict, 1848–1894* (1938), and R. J. S. Hoffmann, *The Anglo-German Trade Rivalry, 1875–1914* (1933), deal with the growing friction between these powers. R. W. Seton-Watson's *Disraeli, Gladstone and the Eastern Question* (1935) and A. L. Kennedy's *Salisbury, 1830–1903* (1953) throw light on Britain's policy in the Balkans and at the Straits. J. A. S. Grenville, *Lord Salisbury and Foreign Policy* (1963), is a perceptive work that emphasizes the end of its subject's career. In addition to B. H. Sumner, *Russia and the Balkans* (1937), an impressive work that has become a classic, three recent volumes are helpful on Russian policy: M. B. Petrovich, *The Emergence of Russian Pan Slavism, 1856–1870* (1956); Hans Kohn, *Pan Slavism* (1953); and Charles Jelavich, *Tsarist Russia and Balkan Nationalism: Russian Influence in the Internal Affairs of Bulgaria and Serbia* (1958). On economic influences, see, *inter alia*, L. C. Robbins, *The Economic Causes of War* (1939), and A. H. Imlah, *Economic Elements in the Pax Britannica* (1958). On military influence, see Alfred Vagts, *Defense and Diplomacy* (1956), and the books cited under General Works.

Chapter 12   **The Evolution of Capitalism and the Spread of Socialism, 1871–1914**

On some characteristic features of late nineteenth-century capitalism, see Joseph A. Schumpeter, *Capitalism, Socialism and Democracy* (3d ed., 1950); Robert Liefmann, *International Cartels, Combines and Trusts* (1927); Jacob Riesser, *The German Great Banks* (1911); and G. W. Edwards, *The Evolution of Finance Capitalism* (1938). W. W. Rostow's *Stages of Economic Growth* (1960) is a challenging analysis of mature capitalism with the sub-title "A Non-Communist Manifesto." Its basic thesis is accepted in Charles P. Kindleberger, *Economic Growth in France and Britain, 1851–1950* (1964).

In addition to works already cited, G. D. H. Cole's *A History of Socialist Thought* (3 vols., 1953 ff.) should be mentioned. Excerpts from basic works of Marxist literature will be found in Emile Burns, *Handbook of Marxism* (1935) and *Karl Marx and Friedrich Engels: Selected Works* (2 vols., 1951). The best biographies of Marx are those of Isaiah Berlin (1939), E. H. Carr (1934), and Franz Mehring (Eng. trans., 1936), and the most satisfactory analyses are M. Bober, *Karl Marx's Interpretation of History* (rev. ed., 1948), George Lichtheim, *Marxism: An Historical and Critical Study* (1961), and Bertram D. Wolfe, *Marxism: 100 Years in the Life of a Doctrine* (1965). An interesting account of his early philosophical ideas is Robert C. Tucker, *Philosophy and Myth in Karl Marx* (1961). See also Edmund Wilson, *To the Finland Station* (rev. ed., 1953). On Engels, see G. Mayer, *Friedrich Engels* (abridged ed., 1936); on anarchism, James Joll, *The Anarchists* (1964), George Woodcock, *Anarchism* (1964), and Barbara Tuchman, *The Proud Tower* (1962); on Proudhon, E. H. Carr, *Studies in Revolution* (1950); on Bakunin, E. H. Carr, *Michael Bakunin* (1937), and E. Lampert, *Studies in Rebellion: Belinsky, Bakunin, Herzen* (1957); on revisionism, Peter Gay, *The Dilemma of Democratic Socialism: Eduard Bernstein's Challenge to Marx* (1952), a thoughtful volume; on syndicalism, R. Humphrey, *Georges Sorel: Prophet without Honor* (1951); on the international organization of socialism, G. M. Stekloff, *History of the First International* (1928), and James Joll, *The Second International, 1889–1914* (1955), and Milorad Drachkovich, ed., *The Revolutionary Internationals, 1864–1943* (1966).

Chapter 13 From Liberalism to Democracy: Political Progress in Western Europe, 1871–1914

R. C. K. Ensor's *England, 1870–1914* (1936) is a reliable and comprehensive survey. Walt Whitman Rostow, *British Economy in the Nineteenth Century* (1948), analyzes the long depression, and Helen Lynd's *England in the Eighteen-Eighties: Toward a Social Basis for Freedom* (1945) some of its consequences. E. F. Benson, *As We Were: A Victorian Peepshow* (1930), is amusing and provocative, while *Edwardian England, 1901–1914,* edited by Simon Nowell-Smith (1964), is a handsome volume that includes essays by acknowledged experts on every aspect of English life from politics and economic growth to domestic life, science, and literature. On the court, see Lady Longford's *Queen Victoria* (1965), Philip Magnus, *King Edward the Seventh* (1964), and the first half of Harold Nicolson, *King George the Fifth: His Life and Reign* (1953), all based upon research in the Royal Archives at Windsor, as well as the immensely readable *Recollections of Three Reigns* by Lord Ponsonby (1951). Conservative politics receive attention in R. B. McDowell, *British Conservatism* (1959), W. S. Churchill, *Lord Randolph Churchill* (1906), and J. L. Garvin, *Life of Joseph Chamberlain* (3 vols., 1932–1934), now completed in three additional volumes by Julian Amery (1951–1969). Gladstone's successor is treated at length in Robert Rhodes James, *Rosebery* (1962), and the Liberal floodtide after 1905 in Colin Cross, *The Liberals in Power, 1905–1914* (1962). The struggle with the House of Lords is analyzed in *Mr. Balfour's Poodle* (1954) by Roy Jenkins, who has also written the definitive biography, *Asquith: Portrait of a Man and an Era* (1964). On Asquith's colleagues, see Violet Bonham Carter, *Winston Churchill as I Knew Him* (1964), the two volumes of Randolph Churchill's unfinished life of his father (1966, 1967), John Edwards, *David Lloyd George: The Man and the Statesman* (2 vols., 1929), Frank Owen, *Tempestuous Journey: Lloyd George, His Life and Times* (1954), Thomas Jones, *Lloyd George* (1951), the biographies of Haldane by Sir Frederick Maurice (2 vols., 1937–1939), and Dudley Sommer (1960) and A. J. Marder, *From the Dreadnought to Scapa Flow: The Royal Navy in the Fisher Era,* vol. I, *1904–1914* (1961).

Henry Pelling, *Origins of the Labour Party, 1880–1900* (1954), is the most useful and reliable account of its subject. Fabianism is examined in E. R. Pease's history of the society (1916), in A. M. McBriar, *Fabian Socialism and English Politics, 1884–1918* (1962), a comprehensive analysis of the society's ideas and particularly those of Sidney Webb and Bernard Shaw, and, in a lighter vein, in Anne Fremantle, *This Little Band of Prophets* (1960). The new unionism and the Taff Vale decision and its consequences are discussed in H. A. Clegg, Alan Fox, and A. F. Thompson, *A History of British Trade Unions since 1889,* vol. I, *1889–1910* (1964). See also Henry Pelling, *A History of British Trade Unionism* (1963), and E. J. Hobsbawm, *Labouring Men* (1964), selected essays by a leading Marxist historian. On the Irish question, see J. L. Hammond, *Gladstone and the Irish Nation* (1938), John E. Pomfret, *The Struggle for Land in Ireland, 1880–1892* (1930), and the studies of Parnell by R. Barry O'Brien (1899) and J. Haslip (1937). The troubles in Ulster are treated in A. P. Ryan, *The Mutiny at the Curragh* (1955) and, as seen from the War Office, in James Fergusson, *The Curragh Incident* (1963). A stimulating account of social unrest on the eve of the war is George Dangerfield, *The Strange Death of Liberal England* (1936), but see also Henry Pelling, *Popular Politics and Society in Late Victorian Britain* (1960).

On the lesser states of Western Europe, Adrian Barnouw, *The Dutch: A Portrait Study* (1940), G. Edmundson, *History of Holland* (1922), Emile Cammaerts *The Keystone of Europe: History of the Belgian Dynasty, 1830–1939* (1939), and Johannes Gous, ed., *Belgium* (1945), are all useful guides. William Rappard, *The Government of Switzerland* (1936), is written by an outstanding Swiss scholar; and E. Bonjour and others, *A Short History of Switzerland* (1952), is reliable but regrettably brief. Robert Bain's *Scandinavia: A Political History* (1905) has basic facts but is less searching in its analysis of motive forces than R. E. Lindgren's *Norway-Sweden: Union, Disunion, and Scandinavian Integration* (1959). See also R. Svanström and C. F. Palmstierna, *Short History of Sweden* (1934), John Danstrup, *The History of Denmark* (1948), and O. J. Falnes, *National Romanticism in Norway* (1933).

H. V. Livermore's *History of Portugal* (1947) is a general survey and V. de Bragança Cunha's *Revolutionary Portugal, 1910–1936* (1938) a more detailed account of political movements. The troubled history of Spain is treated with balance and perspective by Raymond Carr, *Spain, 1808–1939* (1966). See also Salvador de Madariaga, *Spain* (2d ed., 1946), and Stanley G. Payne, *Politics and the Military in Modern Spain* (1967). The religious question is the subject of Edgar Peers, *The Church in Spain, 1739–1937* (1938), and is handled somewhat differently in Gerald Brenan, *The Spanish Labyrinth* (1943), a work that also sheds light on the agrarian problem and on varieties of socialism. On cultural history, J. B. Trend's *The Civilization of Spain* (1944) and Jose Castillejo's *The War of Ideas in Spain* (1937) are important.

The best history of Italy for this period is that of Christopher Seton-Watson, *Italy from Liberalism to Fascism, 1870–1925* (1967), a mine of information on all aspects of the period, but particularly interesting for the Giolitti years. Benedetto Croce, *A History of Italy, 1871–1915* (1929), is a concise survey by one of Italy's greatest modern thinkers. Denis Mack Smith's *Italy: A Modern History* (1959) embodies the result of modern scholarship and is well written. Cecil Sprigge, *The Development of Modern Italy* (1944), is a good short account which is

Bibliography

perhaps too intent on showing roots of fascism, and M. Hentze, *Pre-Fascist Italy* (1939), suffers from the same fault but is equally useful. A. W. Salomone, *Italian Democracy in the Making* (1945), concentrates on the Giolitti period. Useful and amusing is Luigi Barzini, *The Italians* (1964), a collection of essays on national character. Good histories of socialism are Richard Hostetter, *The Italian Socialist Movement,* vol. I, *Origins* (1958); H. L. Gualtieri, *The Labor Movement in Italy, 1848–1904* (1946); and W. Hilton Young, *The Italian Left* (1949).

Chapter 14   France: The Divided Republic, 1871–1914

Reliable basic surveys are D. W. Brogan, *France under the Republic: The Development of Modern France, 1870–1939* (1940), and David Thomson, *Democracy in France: The Third Republic* (rev. ed., 1952), the latter somewhat more analytical. See also Guy Chapman, *The Third Republic of France: The First Phase, 1871–1894* (1962), a disjointed and often disappointing book.

Articles on various political and social problems by outstanding students of French affairs are found in *Modern France,* edited by Edward Mead Earle (1951). C. J. H. Hayes, *France: A Nation of Patriots* (1931), includes a fascinating analysis

Camille Pissarro (1830–1903), "Place du Théatre Français, Soleil d'Après-Midi en Hiver."
Mr. and Mrs. Norton Simon, Los Angeles.

of the teaching of history in elementary schools; and C. S. Philips, *Church in France*, vol. II, gives the main outlines of the thorny religious question. The most balanced work on the Commune is E. S. Mason, *The Paris Commune* (1930), but see also the study of Frank Jellinek (1937) and, more recently, Alistair Horne, *The Fall of Paris* (1965). On the equally controversial "affair," A. Charpentier, *The Dreyfus Affair* (1935), and Guy Chapman, *The Dreyfus Case* (1955), are sane reconstructions. See also Nicholas Halasz, *Captain Dreyfus* (1955), and, for international repercussions, Thomas M. Ilams, *Dreyfus, Diplomats and the Dual Alliance* (1962). Civil-military relations are the subject of David B. Ralston, *The Army of the Republic: The Place of the Military in the Political Evolution of France, 1871–1914* (1967). Good studies of individuals include Geoffrey Bruun, *Clemenceau* (1943); T. F. Power, *Jules Ferry and the Renaissance of French Imperialism* (1944); J. P. T. Bury, *Gambetta and the National Defence* (1936); J. Hampden Jackson, *Jean Jaurès, His Life and Work* (1934), H. R. Weinstein, *Jean Jaurès* (1936), which emphasizes the Socialist leader's patriotism, and, a much more solid work, Harvey Goldberg, *The Life of Jean Jaurès* (1962). Recent studies of French nationalism are Michael Curtis, *Three against the Third Republic: Sorel, Barrès and Maurras* (1959), and the more solid works of Eugen Weber, *The Nationalist Revival in France, 1905–1914* (1959) and *Action Française: Royalism and Reaction in Twentieth Century France* (1962). On the last subject, Edward R. Tannenbaum, *The Action Française* (1962), is also important. Herbert Tint, *The Decline of French Patriotism, 1870–1940* (1964), discusses Gambetta, Déroulède, Boulanger, Dreyfus, Barrès, and much else but is unsystematic and frequently inaccurate. The contradictions in the personality and thought of Péguy are skillfully treated in Hans Schmitt's essay *Charles Péguy: The Decline of an Idealist* (1967). See also Marjory Villiers' biography (1965) and the older study by Alexander Dru (1952). On colonial affairs, H. I. Priestley, *France Overseas, A Study of Modern Imperialism* (1938), is useful.

Chapter 15 The German Empire: Pseudo-Constitutional Absolutism, 1871–1914

To general political histories already cited may be added W. S. Dawson, *The German Empire and the Unity Movement* (2 vols., 1919), still good on constitutional aspects, and, briefer but more suggestive, Arthur Rosenberg, *The Birth of the German Republic* (1931), and, more recently, W. M. Simon, *Germany in the Age of Bismarck* (1968). Michael Balfour, *The Kaiser and His Times* (1964), is a comprehensive and beautifully written account of the Wilhelmine period, superior to Virginia Cowles, *The Kaiser* (1963). Much new light is thrown on the Bismarck and Wilhelmine periods by Norman Rich's two-volume biography of Friedrich von Holstein (1965). The author is the editor, with M. Fisher, of *The Holstein Papers* (4 vols., 1955–1963). Economic developments are treated well in G. Stolper, *German Economy, 1870–1940* (1940), Werner Bruck, *Social and Economic History of Germany from William II to Hitler, 1888–1938* (1938), and Lamar Cecil, *Albert Ballin* (1967). A study of the political influence of economic groups is Alexander Gershenkron, *Bread and Democracy in Germany* (1943). J. Alden Nichols, *Germany after Bismarck* (1958), and J. C. G. Röhl, *Germany without*

Bismarck: The Crisis of Government in the Second Reich (1967), give a good picture of the competition of irresponsible agencies in the Caprivi era. Of sociological interest is Martin Kitchen, *The German Officer Corps, 1890–1914* (1968). On the rise of socialism, see Evelyn Anderson, *Hammer and Anvil: The Story of the German Working Class Movement* (1945); W. S. Dawson, *German Socialism and Ferdinand Lassalle* (1899), David Footman, *Ferdinand Lassalle: Romantic Revolutionary* (1947), and, especially, the treatment of Lassalle in Wilson, *To the Finland Station;* and Roger Morgan, *The German Social Democrats and the First International, 1864–1872* (1965). Vernon L. Lidtke, *The Outlawed Party: Social Democracy in Germany, 1878–1890* (1966), is a thorough analysis of the experience of the party during the Bismarck repression; Carl W. Schorske, *German Social Democracy, 1905–1917* (1955), analyzes the divisive forces in the movement and gives a convincing portrait of Bebel as party leader and J. P. Nettl discusses the problems of the left exhaustively in his *Rosa Luxemburg* (2 vols., 1966). See also Guenther Roth, *The Social Democrats in Imperial Germany: A Study in Working Class Isolation and National Integration* (1963), which discusses the effects of the deliberate policy of excluding the highly developed labor movement from social and political power. Andreas Dorpalen's *Heinrich von Treitschke* (1957) is a full-scale treatment of one of the leading voices of strident nationalism. Two important works on anti-Semitism are Peter G. J. Pulzer, *The Rise of Political Anti-Semitism in Germany and Austria* (1964), which has a good discussion of Stoecker's movement, and George L. Mosse, *The Crisis of German Ideology: Intellectual Origins of the Third Reich* (1965), the latter stressing the *Voelkisch* tradition. Aspects of the cultural history of the period are to be found in Hans Kohn, *The Mind of Germany* (1960); Harry F. Young, *Maximilian Harden, Censor Germaniae* (1959); Fritz Stern, *The Politics of Cultural Despair* (1961), which discusses such outstanding *Kulturpessimisten* as Paul de Lagarde and Julius Langbehn; and Walter Laqueur, *Young Germany: A History of the German Youth Movement* (1962). See also James J. Sheehan, *The Career of Lujo Brentano* (1966), very good on economic problems and social reform; and Fritz K. Ringer's study of the academic community between 1890 and 1933, *The Decline of the German Mandarins* (1969).

Ralf Dahrendorf, *Society and Democracy in Germany* (1968), is almost as valuable in its analysis of this period as it is for the Bonn Republic.

Chapter 16   Austria-Hungary, the Balkan States, and Turkey, 1871–1914

O. Jaszi, *The Dissolution of the Habsburg Monarchy* (1929), is still useful, but see A. J. May, *The Habsburg Monarchy, 1867–1914* (1951), and, most recently, C. A. Macartney, *The Habsburg Monarchy, 1790–1918* (1968) and *The Nationality Problem in the Habsburg Monarchy in the Nineteenth Century* (Austrian History Yearbook, III, 1967). Valuable on the same subject is Robert Kann, *The Multinational Empire: Nationalism and National Reform in the Habsburg Monarchy, 1848–1918* (2 vols., 1950). Edward Crankshaw, *The Fall of the House of Habsburg* (1963), is very readable but often oversimplified. D. C. Kosáry, *History of Hungary* (1941), C. H. Macartney, *Hungary, A Short History* (1962), and R. W. Seton-Watson, *Racial Problems in Hungary* (1908), are sound accounts, and the latter work is supplemented by the same author's authoritative *The Southern Slav Question and the Habsburg Monarchy* (1911), *The Rise of Nationality in the Balkans* (1917), and *History of the Czechs and Slovaks* (1943). The problems of Bohemia within the empire are also discussed in S. Harrison Thomson, *Czechoslovakia in European History* (2d ed., 1953). Austrian politics in this period have attracted relatively little attention from Western scholars, but see W. A. Jenks, *The Austrian Electoral Reform of 1907* (1950), Peter Pulzer's *The Rise of Political Anti-Semitism in Germany and Austria* (1964), and *The Diaries of Theodor Herzl*, edited and translated by Marvin Löwenthal (1956).

Notable books on the Balkan countries are C. Jelavich and B. Jelavich, eds., *The Balkans in Transition* (1963), C. E. Black, *The Establishment of Constitutional Government in Bulgaria* (1943), R. W. Seton-Watson, *History of the Roumanians* (1934), David Mitrany, *The Land and the Peasant in Rumania* (1930), E. S. Forster, *A Short History of Modern Greece* (1941), H. W. V. Temperley, *History of Serbia* (1917), and, also on Serbia and Montenegro, the beautifully written *Black Lamb and Grey Falcon* by Rebecca West (2 vols., 1941). Joan Haslip, *The Sultan: The Life of Abdul Hamid* (1958), is also eminently readable. On internal conditions in the Ottoman Empire, see Roderic H. Davison's masterful *Reform in the Ottoman Empire, 1856–1876* (1964). The internal situation at a later stage is described in E. E. Ramsaur, Jr., *The Young Turks* (1957).

Chapter 17   Imperial Russia, 1871–1914

Hugh Seton-Watson's *The Decline of Imperial Russia* (1952) is a survey that gives satisfactory treatment of economic growth, labor policy, and local government problems in addition to the larger issues of foreign and domestic policy, and includes sections on Poland and Finland. Richard Charques, *The Twilight of Imperial Russia* (1959), is also notable. Wayne S. Vucinich, ed., *The Peasant in Nineteenth Century Russia* (1968), is a successful collection of essays by different hands.

Intellectual movements are examined in S. R. Tompkins, *The Russian Intelligentsia* (1957), which covers the period between the Crimean War and the revolution, and Walter Bruford, *Chekhov and His Russia* (1948), a sociological study. For the revolutionary movement, see Avrahm Yarmolinsky, *Road to Revolution: A Century of Russian Radicalism* (1959), which deals with early underground movements; E. Lampert, *Sons against Fathers: Studies in Russian Radicalism and Revolution* (1964), which concentrates on figures like Chernyshevsky, Dobrolyubov, and Pisarev; J. H. Billington, *Mikhailovsky and Russian Populism* (1958); the indispensable work of Franco Venturi, *Roots of Revolution: A History of the Populist and Socialist Movements in Nineteenth Century Russia* (1960); Samuel H. Baron, *Plekhanov: The Father of Russian Marxism* (1962); L. H. Haimson, *The Russian Marxists and the Origins of Bolshevism* (1955); and the brilliantly conceived work of B. Wolfe, *Three Who Ruled: A Biographical History* (1948), which treats the early careers of Lenin, Trotsky, and Stalin. Of the recent biographies of Lenin, the best is that of Louis Fischer (1964), which gives a thorough discussion of the development of his thought before 1914. For the Russian right, see Robert E. McMaster, *Danilevsky* (1967), and Martin Karz, *Mikhail N. Katkov: A*

Political Biography, 1818–1887 (1966). John S. Curtiss, Church and State in Russia, 1900–1917 (1940), is a reliable guide, and Robert Byrnes, Pobodonostsev: His Life and Thought (1968), is a full-scale treatment of the procurator of the Holy Synod who symbolized the repressiveness of the regime. Alfred Levin, The Second Duma (1940), is a useful special study. The economic accomplishments of Witte are treated in Theodore Von Laue's basic study, Sergei Witte and the Industrialization of Russia (1963).

A fascinating volume on the development of Siberia is Yuri Semyonov, Siberia: Its Conquest and Development (1963). O. Halecki, Poland (rev. ed., 1955), J. Hampden Jackson, Finland (2d ed., 1940) and Estonia (1941), J. H. Wuorinen, Nationalism in Modern Finland (1931), and L. S. Greenberg, The Jews in Russia (1944), all deal with the nationalities problem within the empire.

Chapter 18 Imperial Expansion, 1871–1914

The origins and uses of the term imperialism are exhaustively explored in Richard Koebner and Helmut Dan Schmidt, Imperialism: The Story and Significance of a Political Word, 1840–1960 (1963). Two classical critiques of imperialism are J. A. Hobson, Imperialism: A Study (3d ed., 1938), and V. I. Lenin, Imperialsim, the Highest Stage of Capitalism (1916). More recent analyses are E. M. Winslow, The Pattern of Imperialism (1948), and E. Staley, War and the Private Investor (1935). An account of British critics of colonial expansion is to be found in A. P. Thornton, The Imperial Idea and Its Critics (1959), and the reflections of one of the most outspoken anti-imperialists in W. S. Blunt, My Diaries, 1888–1914 (one-vol. ed., 1932). On the intellectual impact, see Bernard Semmel, Imperialism and Social Reform: English Social-Imperial Thought, 1895–1914 (1960). An important monograph is Jeffrey Butler, The Liberal Party and the Jameson Raid (1968).

The spread and the consequences of imperial activity are described in W. L. Langer, The Diplomacy of Imperialism (2d ed., 1951), Herbert Feis, Europe, the World's Banker, 1870–1914 (1930). David S. Landes, Bankers and Pashas: International Finance and Economic Imperialism in Egypt (1958), the important study of E. J. Hobsbawm, Industry and Empire (1968), and the collection of essays edited by Prosser Gifford and William R. Louis, Britain and Germany in Africa (1967). See also D. C. M. Platt, Finance, Trade and Politics in British Foreign Policy, 1815–1914 (1968). A romanticized view of the British empire at its height is James Morris, Pax Britannica (1968), but see Max Beloff, Imperial Sunset. vol. I: Britain's Liberal Empire, 1897–1921 (1969) as a corrective. Notable books on empire-builders are Neil Ascherson, The King Incorporated: Leopold II in the Age of Trusts (1963); the biographies of Cecil Rhodes by S. G. Millin (1933), Basil Williams (1938), Felix Gross (1957), and, especially, J. G. Lockhart and C. M. Woodhouse (1963); Margery Perham, Lugard: The Years of Adventure, 1858–1898 (1956) and Lugard: The Years of Authority (1960), as well as her edition of The Diaries of Lord Lugard (4 vols., 1959–1962); Richard Oliver, Sir Harry Johnston and the Scramble for Africa (1958); Philip Magnus, Kitchener: Portrait of an Imperialist (1958); and the studies of Lord Milner by Edward Crankshaw (1952), Vladimir Halperin (1952), John Evelyn Wrench (1958), and A. M. Gollin (1964).

Bibliography

Accounts of national expansion are A. J. P. Taylor, *Germany's First Bid for Colonies, 1884–1885* (1938), W. O. Aydelotte, *Bismarck and British Colonial Policy* (1937), M. E. Townsend, *The Rise and Fall of Germany's Colonial Empire* (1930), D. J. Dallin, *The Rise of Russia in Asia* (1950), B. H. Sumner, *Tsardom and Imperialism in the Far East and Middle East* (1942), a series of excellent studies, E. M. Earle, *Turkey, the Great Powers and the Bagdad Railway* (1923), and Firuz Kazamzedeh, *Russia and Britain in Persia, 1864–1914* (1968). On the Zulu wars, see C. T. Binns, *The Last Zulu King* (1962), Rupert Furneaux, *The Zulu War: Isandhlwana and Rorke's Drift* (1963), and the splendid work of Donald R. Morris, *The Washing of the Spears: The Rise and Fall of the Zulu Nation* (1965). W. S. Churchill, *A Roving Commission* (1930), tells the story of the defeat of the Dervishes. Edgar Holt, *The Boer War* (1958), and Rayne Kruger, *Goodbye Dolly Gray* (1960), discuss the military aspects of that conflict; W. S. Hancock, *Smuts*, vol. I, *The Sanguine Years, 1870–1919* (1962), takes a broader view. Frank Thiess, *The Voyage of Forgotten Men* (1937), gives a dramatic description of the Russian disaster at Tsushima. See also Reginald Hargreaves, *Red Sun Rising: The Siege of Port Arthur* (1962).

Chapter 19   **International Politics and the Coming of War, 1890–1914**

Since the publication of Fritz Fischer's *Griff nach der Weltmacht* in Germany in 1962, the whole question of the origins of, and the responsibility for, the war has been reopened, and many new studies have been written. Fisher's book is now available in English, *Germany's Aims in the First World War* (1967), and so is the useful compilation of his student Emanuel Geiss, *1914: A Documentary Survey* (1968). Some of the controverted issues are discussed in "1914," *Journal of Contemporary History*, I, 3 (1966), and in the highly readable book of Lawrence Lafore, *The Long Fuse: An Interpretation of the Origins of World War I* (1965).

Among the older works, the most comprehensive is L. Albertini, *The Origins of the War of 1914* (3 vols., 1952 ff.), by a former Italian newspaperman. Still standard are S. B. Fay, *The Origins of the World War* (2 vols., 1930), and Bernadotte Schmitt, *The Coming of the War* (2 vols., 1930). Nicholas Mansergh, *The Coming of the First World War* (1949), lacks balance. G. P. Gooch, *Before the War* (2 vols., 1936–1938), focuses on the leading statesmen of the Great Powers in separate essays and is particularly incisive on Delcassé, Bülow, Aehrenthal, and Izvolsky. On Bethmann Hollweg, see especially Fritz Stern's essay in *The Responsibility of Power* (cited above under General Works). E. Brandenburg, *From Bismarck to the World War* (1927), is a critical account of German policy by a German historian, and G. W. Monger, *The End of Isolation: British Foreign Policy, 1900–1907* (1963), an equally critical view of British policy by an English historian who believes that Grey destroyed Britain's freedom of action. Aspects of Anglo-German relations are discussed in P. R. Anderson, *The Background of Anti-English Feeling in Germany* (1939), E. L. Woodward, *Great Britain and the German Navy* (1935), Jonathan Steinberg, *Yesterday's Deterrent: Tirpitz and the Birth of the German Battle Fleet* (1965), and A. J. Marder, *The Anatomy of British Sea Power* (1940), as well as in Hoffmann's

Bibliography

Anglo-German Trade Rivalry, cited in Chapter 11. Military influence is described in J. E. Tyler, *The British Army and the Continent, 1904–1914* (1938), and Craig, *Politics of the Prussian Army.* Compare Gerhard Ritter's *The Schlieffen Plan* (1958). Studies of single crises are E. N. Anderson, *The First Moroccan Crisis* (1930), Irma Barlow, *The Agadir Crisis* (1940), and Alfred Francis Pribram, *Austro-Hungary and Great Britain, 1908–1914* (1950), a somewhat uneven book with sections on the Bosnian crisis and the Balkan wars. Harold Nicolson's *Portrait of a Diplomatist* (1930) and Zara S. Steiner *This Foreign Office and Foreign Policy, 1898–1914* (1969) give intimate glimpses of British diplomacy on the eve of war.

The incident that set the tragedy in train is analyzed in Joachim Remak, *Sarajevo* (1959), and, more recently and at greater length, in Vladimir Dedijer, *The Road to Sarajevo* (1966).

INDEX

Index

Index

Index

Index

Index

Index

Index

Index

Index

Index

Index

Index

Index

Index